INDOOR
GRILLING

GRILL PAN

When you want to mark meat with a perfect crosshatch of razor-sharp grill marks, nothing beats a grill pan. At least two great food cultures back me on this—French and American. Grill pans have been used on both sides of the Atlantic for centuries to give steaks, chops, and chicken breasts the handsome look of food cooked on an outdoor grill—with a corresponding seared flavor. To this add their ease of use, affordable price, and the fact that they require virtually no storage space, and you'll understand why grill pans are so well suited to even a small kitchen. So whether you're grilling the chicken paillards pictured on the facing page or the Portobello "Bool Kogi" shown here, the grill pan gives you compelling results.

Portobello "bool kogi," PAGE 335

chicken paillards with "virgin" sauce, PAGE 195

A meal in a grill pan—
camembert to start,
beef with an herb salad
for a main dish, and
luscious grilled bananas
with a scoop of (ungrilled)
ice cream to finish.

grilled camembert with grilled tomato sauce, PAGE 27

maple-glazed bananas, PAGE 376

beef paillards with fresh herb salad, PAGE 73

CONTACT GRILL

hanks to George Foreman, the contact grill has become America's favorite indoor grilling device. The inspiration for the contact grill may have been the Italian *panini* machine. But *panini* (Italian sandwiches) are just a start, because you can also use this ingenious device to create some of the world's greatest grilled sandwiches, from Cuban *medianoches* to French *croque monsieurs*.

rosemary salmon,
PAGE 227

ON THE PANINI MACHINE:
TOP: paninis with goat cheese, capers, and roasted peppers, PAGE 306;
BOTTOM: croque bernardin,
PAGE 298

ON THE FOREMAN:
bacon and smoked cheddar stuffed new cheeseburgers, PAGE 160

sesame seared tuna, PAGE 240

wrapped asparagus with provolone & prosciutto, PAGE 22

The contact grill turns out a formidable hamburger (don't forget to grill the buns, too), and its nonstick grill plates are perfect for grilling sesame-crusted tuna steaks and prosciutto-wrapped asparagus. In the chapters that follow, you'll push the limits of your contact grill, with dishes ranging from artichoke "sunflowers" to pound cake "s'mores."

ROTISSERIE

hamersley's
lemon mustard
chicken,
PAGE 176;
spit-roasted
onions with
balsamic honey
glaze, PAGE 336

When it comes to turning out crisp, moist chickens and succulent, crusty roasts, few methods beat spit roasting.

spit-roasted prime rib with garlic and herbs, PAGE 54

When cooking one chicken, skewer it lengthwise on the rotisserie spit.

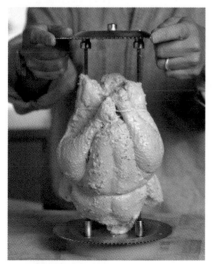

Place the geared rotisserie wheel on the spit, firmly seating the metal ends in the sockets.

The countertop rotisserie makes the process virtually foolproof, with an advance preparation time that's often measured in minutes. I'll show you how to spit roast both the old standbys and foods you may never have dreamed you could cook this way.

Quartered onions in the rotisserie basket, spit-roasted until golden with deeply browned edges.

BUILT-IN GRILL

The built-in grill functions like an outdoor gas grill—some even have the ceramic briquettes or metal bottles you find in outdoor models. What all built-ins offer is the inviting sizzle you get when the meat hits the hot grill. Which makes them great for grilling lamb chops, shish kebabs, steaks, seafood, and vegetables.

rosemary grilled lamb chops, PAGE 145, with sage and garlic grilled tomatoes, PAGE 353

GRILLED KEBABS,
LEFT TO RIGHT:
cyprus souvlaki, PAGE 112;
curry grilled chicken
kebabs, TIP, PAGE 151; and
raznjici, PAGE 115

FIREPLACE

The fireplace was likely man's first grill (remember our cave-dwelling forebears), and the experience of cooking in the fireplace most closely resembles grilling over charcoal or wood outdoors. Whether you're charring bell peppers in the style of an Argentinean pit master or sizzling a rib eye steak, the fireplace makes winter a season grill masters look forward to.

A fireplace grill gives you an irresistible wood-smoke flavor.

buenos aires grilled bell peppers, PAGE 328

Hold your hand 2 to 3 inches above the grill grate and start counting, one Mississippi, two Mississippi . . . If at two to three Mississippi, the heat forces you to move your hand, the embers are hot enough to begin cooking.

You can grill on a gridiron or a Tuscan grill, or even set up a rotisserie in front of the fire.

prosciutto-grilled figs, PAGE 25

Shovel fresh embers under the gridiron as needed to sustain the requisite heat.

spit-roasted lamb with berber spices, PAGE 132

"barbecued" baby backs, PAGE 125

sunday morning smoked salmon,
PAGE 233

SMOKER

As any Kansas City pit master knows, the essence of true barbecue is wood smoke. A stove-top smoker makes it possible, and even easy to accomplish indoors. By varying the type of sawdust you use, you can create an intense hickory, cherry, apple, or mesquite flavor.

A stove-top smoker works great for making "barbecued" ribs and kipper-style salmon. Use it to smoke brisket and beer-can chicken. By smoking tomatoes and other vegetables, you can create an unforgettable gazpacho.

smoked gazpacho, PAGE 51

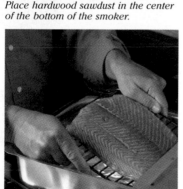

Place hardwood sawdust in the center of the bottom of the smoker.

Place the food, in this case salmon, on the wire rack over the aluminum foil–lined drip pan.

Place the smoker with the lid ajar over high heat. When you start to see smoke, close the lid tightly and reduce the heat to medium.

chile-rubbed shrimp with avocado corn cocktail, PAGE 46

FREE-STANDING GRILL

The freestanding grill enables you to bring the grilling experience right to the table. These highly portable grills are well suited to small, quick-cooking foods, like shrimp or fruit kebabs. Some models are even powerful enough to grill steaks.

vanilla-grilled pineapple
with dark rum glaze, PAGE 385;
cinnamon plums with
port sauce, PAGE 380

"Cooks are made,
but grill masters
are born."

—BRILLAT-SAVARIN

"If something tastes
good baked, fried, or sautéed,
it probably tastes
better grilled."

—STEVEN RAICHLEN

RAICHLEN'S Indoor! GRILLING

by Steven Raichlen

Photography by Susan Goldman
Illustrations by Ron Tanovitz

workman publishing • new york

Library of Congress Cataloging-in-Publication Data is available.
ISBN 0-7611-3335-6 (pb)
ISBN 0-7611-3588-X (hc)

Cover design by Paul Hanson
Book design by Lisa Hollander with Lori S. Malkin
Color photography (cover and interior) by Susan Goldman
Illustrations by Ron Tanovitz
Photography locations: Manhattan Center for Kitchen & Bath (all kitchen photos);
    Julie Killian (fireplace)

Workman books are available at special discounts when purchased in bulk
for premiums and sales promotions as well as for fund-raising or educational use.
Special editions or book excerpts can be created to specification.
For details, contact the Special Sales Director at the address below.

Workman Publishing Company, Inc.
708 Broadway
New York, NY 10003-9555
www.workman.com

Printed in the U.S.A.
First printing October 2004
10 9 8 7 6 5 4 3 2 1

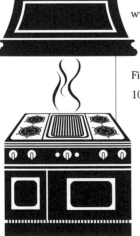

to suzanne rafer,
editor and
friend extraordinaire

acknowledgments

This book began with a simple idea, but it took the hard work of a small army to march it into print. I'd like to salute the troops who helped make it possible:

ON THE HOME FRONT: Barbara Raichlen (chief of staff, pit mistress, best friend, second in command, and second to none) and Jake and Betsy Klein (grill soldiers and super step-kids).

AT WORKMAN PUBLISHING: Peter Workman (commander in chief); Suzanne Rafer (commanding editorial general); Barbara Mateer (sharpshooter and copy editor); Beth Doty (assistant editor); Robyn Schwartz (editorial assistant); Lisa Hollander and Paul Hanson (art directors); Lori Malkin (layout); Barbara Peragine (pre-press); Carolan Workman (international sales); Katie Workman (associate publisher and marketing); and Kate Tyler (publicity).

PHOTOGRAPHY AND ILLUSTRATION: Susan Goldman (photographer extraordinaire); Andrea Carson (technology expert); Linda Romero (photographer's assistant); Grady Best and Marianne Sauvion (food styling), and Rebecca Adams (assistant food stylist). Ron Tanovitz (illustrator extraordinaire).

For sharing their lovely showroom, Sol Kassorla, Sol Drimmer, and Fran Asaro of the Manhattan Center for Kitchen & Bath.

For sharing her home and lovely fireplace, Julie Killian. For sharing her sister, Sarah Powers; and for providing the fireplace rotisserie, Bruce Frankel.

For recipe testing (done at Barbecue University at the Greenbrier resort in White Sulphur Springs, West Virginia) Eve Cohen (cooking school director) and Sue Moats and Stacy Adwell (recipe testing).

GRILL MANUFACTURERS: Camerons Smoker Cooker; Jenn-Air; Le Creuset; Ronco (manufacturers of the Showtime Rotisserie); Salton (manufacturers of the George Foreman grill); T-Fal; Thermidor; Viking; and VillaWare.

And thanks, too, to Chuck Adams (logistics), Allan Dresner (information technology), Mark Fischer (legal eagle), Fred Plotkin (Italian food mavin), and Bepi Pucciarella (who introduced me to the *fogolar*).

contents

indoor grills 1

The machines and the mechanics: How to make the most of contact grills, grill pans, built-in grills, freestanding grills, the fireplace, the countertop rotisserie, and the stove-top smoker.

appetizers . . 17

Heat up the grill and start the meal off right: Serve Artichoke "Sunflowers," Ginger and Sesame Stuffed Mushrooms, Prosciutto Grilled Figs, three different kinds of chicken wings, or a Smoked Shrimp Cocktail.

beef 53

What's more natural than beef on the grill? Sizzle steak au poivre or Filipino-Style London Broil in the grill pan or on a built-in grill. Spit-roast prime ribs and beef ribs in the rotisserie and smoke pastrami on top of the stove. Indoor grilling gives beef an invigorating new spin.

pork 93

Outdoor favorites come indoors with flavorful results: Cases in point are the Garlicky Spit-Roasted Pork, Kansas City Barbecue Ribs, and Chinatown Barbecued Pork Tenderloins. And for something really different, a Cyprus Souvlaki, redolent of cinnamon and fresh mint.

lamb 131

Beef and pork move over and make room on the grill for lamb. Shish kebabs and more: Lamb Steaks with Mint Chimichurri, lamb with a Berber spice paste, Espresso-Crusted Lamb Shanks, and Lamb Chops with Lavender and Cardamom. Exotic and delicious.

burgers 155

A burger on any indoor grill is a hit, and wait till you taste these: Spice up your repertory with hamburgers stuffed with bacon and cheese; New Mexican Green Chile Burgers; Barbecue Pork Burgers with Honey Mustard Sauce; Oaxacan-Spiced Turkey Burgers; and Thai Tuna Burgers.

poultry 173

The Perfect Roast Chicken—crisp-skinned and succulent. Chicken breasts, cumin-crusted or pounded thin and grilled Central American–style. Rum-Brined Turkey Breast, Spit-Roasted Duck, Piri-Piri Game Hens. Plus beer-can chicken in a stove-top smoker. Birds have never been better.

seafood 225

Fire up the Foreman for Moroccan Salmon, Grilled Tuna with Green Peppercorn Sauce, and Ginger Lime Halibut. Barbecue shrimp in a stove-top smoker. Blacken tuna on the built-in and grill swordfish in the fireplace. Seafood grilled indoors is seafood at its best.

breads and sandwiches

.... 279

The Real Bruschetta. Parmesan and Rosemary Lavash. A New Panini Caprese. Plus a Cuban Roast Pork Sandwich, Lobster Reubens, five variations on the *croque monsieur,* and more. Step aside, toaster—sandwiches demand an indoor grill.

vegetables and sides .. 325

Potatoes and onions and bell peppers roasted in the fireplace. Tomatoes flavored with sage and garlic prepared in a Foreman, a built-in grill, or a grill pan. Artichoke quarters singed crisp and waferlike in the rotisserie. Plus Portobello "Bool Kogi," Grilled Squash with Herbes de Provence, and Grilled Corn with Soy Butter and Sesame.

basics 361

Rubs, compound butters, and sauces—whether you're grilling indoors or out, these essential seasonings add character, even soul, to your food.

desserts ... 375

The Ultimate S'mores. Grilled Pound Cake. Banana "Tostones" with Cinnamon Rum Whipped Cream, Grilled Peaches with Bourbon Caramel Sauce, and Pears Belle Hélène on the Grill—now *these* are desserts!

bringing the grill indoors

There are lots of places I could start this book.

At the rugged stone hearth at Randall's Ordinary in Stonington, Connecticut, a country inn where dinner is cooked nightly in an antique fireplace—almost exactly as it has been since Colonial times.

In the "green room" of a television station, where I met boxer turned indoor grill champ—and the personality behind one of the most widely sold cooking devices in human history—George Foreman. (It was a great and validating moment—the champ gave me the perfunctory smile, walked halfway down the hall, then turned and shouted: "Hey, you're the guy that wrote *How to Grill!*")

On the set of the QVC, where, a few years back, an inventor and marketing genius named Ron Popiel made retailing history by selling $1 million worth of his Showtime rotisseries in a single hour.

But the most appropriate place to begin might be at the restaurant Da Toso in the hamlet of Leonacco in the province of Friuli, northeastern Italy.

Da Toso is a 'que hound's dream come true—a third-generation family-run restaurant in an out-of-the-way village with a strictly local clientele, and absolutely terrific, authentic live-fire-cooked food. I'd been brought here by Friuli gastronomy expert Bepi Pucciarella to experience a highly distinctive style of Italian barbecue— grilling on a *fogolar*—a freestanding hearth located not outdoors or even in a fireplace, but in the center of a dining or living room.

The *fogolar* is remarkable for the ingenuity of the setup—a raised stone hearth on stout wooden legs with a charcoal-burning, slanted metal grill positioned under an onion-shaped copper chimney (also freestanding) to carry away the smoke. Da Toso's food was remarkable, too, for its simplicity and forthright flavors—lamb chops grilled with garlic and rosemary, for example, or grilled calf's liver carpeted with paper-thin slices of white truffle.

But what struck me the most was how warm and comforting the arrangement was. It combined the sights, sounds, smells, and of course flavors of live-fire cooking with the inimitable sense of comfort you get when you stand in front of a fireplace on a cold or rainy day. From the dawn of humankind, the fire has provided light, warmth, cooking, and a sense of security, and all were abundantly present in Da Toso's unassuming dining room.

It was here that the vision for this book began to take shape, for while I had experimented with grilling in the massive fireplace at my grilling seminar, Barbecue University at the Greenbrier, and tinkered with grill pans and stove-top smokers, I'd never thought of indoor grilling as an area I'd be interested in pursuing. My lunch at Da Toso convinced me that one could grill indoors with passion and finesse—even soul.

Thus began an adventure that led me from the venerable art of fireplace cookery to the high-tech convenience of contact grills like the George Foreman and panini machines, and built-in grills like the Jenn-Air. I decided that the book would include an indoor equivalent for every sort of outdoor live-fire cooking experience: direct grilling, indirect grilling, spit-roasting, smoking, and even roasting in the embers.

To this end, I resolved to cover all the major types of indoor grills, from a gridiron in the fireplace to a built-in grill in your stove to a grill pan, contact grill, freestanding electric grill, stove-top smoker, and even countertop rotisserie. (See box on this page.)

I began to experiment with these devices—sometimes with felicitous results, sometimes with disappointment. The contact grill, for example, turned out middling steaks at best. (However, I did figure out some techniques for improving the performance of a contact grill for meat—see page 81.) On the other hand, it proved terrific for making *panini* and other pressed sandwiches—a category I had been unable to include in previous books. The contact grill also proved

surprisingly effective for grilling seafood, vegetables, and even fruit for dessert.

For decades I've used my Camerons stove-top smoker cooker to prepare delicious kipper-style smoked salmon. In the course of writing this book, I discovered you could also use it to make delectable barbecued ribs, smoked turkey, Texas-style brisket, and even an indoor beer-can chicken.

Grill pans have been part of my *batterie de cuisine* since my student days in Paris. Back then, French chefs didn't grill over live fire (most still don't), but they often used grill pans to give steaks, chops, and chicken breasts a seared flavor and a handsome cross-hatch of grill marks.

The countertop rotisserie, on the other hand, was a new piece of cookware for me, and I must confess I was skeptical the first time I plugged one in. It lived up to its impressive sales figures, however, turning out crisp-skinned succulent chickens, handsome roasted ducks, and even many foods

outdoor vs. indoor

OUTDOOR GRILLING METHOD	INDOOR EQUIVALENT
Direct grilling over wood or charcoal	Fireplace grill
Direct grilling over gas	Built-in grill, freestanding grill, grill pan
Indirect grilling	Countertop rotisserie
Spit-roasting	Countertop rotisserie
Smoking	Stove-top smoker
Grilling in the embers	Fireplace grill

how to use this book

In writing this book, I've tried to make the recipes as versatile and user-friendly as possible. There are dozens of different indoor grilling devices on the market, and beginning on the next page, you'll find descriptions of the major types and brands.

In terms of sheer number sold, the George Foreman contact grill is probably the most popular, followed by the countertop rotisserie, grill pan, and built-in grill.

To bring everyone under the tent, I've tried to provide instructions for preparing a particular recipe on as many different types of indoor grills as possible. The body of the recipe outlines the basic preparation, marinating, and seasoning instructions. The box that accompanies most recipes, entitled "If you have a . . .," will tell you how to cook the dish on the various types of indoor grills, while Tips and Notes highlight special ingredients or cooking strategies.

For some recipes, particularly those that are smoked or spit-roasted, only one type of indoor grilling device will work. In these instances, only one device is listed.

you wouldn't normally think of spit-roasting, from tuna "roasts" to lamb shanks to corn on the cob.

The shortest leap from outdoor to indoor grills came with fireplace grills and built-in grills (built into your stove). Grilling in a fireplace most closely resembles grilling on charcoal outdoors—with one added advantage—wood embers produce a lot more flavor than charcoal. Built-in grills powered by gas or electricity function very much like outdoor gas grills.

one final note

Although there's nothing like the thrill of cooking over live fire outdoors, or the inimitable flavor that results when foods are sizzled over glowing embers or slow-smoked over smoldering wood, you can grill very tasty and righteous food indoors. This book was written to help you bring those robust, soul-satisfying flavors from the outdoors indoors. (In fact, if you're a diehard outdoor griller, be assured that most of the marinades, rubs, basting sauces, indeed, entire recipes in this book can be made outdoors.)

So happy grilling and warmest wishes.

—Steven Raichlen

There are five basic types of indoor grills: the contact grill, the grill pan, the built-in grill, the freestanding grill, and the fireplace grill. Add to those two other ingenious devices, the countertop rotisserie and the stove-top smoker. Some function like outdoor charcoal or gas grills; others use technologies that produce results comparable to various grilling methods. All can be useful tools in the indoor griller's arsenal, although each also has limitations. Here's a

indoor grills

scorecard to help you understand the players, beginning with the popular contact grill. My favorite indoor method—and the one that's most comparable to outdoor live-fire cooking—is the fireplace. If you want to check that out first, turn to page 10.

contact grills

The contact grill, which most people are familiar with in the form of the very popular George Foreman, works something like a waffle iron or sandwich press. Its ridged grilling plates heat up to cook food from the top and the bottom simultaneously. The weight of the lid presses down on the food, creating an inviting crust, and the raised ridges on the best models leave well-defined grill marks. *Panini* machines are also contact grills.

If you're a hardcore barbecue traditionalist, you may have doubts about contact grills and how their results compare with outdoor grills. It's not the same, of course, but when it comes to what contact grills do well, they can be handy. They preheat quickly and, since you don't have to turn most food cooked in them, cooking generally takes less than half the time as on an outdoor grill. And contact grills are terrific for making hot sandwiches, such as Italian *panini* (see pages 300 through 307), Cuban sandwiches like the *medianoche* (page 308), a French *croque*

monsieur (page 292), and the classic Reuben (page 319).

Along with the weight of the grill's lid, the top and bottom heat sources produce exceptionally satisfying exteriors on seafood, especially fatty salmon and bluefish. The moderate heat enables you to grill delicate foods that would normally be off-limits to outdoor grills, such as thin fish fillets or shad roe. Contact grills are also good for cooking foods crusted with ground nuts, seeds, or bread crumbs. And the nonstick surface that's a feature of most contact grills makes them a dream for grilling sticky foods like polenta and cheese. If you believe (and I do, Dr. Atkins notwithstanding) that a reduced-fat diet is generally good for you, the contact grill can have powerful health benefits, since fat drains off as the lid presses down on the food while it cooks. As the mighty George Foreman says, "Knock out the fat."

Another advantage of contact grills, however, is that they're fairly compact. They don't take up a lot of space, and they're well suited to cooking for one or two people.

Most contact grills, however, do a middling job of cooking steaks and other red meats—indeed, any food that needs to be seared over high heat. This brings us to the main drawback of contact grills: Because the meat is sandwiched between the two metal plates, it tends to stew in its own steam rather than grill. And as for those grill marks, models vary widely in their ability to create well-defined ones and to properly cook food through, so ample wattage is essential.

One improvement I'd like to see for all contact grills is an on/off switch. Many models turn on when you plug them in. I'd also like to see more power and a higher heat capacity controlled by a thermostat on even the smallest machines.

WHAT TO LOOK FOR WHEN BUYING A CONTACT GRILL

■ A grill with enough power to brown and sear food. Buy one that can cook at least four burgers at a time, and preferably one that cooks six. Two-burger grills just don't get hot enough. For more about contact grill sizes, see the box on page 4.

■ An adjustable temperature control—many contact grills lack this, but it's a feature I appreciate, even though ninety-nine percent of the time, I run the grill on the highest setting.

■ An on light to let you know the grill is in operation.

■ A nonstick coating on the cooking surface to prevent food from sticking to it.

■ Raised parallel ridges on the cooking surface to give you well-defined grill marks.

■ A drip pan to catch the fat.

■ Easy cleanup. Ideally, you should be able to immerse the grilling plates in water, but only one contact grill I know of lets you do this, and it's a loser on other accounts. Many contact grills come with plastic "combs" or "rakes" to enable you to scrape clean between the grill ridges.

preheating times

TYPE OF GRILL	PREHEATING TO HIGH
Contact grills	3 to 5 minutes
Grill pans	3 to 5 minutes
Built-in grills	5 to 8 minutes
Freestanding grills	5 minutes
Countertop rotisseries	0 to 5 minutes
Stove-top smokers	3 to 5 minutes

■ Sturdy construction, particularly with regards to the handle. Some recipes occasionally require you to exert extra pressure on the food as it cooks by pressing down on the top grill plate.

■ A floating hinge, which enables the top grill plate to sit higher or lower depending on the thickness of the food underneath it. This promotes even grilling, while a fixed hinge causes the food closer to the hinge to cook faster and hotter than the food farther from it.

■ A latch so you can fasten the grill closed when you put it away.

■ Finally, a cool-looking design. I love the ribbed chrome look of *panini* machines, such as VillaWare's Uno ProPress (for more about *panini* machines, see the box on page 302).

TIPS FOR COOKING IN A CONTACT GRILL

■ Don't forget to put the drip pan under the front of the contact grill before you start cooking. Rendered fat can flow quickly, so you may need to replace the

safety tip

To reduce the likelihood of setting off your smoke alarm, grill under or as close to your stove hood as possible and run the exhaust fan on high.

is bigger better?

The shopper buying a contact grill is faced with a daunting selection—even from a single manufacturer. Consider the broad product line of George Foreman grills, which are manufactured by Salton.

It turns out that not all contact grills are equal, and that with the popular Foreman grill, at least, bigger is better. Foreman grills come with varying wattages—from 760 watts to 1,500. The lower-wattage machines may fit handily on the counter of a small kitchen, but they have a hard time getting hot enough to brown food and apply grill marks.

So when you buy a contact grill, look for the highest available wattage—at least 1,000 watts, ideally 1,500. Unfortunately, while this is marked on the bottom of the machine, it may be not be marked on the box. It's best to check the label on the underside of the machine before buying. That's easy in stores with display models. In smaller stores, ask a salesperson to open the box so you can double-check.

drip pan with a clean one. You may even want to set the whole grill on a rimmed baking sheet.

■ To grill, plug in the machine, and if your model has one, set the thermostat to the desired temperature—most often high. When the power light goes from red to green (or from off to on), the grill is ready. If you don't have a thermostat, preheat the grill for three to five minutes.

■ Despite their name, *panini* machines are good for grilling much more than sandwiches. Their high wattage and heavy lids make them ideal for chicken breasts, for example, and even steak. But that heavy lid can wreak havoc on delicate foods; when cooking these, lower the lid gently. For all intents and purposes *panini* machines and Foreman grills are interchangeable.

■ In the best of all possible worlds, you'd buy a high-powered contact grill to start with. If you own a lower-power model, preheat it well, and use it for seafood, burgers, sandwiches, and vegetables—not steaks or chops.

■ Contact grills do a good job with bone-in chicken breasts, but other meats, such as pork and veal chops, turn out best when they're boneless.

■ One of the advantages of the contact grill is its ability to apply pressure as well as heat. This is great when making dishes like *pollo al mattone* (chicken under a brick; see page 190) or pressed sandwiches, like *panini*. As a general rule, as you cook, press down hard from time to time on sturdy foods, such as steaks and chops, or foods that are supposed to be flattened, like sandwiches. Pressing down on the lid one or two times during the grilling process ensures good grill marks and a crusty exterior.

■ Gently lower the lid and don't press on it when grilling delicate foods, like fragile fish fillets, delicate vegetables, and pound cake. You don't want to crush them.

■ Grilling fish indoors can create aromas that some people wish had remained outdoors. To minimize this, set up your contact grill on the stove under your stove hood and run the exhaust fan on high, or place the grill next to an open kitchen window.

■ It's easier to clean a contact grill when it's hot than when it's cold. Let it cool slightly, then use the plastic comb or rake it comes with to scrape large pieces of food off the grilling surfaces and between the ridges. Wipe the grill plates and outside of the grill with damp paper towels. Wash dishwasher-proof parts, such as the drip pan, in the dishwasher. (If you turn off the grill while you eat your dinner, plug it in again afterward to reheat. Then, let the grill cool slightly before cleaning it.)

grill pans

Next to the fireplace (see page 10), the grill pan is probably the oldest type of indoor grill. It's widely used in France (indeed, throughout Europe) and has become a classic culinary tool (when I attended cooking school in Paris in the 1970s, we cooked steaks in grill pans). Grill pans are great for preparing steaks, chops, chicken breasts, and thinly sliced vegetables—good ones apply dark, tack-sharp grill marks. Indeed, food stylists often use grill pans to cook steaks and vegetables that look as if they were cooked over live fire.

A grill pan is nothing more than a frying pan with raised parallel ridges on the bottom; these ridges create the charred parallel grill marks. Like all true grills, and unlike skillets, grill pans have the advantage of draining off excess fat. Unlike cooking on a true grill, you get to collect the pan juices, which make a good base for sauces.

The jury is out on the ultimate superiority of plain or stick-resistant cooking surfaces. (Stick-resistant surfaces are increasingly replacing the less satisfactory nonstick surfaces once so common.) I personally like cast-iron grill pans without any special finish, but you need to season these well and keep them

seasoned (see page 6). If you prefer to use an enameled, stick-resistant grill pan, like Le Creuset's, just remember they should not be subjected to sudden changes of temperature—for example, by rinsing a hot grill pan under cold water. This can crack the enamel, even though it's the most effective way to clean the pan.

Grill pans come in a variety of shapes and sizes—round, square, rectangular; small enough to fit on one burner or large enough to straddle two. I use a basic 10-inch square pan. Rectangular pans are good for long, slender foods, like whole trout. For one or two people, a 9- to 12-inch square grill pan is fine. For larger families, you may want to invest in a grill pan large enough to cover two burners. If your main goal is to grill steaks and chops, any grill ridge configuration will do. If you mostly want to cook small pieces of food, such as scallops, shrimp, and sliced vegetables, buy a grill pan with closely spaced ridges.

seasoning a cast-iron grill pan

It's my opinion that cast iron makes the best grill pans. It's sturdy and heavy; it conducts and retains heat well; and there's nothing like cast iron for branding in grill marks. However, it does require a little extra care, namely in the washing and seasoning. (Seasoning cast iron with vegetable oil or shortening creates a rust-proof, nonstick finish.) Here's how the Lodge Manufacturing Company, one of America's oldest cast-iron cookware companies, suggests you do it.

1. Place an oven rack in the highest position in the oven and another in the lowest. Line the lower rack with aluminum foil to catch any drippings. Preheat the oven to 350°F.

2. Wash a brand-new cast-iron grill pan with hot soapy water and a stiff brush. This removes any oil or metal shavings left from the factory.

3. Rinse and dry the pan completely with paper towels.

4. Apply a thin coat of melted solid vegetable shortening (for example, Crisco) to the entire surface, both inside and out. A pastry brush works well for this.

5. Place the grill pan upside down on the upper oven rack and bake it for one hour.

6. Turn off the oven and let the pan cool before removing it from the oven.

7. Store the pan in a cool, dry place.

The more you use a cast-iron grill pan, the better seasoned it will become.

After each use, clean the pan using a stiff brush and hot water only. Do not use soap. Towel dry the pan immediately and apply a light coating of vegetable oil to it while still warm. Never wash a cast-iron grill pan in the dishwasher.

If the pan develops a metallic smell or leaves a metallic taste or shows signs of rust, don't worry. Wash the pan with soap and hot water, scour off the rust with steel wool, and reseason.

WHAT TO LOOK FOR WHEN BUYING A GRILL PAN

■ A thick, heavy metal, stick-resistant, or cast-iron body that absorbs heat and distributes it evenly.

■ High, sharp ridges that will produce clean grill marks.

TIPS FOR COOKING IN A GRILL PAN

■ To preheat the grill pan, place it over medium, rather than high, heat. You want the pan hot but not superheated. A superheated grill pan will burn the food before it has cooked through.

■ To test whether the grill pan is properly preheated, sprinkle a few drops of water over it. On a hot grill, they will skitter and evaporate in two seconds; on a medium-hot grill, this will take four to six seconds.

■ To prevent food from sticking, lightly oil the tops of the ridges of the grill pan. Fold a paper towel into a tight pad, then dip it in a small bowl of oil, shaking off any excess. Holding the folded paper towel with tongs, run it over the top of the ridges, taking care not to dribble oil between the ridges; any excess oil will burn on the pan.

■ Grill pans are best for grilling dry foods—unmarinated steaks, chops, and fish fillets and thinly sliced vegetables. When grilling marinated foods, drain them well, scraping off bits of minced onion or garlic; these can fall into the pan and burn.

■ If a handsome crosshatch of grill marks is desired, rotate each piece of food a quarter turn halfway through the grilling process.

■ Let enameled or stick-resistant grill pans cool to warm before immersing them in soapy water to wash. If your grill pan is cast iron, don't add soap to the soaking water. Soak all pans for five to ten minutes, then use a stiff natural- or plastic-bristled brush to scrub enameled or stick-resistant pans; use a wire brush on cast-iron pans.

built-in grills

If the fireplace grill is the indoor equivalent of a wood-burning or charcoal grill, the built-in grill is designed to perform like a gas grill. As its name suggests, the built-in grill is a permanent feature of some gas or electric ranges. Good ones enable you to do any sort of direct grilling that you would do on an outdoor gas grill. Bad ones lure you with the promise of indoor grilling but don't really get hot enough to do the job.

The first built-in grill that had wide commercial success was the Jenn-Air, pioneered by the Maytag appliance company. The grill offered two important innovations: It functioned like an inverted broiler, thanks to an electric heating element positioned under the grate, and it had a powerful downdraft exhaust system that sucked away smoke through a vent next to the grill. These two features made it possible to grill indoors using the direct method without having a massive space-gobbling overhead hood and yet not have the kitchen fill up with smoke.

Today many big-name appliance companies make stoves with built-in grills, including Jenn-Air, Thermador, Viking, and Wolf. They are available heated by both gas and electricity, using a variety of heat-diffusing systems, including metal baffles and ceramic briquettes. Some have nonstick grill grates. Others come with rotisserie attachments.

In the course of teaching cooking classes around the country, I've worked on some pretty terrific built-in grills and some fairly awful ones. If you're considering buying a stove with one, I suggest you go to an appliance store or cooking school where you can actually watch the grill being used or, better still, try grilling on it yourself.

WHAT TO LOOK FOR WHEN BUYING A BUILT-IN GRILL

■ Check the heat output. Steaks should be grilled over a 600° to 800°F "fire." Turn the heat to high and wait about five minutes, then use the Mississippi test (see right) to check the heat of the grill.

■ Check the evenness of the heat: Does the grill burn as hot in the back as in the front? To some extent all grills have hot spots and cool spots, but the overall heat distribution should be consistent.

■ Does the heat respond to and correspond to the temperature control? Set the grill heat to high and let it run for a few minutes. Then lower the heat to medium. Does the temperature drop noticeably? Turn the heat down to low and test it again. Each time you lower the temperature control you should feel a drop in the heat coming off of the grill.

MISSISSIPPI TEST

Hold your hand 2 to 3 inches above the grate and start counting: "One Mississippi, two Mississippi, three Mississippi," and so on. When the grill is heated to high, you'll be able to get to two to three Mississippi before the heat forces you to pull your hand away. When the grill is heated to medium, you'll be able to get to five to six Mississippi. When the grill is heated to low, you'll be able to get to ten to twelve Mississippi.

don't burn the skewer!

Kebabs on bamboo or wooden skewers present the same challenge whether you're grilling indoors or outdoors: How do you cook the meat without burning the exposed part of the skewers? Here are three solutions.

■ Position the kebabs on the grate so the exposed ends of the skewers extend off the edge of the grill. This is easy to do on the narrow built-in grills found in many stoves.

■ Use an aluminum foil shield. This method is good for fireplace grills and some built-in grills. Check the manufacturer's instructions; in some cases, such as with Jenn-Air built-ins, covering a portion of the grate may interfere with the grill's thermostat and ventilation system. To make a shield, tear off a sheet of aluminum foil that's about three times as long as the exposed part of a skewer and fold it in three, as you would a business letter. Place the foil shield on the grate under the bare part of the skewers.

■ Opt for a contact grill, free-standing grill, or grill pan. These grills naturally shield the skewers from the heat.

easily, and are at least some of the pieces (particularly the drip pan) dishwasher safe?

■ Finally, how's the exhaust system? Is it powerful enough to remove the smoke, or will you set off your smoke alarm every time you grill?

TIPS FOR GRILLING ON BUILT-IN GRILLS

■ Before grilling, make sure you've read the grill instructions that come from the manufacturer.

■ Some models come with nonstick or stick-resistant grill grates. Other built-in grill grates should be brushed and oiled prior to grilling.

■ To preheat the grill, turn the heat to high. To test the heat use the Mississippi test. Hold your hand 2 to 3 inches above the grate and start counting: "One Mississippi, two Mississippi, three Mississippi," and so on. When the grill is heated to high, you'll be able to get to two to three Mississippi before the heat forces you to pull your hand away. When the grill is heated to medium, you'll be able to get to five to six Mississippi. When the grill is heated to low, you'll be able to get to ten to twelve Mississippi. Heating a built-in grill to high will take between five and eight minutes.

■ To oil the grate, fold a paper towel into a small pad and lightly dip it in oil, shaking off the excess. Hold the paper towel with tongs and draw it across the bars of the grate.

■ To minimize drips and residue on a built-in grill, drain marinated meats and

■ Does the size of the grill meet your needs? Because built-in grills share the stove-top with the range burners and sometimes a griddle, many have a relatively small cooking surface. If you're grilling for yourself and your spouse or companion, the average-size built-in grill will be ample. If, on the other hand, you like to entertain, you'll want to look for a built-in with a large cooking area or choose another type of grill.

■ Is the grill grate nonstick or stick-resistant? Are the bars of the grate thick enough to create respectable grill marks? Is there a drip pan, and can you line it with aluminum foil?

■ How easy is the grill to clean? This is a biggie. It's no fun using a system that does the grilling in ten minutes but requires an hour to clean. Does the grill come apart seafood well before placing them on the grill. You may even want to blot them dry with paper towels.

■ Clean or change your grill exhaust system filter often.

■ To clean the grate, soak it in hot soapy water. Then, if it does not have a nonstick surface, brush the grate with a natural- or plastic-bristled brush or a ball of crumpled aluminum foil held with tongs.

freestanding grills

The freestanding grill functions like a built-in grill, but it's self-contained and small enough to sit on a countertop. Most work like inverted broilers, with an electric heating element under the grate. (Some models, like those from T-Fal and Zojirushi, have the heating element built right into the grate. This tends to give these grills a bit more firepower.) Thus, in design at least, the freestanding grill functions similarly to an outdoor gas or electric grill. And, you have the theatrical advantage of being able to grill at tableside or even right on the table, should you desire.

Unfortunately, many freestanding grills are woefully underpowered—they can take almost forever to produce anemic-looking food that has little in common with the glories of the grill. Nonetheless, there are a few freestanding grills that can turn out a respectable steak for one or two people. Generally use freestanding grills to cook small or thin pieces of food that are done quickly.

WHAT TO LOOK FOR WHEN BUYING A FREESTANDING GRILL

■ Sufficient wattage to achieve a grilling temperature that is hot enough. Buy one from a cookware store where you can actually see the grill in action.

■ A temperature control and an on light.

■ A drip pan you can fill with water or line with aluminum foil for easy cleaning.

■ Easy to remove, dishwasher-safe parts, for easy cleanup.

TIPS FOR GRILLING ON A FREESTANDING GRILL

■ Most freestanding grills have built-in shielding to protect countertops and work surfaces from excess heat. However, it's a good idea to play it safe and place the device on a baking sheet; this will also collect any splatters or drips.

■ To preheat the grill, turn the heat to high. To test for heat, hold your hand 2 to 3 inches above the grate and start counting: "One Mississippi, two Mississippi, three Mississippi," and so on. When the grill is heated to high, you'll be able to get to two to three Mississippi before the heat forces you to pull your hand away. When the grill is heated to medium, you'll be able to get to five to six Mississippi. When the grill is heated to low,

THE FOGOLAR

The ultimate fireplace for indoor grilling is the *fogolar* of Friuli in northeastern Italy. This traditional freestanding hearth is often located in the middle of a home living room or restaurant dining room, so it truly serves as the focal point of the meal (not to mention the local social life). The raised hearth allows you to grill standing upright— much easier on the back than cooking in a floor-level fireplace. Suspended from the ceiling above a traditional *fogolar* is a distinctive onion- shaped chimney hood, which carries away the smoke and food fumes. Elaborate models may even have built- in rotisseries. The *fogolar* is the most perfect indoor grilling setup I've encountered.

you'll be able to get to ten to twelve Mississippi. Heating a freestanding grill to high should take five minutes, but may take longer. Some do not ever get all that hot.

■ Most foods will take slightly longer to grill on freestanding grills than they would on other indoor grills. While I've made the cooking times 1 minute longer per side, you may need several extra minutes per side, depending on your machine.

■ Never submerge a freestanding grill in water unless the manufacturer's instructions specifically say it is safe to do this.

fireplace grill

The fireplace is the oldest indoor grill. The Romans called it a *focus* (hearth), and its central role in cooking, domestic well-being, and promoting general human happiness made it the literal and spiritual focal point of the home. In Colonial America, most cook- ing was done in the fireplace, and grilling on a gridiron (a sort of square

metal grate on legs) was a popular way to cook meat. While this practice has all but disappeared in the United States, it is still common in Italy, France, Argentina, and India.

There are at least five benefits to grilling in a fireplace. First, it is the indoor grilling method most like grilling outdoors, particularly like grilling on a wood-burning or charcoal grill. Second, you can cook over as hot a fire as you desire. Third, you get to grill with wood, which provides a subtle but unmistak- able smoke flavor. Fourth, if you happen to live in the Frost Belt, it lets you grill in the winter without having to brave the elements. Best of all, you get the primal sense of well-being that comes from gathering in front of a fire—an experi- ence that marked the transition of pre- historic man from bipedal animals to human beings.

To grill in a fireplace, you need a fire and a gridiron or a Tuscan grill. A grid- iron is a square or rectangular grill, often made of cast iron, with a grate that can be positioned 3 to 6 inches above the fire. (The white markings on a football field resemble the parallel metal bars, hence the football term *gridiron*.) It doesn't need to be fancy. I've seen fireplace grills made by laying a wire refrigerator shelf over a couple of bricks positioned at opposite sides of the fire.

The basic procedure for fireplace grilling is to light a log fire and let it burn down to glowing orange embers. Then you rake the embers into a pile about 1 inch deep (or into a two-zone fire—a taller pile on one side for high- heat searing and a shallower pile on the other to provide a more moderate cook- ing heat). Position the gridiron or grate of the Tuscan gill over the coals and preheat it for three to five minutes before grilling. In some bigger fireplaces (especially in restaurants), the fire is built on one side of the hearth or in the center and the embers are raked or shoveled under one or more gridirons on the side.

WHAT TO LOOK FOR WHEN BUYING A FIREPLACE GRILL

■ I like a heavy cast-iron gridiron with bars that are at least ¼ inch thick and legs that are at least 3 inches tall. Some models have a handle, which makes them easy to move, and some have widely spaced bars at one end for grilling larger things like steaks and more narrowly spaced bars at the other end for vegetables.

■ Some Tuscan grills have a notched frame into which the grate fits. This allows you to raise or lower the grate as needed.

■ Also available are Tuscan grills that come with two gridirons attached by a floating hinge and featuring legs on both the top and bottom. To use this ingenious device, sandwich steaks, vegetables, or other foods, especially more delicate ones, between the grates; then, once the food has grilled on one side, you turn over the entire grill to cook the second side.

TIPS FOR GRILLING IN A FIREPLACE

■ It's best if the fireplace is large enough to build a fire on one side or in the back while allowing you to position the gridiron on the other side or in the front.

the fireplace rotisserie

I have in my collection of grilling memorabilia a copy of a page from a medieval illuminated manuscript. The picture shows a brace of ducks turning on a spit in a fireplace. The spit is driven by a simple clockwork mechanism, which one of the kitchen scullions was undoubtedly charged with rewinding every fifteen minutes. It's a device that dates back to the ancient Romans (remember Trimalchio's feast in Fellini's *Satyricon*?) and in this high-tech world, this ingeniously low-tech machine not only sets my mouth watering but satisfies my soul.

Enter the SpitJack, a fireplace rotisserie manufactured in Italy that has the brass and handsome black metal look of nineteenth-century cookware. The machine has just four basic parts: a steel turnspit; an upright metal brace to hold the spit on one end; a metal box with a clockwork mechanism to hold and turn the spit on the other; and a long flat metal pan you place under the spit to catch the drippings.

A SpitJack is perfect for cooking large pieces of meat, like the leg of lamb shown in the color section at the front of the book. Since there is no rotisserie basket, it can't be used for smaller cuts of meat or vegetable pieces. To operate the SpitJack, you stick a roast or bird on the spit, securing it with the metal prongs provided. (The model I have comes with two spits, so you can cook a chicken on the top rod and spit roast vegetables beneath it.) Place the box with the clockwork mechanism in front of the fire at one side of the fireplace and the spit holder on the opposite side. Insert one end of the spit in the clockwork mechanism; insert the other end in the hole in the spit holder. Then place the drip pan underneath the turnspit. You want to position the rotisserie far enough away from the fire so the meat is exposed to a medium to high, but not scorching, heat. Wind up the clockwork, and the rotisserie will spring into action. To control the heat, move the SpitJack deeper into your fireplace or farther away from the fire. Rewind the mechanism as necessary to keep the spit turning. (The SpitJack also comes in a model with an electric motor.) Although the clockwork mechanism is usually far enough away from the fire to prevent it from getting unbearably hot, be sure to wear oven mitts to protect your hands when winding it.

Why would you want to use a fireplace rotisserie instead of a countertop model? Well, first, there's the pleasure of huddling in front of a fireplace and cooking over live fire. Then there's the flavor—the food picks up a whiff of wood smoke. There's something mesmerizing about watching food turn slowly in front of a flickering fire. And something soul satisfying about using a cooking method that's almost as old as civilization itself.

To order the SpitJack, see Mail-Order Sources, page 396.

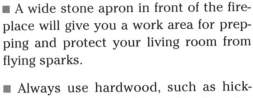

safety tips

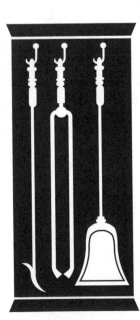

■ Have a dry chemical fire extinguisher on hand. Take it to your local fire department once a year to make sure it's fully loaded and operational.

■ Minor flare-ups can be extinguished with a handful of salt. Keep a carton nearby when grilling.

■ A wide stone apron in front of the fireplace will give you a work area for prepping and protect your living room from flying sparks.

■ Always use hardwood, such as hickory, oak, cherry, apple, or alder logs for fireplace grilling. Never use soft woods, like pine or spruce. They emit a tarry, sooty residue and increase the risk of chimney fires. *Warning:* Never use charcoal in your fireplace. Burning charcoal emits carbon monoxide, which can be lethal.

■ Andirons or a raised fire grate make it easy for the logs to burn down to glowing embers. If you have the room, place the andiron with the logs in the back of the fireplace.

■ To reduce the risk of chimney fires, have your chimney cleaned by a professional chimney sweep at the beginning of the cold weather. You need a fireplace that draws well.

■ Let the fire burn out completely before removing the ashes. Make sure they are no longer warm and douse the ashes with water to kill any unseen sparks. Place the ashes in a metal bucket or trash can (not a plastic container), even if you are cleaning the fireplace the day after cooking.

HOW TO GRILL IN A FIREPLACE

■ Make sure you have plenty of wood on hand. Split logs that are 3 to 4 inches in diameter work best. You'll need somewhere between eight and fifteen logs per recipe and some kindling.

■ Make sure to open the damper.

■ Build the fire in the back of the fireplace, if possible, starting with four to six logs, and do the cooking in the front. It will take between forty minutes and one hour or so to have a good bed of embers. Keep an eye on the fire; you want to start cooking when the embers are at their peak.

■ Use the Mississippi test to check the heat; hold your hand 2 to 3 inches above the grate and start counting: "One Mississippi, two Mississippi, three Mississippi," and so on. When the grill is heated to hot, you'll be able to get to two to three Mississippi before the heat forces you to pull your hand away. When the grill is heated to medium, you'll be able to get to five to six Mississippi. When the grill is heated to low, you'll be able to get to ten to twelve Mississippi.

■ Once you've got a good bed of embers, rake them into a pile about 1 inch deep. Put the Tuscan grill or gridiron in place (preferably in front of the andirons) and preheat it. Cooking times are listed with each of the recipes suitable for fireplace grilling. Depending on the heat of your embers, the time may be a little shorter or longer than the noted times. Don't forget to shovel fresh embers under the gridiron from time to time to keep the bed hot.

■ If practical, keep feeding the fire. I add a fresh log fifteen minutes after lighting the fire and continue adding logs at the rate of one every five minutes. This way I'm assured of a continuous supply of fresh embers.

countertop rotisserie

Like the contact grill, the countertop rotisserie is virtually synonymous with its foremost pitchman. Ron Popeil, who became something of a celebrity hawking the Veg-O-Matic, now touts a device that began as an aquarium fitted with a motor and heating element. "As seen on television," proclaim the bold red letters on the box, and the Showtime Rotisserie and BBQ has sold literally in the millions—thanks in part to the machine's virtues and in part to Popeil's on-air charisma.

Actually, countertop rotisseries have been around for decades. My mother-in-law waxes nostalgic about the Roto-Broil 400 of her younger days on Miami Beach. Today, you can buy countertop rotisseries with horizontal spits or vertical spits; there's even one brought out by George Foreman. But the appeal of the countertop rotisserie lies as much in the nature of the cooking process as the machine itself. One of America's first food writers, Mary Randolph, summed it up in her 1824 cookbook, *The Virginia House-Wife:* "No meat can be well roasted, except on a spit."

A countertop rotisserie functions much like an outdoor one. The food spins slowly (six times per minute in the case of the Showtime) on a turnspit in front of or over an electric heating element (outdoor and commercial models use gas or, occasionally, wood or charcoal). With the Showtime, a metal reflector behind the heating element focuses that heat on the food, while a metal pan in the bottom catches the drippings.

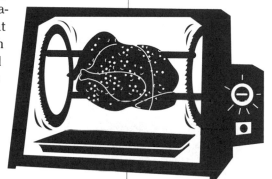

There are at least three advantages to rotisserie cooking. The slow, gentle rotation bastes the meat both internally (with the meat juices) and externally (with the fat). Because it turns slowly, no part of the meat is exposed to the heat too long, preventing scorching or overcooking. Finally, the steady rotation ensures even browning on all sides.

Countertop rotisseries are good for cooking any cylindrical or football-shaped cut of meat, from a whole chicken or turkey to a rib roast or pork loin. Basket attachments make it possible to spit-roast flatter foods, like fish steaks and lobster tails. Tough or fatty cuts of meat, such as ribs or duck, do well in a rotisserie—ribs are tenderized by the slow cooking process; ducks lose their excess fat. One of the major shortcomings of most indoor grills is that they don't make it possible to grill using an indirect heat source. Countertop rotisseries provide many of the advantages of indirect grilling, with the added benefits of spit roasting.

WHAT TO LOOK FOR WHEN BUYING A COUNTERTOP ROTISSERIE

■ A rotisserie with a heavy-duty motor and enough firepower to brown and sear the food.

■ An adjustable temperature control. Some of the best-selling rotisseries lack this with no appreciable detriment to the food, but if you're like me, you'll want to be in control.

■ A turnspit that is thick and heavy enough to hold a 15-pound turkey.

■ Rustproof and easy-to-use meat prongs to hold the food in place (the Showtime rotisserie's double turnspit eliminates the need for prongs).

■ I like horizontal turnspits. Juices and fat drain off food on a vertical spit quickly, so you don't get the continuous basting of a horizontal spit. Two exceptions to this are the Turkish *doner* and the Middle Eastern *shawarma* machines, vertical rotisseries used to cook ground lamb and other fatty meats, where you want to melt off as much fat as possible.

■ Rotisserie baskets for spit roasting odd-shaped foods, like quartered artichokes and ribs.

■ Some rotisseries, like the Showtime, come with a round plastic spit holder that holds the spit upright and stable so you can use both hands to skewer the food. This is a great feature—don't forget to use it.

■ A timer.

■ A glass front so you can monitor the cooking progress.

■ An easy-to-clean drip pan to catch the dripping fat.

■ A rotisserie that's easy to take apart and clean. Ideally, all the parts exposed to food should be dishwasher safe.

■ A convenient size. The rotisserie should be large enough to accommodate the food you want to spit roast but small enough to fit on your counter.

TIPS FOR USING A COUNTERTOP ROTISSERIE

■ There is no need to preheat most countertop rotisseries; you simply turn them on. The manufacturer's instructions will include information about whether preheating is necessary.

■ Line the drip pan with aluminum foil to facilitate cleanup.

■ Truss all poultry before placing it in the rotisserie (you'll find instructions for trussing on page 177). Trussing gives the bird a more compact and attractive shape, promotes even roasting, and prevents loose limbs from brushing against the heating element.

■ When roasting a single chicken, put it on the spit so that the spit runs through it from the neck to the tail. When roasting two chickens, place the birds on the spit so the spit is perpendicular to their back bones, positioning one with the head end up and the other with the tail end up.

■ Skewer food on the spit so that the weight will be as evenly distributed as possible.

■ When carrying the spit, hold it so that the removable gear wheel is slightly elevated, to keep the gear wheel from falling off.

■ When loading a flat rotisserie basket, fill the basket entirely and fasten the lid on as tightly as possible, so the food doesn't move around in the basket.

■ You can use the pause button to brown roasts that have flat surfaces. Press the button to stop the roast with the flat surface directly facing the heating element.

■ To clean a countertop rotisserie, first remove dishwasher-safe parts, such as the front window, the drip pan, grill baskets, spit, and so on. Soak them in soapy water to loosen any spatterings, then wash in the dishwasher or by hand. Do not use abrasive scrubbers on any parts with a nonstick surface. Wipe the inside of the rotisserie with a damp soapy sponge or cloth.

stove-top smokers

The stove-top smoker is one of the most ingenious cooking devices ever invented—elegant in its simplicity and effective in its design. It gives food the smoke flavor of authentic barbecue— indoors, often in ten to twenty minutes. You can customize the smoke flavor simply by varying the type of sawdust you use.

The most widely distributed stove-top smoker is made by Camerons, manufactured in South Africa and distributed by CM International, based in Colorado Springs. The smoker comes in a few sizes, but it basically consists of a rectangular metal box with a flat sliding lid. Inside, there's a drip pan to catch any dripping

juices or fat and a rack to hold the food. The whole contraption is relatively small and easy to store. Camerons also sells sawdust, which it calls smoking chips, in a wide variety of types. You can get apple, mesquite, oak, cherry, maple, pecan, hickory, alder, and corn cob.

The relatively shallow depth of the Camerons smoker makes it ideal for smoking thin foods, like shrimp, chicken breasts, or pork chops. If you're really going to do a lot of smoking of large cuts of meat, like a beer-can chicken (see page 180) or a whole turkey (see page 207), it makes sense to invest in a taller stove-top smoker, like the eight-quart smoker with a domed lid recently introduced by VillaWare. However, you can improvise using the Camerons; see Two-Step Smoking on page 139.

WHAT TO LOOK FOR WHEN BUYING A STOVE-TOP SMOKER

■ Buy a smoker with a sturdy metal body and tight-fitting lid.

■ Make sure it comes with a drip pan and wire food rack.

■ Check to see that the manufacturer offers a selecion of sawdust for smoking. If it doesn't, the booklet included with the smoker should clearly explain what kind of wood to use and where to get it.

TIPS FOR USING A STOVE-TOP SMOKER

■ Unlike smoking outdoors, you don't need to soak the sawdust before smoking on a stove-top.

■ To facilitate cleaning, line the smoker with aluminum foil before adding the sawdust.

■ You can also use hardwood pellets for indoor smoking; use six to eight pellets for every tablespoon of sawdust. One good manufacturer of pellets is BBQr's Delight.

■ Run your stove exhaust fan on high when smoking indoors. If you've got a kitchen window, you may also want to open it. If your smoke detector goes off and you disconnect it (which I don't recommend), make certain you reconnect it when you're done smoking.

■ When emptying the smoker, be sure the sawdust is completely cool. Douse it with a little water and leave it at room temperature for at least an hour. You don't want even the slightest spark in your trash.

■ After several uses, the top of your smoker may warp slightly, allowing a little smoke to escape. Place a heavy object, like a kettle filled with water, on top to restore the seal as soon as you close the lid.

HOW TO USE A STOVE-TOP SMOKER

■ To use most indoor smokers, you simply place the specified number of tablespoons of hardwood sawdust in the bottom of the smoker, then place the drip pan on top of the sawdust. Place the wire rack on top of the drip pan and put the food on it. Slide on the lid until the smoker is closed.

■ Place the smoker over a medium-hot burner. After a few minutes, you're likely to smell and see wisps of smoke. Close the lid and lower the heat to medium. Smoke the food for the suggested amount of time.

Grilling from start to finish—that's how I plan my menus, and when you dine at our home, the appetizer always comes hot off some sort of grill. It could be artichoke "sunflowers," grilled asparagus with prosciutto and Provolone, radicchio-grilled goat cheese, or Japanese-inspired sesame and ginger grilled stuffed mushrooms. Chicken wings are a North American classic, and I'll show you how to sizzle them in a rotisserie, on a contact grill, and in a smoker. Chile-rubbed grilled shrimp makes for the ultimate shrimp cocktail. And even the Swedish meatball gets a makeover when seared on an indoor grill.

appetizers

artichoke "sunflowers" with lemon dipping sauce

■ For the best results, use artichokes with leaves that are beginning to open, not fist-tight globe artichokes. They're easier to spread apart.

■ If you like, you can also cook the artichoke stems. Brush them with the garlic–olive oil mixture along with the artichokes (see Step 6 on the facing page). Cooked on a contact grill, they'll take about 3 minutes. Cooked in a grill pan, on a built-in grill, or in the fireplace, they'll take about 3 minutes per side.

I've long been intrigued by grilled artichokes, so it was only a matter of time before I found a way to take advantage of the simultaneous top and bottom heat sources of a contact grill to produce artichokes similar to Rome's famous *carciofi alla guidia* (artichokes in the Jewish style). In this venerable dish, artichokes are pan-fried in oil while being pressed to flatten them as they cook. The result looks something like a sunflower, with crackling crisp "petals" you can just about eat whole. You can certainly use other indoor grills, but you'll need to weight down the artichokes (see "If you have a . . ." on the facing page). **MAKES 4**

THE RECIPE

FOR THE SAUCE:
1 medium-size lemon
1/2 cup mayonnaise
1/4 cup sour cream
Coarse salt (kosher or sea) and freshly ground white pepper

FOR THE ARTICHOKES:
4 large artichokes with stems attached
1/3 cup extra-virgin olive oil
2 cloves garlic, minced
3 tablespoons finely chopped fresh parsley
Coarse salt (kosher or sea) and freshly ground white pepper

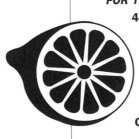

1. Make the sauce: Using a Microplane or the fine side of a box grater, finely grate 1/2 teaspoon lemon zest and place it in a small nonreactive mixing bowl. Cut the lemon in half and squeeze 2 teaspoons of lemon juice into the bowl. Set aside 1 lemon half. Add the mayonnaise and sour cream to the lemon zest and juice and whisk to mix. Season with salt and white pepper to taste. The sauce can be prepared several hours ahead and stored, covered, in the refrigerator. Let it return to room temperature before serving.

2. Prepare the artichokes: Bring 1 gallon salted water to a boil in a large pot.

3. Meanwhile, trim the artichokes: Using a sharp knife, cut off and discard the top inch of each artichoke. Using kitchen shears, cut off and discard the spine tips on the remaining leaves. Trim off and discard ½ inch from the end of each stem. To prevent them from discoloring, rub all of the cut edges of the artichokes with the cut side of the reserved lemon half.

4. Place the artichokes in the pot of boiling water. Place a pot lid or heatproof plate that is slightly smaller than the diameter of the pot on top of the artichokes to keep them submerged. Boil the artichokes until just tender, 15 to 30 minutes, depending on their size and toughness. Drain the artichokes in a colander, rinse them thoroughly with cold water to cool, then place them stem up on a wire rack over a roasting pan or the sink to drain.

5. Using a grapefruit spoon or a melon baller, scrape out the inside leaves and fibrous part in the center of each artichoke, leaving the outer leaves and heart intact. Place your fingers in the cavity in the center of an artichoke, and gently pry the leaves apart to open the artichoke like a flower. Place the artichoke, stem end up, on a work surface and gently press on it to flatten it further. Cut the stem off the artichoke so the bottom of the choke is flat. You can set aside the stem to cook (see Tips on the facing page) or discard it. Repeat with the remaining artichokes, then blot them dry with paper towels. The artichokes can be prepared to this stage several hours ahead and refrigerated, covered with plastic wrap.

6. Place the olive oil, garlic, and parsley in a small bowl and stir to mix. Generously

if you have a...

CONTACT GRILL: Preheat the grill; if your contact grill has a temperature control, preheat the grill to high. Place the drip pan under the front of the grill. When ready to cook, lightly oil the grill surface. Arrange the artichokes on the hot grill, stem side up, then close the lid. The artichokes will be done after cooking 5 to 8 minutes.

GRILL PAN: You can cook the artichokes and stems in a grill pan if its ridges are shallow; a grill pan with deep ridges may not provide enough surface heat. Place the grill pan on the stove and preheat it to medium-high over medium heat. When the grill pan is hot a drop of water will skitter in the pan. When ready to cook, lightly oil the ridges of the grill pan. Arrange the artichokes in the hot grill pan, stem side up. Weight them down with a grill press or heavy

skillet. The artichokes will be done after cooking 4 to 6 minutes per side.

BUILT-IN GRILL: Preheat the grill to medium-high, then, if it does not have a nonstick surface, brush and oil the grill grate. Arrange the artichokes on the hot grate, stem side up. Weight them down with a grill press or heavy skillet. The artichokes will be done after cooking 4 to 6 minutes per side.

FIREPLACE GRILL: Fragrant oak or hickory does wonders for grilled artichokes. Rake red hot embers under the gridiron and preheat it for 3 to 5 minutes; you want a hot, 2 to 3 Mississippi fire. When ready to cook, brush and oil the gridiron. Arrange the artichokes on the hot grate, stem side up. Weight them down with a grill press or heavy skillet. The artichokes will be done after cooking 4 to 6 minutes per side.

brush the artichokes and stems on all sides with the olive oil mixture, taking pains to dab plenty between the leaves. Season the artichokes generously on all sides with salt and white pepper.

7. Cook the artichokes, following the instructions for any of the grills in the box above, until the leaves are browned and crackling crisp.

8. To serve, arrange the artichokes on plates, stem side down. Spoon some of the sauce into the center of each artichoke, then place a stem, if using, on top.

ginger and sesame stuffed mushrooms

Stuffed mushrooms turn up as appetizers all over the world— from Mexico to Italy to Japan. Here's a grilled version, inspired by a dish served at the popular sushi bar and Japanese grill parlor Kirala in Berkeley, California. If you're used to the Italian-American stuffing of bread crumbs and cheese, the sizzling ginger, scallion, and sesame mixture here will be an inspiration. **MAKES 12**

tip

Most of the world uses dark-meat chicken for grilling—it's moister and richer than the breast—but you can certainly use breast meat if you prefer. The stuffing for the mushrooms would be equally rich made with pork or shrimp in place of the chicken.

THE RECIPE

¹/₂ pound skinless, boneless chicken
  thighs or breasts, cut into ¹/₂-inch pieces
1 clove garlic, minced
1 scallion, both white and green parts,
  trimmed and minced (reserve
  1 tablespoon minced scallion greens
  for garnish)
1 teaspoon finely chopped peeled
  fresh ginger
3 teaspoons toasted sesame seeds (see Note)
¹/₄ teaspoon coarse salt (kosher or sea),
  or more to taste
¹/₄ teaspoon freshly ground black pepper
1 tablespoon soy sauce, or more to taste
2 teaspoons Asian (dark) sesame oil
12 large white mushroom caps
  (about 12 ounces total)

1. Place the chicken, garlic, scallion, ginger, 1 teaspoon of the sesame seeds, and the salt and pepper in a food processor. Process to finely chop, running the machine in short bursts; do not purée the stuffing mixture. Add the soy sauce and the sesame oil. Taste the chicken mixture for seasoning by grilling or cooking a tiny patty in a nonstick skillet. Add more salt and/or soy sauce as necessary; the mixture should be highly seasoned.

2. Cut the mushroom stems off flush with the caps. Using a grapefruit spoon or a melon baller, hollow out the mushroom caps (set aside the mushroom scraps for making broth or another use). Spoon the stuffing into the mushroom caps, mounding it in the center of each.

3. Cook the mushrooms, following the instructions for any of the grills in the box on the facing page, until the mushrooms are browned and tender and the stuffing is sizzling. Use the "Charmin test" to check for doneness; the sides of the mushrooms should yield gently when squeezed with your fingers.

4. Sprinkle the reserved tablespoon of scallion greens and the remaining 2 teaspoons of sesame seeds over the mushrooms and serve at once.

NOTE: To toast sesame seeds, place them in a dry cast-iron or other heavy skillet (don't use a nonstick skillet for this). Cook the sesame seeds over medium heat until lightly browned, about 3 minutes, shaking the skillet to ensure that they toast evenly. Transfer the toasted sesame seeds to a heatproof bowl to cool.

if you have a...

CONTACT GRILL: Preheat the grill; if your contact grill has a temperature control, preheat the grill to high. Place the drip pan under the front of the grill. When ready to cook, lightly oil the grill surface. Place the stuffed mushrooms on the hot grill, then close the lid. The mushrooms will be done after cooking 3 to 5 minutes.

BUILT-IN GRILL: Preheat the grill to high, then, if it does not have a nonstick surface, brush and oil the grill grate. Place the mushrooms on the hot grate, stuffing side down. The mushrooms will be done after cooking 3 to 5 minutes per side.

FREESTANDING GRILL: Preheat the grill to high; there's no need to oil the grate. Place the mushrooms on the hot grill, stuffing side down. The mushrooms will be done after cooking 4 to 6 minutes per side.

FIREPLACE GRILL: Rake red-hot embers under the gridiron and preheat it for 3 to 5 minutes; you want a hot, 2 to 3 Mississippi fire. When ready to cook, brush and oil the gridiron. Place the mushrooms on the hot grate, stuffing side down. The mushrooms will be done after cooking 3 to 5 minutes per side.

contact grill

poppers on the grill

Poppers (in culinary circles, at least) are cheese-stuffed, deep-fried jalapeño peppers. There are at least two reasons to make them on a contact grill: There's a lot less fat and they taste a lot less oily. Not surprisingly, this dish was inspired by one made by a Texan, Jerry Lawson, president of the largest supplier of grilling woods in the United States, W W Wood. Serve these bad boys to a crowd that can handle the heat. **MAKES 24**

tip

For a meaty alternative, wrap the poppers in strips of thinly sliced flank steak that has been seasoned with salt and pepper. You'll need about 8 ounces of flank steak, and the cooking time will be about the same.

THE RECIPE

6 ounces (¾ cup) soft goat cheese
    or herbed cream cheese,
    at room temperature
12 jalapeño peppers, stemmed,
    cut in half lengthwise, and seeded
Ground cumin
24 sprigs fresh cilantro
8 slices bacon, each cut crosswise
    into thirds
Cooking oil spray

YOU'LL ALSO NEED:
24 wooden toothpicks

1. Place a spoonful of cheese in a jalapeño half. Lightly sprinkle some cumin over it and place a cilantro sprig on top. Wrap a piece of bacon around the jalapeño, securing it through the side with a tooth-pick. Repeat with the remaining jalapeño halves. The recipe can be prepared several hours ahead to this stage and refrigerated, covered.

2. Preheat the grill (for instructions for using a contact grill, see page 3); if your contact grill has a temperature control, preheat the grill to high. Place the drip pan under the front of the grill.

3. When ready to cook, lightly coat the grill surface with cooking oil spray. Arrange the poppers on the grill, cut side up. Gently close the lid and grill the jalapeños until the bacon is browned and the cheese is sizzling, 2 to 4 minutes. Transfer the jalapeños to a platter and serve at once.

wrapped asparagus
with provolone and prosciutto

tip

Buy the fattest asparagus stalks you can find—ideally ones as thick as your little finger. As for the cheese, choose an aged Provolone, pepper Provolone, or truffled Provolone.

Asparagus and ham hors d'oeuvres are surprisingly universal. In the past year, I've had variations on the theme at a Japanese *robatayaki* (grill) parlor in Oakland, California, and at a Relais & Château temple of haute cuisine in Edgartown, on Martha's Vineyard. You can grill single asparagus stalks in prosciutto to pass around or gang four of the prosciutto-wrapped spears together with a couple of bamboo skewers inserted crosswise to form a sort of raft. **MAKES 16**

1 bunch chives or scallions, green part only
  (see Note)
16 thick asparagus stalks (about 1 pound)
2 slices (¼ inch thick, about 4 ounces total)
  Provolone cheese
8 thin slices prosciutto (about 4 ounces),
  cut crosswise in half

1. Snap the fibrous ends off the asparagus; the easiest way to do this is to grab a stalk by its base with one hand and bend the stalk with your other hand. The asparagus will snap where the woody part ends. Discard the fibrous ends.

2. Cut each slice of Provolone into ¼-inch strips. Place a piece of prosciutto on a work surface with the cut end toward you. Place an asparagus stalk on top of the prosciutto at the edge of and parallel to the cut end. Place a strip of Provolone alongside the asparagus stalk on top of the prosciutto. Roll up the asparagus and Provolone in the prosciutto, then tie the bundle together with 1 or 2 pieces of chive. Repeat until all the remaining pieces of prosciutto and asparagus stalks have been used. The asparagus bundles can be prepared to this stage several hours ahead and refrigerated, covered.

3. Cook the asparagus, following the instructions for any of the grills in the box at right, until the prosciutto is browned, the Provolone is melted, and the asparagus is tender. You may need to cook the asparagus in more than one batch.

4. Transfer the asparagus bundles to a platter and serve at once.

NOTE: If you use scallion greens, you'll need to blanch them so that they are pliable enough to tie without breaking (you probably won't need to do this with chives). Cut the scallion greens into pieces about 3 inches long. Bring 2 quarts well-salted water to a boil in a saucepan over medium-high heat. Add the scallion greens and let them boil for 10 seconds. Drain the blanched scallion greens in a colander, rinse them under cold running water until cool, then transfer them to paper towels and blot dry.

if you have a...

CONTACT GRILL: Preheat the grill; if your contact grill has a temperature control, preheat the grill to high. Place the drip pan under the front of the grill. When ready to cook, lightly oil the grill surface. Place the asparagus on the hot grill, then gently close the lid. The asparagus will be done after cooking 2 to 4 minutes.

GRILL PAN: Place the grill pan on the stove and preheat it to medium-high over medium heat. When the grill pan is hot a drop of water will skitter in the pan. When ready to cook, lightly oil the ridges of the grill pan. Arrange the asparagus in the hot grill pan so that the stalks are perpendicular to the ridges. The asparagus will be done after cooking 2 to 3 minutes per side.

BUILT-IN GRILL: Preheat the grill to high, then, if it does not have a nonstick surface, brush and oil the grill grate. Arrange the asparagus on the hot grate so that the stalks are perpendicular to the ridges. The asparagus will be done after cooking 2 to 3 minutes per side.

FREESTANDING GRILL: Preheat the grill to high; there's no need to oil the grate. Arrange the asparagus on the hot grill so that the stalks are perpendicular to the ridges. The asparagus will be done after cooking 3 to 4 minutes per side.

FIREPLACE GRILL: Rake red hot embers under the gridiron and preheat it for 3 to 5 minutes; you want a hot, 2 to 3 Mississippi fire. When ready to cook, brush and oil the gridiron. Arrange the asparagus on the hot grate so that the stalks are perpendicular to the ridges. The asparagus will be done after cooking 2 to 3 minutes per side.

radicchio-grilled goat cheese

Grilling in leaves is one of the world's oldest live-fire cooking techniques, practiced by pit masters in lands as diverse as Thailand, Sri Lanka, and the Yucatán. The advantages are many—the leaves (banana, pumpkin, or grape, to name a few) protect delicate foods from the searing heat of the fire while imparting a distinctive smoky, herbaceous flavor all their own. It looks cool as all get out, and there's the primal pleasure of opening an edible package. This offbeat version, inspired by Portland, Oregon, chefs and PBS TV hosts Caprial and John Pense, features a distinctive interplay of flavors: salty pancetta, bitter radicchio, and earthy goat cheese. The bruschetta on page 280 or another grilled bread would make a good accompaniment. **MAKES 8**

tips

■ Radicchio, a type of chicory with dark red leaves with creamy white veins and a pleasantly bitter flavor, is available in specialty food stores and many supermarkets. You can substitute Boston lettuce or collard greens. Neither tastes quite like radicchio, but both work well for wrapping the cheese.

■ As for the goat cheese, use a soft, white log-shaped goat cheese, like Montrachet.

■ Pancetta is a sort of unsmoked Italian bacon. Substitute regular bacon if you prefer.

THE RECIPE

1 large head radicchio
8 ounces soft, mild goat cheese
1 tablespoon toasted pine nuts
　　(see Note), or 1 tablespoon
　　chopped pecans
8 thin slices pancetta or bacon
　　(6 to 8 ounces total)
Coarse salt (kosher or sea) and
　　freshly ground black pepper
Well-aged balsamic vinegar,
　　for drizzling

YOU'LL ALSO NEED:
Butcher's string or 8 wooden toothpicks

1. Cut the stem and core out of the head of radicchio and discard them. Tear off 8 of the largest radicchio leaves; set the rest of the radicchio aside for another use. Place the leaves on a work surface, hollow side up. Cut the goat cheese into

8 equal slices and place a slice in the center of each radicchio leaf. Place some pine nuts on top of the cheese.

2. Fold the stem end of a radicchio leaf into the center, over the cheese, then fold the sides of the leaf into the middle. Roll the leaf up. Wrap a slice of pancetta around the radicchio leaf packet and tie the radicchio packet together with butcher's string or secure it with a toothpick. Repeat with the remaining cheese-filled leaves and pancetta slices. The radicchio packets can be prepared to this stage up to 24 hours ahead.

3. Cook the radicchio packets, following the instructions for any of the grills in the box at right, until they are browned and soft.

4. Transfer the radicchio packets to a platter or plates and snip off the strings or remove and discard the toothpicks. Season the packets with salt and pepper and drizzle a little balsamic vinegar over each, then serve at once.

if you have a...

CONTACT GRILL: Preheat the grill; if your contact grill has a temperature control, preheat the grill to high. Place the drip pan under the front of the grill. When ready to cook, lightly oil the grill surface. Place the radicchio packets on the hot grill, then close the lid. The radicchio packets will be done after cooking 3 to 5 minutes.

GRILL PAN: Place the grill pan on the stove and preheat it to medium-high over medium heat. When the grill pan is hot a drop of water will skitter in the pan. When ready to cook, lightly oil the ridges of the grill pan. Place the radicchio packets in the hot grill pan. They will be done after cooking 3 to 5 minutes per side.

BUILT-IN GRILL: Preheat the grill to high, then, if it does not have a nonstick surface, brush and oil the grill grate. Place the radicchio packets on the hot grate. They will be done after cooking 3 to 5 minutes per side.

FREESTANDING GRILL: Preheat the grill to high; there's no need to oil the grate. Place the radicchio packets on the hot grill. They will be done after cooking 4 to 6 minutes per side.

NOTE: To toast pine nuts, place them in a dry cast-iron or other heavy skillet. Cook the pine nuts over medium heat until they begin to brown, 3 to 5 minutes, shaking the skillet to ensure that they toast evenly. Transfer the toasted pine nuts to a heatproof bowl to cool.

prosciutto-grilled figs

Prosciutto and figs is one of many variations on the Italian pairing of sweet with salty, exemplified by the popular appetizer of melon and cured ham. This rendition introduces another element, the creamy delicacy of Lombardy's famous mascarpone cheese. The recipe is extremely flexible: The figs can be sizzled on a contact grill, seared on a built-in grill, cooked in a grill pan, or even grilled in a fireplace—in the unlikely event that you'd fire yours up in the summer, when fresh figs are in season. **MAKES 12**

THE RECIPE

6 large ripe figs
6 tablespoons mascarpone or cream cheese
(about 3 ounces)
6 thin slices prosciutto (about 3 ounces total),
cut in half lengthwise
Cooking oil spray

YOU'LL ALSO NEED:
12 wooden toothpicks or butcher's string

1. Rinse the figs under cold running water and blot them dry with paper towels. Remove the stems and cut each fig in half lengthwise. Spoon 1½ teaspoons of mascarpone on the cut side of each fig half. Wrap each fig half in a piece of prosciutto and secure it with a toothpick or tie it onto the fig with a piece of butcher's string. The figs can be prepared to this stage several hours ahead and refrigerated, covered.

2. Cook the prosciutto-wrapped figs, following the instructions for any of the grills in the box at left, until the prosciutto is browned and the figs are cooked through.

3. Transfer the figs to a platter and warn everyone to remove the toothpicks or cut off the strings.

NOTE: The soft, white Italian mascarpone cheese is sold in plastic tubs at Italian markets and many specialty food stores. If you can't find it, you can substitute cream cheese or, for an interesting alternative, use Gorgonzola. You can also use pancetta (Italian bacon) in place of the prosciutto.

if you have a...

CONTACT GRILL: Preheat the grill; if your contact grill has a temperature control, preheat the grill to high. Place the drip pan under the front of the grill. When ready to cook, lightly oil the grill surface. Place the prosciutto-wrapped figs on the hot grill, then very gently close the lid. The figs will be done after cooking 2 to 4 minutes.

GRILL PAN: Place the grill pan on the stove and preheat it to medium-high over medium heat. When the grill pan is hot a drop of water will skitter in the pan. When ready to cook, lightly oil the ridges of the grill pan. Place the prosciutto-wrapped figs in the hot grill pan. The figs will be done after cooking 2 to 4 minutes per side.

BUILT-IN GRILL: Preheat the grill to high, then, if it does not have a nonstick surface, brush and oil the grill grate. Place the prosciutto-wrapped figs on the hot grate. The figs will be done after cooking 2 to 4 minutes per side.

FREESTANDING GRILL: Preheat the grill to high; there's no need to oil the grate. Place the prosciutto-wrapped figs on the hot grill. The figs will be done after cooking 3 to 5 minutes per side.

FIREPLACE GRILL: Rake red hot embers under the gridiron and preheat it for 3 to 5 minutes; you want a hot, 2 to 3 Mississippi fire. When ready to cook, brush and oil the gridiron. Place the prosciutto-wrapped figs on the hot grate. The figs will be done after cooking 2 to 4 minutes per side.

grill pan

grilled camembert
with grilled tomato sauce

Cheese acquires an alter ego when grilled. If you don't believe me, ask Greeks about *saganaki,* Argentineans about *provoleta,* or the Swiss about raclette. True Camembert is a soft-ripened cow's milk cheese from Normandy (a soft-ripened cheese has had its exterior exposed to molds so it ripens from the outside in, producing a thin downy rind and a soft interior). I'm not sure anyone has tried to grill Camembert before, but a grill pan gives you killer grill marks that really pop against the snowy white rind, and the cheese becomes even more oozing and pungent inside. It's delectable served with grilled tomato sauce or smoked tomato salsa and grilled bread. **SERVES 4 TO 6**

tip

I've made this recipe with several types of Camemberts, including the classic 8-ounce disk from Normandy and an interesting square sheep's milk Camembert from the Old Chatham Sheepherding Company in upstate New York (see Mail-Order Sources on page 396). The grill pan works its magic no matter what sort of Camembert you use.

THE RECIPE

1 large Camembert (about 8 ounces), or
    2 small Camemberts (each about 5 ounces)
2 teaspoons extra-virgin olive oil
Grilled Tomato Sauce (page 372),
    or Smoked Tomato Salsa (page 369)
Bruschetta (page 280)

1. Place the grill pan on the stove and preheat it to medium-high over medium heat (for instructions for using a grill pan, see page 6).

2. When ready to cook, lightly oil the raised ridges of the grill pan with a paper towel that has been folded and dipped in oil. Brush the top and bottom of the Camembert(s) with the olive oil. Place the Camembert(s) in the hot grill pan, gently pressing the cheese onto the raised ridges. Grill the cheese until dark grill marks appear on the bottom, 1 to 2 minutes. Carefully turn the cheese over with a spatula and grill on the other side until it has grill marks, 1 to 2 minutes. Don't overgrill the cheese or it will become too runny inside and may leak out of the rind.

3. Spoon the tomato sauce into the well of a platter or plate. Using a spatula, carefully set the grilled Camembert in the center (you can also place the cheese in the center of the platter and spoon the sauce around it). Serve at once, with a spoon for spreading the runny cheese and sauce on the bread.

grilled provoleta

When Argentineans say grilled cheese, they really mean it. Not cheese sandwiches browned in butter on the griddle, but thick slabs of *provoleta* (a firm cow's milk cheese similar to Provolone) seared on the gridiron until they are partially melted and lightly browned. It's mandatory fare at any Argentinean steakhouse. You can achieve similar results on an indoor grill. When I tested this recipe at the Greenbrier, the whole kitchen staff came running—it's amazing how a few simple ingredients grilled indoors can produce billboard-size flavors.

The key to grilling Provolone successfully is to choose a firm, well-aged cheese that will hold its shape when grilled. If you live in a community with a large Argentinean population, like Miami, you may be able to find *provoleta* at a grocery store. Otherwise, use a hard, aged Italian Provolone or, for even more flavor, Provolone laced with peppercorns. **SERVES 4 TO 6**

if you have a...

CONTACT GRILL: The cheese melts well on a contact grill, but won't brown very much. Use this method only as a last resort. To keep the cheese from sticking to the grill, once you have sprinkled the cracked pepper and oregano over it, lightly dust the slices of cheese with flour. Preheat the grill; if your contact grill has a temperature control, preheat the grill to high. Place the drip pan under the front of the grill. When ready to cook, lightly oil the grill surface. Place the cheese slices on the hot grill, then close the lid. The cheese will be done after cooking 2 to 4 minutes.

GRILL PAN: Place the grill pan on the stove and preheat it to high over medium heat. When the grill pan is hot a drop of water will skitter in the pan. When ready to cook, lightly oil the ridges of the grill pan. Place the cheese slices in the hot grill pan. The cheese will be done after cooking 2 to 4 minutes per side.

BUILT-IN GRILL: Preheat the grill to high, then, if it does not have a nonstick surface, brush and oil the grill grate. Place the cheese slices on the hot grate. The cheese will be done after cooking 2 to 4 minutes per side. Take care to remove it from the grate before the cheese melts into the grill.

FREESTANDING GRILL: Preheat the grill to high; there's no need to oil the grate. Place the cheese slices on the hot grill. The cheese will be done after cooking 2 to 4 minutes per side.

FIREPLACE GRILL: Rake red hot embers under the gridiron and preheat it for 3 to 5 minutes; you want a hot, 2 to 3 Mississippi fire. When ready to cook, brush and oil the gridiron. Place the cheese slices on the hot grate. The cheese will be done after cooking 2 to 4 minutes per side. Take care to remove it from the grate before the cheese melts onto the embers.

2 thick slices provoleta or Provolone
(each about ¾ inches thick and
8 ounces)

1 tablespoon extra-virgin olive oil

2 teaspoons cracked black peppercorns

2 teaspoons dried oregano

Crusty bread or bruschetta (page 280),
for serving

1. Brush each slice of cheese on both sides with 1½ teaspoons of the olive oil and sprinkle ½ teaspoon of cracked pepper and oregano on each side of the slices.

2. Cook the cheese slices, following the instructions for any of the grills in the box on the facing page, until they are browned and partially melted. The idea is to grill the cheese enough so that the exterior is brown but not so much that the slices melt into gooey puddles.

3. Transfer the grilled cheese to a platter or plates and serve with bread.

cypriot grilled cheese flambéed with ouzo

"The cheese that grills" is the slogan of the Pittas Dairy Industries of Cyprus, and their salty, bone-white Halloumi is indeed perfect for grilling, possessing a firm, tooth-squeaking texture that can face down the heat of the fire and a dousing with flaming brandy. I cut the brandy with an anise-flavored liquor called ouzo in Greece and raki in Turkey. I love the way the sweet licorice taste of the spirit complements the salty, minty cheese. Best of all, flambéing the cheese is dramatic, to say the least. **SERVES 4**

8 ounces Halloumi, cut crosswise
into ¹/₂-inch-thick slices
Olive oil
Freshly ground black pepper
3 tablespoons ouzo or other
anise-flavored spirit
3 tablespoons Metaxa or brandy
Crusty bread or bruschetta (page 280),
for serving

1. Lightly brush each slice of cheese on both sides with olive oil and season both sides with pepper.

2. Place the ouzo and Metaxa in a small bowl and stir to mix.

3. Cook the cheese slices, following the instructions for any of the grills in the box at left, until they are sizzling.

4. Transfer the grilled cheese to a platter. Warm the ouzo and Metaxa in a small saucepan over low heat (don't let it boil or you'll cook off the alcohol). Remove the saucepan from the heat and, working away from anything flammable and making sure that your sleeves are rolled up and your hair is tied back, ignite the warm ouzo mixture with a long kitchen match, then carefully pour the flaming liquid over the cheese. Serve the cheese as soon as the flames go out.

if you have a...

CONTACT GRILL: Preheat the grill; if your contact grill has a temperature control, preheat the grill to high. Place the drip pan under the front of the grill. When ready to cook, lightly oil the grill surface. Place the cheese slices on the hot grill, then close the lid. The cheese will be sizzling and lightly browned after cooking 2 to 4 minutes.

GRILL PAN: Place the grill pan on the stove and preheat it to medium-high over medium heat. When the grill pan is hot a drop of water will skitter in the pan. When ready to cook, lightly oil the ridges of the grill pan. Place the cheese slices in the hot grill pan so that they are on a diagonal to the ridges. The cheese will be sizzling and lined with dark grill marks after cooking 2 to 4 minutes per side. You can flambé the ouzo and Metaxa right in the grill pan.

BUILT-IN GRILL: Preheat the grill to high, then, if it does not have a nonstick surface, brush and oil the grill grate. Place the cheese slices on the hot grate. The cheese will be sizzling and lightly browned after cooking 2 to 4 minutes per side. Take care to remove it from the grate before the cheese melts into the grill.

FREESTANDING GRILL: Preheat the grill to high; there's no need to oil the grate. Place the cheese slices on the hot grill. The cheese will be done after cooking 3 to 5 minutes per side.

FIREPLACE GRILL: Rake red hot embers under the gridiron and preheat it for 3 to 5 minutes; you want a hot, 2 to 3 Mississippi fire. When ready to cook, brush and oil the gridiron. Place the cheese slices on the hot grate. The cheese will be done after cooking 2 to 4 minutes per side. Take care to remove it from the grate before the cheese melts onto the embers.

NOTES:
■ Halloumi is available at Lebanese, Greek, Turkish, and Middle Eastern markets. You may notice green flecks in the cheese; these are bits of the mint leaves that are traditionally added as a flavoring. If Halloumi is unavailable, you can use the similar Greek cheese kasseri.

■ To flambé the cheese I'm calling for equal parts ouzo and the Greek brandy Metaxa. If you can't find these spirits, flambé the cheese with straight brandy, Cognac, or even vodka.

chicken scallion yakitori

Yakitori is more than one of Japan's most popular snacks, it's a veritable way of life. Each afternoon after work, Tokyo's thousands of yakitori parlors fill up with tens of thousands of office workers, who stop by for a quick snack of tiny grilled chicken kebabs before starting the long commute home. Yakitori parlors range from rough-and-tumble joints to chic restaurants that are nearly impossible to get into. Traditionally, yakitori are grilled plain to start with, then dipped in a dark, syrupy, sweet-salty sauce called *tare* halfway through the cooking process to give them a lacquered finish. The sauce is boiled, replenished with fresh ingredients as needed, and reused the next day. Some yakitori sauces go back years, even decades, and each freshly dipped chicken kebab adds more flavor. **MAKES ABOUT 20**

tip

To keep the sauce going at home, boil it for 3 minutes when you've finished grilling. Let the sauce cool to room temperature, then refrigerate it until the next time you want to use it. Add more soy sauce, mirin, sake, sugar, and honey as needed in the proportions you'll find here and cook as described in Step 3 on page 32.

THE RECIPE

FOR THE YAKITORI:
2 pounds chicken thighs (see Notes)
1 bunch scallions, both white and
    green parts, trimmed
Coarse salt (kosher or sea)

FOR THE SAUCE:
2 cups soy sauce
2 cups mirin (Japanese sweet rice wine)
1 cup sake
6 tablespoons sugar, or more to taste
2 tablespoons honey

YOU'LL ALSO NEED:
About 20 bamboo skewers
    (about 8 inches long)

if you have a . . .

CONTACT GRILL: Preheat the grill; if your contact grill has a temperature control, preheat the grill to high. Place the drip pan under the front of the grill. When ready to cook, lightly oil the grill surface. Place the yakitori on the hot grill, then close the lid. The yakitori will be done after cooking 2 to 4 minutes.

GRILL PAN: I generally don't like to cook foods that have syrupy glazes in a grill pan—the glaze tends to burn on the bottom of the pan. However, if you dip the yakitori in the sauce only briefly and let the excess sauce drain off, you can cook them in a grill pan. Place the grill pan on the stove and preheat it to medium-high over medium heat. When the grill pan is hot a drop of water will skitter in the pan. When ready to cook, lightly oil the ridges of the grill pan. Place the yakitori in the hot grill pan. They will be done after cooking 2 to 3 minutes per side. After it has cooled down, soak the grill pan in hot water to loosen any burnt-on sauce.

BUILT-IN GRILL: Preheat the grill to high, then, if it does not have a nonstick surface, brush and oil the grill grate. Arrange the yakitori on the hot grill so that the exposed ends of the skewers extend off the grate. The yakitori will be done after cooking 2 to 3 minutes per side.

FREESTANDING GRILL: Preheat the grill to high; there's no need to oil the grate. Place the yakitori on the hot grill. They will be done after cooking 3 to 5 minutes per side.

FIREPLACE GRILL: Rake red hot embers under the gridiron and preheat it for 3 to 5 minutes; you want a hot, 2 to 3 Mississippi fire. Make an aluminum foil shield for the skewers by folding an 18-by-12-inch piece of heavy-duty aluminum foil into thirds like a business letter. When ready to cook, brush and oil the gridiron. Place the aluminum foil shield at the edge of the grate. Arrange the yakitori on the grate so that they are over the fire but the exposed ends of the skewers are on the foil shield. The yakitori will be done after cooking 2 to 3 minutes per side.

1. Make the yakitori: Rinse the chicken thighs under cold running water and blot them dry with paper towels. Remove the skin from the chicken thighs (if you like, set aside the skin to skewer and grill as chicken skin yakitori). Using a sharp knife, cut the meat off the bones in pieces as large as possible. Set aside the bones.

Cut the chicken into pieces that are roughly 1½ inches long and ½ inch wide and thick.

2. Cut the scallions crosswise into 1½-inch pieces. Skewer 3 pieces of chicken and 2 pieces of scallion on a bamboo skewer, alternating pieces of chicken and scallion. Repeat with the remaining chicken and scallions. Refrigerate the yakitori, covered, until ready to cook.

3. Make the sauce: Place the soy sauce, mirin, sake, sugar, and honey in a deep, heavy, nonreactive saucepan over medium-high heat and stir to mix. Add the chicken bones. Gradually bring the sauce to a boil, stirring with a wooden spoon. Taste for sweetness, adding more sugar as necessary. Reduce the heat to medium and let the sauce simmer until thick and syrupy, 10 to 15 minutes; it should be the consistency of heavy cream. Remove the saucepan from the heat and let the sauce cool slightly. Set some of the sauce aside to use in Step 5.

4. Season the yakitori with salt, then cook them, following the instructions for any of the grills in the box at left, until they begin to brown, about 1½ minutes on a contact grill, 1½ minutes per side on any of the other indoor grills. Dip each yakitori in the sauce, then return it to the grill and continue cooking until the chicken is golden brown and cooked through. You may need to cook the yakitori in more than one batch; transfer the cooked yakitori to a platter and cover them loosely with aluminum foil to keep warm until all are done.

5. Dip the yakitori in the reserved sauce, then arrange them on a platter. Serve at once.

NOTES:

■ The Japanese prefer to make yakitori with chicken thighs—the meat has a richer flavor than breast meat and more fat, which keeps it from drying out as it grills. If you prefer white meat, this is a great way to use chicken tenders.

■ It's a little more work, but you'll get even more flavor if you grill the chicken bones before adding them to the yakitori sauce. Preheat the grill to medium-high, then grill the thigh bones until golden brown, 4 to 6 minutes on a contact grill, 4 to 6 minutes per side on any of the other indoor grills.

chicken wings
with jamaican seasoning

Here's what Buffalo wings would taste like if they had been invented by a Jamaican. The Tabasco sauce of conventional Buffalo wings gives way to jerk seasoning—a paste of garlic, thyme, allspice, and many other aromatics made fiery by incendiary Scotch bonnet chiles. Jerk is believed to have originated with the Maroons, runaway slaves of the seventeenth and eighteenth centuries, who used the strong seasoning to preserve meats in their mountain hideouts. I've given a range of Scotch bonnet chiles: Two will give you moderately hot wings; four would be more typical of the way they do it in Jamaica. **MAKES 12**

tip

You'll find instructions for cooking wings in a rotisserie on the facing page.

2 to 4 Scotch bonnet chiles, stemmed and
seeded (for hotter wings, leave the seeds in)

1 small onion, coarsely chopped (about 1/2 cup)

4 scallions, both white and green parts,
trimmed and coarsely chopped

3 cloves garlic, coarsely chopped

1 piece (1 inch) fresh ginger, peeled and
coarsely chopped

1 tablespoon brown sugar

1 tablespoon coarse salt (kosher or sea)

1 tablespoon fresh thyme leaves,
or 1 teaspoon dried thyme

1/2 teaspoon ground allspice

1/2 teaspoon freshly ground black pepper

1/4 teaspoon ground nutmeg

1/4 teaspoon ground cinnamon

3 tablespoons vegetable oil

2 tablespoons fresh lime juice

1 tablespoon soy sauce

12 whole chicken wings (about 2 pounds)

Peppa Cream Sauce (recipe follows)

1. Place the chiles, onion, scallions, garlic, ginger, brown sugar, salt, thyme, allspice, pepper, nutmeg, and cinnamon in a food processor and finely chop, running the machine in short bursts. Gradually add the oil, lime juice, and soy sauce. Transfer the jerk seasoning to a nonreactive mixing bowl.

2. Rinse the chicken wings under cold running water and blot them dry with paper towels. Cut the tips off the wings and discard them. Cut each wing into 2 pieces through the joint. Add the chicken wings to the jerk seasoning and stir to coat evenly. Let the wings marinate in the refrigerator, covered, for at least 6 hours, preferably overnight.

3. Drain the chicken wings and discard the marinade. Cook the wings, following the instructions for any of the grills in the box at left, until the skin is browned and crisp and the meat is cooked through. To test for doneness, make a tiny cut in the thickest part of one of the larger wing halves: There should be no trace of red at the bone.

4. Transfer the wings to a platter or plates and serve at once with the Peppa Cream Sauce for dipping.

peppa cream sauce

Tamarind is a tropical seed pod with a pulp that's sweet and smoky, like a good prune, and agreeably sour, like fresh lime. If you live in an area with a

if you have a...

CONTACT GRILL: Preheat the grill; if your contact grill has a temperature control, preheat the grill to high. Place the drip pan under the front of the grill. When ready to cook, lightly oil the grill surface. Place the wings on the hot grill, then close the lid. The wings will be done after cooking 4 to 6 minutes.

BUILT-IN GRILL: Preheat the grill to medium-high, then, if it does not have a nonstick surface, brush and oil the grill grate. Place the wings on the hot grate. They will be done after cooking 6 to 8 minutes per side.

FREESTANDING GRILL: Preheat the grill to high; there's no need to oil the grate. Place the wings on the hot grill. The wings will be done after cooking 7 to 9 minutes per side.

FIREPLACE GRILL: Rake red hot embers under the gridiron and preheat it for 3 to 5 minutes; you want a medium-high, 4 Mississippi fire. When ready to cook, brush and oil the gridiron. Place the wings on the hot grate. To prevent flare-ups, don't crowd the grill. The wings will be done after cooking 6 to 8 minutes per side.

large West Indian, East Indian, or Hispanic community, you can probably find fresh tamarind pods or frozen pulp at an ethnic market. I've made this recipe really easy for you instead by calling for the Jamaican Pickapeppa sauce, which is made from tamarinds and is widely available. The sauce would be good served with any sort of grilled fish or poultry. **MAKES 1 CUP**

½ cup mayonnaise
¼ cup sour cream
¼ cup Pickapeppa sauce

Combine the mayonnaise, sour cream, and Pickapeppa sauce in a small nonreactive bowl and whisk to mix. The sauce can be refrigerated, covered, for up to 4 days. Let it come to room temperature before serving.

calgary hot wings

Barbecue without beer is, well, too depressing to contemplate, and I'm not just talking about to drink. Beer's malty sweetness and pleasantly bitter edge of hops make for an interesting marinade. These Calgary Hot Wings, were inspired by the Big Rock Brewery, in Calgary, Alberta, Canada. I taught a memorable cooking class at Big Rock—memorable not only for the impressive assortment of interesting beers on tap but also for the fact that it snowed 3 inches during my outdoor class, a first for this Miami-based grill guy. **MAKES 12**

THE RECIPE

12 whole chicken wings (about 2 pounds)
2 cups wheat beer
2 teaspoons coarse salt (kosher or sea)
1 teaspoon freshly ground black pepper
1 teaspoon sweet paprika
1 teaspoon chili powder
½ teaspoon celery seed
1 tablespoon extra-virgin olive oil

Cooking oil spray
4 tablespoons (½ stick) unsalted butter, melted
¼ cut Sriracha (Thai hot sauce)
½ cup Crystal hot sauce or Tabasco sauce
2 tablespoons chopped fresh cilantro or flat-leaf parsley (optional)

WINGS IN THE ROTISSERIE

It's easy to cook chicken wings in a rotisserie basket (on page 33 and this page you'll find recipes for chicken wings that can be cooked this way). Use a flat rotisserie basket, if possible, and arrange the wings in it so that nothing sticks out, then close the basket tightly. The basket will hold about a dozen whole chicken wings. Place the drip pan in the bottom of the rotisserie. Attach the basket to the rotisserie spit, attach the spit to the rotisserie, and turn on the motor. If your rotisserie has a temperature control, set it to 400°F. The wings will be golden brown and cooked through after spit-roasting for 30 to 40 minutes. To test for doneness, make a tiny cut in the thickest part of one of the larger wing halves: There should be no trace of red at the bone.

if you have a...

CONTACT GRILL: Preheat the grill; if your contact grill has a temperature control, preheat the grill to high. Place the drip pan under the front of the grill. When ready to cook, lightly oil the grill surface. Place the wings on the hot grill, then close the lid. The wings will be done after cooking 4 to 6 minutes.

BUILT-IN GRILL: Preheat the grill to medium-high, then, if it does not have a nonstick surface, brush and oil the grill grate. Place the wings on the hot grate. They will be done after cooking 6 to 8 minutes per side.

FREESTANDING GRILL: Preheat the grill to high; there's no need to oil the grate. Place the wings on the hot grill. The wings will be done after cooking 7 to 9 minutes per side.

FIREPLACE GRILL: Rake red hot embers under the gridiron and preheat it for 3 to 5 minutes; you want a medium-high, 4 Mississippi fire. When ready to cook, brush and oil the gridiron. Place the wings on the hot grate. To prevent flare-ups, don't crowd the grill. The wings will be done after cooking 6 to 8 minutes per side.

tip

You'll find instructions for cooking wings in a rotisserie on page 35.

1. Rinse the chicken wings under cold running water and blot them dry with paper towels. Cut the tips off the wings and discard them. Cut each wing into 2 pieces through the joint. Place the wings in a large nonreactive bowl or resealable plastic bag and add the beer. Let the wings marinate for 12 to 24 hours; the longer the wings marinate, the more pronounced the beer flavor will be.

2. Place the salt, pepper, paprika, chili powder, and celery seed in a small bowl and whisk to mix. Set the rub aside.

3. Drain the wings in a colander and blot them dry with paper towels, then place them in a large mixing bowl. Add the rub and toss to coat the wings evenly. Add the olive oil and toss well to mix.

4. Cook the wings, following the instructions for any of the grills in the box above, until the skin is browned and crisp and the meat is cooked through. To test for doneness, make a tiny cut in the thickest part of one of the larger wing halves: There should be no trace of red at the bone.

5. Transfer the wings to a clean shallow serving bowl. Pour the butter, Sriracha, and hot sauce over them and stir to mix. Sprinkle the cilantro over the wings, if desired, and serve at once. You'll need to provide plenty of napkins.

NOTES:

■ Big Rock Grill chef Klaus Wöckinger uses a wheat ale called Grasshopper. If you live in many parts of Canada, California, or the Northwest you'll probably be able to find Big Rock Grasshopper. Otherwise, use an imported or domestic wheat beer like Capital Brewery's Weizen Doppelbock or Celis White.

■ Sriracha is a sweet Thai hot sauce—think turbocharged ketchup, rather than tongue-blistering hot sauce. If you'd like sweeter wings, you can use sweet Thai chile sauce.

stove-top smoker

bayou wings

What would happen if a Cajun pit master reinvented the Buffalo wing? Pan-blackening spices would replace the traditional seasonings, and the wings might be cooked in a smoker. This has at least three advantages: It produces a crisp skin without deep-fat frying. The smoke adds an incredible depth of flavor. And you're looking at only about ten minutes of prep time. Sounds like a winner in my book. **MAKES 12**

tips

- Pan-blackening, a.k.a. Cajun spice, rub is easy to make from scratch (see page 364), but you can certainly use a good commercial brand instead.

- You can also smoke the chicken wings on the stove-top in a wok. You'll find instructions for doing this on page 234.

THE RECIPE

12 whole chicken wings (about 2 pounds)
3 tablespoons Cajun spice rub (see Tips)
Cooking oil spray (optional)
4 tablespoons (½ stick) unsalted butter
½ cup Crystal hot sauce or another
    Louisiana hot sauce

YOU'LL ALSO NEED:
1½ tablespoons hickory sawdust

1. Rinse the chicken wings under cold running water and blot them dry with paper towels. Cut the tips off the wings and discard them (or leave the tips on if you don't mind munching on a morsel that's mostly skin and bones). Cut each wing into 2 pieces through the joint closest to the body. Place the wings in a large bowl and sprinkle the rub over them, then toss to coat on all sides.

2. When ready to cook, set up the smoker (for instructions for using a stove-top smoker, see page 16). Place the sawdust in the center of the bottom of the smoker. Line the drip pan with aluminum foil and place it in the smoker. Lightly coat the smoker rack with cooking oil spray, or use a paper towel dipped in oil, and place the rack in the smoker. Arrange the wings on the rack at least ½ inch apart. Cover the smoker and place it over high heat for 3 minutes, then reduce the heat to medium. Smoke the wings until crisp, browned, and cooked through, about 20 minutes. To test for doneness, make a tiny cut in the thickest part of one of the larger wing halves: There should be no trace of red at the bone.

3. Meanwhile, melt the butter in a small saucepan over medium-high heat. Add the hot sauce and bring to a boil.

4. Transfer the wings to a serving bowl or platter. Pour the hot sauce mixture over the wings and stir until coated. Serve at once, with plenty of cold beer.

chicken liver yakitori

Birdland is an upscale yakitori bar in the glittering Ginza section of Tokyo. Its owner is Toshihiro Wada, a marquee chef who caters to an equally marquee clientele that includes the likes of chefs Joël Robuchon and Jamie Oliver. A spirit of cosmopolitanism has led Chef Wada to use Western ingredients like grilled cheese to jazz up traditional Japanese grilling. Just wait until you try his chicken liver yakitori, with a soy sauce and balsamic vinegar glaze. **MAKES 16**

if you have a...

CONTACT GRILL: Preheat the grill; if your contact grill has a temperature control, preheat the grill to high. Place the drip pan under the front of the grill. When ready to cook, lightly oil the grill surface. Place the chicken livers on the hot grill, then close the lid. The chicken livers will be done after cooking 2 to 3 minutes for medium. You will need to turn the chicken livers so that you can baste both sides.

GRILL PAN: Place the grill pan on the stove and preheat it to medium-high over medium heat. When the grill pan is hot a drop of water will skitter in the pan. When ready to cook, lightly oil the ridges of the grill pan. Place the chicken livers in the hot grill pan. They will be done after cooking about 2 minutes per side for medium. Use the glaze sparingly when basting, taking care not to drip a lot of glaze into the grill pan. After it has cooled down, soak the grill pan in hot water to loosen any burnt-on glaze.

BUILT-IN GRILL: Preheat the grill to high, then, if it does not have a nonstick surface, brush and oil the grill grate. Place the chicken livers on the hot grate. They will be done after cooking about 2 minutes per side for medium.

FREESTANDING GRILL: Preheat the grill to high; there's no need to oil the grate. Place the chicken livers on the hot grill. They will be done after cooking 3 to 5 minutes per side for medium.

FIREPLACE GRILL: Rake red hot embers under the gridiron and preheat it for 3 to 5 minutes; you want a hot, 2 to 3 Mississippi fire. When ready to cook, brush and oil the gridiron. Place the chicken livers on the hot grate. They will be done after cooking about 2 minutes per side for medium.

THE RECIPE

1/2 cup soy sauce
1/2 cup balsamic vinegar
16 chicken livers (about 1 pound)
Coarse (kosher or sea) salt and freshly ground white pepper

YOU'LL ALSO NEED:
16 bamboo skewers (about 8 inches long), for serving

1. Place the soy sauce and balsamic vinegar in a heavy saucepan over high heat and stir to mix. Bring to a boil, reduce the heat to medium-high, and let simmer briskly until thickened to the consistency of maple syrup, about 5 minutes, stirring with a wooden spoon. Remove the saucepan from the heat and set the balsamic soy glaze aside.

2. Trim any fat, sinews, or green spots off the chicken livers. Keep refrigerated, covered, until ready to grill.

3. Cook the chicken livers, following the instructions for any of the grills in the box on the facing page, until cooked to taste. To test for doneness, squeeze a chicken liver between your thumb and forefinger; it should be gently yielding, not soft and squishy. Turn the chicken livers over after they have cooked for 1 minute and baste them with the balsamic soy glaze. Baste each side once or twice more with the glaze.

4. Transfer the grilled chicken livers to a platter or plates and season them on both sides with salt and white pepper to taste. Stick a bamboo skewer in each chicken liver and serve at once.

tip

Wada grills chicken livers over a very hot fire and serves them quite rare in the center. Most indoor grills can't duplicate the searing heat of a Japanese yakitori grill, so the chicken livers will cook longer and turn out medium or medium-well. This is actually a plus, as most people I know tend to prefer their chicken livers thoroughly cooked through.

frikadeller
(grilled swedish meatballs)

Grilled meatballs show up all along the world's barbecue trail. Bulgaria has *kyutfte;* Yugoslavia its *cevapcici;* and Romania its garlicky *karnatzlach.* Of course, the Swedish also have meatballs—*frikadeller.* Grilling isn't the traditional cooking method, but the high dry heat of a grill can give the meat, a rich combination of veal and pork perfumed with dill and nutmeg, a sizzling, caramelized, flavorful crust. **MAKES 36 TO 40**

THE RECIPE

2 slices white bread, torn into 1-inch pieces
1/2 cup milk
12 ounces ground veal
12 ounces ground pork
1/2 medium-size onion, minced
1 tablespoon chopped fresh dill
1 1/2 teaspoons coarse salt (kosher or sea)
1/2 teaspoon freshly ground black pepper

1/2 teaspoon ground allspice
1/2 teaspoon ground nutmeg
1 large egg
Caper and Dill Sauce (recipe follows)

YOU'LL ALSO NEED:
36 to 40 small bamboo skewers
    (6 inches long), for serving

tip

This is a good place to use up stale bread; the mixture of bread and milk gives the meatballs a surprisingly light consistency.

1. Place the bread in a large mixing bowl and stir in the milk. Let the bread soak until it is very soft, about 5 minutes. Drain the bread in a strainer over the sink, then squeeze it with your fingers to extract as much liquid as possible. Return the bread to the mixing bowl.

2. Add the veal, pork, onion, dill, salt, pepper, allspice, nutmeg, and egg to the bowl with the bread. Stir with a wooden spoon until the mixture is well mixed. Refrigerate the meat mixture for 1 hour to make it easier to form the meatballs.

3. Spread plastic wrap over a large plate and place a bowl of water next to it. Wet your hands in the water, then pinch off a 1-inch piece of the meatball mixture and roll it into a ball. Place the meatball on the plate. Continue making meatballs until all of the meat mixture is used up. Wet your hands as needed to help form the meatballs. The *frikadeller* can be prepared up to 2 hours ahead to this stage. Cover them with plastic wrap and refrigerate until ready to grill.

4. Cook the *frikadeller* following the instructions for any of the grills in the box below, until browned on the outside and cooked through. Use the poke test to check for doneness: The meatballs should feel firm when pressed. You may need to cook the meatballs in batches.

5. Transfer the *frikadeller* to a platter or plates. Stick a bamboo skewer in each and serve with the Caper and Dill Sauce.

if you have a...

CONTACT GRILL: Preheat the grill; if your contact grill has a temperature control, preheat the grill to high. Place the drip pan under the front of the grill. When ready to cook, lightly oil the grill surface. Place the *frikadeller* on the hot grill, then close the lid. The *frikadeller* will be done after cooking 3 to 4 minutes.

GRILL PAN: Place the grill pan on the stove and preheat it to medium-high over medium heat. When the grill pan is hot a drop of water will skitter in the pan. When ready to cook, lightly oil the ridges of the grill pan. Place the *frikadeller* in the hot grill pan. They will be done after cooking 3 to 4 minutes per side (12 to 16 minutes in all).

BUILT-IN GRILL: Preheat the grill to high, then, if it does not have a nonstick surface, brush and oil the grill grate. Place the *frikadeller* on the hot grate. They will be done after cooking 3 to 4 minutes per side (12 to 16 minutes in all).

FREESTANDING GRILL: Preheat the grill to high; there's no need to oil the grate. Place the *frikadeller* on the hot grill. They will be done after cooking 4 to 5 minutes per side (16 to 20 minutes in all).

FIREPLACE GRILL: Rake red hot embers under the gridiron and preheat it for 3 to 5 minutes; you want a hot, 2 to 3 Mississippi fire. When ready to cook, brush and oil the gridiron. Lightly flatten the *frikadeller,* then place them on the hot grate. The meatballs will be done after cooking about 3 to 4 minutes per side (12 to 16 minutes in all).

caper and dill sauce

Here's a simple dill sauce to serve with the *frikadeller.* For a sweeter sauce in the Scandinavian style, substitute a tablespoon of light brown sugar for the capers. Either sauce would be great with grilled salmon or arctic char, too. **MAKES ABOUT 1 CUP**

1/3 cup mayonnaise

1/3 cup sour cream, or 1/3 cup more
    mayonnaise

1/3 cup Dijon mustard

2 tablespoons finely chopped fresh dill

1 tablespoon drained capers

Coarse salt (kosher or sea) and freshly
    ground black pepper

Place the mayonnaise, sour cream, mustard, dill, and capers in a nonreactive bowl and whisk to mix. Season with salt and pepper to taste. The sauce can be refrigerated, covered, for up to 3 days.

greek lamb meatballs
with yogurt dill sauce

Make *frikadeller* substituting lamb for the pork and Peloponnesian seasonings for the Scandinavian ones and you get grilled Greek meatballs, fragrant with dill and mint. Serve them with a yogurt dill sauce. For a more intense flavor, substitute an equal amount of ground lamb for the veal. **MAKES 36 TO 40**

tip

I've called for equal amounts of fresh mint and dill in this recipe. Both are typical Greek seasonings, but the meatballs will be equally tasty made with all fresh mint or dill or with 1 teaspoon each of dried mint and dill.

THE RECIPE

12 ounces ground lamb

12 ounces ground veal

3 scallions, both white and green parts,
    trimmed and finely chopped

1 to 2 cloves garlic, minced

2 tablespoons chopped fresh mint

2 tablespoons chopped fresh dill

1 1/2 teaspoons coarse salt
    (kosher or sea)

1/2 teaspoon freshly ground black pepper

Yogurt Dill Sauce (recipe follows)

YOU'LL ALSO NEED:

**36 to 40 small bamboo skewers
    (6 inches long), for serving**

1. Place the lamb, veal, scallions, garlic, mint, dill, salt, and pepper in a large mixing bowl. Stir with a wooden spoon until well mixed. If you are tech minded, you can also mix the meatballs in a food processor; run the machine in brief bursts. Refrigerate the meat mixture for 1 hour to make it easier to form the meatballs.

if you have a...

CONTACT GRILL: Preheat the grill; if your contact grill has a temperature control, preheat the grill to high. Place the drip pan under the front of the grill. When ready to cook, lightly oil the grill surface. Place the meatballs on the hot grill, then close the lid. The meatballs will be done after cooking 3 to 4 minutes.

GRILL PAN: Place the grill pan on the stove and preheat it to medium-high over medium heat. When the grill pan is hot a drop of water will skitter in the pan. When ready to cook, lightly oil the ridges of the grill pan. Place the meatballs in the hot grill pan. They will be done after cooking 3 to 4 minutes per side (12 to 16 minutes in all).

BUILT-IN GRILL: Preheat the grill to high, then, if it does not have a nonstick surface, brush and oil the grill grate. Place the meatballs on the hot grate. They will be done after cooking 3 to 4 minutes per side (12 to 16 minutes in all).

FREESTANDING GRILL: Preheat the grill to high; there's no need to oil the grate. Place the meatballs on the hot grill. They will be done after cooking 4 to 5 minutes per side (16 to 20 minutes in all).

FIREPLACE GRILL: Rake red hot embers under the gridiron and preheat it for 3 to 5 minutes; you want a hot, 2 to 3 Mississippi fire. When ready to cook, brush and oil the gridiron. Lightly flatten the meatballs, then place them on the hot grate. The meatballs will be done after cooking 3 to 4 minutes per side (12 to 16 minutes in all).

2. Spread plastic wrap over a large plate and place a bowl of water next to it. Wet your hands in the water, then pinch off a 1-inch piece of the meatball mixture and roll it into a ball. Gently flatten the meatball with your fingers. Place the meatball on the plate. Continue making meatballs until the meat mixture is used up. Wet your hands as needed to help form the meatballs. The meatballs can be prepared up to 2 hours ahead to this stage. Cover them with plastic wrap and refrigerate until ready to grill.

3. Cook the meatballs following the instructions for any of the grills in the box above, until browned on the outside and cooked through. Use the poke test to check for doneness: The meatballs should feel firm when pressed. You may need to cook the meatballs in batches.

4. Transfer the meatballs to a platter or plates. Stick a bamboo skewer in each and serve with the Yogurt Dill Sauce.

yogurt dill sauce

This is just one of the dozens, perhaps hundreds, of yogurt-based sauces that are served throughout the world. You can spice the sauce up by adding cumin or coriander seed, chopped chile peppers, or cilantro. Or add diced cucumber and tomatoes and turn it into a salad that's great on pita bread with the meatballs. **MAKES ABOUT 1 CUP**

1 large clove garlic, minced
1/2 teaspoon coarse salt (kosher or sea), or more to taste
1 cup whole-milk yogurt
1 tablespoon fresh lemon juice
1 scallion, both white and green parts, trimmed and finely chopped
2 tablespoons chopped fresh dill, or 1 tablespoon each fresh dill and mint
1/4 teaspoon freshly ground black pepper, or more to taste

Place the garlic and salt in a nonreactive mixing bowl and mash to a paste with the back of a wooden spoon. Add the yogurt, lemon juice, scallion, dill, and pepper and stir to mix. Taste for seasoning, adding more salt and/or pepper as necessary. The sauce can be refrigerated, covered, for several days.

fireplace grill

fired-up beef carpaccio

Carpaccio is raw beef sliced paper-thin, and dressed with Jackson Pollock–esque squiggles of a mayonnaise sauce. It was created in 1950 by the legendary Venetian restaurateur Giuseppe Cipriani for a countess on a diet of raw foods. (The blood-red meat and ghostly white sauce recalled the colors favored by the Venetian Renaissance painter Vittore Carpaccio.) My philosophy is that if something tastes good baked, broiled, fried, or sautéed—or for that matter, raw—it will probably taste even better grilled (briefly). So here's a carpaccio with a whiff of fire and wood smoke. It has the added advantage of appealing to people who don't care for raw beef. **SERVES 4**

tip

The beef will be easier to slice if it has been refrigerated. You can grill it up to one day ahead.

THE RECIPE

1 pound trimmed beef tenderloin (see Notes)
Coarse salt (kosher or sea) and cracked
    black peppercorns
1 tablespoon extra-virgin olive oil
1/2 cup mayonnaise
1 tablespoon Dijon mustard
1/2 teaspoon finely grated lemon zest
2 teaspoons fresh lemon juice, or more
    to taste
1 teaspoon Worcestershire sauce
Freshly ground white pepper
1 tablespoon chopped fresh chives
    (optional)

YOU'LL ALSO NEED:
Squirt bottle (optional)

1. Light wood in the fireplace and let it burn down to glowing embers (for instructions for grilling in a fireplace, see page 12). Rake a layer of embers into the center of the fireplace, then place the gridiron over them and preheat it for 3 to 5 minutes. You want a hot, 2 to 3 Mississippi fire.

2. Generously season the beef on all sides with salt and peppercorns. Drizzle the olive oil all over the meat and rub the oil and seasonings onto it.

3. When ready to cook, brush and oil the grill grate and place the meat on top. Grill the beef until the outside is charred but the inside remains raw, 1 to 2 minutes per side (4 to 8 minutes in all). Transfer the beef to a plate to cool to room temperature, then chill in the freezer until very cold but not frozen, about 1 hour.

4. Meanwhile, place the mayonnaise in a nonreactive bowl. Add the mustard, lemon zest, lemon juice, and Worcestershire sauce and whisk to mix. Season with salt and white pepper to taste; the sauce should be highly seasoned. Transfer the sauce to a squirt bottle, if desired.

5. Using the sharpest possible knife, slice the beef crosswise against the grain into the thinnest possible slices. Use these to cover 4 ice-cold plates. If using a squirt bottle, squirt the sauce over the meat in decorative squiggles or, using a spoon, drizzle it over the meat. Sprinkle the meat with the chives, if using, and serve at once.

NOTES:

■ You want to use the very best quality meat you can find, since you will be serving it virtually raw. It should be cut from the middle of the tenderloin and all fat should be meticulously trimmed off.

■ Although you won't get the smoke flavor that comes from grilling in the fireplace, you can sear the carpaccio in a grill pan or on a built-in grill (most contact grills don't get hot enough to sear the beef). Cook the tenderloin for 1 to 2 minutes per side (4 to 8 minutes in all).

tip

If you live in south Florida and you know someone with an airboat, you may be able to get a hold of fresh frogs' legs, in which case you won't need to go to heaven when you die, for you'll already have experienced paradise on earth. Barring that, you can buy frogs' legs at a butcher shop, fishmonger, or specialty food store, but try to find the Florida variety, not imported ones. In a pinch, this recipe could be made with 2 pounds of chicken drumsticks.

willy d.'s spice-grilled frogs' legs

The last time I saw Willy D. and Alex P. they were all abuzz about a nocturnal frogging expedition. Seems their boss owns an airboat and makes weekly forays into the wide expanse of swamp and saw grass known as the Everglades. Their quest—besides the general joviality of a night on the water—was the sweetest, meatiest frogs' legs ever tasted, veritable drumsticks that are vastly superior to the puny European variety. Frogs' legs are usually fried, but grilling imparts a seared flavor you just can't achieve with cornmeal and oil. **SERVES 4**

THE RECIPE

2 pounds frogs' legs, thawed if frozen

1 tablespoon hickory-smoked salt
   (see Note)

2 teaspoons freshly ground black pepper

1 teaspoon garlic powder

$1/2$ teaspoon cayenne pepper

3 tablespoons salted butter

3 tablespoons olive oil

3 cloves garlic, minced

5 tablespoons chopped fresh
   flat-leaf parsley

Lemon wedges, for serving

1. Rinse the frogs' legs under cold running water, then blot them dry with paper towels.

2. Place the hickory-smoked salt, black pepper, garlic powder, and cayenne in a small bowl and whisk to mix. Season the frogs' legs all over with this rub.

3. Melt the butter in a small saucepan over medium heat. Add the olive oil, garlic, and 3 tablespoons of the parsley and cook until the garlic has lost its rawness, about 2 minutes. Do not let the garlic brown. Remove the saucepan from the heat and lightly brush the frogs' legs on both sides with some of the garlic mixture.

4. Cook the frogs' legs, following the instructions for any of the grills in the box at right, until golden brown and cooked through, basting them once or twice more with the garlic butter.

5. Transfer the frogs' legs to a platter or plates and pour any remaining garlic butter over them. Sprinkle the remaining 2 tablespoons of parsley over the frogs' legs and serve at once, with lemon wedges.

NOTE: Hickory-smoked salt is available in most supermarkets.

if you have a...

CONTACT GRILL: Preheat the grill; if your contact grill has a temperature control, preheat the grill to high. Place the drip pan under the front of the grill. When ready to cook, lightly oil the grill surface. Place the frogs' legs on the hot grill, then close the lid. The frogs' legs will be done after cooking 3 to 4 minutes.

GRILL PAN: Place the grill pan on the stove and preheat it to medium-high over medium heat. When the grill pan is hot a drop of water will skitter in the pan. When ready to cook, lightly oil the ridges of the grill pan. Place the frogs' legs in the hot grill pan. They will be done after cooking 3 to 5 minutes per side.

BUILT-IN GRILL: Preheat the grill to high, then, if it does not have a nonstick surface, brush and oil the grill grate. Place the frogs' legs on the hot grate. They will be done after cooking 3 to 5 minutes per side.

FREESTANDING GRILL: Preheat the grill to high; there's no need to oil the grate. Place the frogs' legs on the hot grill. They will be done after cooking 4 to 6 minutes per side.

FIREPLACE GRILL: Rake red hot embers under the gridiron and preheat it for 3 to 5 minutes; you want a hot, 2 to 3 Mississippi fire. When ready to cook, brush and oil the gridiron. Place the frogs' legs on the hot grate. They will be done after cooking 3 to 5 minutes per side.

chile-rubbed shrimp
with avocado corn cocktail

I've never quite understood the appeal of the traditional shrimp cocktail. I mean, what could be less interesting than cold boiled shrimp dipped in a lackluster mixture of ketchup and prepared horseradish? Here's a shrimp cocktail with gumption, featuring chile-rubbed, grill-seared shrimp served over a colorful, chunky salsa of avocado and sweet corn. You can chill the grilled shrimp before you serve them, but I like the contrast of hot shrimp and cool salsa. **SERVES 4**

tips

■ The traditional way to devein shrimp is to make a V-shaped cut that runs the length of the back. The advantage of this method is that the shrimp opens up like a butterfly as it grills. A quicker way to devein is to insert the tine of a fork in the back of a shrimp about ¼ inch deep to snag the vein, then slowly and gently pull it out.

■ For a striking presentation, spoon the salsa into oversize martini glasses and drape the shrimp over the side of the glass.

THE RECIPE

16 jumbo shrimp (about 1½ pounds),
    peeled and deveined
1 tablespoon ancho chile powder
1½ teaspoons garlic salt
1 teaspoon ground coriander
1 teaspoon dried oregano
½ teaspoon ground cumin
½ teaspoon freshly ground black pepper
2 tablespoons extra-virgin olive oil
Avocado and Corn Salsa (recipe follows)

1. Rinse the shrimp under cold running water, then blot them dry with paper towels.

2. Place the chile powder, garlic salt, coriander, oregano, cumin, and pepper in a mixing bowl and whisk to mix. Add the shrimp and toss to coat. Stir in the olive oil. Let the shrimp marinate in the refrigerator, covered, for 30 minutes to 1 hour.

3. Cook the shrimp, following the instructions for any of the grills in the box on the facing page, until just cooked through. When done the shrimp will turn pinkish white and will feel firm to the touch.

4. Spoon the Avocado and Corn Salsa into 4 large martini glasses or serving bowls. Drape 4 of the hot shrimp over the edge of each glass or bowl and serve at once. Or for a cold shrimp cocktail, let the cooked shrimp cool to room temperature. Refrigerate the shrimp, covered, until they are chilled before serving them with the salsa. The cooked shrimp can be refrigerated for up to 2 days.

avocado and corn salsa

A salsa this simple lives or dies by the quality of the ingredients—ripe avocado, luscious tomato, and a sweet, crunchy ear of corn. Most of my corn salsa recipes call for grilled corn. This one features the succulent crunch of raw corn to reinforce the sweetness of the fresh avocado. **MAKES 2 TO 3 CUPS**

1 ripe avocado, cut into ¼-inch dice

2 to 3 tablespoons fresh lime juice

1 ripe red tomato, seeded and cut into
   ¼-inch dice

1 ear sweet corn, shucked

1 scallion, both white and green
   parts, trimmed and finely chopped,
   or 3 tablespoons diced sweet
   onion

1 to 2 jalapeño peppers or serrano
   peppers, seeded and minced
   (for a hotter salsa, leave the seeds in)

¼ cup chopped fresh cilantro

Coarse salt (kosher or sea) and freshly
   ground black pepper

1. Place the avocado in the bottom of a nonreactive mixing bowl and gently toss it with 2 tablespoons of the lime juice. Spoon the tomato on top of the avocado.

2. Cut the kernels off the corn. The easiest way to do this is to lay the cob flat on a cutting board and remove the kernels using lengthwise strokes of a chef's knife. Add the corn kernels to the mixing bowl. The salsa can be prepared to this stage up to 2 hours ahead. Refrigerate it, covered.

if you have a...

CONTACT GRILL: Preheat the grill; if your contact grill has a temperature control, preheat the grill to high. Place the drip pan under the front of the grill. When ready to cook, lightly oil the grill surface. Place the marinated shrimp on the hot grill, then close the lid. The shrimp will be done after cooking 1 to 3 minutes.

GRILL PAN: Place the grill pan on the stove and preheat it to high over medium heat. When the grill pan is hot a drop of water will skitter in the pan. When ready to cook, lightly oil the ridges of the grill pan. Place the marinated shrimp in the hot grill pan. They will be done after cooking 1 to 3 minutes per side.

BUILT-IN GRILL: Preheat the grill to high, then, if it does not have a nonstick surface, brush and oil the grill grate. Place the marinated shrimp on the hot grate. They will be done after cooking 1 to 3 minutes per side.

FREESTANDING GRILL: Preheat the grill to high; there's no need to oil the grate. Place the marinated shrimp on the hot grill. They will be done after cooking 2 to 4 minutes per side.

FIREPLACE GRILL: Rake red hot embers under the gridiron and preheat it for 3 to 5 minutes; you want a hot, 2 to 3 Mississippi fire. When ready to cook, brush and oil the gridiron. Place the marinated shrimp on the hot grate. They will be done after cooking 1 to 3 minutes per side.

3. Just before serving, add the jalapeño(s) and cilantro to the mixing bowl and gently toss to mix. Taste for seasoning, adding more lime juice as necessary and season with salt and pepper to taste; the salsa should be highly seasoned.

NOTE: To determine the ripeness of an avocado, give it the "Charmin test"; the flesh should be gently yielding when the sides are squeezed.

stove-top smoker

smoked shrimp cocktail
with horseradish cream

Shrimp has a natural affinity for smoke, a fact appreciated by anyone who has sampled boiled shrimp and smokies (smoked sausage) in the Florida Keys or on the Gulf Coast. And smoked foods have an affinity for horseradish, which appears here in a pugnacious cream sauce. In this recipe, wood smoke gives the shellfish a complex and evocative flavor. The seasonings—salt and a homemade lemon pepper rub—are deliberately simple to keep the focus on the smoky shrimp.

SERVES 4

THE RECIPE

FOR THE SHRIMP AND RUB:
2 strips lemon zest (each about 1/2 by
    2 inches), coarsely chopped
2 teaspoons black peppercorns
2 teaspoons coarse salt (kosher or sea)
1 to 1 1/2 pounds jumbo shrimp, peeled and
    deveined (see Tips on page 46)
2 teaspoons vegetable oil
Cooking oil spray (optional)

FOR THE HORSERADISH CREAM:
1 piece (2 inches; about 2 ounces) fresh
    horseradish root, peeled, or 2 to 3
    tablespoons prepared white horseradish
2/3 cup mayonnaise
1/3 cup sour cream
1/2 teaspoon finely grated lemon zest

2 teaspoons fresh lemon juice
Coarse salt (kosher or sea) and freshly
    ground black pepper

YOU'LL ALSO NEED:
1 tablespoon sawdust

1. Make the rub: Place the lemon zest, peppercorns, and salt in a spice mill or clean coffee grinder and grind to a coarse powder, running the machine in short bursts (you can also make the rub in a mortar using a pestle).

2. Rinse the shrimp under cold running water, then blot dry with paper towels. Place the shrimp and rub in a large mixing bowl and toss to mix. Add the vegetable oil and stir to coat. Let the shrimp marinate in the refrigerator, covered, for 30 minutes to 1 hour.

3. When ready to cook, set up the smoker (for instructions for using a stove-top smoker, see page 16). Place the sawdust in the center of the bottom of the smoker. Line the drip pan with aluminum foil and place the rack in the smoker. Lightly coat the wire rack with cooking oil spray, or use a paper towel dipped in oil, and place the rack in the smoker. Arrange the marinated shrimp on the rack at least ¼ inch apart. Cover the smoker and place it over high heat for 3 minutes, then reduce the heat to medium. Smoke the shrimp until cooked

through, 10 to 12 minutes. When done, the shrimp will turn a pinkish white and will feel firm to the touch. Transfer the shrimp to a wire rack set over a plate to cool, then refrigerate, covered, until ready to serve.

4. Make the horseradish cream: If using fresh horseradish, finely grate it or chop it in a food processor fitted with a metal blade. (If using the food processor, cut the horseradish into ½-inch-thick slices before processing.) Whichever method you use, take care not to breathe the potent horseradish fumes. Transfer the horseradish to a nonreactive mixing bowl, add the mayonnaise, sour cream, lemon zest, and lemon juice and whisk to mix. Season with salt and pepper to taste.

5. To serve, spoon 2 to 3 tablespoons of the horseradish cream into the bottom of each of 4 martini glasses or small stylish bowls. Drape the smoked shrimp over the edge of the glasses or arrange them on a plate and serve with a bowl of the remaining horseradish cream alongside.

tips

- If you're in a hurry and want to use store-bought lemon pepper in the rub, add 1 teaspoon of it to the rub, omit the lemon zest, and reduce the peppercorns to 1 teaspoon.

- The zest is the oil-rich yellow outer rind of the lemon. Remove it in strips with a vegetable peeler, taking pains to leave behind the bitter white pith underneath it.

- For instructions for using a wok as a stove-top smoker, see page 234.

shiso-grilled shrimp rolls

This recipe was inspired by a classic Vietnamese appetizer—rolls of peppery, garlicky ground beef wrapped and grilled in fresh basil leaves. I've added a Japanese twist, using fresh shiso, an aromatic herb that's shaped a bit like the palm of your hand and has a vibrant flavor that's somewhere between fresh basil and mint (but more interesting and electric than either). And I've replaced the beef with ground shrimp in the style of a Japanese dumpling. It all may sound complicated, but the preparation time is less than fifteen minutes. **MAKES 16 TO 20**

THE RECIPE

1/2 pound shrimp, peeled, deveined (see Tips on page 46), and cut into 1/2-inch pieces (see Note)
2 cloves garlic, minced
2 teaspoons finely chopped peeled fresh ginger
2 teaspoons sugar, or more to taste

1 teaspoon freshly ground black pepper
1/4 teaspoon coarse salt (kosher or sea), or more to taste
1 tablespoon soy sauce
16 to 20 shiso leaves or large basil leaves

YOU'LL ALSO NEED:
4 metal skewers (10 to 12 inches long) or 8 to 10 small bamboo skewers (6 inches long)

if you have a...

CONTACT GRILL: Preheat the grill; if your contact grill has a temperature control, preheat the grill to high. Place the drip pan under the front of the grill. When ready to cook, lightly oil the grill surface. Place the shrimp rolls on the hot grill, then close the lid. The shrimp rolls will be done after cooking 2 to 3 minutes.

GRILL PAN: Place the grill pan on the stove and preheat it to medium-high over medium heat. When the grill pan is hot a drop of water will skitter in the pan. When ready to cook, lightly oil the ridges of the grill pan. Place the shrimp rolls in the hot grill pan. They will be done after cooking 2 to 3 minutes per side.

BUILT-IN GRILL: Preheat the grill to high, then, if it does not have a nonstick surface, brush and oil the grill grate. Arrange the shrimp rolls on the hot grill so that the exposed ends of the skewers extend off the grate. The shrimp rolls will be done after cooking 2 to 3 minutes per side.

FREESTANDING GRILL: Preheat the grill to high; there's no need to oil the grate. Place the shrimp rolls on the hot grill. They will be done after cooking 3 to 5 minutes per side.

FIREPLACE GRILL: Rake red hot embers under the gridiron and preheat it for 3 to 5 minutes; you want a hot, 2 to 3 Mississippi fire. When ready to cook, brush and oil the gridiron. Place the shrimp rolls on the hot grate. The shrimp rolls will be done after cooking 2 to 3 minutes per side.

1. Place the shrimp, garlic, ginger, sugar, pepper, salt, and soy sauce in a food processor and finely chop, running the machine in short bursts. Taste the shrimp mixture for seasoning by grilling or cooking a tiny patty in a nonstick skillet. Add more sugar and/or salt as necessary; the mixture should be both salty and sweet.

2. Mound 2 to 3 teaspoons of the shrimp mixture on a shiso leaf and, starting at the stem end, roll it into a compact cylinder. Repeat until all of the shrimp mixture is used up.

3. Skewer the rolls crosswise on bamboo skewers, 2 rolls to a skewer. The rolls can be prepared several hours ahead to this stage and refrigerated, covered.

4. Cook the shrimp rolls, following the instructions for any of the grills in the box on the facing page, until they are browned on the outside and cooked through (they'll be firm and hot to the touch), 2 to 4 minutes per side. Serve at once.

NOTES:

■ Since they're chopped up, the size of the shrimp doesn't matter. You can use medium-size or large shrimp—whichever is less expensive.

■ You could certainly make this recipe with ½ pound ground beef, chicken, or pork.

tip

Fresh shiso (also known as perilla or beefsteak leaf) is available at Japanese markets and many natural food stores. If you can't find it, you can use large fresh basil leaves.

stove-top smoker

smoked gazpacho

My interest (perhaps I should call it an obsession) in grilled and smoked soups was sparked almost the moment I acquired my first stove-top smoker, back when I was writing *Miami Spice*. (My very first smoked gazpacho appeared in that book.) Here's the latest version, made with smoked plum tomatoes, bell pepper, onion, and garlic. On a hot summer day, the curious juxtaposition of cool and smoky, of vegetable and oak, will take your breath away. The grilled garlic bread on page 281 would make a good accompaniment for the gazpacho. **SERVES 4**

THE RECIPE

Cooking oil spray (optional)

6 plum tomatoes (about 1¼ pounds), cut in half lengthwise

1 medium-size red bell pepper, cored, seeded, and quartered

1 medium-size cucumber, peeled, halved, and seeded

¼ large red onion

3 cloves garlic, peeled and skewered on a wooden toothpick

3 tablespoons extra-virgin olive oil

2 tablespoons red wine vinegar, or more to taste

Coarse salt (kosher or sea) and freshly ground black pepper

2 tablespoons finely chopped fresh chives or other fresh herb

YOU'LL ALSO NEED:

1½ tablespoons oak sawdust

tips

■ You want to add a light smoke flavor to the vegetables without cooking them through, hence the high heat for smoking. (You could also smoke the vegetables in a wok; there are instructions for doing this on page 234).

■ For a chunkier gazpacho, purée the soup in a food processor; for a smoother gazpacho, use a blender.

1. Set up the smoker (for instructions for using a stove-top smoker, see page 16). Place the sawdust in the center of the bottom of the smoker. Line the drip pan with aluminum foil and place it in the smoker. Lightly coat the wire rack with cooking oil spray, or use a paper towel dipped in oil, and place the rack in the smoker. Arrange the tomatoes, bell pepper, cucumber, and onion on the rack, cut sides up, then add the garlic. Cover the smoker and place it over high heat for 3 minutes, then reduce the heat to medium. Cook the vegetables until they are heavily smoked (they'll be coated with a light brown film) but still raw in the center, about 8 minutes.

2. Transfer the smoked vegetables to a cutting board and let cool to room temperature. Cut the vegetables into 1-inch pieces and place in a food processor or blender and purée to the desired consistency.

3. With the motor running, add 2 tablespoons of the olive oil, the wine vinegar, and enough water to make a thick but pourable soup. (you'll need between $1/2$ and 1 cup of water). Taste for seasoning, adding more vinegar as necessary, and salt and pepper to taste. If you're making the gazpacho in a blender, you can add all of the ingredients, and $1/2$ cup of water, to it at once; you may need to add a little more water to obtain a pourable consistency. The gazpacho can be prepared up to 8 hours ahead. Refrigerate the gazpacho until chilled before serving. Taste and add more vinegar and salt and pepper, if needed.

4. To serve, ladle the gazpacho into chilled bowls or glasses. Drizzle the remaining 1 tablespoon of olive oil on top and sprinkle with the chives.

In many places—Texas, Tuscany, and just about all of Argentina, to name a few—beef is the soul of barbecue. And grilling beef indoors is a widespread tradition. Think of English spit-roasted prime rib, French steak au poivre, or a rib steak smokily seared in the fireplace. While we're on the subject of smoke, did you know you can prepare pastrami and brisket in a stove-top smoker? Indoor grilling gives a whole new spin to beef and veal dishes, from Magyar beef rolls to Italian saltimbocca. And did I mention three sorts of beef ribs in the rotisserie?

beef

rotisserie

spit-roasted prime rib
with garlic and herbs

Prime rib is a guaranteed showstopper—expensive, impressive, and one of the tastiest roasts from the steer. It turns Saturday night into New Year's. What you may not realize is how unbelievably easy it is to make, especially on a rotisserie. This recipe features a fragrant paste of garlic, fresh herbs, and lemon zest. To make the roast even more flavorful, half of the paste goes in slits in the meat. **SERVES 4 TO 6**

tips

■ A full prime rib has seven ribs and tips the scales at 16 to 18 pounds. This recipe calls for a two-rib roast, which is small enough to fit in most countertop rotisseries but still large enough to make an impressive centerpiece.

■ You can also cook the meat on a fireplace rotisserie (see page 11). Trim off any excess fat before placing it in the spit. Cook over a hot, 2 to 3 Mississippi fire. It will take from 1 to 1¼ hours, depending on your fireplace.

■ For an awesome French dip sandwich, pile thinly sliced roast beef on a French roll or slice of bread, then dip the sandwich in the Garlic Jus.

THE RECIPE

FOR THE HERB PASTE:
4 cloves garlic, coarsely chopped
⅓ packed cup stemmed mixed fresh herbs,
    coarsely chopped
1 tablespoon coarse salt (kosher or sea)
1 tablespoon cracked black peppercorns
2 teaspoons finely grated fresh lemon zest
About 2 tablespoons extra-virgin olive oil

1 prime rib beef roast
    (2 ribs; 4 to 4½ pounds)
Garlic Jus (recipe follows)

1. Make the herb paste: Place the garlic, herbs, salt, peppercorns, and lemon zest in a mortar and, using the pestle, pound them to a coarse paste. Gradually work in the olive oil and pound to a smooth paste. Alternatively, place the garlic, herbs, salt, peppercorns, and lemon zest in a food processor and finely chop. Add enough olive oil to process to a smooth paste, scraping down the side of the bowl with a rubber spatula.

2. Using the tip of a paring knife, make small slits on all sides of the roast about ½ inch deep and 1½ inches apart. Using the tip of your index finger, widen the holes. Place a tiny spoonful of herb paste in each hole, forcing it in with your finger. This will use up about half of the herb paste. Spread the remaining herb paste over the roast on all sides. You can cook the roast right away, but it will have even more flavor if you let it marinate in the refrigerator, covered, for 1 to 2 hours.

3. When ready to cook, place the drip pan in the bottom of the rotisserie.

Skewer the roast on the rotisserie by inserting the spit between the ribs. Attach the spit to the rotisserie and turn on the motor. If your rotisseric has a temperature control, set it to 400°F (for instructions for using a rotisserie, see page 14).

4. Cook the roast until it is darkly browned on all sides and cooked to taste, 1¼ to 1½ hours for medium-rare. Use an instant-read meat thermometer to test for doneness; don't let the thermometer touch the spit or a bone. Medium-rare beef will have an internal temperature of 145°F. If your rotisserie has a pause button, after the roast has cooked for about 1 hour, stop the spit so that a flat side of the roast faces the heating element and let the meat brown for a few minutes. Then advance the spit until the other flat side faces the heating element and let it brown for a few minutes.

5. Transfer the roast to a platter or cutting board, remove the spit, and let the meat rest for about 10 minutes. Reserve the meat drippings for the sauce. To carve, cut the meat off the ribs, running your knife along the inside of the bones. Cut the 2 ribs apart and let people fight over them at the table (or keep them for yourself to gnaw on in the kitchen). Thinly slice the roast crosswise and serve with the Garlic Jus.

garlic jus

A *jus,* from the French word for juice, is nothing more than meat drippings enriched with a little veal or beef stock. This one is flavored with fragrant chips of fried garlic. It's heaven-sent with beef (for the best results, use homemade stock). **MAKES ABOUT 1½ CUPS**

**Drippings from the Spit-Roasted
     Prime Rib with Garlic and Herbs
     (facing page)**
6 cloves garlic, thinly sliced crosswise
**1 tablespoon finely chopped fresh rosemary
     or flat-leaf parsley**
**About 1 cup veal, beef, or chicken stock,
     or more as needed**
**Coarse salt (kosher or sea) and
     freshly ground black pepper**

1. Pour the drippings from the roast into a fat separator (see sidebar on page 178). Let stand for 5 minutes. Spoon 2 tablespoons of the beef fat from the top of the separator into a saucepan and place over medium heat. Add the garlic and rosemary and cook until lightly browned, stirring with a wooden spoon, 3 to 4 minutes. Do not let the garlic burn.

2. Pour the meat juices from the bottom of the fat separator through a strainer into a large measuring cup, stopping when the fat starts to come out. Add enough veal stock to obtain 1½ cups. Add the meat juice mixture to the saucepan. Increase the heat to high, bring to a boil, and let boil about 1 minute. Season with salt and pepper to taste.

THE PAUSE BUTTON

Countertop rotisseries are great for cooking cylindrical roasts, like leg of lamb, and whole chickens. But what about flat cuts of meat, like a two-bone rib roast? That's where the pause button found on rotisseries like the Showtime comes in. The pause button enables you to stop the rotation of the spit and expose a flat side of a roast to the heating element so it can brown. This turns the rotisserie into a sort of lateral broiler.

Simply wait for one side of the roast to line up with the heating element, then push the pause button. Generally 3 to 5 minutes per side is enough to achieve the requisite browned crust. Then, let the spit make a half turn to line up the other side of the roast with the heat and press the pause button again. This is best done toward the end of the cooking process, so you can control the degree of browning.

stove-top smoker

texas brisket indoors

OK, it may smack of heresy, especially if you're a Texan, but it *is* possible to make a credible—even delectable— Texas-style brisket indoors. The secret is to use a stove-stop smoker to lay on the smoke flavor, then slow roast the brisket in the oven until it's tender enough to cut with the side of a fork. Despite the general association of mesquite with Texas, the preferred wood for smoking brisket in the state is actually oak, what's called for here. If you like your brisket smoky and tender, with not one iota of sugar but plenty of spice, this one's just about as good as what comes off a pit. **SERVES 6 TO 8**

tip

The recipe calls for a piece of brisket cut from the "flat," the flat rectangular center portion. It's the part of the brisket most commonly sold at supermarkets. Most of the fat will probably have been trimmed off, but try to find a piece that has at least 1/8 inch. The fat melts during cooking, basting the meat and keeping it moist.

T H E   R E C I P E

1 tablespoon sweet paprika
2 teaspoons chili powder
2 teaspoons coarse salt (kosher or sea)
1 teaspoon freshly ground black pepper
1 teaspoon ground cumin
1/4 to 1/2 teaspoon cayenne pepper
1/4 teaspoon ground cinnamon
1 center-cut piece beef brisket
   (3 1/2 to 4 pounds)
Cooking oil spray (optional)
Texas Barbecue Sauce (recipe follows)

YOU'LL ALSO NEED:
3 tablespoons oak sawdust

1. Place the paprika, chili powder, salt, black pepper, cumin, cayenne, and cinnamon in a small bowl and whisk to mix.

2. Place the brisket on a baking sheet and sprinkle the rub over both sides, patting it onto the meat with your fingertips. You can smoke the brisket right away, but it will have even more flavor if you let it cure in the refrigerator, covered, for 2 to 4 hours before smoking.

3. When ready to cook, set up the smoker (for instructions for using a stove-top smoker, see page 16). Place the sawdust in the center of the bottom of the smoker. Line the drip pan with aluminum foil and place it in the smoker. Lightly coat the smoker rack with cooking oil spray, or use a paper towel dipped in oil, and place the rack in the smoker. Place the brisket, fat side up, on the rack. Cover the smoker and place the rack over high heat for 3 minutes, then reduce the heat to medium. Smoke the brisket until it has a good smoke flavor, about 30 minutes.

4. Meanwhile, preheat the oven to 275°F.

5. Spread out a large piece of heavy-duty aluminum foil shiny side down on a work surface. Place the brisket on the foil. Reserve any juices in the smoker drip pan for the Texas Barbecue Sauce. Tightly wrap the brisket in the foil, pleating the edges to make a tight seal. Place the foil-wrapped brisket on a baking sheet with the seam on top and bake until very tender, 2½ to 3 hours. When done the internal temperature will be about 190°F (unwrap one end of the brisket and insert an instant-read meat thermometer in the side of the brisket).

6. Transfer the brisket in the foil to a cutting board and carefully unwrap it. Pour the juices that have collected in the foil and those in the smoker drip pan into a fat separator (you'll have about 1¼ cups). Set the drippings aside for the Texas Barbecue Sauce. Rewrap the brisket and let it rest for about 10 minutes while you make the barbecue sauce.

7. Unwrap the brisket and add any additional juices to the barbecue sauce. Place the brisket on a cutting board and thinly slice it across the grain. Serve the barbecue sauce on the side, please; no self-respecting Texan would drown his brisket in barbecue sauce.

texas barbecue sauce

Texas barbecue sauce is more about what it isn't than what it is—not thick, not overly sweet, and not particularly complex. Traditional barbecue sauce in the Lone Star State is more of an afterthought, just meat drippings reddened with a little tomato sauce or ketchup. This sauce is a little more elaborate (just a little). It won't distract you from the flavor of the brisket, living proof of the adage that sometimes less *is* more.

MAKES ABOUT 2¼ CUPS

1 tablespoon butter
1 slice bacon, cut crosswise into
    ¼-inch slivers
1 small onion, finely chopped
Drippings from Texas Brisket Indoors
    (facing page)
½ to 1 cup beef or veal stock
    (preferably homemade)
⅓ cup ketchup or tomato sauce
2 tablespoons dark corn syrup,
    or more to taste
1 tablespoon fresh lemon juice,
    or more to taste
1 tablespoon distilled white vinegar
    or cider vinegar
2 teaspoons Worcestershire sauce
Coarse salt (kosher or sea) and freshly
    ground black pepper

1. Melt the butter in a saucepan over medium heat. Add the bacon and onion and cook until both are lightly browned, 4 to 5 minutes.

2. Pour the drippings into a fat separator. After the drippings have stood for at least 3 minutes, pour the meat juices from the bottom of the separator through a strainer into a 2-cup measuring cup, stopping when the fat starts to come out. Add enough beef stock to obtain 2 cups. Add the meat juice mixture to the bacon and onions, increase the heat to high, and bring to a brisk simmer.

3. Add the ketchup, corn syrup, lemon juice, vinegar, and Worcestershire sauce to the saucepan, bring to a simmer, and let the sauce cook until slightly thickened, 6 to 8 minutes. The sauce should remain fairly liquid and be thinner than conventional barbecue sauce, about the consistency of half-and-half. Season with salt and pepper to taste. If a sweeter sauce is desired, add a little more corn syrup. For a more tart sauce, add a little more lemon juice.

stove-top smoker

pastrami-style brisket

Pastrami is such a mainstay of American delicatessens that you may be surprised to learn it originated in central Asia, where it goes by the name of *pastirma* or *basturma*. Visit a market in Turkey or Aleppo, Syria, and you'll find long, fragrant orange strips of spice-crusted beef hanging from the rafters of market stalls. From the Near East, *basturma* migrated to eastern Europe, and from there to America. Somewhere along the way, it came to be made with brisket and, more important, it began to be smoked. For me, pastrami is less a particular dish than a process—curing meat, poultry, or even seafood with a pungent sweet-salty blend of aromatics, principally garlic, coriander, mustard, and pepper, and then smoking the cured meat over hardwood. **SERVES 6 TO 8**

tips

■ I've streamlined this pastrami recipe, making it practical for the indoor pit master by calling for a 3½- to 4-pound piece of brisket cut from the "flat" rather than a full 18-pound brisket. This is the cut and weight you're most likely to find at the supermarket.

■ You may be surprised by the color of the pastrami after it's smoked. It won't have a reddish hue like delicatessen pastramis. That color comes from the nitrates commercial meat processors use; this pastrami will taste just fine without them.

1 tablespoon coarse salt (kosher or sea)

1 tablespoon dark brown sugar

1 tablespoon sweet paprika

1¹/₂ teaspoons cracked black peppercorns

1¹/₂ teaspoons ground coriander

1 teaspoon ground ginger

1 teaspoon yellow mustard seeds

¹/₂ teaspoon ground mace (see Note)

3 cloves garlic, minced

1 center-cut piece beef brisket
   (3¹/₂ to 4 pounds; leave the fat on)

Cooking oil spray (optional)

YOU'LL ALSO NEED:

3 tablespoons oak or hickory sawdust

1. Place the salt, brown sugar, paprika, peppercorns, coriander, ginger, mustard seeds, mace, and garlic in a small bowl and whisk to mix. Set the rub aside.

2. Lightly score the brisket on both sides in a crosshatch pattern, making very shallow (¹/₁₆ inch deep) cuts about ¹/₄ inch apart (this helps the meat absorb the spices). Place the brisket on a baking sheet and sprinkle the rub over both sides, patting it onto the meat with your fingertips. Let the brisket cure in the refrigerator, covered, for 12 to 24 hours. You can also cure the brisket in a resealable plastic bag.

3. When ready to cook, set up the smoker (for instructions for using a stove-top smoker, see page 16). Place the sawdust in the center of the bottom of the smoker. Line the drip pan with aluminum foil and place it in the smoker. Lightly coat the smoker rack with cooking oil spray, or use a paper towel dipped in oil, and place the rack in the smoker. Place the brisket, fat side up, on the rack. Cover the smoker and place it over high heat for 3 minutes, then reduce the heat to medium. Smoke the brisket until it has a good smoke flavor, about 30 minutes.

4. Meanwhile, preheat the oven to 275°F.

5. Spread out a large piece of heavy-duty aluminum foil shiny side down on a work surface. Place the brisket on the foil. Tightly wrap the brisket in the foil, pleating the edges to make a tight seal. Place the foil-wrapped brisket on a baking sheet and bake until very tender, 2¹/₂ to 3 hours. When done the internal temperature of the brisket will be about 190°F (unwrap one end of the brisket and insert an instant-read meat thermometer in the side of the brisket).

6. Transfer the brisket in the foil to a cutting board and let it rest for 5 minutes. If you like your pastrami hot, unwrap the brisket and thinly slice it crosswise. If you prefer your pastrami cold, let it cool to room temperature, then refrigerate it until ready to serve.

NOTE: Mace is an orangish-brown spice that grows as a lacelike covering on the outer shell of nutmeg. You can use ¹/₂ teaspoon of ground nutmeg as a substitute.

VARIATIONS: Once you get the hang of making pastrami, just about any food is fair game, including turkey breast, salmon fillet, and tofu. Each of these is smaller and doesn't have as much fat as brisket, so you'll need to use less rub and add some canola oil to it. And, they'll be done right out of the smoker—you don't need to bake them, the way you do with brisket. Follow the instructions in Step 1 on page 59 for making the rub. The leftover rub will keep well in the refrigerator for several weeks and make a great seasoning for meats, poultry, even seafood.

To make turkey pastrami, start with a 1¹⁄₂- to 2-pound boneless turkey breast half. Make the rub as described in Step 1 on page 59. Mix about 2 tablespoons of the rub with 2 tablespoons of canola oil, spread this all over the turkey breast, and let it cure in the refrigerator, covered, for 6 to 12 hours. The turkey breast will be done after it smokes for 25 to 30 minutes; the internal temperature on an instant-read meat thermometer will be about 160°F when the turkey is fully cooked.

To make salmon pastrami, substitute a 1¹⁄₂-pound piece of skinless salmon fillet for the brisket. Run your fingers over the top of the salmon and, using tweezers or needle-nose pliers, pull out any bones you find, then rinse the salmon under cold running water and pat it dry with paper towels. Make the rub as described in Step 1 on page 59. Mix about 1¹⁄₂ tablespoons of the rub with 1¹⁄₂ tablespoons of canola oil, spread this all over the salmon, and let it cure in the refrigerator, covered, for 4 to 6 hours. The salmon will be done after it smokes for about 18 minutes.

To make tofu pastrami, use 2 pounds of extra-firm or firm tofu. Make the rub as described in Step 1 on page 59. Mix about 1¹⁄₂ tablespoons of the rub with 1¹⁄₂ tablespoons of canola oil, spread this all over the tofu, and let it cure in the refrigerator, covered, for 4 to 8 hours. The tofu will be done after it smokes for about 20 minutes.

tip

Finding a tri-tip can be a challenge. If you live in central or southern California, it will require nothing more than a trip to your local supermarket meat department. If you live elsewhere, you can special order it from your local butcher. Tri-tips are cut from the bottom sirloin. There's no exact substitute, but a 2-inch-thick slab of sirloin or bottom round will get you in the ballpark.

rotisserie

garlic pepper rotisserie tri-tip

The elusive tri-tip is popular barbecue in California, and virtually ignored in the rest of the United States. The roast takes its name from its distinctive shape, a triangular slab of beef sirloin that slices like brisket and cooks up and eats like steak. Its birthplace is the town of Santa Maria, situated between

Los Angeles and San Francisco. These days most of the tri-tip at barbecue joints is grilled over oak embers, but the original version was spit roasted. That's how a butcher named Bob Schutz did it back in 1952, and he's the man credited with popularizing this California classic. A countertop rotisserie produces a superb tri-tip, but you can also grill it using the methods in the box below. Tri-tip is traditionally served with a flavorful salsa and garlic bread (see page 281). **SERVES 4 TO 6**

THE RECIPE

Garlic powder
Coarse salt (kosher or sea)
Cracked black peppercorns or
        freshly ground black pepper
1 tri-tip (2 to 2½ pounds)
Santa Maria Salsa (recipe follows)

1. Generously sprinkle the garlic powder, salt, and pepper on both sides of the tri-tip.

2. When ready to cook, place the tri-tip in the rotisserie basket. Place the drip pan in the bottom of the rotisserie. Attach the basket to the rotisserie, then attach the spit to the rotisserie and turn on the motor. If your rotisserie has a temperature control, set it to 400°F (for instructions for using a rotisserie, see page 14).

3. Cook the tri-tip until it is darkly browned on the outside and cooked to taste, about 40 minutes for medium-rare. To test for doneness, insert an instant-read meat thermometer through the side of the tri-tip but not so that it touches the spit. The internal temperature should be about 145°F for medium-rare. If your

if you have a...

CONTACT GRILL: The smaller and thinner the tri-tip, the better the results you'll get on a contact grill (thick pieces of meat tend to burn on the outside before becoming fully cooked in the center). Preheat the grill; if your contact grill has a temperature control, preheat the grill to high. Place the drip pan under the front of the grill. When ready to cook, lightly oil the grill surface. Arrange the tri-tip on the hot grill, placing pieces of aluminum foil between the grill plates and the meat; this will slow the burning process. Close the lid. The tri-tip will be cooked to medium-rare after 8 to 10 minutes.

BUILT-IN GRILL: Preheat the grill to medium-high, then, if it does not have a nonstick surface, brush and oil the grill grate. Place the tri-tip on the hot grate. It will be cooked to medium-rare after 8 to 10 minutes per side.

FREESTANDING GRILL: If you like your tri-tip very rare, you can cook it on a freestanding grill. Preheat the grill to high; there's no need to oil the grate. Place the tri-tip on the hot grill, then place a heavy skillet on top of the meat to keep it flat. The tri-tip will be cooked to rare after 10 to 12 minutes per side (it takes forever to get to medium or well done).

FIREPLACE GRILL: Tri-tip is great grilled in the fireplace, especially over red oak or post oak. Rake red hot embers under the gridiron and preheat it for 3 to 5 minutes; you want a medium-high, 4 Mississippi fire. When ready to cook, brush and oil the gridiron. Place the tri-tip on the hot grate. It will be cooked to medium-rare after 8 to 10 minutes per side.

rotisserie has a pause button, after the tri-tip has cooked for 30 minutes, stop the spit so that a flat side of the tri-tip faces the heating element and let the meat brown for 5 minutes. Then, advance the spit a half turn and brown the other side for 5 minutes.

4. Transfer the tri-tip to a platter or cutting board, remove the spit, and let the meat rest for 5 minutes (loosely cover it with aluminum foil to keep it warm). Thinly slice the tri-tip crosswise, across the grain, and serve with the Santa Maria Salsa.

santa maria salsa

In true Californian fashion, tri-tip is served with salsa. Italian immigrants succeeded the Mexicans in these parts. Their influence can be seen in the use of celery, oregano, and red wine vinegar here. **MAKES ABOUT 3 CUPS**

3 scallions, trimmed and coarsely chopped

2 celery ribs, peeled with a vegetable peeler and coarsely chopped

2 to 4 jalapeño peppers, seeded and coarsely chopped (for a hotter salsa, leave the seeds in)

2 cloves garlic, coarsely chopped

1/2 teaspoon dried oregano

6 to 8 ripe plum tomatoes (1 1/4 to 1 1/2 pounds), coarsely chopped, with their juices

3 tablespoons chopped fresh cilantro

1 tablespoon red wine vinegar

1 tablespoon fresh lime juice

Coarse salt (kosher or sea) and freshly ground black pepper

Place the scallions, celery, jalapeños, garlic, and oregano in a food processor fitted with a chopping blade and finely chop. Add the tomatoes, running the processor in short bursts so as not to purée the salsa too finely. Add the cilantro, vinegar, and lime juice, then season with salt and pepper to taste; the salsa should be highly seasoned. The salsa can be made up to 2 hours ahead.

the original italian "cheese steak"

Here's an Italian "cheese steak" for the low-carb generation. There's no roll—the "sandwich" consists of two broad thin pieces of bottom round stuffed with Fontina cheese and prosciutto. *Thin* is the operative word here, as the thinness is what makes a normally tough steak tender. **SERVES 2**

tip

If you are shopping at an Italian meat market, ask for a *braciole* steak—a broad thin slice of bottom round. You could also use thinly sliced top round, beef round tips, or sirloin. The key is to have a butcher slice it thinly across the grain on a meat slicer.

2 pieces thinly sliced beef top or bottom
   round, or sirloin (each 6 ounces and about
   8 inches long, 4 inches wide, and just shy
   of 1/4 inch thick)
Coarse salt (kosher or sea) and freshly ground
   black pepper
2 ounces thinly sliced imported Italian
   Fontina cheese
2 slices prosciutto (about 1 1/2 ounces in all)
3 tablespoons freshly grated Parmesan cheese

YOU'LL ALSO NEED:
Wooden toothpicks

1. Place a steak on a work surface with a
long edge toward you. Using a sharp knife
and making a cut that is perpendicular to
the long edge, score the steak down the
middle by cutting about halfway through
the meat (this will enable you to fold the
steak closed like a book). Repeat with the
remaining steak. Season the steaks on
both sides with salt and pepper.

2. Place a steak on the work surface, cut
side down. Arrange half of the slices of
Fontina on top of one half of the steak so
that they are parallel to the cut. Top the
Fontina with a slice of prosciutto, then
sprinkle 1 1/2 tablespoons of the Parmesan
over it. Folding the steak along the cut
edge, cover the cheese and prosciutto
with the bare half of the steak. Secure the
open end with toothpicks. Repeat with
the remaining steak, Fontina, prosciutto,
and Parmesan. The steaks can be prepared up to this stage several hours
ahead and refrigerated, covered.

3. Cook the stuffed steaks, following the
instructions for any of the grills in the
box below, until the cheese is melted and
the steaks are nicely browned on the outside and cooked through.

4. Transfer the stuffed steaks to a platter
or plates. Remove and discard the toothpicks, then serve the steaks at once.

VARIATION: To make an Alpine
cheese steak, substitute thinly sliced
Gruyère, Appenzeller, or a raclette cheese
for the Fontina and *bresaola,* salt-cured,
air-dried beef, for the prosciutto.

if you have a...

CONTACT GRILL: Preheat
the grill; if your contact grill has a
temperature control, preheat the
grill to high. Place the drip pan
under the front of the grill. When
ready to cook, lightly oil the grill
surface. Place the stuffed steaks
on the hot grill, then close the
lid. The steaks will be done after
cooking 4 to 6 minutes.

GRILL PAN: Place the grill
pan on the stove and preheat it to
medium-high over medium heat.
When the grill pan is hot a drop of
water will skitter in the pan. When
ready to cook, lightly oil the ridges
of the grill pan. Place the stuffed
steaks in the hot grill pan. They
will be done after cooking 2 to 3
minutes per side.

BUILT-IN GRILL: Preheat
the grill to medium-high, then, if
it does not have a nonstick surface,
brush and oil the grill grate. Place
the stuffed steaks on the hot grate.
They will be done after cooking
2 to 3 minutes per side.

FREESTANDING GRILL:
Preheat the grill to high; there's
no need to oil the grate. Place
the stuffed steaks on the hot grill.
They will be done after cooking
3 to 5 minutes per side.

FIREPLACE GRILL: Rake
red hot embers under the gridiron
and preheat it for 3 to 5 minutes;
you want a hot, 2 to 3 Mississippi
fire. When ready to cook, brush and
oil the gridiron. Place the stuffed
steaks on the hot grate. The steaks
will be done after cooking 2 to 3
minutes per side.

magyar beef rolls

The stuffed beef roll is a staple throughout eastern Europe—to the point where it played a leading role in a haunting movie called *Gloomy Sunday,* set at a Budapest restaurant during World War II. The recipe varies from country to country and kitchen to kitchen: here the steaks might be stuffed with ham (cured, smoked, or cooked) and/or cheese; there filled with bacon, pickles, capers, or wedges of onion. Being a "more is more" sort of guy, I've created a super beef roll by incorporating most of these ingredients into the filling. You can certainly opt for fewer ingredients or vary the filling to suit your taste. In eastern Europe, they'd pan-fry the rolls, but an indoor grill can do a great job of searing the crust and melting the filling. **SERVES 4**

tip

You don't need an expensive steak for these beef rolls. Top or bottom round or sirloin will work fine. What you do need is an extremely thin steak, which is best cut on a meat slicer by a butcher. When I make this dish, I use beef round tips sliced slightly under ¼ inch thick.

THE RECIPE

8 pieces thinly sliced beef top round, bottom round, or sirloin (each about 4 ounces, 4 inches square, and just shy of ¼ inch thick)

1 tablespoon sweet Hungarian paprika

Coarse salt (kosher or sea) and freshly ground black pepper

1 tablespoon Dijon mustard

8 thin slices Provolone or Cheddar cheese (about 6 ounces), cut into 3-by-3-inch pieces

8 thin slices smoked ham, such as Westphalian ham (4 to 6 ounces), cut into 3-by-4-inch pieces

1 dill pickle, cut into 8 thin wedges

8 slices bacon

Cooking oil spray

YOU'LL ALSO NEED:
Wooden toothpicks or butcher's string

1. Place the pieces of beef on a work surface. Season each on both sides with the paprika and salt and pepper. Spread the mustard over the tops of the meat. Arrange a slice of cheese on each piece and top with a slice of ham. Place a pickle wedge at the widest end of once piece and roll up the beef, cheese, and ham around it to form a sort of mini jelly roll. Repeat with the remaining pieces of beef. Wrap a slice of bacon around each beef roll, angling it on a diagonal, like the stripe on a candy cane.

2. Cook the beef rolls, following the instructions for any of the grills in the box at right, until the cheese is melted and the meat is nicely browned on the outside and cooked through (you may need to do this in batches). Serve at once, removing and discarding the toothpicks or string.

if you have a...

CONTACT GRILL: Preheat the grill; if your contact grill has a temperature control, preheat the grill to high. Place the drip pan under the front of the grill. When ready to cook, lightly oil the grill surface. Place the beef rolls on the hot grill, then close the lid. The beef rolls will be done after cooking 5 to 8 minutes.

GRILL PAN: Place the grill pan on the stove and preheat it to medium-high over medium heat. When the grill pan is hot a drop of water will skitter in the pan. When ready to cook, lightly oil the ridges of the grill pan. Place the beef rolls in the hot grill pan. They will be done after cooking 1½ to 2 minutes per side (6 to 8 minutes in all).

BUILT-IN GRILL: Preheat the grill to medium-high, then, if it does not have a nonstick surface, brush and oil the grill grate. Arrange the beef rolls on the hot grate; to avoid flare-ups, don't crowd the grill. The beef rolls will be done after cooking 1½ to 2 minutes per side (6 to 8 minutes in all).

FREESTANDING GRILL: Preheat the grill to high; there's no need to oil the grate. Place the beef rolls on the hot grill. They will be done after cooking 2½ to 3 minutes per side (10 to 12 minutes in all).

FIREPLACE GRILL: Rake red hot embers under the gridiron and preheat it for 3 to 5 minutes; you want a medium-high, 4 Mississippi fire. When ready to cook, brush and oil the gridiron. Place the beef rolls on the hot grate; to avoid flare-ups, don't crowd the grill. They will be done after cooking 1½ to 2 minutes per side (6 to 8 minutes in all). Should flare-ups occur, move the beef rolls to another section of the grill.

ROTISSERIE: Place the beef rolls in the rotisserie basket. Place the drip pan in the bottom of the rotisserie. Attach the basket to the spit, then attach the spit to the rotisserie and turn it on (if your rotisserie has a temperature control, set it to 400°F). The beef rolls will be done after 20 to 30 minutes.

lemon pepper london broil

Food, like fashion, has its rising and falling hemlines. Take London broil: When I was growing up, it was common currency at local restaurants. But I can't remember seeing London broil on a menu in a while. This is a shame, as it's an excellent way of preparing economical cuts of beef. Slicing the meat thinly on the diagonal produces tender slices of steak. So, in the interests of reviving this chophouse classic, here's a London broil with an East-West marinade. **SERVES 4**

THE RECIPE

1 flank steak or piece of sirloin or top or bottom round steak (1¹/₂ to 1³/₄ pounds)

1 tablespoon cracked black peppercorns
2 teaspoons finely grated lemon zest
3 cloves garlic, coarsely chopped
1 shallot, coarsely chopped
3 tablespoons soy sauce
1 tablespoon Dijon mustard
1 tablespoon fresh lemon juice
2 tablespoons vegetable oil

if you have a...

CONTACT GRILL: When cooking on a contact grill, you're best off using a thick cut of steak, like sirloin or round (flank steak will most likely turn out well-done). Preheat the grill; if your contact grill has a temperature control, preheat the grill to high. Place the drip pan under the front of the grill. When ready to cook, lightly oil the grill surface. Place the beef on the hot grill, then close the lid. A thick slab of sirloin or round steak will be cooked to medium-rare after 7 to 10 minutes; flank steak will be cooked to medium after 3 to 5 minutes.

GRILL PAN: Place the grill pan on the stove and preheat it to medium-high over medium heat. When the grill pan is hot a drop of water will skitter in the pan. When ready to cook, lightly oil the ridges of the grill pan. Place the beef in the hot grill pan. Sirloin or round steak will be cooked to medium-rare after 5 to 8 minutes per side; flank steak will be cooked to medium-rare after 4 to 6 minutes per side.

BUILT-IN GRILL: Preheat the grill to high, then, if it does not have a nonstick surface, brush and oil the grill grate. Place the beef on the hot grate. Sirloin or round steak will be cooked to medium-rare after 5 to 8 minutes per side; flank steak will be cooked to medium-rare after 4 to 6 minutes per side.

FREESTANDING GRILL: Preheat the grill to high; there's no need to oil the grate. Place the beef on the hot grill. Sirloin or round steak will be cooked to medium-rare after 6 to 9 minutes per side; flank steak will be cooked to medium-rare after 5 to 7 minutes per side.

FIREPLACE GRILL: Rake red hot embers under the gridiron and preheat it for 3 to 5 minutes; you want a hot, 2 to 3 Mississippi fire. When ready to cook, brush and oil the gridiron. Place the beef on the hot grate. Sirloin or round steak will be cooked to medium-rare after 5 to 8 minutes per side; flank steak will be cooked to medium-rare after 4 to 6 minutes per side.

1. If using flank steak, score it on both sides in a crosshatch pattern, making shallow cuts on the diagonal no deeper than ¹/₈ inch and about ¹/₄ inch apart. This will keep the flank steak from curling as it cooks; you don't have to score sirloin or top or bottom round.

2. Place the peppercorns, lemon zest, garlic, and shallot in a food processor and process to a coarse paste. Add the soy sauce, mustard, lemon juice, and 1 tablespoon of the oil. Spread half of the soy sauce mixture in the bottom of a nonreactive baking dish just large enough to hold the beef. Place the meat on top and spread the remaining soy sauce mixture over it. Let the meat marinate for at least 4 hours or as long as overnight. You can also marinate the beef in a resealable plastic bag.

3. When ready to cook, drain the meat, scraping off most of the marinade with a rubber spatula. (Scraping off the marinade will help the steak to sear better and makes less of a mess on the grill.) Drizzle the remaining 1 tablespoon of oil over the beef on both sides, spreading it over the meat with your fingertips.

4. Cook the beef, following the instructions for any of the grills in the box on the facing page, until cooked to taste. To test for doneness, use the poke method; when cooked to medium-rare the meat should be gently yielding.

5. Transfer the meat to a cutting board and let rest for 3 minutes. To serve, thinly slice the meat against the grain on a

sharp diagonal. Fan out the slices on a platter or plate and serve at once.

NOTE: You won't find London broil on a meat cutter's chart—it can refer to any of four beef steaks that ordinarily tend to be on the tough side: flank steak, sirloin, top round, or bottom round. When thinly sliced against the grain on a sharp diagonal, all of these give you tender ribbons of meat. To make London broil with a flank steak, pick one that's about ¾ inch thick. If you prefer sirloin or top or bottom round, it should be between 1 and 1½ inches thick.

filipino-style london broil

Rodolfo Lagua, a thirty-year California barbecue veteran of Filipino heritage, was the inspiration for this recipe. Lagua learned this way of preparing tri-tips from his friend Sammy Ariola, one of the area's first Filipino immigrants. "I have no money for you to inherit," said Ariola, as he lay on his deathbed, "but I'll give you the recipe for my marinade." Since then Lagua has won numerous barbecue contests with his Filipino-style tri-tips, raising thousands of dollars for Filipino community charities. He's now working on bottling the sauce commercially, once again as a fund-raiser. The interplay of salty, sweet, and sour is pure Filipino, and the lemon rind adds an intense blast of citrus flavor. I've adapted my approximation of Lagua's recipe to London broil; in the Tip you'll find instructions for making tri-tips with this marinade. Lagua would serve the meat with boiled rice. **SERVES 4 TO 6**

THE RECIPE

2 medium-size lemons
1 cup soy sauce
1/2 cup distilled white vinegar

1/2 cup vegetable oil
1 medium-size onion, finely chopped
3 cloves garlic, finely chopped
3 bay leaves, crumbled
1 tablespoon coriander seed
1 teaspoon black pepper
1 flank steak or piece of sirloin or top or
   bottom round steak (1 1/2 to 1 3/4 pounds;
   see Note on page 67)

1. Rinse the lemons. Cut each in half and squeeze out the juice with a citrus press. Place the lemon juice in a large nonreactive mixing bowl. Cut the rind of 1 lemon into 1/4-inch dice and add it to the juice. Add the soy sauce, vinegar, oil, onion, garlic, bay leaves, coriander seed, and pepper and whisk to mix. Set aside half of the lemon juice mixture to use as a sauce.

2. If using flank steak, score it on both sides in a crosshatch pattern, making shallow cuts on the diagonal no deeper than 1/8 inch and about 1/4 inch apart. This will keep the flank steak from curling as it cooks; you don't have to score sirloin or top or bottom round.

3. Spread half of the remaining lemon juice mixture in the bottom of a nonreactive baking dish just large enough to hold the meat. Place the meat on top and spread the other half of the lemon juice mixture over it. Let the steak marinate for

if you have a...

CONTACT GRILL: When cooking on a contact grill, you're best off using a thick cut of steak, like sirloin or round (flank steak will most likely turn out well-done). Preheat the grill; if your contact grill has a temperature control, preheat the grill to high. Place the drip pan under the front of the grill. When ready to cook, lightly oil the grill surface. Place the beef on the hot grill, then close the lid. A thick slab of sirloin or round steak will be cooked to medium-rare after 7 to 10 minutes; flank steak will be cooked to medium after 3 to 5 minutes.

GRILL PAN: Place the grill pan on the stove and preheat it to medium-high over medium heat. When the grill pan is hot a drop of water will skitter in the pan. When ready to cook, lightly oil the ridges of the grill pan. Place the beef in the hot grill pan. Sirloin or round steak will be cooked to medium-rare after 5 to 8 minutes per side; flank steak will be cooked to medium-rare after 4 to 6 minutes per side.

BUILT-IN GRILL: Preheat the grill to high, then, if it does not have a nonstick surface, brush and oil the grill grate. Place the beef on the hot grate. Sirloin or round steak will be cooked to medium-rare after 5 to 8 minutes per side; flank steak will be cooked to medium-rare after 4 to 6 minutes per side.

FREESTANDING GRILL: Preheat the grill to high; there's no need to oil the grate. Place the beef on the hot grill. Sirloin or round steak will be cooked to medium-rare after 6 to 9 minutes per side; flank steak will be cooked to medium-rare after 5 to 7 minutes per side.

FIREPLACE GRILL: Rake red hot embers under the gridiron and preheat it for 3 to 5 minutes; you want a hot, 2 to 3 Mississippi fire. When ready to cook, brush and oil the gridiron. Place the beef on the hot grate. Sirloin or round steak will be cooked to medium-rare after 5 to 8 minutes per side; flank steak will be cooked to medium-rare after 4 to 6 minutes per side.

at least 6 hours, ideally overnight. The beef can also be marinated in a resealable plastic bag.

4. When ready to cook, drain the meat, scraping off most of the marinade with a rubber spatula. Cook the beef, following the instructions for any of the grills in the box on the facing page, until cooked to taste. To test for doneness, use the poke method; when cooked to medium-rare the meat should be gently yielding.

5. Transfer the meat to a cutting board and let sit for 5 minutes. Cut the meat into broad thin slices, holding a sharp knife blade at a 45-degree angle to the top of the meat. Spoon the reserved sauce over the slices and serve at once.

rotisserie

braciole
sicilian-style stuffed flank steak

This Sicilian-style stuffed beef roll takes me back to my restaurant reviewing days, when I was the restaurant critic for *Boston* magazine. One of my beats was Boston's North End or Little Italy, where I would do an annual roundup of the best places to eat and grocery shop. It was there, at a butcher shop that's long since defunct, that I first found *braciole,* which the locals pronounced "brash-ohl." What you got was a roll of beef stuffed with prosciutto, salami, mortadella, and other Italian cold cuts, not to mention Italian hot peppers and Provolone cheese. You'd buy it already stuffed and bake it at home according to the butcher's instructions. What emerged from the oven was about the tastiest dish ever to clog your arteries. It was great hot.

tip

Rodolfo Lagua uses a marinade like this one when preparing tri-tips. To do this, start with a tri-tip that's between 2 and 2½ pounds. Make the marinade following the directions in Step 1, then let the meat marinate for 12 to 24 hours. You can grill the tri-tip in the rotisserie following Steps 2 and 3 in the tri-tip recipe on page 61 or use one of the alternative grilling methods on page 61.

It was great cold. It was great served as an appetizer or main course. Here's a not strictly traditional *braciole* made with flank steak and cooked on a rotisserie. **SERVES 8 TO 10 AS AN APPETIZER; 4 TO 6 AS A MAIN COURSE**

tips

THE RECIPE

1 flank steak (1½ to 1¾ pounds)
Coarse salt (kosher or sea) and freshly
    ground black pepper
1 tablespoon dried oregano
4 ounces thinly sliced aged Provolone cheese
1½ ounces thinly sliced prosciutto
1½ ounces thinly sliced Genoa salami or
    other Italian salami
1½ ounces thinly sliced pepperoni
1½ ounces thinly sliced mortadella (optional)
½ cup Italian pickled hot peppers (optional),
    drained and finely chopped
4 slices pancetta (3 to 4 ounces) unrolled,
    or 4 slices bacon

YOU'LL ALSO NEED:
Butcher's string

1. Butterfly the flank steak: Trim the edges of the flank steak so that they are straight and the meat is an even rectangle. Position the flank steak lengthwise along the edge of the cutting board. Using a very sharp, long, slender knife, make a horizontal cut through a long side, slicing the meat almost in half (stop about ½ inch from the opposite side). Open the flank steak up like a book, then pound the center flat with a meat pounder or the side of a cleaver. The idea is to create a piece of meat that's 12 to 15 inches long and wide.

2. Season the meat on both sides with salt and pepper. Arrange the butterflied flank steak cut side up on the work surface so that a short side is closest to you. Sprinkle the oregano over the meat.

3. Arrange the slices of Provolone, prosciutto, salami, pepperoni, and mortadella, if using, in layers on top of the flank steak, placing them ½ inch from the bottom and sides of the meat. Leave the top 2 inches of the flank steak bare. Sprinkle the peppers, if using, on top. Starting with the edge of the flank steak closest to you, roll up the meat into a tight cylinder. Carefully move it to the side.

4. Cut four 15-inch-long pieces of butcher's string. Position the strings on the cutting board so that they are parallel to each other and roughly 2 inches apart. Place 1 slice of pancetta across the center of the strings so that it is perpendicular to them.

5. Place the rolled-up meat on top of the slice of pancetta so that it is perpendicular to the strings. Place a slice of pancetta lengthwise on top of the rolled meat. Press the remaining 2 slices of pancetta against either side of the rolled flank steak. Tie the pieces of string together around the meat so that they hold the slices of pancetta tightly against it. The *braciole* can be prepared up to this stage several hours ahead and refrigerated, covered.

6. When ready to cook, place the drip pan in the bottom of the rotisserie. Gently flatten the flank steak roll with your hand so that it will fit in the rotisserie basket, then place it in the basket so that the spit will pass through it crosswise. Close the basket tightly and attach it to the rotisserie spit. Attach the spit to the rotisserie, then turn on the motor. If your rotisserie has a temperature control, set it to 400°F (for instructions for using a rotisserie, see page 14). Cook the *braciole* until crusty and brown on the outside and cooked through. To test for doneness, use an instant-read meat thermometer: Insert it into the center of the

braciole but not so that it touches the spit. The internal temperature should be about 190°F.

7. Transfer the *braciole* to a cutting board and let cool for a few minutes. Remove and discard the strings. Cut the roll crosswise into ½-inch slices and serve. The braciole is also pretty tasty served at room temperature or even cold.

skirt steaks
with cotija cheese and two-pepper salsa

Steak, cheese, and peppers. It's a time-honored combination that turns up in the Old World as well as in the New: Italians have *braciole* (page 69); in Philadelphia it's cheese steak. Here's the Mexican version—or I should say one of the Mexican versions—as in many regions there grilled beef is topped with roasted peppers and cheese. The steak in question here is skirt steak. The peppers are fresh and smoked jalapeños (called chipotles), while the cheese is a salty, sharp-flavored one called *cotija*. Put them all together and you get a dish with shockingly vivid colors, textures, and tastes. **SERVES 4**

tip

Cotija cheese (pronounced "ko-TEE-ha") is available at Mexican and Hispanic markets. In a pinch you can substitute feta cheese.

1½ pounds skirt steaks,
    cut into 4 even portions
Garlic salt
Freshly ground black pepper
Two-Pepper Salsa (recipe follows)
2 ounces cotija cheese
4 fresh cilantro sprigs, for garnish

1. Season the skirt steaks on both sides with garlic salt and black pepper. Cook the steaks, following the instructions for any of the grills in the box below, until cooked to taste, rotating each a quarter turn after 1½ minutes to create a handsome crosshatch of grill marks. To test for doneness, use the poke method; when cooked to medium-rare the meat should be gently yielding.

2. Spoon the Two-Pepper Salsa onto a platter or plates. Arrange the steaks on top. Coarsely grate or crumble some of the *cotija* cheese on top of each steak and garnish with a sprig of cilantro. Serve at once.

two-pepper salsa

Tomatillos look like green cherry tomatoes that are covered with a tan papery husk. They have a tart and fruity flavor. You can grill them and the other vegetables for the salsa a day or two ahead of when you plan to serve the skirt steaks. Or, if you prefer, rather than grill them, roast the vegetables in a cast-iron skillet. **MAKES ABOUT 1½ CUPS**

4 large tomatillos (5 to 6 ounces total),
    husked
3 plum tomatoes (8 to 10 ounces total)
2 jalapeño peppers
4 scallions, both white and green parts,
    trimmed
3 cloves garlic, skewered on a wooden
    toothpick
1 to 2 canned chipotle peppers (see Note),
    coarsely chopped, with 1 tablespoon of
    their adobo sauce, or more to taste
3 tablespoons chopped fresh cilantro
1 tablespoon fresh lime juice, or more as
    necessary
A pinch of sugar
Coarse salt (kosher or sea) and freshly
    ground black pepper

if you have a...

CONTACT GRILL: Preheat the grill; if your contact grill has a temperature control, preheat the grill to high. Place the drip pan under the front of the grill. When ready to cook, lightly oil the grill surface. Place the strip steaks on the hot grill, then close the lid. The steaks will be cooked to medium after 3 to 4 minutes.

GRILL PAN: Place the grill pan on the stove and preheat it to medium-high over medium heat. When the grill pan is hot a drop of water will skitter in the pan. When ready to cook, lightly oil the ridges of the grill pan. Place the strip steaks in the hot grill pan. They will be cooked to medium-rare after 3 to 4 minutes per side.

BUILT-IN GRILL: Preheat the grill to high, then, if it does not have a nonstick surface, brush and oil the grill grate. Place the strip steaks on the hot grate. They will be cooked to medium-rare after 3 to 4 minutes per side.

FREESTANDING GRILL: Preheat the grill to high; there's no need to oil the grate. Place the strip steaks on the hot grill. They will be cooked to medium-rare after about 4 minutes per side.

FIREPLACE GRILL: Rake red hot embers under the gridiron and preheat it for 3 to 5 minutes; you want a hot, 2 to 3 Mississippi fire. When ready to cook, brush and oil the gridiron. Place the strip steaks on the hot grate. They will be cooked to medium-rare after 3 to 4 minutes per side.

1. Cook the tomatillos, plum tomatoes, jalapeños, scallions, and garlic, following the instructions for any of the grills in the box at right, until partially browned on all sides, turning with tongs.

2. Transfer the grilled vegetables to a plate to cool, then, if a milder salsa is desired, seed the jalapeños.

3. Cut the vegetables into 1-inch pieces and place in a food processor. Add the chipotle(s) with the 1 tablespoon of adobo sauce and the cilantro and process to a coarse paste. Add the lime juice and sugar. Taste for seasoning, adding more adobo sauce as necessary and salt and black pepper to taste; the salsa should be highly seasoned. If necessary, add 1 to 2 tablespoons of water; the salsa should be thick but pourable. The salsa can be made up to 2 days ahead of time and refrigerated, covered, in a nonreactive container. Let it return to room temperature, then taste for seasoning, adding more lime juice and/or salt as necessary.

if you have a...

CONTACT GRILL: Preheat the grill; if your contact grill has a temperature control, preheat the grill to high. Place the drip pan under the front of the grill. When ready to cook, lightly oil the grill surface. Place the vegetables on the hot grill, then close the lid (see Timing, below).

GRILL PAN: Place the grill pan on the stove and preheat it to medium-high over medium heat. When the grill pan is hot a drop of water will skitter in the pan. When ready to cook, lightly oil the ridges of the grill pan, then place the vegetables in the hot grill pan (see Timing, below).

BUILT-IN GRILL: Preheat the grill to high, then, if it does not have a nonstick surface, brush and oil the grill grate and place the vegetables on the hot grate (see Timing, below).

FREESTANDING GRILL: Preheat the grill to high, then place the vegetables on the hot grill; there's no need to oil the grate (see Timing, below).

FIREPLACE GRILL: Rake red hot embers under the gridiron and preheat it for 3 to 5 minutes; you want a hot, 2 to 3 Mississippi fire. When ready to cook, brush and oil the gridiron, then place the vegetables on the hot grate (see Timing, below).

TIMING: On all grills the tomatillos, plum tomatoes, and jalapeños will be done in 6 to 8 minutes; the scallions and garlic will take 4 to 5 minutes.

NOTE: Chipotle peppers (smoked jalapeño peppers) come both dried and canned. I recommend using canned chipotles because their juices, called adobo, are loaded with flavor.

beef paillards
with fresh herb salad

A paillard is a steak that has been pounded paper-thin and flash grilled. (You can also do this with chicken breasts; there's a recipe for these on page 195.) The pounding achieves several things: It increases the surface area exposed to the heat so the meat can sear better. It shortens the cooking time to a minute or two. It also tenderizes the meat. This is not an issue here, as I call for beef tenderloin, but it's a bonus if you want to use a tougher cut of meat, like top or bottom round steak. And paillards certainly look impressive. These are topped with a fresh herb and asparagus salad. **SERVES 4**

THE RECIPE

1 piece trimmed center-cut beef tenderloin
    (about 1½ pounds)
8 asparagus stalks
2 cups fresh herbs, including whole tarragon,
    chervil, mint, flat-leaf parsley, and/or
    cilantro leaves and/or torn basil leaves

1 tablespoon finely chopped fresh chives
1 bunch arugula, rinsed, spun dry,
    and torn into 2-inch pieces
16 grape tomatoes, or 8 cherry tomatoes,
    cut in half
3½ tablespoons extra-virgin olive oil
Coarse salt (kosher or sea) and freshly
    ground black pepper
2 tablespoons fresh lemon juice
Lemon wedges, for serving

if you have a...

CONTACT GRILL: Preheat the grill; if your contact grill has a temperature control, preheat the grill to high. Place the drip pan under the front of the grill. When ready to cook, lightly oil the grill surface. Place the beef slices on the hot grill, then close the lid. The paillards will be cooked to medium after 2 to 3 minutes.

GRILL PAN: Place the grill pan on the stove and preheat it to medium-high over medium heat. When the grill pan is hot a drop of water will skitter in the pan. When ready to cook, lightly oil the ridges of the grill pan. Place the beef slices in the hot grill pan. They will be cooked to medium-rare after 1 to 2 minutes per side.

BUILT-IN GRILL: Preheat the grill to high, then, if it does not have a nonstick surface, brush and oil the grill grate. Place the beef slices on the hot grate. They will be cooked to medium-rare after 1 to 2 minutes per side.

FREESTANDING GRILL: Preheat the grill to high; there's no need to oil the grate. Place the beef slices on the hot grill. They will be cooked to medium-rare after 2 to 3 minutes per side.

FIREPLACE GRILL: Rake red hot embers under the gridiron and preheat it for 3 to 5 minutes; you want a hot, 2 to 3 Mississippi fire. When ready to cook, brush and oil the gridiron. Place the beef slices on the hot grate. They will be cooked to medium-rare after 1 to 2 minutes per side.

1. Place the tenderloin flat on a work surface. Using a sharp carving knife held parallel to the work surface, cut the tenderloin into four even flat slices. You can hold the meat steady by pressing on it with the palm of one hand. (If you prefer, ask the butcher to do this for you.) Place a slice of beef between 2 pieces of plastic wrap and gently pound it with a meat pounder or the side of a cleaver until it is about ¼ inch thick. Repeat with the remaining slices of beef.

2. Snap the fibrous ends off the asparagus. The easiest way to do this is to hold an asparagus stalk at the base with one hand and bend it with your other hand. The asparagus will snap where the woody part ends. Slice the asparagus as thinly as possible on the diagonal.

3. Place the sliced asparagus and the herbs, chives, arugula, and tomatoes in a nonreactive mixing bowl and set aside without tossing.

4. Brush the slices of beef on both sides with 1½ tablespoons of the olive oil and

Parsley Chives Rosemary Cilantro

season them on both sides with salt and pepper. Cook the beef slices, following the instructions for any of the grills in the box on the facing page, until cooked to taste (you may need to cook the paillards in more than one batch). To test for doneness, use the poke method; when cooked to medium-rare the meat should be gently yielding. This is so quick, the paillards will be done before you know it.

5. Transfer the paillards to a platter or plates. Add the lemon juice and remaining 2 tablespoons of olive oil to the salad and toss it. Mound the salad on top of the paillards and serve at once, with lemon wedges.

rib steak
with shiitake syrah sauce

The rib steak is for the true beef lover, combining the meaty chew of an expertly grilled steak and the sanguine succulence of roast beef. It's a monster consisting of a Bible-thick rib eye with a whole rib attached. A typical rib steak tips the scales at around 2 pounds and will comfortably serve two to three. I always think of rib steak as fireplace fare, since the first one I ever tasted was cooked over wood embers in a fireplace in France. At Barbecue University at the Greenbrier, we prepare it in the manorial hearth of our mountainside "campus," Kate's Mountain Lodge. Everyone loves the gutsy presentation and robust flavor—not to mention the drama of grilling in the fireplace. The steak is particularly good when grilled over oak or hickory logs, but the other indoor grills handle the job well too. **SERVES 2 OR 3**

T H E   R E C I P E

1 bone-in beef rib steak (1½ to 2 inches
    thick; about 2 pounds; see Note)
1 tablespoon extra-virgin olive oil
2 cloves garlic, minced
2 tablespoons crumbled dried rosemary
    (crumble it between your fingers)

Coarse salt (kosher or sea) and cracked
    black peppercorns
Shiitake Syrah Sauce (recipe follows)
2 tablespoons finely chopped fresh
    flat-leaf parsley

if you have a...

CONTACT GRILL: The rib makes it tough to cook this steak on a contact grill. Pick 2 boneless rib-eye steaks that are 1 to 1¼ inches thick instead. The bigger your machine and the higher its wattage, the better your chance of getting proper searing. Preheat the grill; if your contact grill has a temperature control, preheat the grill to high. Place the drip pan under the front of the grill. When ready to cook, lightly oil the grill surface. Place the steaks on the hot grill, then close the lid. They will be cooked to medium-rare after 7 to 10 minutes.

GRILL PAN: You're better off using thinner steaks here; choose 2 boneless rib eyes that are about ¾ inch thick. Place the grill pan on the stove and preheat it to medium-high over medium heat. When the grill pan is hot a drop of water will skitter in the pan. When ready to cook, lightly oil the ridges of the grill pan. Place

the steaks in the hot grill pan. They will be cooked to medium-rare after 4 to 6 minutes per side. To create a crosshatch of grill marks, rotate the steaks after 2 minutes on each side. These steaks can be served whole.

BUILT-IN GRILL: Although a built-in grill won't give you the heady flavor of wood smoke, it will give you a nice crust. Preheat the grill to medium-high, then, if it does not have a nonstick surface, brush and oil the grill grate. Place the steak on the hot grate. It will be cooked to medium-rare after 7 to 9 minutes per side.

FIREPLACE GRILL: Rake red hot embers under the gridiron and preheat it for 3 to 5 minutes; you want a medium-hot, 4 Mississippi fire. When ready to cook, brush and oil the gridiron. Place the steak on the hot grate. It will be cooked to medium-rare after 7 to 9 minutes per side.

1. Brush the steak on both sides with the olive oil. Thickly crust each side with the garlic and rosemary, then season it with salt and cracked peppercorns. Refrigerate the seasoned steak, covered, until ready to cook.

2. Cook the steak following the instructions for any of the grills in the box at left, until cooked to taste. To test for doneness, use the poke method; when cooked to medium-rare the meat should be gently yielding. Or use an instant-read meat thermometer: Insert it in the side of the steak but not so that it touches the bone. The internal temperature should be about 145°F for medium-rare. Turn the steak over when the bottom side is darkly browned and beads of juice begin to appear on top and rotate it a quarter turn after cooking 3 minutes on each side to create a handsome crosshatch of grill marks.

3. Transfer the steak to a platter or cutting board and let it rest for 3 minutes. Cut off the bone and set it aside (if the meat on the bone is too rare, put the bone back on the grill to cook a little more). Thinly slice the steak crosswise. Serve the steak fanned out on plates with the Shiitake Syrah Sauce spooned on top. Sprinkle the parsley over the steak and serve at once.

NOTE: You'll probably need to buy the rib steak at a butcher shop or order it ahead from the supermarket meat cutter, as most prime rib in the United States is sold in the form of roasts, not steaks.

shiitake syrah sauce

Beef and mushrooms are made for each other. Here they come together in a rich, meaty sauce that's robust enough to stand up to the rib eye. Feel free to substitute different kinds of wild mushrooms. **MAKES ABOUT 1¼ CUPS**

3 tablespoons unsalted butter

3 to 4 shallots, minced (about ¾ cup)

6 ounces shiitake or other mushrooms, stemmed, caps wiped clean with a damp paper towel and thinly sliced

About 2 cups syrah or other full-bodied dry red wine

1 cup beef, veal, or chicken stock (preferably homemade)

1 teaspoon cornstarch (optional)

Coarse salt (kosher or sea) and freshly ground black pepper

1. Melt 2 tablespoons of the butter in a heavy nonreactive saucepan over medium heat. Add the shallots and cook until soft but not brown, about 3 minutes, stirring often. Add the shiitakes and cook until browned and most of the mushroom liquid has evaporated, about 3 minutes. Add 2 cups of the wine, increase the heat to high, and bring to a boil. Let simmer briskly until the liquid is reduced by half, about 5 minutes.

2. Add the stock to the saucepan. Let the mixture simmer briskly until it is reduced to about 1¼ cups, 5 to 10 minutes. If you start with very good homemade stock, the mixture may be thick enough to serve as a sauce without adding the cornstarch. If not, place the cornstarch and 1 tablespoon of wine in a small nonreactive bowl and stir until the cornstarch dissolves. Whisk the cornstarch mixture into the sauce, let come to a boil, and cook until the sauce is slightly thickened, about 1 minute.

3. Remove the saucepan from the heat and whisk in the remaining 1 tablespoon of butter. Season the sauce with salt and pepper to taste; it should be highly seasoned.

my mother's "pittsburgh rare" t-bone steaks

Impetuous. Bold. Extreme. These may be odd words to use to describe a steak, but they certainly describe my mother, who was a ballet dancer. Whatever she did, she did boldly, even recklessly. Whether executing a complicated dance routine or grilling a steak, she did it with grand gestures and a blithe disregard for convention. No handsome crosshatch of grill marks. No carefully monitored cooking times or instant-read meat thermometers. She'd throw the meat on the grill, char it until the outside was only a little paler than the color of coal and the inside was just shy of still mooing, and slap it onto a plate. The name for this style of steak in the 1950s was Pittsburgh rare: The black outside evoked the smoke or perhaps coal of the Pittsburgh steel mills. If you love the sanguine flavor of beef, there's no better way to grill it—carcinogens be

if you have a . . .

CONTACT GRILL: The bone makes it tough to cook these steaks on a contact grill. Pick boneless rib-eye steaks that are about 1 to 1¼ inches thick instead. Preheat the grill; if your contact grill has a temperature control, preheat the grill to high. Place the drip pan under the front of the grill. When ready to cook, lightly oil the grill surface. Place the steaks on the hot grill, then close the lid. They will be cooked to rare after 5 to 8 minutes.

GRILL PAN: You're better off using thinner steaks here, ones that are about ¾ inch thick. Place the grill pan on the stove and preheat it to medium-high over medium heat. When the grill pan is hot a drop of water will skitter in the pan. When ready to cook, lightly oil the ridges of the grill pan. Place the steaks in the hot grill pan. They will be cooked to rare after about 3 minutes per side.

BUILT-IN GRILL: Preheat the grill to high, then, if it does not have a nonstick surface, brush and oil the grill grate. Place the steaks on the hot grate. They will be cooked to rare after about 4 minutes per side.

FIREPLACE GRILL: Rake red hot embers under the gridiron and preheat it for 3 to 5 minutes; you want a very hot, 2 Mississippi fire. When ready to cook, brush and oil the gridiron. Place the steaks on the grate. They will be cooked to rare after about 4 minutes per side.

damned. My mother used nothing more than salt and pepper for seasoning, but I think she would have approved of the brash Roquefort butter I've added. **SERVES 2**

THE RECIPE

1 ounce Roquefort cheese, at room
    temperature
2 tablespoons (¼ stick) unsalted butter,
    at room temperature
2 T-bone steaks (each 1 to 1¼ inch thick
    and 10 to 12 ounces)
Coarse salt (kosher or sea) and cracked
    black peppercorns

1. Place the Roquefort in a bowl and mash it to a paste with the back of a fork. Add the butter and stir to mix. Set the Roquefort butter aside.

2. Very generously season the steaks on both sides with salt and peppercorns. Cook the steaks, following the instructions for any of the grills in the box on the facing page, until darkly browned, even charred black on the outside but still very rare in the center. To test for doneness, use the poke method; when cooked to rare the meat should be soft.

3. Transfer the steaks to a platter or plates and let rest for 2 minutes. Place a dollop of Roquefort butter in the center of each and serve at once.

tip

To get a proper Pittsburgh char on a 1-inch T-bone steak, you need a fireplace grill or a built-in grill that delivers a lot of heat. If you're using a grill pan or freestanding grill, select a thinner steak. A contact grill won't really give you a Pittsburgh char, but there's still something to be said for steak and Roquefort.

sesame soy rib eyes

Contact grills are well suited to cooking many foods. Steak is not normally one of them. Few models get hot enough, and the meat tends to stew and overcook between the plates of the grill. One way to avoid this is to start with a thick steak, so the meat retains its sanguine succulence in the center. Another way is to use a sweetish rub or marinade to speed up the browning. That's what I've done with this sesame and soy flavored steak, which takes its flavorings from the *bool kogi*—flash-seared beef— of Korea. Of course if you have access to a fireplace grill or a good built-in, your steaks will sear all the better. I've called for rib eyes here, but any steak will benefit from this treatment, from New York strip to filet mignon. **SERVES 2**

THE RECIPE

2 rib-eye steaks (each 1 to 1¼ inches thick, the thicker the better, and 8 to 10 ounces)

Coarse salt (kosher or sea) and freshly ground black pepper

2 tablespoons dark brown sugar

About 3 tablespoons soy sauce

3 tablespoons Asian (dark) sesame oil

if you have a...

CONTACT GRILL: Preheat the grill; if your contact grill has a temperature control, preheat the grill to high. Place the drip pan under the front of the grill. When ready to cook, lightly oil the grill surface. Place the steaks on the hot grill, then close the lid. They will be cooked to medium-rare after 6 to 10 minutes.

GRILL PAN: Place the grill pan on the stove and preheat it to medium-high over medium heat. When the grill pan is hot a drop of water will skitter in the pan. When ready to cook, lightly oil the ridges of the grill pan. Place the steaks in the hot grill pan. They will be cooked to medium-rare after 4 to 6 minutes per side.

BUILT-IN GRILL: Preheat the grill to high, then, if it does not have a nonstick surface, brush and oil the grill grate. Place the steaks on the hot grate. They will be cooked to medium-rare after 4 to 6 minutes per side.

FREESTANDING GRILL: You're better off using thinner steaks here, ones that are ¾ inch thick. Preheat the grill to high; there's no need to oil the grate. Place the steaks on the hot grill. They will be cooked to medium-rare after 4 to 6 minutes per side.

FIREPLACE GRILL: Rake red hot embers under the gridiron and preheat it for 3 to 5 minutes; you want a hot, 2 to 3 Mississippi fire. When ready to cook, brush and oil the gridiron. Place the steaks on the hot grate. They will be cooked to medium-rare after about 4 to 6 minutes per side.

1. Place the steaks in a baking dish just large enough to hold them. Season them on both sides with salt and pepper (somewhat sparingly with the salt, very generously with the pepper). Sprinkle 1½ teaspoons of the brown sugar on each side of the steaks, patting it onto the meat with the back of a fork. Drizzle a little soy sauce over one side of each steak and pat it onto the meat with the fork to make a paste with the brown sugar. Repeat on the other side, then let stand for 5 minutes. Pour 3 tablespoons of soy sauce and the sesame oil over the steaks and turn them several times to coat both sides. Let the steaks marinate in the refrigerator, covered, for 1 to 4 hours, turning them once or twice; the longer they marinate, the richer the flavor will be.

2. Drain the steaks well, then cook them, following the instructions for any of the grills in the box at left, until cooked to taste. To test for doneness, use the poke method; when cooked to medium-rare the meat should be gently yielding.

3. Transfer the steaks to a platter or plates and serve at once.

steak au poivre

Steak au poivre is one of the glories of the French bistro. In recent years, there's been a tendency to gussy it up, to see, for example, how many different kinds of peppercorns you can fit on a steak. (Black, white, green, pink, cayenne, Szechuan, anyone?) This is all well and good unless you lose sight of just what steak au poivre is supposed to be—a great slab of meat in a flavorful peppery crust, not the edible equivalent of napalm. You may be intrigued to learn that this is the first of my barbecue books to feature steak au poivre. The reason is simple: The dish is traditionally cooked in a frying pan, which presses the peppercorns into the meat (they tend to fall off on a grill grate). A contact grill achieves a similar effect and gives you handsome grill marks to boot. You can certainly cook steak au poivre on other kinds of indoor grills. You may lose some of the peppercorns, but you'll still get a pronounced pepper flavor coupled with the sophisticated Cognac cream sauce. **SERVES 2; CAN BE MULTIPLIED AS DESIRED**

contact grilling a steak...

Contact grills cook many things well, including fish, burgers, and sandwiches.

Unfortunately, steak isn't one of them. The low heat and confined grilling environment tend to stew steaks rather than sear them, resulting in meat that's overcooked and gray.

There are a few exceptions. The contact grill does an acceptable job with steak dishes where the meat is traditionally cooked until relatively well done, like the Italian cheese steak on page 62 or the Magyar Beef Rolls on page 64. But if you crave a rare, juicy T-bone, it's best to cook it on another type of indoor grill, like a fireplace grill, a built-in grill, or a grill pan.

If you're using a contact grill, be mindful of the following:

1. You'll need one with the highest wattage possible, ideally 1,400 watts. (Low-wattage models simply don't get hot enough.)

2. It's good if the grill has sharply defined grill ridges (the sort you find in a panini machine). These are more likely to sear the meat and reduce the tendency to stew.

3. Preheat the grill well.

4. Grill a thick steak, preferably one that's 1 to 1½ inches thick. That way, the center will stay red and juicy, even with the slow searing of the exterior.

5. Sprinkle a little sugar or sweet barbecue rub on the steak just before you grill it. As the sugar caramelizes, it will help brown the crust.

THE RECIPE

2 New York strip steaks (each about
   1¼ inches thick and 10 to 12 ounces),
   or 4 thick filets mignons (each about
   1¼ inches thick and about 6 ounces)

Coarse salt (kosher or sea)

1 tablespoon extra-virgin olive oil

1 tablespoon dry mustard

2 to 4 tablespoons cracked black
   peppercorns

Cognac Sauce (recipe follows)

1. Season the steaks with salt generously on both sides, then brush both sides with the olive oil. Sprinkle the mustard over the steaks, patting it onto the meat with a fork. Sprinkle the peppercorns over the steaks, then press them into the meat.

2. Cook the steaks, following the instructions for any of the grills in the box at left, until cooked to taste (you may need to work in batches). To test for doneness, use the poke method; when cooked to medium-rare the meat should be gently yielding.

3. Transfer the steaks to a platter or plates. Pour the Cognac Sauce over them and serve at once.

if you have a...

CONTACT GRILL: Preheat the grill; if your contact grill has a temperature control, preheat the grill to high. Place the drip pan under the front of the grill. When ready to cook, lightly oil the grill surface. Place the steaks on the hot grill, then close the lid. Both strip steaks and fillets will be medium-rare after 6 to 10 minutes.

GRILL PAN: You'll need thinner steaks if you are cooking in a grill pan; buy ones that are 3/4 inch thick. Place the grill pan on the stove and preheat it to medium-high over medium heat. When the grill pan is hot a drop of water will skitter i:. the pan. When ready to cook, lightly oil the ridges of the grill pan. Place the steaks in the hot grill pan. Both strip steaks and fillets will be medium-rare after about 4 minutes per side.

BUILT-IN GRILL: Preheat the grill to high, then, if it does not have a nonstick surface, brush and oil the grill grate. Place the steaks on the hot grate. Both strip steaks and fillets will be medium-rare after 6 to 8 minutes per side.

FREESTANDING GRILL: You're better off using thinner steaks here, ones that are 3/4 inch thick. Preheat the grill to high; there's no need to oil the grate. Place the steaks on the hot grill. Both strip steaks and fillets will be medium-rare after about 5 minutes per side.

FIREPLACE GRILL: Rake red hot embers under the gridiron and preheat it for 3 to 5 minutes; you want a hot, 2 to 3 Mississippi fire. When ready to cook, brush and oil the gridiron. Place the steaks on the hot grate. Both strip steaks and fillets will be medium-rare after 6 to 8 minutes per side.

cognac sauce

Cognac, cream, and shallots make the French roots of this sauce unmistakable. For the best results, use a homemade stock (canned stocks and broths tend to be high in sodium, so by the time they cook down, the sauce becomes unpalatably salty). Veal, beef, or chicken stock will all work. The Cognac Sauce would be pretty terrific over grilled chicken or pork, too. It's so tasty, you'll want extra for dunking your bread. **MAKES ABOUT ¾ CUP**

1½ tablespoons unsalted butter

2 shallots, peeled and minced (about ½ cup)

3 tablespoons Cognac

1 cup veal, beef, or chicken stock
    (preferably homemade)

1 cup heavy (whipping) cream

2 teaspoons Dijon mustard

Coarse salt (kosher or sea) and freshly
    ground black pepper

1. Melt the butter in a saucepan (see Note) over medium heat. Add the shallots and cook until soft and translucent but not brown, about 3 minutes.

2. Add the Cognac and increase the heat to high. Let boil until only about 1 tablespoon of the liquid remains, about 2 minutes. Add the stock, let come to a boil, and cook until only about ⅓ cup of the liquid remains, 5 to 8 minutes. Add the cream, let come to a boil, and cook until the sauce is thick and creamy and reduced to about ¾ cup, 5 to 8 minutes. Whisk in the mustard and season the sauce with salt and pepper to taste. The sauce can be made up to a day ahead and refrigerated, covered. Reheat it over low heat just before serving.

NOTE: If you're cooking the steaks in a grill pan, you can make the sauce right in the pan and take advantage of the meat juices.

tip

Some people prefer to make steak au poivre with filet mignon. Personally, I like a steak with more chew to it, but you can certainly use filet mignon if you prefer. And, it's not traditional, but thick pork loin chops prepared this way are terrific; you'll need 1½ to 1¾ pounds.

filets mignons
with gaucho seasonings

Argentinean grilling burst onto the North American dining scene in the 1990s. The bold use of fire and robustly grilled beef struck a sympathetic cord among steak lovers. So did a family of simple, vibrant garlic, herb, and vinegar sauces known collectively as *chimichurri*. In its country of origin (unlike the *chimichurri* you'll find at most restaurants in the States), the gaucho *chimichurri* is made with dried, not fresh, herbs and it is spooned somewhat sparingly over all manner of grilled meats. Here this simple "cowboy" sauce accompanies lavish grilled filets mignons. **SERVES 4**

THE RECIPE

1 clove garlic, minced

Coarse salt (kosher or sea) and freshly ground black pepper

1 tablespoon dried oregano

1 teaspoon dried sage

2 tablespoons distilled white vinegar or wine vinegar, or more to taste

2 tablespoons extra-virgin olive oil

2 tablespoons boiling water

1½ pounds filet mignon (see Note)

1. Place the garlic, 1 teaspoon of salt, and ½ teaspoon of pepper in a small, heat-proof, nonreactive bowl and mash to a paste with the back of a spoon. Add the oregano and sage and continue mashing until combined. Add the vinegar and whisk to mix. Whisk in the olive oil, followed by the boiling water. Taste for seasoning, adding more salt, pepper, and/or vinegar as necessary; the sauce should be highly seasoned.

2. Season the fillets with salt and pepper, then cook them, following the instructions for any of the grills in the box at left, until cooked to taste. To test for doneness, use the poke method; when cooked to medium-rare the meat should be gently yielding.

NOTE: The thickness of the filets mignons will depend on your choice of indoor grill. Choose 1¼- to 1½-inch-thick fillets if you are cooking on a contact grill. When cooking in a grill pan, you want fillets that are about ¾ inch thick. If you are using a built-in grill or fireplace grill, select fillets that are 1 to 1¼ inches thick.

if you have a...

CONTACT GRILL: Preheat the grill; if your contact grill has a temperature control, preheat the grill to high. Place the drip pan under the front of the grill. Place the fillets on the hot grill, then close the lid. They will be cooked to medium-rare after 6 to 10 minutes. (You will get the best results with a powerful *panini* machine.)

GRILL PAN: Place the grill pan on the stove and preheat it to medium-high over medium heat. When the grill pan is hot a drop of water will skitter in the pan. When ready to cook, lightly oil the ridges of the grill pan. Place the fillets in the hot grill pan. They will be cooked to medium-rare after about 4 minutes per side.

BUILT-IN GRILL: Preheat the grill to high, then, if it does not have a nonstick surface, brush and oil the grill grate. Place the fillets on the hot grate. They will be cooked to medium-rare after 6 to 8 minutes per side. You'll probably need to turn the fillets on their sides to grill the edges.

FIREPLACE GRILL: Rake red hot embers under the gridiron and preheat it for 3 to 5 minutes; you want a high, 2 to 3 Mississippi fire. When ready to cook, brush and oil the gridiron. Place the fillets on the hot grate. They will be cooked to medium-rare after 6 to 8 minutes per side. You'll probably need to turn the fillets on their sides to grill the edges.

rotisserie

dry rub beef ribs

As a rule, ribs are grilled or smoked, but they're also great for spit roasting, a fact that is much appreciated by the French, Italians, and Chinese. The gentle heat cooks the meat without making it tough, and as the ribs slowly rotate the fat melts, basting the ribs and forming a crackling crisp crust. Case in point, these ribs, seasoned with a classic American barbecue rub and served "dry" (not slathered with sauce), in the style of Memphis. You even get a hint of smoke flavor, thanks to a shot of liquid smoke. You'll find two more ways to spit roast beef ribs on pages 86 and 87. **SERVES 2 TO 3**

tip

Choose the long slender back ribs, not short ribs, for this recipe—they're more tender. You can use the basket attachment of the rotisserie to hold the ribs as they cook.

T H E   R E C I P E

3 pounds beef back ribs
(1 rack or 6 to 8 individual ribs)
3 tablespoons Basic Barbecue Rub (page 362)
or your favorite barbecue rub
1½ tablespoons liquid smoke
1 tablespoon vegetable oil
Your favorite barbecue sauce (optional),
for serving

1. Rinse the ribs under cold running water and blot dry with paper towels. Sprinkle the rub all over the ribs on both sides, patting it onto the meat with your fingertips.

2. Place the liquid smoke and the oil in a small bowl and whisk to mix. Brush the mixture all over the ribs on both sides. You can cook the ribs right away and they'll taste great, but they'll have even

more flavor if you let them cure in the refrigerator for 2 to 4 hours.

3. When ready to cook, place the drip pan in the bottom of the rotisserie. Place the ribs in the rotisserie basket and tightly close the lid. Attach the basket to the rotisserie spit, then attach the spit to the rotisserie and turn on the motor. If your rotisserie has a temperature control, set it to 400°F (for instructions for using a rotisserie, see page 14). Cook the ribs until they are dark brown and crusty and the meat has shrunk back about ½ inch from the ends of the bones, about 40 minutes.

4. Transfer the ribs to a platter and serve at once with your favorite barbecue sauce on the side, if desired.

rotisserie

lemongrass beef ribs

Here's a Southeast Asian version of a spit-roasted beef rib. It takes advantage of beef's affinity for the herbaceous, lemony flavor of lemongrass. To complete the Southeast Asian theme, sprinkle the ribs with chopped roasted peanuts. The combination will be familiar to anyone who's eaten Vietnam's national grilled beef dish, *bo bun*. **SERVES 4**

THE RECIPE

2 stalks fresh lemongrass, trimmed and
    coarsely chopped
1 shallot, peeled and coarsely chopped
2 cloves garlic, peeled and coarsely chopped
1 to 2 jalapeño peppers or serrano peppers,
    seeded and coarsely chopped
    (for hotter ribs, leave the seeds in)
3 tablespoons chopped fresh cilantro leaves,
    plus $1/4$ cup finely chopped fresh cilantro,
    for serving
2 tablespoons Asian fish sauce or soy sauce
1 tablespoon fresh lemon juice
1 tablespoon vegetable oil
$1/2$ teaspoon freshly ground black pepper
3 pounds beef back ribs
    (1 rack or 6 to 8 individual ribs)
$1/4$ cup finely chopped roasted peanuts,
    for serving

1. Place the lemongrass, shallot, garlic, jalapeño(s), and 3 tablespoons of chopped cilantro in a food processor and finely chop. Add the fish sauce, lemon juice, oil, and black pepper and process to a smooth paste.

2. Rinse the ribs under cold running water and blot dry with paper towels, then place in a large nonreactive bowl. Spread the lemongrass mixture all over the ribs. Let the ribs marinate in the refrigerator, covered, for at least 6 hours, preferably overnight.

3. When ready to cook, place the drip pan in the bottom of the rotisserie. Place the ribs in the rotisserie basket and tightly close the lid. Attach the basket to the rotisserie spit, then attach the spit to the rotisserie and turn on the motor. If your rotisserie has a temperature control, set it to 400°F (for instructions for using a rotisserie, see page 14). Cook the ribs until they are dark brown and crusty and the meat has shrunk back about $1/2$ inch from the ends of the bone, about 40 minutes.

4. Transfer the ribs to a platter, sprinkle the peanuts and the $1/4$ cup cilantro over them, and serve at once.

rotisserie

spit-roasted beef ribs
with smoky spanish paprika

Being an outdoor barbecue guy at heart, I'm obsessed with how to obtain a similar smoke flavor when grilling or spit-roasting indoors. In Dry Rub Beef Ribs (page 85), I resorted to an American solution—a shot of liquid smoke. This recipe features one of the hottest ingredients to be imported from Spain: *pimentón,* smoked paprika. The peppers are smoked over smoldering oak before being ground, and they impart an utterly delicious flavor. **SERVES 4**

SMOKED PAPRIKA

Smoked paprika is available at Spanish markets and gourmet shops; one good brand is La Chinata. Or you can order it online from companies like Tienda (see Mail-Order Sources on page 396). There are at least three different types: sweet smoked paprika, bittersweet smoked paprika, and hot smoked paprika. The choice is up to you.

THE RECIPE

3 pounds beef back ribs
    (1 rack or 6 to 8 individual ribs)
1 tablespoon smoked paprika
1 1/2 teaspoons coarse salt (kosher or sea)
1 teaspoon freshly ground black pepper
1 teaspoon onion powder
1 teaspoon garlic powder
1/2 teaspoon ground cumin
1/2 teaspoon ground coriander
1/2 teaspoon dried oregano
1/2 teaspoon ground ginger
1/4 teaspoon hot red pepper flakes
1 tablespoon extra-virgin olive oil
Smoked Paprika Sauce
    (optional; recipe follows)

1. Rinse the ribs under cold running water and blot dry with paper towels.

2. Place the paprika, salt, pepper, onion and garlic powders, cumin, coriander, oregano, ginger, and hot pepper flakes in a small bowl and whisk to mix. Sprinkle the rub all over the ribs on both sides, patting it onto the meat with your fingertips. Brush the olive oil all over the ribs on both sides. You can cook the ribs right away and they'll taste great, but they'll have even more flavor if you let them cure in the refrigerator, covered, overnight.

3. When ready to cook, place the drip pan in the bottom of the rotisserie. Place the ribs in the rotisserie basket and tightly close the lid. Attach the basket to the rotisserie spit, then attach the spit to the rotisserie and turn on the motor. If your rotisserie has a temperature control, set it to 400°F (for instructions for using a rotisserie, see page 14). Cook the ribs until they are dark brown and crusty and the meat has shrunk back about

½ inch from the ends of the bones, about 40 minutes.

4. Transfer the ribs to a platter and serve at once with the Smoked Paprika Sauce, if desired.

smoked paprika sauce

Catalans call it *allioli*. The French call it *aïoli*. Whatever you call it, this garlicky mayonnaise is irresistible. And, when spiked with smoked paprika,

it makes an unexpected and delectable dip for ribs. You can use sweet, bittersweet, or hot smoked paprika in the sauce. **MAKES ABOUT 1 CUP**

3 cloves garlic, minced
½ teaspoon coarse salt (kosher or sea)
1 cup mayonnaise
½ teaspoon freshly ground white pepper
2 teaspoons smoked paprika
1 tablespoon fresh lemon juice,
**   or more to taste**

Place the garlic and salt in a nonreactive mixing bowl and mash to a paste with the back of a spoon. Stir in the mayonnaise, white pepper, paprika, and lemon juice. Taste for seasoning, adding more lemon juice as necessary. For the best flavor, let the sauce stand for 30 minutes before serving. The sauce can be refrigerated, covered, for several days.

tips

■ You may be surprised to see gin listed as a substitute for juniper, but this purple-blue berry is the spirit's most prominent flavoring.

■ When buying venison, the leg is probably the most economical cut, the back strap or tenderloin the most tender. If you can't find venison, you can marinate and grill beef, pork, or lamb the same way.

juniper-marinated venison kebabs

Grilling venison presents an interesting challenge to the grill jockey. The rich meat benefits from a high, dry heat, but because like most game it's quite lean, it has a tendency to dry out. That's where the marinade and a few slices of bacon come in—both add flavor (in this case a piquant mix of juniper and spices) and help to keep the meat moist. **SERVES 4**

1 tablespoon juniper berries,
    or 2 tablespoons gin

2 teaspoons black peppercorns

1 teaspoon allspice berries

2 sprigs fresh rosemary, chopped,
    or 1 tablespoon dried rosemary

3 cloves garlic, peeled and gently crushed
    with the side of a cleaver

3 strips lemon zest (each $1/2$ by $1^1/2$ inches)

3 tablespoons fresh lemon juice

3 tablespoons dry white vermouth or white wine

$1/4$ cup extra-virgin olive oil

2 medium-size onions

$1^1/2$ pounds venison, cut into 1-inch cubes

4 thick slices bacon, cut into 1-inch pieces

Coarse salt (kosher or sea) and freshly ground
    black pepper

YOU'LL ALSO NEED:
8 metal or bamboo skewers (8 inches long)

1. Place the juniper berries, peppercorns, allspice berries, and rosemary in a large nonreactive bowl and crush them with the back of a wooden spoon to release the aromatic oils. Add the garlic, lemon zest, lemon juice, vermouth, and olive oil and stir to mix. Set the marinade aside.

2. Cut each onion lengthwise into quarters, then cut each quarter in half crosswise. Add the smallest center pieces to the marinade. Set the remaining pieces of onion aside.

3. Add the venison to the bowl with the marinade and stir to coat evenly. Let the venison marinate in the refrigerator, covered, for at least 4 hours or as long as overnight.

4. Drain the venison in a strainer over a small nonreactive saucepan. Bring the marinade to a boil over high heat and let boil briskly until the flavors are concentrated, about 3 minutes. Thread the venison onto skewers, placing a piece of reserved onion and a piece of bacon

if you have a...

CONTACT GRILL: Preheat the grill; if your contact grill has a temperature control, preheat the grill to high. Place the drip pan under the front of the grill. When ready to cook, lightly oil the grill surface. Place the kebabs on the hot grill, then close the lid. Give each kebab a quarter turn after 2 minutes. The kebabs will be cooked to medium-rare after 3 to 4 minutes; they will be cooked to medium after 5 to 6 minutes.

GRILL PAN: Place the grill pan on the stove and preheat it to medium-high over medium heat. When the grill pan is hot a drop of water will skitter in the pan. When ready to cook, lightly oil the ridges of the grill pan. Place the kebabs in the hot grill pan. The kebabs will be cooked to medium-rare after about $1^1/2$ minutes per side (6 minutes in all); they will be cooked to medium after 2 to 3 minutes per side (8 to 12 minutes in all). Use the boiled marinade sparingly when basting, taking care not to drip a lot of it into the grill pan. After it has cooled down, soak the grill pan in hot water to loosen any burnt-on marinade.

BUILT-IN GRILL: Preheat the grill to high, then, if it does not have a nonstick surface, brush and oil the grill grate. Place the kebabs on the hot grate so that the exposed ends of the skewers extend off the grate. The kebabs will be cooked to medium-rare after about $1^1/2$ minutes per side (6 minutes in all); they will be cooked to medium after 2 to 3 minutes per side (8 to 12 minutes in all).

FREESTANDING GRILL: Preheat the grill to high; there's no need to oil the grate. Place the kebabs on the hot grill. They will be cooked to medium-rare after about $2^1/2$ minutes per side (10 minutes in all); they will be cooked to medium after 3 to 4 minutes per side (12 to 16 minutes in all).

FIREPLACE GRILL: Rake red hot embers under the gridiron and preheat it for 3 to 5 minutes; you want a hot, 2 to 3 Mississippi fire. When ready to cook, brush and oil the gridiron. Place the kebabs on the hot grate. The kebabs will be cooked to medium-rare after about $1^1/2$ minutes per side (6 minutes in all); they will be cooked to medium after 2 to 3 minutes per side (8 to 12 minutes in all).

between each cube of meat. The kebabs can be prepared up to this stage several hours ahead and refrigerated, covered.

5. Season the kebabs generously with salt and pepper, then cook them, following the instructions for any of the grills in the box on the previous page, until the meat is nicely browned and cooked to taste. For medium-rare, a meat cube will feel gently yielding when squeezed between thumb and forefinger; medium will feel firmly yielding. Once the kebabs have begun to brown, baste them with the boiled marinade (if you are using a contact grill, there is no need to baste the kebabs).

6. Transfer the grilled kebabs to a platter or plates and serve at once. If you have used metal skewers, warn everyone to take the kebabs off the skewers before eating, as they will be very hot.

saltimbocca

Saltimbocca, small rolls of veal stuffed with fresh sage leaves and slices of prosciutto, is one of Rome's great gifts to veal lovers. Traditionally it's sautéed, but grilling produces crusty roulades with considerably less fat and effort, and it can give you grill marks to boot. The result lives up to the dish's name—so delectable, it literally leaps into (*salt im*) your mouth (*bocca*). **SERVES 4**

THE RECIPE

1¹/₂ pounds thinly sliced veal cutlets
Coarse salt (kosher or sea) and freshly
    ground black pepper
4 thin slices prosciutto (about 3 ounces total),
    each cut crosswise into 4 pieces
1 bunch fresh sage leaves, rinsed, stemmed,
    and blotted dry
3 ounces Taleggio or other cheese,
    cut into ¹/₄-by-¹/₄-by-1-inch strips
Olive oil

YOU'LL ALSO NEED:
About 16 wooden toothpicks

1. Place a piece of veal between 2 pieces of plastic wrap and, using a meat pounder or the side of a heavy cleaver, pound it until it is about ¹/₈ inch thick. Repeat with the remaining pieces of veal, then cut each into pieces that are about 3 inches long and 2 inches wide. Season the veal on both sides with salt and pepper.

2. Place a piece of veal on a work surface and top it with a piece of prosciutto. Place a whole sage leaf and a piece of cheese at one short end and roll up the veal to make a small roulade. Secure the roll closed with a toothpick. Repeat with the remaining pieces of veal; you should have about 16 rolls. The roulades can be prepared up to this stage several hours ahead and refrigerated, covered.

3. Brush the veal rolls all over with olive oil and season them with salt and pepper. Cook the roulades, following the instructions for any of the grills in the box at right, until nicely browned on the outside and cooked through. Unless you are cooking the roulades on a contact grill, you'll need to turn them with tongs often so that they brown evenly.

4. Transfer the saltimbocca to a platter or plates, remove and discard the toothpicks, then serve at once.

if you have a...

CONTACT GRILL: Preheat the grill; if your contact grill has a temperature control, preheat the grill to high. Place the drip pan under the front of the grill. When ready to cook, lightly oil the grill surface. Place the roulades on the hot grill, then close the lid. The saltimbocca will be done after cooking 3 to 5 minutes.

GRILL PAN: Place the grill pan on the stove and preheat it to medium-high over medium heat. When the grill pan is hot a drop of water will skitter in the pan. When ready to cook, lightly oil the ridges of the grill pan. Place the roulades in the hot grill pan. They will be done after cooking 2 to 3 minutes per side (4 to 6 minutes in all).

BUILT-IN GRILL: Preheat the grill to medium-high, then, if it does not have a nonstick surface, brush and oil the grill grate. Place the roulades on the hot grate. They will be done after cooking 2 to 3 minutes per side (4 to 6 minutes in all).

FREESTANDING GRILL: Preheat the grill to high; there's no need to oil the grate. Place the roulades on the hot grill. They will be done after cooking 3 to 4 minutes per side (6 to 8 minutes in all).

FIREPLACE GRILL: Rake red hot embers under the gridiron and preheat it for 3 to 5 minutes; you want a hot, 2 to 3 Mississippi fire. When ready to cook, brush and oil the gridiron. Place the roulades on the hot grate. They will be done after cooking 2 to 3 minutes per side (4 to 6 minutes in all).

grilled calf's liver
with truffles and sage

Mild and tender, with just a hint of sweetness, calf's liver is delicious when quickly seared over a wood fire. That's the way they prepare it at Da Toso, a nearly century-old restaurant in the town of Leonacco near Udine in the northwestern Italian region of Friuli. The centerpiece of the restaurant is the *fogolar,* or freestanding hearth. Once off the grill, the liver is topped with another Italian delicacy—paper-thin shavings of white truffle. This could be the most elegant calf's liver you'll ever taste. **SERVES 4**

T H E R E C I P E

4 thin slices calf's liver
(no less than 1/4 inch and no more than
1/2 inch thick; about 1 1/2 pounds total)
Coarse salt (kosher or sea) and freshly
ground black pepper
1 to 2 tablespoons extra-virgin olive oil
1 small white truffle (1/2 to 1 ounce),
wiped clean with a damp paper towel
(see Notes)

1. Generously season each piece of liver on both sides with salt and pepper. Cook the liver, following the instructions for any of the grills in the box below, until cooked to taste. To test for doneness, use the poke method; when cooked to medium-rare the meat should be gently yielding.

2. Transfer the grilled liver to a platter or plates. Drizzle olive oil over each slice and shave paper-thin slices of truffle on top. Serve at once.

NOTES:

■ The best place to buy calf's liver is from a butcher shop. Be sure it's real calf's liver, not strong-flavored beef liver.

■ Intensely aromatic, scarce white truffles cost a proverbial king's ransom and are served sliced tissue thin (there are truffle shavers specifically for this purpose). The truffles are in season in the fall. If you're not feeling quite so indulgent—or wealthy—you can sprinkle the liver with a few drops of truffle oil, which is available at specialty food stores. To substitute truffle oil for the truffle, omit the olive oil and drizzle 1/2 teaspoon truffle oil over each slice of liver.

if you have a...

CONTACT GRILL: Preheat the grill; if your contact grill has a temperature control, preheat the grill to high. Place the drip pan under the front of the grill. When ready to cook, lightly oil the grill surface. Place the slices of liver on the hot grill, then close the lid. They will be cooked to medium-rare after 2 to 3 minutes.

GRILL PAN: Place the grill pan on the stove and preheat it to medium-high over medium heat. When the grill pan is hot a drop of water will skitter in the pan. When ready to cook, lightly oil the ridges of the grill pan. Place the slices of liver in the hot grill pan. They will be cooked to medium-rare after 2 to 3 minutes per side.

BUILT-IN GRILL: Preheat the grill to high, then, if it does not have a nonstick surface, brush and oil the grill grate. Place the slices of liver on the hot grate. They will be cooked to medium-rare after 2 to 3 minutes per side.

FREESTANDING GRILL: Preheat the grill to high; there's no need to oil the grate. Place the slices of liver on the hot grill. They will be cooked to medium-rare after 3 to 4 minutes per side.

FIREPLACE GRILL: Rake red hot embers under the gridiron and preheat it for 3 to 5 minutes; you want a hot, 2 to 3 Mississippi fire. When ready to cook, brush and oil the gridiron. Place the slices of liver on the hot grate. They will be cooked to medium-rare after 2 to 3 minutes per side.

Go on—make a perfect hog of yourself. Pork is great for indoor grilling. If smoke is your thing, you'll love the North Carolina pulled pork. If you fancy shish kebab, check out the mint-scented pork souvlaki. The grill pan is perfect for pork chops (you'll find seasonings ranging from Greek oregano to a Southeast Asian lemongrass marinade). A countertop rotisserie turns out wondrous ginger and garlic scented Chinese barbecued ribs. From Kansas City–style rotisserie baby backs to pork *paprikás,* the indoor grill makes it easy to live—and eat—high on the hog.

pork

rotisserie

garlicky spit-roasted pork

Every region in Latin America has its version of roast pork. Here's the Spanish Caribbean version, fragrant with garlic, cilantro, cumin, oregano, onion, and freshly squeezed lime juice. The preferred cooking method, in Miami at least, is baked in the oven or pit roasted. While locally I've never seen a pork shoulder cooked in a countertop rotisserie, the slow, gentle rotation turns out a textbook specimen—beautifully browned on the outside, succulent inside, and so tender you can literally pull it apart with your fingers. If you want to serve the roast with a sauce, try the Cuban sauce on page 312. **SERVES 8 TO 10**

tips

■ This recipe calls for a 5-pound pork shoulder roast. Choose one that's well marbled; the melting fat will baste the meat.

■ You can also cook the meat on a fireplace rotisserie (see page 11). Trim off any excess fat before placing it on the spit. Cook over a hot, 2 to 3 Mississippi fire. It will take from 1½ to 2 hours, depending on your fireplace.

THE RECIPE

4 cloves garlic, coarsely chopped
¼ cup fresh cilantro leaves, coarsely chopped
1 teaspoon ground cumin
1 teaspoon dried oregano
Coarse salt (kosher or sea) and freshly ground black pepper
1 tablespoon vegetable oil
2 to 3 tablespoons fresh lime juice, plus ¾ cup for marinating the pork
1 pork shoulder roast (about 5 pounds)
1 small sweet onion, thinly sliced

1. Place the garlic, cilantro, cumin, and oregano in a mortar. Add 1 tablespoon of salt and 2 teaspoons of pepper and, using the pestle, pound to a coarse paste. Gradually work in the vegetable oil and enough lime juice to obtain a thick

paste (you'll need 2 to 3 tablespoons). Alternatively, place the garlic, cilantro, cumin, oregano, 1 tablespoon of salt, and 2 teaspoons of pepper in a food processor and finely chop. Add the vegetable oil and enough lime juice to process to a coarse paste, scraping down the side of the bowl with a rubber spatula.

2. Using the tip of a paring knife, make small slits on all sides of the roast about 1½ inches apart. Using the tip of your index finger, widen the holes. Using about half of the garlic and cilantro paste, place a tiny spoonful in each hole, forcing it in with your finger. Season the roast with salt and pepper, then spread the remaining garlic and cilantro paste all over the pork. Place the roast in a large resealable plastic bag or in a large nonreactive bowl and add the sliced onion. Pour the ¾ cup of lime juice on top. Let the pork shoulder marinate for at least 4 hours or as long as overnight, turning it several times; the longer it marinates, the richer the flavor will be.

3. When ready to cook, place the drip pan in the bottom of the rotisserie. Skewer the pork shoulder lengthwise on the rotisserie spit. Attach the spit to the rotisserie and turn on the motor. If your rotisserie has a temperature control, set it to 400°F (for instructions for using a rotisserie, see page 14). Cook the pork shoulder until it is darkly browned on all sides and well-done,

2 to 2½ hours. Use an instant-read meat thermometer to test for doneness; don't let the thermometer touch the spit or a bone. Well-done pork will have an internal temperature of between 190° and 195°F. This may be more done than you usually cook pork shoulder, but this internal temperature is necessary to produce the requisite fall-off-the-bone tenderness.

4. Transfer the pork shoulder to a platter or cutting board, remove the spit, and let the meat rest for 10 minutes before serving. The meat can be thinly sliced or chopped.

rotisserie

puerto rican pork
with annatto oil

A whole hog or pork shoulder, roasted crackling crisp on a turnspit, perfumed with garlic and Caribbean herbs, and basted with annatto oil till it's the color of gold—if this is your idea of heaven, you'll find paradise in Puerto Rico, where barbecued pork lies somewhere between culinary art and cultural icon. In the countryside, whole hogs are cooked over ember-filled pits. City dwellers can make do with pork shoulder. This isn't a half-bad substitute, for what gives Puerto Rican–style barbecued pork its character is a uniquely fragrant spice paste made of garlic, the herb *culentro, naranja agria* (sour orange), and that golden-colored annatto oil. Annatto oil is one of the most distinctive seasonings in the Caribbean, imparting not just a golden hue but a haunting aromatic flavor. The countertop rotisserie produces a pork shoulder that's dark and crusty on the outside and moist and succulent within. **SERVES 8 TO 10**

THE RECIPE

⅔ cup vegetable oil
⅓ cup annatto seeds, or 3 tablespoons sweet paprika
1 bunch culentro (see Note), rinsed, dried, stemmed, and coarsely chopped (about ½ cup loosely packed)
8 cloves garlic, coarsely chopped
Coarse salt (kosher or sea) and freshly ground black pepper
¼ cup fresh sour orange juice, or
   2 tablespoons fresh lime juice plus
   2 tablespoons fresh orange juice
1 pork shoulder roast (about 5 pounds)

1. Heat the oil in a small skillet over medium heat until it is hot enough that an annatto seed dropped in the oil will dance and sizzle. Add the annatto seeds to the skillet and cook until they start to crackle and the oil is golden brown, 3 to 5 minutes, gently shaking the skillet. Pour the oil through a strainer into a heatproof bowl and discard the annatto seeds. (If using paprika, cook it in the oil for 15 seconds, then pour the oil through a metal strainer lined with a coffee filter.) Let the flavored oil cool to room temperature.

2. Place the *culentro,* garlic, 1 tablespoon of salt, and 2 teaspoons of pepper in a food processor and finely chop. Add ¼

cup of the flavored oil and the sour orange juice and process to a coarse paste, scraping down the side of the bowl with a rubber spatula. Set the remaining flavored oil aside.

3. Using the tip of a paring knife, make small slits on all sides of the roast about 1½ inches apart. Using the tip of your index finger, widen the holes. Using about half of the *culentro* paste, place a tiny spoonful in each hole, forcing it in with your finger. Season the roast with salt and pepper, then spread the remaining *culentro* paste all over the pork. Place the roast in a large resealable plastic bag or in a large nonreactive bowl. Let the pork shoulder marinate for at least 4 hours or as long as overnight, turning it several times; the longer it marinates, the richer the flavor will be.

4. When ready to cook, place the drip pan in the bottom of the rotisserie. Skewer the pork shoulder lengthwise on the rotisserie spit. Attach the spit to the rotisserie and turn on the motor. If your rotisserie has a temperature control, set it to 400°F (for instructions for using a rotisserie, see page 14). Cook the pork shoulder until it is darkly browned on all sides and well-done,

2 to 2½ hours. Use an instant-read meat thermometer to test for doneness; don't let the thermometer touch the spit or a bone. Well-done pork will have an internal temperature of between 190° and 195°F. This may be more done than you usually cook pork shoulder, but this internal temperature is necessary to produce the requisite fall-off-the-bone tenderness. Baste the roast with the remaining flavored oil every 20 minutes.

5. Transfer the pork shoulder to a platter or cutting board, remove the spit, and let the meat rest for 10 minutes before serving. The meat can be thinly sliced or chopped.

NOTE: You can substitute ½ bunch of cilantro that has been rinsed, dried, stemmed, and coarsely chopped (about ½ cup) and ½ cup chopped fresh flat-leaf parsley for the *culentro*.

stove-top smoker

pulled pork indoors

Cooking North Carolina–style pulled pork indoors may well feel right at home. That's because so many Tar Heel pit masters have switched to gas and electric cookers, which are no different, really, than baking pork in the oven. This recipe imbues the pork with a traditional smoke flavor, in the style of the shoulders cooked by legends like Wayne Monk at Lexington Barbecue in Lexington, North Carolina. It all starts with a stove-top smoker—and the mystical properties of hickory smoke. So why is it called pulled pork? The customary way to serve the dark, shiny, smoke-perfumed, fall-off-the-bone tender pork roast is "pulled" or torn into thin meaty shreds (some pit masters chop the meat with a cleaver). The shredded pork is tossed with vinegar sauce, then piled onto hamburger buns with mounds of vinegary coleslaw. When push comes to shove, I doubt there's a better way to enjoy this rich, meaty cut of pork. **SERVES 10 TO 12**

tip

Because of the size of a pork shoulder, you'll need to tent the smoker with a large piece of aluminum foil rather than covering it with its lid.

tip

There are several options for rubs here. To be strictly authentic, you'd season the pork with nothing but salt and pepper. I like to use the All-Purpose Smoky Barbecue Rub on page 362 or even the 5-4-3-2-1 Rub in Step 1 on page 126.

THE RECIPE

1 Boston butt (bone-in pork shoulder roast; 5 to 6 pounds)
1/3 cup of your favorite barbecue rub, or plenty of coarse salt (kosher or sea) and freshly ground black pepper
Cooking oil spray (optional)
Carolina Vinegar Sauce (recipe follows)
10 to 12 hamburger buns
3 tablespoons butter (optional), melted
Vinegar Slaw (recipe follows)

YOU'LL ALSO NEED:
3 tablespoons hickory sawdust

1. Place the pork roast on a baking sheet and sprinkle the barbecue rub on all sides, rubbing it onto the meat with your fingertips, or season the roast very generously with salt and pepper. You can smoke the pork shoulder right away, but it will have even more flavor if you let it cure in the refrigerator, covered, for 4 to 12 hours.

2. When ready to cook, set up the smoker (for instructions for using a stove-top smoker, see page 16). Place the sawdust in the center of the bottom of the smoker. Line the drip pan with aluminum foil and place it in the smoker. Lightly coat the smoker rack with cooking oil spray, or use a paper towel dipped in oil, and place the rack in the smoker. Place the pork shoulder, fat side up, on the rack. Tent the pork with a long sheet of heavy-duty aluminum foil, crumpling and crimping the edges over the outside rim of the smoker bottom to make a tight seal. Try not to let the foil come in contact with the roast.

3. Place the smoker over high heat for 3 minutes, then reduce the heat to medium. Smoke the pork until it has absorbed the maximum amount of smoke, about 40 minutes.

4. Meanwhile, preheat the oven to 325°F.

5. Unwrap the pork shoulder and discard the aluminum foil. Place the pork still on the smoker bottom in the oven and bake it until very darkly browned and well-done, 2½ to 3 hours. Use an instant-read meat thermometer to test for doneness. Well-done pork will have an internal temperature of between 190° and 195°F (this may sound high for pork, but you need this degree of doneness for the pork to shred properly).

6. Transfer the pork to a cutting board, cover it loosely with aluminum foil, and let it rest for 10 minutes. Then, wearing heavy, insulated rubber gloves (you'll probably have these from your indoor rotisserie), pull off the skin and dark crust (these are called the "brownies" and they are considered the connoisseur's morsels) and, if desired, finely chop them. Pull out and discard any bones and lumps of fat. Using your fingertips or a fork, pull each piece of pork into thin shreds. Or use a cleaver to finely chop it. Transfer the pork to a large aluminum foil pan or serving bowl and toss it with 1 cup or so of the vinegar sauce.

7. Just before serving, brush the top, bottom, and insides of the buns with melted butter, if using, and toast them in a contact grill or on a griddle until lightly browned, 2 to 4 minutes. This step is optional; it takes a highly respectable pulled pork sandwich and transports it to the realm of the extraordinary.

8. To serve, place a mound of pork on each bun and add some "brownies," if desired. Top the pork with some Vinegar Slaw and a little more vinegar sauce, if desired. Top with the other half of the bun and serve at once.

carolina vinegar sauce

Red or clear? Sweet-sour or simply sour-sour? These are two of the great debates in North Carolina barbecue, and depending on where you're from you'll advocate one or the other with a loyalty bordering on fanaticism. What you'll find here is a western North Carolina–style sauce, recognizable by the touch of red and sweetness provided by a shot of ketchup and brown sugar. In the eastern part of the state, the sauce would lack these ingredients and would probably be a touch saltier, hotter, and more vinegary. You'll have enough vinegar sauce to toss with the pulled pork and make the coleslaw—and still have some left to pour on the sandwiches before serving. **MAKES ABOUT 3 CUPS**

2 cups cider vinegar
1/3 cup ketchup
**1 to 2 tablespoons hot sauce,
    such as Crystal**
3 tablespoons brown sugar, or more to taste
**4 teaspoons coarse salt (kosher or sea),
    or more to taste**
**1 tablespoon of your favorite barbecue rub,
    such as the All-Purpose Smoky Barbecue
    Rub (page 362) or the 5-4-3-2-1 Rub
    (page 126, Step 1)**
2 to 3 teaspoons hot red pepper flakes
1 teaspoon freshly ground black pepper

Place the vinegar, ketchup, hot sauce, brown sugar, salt, barbecue rub, hot pepper flakes, and black pepper in a nonreactive bowl. Add 1/2 cup of water and whisk until the brown sugar and salt dissolve. Taste for seasoning, adding more brown sugar and/or salt to taste; the sauce should be piquant but not quite sour. Stored in a jar in the refrigerator the sauce will keep for several weeks. Let it return to room temperature before using.

vinegar slaw

North Carolina slaw may seem minimalist, lacking the mayonnaise, carrots, and bell peppers most people associate with coleslaw. But, when it comes to a counterpoint for the richness of pork shoulder, nothing can beat it. **MAKES 6 TO 7 CUPS**

**1 small or 1/2 large green cabbage
    (about 11/2 pounds)**
**1 cup Carolina Vinegar Sauce,
    or more to taste**
**Coarse salt (kosher or sea) and
    freshly ground black pepper**

1. Cut the cabbage in half and remove and discard the core. Cut each half into 5 chunks. Place the cabbage in a food processor fitted with a metal chopping blade and finely chop it, running the machine in short bursts. Work in several batches so as not to overcrowd the processor bowl.

2. Transfer the chopped cabbage to a large nonreactive mixing bowl. Add 1 cup of vinegar sauce and toss to mix. Let the slaw sit for a few minutes, then stir it and taste for seasoning, adding salt and pepper to taste and more vinegar sauce as necessary. The slaw can be refrigerated, covered, for up to 2 days.

rotisserie

asian spit-roasted rack of pork

Rack of pork (also known as a pork rib roast) is one of the best-kept secrets in the meat department—impressive to look at and incredibly flavorful, in the way meat with bones always is, at a price that's a fraction of what you'd pay for a showy prime rib or rack of lamb. This pork roast goes Asian, featuring a seasoning paste made with the "Holy Trinity" of Asian seasonings (fresh ginger, scallions, and garlic). It's cooked in a rotisserie until it turns the color of polished mahogany. While the prep time is measured in minutes, the impact will be remembered for days. **SERVES 6**

tips

■ Rack of pork is how pork chops come before they're cut into individual chops. You can buy either a rack of rib chops or a rack of loin chops. This recipe calls for a six-chop rack that weighs 5 to 5½ pounds. You may need to order it ahead from your butcher shop.

■ For a Southeast Asian twist, add a couple of Thai chiles, a trimmed chopped stalk of lemongrass, and a handful of chopped cilantro to the seasoning paste.

THE RECIPE

FOR THE SEASONING PASTE:
2 tablespoons coarsely chopped peeled
    fresh ginger
2 scallions, both white and green parts,
    trimmed and finely chopped
4 cloves garlic, coarsely chopped
½ teaspoon freshly ground white pepper

2 tablespoons Asian (dark) sesame oil
2 tablespoons soy sauce

1 rack of pork (5 to 5½ pounds;
    see Note)
Ginger Sesame Vinaigrette
    (optional; recipe follows)

1. Make the seasoning paste: Place the ginger, scallions, garlic, and white pepper in a mortar and, using the pestle, pound to a coarse paste. Gradually work in the sesame oil and soy sauce and pound to a smooth paste. Alternatively, place the ginger, scallions, garlic, and white pepper in a food processor and finely chop. Add the sesame oil and soy sauce and process to a coarse paste, scraping down the side of the bowl with a rubber spatula.

2. Using the tip of a paring knife, make small ½-inch-deep slits on all sides of the roast about 1½ inches apart. Using the tip of your index finger, widen the holes. Using about half of the seasoning paste, place a tiny spoonful in each hole, forcing it in with your finger. Spread the remaining seasoning paste all over the pork. You can cook the pork right away, but it will have even more flavor if you let it marinate in the refrigerator, covered, for 1 to 2 hours.

3. When ready to cook, place the drip pan in the bottom of the rotisserie. Skewer the pork on the rotisserie by inserting the spit through the meat so that it is perpendicular to the bones. Attach the spit to the rotisserie and turn on the motor (for instructions for using a rotisserie, see page 14). Cook the pork until it is darkly browned on all sides and cooked to taste, 1½ to 2 hours for medium. Use an instant-read meat thermometer to test for doneness; don't let the thermometer touch the spit or a bone. Medium pork will have

an internal temperature of about 160°F. You can remove the roast from the rotisserie when it has reached 155°F; it will continue cooking.

4. Transfer the pork to a platter or cutting board, remove the spit, and let the meat rest for 5 minutes. Cut the rack into chops and serve at once with the Ginger Sesame Vinaigrette, if desired.

NOTE: Ask the butcher to cut through the chine bone between the pork chops to facilitate carving when the rack is cooked.

ginger sesame vinaigrette

This striking vinaigrette does what any sauce should—provides a little extra flavor and moistness without taking attention away from the pork roast. As you can imagine, it's also great with grilled poultry, seafood, or beef.
MAKES ABOUT 1 CUP

½ **clove garlic, minced**
1 **scallion, both white and green parts,**
   trimmed and minced
½ **teaspoon freshly ground black pepper**
2 **tablespoons rice vinegar, or more to taste**
¼ **cup soy sauce, or more to taste**
¼ **cup Asian (dark) sesame oil**
½ **cup unsalted chicken stock**
   (preferably homemade),
   at room temperature
1 **piece (1 inch) fresh ginger, peeled and**
   cut into matchstick slivers
1 **tablespoon black or toasted white sesame**
   seeds (see Note)

tip

You can also cook the meat on a fireplace rotisserie (see page 11). Trim off any excess fat before placing it on the spit. Cook over a hot, 2 to 3 Mississippi fire. It will take from 1 to 1½ hours, depending on your fireplace.

Place the garlic, scallion, and pepper in a nonreactive mixing bowl and mash to a coarse paste with the back of a wooden spoon. Add the rice vinegar and soy sauce and whisk to mix. Gradually whisk in the sesame oil and chicken stock, followed by the ginger and sesame seeds. Taste for seasoning, adding more vinegar and/or soy sauce as necessary; the mixture should be highly seasoned.

NOTE: To toast sesame seeds, place them in a dry cast-iron or other heavy skillet (don't use a nonstick skillet for this). Cook the sesame seeds over medium heat until lightly browned, about 3 minutes, shaking the skillet to ensure that they toast evenly. Transfer the toasted sesame seeds to a heatproof bowl to cool.

tip

When cooking pork chops on a contact grill, be sure they are at least 1/2 inch thick. Any less and the chop won't make proper contact with the grill plates.

pork loin chops
with caraway, cumin, and garlic

If you like your pork chops small on bone and big on meat, check out the following loin chops. Quick and easy to cook and extremely lean, the loin chop is a perfect parcel of protein—not to mention a ready absorber of flavor. The caraway seeds add a central European touch. To complete the theme, serve the chops with hot sauerkraut. **SERVES 4**

THE RECIPE

4 boneless pork loin chops (each 1/4 to 1/2 inch thick; about 1 1/2 pounds total; see box on page 105)
1 tablespoon extra-virgin olive oil
Coarse salt (kosher or sea) and freshly ground black pepper
2 cloves finely chopped garlic
1 teaspoon caraway seeds
1 teaspoon cumin seeds or ground cumin
Lemon wedges, for serving

1. Arrange the pork chops in a baking dish and brush both sides of each with the olive oil. Generously season each chop on both sides with salt and pepper, then sprinkle the garlic, caraway seeds, and cumin all over them, patting the seasonings onto the meat with your fingertips. Let the chops cure in the refrigerator, covered, for 10 minutes.

2. Cook the pork chops, following the instructions for any of the grills in the box at right, until nicely browned and cooked through. To test for doneness, use the poke method; the meat should be firm but gently yielding. If desired, rotate each chop a quarter turn after 1½ minutes to create a handsome crosshatch of grill marks.

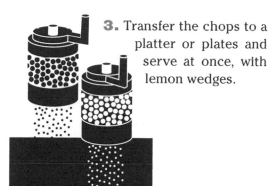

3. Transfer the chops to a platter or plates and serve at once, with lemon wedges.

if you have a...

CONTACT GRILL: Preheat the grill; if your contact grill has a temperature control, preheat the grill to high. Place the drip pan under the front of the grill. When ready to cook, lightly oil the grill surface. Place the pork chops on the hot grill, then close the lid. The chops will be done after cooking 3 to 5 minutes.

GRILL PAN: Place the grill pan on the stove and preheat it to medium-high over medium heat. When the grill pan is hot a drop of water will skitter in the pan. When ready to cook, lightly oil the ridges of the grill pan. Place the pork chops in the hot grill pan.

They will be done after cooking 3 to 4 minutes per side.

BUILT-IN GRILL: Preheat the grill to high, then, if it does not have a nonstick surface, brush and oil the grill grate. Place the pork chops on the hot grate. They will be done after cooking 3 to 4 minutes per side.

FIREPLACE GRILL: Rake red hot embers under the gridiron and preheat it for 3 to 5 minutes; you want a hot, 2 to 3 Mississippi fire. When ready to cook, brush and oil the gridiron. Place the pork chops on the hot grate. They will be done after cooking 3 to 4 minutes per side.

pork chops
with greek oregano

In the United States, pork generally receives a sweet, smoky barbecue treatment, with the sweetness coming from a sugar-based rub and barbecue sauce, and the smoke supplied by smoldering hickory and/or liquid smoke. When Europeans grill pork they tend to use more Mediterranean seasonings, keeping the emphasis on the flavor of the meat. In this Greek recipe pork is marinated in and basted with an oregano-scented vinaigrette, which doubles as a sauce. You can use this marinade and baste when grilling beef or lamb, poultry, and even seafood. **SERVES 4**

A NEW WAY TO BASTE

For an aromatic basting brush you don't have to wash, buy a bunch of fresh oregano, tie the stems together with butcher's string, and trim the leafy ends straight across.

tip

Greek oregano has a more pungent, more aromatic, and mintier flavor than the Italian or Mexican varieties— look for it at Greek markets and specialty food stores.

4 boneless pork loin chops
   (each about 1/4 to 1/2 inch thick;
   about 11/2 pounds total; see box on
   facing page and Tip on page 102)
1 to 2 cloves garlic, minced
1 teaspoon coarse salt (kosher or sea),
   or more to taste
1/4 cup red wine vinegar, or more to taste
1/2 teaspoon finely grated lemon zest
2 tablespoons fresh lemon juice
1 cup extra-virgin olive oil (preferably Greek)
2 teaspoons dried Greek oregano
1/2 teaspoon cracked black peppercorns

1. Arrange the pork chops in a single layer in a nonreactive baking dish or roasting pan.

if you have a...

CONTACT GRILL: Preheat the grill; if your contact grill has a temperature control, preheat the grill to high. Place the drip pan under the front of the grill. When ready to cook, lightly oil the grill surface. Place the pork chops on the hot grill, then close the lid. The chops will be done after cooking 4 to 6 minutes. You will need to turn the chops so that you can baste both sides; use the baste sparingly.

GRILL PAN: Place the grill pan on the stove and preheat it to medium-high over medium heat. When the grill pan is hot a drop of water will skitter in the pan. When ready to cook, lightly oil the ridges of the grill pan. Place the pork chops in the hot grill pan. They will be done after cooking 3 to 4 minutes per side. Baste sparingly,

taking care not to drip a lot of marinade into the grill pan. After it has cooled down, soak the grill pan in hot water to loosen any burnt-on baste.

BUILT-IN GRILL: Preheat the grill to high, then, if it does not have a nonstick surface, brush and oil the grill grate. Place the pork chops on the hot grate. They will be done after cooking 4 to 6 minutes per side.

FIREPLACE GRILL: Rake red hot embers under the gridiron and preheat it for 3 to 5 minutes; you want a hot, 2 to 3 Mississippi fire. When ready to cook, brush and oil the gridiron. Place the pork chops on the hot grate. They will be done after cooking 3 to 4 minutes per side.

2. Place the garlic and salt in a nonreactive mixing bowl and mash with the back of a spoon. Add the wine vinegar, lemon zest, and lemon juice and whisk until the salt dissolves. Gradually whisk in the olive oil, oregano, and peppercorns. Taste for seasoning, adding more salt and/or vinegar as necessary; the marinade should be highly seasoned.

3. Pour 1/2 cup of the marinade over the pork, turning the chops to coat both sides evenly. Pour 1/4 cup of the marinade into a small nonreactive bowl and set aside to use for basting. Pour the rest of the marinade into a nonreactive bowl and set aside for serving. Let the chops marinate in the refrigerator, covered, for 1 to 2 hours.

4. When ready to cook, drain the pork chops well and discard the marinade. Cook the pork chops, following the instructions for any of the grills in the box at left, until nicely browned and cooked through. To test for doneness, use the poke method; the meat should be firm but gently yielding. If desired, rotate each chop a quarter turn after 11/2 minutes to create a handsome crosshatch of grill marks.

5. Stir the 1/4 cup of reserved marinade with a fork to recombine and use it to baste the chops as they grill (apply it only to cooked meat, not raw, to avoid cross-contamination).

6. Transfer the pork chops to a platter or plates. Stir the remaining marinade with a fork, spoon it over the chops, and serve at once.

deconstructed pork paprikás

I've deconstructed *paprikás,* one of the glories of Hungarian cuisine, to make a pork version you can cook on an indoor grill. The paprika, garlic, and onion become a rub; the sour cream traditionally used to make the sauce becomes a drizzle. Put it in a plastic squirt bottle, if you have one, and you can make decorative zigzags. If not, just spoon a small dollop of sour cream onto each chop.

SERVES 4

pork chops

I've called for boneless pork loin chops in the recipe here and in those on pages 102, 103, and 106. Cut from the "eye" of the loin, they're a good chop to cook on contact grills that don't have a floating hinge because there's no bone to get in the way. Boneless loin chops are also the best choice for cooking in a grill pan; bone-in chops have a tendency not to cook evenly, remaining too rare by the bone in the center when the outside is thoroughly done.

If you have a *panini* machine or want to use a built-in grill or cook in the fireplace, you can certainly grill rib chops. They will take a little longer because of the bone; figure on 4 to 6 minutes per side. You can also grill a pork "porterhouse," a mighty chop that has both some loin and tenderloin attached to the T-bone. These weigh about 10 ounces each and will be 1 to 1½ inches thick. They'll take 5 to 8 minutes per side to cook and are perfect for grilling over wood in the fireplace.

Another option is small pork tenderloins. They will take 4 to 8 minutes on a contact grill or about 4 minutes per side—about 16 minutes in all—on any of the other indoor grills.

THE RECIPE

4 boneless pork loin chops
   (each ¼ to ½ inch thick; about
   1½ pounds total; see Tip on page 102)
1 tablespoon extra-virgin olive oil
Garlic salt
Onion powder
Freshly ground black pepper
Sweet or hot paprika (see Note)
½ cup sour cream

YOU'LL ALSO NEED:
Plastic squirt bottle (optional)

1. Arrange the pork chops in a baking dish. Lightly brush each on both sides with the olive oil. Generously—and I mean generously—season each chop on both sides with garlic salt, onion powder, pepper, and paprika. Let the chops cure in the refrigerator, covered, for at least 20 minutes.

2. Cook the pork chops, following the instructions for any of the grills in the box on the following page, until nicely

if you have a...

CONTACT GRILL: Preheat the grill; if your contact grill has a temperature control, preheat the grill to high. Place the drip pan under the front of the grill. When ready to cook, lightly oil the grill surface. Place the pork chops on the hot grill, then close the lid. The chops will be done after cooking 3 to 4 minutes.

GRILL PAN: Place the grill pan on the stove and preheat it to medium-high over medium heat. When the grill pan is hot a drop of water will skitter in the pan. When ready to cook, lightly oil the ridges of the grill pan. Place the pork chops in the hot grill pan. They

will be done after cooking 3 to 4 minutes per side.

BUILT-IN GRILL: Preheat the grill to high, then, if it does not have a nonstick surface, brush and oil the grill grate. Place the pork chops on the hot grate. They will be done after cooking 3 to 4 minutes per side.

FIREPLACE GRILL: Rake red hot embers under the gridiron and preheat it for 3 to 5 minutes; you want a hot, 2 to 3 Mississippi fire. When ready to cook, brush and oil the gridiron. Place the pork chops on the hot grate. They will be done after cooking 3 to 4 minutes per side.

browned and cooked through. To test for doneness, use the poke method; the meat should be firm but gently yielding.

3. Transfer the chops to a platter or plates. If using a squirt bottle, squirt zig-zags of sour cream over each chop; otherwise place a spoonful of sour cream in the center of each. Serve at once.

NOTE: The quality of the paprika is paramount here. Use imported paprika—sweet Hungarian paprika if you want a milder dish; hot paprika if you crave some fire. The best Hungarian paprika comes from Szeged, and you can likely find it at your supermarket. For an interesting and esoteric twist, you could use *pimentón,* a Spanish smoked paprika.

sweet and salty lemongrass pork chops

Turn in at 1007 Clay Street in downtown Oakland, California, and you'll find a long line of people waiting and a cavernous dining room filled to capacity. There are at least three reasons for Le Cheval's success: authentic and intensely flavorful Vietnamese food, mercifully affordable prices, and the watchful management of the Saigon-born Tran family, which opened the popular restaurant in 1985. These pork chops epitomize Le Cheval's cooking. They're crusty and succulent, fragrant with garlic and lemongrass, and grilled over a heat that's high enough to caramelize the oyster sauce and sugar. In short, they're everything a pork chop should be and more. Here's my interpretation adapted for indoor grills. **SERVES 4**

T H E   R E C I P E

¼ cup sugar

¼ cup oyster sauce

¼ cup soy sauce

1 teaspoon freshly ground black pepper

2 stalks lemongrass, or 2 strips of lemon zest
   (see Notes)

4 cloves garlic, peeled and gently crushed
   with the side of a cleaver

4 boneless pork loin chops
   (each ¼ to ½ inch thick, and about
   1½ pounds total; see box on page 105)

1. Place the sugar, oyster sauce, soy sauce, and pepper in a large shallow mixing bowl and whisk until the sugar dissolves.

2. Trim the lemongrass, removing the root ends and flexible green stalks. You should be left with a cream-colored core that is 3 to 4 inches long. Cut this into 1-inch pieces and gently crush them with the side of a cleaver to release the aroma. Stir the lemongrass and garlic into the marinade.

3. Add the pork chops to the marinade, turning to coat both sides. Cover the bowl with plastic wrap and let the pork chops marinate in the refrigerator for at least 2 hours or as long as overnight, turning them several times; the longer the chops marinate, the richer the flavor will be. You can also marinate the chops in a resealable plastic bag.

if you have a...

CONTACT GRILL: Preheat the grill; if your contact grill has a temperature control, preheat the grill to high. Place the drip pan under the front of the grill. When ready to cook, lightly oil the grill surface. Place the pork chops on the hot grill, then close the lid. The chops will be done after cooking 2 to 4 minutes.

GRILL PAN: Place the grill pan on the stove and preheat it to medium-high over medium heat. When the grill pan is hot a drop of water will skitter in the pan. When ready to cook, lightly oil the ridges of the grill pan. Place the pork chops in the hot grill pan. They will be done after cooking 3 to 4 minutes per side.

BUILT-IN GRILL: Preheat the grill to high, then, if it does not have a nonstick surface, brush and oil the grill grate. Place the pork chops on the hot grate. They will be done after cooking 3 to 4 minutes per side.

FREESTANDING GRILL: Preheat the grill to high; there's no need to oil the grate. Place the pork chops on the hot grill. They will be done after cooking 4 to 5 minutes per side.

FIREPLACE GRILL: Rake red hot embers under the gridiron and preheat it for 3 to 5 minutes; you want a hot, 2 to 3 Mississippi fire. When ready to cook, brush and oil the gridiron. Place the pork chops on the hot grate. They will be done after cooking 3 to 4 minutes per side.

4. Cook the pork chops, following the instructions for any of the grills in the box below, until nicely browned and cooked through. To test for doneness, use the poke method; the meat should be firm but gently yielding.

5. Transfer the pork chops to a platter or plates and serve at once.

NOTES:

■ Lemongrass is an aromatic Asian grass with a lemony flavor but no tartness. Look for it at Asian and natural markets and many supermarkets. If you don't find it, lemon zest (the yellow oil-rich outer rind of the lemon) makes an acceptable substitute.

■ You can use a vegetable peeler to remove the lemon zest in strips. Be careful to leave behind the bitter white pith. You'll need strips that are about 1/2 by 2 inches.

tip

Oyster sauce is a thick, sweet-salty condiment made from oysters and soybeans, among other things.

rotisserie

chinatown barbecued pork tenderloins

You've seen them hanging in the kitchen windows of Chinese restaurants—pork tenderloins roasted until they're dark and crusty, glistening with honey and hoisin sauce, and perfumed with garlic and five-spice powder, a mix of spices including star anise, fennel seeds, cinnamon, cloves, and pepper. This is Chinese "barbecue" at its best and it's easy to make at home. The combination of garlic and sugar with pork, widespread in Asia, may sound a bit odd, until you pause to think of the many sweet American barbecue sauces that contain garlic. Traditionally, Chinese pork is roasted suspended in a special oven. However, the rotisserie turns out a spectacular tenderloin that's succulent, and candy sweet. **SERVES 4**

THE RECIPE

2 teaspoons Chinese five-spice powder

1 teaspoon sugar

1 teaspoon coarse salt (kosher or sea)

1 teaspoon freshly ground black pepper

1½ pounds pork tenderloin
     (2 to 3 tenderloins)

4 cloves garlic, thinly sliced

1 piece (2 inches) fresh ginger, peeled and
     thinly sliced

3 tablespoons char siu sauce (see Note)
     or hoisin sauce

3 tablespoons rice wine or dry sherry

3 tablespoons honey

2 tablespoons soy sauce

1. Place the five-spice powder, sugar, salt, and pepper in a small bowl and stir to mix. Sprinkle this rub over the tenderloins on all sides, patting it onto the meat with your fingertips.

2. Remove the silver skins (the sinewlike covering) from the tenderloins by trimming them off with a knife. Place the pork in a nonreactive baking dish or resealable plastic bag and add the garlic and ginger. Place the *char siu* sauce, rice wine, honey, and soy sauce in a small nonreactive bowl and whisk to mix. Pour this mixture over the pork and turn it to coat on all sides. Let the pork marinate in the refrigerator, covered, for at least 6 hours or as long as overnight.

3. When ready to cook, drain the pork in a strainer over a nonreactive saucepan and set the marinade aside. Place the drip pan in the bottom of the rotisserie. Skewer the tenderloins onto the rotisserie spit (ideally, they should be posi-

tioned so that they will be perpendicular to the spit). Attach the spit to the rotisserie and turn on the motor. If your rotisserie has a temperature control, set it to 400°F (for instructions for using a rotisserie, see page 14). Cook the pork until golden brown and cooked through, 40 minutes to 1 hour. Use an instant-read meat thermometer to test for doneness; don't let the thermometer touch the spit. When done the internal temperature of the meat should be about 160°F.

4. Meanwhile, as the pork cooks, bring the reserved marinade to a boil over high heat and let boil until thick and syrupy, 2 to 4 minutes. Baste the pork tenderloins with the boiled marinade after they have cooked for 30 minutes and again once or twice more before removing them from the rotisserie.

5. Transfer the pork tenderloins to a platter or cutting board and let rest for 3 minutes, then thinly slice them crosswise. Pour any remaining marinade over the pork and serve at once.

NOTE: *Char siu* (sometimes spelled *chu hou*) sauce is a dark red Chinese barbecue sauce sold in jars in Asian markets and many specialty food stores.

tip

You can also cook the meat on a fireplace rotisserie (see page 11). Cook over a hot, 2 to 3 Mississippi fire. It will take from 30 to 45 minutes, depending on your fireplace.

"wild boar" (juniper-scented pork medallions)

Back in the Dark Ages, when I attended cooking school in Paris, we often used a red wine and juniper berry marinade to give commonplace meats the taste of wild game. With a little imagination, the sharp-flavored marinade transformed beef into "venison," lamb into "bighorn sheep," and pork into "wild boar"—especially when the meat was served with a traditional *grand veneur* (huntsman) or St. Hubert sauce, both of which are flavored with sweet-sour red currant jelly. The sweetness of the cream sauce here counterbalances the acidity of the marinade for the pork. Best of all, you can experience the full-flavored pleasures of "wild game" without having to bag it yourself.

SERVES 4

tips

■ Juniper berries are the small, round blueish fruit of the juniper tree, and the predominant flavoring in gin (the spirit takes its name from *genièvre*, the French word for juniper). You can frequently find juniper berries at specialty food stores or some supermarkets. You can also substitute a shot of gin.

■ The marinade and sauce are also good with beef tenderloin or lamb chops. There will be enough for 1½ pounds of beef tenderloin or 1¾ pounds of lamb chops.

THE RECIPE

1 center-cut piece of pork loin, or 2 to 3 pork tenderloins (about 1½ pounds; see Note)

3 cups dry red wine

About ⅔ cup red wine vinegar, or more to taste

2 tablespoons extra-virgin olive oil

1 small onion, finely chopped

1 medium-size carrot, finely chopped

1 rib celery, finely chopped

2 cloves garlic, finely chopped

20 black peppercorns

10 juniper berries, or ¼ cup gin

3 bay leaves

3 whole cloves

1 teaspoon fresh thyme or dried thyme

1 cup beef or veal stock

3 tablespoons heavy (whipping) cream

3 tablespoons red currant jelly, or more to taste

1½ teaspoons cornstarch

1 tablespoon port or water

Coarse salt (kosher or sea) and freshly ground black pepper

1 tablespoon unsalted butter

Fresh flat-leaf parsley or cilantro sprigs, for garnish

1. Cut the pork crosswise into ½-inch-thick medallions. Arrange them in a nonreactive baking dish just large enough to hold them in one layer.

2. Place the wine, wine vinegar, olive oil, onion, carrot, celery, garlic, peppercorns, juniper berries, bay leaves, cloves, and thyme in a nonreactive bowl and stir to mix. Pour the wine mixture over the pork and let marinate in the refrigerator, covered, for at least 3 hours, preferably overnight, turning the medallions several times so that they marinate evenly. You can also marinate the pork in a resealable plastic bag.

3. Drain the pork in a strainer over a large nonreactive saucepan. Add the vegetables from the marinade to the saucepan and set the pork aside. Bring the marinade to a boil over high heat and let boil until the liquid is reduced to 1 cup, 7 to 10 minutes. Add the stock, let come to a boil, and boil until the liquid is reduced to 1 cup, 7 to 10 minutes.

4. Strain the marinade mixture into another nonreactive saucepan, pressing on the vegetables with the back of a spoon to extract the juices (discard the vegetables). Whisk the cream and red currant jelly into the marinade mixture. Let come to a simmer and cook the sauce until the jelly melts, about 3 minutes.

5. Dissolve the cornstarch in the port, then whisk it into the sauce. Let simmer until thickened, about 1 minute. Season with salt and pepper to taste. If a sweeter sauce is desired, add a little more currant jelly. For a more tart sauce, add a few drops of vinegar. The sauce should be

if you have a...

CONTACT GRILL: Preheat the grill; if your contact grill has a temperature control, preheat the grill to high. Place the drip pan under the front of the grill. When ready to cook, lightly oil the grill surface. Place the medallions on the hot grill, then close the lid. The medallions will be done after cooking 3 to 5 minutes.

GRILL PAN: Place the grill pan on the stove and preheat it to medium-high over medium heat. When the grill pan is hot a drop of water will skitter in the pan. When ready to cook, lightly oil the ridges of the grill pan. Place

the medallions in the hot grill pan. They will be done after cooking 2 to 3 minutes per side.

BUILT-IN GRILL: Preheat the grill to high, then, if it does not have a nonstick surface, brush and oil the grill grate. Place the medallions on the hot grate. They will be done after cooking 3 to 4 minutes per side.

FREESTANDING GRILL: Preheat the grill to high; there's no need to oil the grate. Place the medallions on the hot grill. They will be done after cooking 4 to 5 minutes per side.

highly seasoned. Keep the sauce warm over low heat.

6. Blot the pork medallions dry with paper towels and season them generously with salt and pepper. Cook the medallions, following the instructions for any of the grills in the box above, until just cooked through. To test for doneness, use the poke method; the pork should be gently yielding. If desired, rotate each medallion a quarter turn after 1 minute to create a handsome crosshatch of grill marks.

7. Just before serving, whisk the butter into the sauce, then spoon it onto a platter or plates. Arrange the medallions on top of the sauce. Garnish each with a sprig of parsley and serve at once.

NOTE: If you use pork tenderloin, remove the silver skin (the thin, translucent, sinewlike covering) by using a knife to trim it off the meat.

cyprus souvlaki

Located in the northeastern corner of the Mediterranean, Cyprus is home to two great grilling cultures, Greek and Turkish. According to my Cypriot grilling connection Stelios Stylianou, the traditional meat for souvlaki (shish kebab) there is pork, not the region's ubiquitous lamb, and it's perfumed with two unexpected seasonings: cinnamon and fresh mint. The kebabs here call for commonplace ingredients, but I'll wager they'll taste nothing like the souvlaki you may have sampled at a typical Greek restaurant in the States. **SERVES 4**

THE RECIPE

1¹⁄₂ **pounds boneless pork shoulder**
1¹⁄₂ **teaspoons coarse salt (kosher or sea)**
¹⁄₂ **teaspoon freshly ground black pepper,**
    or more to taste
2 **bunches fresh mint, rinsed and stemmed,**
    1 bunch coarsely chopped
4 **cinnamon sticks (each 3 inches)**
1 **cup dry red wine**
¹⁄₄ **cup extra-virgin olive oil**
4 **pita breads (optional)**
Cyprus Salad (optional; recipe follows)

YOU'LL ALSO NEED:
4 **metal skewers**
    (10 to 12 inches long),
    or 8 bamboo skewers
    (6 to 8 inches long)

1. Cut the pork into 1-inch cubes, leaving a little of the fat on. Place the pork in a large nonreactive bowl. Sprinkle the salt and pepper over the meat, tossing it to coat all sides well. Stir in the chopped mint, followed by the cinnamon sticks, wine, and olive oil. Let the pork marinate in the refrigerator, covered, for 3 to 4 hours. You can also marinate the pork in a resealable plastic bag.

2. Drain the pork well and discard the marinade. Thread the pork onto skewers, placing a whole mint leaf between each piece of meat.

tips

■ The secret to great souvlaki is to use meat that's not too lean—in this case, pork shoulder rather than the leaner pork loin or tenderloin. Ideally, each cube of pork should have a little fat in it. The fat sizzles and melts as it grills, basting the meat and keeping it moist.

■ You can also make these souvlaki with beef, lamb, or chicken.

■ If you like, warm the pita bread on the grill for 30 seconds to 1 minute.

3. Cook the kebabs, following the instructions for any of the grills in the box at right, until nicely browned and cooked through. To test for doneness, squeeze a meat cube between your thumb and forefinger. It should feel firm.

4. Transfer the kebabs to a platter or plates and serve with the pita breads and the Cyprus Salad, if desired. If you have used metal skewers, warn everyone to take the kebabs off the skewers before eating, as they will be very hot.

cyprus salad

Variations of this salad turn up throughout the eastern Mediterranean. Cut the vegetables into larger pieces to make a salad or finely dice them to make a sort of salsa. **MAKES ABOUT 3 CUPS**

2 medium-size luscious ripe red tomatoes, cut into 1/2-inch dice, with their juices and seeds

1 small cucumber, peeled, seeded, and cut into 1/2-inch dice

1/2 medium-size green bell pepper, cut into 1/2-inch dice

1/2 cup kalamata olives

4 ounces feta cheese, drained and crumbled (about 2/3 cup)

3 scallions, both white and green parts, trimmed and finely chopped

3 tablespoons chopped fresh mint

3 tablespoons extra-virgin olive oil

2 tablespoons fresh lemon juice or red wine vinegar, or more to taste

Coarse salt (kosher or sea) and freshly ground black pepper

Place the tomatoes, cucumber, bell pepper, olives, feta, scallions, mint, olive oil, and lemon juice in a large nonreactive bowl, but don't toss the salad until 15 minutes before serving. Taste for seasoning, adding more lemon juice, if necessary, and salt and pepper to taste.

if you have a...

CONTACT GRILL: Preheat the grill; if your contact grill has a temperature control, preheat the grill to high. Place the drip pan under the front of the grill. When ready to cook, lightly oil the grill surface. Place the kebabs on the hot grill, then close the lid. The kebabs will be done after cooking 4 to 6 minutes. Give each kebab a quarter turn after 2 minutes so that all of the sides are exposed to the heat.

GRILL PAN: Place the grill pan on the stove and preheat it to medium-high over medium heat. When the grill pan is hot a drop of water will skitter in the pan. When ready to cook, lightly oil the ridges of the grill pan. Place the kebabs in the hot grill pan. They will be done after cooking 2 to 3 minutes per side (8 to 12 minutes in all).

BUILT-IN GRILL: Preheat the grill to high, then, if it does not have a nonstick surface, brush and oil the grill grate. Arrange the kebabs on the hot grill so that the exposed ends of the skewers extend off the grate. The kebabs will be done after cooking 2 to 3 minutes per side (8 to 12 minutes in all).

FREESTANDING GRILL: Preheat the grill to high; there's no need to oil the grate. Place the kebabs on the hot grill. They will be done after cooking 3 to 4 minutes per side (12 to 16 minutes in all).

FIREPLACE GRILL: Rake red hot embers under the gridiron and preheat it for 3 to 5 minutes; you want a hot, 2 to 3 Mississippi fire. When ready to cook, brush and oil the gridiron. Place the kebabs on the hot grate. The kebabs will be done after cooking 2 to 3 minutes per side (8 to 12 minutes in all).

pork kebabs
with haitian seasonings

Say *grillot* to Haitians and their mouths will water and their eyes will light up with pleasure. These crusty pork bites— spiced with garlic, Scotch bonnet chiles, and sour orange juice—are a national snack. Traditionally they're deep-fried, but you know Raichlen's rule: If something tastes good fried, baked, stewed, or sautéed, it probably tastes even better grilled. Red beans and rice would make a great accompaniment for the *grillot*. **SERVES 4**

if you have a...

CONTACT GRILL: Preheat the grill; if your contact grill has a temperature control, preheat the grill to high. Place the drip pan under the front of the grill. When ready to cook, lightly oil the grill surface. Place the kebabs on the hot grill, then close the lid. The kebabs will be done after cooking 4 to 6 minutes. Give each kebab a quarter turn after 2 minutes so that all of the sides are exposed to the heat.

GRILL PAN: Place the grill pan on the stove and preheat it to medium-high over medium heat. When the grill pan is hot a drop of water will skitter in the pan. When ready to cook, lightly oil the ridges of the grill pan. Place the kebabs in the hot grill pan. They will be done after cooking 2 to 3 minutes per side (8 to 12 minutes in all).

BUILT-IN GRILL: Preheat the grill to high, then, if it does not have a nonstick surface, brush and oil the grill grate. Arrange the kebabs on the hot grill so that the exposed ends of the skewers extend off the grate. The kebabs will be done after cooking 2 to 3 minutes per side (8 to 12 minutes in all).

FREESTANDING GRILL: Preheat the grill to high; there's no need to oil the grate. Place the kebabs on the hot grill. They will be done after cooking 3 to 4 minutes per side (12 to 16 minutes in all).

FIREPLACE GRILL: Rake red hot embers under the gridiron and preheat it for 3 to 5 minutes; you want a hot, 2 to 3 Mississippi fire. When ready to cook, brush and oil the gridiron. Place the kebabs on the hot grate. The kebabs will be done after cooking 2 to 3 minutes per side (8 to 12 minutes in all).

THE RECIPE

- 1 1/2 pounds pork loin, tenderloin, or boneless pork shoulder (see Note)
- 3 cloves garlic, minced
- 1 Scotch bonnet chile or habañero pepper, seeded and minced (for hotter pork kebabs, leave the seeds in)
- 2 tablespoons finely chopped fresh flat-leaf parsley
- 2 teaspoons fresh thyme, or 1 teaspoon dried thyme
- 1 teaspoon coarse salt (kosher or sea)
- 1/2 teaspoon freshly ground black pepper
- 1/2 cup fresh sour orange juice, or 1/4 cup each fresh lime juice and fresh orange juice
- 1 tablespoon vegetable oil

YOU'LL ALSO NEED:
- 4 metal skewers (10 to 12 inches long), or 8 bamboo skewers (6 to 8 inches long)

1. Cut the pork into 1-inch pieces and place it in a nonreactive bowl. Add the garlic, Scotch bonnet, parsley, thyme, salt, and pepper and stir to coat evenly. Let stand for 5 minutes. Add the sour orange juice and stir to mix. Let the pork marinate in the refrigerator, covered, for at least 2 hours or as long as overnight; the longer the pork marinates, the richer the flavor will be.

2. Cook the kebabs, following the instructions for any of the grills in the box on the facing page, until nicely browned and cooked through. To test for doneness, squeeze a meat cube between your thumb and forefinger. It should feel firm.

3. Transfer the kebabs to a platter or plates and serve at once. If you have used metal skewers, warn everyone to take the kebabs off the skewers before eating, as they will be very hot.

NOTE: If you use pork tenderloin, remove the silver skin (the thin, translucent, sinewlike covering) by using a knife to trim it off the meat.

tips

- For lean *grillots,* start with pork loin or tenderloin. For richer kebabs, use cubed pork shoulder.

- The sour orange (*narnaja agria*) is a Caribbean citrus fruit available in West Indian and Spanish Caribbean markets and some supermarkets. If it's unavailable, you can use a mixture of half fresh lime juice and half fresh orange juice.

raznjici
(pork, veal, and bay leaf kebabs)

Kebabs made from a mix of different meats are common currency in the Balkans. These Yugoslavian kebabs combine cubes of pork and veal that are marinated with onions and vinegar, then grilled on skewers with bay leaves. The ends of the bay leaves burn as the kebabs cook, imparting an incredible herbal smoke flavor. The traditional way to serve *raznjici* is with a mixture of parsley and diced onion on top. And just how do you wrap your tongue around the name of this dish? It's pronounced "raj-NEE-kee." **SERVES 4**

THE RECIPE

12 ounces pork, cut into 1-inch cubes
12 ounces veal, cut into 1-inch cubes
1½ teaspoons coarse salt (kosher or sea)

½ teaspoon freshly ground black pepper
2 tablespoons extra-virgin olive oil
2 tablespoons red wine vinegar
1 medium-size sweet onion
6 tablespoons finely chopped fresh flat-leaf parsley
10 to 12 bay leaves, broken in half crosswise

YOU'LL ALSO NEED:
4 metal skewers (10 to 12 inches long),
    or 8 bamboo skewers (6 to 8 inches long)

if you have a...

CONTACT GRILL: Preheat the grill; if your contact grill has a temperature control, preheat the grill to high. Place the drip pan under the front of the grill. When ready to cook, lightly oil the grill surface. Place the kebabs on the hot grill, then close the lid. The kebabs will be done after cooking 4 to 6 minutes. Give each kebab a quarter turn after 2 minutes so that all of the sides are exposed to the heat.

GRILL PAN: Place the grill pan on the stove and preheat it to medium-high over medium heat. When the grill pan is hot a drop of water will skitter in the pan. When ready to cook, lightly oil the ridges of the grill pan. Place the kebabs in the hot grill pan. They will be done after cooking 2 to 3 minutes per side (8 to 12 minutes in all).

BUILT-IN GRILL: Preheat the grill to high, then, if it does not have a nonstick surface, brush and oil the grill grate. Arrange the kebabs on the hot grill so that the exposed ends of the skewers extend off the grate. The kebabs will be done after cooking 2 to 3 minutes per side (8 to 12 minutes in all).

FREESTANDING GRILL: Preheat the grill to high; there's no need to oil the grate. Place the kebabs on the hot grill. They will be done after cooking 3 to 4 minutes per side (12 to 16 minutes in all).

FIREPLACE GRILL: Rake red hot embers under the gridiron and preheat it for 3 to 5 minutes; you want a hot, 2 to 3 Mississippi fire. When ready to cook, brush and oil the gridiron. Place the kebabs on the hot grate. The kebabs will be done after cooking 2 to 3 minutes per side (8 to 12 minutes in all).

1. Place the pork and veal in a large non-reactive mixing bowl. Sprinkle the salt and pepper over the meat and stir to mix. Stir in the olive oil and wine vinegar. Thinly slice two thirds of the onion and add the slices to the meat mixture. Set the remaining piece of onion aside; you'll use it when serving. Add 3 tablespoons of the parsley to the meat mixture and stir to coat evenly. Let the meat marinate in the refrigerator, covered, for at least 4 hours, or as long as overnight, stirring once or twice.

2. When ready to cook, finely chop the remaining onion third and mix it with the remaining 3 tablespoons of parsley. Place the onion and parsley mixture in an attractive bowl for serving.

3. Drain the meat, discarding the marinade. Thread the meat onto skewers, alternating pieces of pork and veal and placing a bay leaf half between the pieces of meat.

4. Cook the kebabs, following the instructions for any of the grills in the box on the facing page, until nicely browned and just cooked through. To test for doneness, squeeze a meat cube between your thumb and forefinger. It should feel firm.

5. Transfer the kebabs to a platter or plates and serve at once with the onion and parsley mixture on the side. If you've used metal skewers, warn everyone to take the meat off the skewers before serving, as they will be very hot.

tip

Use veal and pork shoulder or leg for these kebabs and look for meat with a little fat to keep them moist as they grill.

rotisserie

dry rub ribs on a spit

Wet or dry? Three simple words, but to barbecue fanatics they speak volumes. Wet is the way most Americans eat ribs—smoky, tender, and dripping with sweet, sticky barbecue sauce. But if you really want to savor pork bones in all their primal glory, you must journey to Memphis to sample the dry rub ribs, all spice and vinegar, at the Rendezvous. For more than half a century, the Vergos (pronounced "Vargus") family has been dishing up baby back ribs that are mopped with vinegar sauce and thickly crusted with a dry rub just before serving. But the most famous ribs in Memphis may, technically speaking, not be barbecued at all—not if you define barbecuing as slowly cooking meat at a low temperature in a pit with plenty of wood smoke. The Rendezvous grills its ribs over an open charcoal fire, with nary a log or hickory chip in sight. Well, if you're not going to smoke the ribs, why not cook them on a rotisserie? I think you'll find that the result is highly satisfactory. **SERVES 2**

tip

Baby backs are
the best ribs for spit
roasting. They're
quick cooking,
naturally tender,
and well marbled,
so they stay moist
as they cook.

THE RECIPE

FOR THE RUB AND RIBS:

1½ tablespoons sweet paprika

1 tablespoon chili powder

2 teaspoons salt

1 teaspoon freshly ground black pepper

1 teaspoon garlic powder

1 teaspoon onion powder

1 teaspoon dried thyme

1 teaspoon dried oregano

1 teaspoon yellow mustard seeds

½ teaspoon ground coriander

½ teaspoon celery seed

¼ teaspoon cayenne pepper

1 rack baby back pork ribs
  (2 to 2½ pounds), peeled
  (see box on facing page)

FOR THE MOP SAUCE:

¼ cup distilled white vinegar

¾ teaspoon salt

1½ teaspoons rub (reserved from above)

1. Make the rub: Place the paprika, chili powder, salt, black pepper, garlic and onion powders, thyme, oregano, mustard seeds, coriander, celery seed, and cayenne in a small bowl and whisk to mix. Place 1½ teaspoons of the rub in a medium-size nonreactive mixing bowl and set aside for the mop sauce. (This may make more rub than you need for the ribs; don't worry, you'll find plenty of other uses for it. Stored in an airtight jar away from heat or light, it will keep for several months.)

2. Place the ribs on a baking sheet. Sprinkle both sides all over with barbecue rub, 2 to 3 teaspoons per side, rub-bing it onto the meat with your fingertips. Set the remaining rub aside. You can cook the ribs right away, but they will have even more flavor if you let them cure for 4 hours, covered, in the refrigerator.

3. When ready to cook, place the drip pan in the bottom of the rotisserie. Place the ribs in the rotisserie basket (see box on page 121) and close it tightly. Attach the basket to the rotisserie spit, then attach the spit to the rotisserie and turn on the motor. If your rotisserie has a temperature control, set it to 400°F (for instructions for using a rotisserie, see page 14). Cook the ribs until they are dark brown and crusty and the meat has shrunk back about ¼ inch from the ends of the bones, 40 to 50 minutes.

4. Meanwhile, make the mop sauce: Place the vinegar and salt in the bowl with the 1½ teaspoons of rub. Add ¼ cup of water and whisk until the salt dissolves.

5. Transfer the ribs to a cutting board. Generously brush the ribs on both sides with the mop sauce. Thickly sprinkle some of the remaining rub over the meat side of the ribs to form a ⅛-inch crust. Cut the rack in half or into individual ribs and serve.

NOTE: You can also smoke these ribs in a stove-top smoker. You'll find instructions for doing this on page 122.

how to skin a rack of ribs

Ribs come with a thin, translucent, papery membrane on the inside (convex) side of the bones. This membrane is perfectly edible, but it's a little tougher than the rest of the meat. Also, it forms a barrier to rubs, preventing the seasonings from penetrating one side of the meat. For this reason, and for general pride of workmanship, I like to remove the membrane.

To do this, first place the rack on a cutting board, meat side down. Insert a sharp implement, such as the tip of a meat thermometer or a Phillips head screwdriver, under the membrane (the best place to start is right next to the first rib bone). Gently pry off the membrane to loosen about an inch of it from the bone. Using a dishcloth or paper towel to gain a secure grip, gently but firmly pull the membrane off the bones. When removing the membrane from baby back ribs, it will most likely come off in a single piece. The membrane is a little harder to remove from spareribs. You may need to pry it off the ribs with a sharp implement in several places.

Beef ribs have a similar membrane. It should also be removed.

rotisserie

kansas city barbecue ribs

The notion of a rotisserie rib may seem strange to many Americans, but in other parts of the world—in Europe and Asia, for example—pit masters often cook ribs on a spit. One advantage to using a countertop rotisserie is that you can cook a small quantity of ribs, enough for one or two people, something that would be impractical in a large grill or a smoker. Here's how a Kansas City pit master might make ribs if he used a rotisserie instead of a barbecue pit. **SERVES 2**

1 rack baby back pork ribs (2 to 2½ pounds), peeled (see box on page 119)
About 2 tablespoons Basic Barbecue Rub (page 362) or your favorite commercial rub
1 cup Kansas City–Style Sweet and Smoky Barbecue Sauce (page 374) or your favorite commercial sauce

tip

These ribs come slathered with a smoky red barbecue sauce. If you wish to accentuate the smoke flavor, brush the ribs with a mixture of 2 teaspoons vegetable oil and 2 teaspoons liquid smoke before sprinkling on the rub.

1. Place the ribs on a baking sheet. Sprinkle both sides all over with barbecue rub, 2 to 3 teaspoons per side, rubbing it onto the meat with your fingertips. You can cook the ribs right away, but they will have even more flavor if you let them cure in the refrigerator, covered, for up to 4 hours.

2. When ready to cook, place the drip pan in the bottom of the rotisserie. Place the ribs in the rotisserie basket (see box on facing page) and close it tightly. Attach the basket to the rotisserie spit, then attach the spit to the rotisserie and turn on the motor. If your rotisserie has a temperature control, set it on 400°F (for instructions for using a rotisserie, see page 14). Cook the ribs until they are dark brown and crusty and the meat

has shrunk back about ¼ inch from the end of the bones, 40 to 50 minutes (see Notes).

3. Transfer the rack to a platter or cutting board and cut it in half or into individual ribs. Generously baste with barbecue sauce and serve at once with the remaining sauce on the side.

NOTES:

■ For the best results, you'd baste the ribs with barbecue sauce on both sides after they have cooked for 30 minutes, then continue spit roasting them until they're done. This has the advantage of caramelizing some of the sugar in the barbecue sauce and cooking the sauce into the meat. But to do this you need to remove the spit from the rotisserie, remove the basket from the spit, and open the basket to baste the ribs. This is time-consuming and somewhat messy, so we'll leave it to fanatics only.

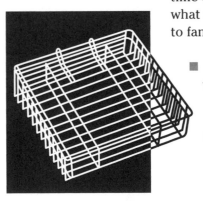

■ You can also smoke these ribs in a stove-top smoker. You'll find instructions for doing this on page 122.

rotisserie

tunnel bar-b-q ribs

How far would you go for great ribs? To another country? Every day legions of Detroiters take the quick trip through the Windsor Tunnel under the Detroit River to enjoy some of the most famous spit-roasted ribs in Canada. They don't have far to go, for the minute they emerge from the tunnel, the neon lights of the Tunnel Bar-B-Q are visible on the right. Once there, they watch glistening racks of ribs and sizzling whole chickens rotate slowly on spits before the leaping flames of a gas-fired rotisserie, just as I did twenty years ago, when I first visited the Tunnel Bar-B-Q. Ribs have probably been spit roasting here since 1941, when a Greek immigrant couple, Harry and Helen Racovitis, borrowed $500 to open a small eatery. It's now a third-generation barbecue emporium that serves literally thousands of people a week. In terms of barbecue, Tunnel Bar-B-Q is a two-trick pony—ribs and chicken—both seasoned with a simple rub and roasted until sizzling, crisp, brown, and delicious. The Tunnel rub is a proprietary secret. What you'll find here is how I imagine they make it. **SERVES 2**

ribs in the rotisserie

The French do it. So do the Italians, Spaniards, and Turks. I'm talking about one of the oldest and most effective ways to cook ribs—on the rotisserie. The gentle heat reduces tough meat to pull-apart-with-your-fingers tenderness and melts out the excess fat. The slow rotation bastes the ribs both internally and externally, so the meat never dries out.

The chief challenge is attaching the ribs to the rotisserie. Various manufacturers have come up with different ways to do this. With my Showtime rotisserie, for example, the easiest way is to place the ribs in the flat rotisserie basket. The instruction manual also explains how you can weave racks of ribs onto the shish kebab attachment or even between the two central spits.

To attempt to cover all the methods of other manufacturers would be confusing and probably incomplete. Consult the manufacturer's instructions for the best way to cook ribs in your particular rotisserie. You may need to cut the rack of ribs into more than one piece to get it to fit in a rotisserie basket.

One final note: Most rotisserie baskets come coated with a non-stick finish, so technically there's no need to oil them before adding ribs or other meat. However, it never hurts to give the basket a quick squirt of cooking oil spray just to play it safe.

4 teaspoons sweet paprika

2 teaspoons coarse salt (kosher or sea)

2 teaspoons freshly ground black pepper

2 teaspoons garlic powder

2 teaspoons dried oregano

1 teaspoon celery seed

1 rack baby back pork ribs (2 to 2½ pounds), peeled (see box on page 119)

Your favorite tomato or mustard barbecue sauce, for serving

1. Place the paprika, salt, pepper, garlic powder, oregano, and celery seed in a small bowl and whisk to mix the rub.

2. Place the ribs on a baking sheet. Sprinkle both sides all over with the rub, 2 to 3 teaspoons per side, rubbing it onto the meat with your fingertips. You can cook the ribs right away, but they will have even more flavor if you let them cure in the refrigerator, covered, for 4 hours.

3. When ready to cook, place the drip pan in the bottom of the rotisserie. Place the ribs in the rotisserie basket (see box on page 121) and close it tightly. Attach the basket to the rotisserie spit, then attach the spit to the rotisserie and turn on the motor. If your rotisserie has a temperature control, set it on 400°F (for instructions for using a rotisserie, see page 14). Cook the ribs until they are dark brown and crusty and the meat has shrunk back about ¼ inch from the ends of the bones, 40 to 50 minutes.

4. Transfer the rack to a platter or cutting board and cut it in half or into individual ribs. Serve at once, with the barbecue sauce on the side.

NOTES:

■ You can also smoke these ribs in a stove-top smoker. You'll find instructions for doing this at left.

■ You can also cook the meat on a fireplace rotisserie (see page 11). Trim off any excess fat before placing it on the spit. Cook over a hot, 2 to 3 Mississippi fire. It will take from 30 to 40 minutes, depending on your fireplace.

stove-top smoker ribs

You can prepare Dry Rub Ribs on a Spit (page 117), Kansas City Barbecue Ribs (page 119), and Tunnel Bar-B-Q Ribs (this page) in a stove-top smoker instead of a rotisserie. Perfuming them with wood smoke will give you totally different ribs. Follow the directions for spreading the rub on the rack of ribs, then set up the smoker (you'll find instructions for using a smoker on page 16). Place 1½ tablespoons hickory or oak sawdust in the center of the bottom of the smoker. Line the drip pan with aluminum foil and place it in the smoker. Lightly coat the smoker rack with cooking oil spray or use a paper towel dipped in oil, and place the rack in the smoker. Place the ribs on the rack; if you are smoking individual ribs, try to leave at least ½ inch between each.

Cover the smoker and place it over high heat for 3 minutes, then reduce the heat to medium. Smoke the ribs until they are cooked through, 20 to 30 minutes. When cooked, the meat will have shrunk about ¼ inch from the ends of the ribs and the ribs will be tender enough to pull apart with your fingers. Transfer the ribs to a cutting board. Generously brush the Dry Rub Ribs on both sides with mop sauce and thickly sprinkle rub over them. Brush Kansas City Barbecue Ribs with barbecue sauce. Serve Tunnel Bar-B-Q Ribs with barbecue sauce on the side.

rotisserie

tuscan-style ribs on a spit

In North America and Asia, ribs are treated as something of a blank canvas. The color comes from seasoning with rubs, marinades, mops, and/or sauces. Europeans take a different approach: They spit roast ribs with a minimum of seasonings—salt, pepper, maybe a little garlic, rosemary, or sage. The idea is to keep the focus on the flavor of the pork ribs themselves. **SERVES 2**

THE RECIPE

1 rack baby back pork ribs (2 to 2¹/₂ pounds), peeled (see box on page 119)
1 tablespoon extra-virgin olive oil
Coarse salt (kosher or sea) and freshly ground black pepper
2 cloves garlic, minced
2 tablespoons chopped fresh rosemary
2 tablespoons chopped fresh sage or more rosemary
Lemon wedges, for serving

1. Place the ribs on a baking sheet. Brush both sides with the olive oil. Generously season both sides with salt and pepper and sprinkle the garlic, rosemary, and sage over them, patting them onto the meat with your fingertips. You can cook the ribs right away, but they will have even more flavor if you refrigerate them, covered, for 2 to 4 hours.

2. When ready to cook, place the drip pan in the bottom of the rotisserie. Place the ribs in the rotisserie basket (see box on page 121) and close it tightly. Attach the basket to the rotisserie spit, then attach the spit to the rotisserie and turn on the motor. If your rotisserie has a temperature control, set it to 400°F (for instructions for using a rotisserie, see page 14). Cook the ribs until they are dark brown and crusty and the meat has shrunk back about ¹/₄ inch from the ends of the bones, 40 to 50 minutes.

3. Transfer the rack to a platter or cutting board and cut it in half or into individual ribs. Serve at once, with lemon wedges.

NOTE: To prepare these ribs on a fireplace rotisserie, see Notes, facing page.

RIB RAP

Also referred to as top loin ribs, pork baby back ribs are cut from the center part of the loin, next to the backbone. They're well marbled with fat and very tender, which makes them perfect for indoor grilling. You'll find them in two sizes. A rack of baby backs imported from Denmark weighs about 1 pound. Domestic baby backs tend to be larger, weighing from 2 to 2³/₄ pounds per rack.

For the sake of brevity, in the recipes here I've called for larger American-style racks of 2 to 2¹/₂ pounds. You can certainly use two of the smaller 1-pound racks in place of the larger rack. The cooking time will be about 30 minutes.

rotisserie

chinese barbecue "spare" ribs on the rotisserie

Consider the spare ribs served at your local Chinese restaurant. Chances are they're crusty on the outside and tender but not soft, with a complex flavor that ricochets from the salty tang of soy and hoisin sauce to the sweetness of sugar or honey to the pungency of garlic and perfume of five-spice powder. The one thing they're probably *not* is smoky, as the Chinese don't generally smoke ribs. The rotisserie turns out delicious Chinese-style ribs, with a lot less fat than the original, which are often deep-fried just before serving. The rib of choice for most Chinese is the pork spare rib. I call for smaller, more tender baby back ribs, which are better suited to the rotisserie. **SERVES 2**

THE RECIPE

1/3 cup hoisin sauce

3 tablespoons sugar

3 tablespoons soy sauce

2 tablespoons Chinese rice wine or dry sherry

1 tablespoon Asian (dark) sesame oil

2 cloves garlic, peeled and gently crushed with the side of a cleaver

2 slices ginger (each 1/4 inch thick), peeled and gently crushed with the side of a cleaver

1 rack baby back pork ribs (2 to 2 1/2 pounds), peeled (see box on page 119)

1. Place the hoisin sauce, sugar, soy sauce, rice wine, and sesame oil in a nonreactive mixing bowl and whisk until the sugar dissolves. Stir in the garlic and ginger.

2. Place the ribs in a nonreactive baking dish just large enough to hold them or in a large resealable plastic bag. Add the hoisin sauce mixture. Let the ribs marinate in the refrigerator, covered, for at least 6 hours, or as long as overnight, turning several times.

tip

You can also cook the meat on a fireplace rotisserie (see page 11). Trim off any excess fat before placing it on the spit. Cook over a hot, 2 to 3 Mississippi fire. It will take from 30 to 40 minutes, depending on your fireplace.

3. When ready to cook, place the drip pan in the bottom of the rotisserie. Place the ribs in the rotisserie basket (see box on page 121) and close it tightly. Attach the basket to the rotisserie spit, then attach the spit to the rotisserie and turn on the motor. If your rotisserie has a temperature control, set it on 400°F (for instructions for using a rotisserie, see page 14). Cook the ribs until they are dark brown and crusty and the meat has shrunk back about ¼ inch from the ends of the bones, 40 minutes to 1 hour.

4. Transfer the rack to a platter or cutting board and cut it in half or into individual ribs. Serve at once.

tip

■ Hoisin sauce is a thick, purplish brown, sweet-salty condiment made from fermented soy beans, vinegar, garlic, sugar, and Chinese five-spice powder. You can find it in jars in the ethnic food section of your supermarket.

■ Chinese five-spice powder is a spice mix frequently made with star anise, fennel seeds, cinnamon, cloves, and pepper.

stove-top smoker

"barbecued" baby backs

Ask barbecue fanatics about the nature of true 'que and they'll tell you it's all in the wood smoke. Now, there are many perfectly good ways to cook ribs indoors (several of them in this book on pages 117 through 124), but only one approximates the glory of true pit-cooked ribs: roasting in a stove-top smoker. The seasoning here is a simple 5-4-3-2-1 Rub (you'll soon see why it has this curious name). The goal is to keep the focus on the meat and wood smoke. **SERVES 4**

tip

This rub is so versatile (and downright good) that you'll want to keep a supply on hand. To make a larger batch, for every teaspoon of an ingredient called for, substitute one tablespoon—for example, use 5 tablespoons of sweet paprika instead of 5 teaspoons. Be sure to store the rub in an airtight container away from heat or light. It will keep for several months and is good on just about everything.

THE RECIPE

FOR THE 5-4-3-2-1 RUB:
5 teaspoons sweet paprika
4 teaspoons dark brown sugar
3 teaspoons coarse salt (kosher or sea)
2 teaspoons freshly ground black pepper
1 teaspoon dry mustard

2 large racks (2 to 2½ pounds each)
   baby back pork ribs, peeled
   (see box on page 119)
Cooking oil spray (optional)
1 cup of your favorite barbecue sauce
   (optional; for a good made-from-scratch
   candidate, see page 374)

YOU'LL ALSO NEED:
2 tablespoons hickory wood sawdust

1. Make the 5-4-3-2-1 Rub: Place the paprika, brown sugar, salt, pepper, and mustard in a small bowl and whisk to mix, breaking up any lumps of brown sugar with your fingers.

2. Place the ribs on a baking sheet. Sprinkle both sides of the racks all over with the 5-4-3-2-1 Rub, rubbing it onto the meat with your fingertips. Use 2 to 3 teaspoons of rub per side. You can smoke the ribs right away, but they will have even more flavor if you let them cure in the refrigerator, covered, for 4 hours before smoking.

3. When ready to cook, set up the smoker (for instructions for using a stove-top smoker, see page 16). Place the sawdust in the center of the bottom of the smoker. Line the drip pan with aluminum foil and place it in the smoker. Lightly coat the smoker rack with cooking oil spray, or use a paper towel dipped in oil, and place the rack in the smoker. Place the ribs on the rack; try to leave at least ½ inch between each rack of ribs. Cover the smoker and place it over high heat for 3 minutes, then reduce the heat to medium.

4. Smoke the ribs until cooked though, 20 to 30 minutes. When cooked, the meat will have shrunk about ¼ inch from the ends of the bones and will be tender enough to pull apart with your fingers.

5. Transfer the ribs to a platter or cutting board and cut large racks in half. There are two ways to serve the ribs: For Memphis-style (dry ribs), sprinkle each rack with an additional 1 to 2 tablespoons of rub (if you want to serve the ribs this way, make extra rub following the instructions in the Tip at left). For Kansas City–style (wet ribs), brush each rack with 2 to 3 tablespoons of barbecue sauce, serving the remainder on the side.

rotisserie

rotisserie "brat fry"

A brat fry is a Wisconsin barbecue. More specifically, it's a feast of bratwurst served with onions and Sheboygan hard rolls, which are similar to kaiser rolls. It's customary for German Americans all across Wisconsin to grill the bratwursts and onions, but the rotisserie produces crisp-skinned, succulent sausages and sweet roasted vegetables— without the risk of flare-ups. OK, so the bell peppers are more of an Italian than a Wisconsin touch, but they make a nice combo. The bratwursts are particularly good served with Wisconsin brewery Leinenkugel's wheat beer. **SERVES 4**

THE RECIPE

**4 uncooked bratwursts
    (about 1 pound)**
**1 large red bell pepper, cored,
    seeded, and quartered**
**1 to 2 tablespoons extra-virgin
    olive oil**
1 medium-size onion, quartered
**Coarse salt (kosher or sea) and
    freshly ground black pepper**
**4 hard rolls or kaiser rolls,
    cut almost in half through one side**
1 cup sauerkraut, drained
**German-style mustard or horseradish
    mustard**

1. Lightly brush the bratwursts and bell pepper with olive oil, then brush the onion quarters more generously with olive oil. Season the bell pepper and onion with salt and pepper.

2. Arrange the bratwursts, bell pepper, and onion in the rotisserie basket (if possible, use a flat basket). Ideally, the bratwursts should be positioned so that they will be perpendicular to the rotisserie spit and the bell pepper and onion quarters should be placed in rows between the sausages. Close the basket lid tightly.

tip

You can cook just about any fresh sausage on the rotisserie. You'll find a Variation using Italian sausage on page 128.

tips

Bratwurst is a coarsely ground, mildly seasoned pork sausage of German–Austrian heritage. The Wisconsin firm Johnsonville makes some of the best. Its bratwurst is distributed nationally.

3. When ready to cook, place the drip pan in the bottom of the rotisserie. Attach the basket to the rotisserie spit, then attach the spit to the rotisserie and turn the motor on. If your rotisserie has a temperature control, set it to 400°F (for instructions for using a rotisserie, see page 14). Cook the sausages, bell pepper, and onion until the sausages are dark brown and cooked through, 30 to 40 minutes.

4. To serve, thinly slice the bell pepper and onion. Cut each bratwurst in half lengthwise and place it in a roll. Top each sausage with a quarter of the spit-roasted bell pepper and onion and ¼ cup of sauerkraut. Slather the remaining halves of the rolls with mustard, put them on top of the sandwiches, and serve at once.

VARIATION: A favorite at street fairs and block parties in Little Italys across the country, Italian sausages can also be cooked in the rotisserie along with bell pepper and onion. Just substitute 1 pound of fresh sweet or hot Italian sausage for the bratwurst. You can use either links or coil sausage. The cooking time will be the same.

grilled ham steaks
with apple and pecan salsa

When I was growing up, ham steaks appeared on our table fortnightly—invariably served with applesauce. Here's an update on this classic combination, featuring a fresh, quick-to-make apple salsa. I think you'll like the way the apples counterpoint the saltiness of the ham. It should come as no surprise that, like steaks and chops, ham steaks taste best when seared on the grill.

SERVES 2 AND CAN BE MULTIPLIED AS DESIRED

if you have a...

FOR THE APPLE AND PECAN SALSA:

1 large, crisp, sweet-tart apple,
   such as a Fuji or Braeburn

2 tablespoons fresh lime juice,
   or more to taste

3 tablespoons coarsely chopped toasted
   pecans (see Notes)

3 tablespoons finely chopped fresh mint
   or cilantro

1 to 2 jalapeño peppers, seeded and
   finely chopped (for a hotter salsa,
   leave the seeds in)

1 tablespoon finely chopped
   candied ginger

2 tablespoons finely chopped sweet onion
   (optional)

1 to 2 tablespoons light brown sugar

FOR THE HAM STEAKS:

1 large or 2 small ham steaks
   (¾ to 1 pound in all; see Notes)

1 tablespoon butter, melted, or
   1 tablespoon extra-virgin olive oil

Freshly ground black pepper

CONTACT GRILL: Preheat the grill; if your contact grill has a temperature control, preheat the grill to high. Place the drip pan under the front of the grill. When ready to cook, lightly oil the grill surface. Place the ham steak(s) on the hot grill, then close the lid. The ham will be done after cooking 3 to 5 minutes.

GRILL PAN: Place the grill pan on the stove and preheat it to medium-high over medium heat. When the grill pan is hot a drop of water will skitter in the pan. When ready to cook, lightly oil the ridges of the grill pan. Place the ham steak(s) in the hot grill pan. The ham will be done after cooking 3 to 5 minutes per side.

BUILT-IN GRILL: Preheat the grill to high, then, if it does not have a nonstick surface, brush and oil the grill grate. Place the ham steak(s) on the hot grate. The ham will be done after cooking 3 to 5 minutes per side.

FREESTANDING GRILL: Preheat the grill to high; there's no need to oil the grate. Place the ham steak(s) on the hot grill. The ham will be done after cooking 4 to 6 minutes per side.

FIREPLACE GRILL: Rake red hot embers under the gridiron and preheat it for 3 to 5 minutes; you want a hot, 2 to 3 Mississippi fire. When ready to cook, brush and oil the gridiron. Place the ham steak(s) on the hot grate. The ham will be done after cooking 3 to 5 minutes per side.

1. Make the apple and pecan salsa: Core the apple and cut it into fine dice (I don't bother peeling the apple; the skin adds color and texture). Place the apple in a nonreactive mixing bowl, add the lime juice, and toss to coat. Add the pecans, mint, jalapeño(s), candied ginger, onion, if using, and 1 tablespoon brown sugar, but don't mix the salsa until right before you are ready to serve it. The salsa can be prepared up to this stage several hours ahead of time and refrigerated, covered.

2. Cook the ham steak(s), following the instructions for any of the grills in the box above, until cooked through. Rotate the ham steak(s) a quarter turn after 1½ minutes to create a handsome cross-hatch of grill marks.

3. Transfer the ham steak(s) to a platter or plates. Stir the salsa, then taste for seasoning, adding more lime juice and/or brown sugar as necessary; the salsa should be highly seasoned. Spoon the salsa over the ham, or serve it on the side, and serve at once.

NOTES:

■ To toast pecans, place them in a dry cast-iron or other heavy skillet (don't use a nonstick skillet for this). Cook the pecans over medium heat until fragrant and lightly browned, 3 to 6 minutes, shaking the skillet to ensure that they toast evenly. Transfer the toasted pecans to a heatproof bowl to cool.

■ For the absolute best results, take the time to find a Smithfield or other dry-cured ham steak; they're frequently available at specialty food stores and some supermarkets. They're quite salty, so you'll probably want to soak the ham steaks in a baking dish filled with cold water for a couple hours, changing the water 2 or 3 times. Blot the ham steaks dry with paper towels before you grill them. If this seems like too much trouble, you can use regular, baked ham steaks.

From as far west as North Africa to as far east as Indonesia, the meat of choice is lamb. Just consider the sheer diversity of lamb dishes you can cook on an indoor grill: spit-roasted leg of lamb with Berber spices from Morocco; garlic and rosemary perfumed lamb chops from Friuli in northern Italy; and shish kebab from the Middle East. Hunger for something more exotic? How about lamb steaks with a feta cheese sauce or a spit-roasted kid inspired by Piedmont chef Cesare Giaccone? You can even barbecue leg of lamb, like they do in Owensboro, Kentucky.

lamb

rotisserie

spit-roasted lamb
with berber spices

The Berbers are a largely nomadic people of northwestern Africa, and while this particular recipe comes from Morocco, you'll find Berber-spiced grilled meats as far afield as Israel and Ethiopia. Like Jamaica's jerk seasoning, the spice paste likely originated as a preservative. It's loaded with complex aromatic notes coming from coriander, cumin, and ginger and a sweetish touch in the form of cinnamon, cloves, and allspice. In Morocco, the meat of choice for Berber seasoning is lamb, but the spice paste is also compelling used with chicken, beef, and whole fish.

SERVES 6 TO 8

tips

■ Fenugreek (literally Greek hay) is a small rectangular seed with an earthy, pleasantly bitter flavor. There's certainly plenty going on in the spice paste without it, but if you can find fenugreek (look for it at Indian markets, where it goes by the name *methi*), your lamb will be all the more authentic.

■ You can also cook the meat on a fireplace rotisserie (see page 11). Trim off any excess fat before placing it on the spit. Cook over a hot, 2 to 3 Mississippi fire. It will take from 1 to 1¼ hours for medium-rare and 1½ hours for medium, depending on your fireplace.

THE RECIPE

FOR THE SPICE PASTE:
1 small onion, coarsely chopped
1 piece (2 inches) fresh ginger, peeled and coarsely chopped
2 cloves garlic, coarsely chopped
1 to 2 jalapeño peppers, seeded and coarsely chopped (for a hotter spice paste, leave the seeds in)
¼ cup sweet paprika
1 tablespoon coarse salt (kosher or sea), or more to taste
2 teaspoons cracked black peppercorns
2 teaspoons ground coriander
1 teaspoon ground cumin
½ teaspoon ground cardamom
½ teaspoon ground cinnamon
½ teaspoon ground fenugreek (optional)
¼ teaspoon ground allspice

⅛ teaspoon ground cloves
⅓ cup olive oil
3 tablespoons fresh lemon juice, or more to taste

1 bone-in leg of lamb (4 to 5 pounds)
2 tablespoons (¼ stick) unsalted butter (optional), melted

YOU'LL ALSO NEED:
Butcher's string

1. Make the spice paste: Place the onion, ginger, garlic, and jalapeño(s) in a food processor and finely chop, running the machine in short bursts. Add the paprika, salt, cracked pepper, coriander, cumin, cardamom, cinnamon, fenugreek, if using, allspice, and cloves and process until smooth. Gradually add the olive oil and lemon juice. Taste for seasoning, adding more salt and/or lemon juice as necessary; the mixture should be highly seasoned.

2. Using the tip of a paring knife, make small slits on all sides of the roast about 1½ inches apart. Using the tip of your index finger, widen the holes slightly. Place a tiny spoonful of spice paste in each slit, forcing it in with your finger. Spread the remaining spice paste over the roast. Tie the lamb into a tight cylinder with butcher's string. You can cook the lamb right away, but it will have even more flavor if you let it marinate in the refrigerator, covered, for 4 to 6 hours.

3. When ready to cook, place the drip pan in the bottom of the rotisserie. Skewer the lamb lengthwise on the rotisserie spit. Attach the spit to the rotisserie and turn on the motor. If your rotisserie has a temperature control, set it to 400°F (for instructions for using a rotisserie,

see page 14). Cook the roast until it is dark brown on all sides and cooked to taste, 1¼ to 1½ hours for medium-rare, about 1¾ hours for medium (most Moroccans prefer their lamb medium to well-done). Use an instant-read meat thermometer to test for doneness; don't let the thermometer touch the spit or a bone. Medium-rare lamb will have an internal temperature of about 145°F; medium lamb will be about 160°F.

4. Transfer the roast to a platter or cutting board, remove the spit, and let the meat rest for 5 minutes. Cut off and discard the string. Brush the lamb with butter, if desired (this may seem like gilding the lily, but it makes a luscious dish even richer). Thinly slice the lamb off the bone across the grain and serve at once.

It's useful to know how to cook a bone-in leg of lamb in the event you can't find a butterflied boneless leg of lamb. Try to find a bone-in roast from the loin (the upper) part of the leg; it will have more meat and less sinew than the shank end. You can certainly substitute a 3- to 3½-pound rolled butterflied leg of lamb—you'll find the cooking time for it in the recipe below.

rotisserie

leg of lamb
with garlic mint wet rub

Lamb begs for mint—a fact appreciated by anyone who grew up eating lamb chops with mint jelly in Continental restaurants in the United States (or just about anywhere in England). Some people find mint jelly unpalatably cloying, however, so

**GETTING
A LEG UP**

Abutterflied leg of
lamb is one that
has had the bone
removed. Tying a
butterflied leg of
lamb into a cylinder
makes a boneless
lamb roast.

here's a Mediterranean remake of this classic combination,
featuring a decidedly unsweet wet rub made with fresh mint,
garlic, and lemon. Mint jelly makes a cameo appearance in
the sauce. **SERVES 6**

T H E   R E C I P E

3 cloves garlic, coarsely chopped
2 strips lemon zest (each ¹/₂ by ¹/₂ inch),
    finely chopped
1 to 2 bunches mint, rinsed, shaken dry,
    and stemmed (for about 1 cup loosely
    packed leaves)
1 teaspoon coarse salt (kosher or sea)
¹/₂ teaspoon cracked or coarsely ground
    black peppercorns
2 tablespoons extra-virgin olive oil
1 tablespoon fresh lemon juice
1 butterflied leg of lamb (3 to 3¹/₂ pounds;
    see page 133), tied into a cylindrical
    roast
Sweet-and-Sour Mint Sauce
    (optional; recipe follows)

1. Place the garlic, lemon zest, mint, salt,
and cracked pepper in a food processor
and finely chop. Add the olive oil and
lemon juice and process to a smooth
paste, scraping down the side of the bowl
with a rubber spatula.

2. Using the tip of a paring
knife, make small slits on all
sides of the roast about
1¹/₂ inches apart.
Using the tip of
your index finger,

widen the holes. Place a tiny spoonful of
mint mixture in each slit, forcing it in with
your finger. This will use up a little more
than half of the mint mixture. If you are
feeling ambitious, you can force a little of
the mint mixture between the seams in
the roast. Spread the remaining mint mixture over the roast. You can cook the
lamb right away, but it will have even
more flavor if you let it marinate in the
refrigerator, covered, for 1 to 2 hours.

3. When ready to cook, place the drip
pan in the bottom of the rotisserie.
Skewer the lamb lengthwise on the rotisserie spit. Attach the spit to the rotisserie
and turn on the motor. If your rotisserie
has a temperature control, set it to 400°F
(for instructions for using a rotisserie,
see page 14; for instructions for cooking
the lamb on a fireplace rotisserie, see the
Tips on page 132). Cook the roast until
it is dark brown on all sides and cooked
to taste, 1 to 1¹/₄ hours for medium-rare,
about 1¹/₂ hours for medium. Use an
instant-read meat thermometer to test for
doneness; don't let the thermometer
touch the spit. Medium-rare lamb will
have an internal temperature of about
145°F; medium lamb will be about 160°F.

4. Transfer the roast to a platter or cutting board, remove the spit, and let the meat rest for 5 to 10 minutes. If desired reserve the drippings for making the Sweet-and-Sour Mint Sauce. Cut off and discard the string. Thinly slice the lamb crosswise and serve it at once with Sweet-and-Sour Mint Sauce, if desired.

sweet-and-sour mint sauce

Here's a simple sauce that features mint jelly, along with meat drippings and stock and a fillip of vinegar to counterbalance the jelly's sweetness.
MAKES ABOUT 1¼ CUPS

2 tablespoons drippings from the Leg of Lamb with Garlic Mint Wet Rub (facing page)
1 cup veal, lamb, beef, or chicken stock (preferably homemade)
2 tablespoons dry white wine
2 tablespoons mint jelly
1 tablespoon rice vinegar or distilled white vinegar, or more to taste
Coarse salt (kosher or sea) and freshly ground black pepper

Place the drippings, stock, wine, mint jelly, and rice vinegar in a saucepan over high heat, bring to a boil, and let boil until the mint jelly dissolves and the wine loses its alcohol taste, about 10 minutes.

rotisserie

leg of lamb
with roquefort, spinach, and pine nuts

The inspiration for this dish comes from the Causses—the rocky highlands of southwest France. This stark, seemingly inhospitable region is the source of two great delicacies: Roquefort cheese, which is ripened in the limestone caves that riddle the area, and succulent spring lamb. Put the two together on a spit and you get lamb that's crusty on the outside, moist inside, and bursting with the tangy, salty flavor of Roquefort.

The spinach and pine nuts add an earthy flavor, while the melting cheese bastes the meat from the inside. **SERVES 6**

THE RECIPE

8 ounces fresh spinach, rinsed and
    stemmed (see Notes)
3 ounces Roquefort cheese, crumbled
    (for about 6 tablespoons)
2 tablespoons toasted pine nuts
    (see Notes)
Coarse salt (kosher or sea) and
    freshly ground black pepper
1 butterflied leg of lamb
    (3 to 3½ pounds; see page 133)
About 2 teaspoons extra-virgin olive oil
Minted Tomato Sauce (optional; recipe follows)

YOU'LL ALSO NEED:
Butcher's string

1. Bring 2 cups of salted water to a boil in a large pot over high heat. Add the spinach and cook it until the leaves are limp, 1 to 2 minutes. Drain the spinach in a colander, rinse it with cold water until chilled, then drain it well, grabbing fistfuls of spinach and squeezing them tightly to wring out all water (it's important to extract *all* of the water). Coarsely chop the spinach with a chef's knife and place it in a mixing bowl. Stir in the Roquefort and pine nuts and season with salt and pepper to taste.

2. Spread the lamb open on a work surface and season the top with salt and pepper. Using a spatula, spread the spinach and Roquefort filling over the meat. Roll the lamb into a tight cylinder and tie it in several places with butcher's string. Lightly brush or rub the outside of the lamb roast with the oil and season it very generously with salt and pepper.

3. When ready to cook, place the drip pan in the bottom of the rotisserie. Skewer the lamb lengthwise on the rotisserie spit. Attach the spit to the rotisserie and turn on the motor. If your rotisserie has a temperature control, set it to 400°F (for instructions for using a rotisserie, see page 14). Cook the lamb until it is dark brown on all sides and cooked to taste, 1 to 1¼ hours for medium-rare, about 1½ hours for medium. Use an instant-read meat thermometer to test for doneness; don't let the thermometer touch the spit. Medium-rare lamb will have an internal temperature of about 145°F; medium lamb will be about 160°F.

4. Transfer the roast to a platter or cutting board, remove the spit, and let the meat rest for 5 minutes. If desired, reserve the drippings for making the Minted Tomato Sauce. Cut off and discard the string. Thinly slice the lamb crosswise and serve it at once with the Minted Tomato Sauce, if desired.

NOTES:
■ Being a purist, I've called for fresh spinach here, but no great harm will be done if you use frozen. Prepare a 10-ounce package of frozen chopped spinach according to the instructions on the box and be sure to drain it very well before adding the Roquefort and pine nuts.

tips

■ Sometimes butterflied leg of lamb comes tied up in a string net. You'll need to remove the net to stuff the lamb, then tie the meat back into a roast with butcher's string.

■ For the full effect of this recipe, you must use imported Roquefort cheese, not a domestic blue.

■ You can also cook the leg of lamb on a fireplace rotisserie. For instructions for doing this, see the Tips on page 132.

■ To toast pine nuts, place them in a clean, dry, heavy skillet over medium heat (don't use a nonstick skillet for this). Cook the pine nuts until fragrant and lightly browned, 2 to 4 minutes, shaking the pan to brown the nuts evenly. Immediately transfer them to a small heatproof bowl to cool.

minted tomato sauce

In North America and Great Britain, lamb is often paired with mint. In the Mediterranean and Near East, it's paired with tomato. This recipe brings the two together in a simple sauce that will be good made without lamb drippings and fabulous if you add them. Spoon off most of the fat from the drip pan before adding the drippings to the saucepan. **MAKES ABOUT 1½ CUPS**

1 cup veal, lamb, beef, or chicken stock (preferably homemade)
¼ cup canned tomato sauce
3 tablespoons mint jelly
1 clove garlic, peeled and gently crushed with the side of a cleaver
2 tablespoons drippings from Leg of Lamb with Roquefort, Spinach, and Pine Nuts (optional; facing page)
Coarse salt (kosher or sea) and freshly ground black pepper

Place the stock, tomato sauce, mint jelly, garlic, and lamb drippings, if using, in a heavy nonreactive saucepan over medium heat and stir to mix. Bring the sauce to a simmer, then let cook until slightly thickened and richly flavored, 5 to 8 minutes, whisking from time to time. Season the sauce with salt and pepper to taste.

stove-top smoker

smoked leg of lamb

Lamb is often served grilled and almost never smoked—unless you're in Owensboro, Kentucky. This mellow town on the Ohio River is the birthplace of barbecued mutton, and possibly the only place on the planet where it's popular. But smoked lamb is another story (lamb's much milder than mutton), and if you haven't tried it, you haven't fully lived. Here's a version you can make in a stove-top smoker. There are two options for sauces—a "black" barbecue sauce like they serve in Owensboro or a minted tomato sauce. **SERVES 6**

1 butterflied leg of lamb (3 to 3½ pounds;
   see page 133), tied into a cylindrical roast
Coarse salt (kosher or sea) and freshly ground
   black pepper
Cooking oil spray (optional)
1 tablespoon butter, melted (optional)
Black Barbecue Sauce (recipe follows)
   or Minted Tomato Sauce (page 137)

YOU'LL ALSO NEED:
3 tablespoons hickory or oak sawdust

1. Place the lamb on a baking sheet and season it generously on all sides with salt and pepper.

2. Set up the smoker (for instructions for using a stove-top smoker, see page 16). Place the sawdust in the center of the bottom of the smoker. Line the drip pan with aluminum foil and place it on top. Lightly coat the smoker rack with cooking oil spray, or use a paper towel dipped in oil, and insert the rack in the smoker. Place the leg of lamb, fat side up, on the rack. Tent the lamb with a large sheet of heavy-duty aluminum foil, crumpling and crimping the edges over the outside rim of the smoker bottom to make a tight seal. Try not to let the foil come in contact with the meat.

3. Place the smoker over high heat for 3 minutes, then reduce the heat to medium. Smoke the lamb until it has a good smoke flavor, about 30 minutes.

4. Meanwhile, preheat the oven to 350°F.

5. Unwrap the lamb and discard the aluminum foil. Place the lamb still on the smoker bottom in the oven and bake it until crusty and dark brown on the outside and cooked to the desired degree of doneness inside, about 30 minutes for medium-rare; about 45 minutes for medium. Use an instant-read meat thermometer to test for doneness. Medium-rare lamb will have an internal temperature of about 145°F; medium lamb will be about 160°F.

6. Transfer the lamb to a platter or cutting board, cut off and discard the string, then brush the lamb with the melted butter, if desired. Let the lamb rest for 5 minutes. Cut the lamb into thin slices and serve it at once with Black Barbecue Sauce or Minted Tomato Sauce.

black barbecue sauce

This sauce is unique in the annals of American barbecue sauces—because it's black and because it lacks some of the ingredients so often associated with American sauces: ketchup, liquid smoke, and molasses. It's a terrific condiment—tart, piquant, spicy, and mercifully free of cloying sweetness—with enough gumption to stand up to the rich, smoky taste of the lamb. Be generous when you add the black pepper. **MAKES ABOUT 1½ CUPS**

4 tablespoons (½ stick) unsalted butter
2 cloves garlic, minced
1 shallot, or ½ small onion, minced
¼ cup Worcestershire sauce
¼ cup distilled white vinegar
2 tablespoons fresh lemon juice
1 tablespoon dark brown sugar
¼ teaspoon ground allspice
¾ cup beef, veal, or chicken stock
    (preferably homemade)
Coarse salt (kosher or sea) and freshly ground
    black pepper

1. Melt the butter in a heavy nonreactive saucepan over high heat. Add the garlic and shallot and cook until fragrant but not brown, about 3 minutes.

2. Add the Worcestershire sauce, vinegar, lemon juice, brown sugar, allspice, and beef stock and bring to a boil. Reduce the heat to medium and let the

two-step smoking

The stove-top smoker is great for smoking and cooking relatively small pieces of food, like chicken wings, salmon, tomatoes, and tofu. But what do you do when you want to smoke larger or tougher cuts of meat, like leg of lamb, brisket, turkey, or even beer-can chicken? Well, you can use a stove-top smoker for these foods, too, and still get a satisfying crust, something that's usually a challenge to do in the moist environment of a smoker. The solution is two-step smoking.

The first step is to use the smoker on the stove-top to apply a smoke flavor to the food. When cooking foods that are too tall to fit under the lid of the smoker, like beer-can chickens or turkeys, you can tent the smoker with aluminum foil, tightly crimping the foil at the top edge of the smoker to seal in the smoke. Smoking will take between 30 and 40 minutes.

To finish cooking larger items, place the oven rack on one of the lower shelf settings and preheat the oven. Once the food is smoked, remove and discard the foil. Carefully place the food, still on the smoker, in the oven. Bake the food, uncovered, until it's cooked through. This gives you the best of two methods—smoking and roasting.

sauce simmer until richly flavored, 4 to 6 minutes. Taste for seasoning, adding salt and pepper to taste. You can serve the sauce warm or at room temperature. It can be refrigerated, covered, for several days.

rotisserie

espresso-crusted lamb shanks

'm always looking for new ways to use coffee in barbecue rubs and sauces. The dish here may sound American in inspiration—after all, the United States was the birthplace of redeye gravy. Actually, the idea was sparked by the young turks of nouvelle cuisine I worked with in Paris in the 1970s (the juxtaposition of unexpected ingredients was one of the hallmarks of nouvelle cuisine). Lamb has an assertive flavor, requiring a bold rub to stand up to it. The bittersweet, smoky pungency of ground espresso beans is just the ticket; it minimizes what some people call the gamey taste of lamb. And, since lamb shanks need a slow, gentle heat to melt their tough connective tissue, the rotisserie is the ideal way to cook them. **SERVES 4**

THE RECIPE

2 tablespoons ground espresso beans

1 tablespoon coarse salt (kosher or sea)

1 tablespoon sweet paprika

1 tablespoon brown sugar

2 teaspoons ground coriander

2 teaspoons freshly ground black pepper

1 teaspoon ground cardamom

4 lamb shanks (each 12 to 14 ounces)

1 to 2 teaspoons vegetable oil

Espresso Sauce with Asian Seasonings
(recipe follows)

1. Make the rub: Place the ground espresso beans, salt, paprika, brown sugar, coriander, pepper, and cardamom in a small bowl and stir to mix.

2. Place the lamb shanks in a large mixing bowl. Add the espresso rub and stir to coat evenly. Add the vegetable oil and stir to mix. You can cook the lamb shanks right away, but they'll have a much richer flavor if you let them marinate in the refrigerator, covered, for at least 4 hours or as long as overnight.

3. When ready to cook, place the drip pan in the bottom of the rotisserie. Place

tip

Once a dish of the peasantry and the poor, lamb shanks have acquired a certain cachet. You can probably find them at your supermarket; if not, visit a Greek or Middle Eastern market or a butcher shop.

the lamb shanks in the rotisserie basket or skewer them on the spit, positioning the shanks so that the fat and thin ends alternate and are perpendicular to the spit. Attach the basket, if using, to the rotisserie spit, then attach the spit to the rotisserie and turn on the motor. If your rotisserie has a temperature control, set it to 400°F (for instructions for using a rotisserie, see page 14). Cook the lamb shanks until they are sizzling, dark brown, and crusty and the meat has shrunk back about ½ inch from the ends of the shank bones, 1 to 1¼ hours. Lamb shanks should be served medium-well to well-done, 170° to 190°F on an instant-read meat thermometer inserted in the thickest part of the meat but not so that it touches the spit or bone.

4. Transfer the lamb shanks to a platter or plates and serve with the Espresso Sauce with Asian Seasonings.

espresso sauce with asian seasonings

East meets West in this barbecue sauce, which starts with espresso but finishes with a thoroughly Asian combination of hoisin sauce and ginger, garlic, and scallions. Hoisin sauce is a thick, sweet Chinese condiment made from soybeans and star anise, among other things. **MAKES ABOUT 1 CUP**

2 tablespoons unsalted butter
2 scallions, both white and green parts, trimmed and finely chopped
1 clove garlic, minced
1 jalapeño pepper, seeded and minced
2 teaspoons minced peeled fresh ginger
Drippings from the Espresso-Crusted Lamb Shanks
¾ cup brewed espresso
2 tablespoons hoisin sauce
½ teaspoon finely grated lime zest
1 tablespoon fresh lime juice
1 tablespoon honey
½ teaspoon ground cardamom
½ teaspoon ground coriander
Coarse salt (kosher or sea) and freshly ground black pepper

1. Melt 1 tablespoon of the butter in a small nonreactive saucepan over medium heat. Add the scallions, garlic, jalapeño, and ginger and cook until the scallions, garlic, and ginger are just beginning to brown, 4 to 5 minutes.

2. Add the drippings, espresso, hoisin sauce, lime zest, lime juice, honey, cardamom, and coriander. Let the sauce simmer gently until thick and richly flavored, 4 to 6 minutes, stirring often with a wooden spoon. Season the sauce with salt and pepper to taste. Just before serving, stir in the remaining 1 tablespoon of butter.

tip

You can also cook the meat on a fireplace rotisserie (see page 11). Trim off any excess fat before placing it on the spit. Cook over a hot, 2 to 3 Mississippi fire. It will take from 45 minutes to 1 hour, depending on your fireplace.

lamb steaks
with mint chimichurri

This recipe breathes new life into the hackneyed combination of roast lamb with mint jelly, jazzing up flash-grilled lamb steaks with a mentholated twist on Argentina's fabled *chimichurri,* a garlic and parsley sauce traditionally served with grilled beef. Using fresh mint in place of parsley gives the *chimichurri* a whole new personality, and here it does double duty—as a marinade and as a sauce. **SERVES 4**

THE RECIPE

1 to 2 bunches fresh mint, rinsed and shaken dry (for about 1 cup loosely packed leaves)

3 cloves garlic, coarsely chopped

1 teaspoon coarse salt (kosher or sea), or more to taste

1/2 teaspoon freshly ground black pepper, or more to taste

1/3 cup extra-virgin olive oil (preferably Spanish)

2 tablespoons red wine vinegar

4 lamb steaks (each about 1/2 inch thick and 6 to 8 ounces)

1. Set aside 4 mint sprigs for garnish, then remove the stems from the remaining mint. Place the mint leaves, garlic, salt, and pepper in a food processor and finely chop them, running the machine in short bursts. Add the olive oil and wine vinegar in a thin stream, again running the machine in short bursts. Add 2 to 4 tablespoons of water, enough to thin the mixture to a pourable sauce. Taste for seasoning, adding more salt and/or pepper as necessary; the *chimichurri* should be highly seasoned.

2. Spoon about 1/4 cup of the *chimichurri* into the bottom of a nonreactive baking dish that is just large enough to hold the lamb steaks in a single layer. Arrange the lamb steaks on top and spoon about a third of the remaining *chimichurri* over them, spreading it over the lamb with the back of the spoon. Let the lamb marinate, covered, in the refrigerator for at least 30 minutes or as long as 4 hours; the longer the lamb marinates, the richer the flavor will be. Refrigerate the remaining *chimichurri,* covered; you'll use this as a sauce (let it return to room temperature before serving).

3. When ready to cook, drain the lamb well, scraping off the excess marinade with a rubber spatula. Discard the marinade. Cook the lamb steaks, following the

tip

Your chief challenge in this recipe will be finding lamb steaks. Some supermarkets sell them; if not, try a butcher or Greek market. If you can't find lamb steaks, substitute rib or loin lamb chops. Rib chops that are 1/2 inch thick will be cooked to medium-rare after 3 to 5 minutes per side; 1-inch-thick loin chops will be medium-rare after 4 to 6 minutes.

instructions for any of the grills in the box at right, until nicely browned and cooked to taste. To test for doneness, use the poke method; when cooked to medium-rare the meat should be gently yielding. If desired, rotate each steak a quarter turn after 1½ minutes to create a handsome crosshatch of grill marks.

4. Transfer the lamb steaks to a platter or plates. Garnish each with a sprig of mint and serve the remaining *chimichurri* on the side.

if you have a...

CONTACT GRILL: Preheat the grill; if your contact grill has a temperature control, preheat the grill to high. Place the drip pan under the front of the grill. When ready to cook, lightly oil the grill surface. Place the lamb steaks on the hot grill, then close the lid. They will be cooked to medium-rare after 3 to 4 minutes; they will be medium after 5 to 6 minutes.

GRILL PAN: Place the grill pan on the stove and preheat it to medium-high over medium heat. When the grill pan is hot a drop of water will skitter in the pan. When ready to cook, lightly oil the ridges of the grill pan. Place the lamb steaks in the hot grill pan. They will be cooked to medium-rare after 3 to 4 minutes per side; they will be medium after 5 to 6 minutes per side. After

it has cooled down, soak the grill pan in hot water to clean.

BUILT-IN GRILL: Preheat the grill to high, then, if it does not have a nonstick surface, brush and oil the grill grate. Place the lamb steaks on the hot grate. They will be cooked to medium-rare after 3 to 4 minutes per side; they will be medium after 5 to 6 minutes per side.

FIREPLACE GRILL: Rake red hot embers under the gridiron and preheat it for 3 to 5 minutes; you want a hot, 2 to 3 Mississippi fire. When ready to cook, brush and oil the gridiron. Place the lamb steaks on the hot grate. They will be cooked to medium-rare after 3 to 4 minutes per side; they will be medium after 5 to 6 minutes per side.

lamb steaks
with feta cheese

The lamb steak is one of the best-kept secrets in the meat department—a rich, hearty steak cut crosswise from the leg. Like its beef counterpart, lamb steak has a broad surface that sears quickly and efficiently. It costs a fraction of the price of rack of lamb or lamb chops. To match the robust flavor of the lamb steaks, serve them with a Greek-inspired feta cheese sauce.

SERVES 4

THE RECIPE

4 lamb steaks (each about 1/2 inch thick
    and 6 to 8 ounces)
2 tablespoons olive oil
1 tablespoon dried oregano
    (preferably Greek)
1 tablespoon minced garlic
Coarse salt (kosher or sea) and freshly
    ground black pepper
1/4 cup diced sweet onion
1/4 cup chopped fresh flat-leaf parsley
Feta Cheese Sauce (recipe follows)

1. Place the lamb steaks in a baking dish and brush both sides with the olive oil. Sprinkle the oregano and garlic over both sides of the steaks, then season them with salt and pepper. Let the lamb marinate for 30 minutes.

2. Cook the lamb steaks, following the instructions for any of the grills in the box at left, until nicely browned and done to taste. To test for doneness, use the poke method; when cooked to medium-rare the meat should be gently yielding.

3. Meanwhile, place the onion and parsley in a bowl and stir to mix. Set aside until ready to serve.

4. Transfer the lamb steaks to a platter or plates and let rest for 2 minutes. Sprinkle the onion and parsley mixture over the lamb and serve the Feta Cheese Sauce on the side.

if you have a...

CONTACT GRILL: Preheat the grill; if your contact grill has a temperature control, preheat the grill to high. Place the drip pan under the front of the grill. When ready to cook, lightly oil the grill surface. Place the lamb steaks on the hot grill, then close the lid. The lamp steaks will be cooked to medium-rare after 3 to 4 minutes; they will be medium after 5 to 6 minutes.

GRILL PAN: Place the grill pan on the stove and preheat it to medium-high over medium heat. When the grill pan is hot a drop of water will skitter in the pan. When ready to cook, lightly oil the ridges of the grill pan. Place the lamb steaks in the hot grill pan. They will be cooked to medium-rare after 3 to 4 minutes per side; they will be medium after 5 to 6 minutes per side.

BUILT-IN GRILL: Preheat the grill to high, then, if it does not have a nonstick surface, brush and oil the grill grate. Place the lamb steaks on the hot grate. They will be cooked to medium-rare after 3 to 4 minutes per side; they will be medium after 5 to 6 minutes per side.

FIREPLACE GRILL: Rake red hot embers under the gridiron and preheat it for 3 to 5 minutes; you want a hot, 2 to 3 Mississippi fire. When ready to cook, brush and oil the gridiron. Place the lamb steaks on the hot grate. They will be cooked to medium-rare after 3 to 4 minutes per side; they will be medium after 5 to 6 minutes per side.

feta cheese sauce

The in-your-face flavor of this sauce comes from the strong, sharp tang of feta cheese. This sheep's milk cheese is cured in brine, which gives it its characteristic salty flavor. It's a perfect foil for the rich flavor of any sort of grilled or spit-roasted lamb. **MAKES ABOUT 1 CUP**

3 ounces feta cheese, drained and
   crumbled (about 6 tablespoons; see Note)
¼ cup milk or water
3 tablespoons extra-virgin olive oil
2 tablespoons mayonnaise
2 teaspoons sweet paprika
½ teaspoon hot red pepper flakes
About 3 tablespoons heavy (whipping) cream
1 teaspoon fresh lemon juice, or more to taste
Coarse salt (kosher or sea; optional) and
   freshly ground black pepper

Place the feta, milk, olive oil, mayonnaise, paprika, and hot pepper flakes in a blender and purée until smooth. Add the cream and lemon juice and purée just to mix; overblending the cream may cause it to curdle. The sauce should be thick but pourable. If it's too thick, add up to 1 tablespoon more cream. Taste for seasoning, adding more lemon juice as necessary and salt, if desired, and pepper to taste.

NOTE: Many countries in the eastern Mediterranean and Balkans make feta, from Bulgaria to Turkey and, of course, Greece. Each has its own unique flavor, so keep trying fetas until you find your favorite. The feta sold in sealed plastic packages in many supermarkets is not the exemplar of the species.

tip

You'll find Greek oregano for the lamb steaks at Greek markets and specialty food shops, or order it by mail (see page 396).

rosemary grilled lamb chops
in the style of da toso

If you've ever doubted the authenticity of indoor grilling, consider Da Toso, a restaurant in the town of Leonacco in northeast Italy's Friuli. The region is home to one of the world's most distinctive indoor grills—the *fogolar*—a freestanding, raised stone hearth located in the center of a living room or dining room. It has an onion-shaped hood suspended from the ceiling to remove the smoke (the hood looks like one of the spires of the churches in the Kremlin). Since 1907 the Toso family has grilled steaks, sausages, chicken, and chops on a *fogolar* over blazing oak embers, keeping the seasonings simple—a drizzle of olive oil, a whisper of rosemary or garlic—to focus attention on the quality of the meat. The atmosphere is unbelievably hospitable and comforting, especially on a cold winter day. **SERVES 4**

T H E   R E C I P E

12 lamb rib chops (1/2 to 3/4 inch thick; about 2 pounds total; see Note)
Coarse salt (kosher or sea) and freshly ground black pepper
3 tablespoons extra-virgin olive oil
2 cloves garlic, minced
2 tablespoons finely chopped fresh rosemary, plus 1 long sprig of fresh rosemary

1. Generously season the lamb chops on both sides with salt and pepper. Drizzle a few drops of olive oil over each chop on both sides and rub it onto the meat (you should use about 1 tablespoon in all for the 12 chops). Sprinkle the garlic and chopped rosemary over both sides of the chops. Let the lamb marinate for 20 minutes.

2. Cook the lamb chops, following the instructions for any of the grills in the box at left, until done to taste. To test for doneness, use the poke test; when cooked to medium-rare, the meat should be gently yielding. Use the rosemary sprig to baste the chops with the remaining 2 tablespoons of olive oil as they grill.

3. Transfer the lamb chops to a platter or plates and serve at once.

NOTE: There are two options for lamb chops, rib and loin. At Da Toso they cook rib chops, a practice I recommend, as I like having the longer piece of bone to gnaw on. You can also prepare loin chops in this manner, in which case you'll need eight chops. Loin chops will be medium-rare after 4 to 6 minutes per side.

if you have a . . .

CONTACT GRILL: Preheat the grill; if your contact grill has a temperature control, preheat the grill to high. Place the drip pan under the front of the grill. When ready to cook, lightly oil the grill surface. Place the lamb chops on the hot grill, then close the lid. The chops will be cooked to medium-rare after 3 to 5 minutes. You will need to turn the chops so that you can baste both sides.

GRILL PAN: Place the grill pan on the stove and preheat it to medium-high over medium heat. When the grill pan is hot a drop of water will skitter in the pan. When ready to cook, lightly oil the ridges of the grill pan. Place the lamb chops in the hot grill pan. They will be cooked to medium-rare after 3 to 5 minutes per side.

BUILT-IN GRILL: Preheat the grill to high, then, if it does not have a nonstick surface, brush and oil the grill grate. Place the lamb chops on the hot grate. They will be cooked to medium-rare after 3 to 5 minutes per side.

FIREPLACE GRILL: Rake red hot embers under the gridiron and preheat it for 3 to 5 minutes; you want a hot, 2 to 3 Mississippi fire. When ready to cook, brush and oil the gridiron. Place the lamb chops on the hot grate. They will be cooked to medium-rare after 3 to 5 minutes per side.

Rosemary

lamb chops
with lavender and cardamom

Sandro Gamba may be French—he trained as a chef at Michelin three-star restaurants (his mentors include Alain Ducasse and Joël Robuchon)—but he cooks with an American sensibility. His restaurant, NoMI, at the Chicago Park Hyatt, is equally remarkable for its innovative menu, its refreshing lack of pretension, and its stunning view of the Miracle Mile. The Mediterranean roots of this recipe are apparent in the lavender, fennel seeds, and olive oil, but the sweet touch provided by a honey vinegar glaze is pure American barbecue. **SERVES 4**

THE RECIPE

1 cup extra-virgin olive oil
1 cup plus 2 tablespoons lavender honey
 (see Note)
1½ teaspoons dried lavender
1 teaspoon hot red pepper flakes
1 teaspoon fennel seeds
8 loin lamb chops (each about 1 inch thick;
 1¾ to 2 pounds total)
⅓ cup distilled white vinegar
1 teaspoon ground cardamom
Coarse salt (kosher or sea) and freshly
 ground black pepper

1. Place the olive oil, 2 tablespoons of the honey, the lavender, hot pepper flakes, and fennel seeds in a mixing bowl and whisk until well mixed.

2. Place the lamb chops in a nonreactive baking dish just large enough to hold them in one layer. Pour the olive oil mixture over the chops, turning them once or twice to coat both sides. Let the lamb marinate in the refrigerator, covered, for 24 hours, turning the chops several times.

3. Place the remaining 1 cup of honey and the vinegar and cardamom in a non-reactive saucepan. Bring to a boil over medium-high heat and let boil until the glaze is thick and syrupy, 3 to 6 minutes. It can be made up to 4 hours ahead.

4. When ready to cook, drain the lamb chops well, scraping off most of the

tips

■ I've called for meaty loin lamb chops; you could also cook rib chops in this manner.

■ Sandro originally developed this recipe using racks of lamb cooked on a rotisserie, and you can certainly try this. Place two racks of lamb in the rotisserie basket with the meaty part facing out. The cooking time will be about 40 minutes. Use the pause button to expose the broad sides of the racks to the heating element so they brown.

■ This recipe is super-easy, but for the best results, you do need to let the lamb marinate for 24 hours.

if you have a...

CONTACT GRILL: Preheat the grill; if your contact grill has a temperature control, preheat the grill to high. Place the drip pan under the front of the grill. When ready to cook, lightly oil the grill surface. Place the lamb chops on the hot grill, then close the lid. The chops will be cooked to medium-rare after 4 to 6 minutes. You will need to turn the chops so that you can glaze both sides.

GRILL PAN: Place the grill pan on the stove and preheat it to medium-high over medium heat. When the grill pan is hot a drop of water will skitter in the pan. When ready to cook, lightly oil the ridges of the grill pan. Place the lamb chops in the hot grill pan. They will be cooked to medium-rare after 4 to 6 minutes per side.

BUILT-IN GRILL: Preheat the grill to high, then, if it does not have a nonstick surface, brush and oil the grill grate. Place the lamb chops on the hot grate. The chops will be cooked to medium-rare after 4 to 6 minutes per side.

FREESTANDING GRILL: Preheat the grill to high; there's no need to oil the grate. Place the lamb chops on the hot grill. They will be cooked to medium-rare after 5 to 7 minutes per side.

FIREPLACE GRILL: Rake red hot embers under the gridiron and preheat it for 3 to 5 minutes; you want a hot, 2 to 3 Mississippi fire. When ready to cook, brush and oil the gridiron. Place the lamb chops on the hot grate. They will be cooked to medium-rare after 4 to 6 minutes per side.

marinade with a rubber spatula. Season the chops generously on both sides with salt and pepper. Cook the chops, following the instructions for any of the grills in the box at left, until done to taste. To test for doneness, use the poke test; when cooked to medium-rare, the meat should be gently yielding. If desired, rotate each chop a quarter turn after 2 minutes to create a handsome crosshatch of grill marks. After 3 minutes of cooking on each side, brush the cooked side of the chops with a little of the glaze.

5. Transfer the lamb to a platter or plates. If desired, drizzle a little more of the glaze on top of the chops and serve at once.

NOTE: To be strictly authentic, you need to use lavender honey (available at specialty food stores), but regular honey will give you tasty results too.

shish kebab indoors

Shish kebab may seem like the ultimate outdoor grill fare, yet in Turkey a great deal of lamb is cooked on indoor hearths and in fireplaces. The traditional Turkish seasonings for shish kebab aren't fancy: onion, either diced or puréed; lemon juice; olive oil; parsley; maybe bay leaf; and sometimes yogurt. Yet these simple seasonings make kebabs that are unforgettably flavorful. Rice pilaf makes a good accompaniment. **SERVES 4**

THE RECIPE

1½ pounds leg or shoulder of lamb,
   cut into 1-inch cubes

1½ teaspoons coarse salt (kosher or sea)

½ teaspoon coarsely ground black pepper
   or cracked black peppercorns

2 lemons, 1 cut into wedges for serving

1 medium-size onion, thinly sliced

3 tablespoons chopped fresh flat-leaf parsley

2 bay leaves

3 tablespoons extra-virgin olive oil

2 tablespoons salted butter, melted

YOU'LL ALSO NEED:

4 metal skewers (12 to 14 inches long),
   or 8 bamboo skewers (6 to 8 inches long)

1. Place the lamb in a large nonreactive bowl. Add the salt and pepper and toss to mix. Using a vegetable peeler, remove 4 strips of lemon zest each ½ by 2 inches from the whole lemon and add them to the lamb. Cut the lemon in half and squeeze the juice over the lamb (squeeze it between your fingers to catch the seeds). Add the onion, parsley, bay leaves, and olive oil and stir to mix. Let the lamb marinate in the refrigerator, covered, for 30 minutes to 3 hours, stirring once or twice to mix; the longer the lamb marinates, the richer the flavor will be.

2. Thread the cubes of lamb onto the skewers, discarding the marinade.

3. Cook the kebabs, following the instructions for any of the grills in the box below, until the meat is nicely browned

tip

You can use either lamb leg or shoulder meat for the kebabs. I prefer shoulder because it contains more fat, which keeps the kebabs moist as they grill.

if you have a...

CONTACT GRILL: Preheat the grill; if your contact grill has a temperature control, preheat the grill to high. Place the drip pan under the front of the grill. When ready to cook, lightly oil the grill surface. Place the kebabs on the hot grill, then close the lid. Give the kebabs a quarter turn after 2 minutes and baste again. The kebabs will be cooked to medium after 3 to 5 minutes.

GRILL PAN: Place the grill pan on the stove and preheat it to medium-high over medium heat. When the grill pan is hot a drop of water will skitter in the pan. When ready to cook, lightly oil the ridges of the grill pan. Place the kebabs in the hot grill pan. They will be cooked to medium after 2 to 3 minutes per side (8 to 12 minutes in all).

BUILT-IN GRILL: Preheat the grill to high, then, if it does not have a nonstick surface, brush and oil the grill grate. Arrange the kebabs on the hot grill so that the exposed ends of the skewers extend off the grate. The kebabs will be cooked to medium after 2 to 3 minutes per side (8 to 12 minutes in all).

FREESTANDING GRILL: Preheat the grill to high; there's no need to oil the grate. Place the kebabs on the hot grill. They will be cooked to medium after 3 to 4 minutes per side (12 to 16 minutes in all).

FIREPLACE GRILL: Rake red hot embers under the gridiron and preheat it for 3 to 5 minutes; you want a hot, 2 to 3 Mississippi fire. When ready to cook, brush and oil the gridiron. Place the kebabs on the hot grate. The kebabs will be cooked to medium after 2 to 3 minutes per side (8 to 12 minutes in all).

Shish kebab is quintessentially Turkish, but you may be surprised to learn that in that country meat and vegetables are usually grilled on separate skewers. The rationale is simple: Meat and vegetables have different cooking times, and moist vegetables, such as cherry tomatoes, can cause meat to steam rather than sear when cooked together. Try doing this the next time you make shish kebab.

and cooked through. For medium, a lamb cube will feel firmly yielding when squeezed between thumb and forefinger. During the last 2 minutes of cooking, baste the kebabs with the butter.

4. Serve the lamb kebabs at once with the lemon wedges. If you've used metal skewers, warn everyone to take the meat off of them before eating, as they will be quite hot.

iranian-style shish kebabs

As you travel east from Turkey to Iran, the meat for shish kebabs is often marinated in yogurt and saffron. Yogurt adds an unmistakable richness and its acidity helps tenderize the meat. Use plain whole-milk yogurt, available at natural foods stores, and saffron threads, which have a bolder flavor than saffron powder. **SERVES 4**

THE RECIPE

1¹/₂ pounds leg or shoulder of lamb,
　　cut into 1-inch cubes
1¹/₂ teaspoons coarse salt
　　(kosher or sea)
¹/₂ teaspoon coarsely ground
　　black pepper or cracked black
　　peppercorns
¹/₂ teaspoon saffron threads, crumbled
　　between your thumb and forefinger
1 medium-size onion, thinly sliced
1 cup plain whole-milk yogurt
2 tablespoons extra-virgin olive oil
2 tablespoons salted butter, melted
1 lemon, cut into wedges,
　　for serving

YOU'LL ALSO NEED:
4 metal skewers (12 to 14 inches long), or
　　8 bamboo skewers (6 to 8 inches long)

1. Place the lamb in a large nonreactive bowl. Add the salt, pepper, and saffron

and toss to mix. Add the onion, yogurt, and olive oil and stir to mix. Let the lamb marinate in the refrigerator, covered, for 2 hours or as long as overnight, stirring once or twice to mix; the longer the lamb marinates, the richer the flavor will be.

2. Thread the cubes of lamb onto the skewers, discarding the marinade.

3. Cook the kebabs, following the instructions for any of the grills in the box at right, until the meat is nicely browned and cooked through. For medium, a lamb cube will feel firmly yielding when squeezed between thumb and forefinger. During the last 2 minutes of cooking, baste the kebabs with the butter.

4. Serve the lamb kebabs at once with the lemon wedges. If you've used metal skewers, warn everyone to take the meat off them before eating, as they will be quite hot.

if you have a...

CONTACT GRILL: Preheat the grill; if your contact grill has a temperature control, preheat the grill to high. Place the drip pan under the front of the grill. When ready to cook, lightly oil the grill surface. Place the kebabs on the hot grill, then close the lid. Give the kebabs a quarter turn after 2 minutes and baste. The kebabs will be cooked to medium after 3 to 5 minutes.

GRILL PAN: Place the grill pan on the stove and preheat it to medium-high over medium heat. When the grill pan is hot a drop of water will skitter in the pan. When ready to cook, lightly oil the ridges of the grill pan. Place the kebabs in the hot grill pan. They will be cooked to medium after 2 to 3 minutes per side (8 to 12 minutes in all).

BUILT-IN GRILL: Preheat the grill to high, then, if it does not have a nonstick surface, brush and oil the grill grate. Arrange the kebabs on the hot grill so that the exposed ends of the skewers extend off the grate. The kebabs will be cooked to medium after 2 to 3 minutes per side (8 to 12 minutes in all).

FREESTANDING GRILL: Preheat the grill to high; there's no need to oil the grate. Place the kebabs on the hot grill. They will be cooked to medium after 3 to 4 minutes per side (12 to 16 minutes in all).

FIREPLACE GRILL: Rake red hot embers under the gridiron and preheat it for 3 to 5 minutes; you want a hot, 2 to 3 Mississippi fire. When ready to cook, brush and oil the gridiron. Place the kebabs on the hot grate. The kebabs will be cooked to medium after 2 to 3 minutes per side (8 to 12 minutes in all).

curry-grilled lamb kebabs
with minted yogurt

The Indian inspiration of the kebabs here is apparent in the seasonings (ginger, garlic, curry power) as well as the sauce, a refreshing condiment made from yogurt and mint. The dates aren't particularly traditional, but I like the touch of sweetness they add. **SERVES 4**

THE RECIPE

1½ pounds leg or shoulder of lamb,
   cut into 1-inch cubes
1 tablespoon minced peeled fresh ginger
2 cloves garlic, minced
2 teaspoons curry powder
1½ teaspoons coarse salt (kosher or sea)
½ teaspoon coarsely ground black pepper
¼ to ½ teaspoon cayenne pepper
2 tablespoons mustard oil (see Note)
1 medium-size white onion, peeled

2 medium-size red or yellow bell peppers,
   cored, seeded, and cut into 1-inch squares
12 large pitted dates, cut in half lengthwise
Yogurt Mint Sauce (recipe follows)

YOU'LL ALSO NEED:
4 metal skewers (12 to 14 inches long), or
   8 bamboo skewers (6 to 8 inches long)

if you have a...

CONTACT GRILL: Preheat the grill; if your contact grill has a temperature control, preheat the grill to high. Place the drip pan under the front of the grill. When ready to cook, lightly oil the grill surface. Place the kebabs on the hot grill, then close the lid. Give each kebab a quarter turn after 2 minutes and baste. The kebabs will be cooked to medium after 3 to 5 minutes.

GRILL PAN: Place the grill pan on the stove and preheat it to medium-high over medium heat. When the grill pan is hot a drop of water will skitter in the pan. When ready to cook, lightly oil the ridges of the grill pan. Place the kebabs in the hot grill pan. They will be cooked to medium after 2 to 3 minutes per side (8 to 12 minutes in all).

BUILT-IN GRILL: Preheat the grill to high, then, if it does not have a nonstick surface, brush and oil the grill grate. Arrange the kebabs on the hot grill so that the exposed ends of the skewers extend off the grate. The kebabs will be cooked to medium after 2 to 3 minutes per side (8 to 12 minutes in all).

FREESTANDING GRILL: Preheat the grill to high; there's no need to oil the grate. Place the kebabs on the hot grill. They will be cooked to medium after 3 to 4 minutes per side (12 to 16 minutes in all).

FIREPLACE GRILL: Rake red hot embers under the gridiron and preheat it for 3 to 5 minutes; you want a hot, 2 to 3 Mississippi fire. When ready to cook, brush and oil the gridiron. Place the kebabs on the hot grate. The kebabs will be cooked to medium after 2 to 3 minutes per side (8 to 12 minutes in all).

1. Place the lamb in a bowl, sprinkle the ginger, garlic, curry powder, salt, black pepper, and cayenne over it, and stir to coat. Add the mustard oil and stir to coat evenly. Let the lamb marinate in the refrigerator, covered, for at least 1 hour or as long as overnight, turning it several times so that it marinates evenly.

2. Cut the onion in half crosswise. Cut each half into quarters. Separate each onion quarter into layers.

3. Thread the cubes of lamb onto skewers, alternating them with pieces of onion and bell pepper and dates. The kebabs can be prepared several hours ahead to this stage and refrigerated, covered.

4. Cook the kebabs, following the instructions for any of the grills in the box at left, until the meat is nicely browned and just cooked through. For medium, a lamb cube will feel firmly yielding when squeezed between thumb and forefinger.

5. Serve the lamb kebabs at once with the Yogurt Mint Sauce on the side. If you've used metal skewers, warn everyone to take the meat off them before eating, as they will be quite hot.

NOTE: Mustard oil is a spicy oil available at Indian markets. If you can't find it, you can use 2 tablespoons of vegetable oil and add ½ teaspoon of mustard powder to it.

yogurt mint sauce

Variations of this sauce turn up all over, from the *tzatziki* of Greece to the *raita* of India. For the best results, use plain whole-milk yogurt. If you don't find it at the supermarket, it's available at natural foods stores. **MAKES ABOUT 1¼ CUPS**

1 clove garlic, minced
½ teaspoon coarse salt (kosher or sea), or more to taste
½ teaspoon freshly ground white pepper
½ teaspoon ground coriander
¼ teaspoon ground cumin, or more to taste
½ medium-size cucumber, peeled and seeded
1 cup plain whole-milk yogurt
3 tablespoons finely chopped fresh spearmint, or 1 tablespoon dried spearmint

Place the garlic, salt, white pepper, coriander, and cumin in a mixing bowl and mash with the back of a wooden spoon. Grate the cucumber into the bowl using the coarse side of a grater. Add the yogurt and mint and stir to mix. Taste for seasoning, adding more salt and/or cumin as necessary.

tips

■ The best dates are the soft, sweet Medjool dates sold at Middle Eastern markets, health food stores, and many supermarkets.

■ You can also make these kebabs using 1½ pounds of skinless, boneless chicken. They'll be done after cooking 3 to 5 minutes in a contact grill or 2 to 3 minutes (8 to 12 in all) in a grill pan, on a built-in grill, or on a fireplace grill.

rotisserie
kid or lamb
with salsa verde

Kid—baby goat—is the house specialty of Da Cesare in Albaretto della Torre in northern Italy's Piedmont region. Da Cesare is the sort of restaurant every foodie and grill hound dreams of discovering, a twelve-table dining room in a virtually unmarked house with a fireplace that doubles as a rotisserie. For several decades, chef Cesare Giaccone has spit roasted baby goat over an oak and beech wood fire, and critics on both sides of the Atlantic have proclaimed it some of the best meat in Italy. You can also cook up a credible version in a countertop rotisserie—especially when you pair it with the vibrant herb flavor of *salsa verde*. Lamb is also delicious prepared this way. **SERVES 4 TO 6**

T H E   R E C I P E

Kid or lamb shoulder or leg (2¹/₂ to 3 pounds)
Coarse salt (kosher or sea) and freshly
    ground black pepper
2 cloves garlic, finely chopped
3 tablespoons chopped fresh rosemary leaves
3 tablespoons chopped fresh sage leaves
3 tablespoons chopped fresh flat-leaf parsley
1 cup extra-virgin olive oil

1. Very generously season the kid all over with salt and pepper.

2. When ready to cook, place the drip pan in the bottom of the rotisserie. Skewer the kid lengthwise on the rotisserie spit. Attach the spit to the rotisserie and turn on the motor. If your rotisserie has a temperature control, set it to 400°F (for instructions for using a rotisserie, see page 14). Cook the kid until dark brown and cooked to taste, about 1 hour for medium (I like kid served medium and so does Giaccone). To test for doneness, insert an instant-read meat thermometer into the meat but not so that it touches the spit or a bone. The internal temperature should be about 160°F.

3. Meanwhile, make the *salsa verde:* Place the garlic and ¹/₂ teaspoon of salt in a mixing bowl and mash to a paste with the back of a spoon. Add the rosemary, sage, and parsley and mash slightly with the back of the spoon to release the aromatic oils. Stir in the olive oil and season with more salt as necessary and pepper to taste. For a thicker and smoother sauce, mix the ingredients in a food processor or blender.

4. Transfer the kid to a platter or cutting board, remove the spit, and let the meat rest for 5 minutes. Thinly slice the meat off the bone across the grain or cut it into chunks. Serve the kid with the *salsa verde* on the side.

tips

■ Kid can be tricky to find. Look for it at an Italian or West Indian market. Make sure you're buying kid, not goat, which has a much stronger flavor. Or substitute lamb, either baby lamb (look for it at an Italian market in the springtime) or regular lamb. A 2¹/₂- to 3-pound piece of lamb shoulder or leg will have the same cooking time as the kid.

■ To duplicate Cesare Giaccone's dish on a fireplace rotisserie, see page 11. Trim off any excess fat before placing it on the spit. Cook over a hot, 2 to 3 Mississippi fire. It will take from 45 minutes to 1 hour, depending on your fireplace.

If I were to name the single most popular dish for cooking on a contact grill, I'd say hamburgers. The manufacturers of the Foreman grill seem to back me up on this—they measure the various sizes of their grills by how many burgers you can cook on each at one time. This chapter gets right to the meat of the matter with a bacon and smoked Cheddar cheeseburger, a New Mexican green chile burger, and a South Carolina barbecue pork burger with a mustard barbecue sauce. Looking for something more unusual? How about a Greek-inspired lamb burger or a chile-spiced turkey burger from Oaxaca? Finally, for folks with a hankering for fish, there's a Thai tuna burger.

burgers

grilled steak tartare burgers

Some months ago, I had steak tartare at a restaurant in Buenos Aires. It had been a long while since I'd ordered this dish, and the notion of eating beef raw seemed daring, even audacious. But Argentinean cattle are fed exclusively on grass, so the risks associated with beef in other countries are greatly reduced. Here's a way to enjoy the robust flavor of a steak tartare—the salty tang of capers and anchovies; the pungency of shallots and mustard—without the raw beef. **SERVES 4**

THE RECIPE

if you have a...

CONTACT GRILL: Preheat the grill; if your contact grill has a temperature control, preheat the grill to high. Place the drip pan under the front of the grill. When ready to cook, lightly oil the grill surface. Place the burgers on the hot grill, then gently close the lid. The burgers will be done after cooking 4 to 6 minutes.

GRILL PAN: Place the grill pan on the stove and preheat it to medium-high over medium heat. When the grill pan is hot a drop of water will skitter in the pan. When ready to cook, lightly oil the ridges of the grill pan. Place the burgers in the hot grill pan. They will be done after cooking 4 to 6 minutes per side.

BUILT-IN GRILL: Preheat the grill to high, then, if it does not have a nonstick surface, brush and oil the grill grate. Place the burgers on the hot grate. They will be done after cooking 4 to 6 minutes per side.

FREESTANDING GRILL: Preheat the grill to high; there's no need to oil the grate. Place the burgers on the hot grill. They will be done after cooking about 7 minutes per side.

FIREPLACE GRILL: Rake red hot embers under the gridiron and preheat it for 3 to 5 minutes; you want a hot, 2 to 3 Mississippi fire. When ready to cook, brush and oil the gridiron. Place the burgers on the hot grate. They will be done after cooking 4 to 6 minutes per side.

1½ pounds ground beef sirloin or chuck
1 large shallot, minced
    (3 to 4 tablespoons)
2 tablespoons finely chopped fresh
    flat-leaf parsley
2 tablespoons drained capers
2 to 4 anchovy fillets, drained, blotted dry,
    and finely chopped
1 tablespoon Dijon mustard
1 tablespoon fresh lemon juice
1 teaspoon coarse salt
    (kosher or sea)
½ teaspoon freshly ground black pepper
4 quail eggs (optional; see Note)
Cooking oil spray
1 bunch arugula leaves, rinsed and
    spun dry
4 slices dense white sandwich bread or
    rye bread, grilled or toasted

1. Place the ground beef, shallot, parsley, capers, anchovies, mustard, lemon juice, salt, and pepper in a large mixing bowl and stir with a wooden spoon to mix. Wet your hands with cold water and divide the beef mixture into 4 equal portions. Working quickly and with a light touch, pat each portion into a thick patty. Place the patties on a plate lined with plastic wrap and refrigerate, covered, until ready to grill. The patties can be prepared up to 2 hours ahead.

2. Grill the burgers, following the instructions for any of the grills in the box on the facing page, until cooked through. See the box at right for doneness tests. Remove the burgers and cover to keep warm.

3. Fry the quail eggs in a nonstick pan coated with cooking oil spray.

4. Place some arugula leaves on each slice of toast. Top each with a burger, then slide a fried quail egg onto each burger.

NOTE: Quail eggs are available at many supermarkets and specialty food stores, but I've made them optional here.

Unlike chicken eggs, quail eggs are difficult to crack in half. To do this, hold each egg upright (narrow end up) in one hand. Using the cutting edge of a paring knife, knock off the top ¼ inch of shell (this may take several whacks). Pour the egg into the heated oiled skillet and fry it. It will take 1 to 2 minutes.

burger doneness

If you use commercially ground hamburger meat, I strongly recommend that you cook it through, meaning done to medium so there's no trace of red in the center. But how do you tell when a burger is cooked through? Use one of the following three tests.

1. Use the poke test: Press the center of the burger with the tip of your index finger—it should feel mostly firm, with just the slightest bit of yield in the center.

2. Take the burger's temperature: Insert the probe of an instant-read meat thermometer through the side of the burger (you won't get an accurate reading if the probe is inserted through the top). The internal temperature should be at least 160°F for beef and pork burgers and at least 170°F for poultry burgers. Tuna burgers, when made with sushi-quality tuna, can be served rare or medium-rare.

3. Make a small cut in the center of the burger with the tip of a paring knife. There should be no traces of red and only the faintest blush of pink in the center. Use this method sparingly, as each cut will release tasty juices. When serving the burger, place the cut side down.

Some establishments serve rare hamburgers, but to ensure safety, it's likely they grind their meat fresh daily on the premises. If you're willing to do this, you can cook and serve your burgers to whatever degree of doneness you desire—even rare.

new mexican green chile burgers
with salsa verde

The burger plays an iconic role in American gastronomy. Every region reinterprets the basic recipe—case in point, these green chile burgers from New Mexico. The burgers owe their kick to roasted New Mexican green chiles. There's a double dose of chiles, first in the form of *rajas,* roasted chile strips spooned over the burgers, then in a classic New Mexican *salsa verde*—green chile sauce. **SERVES 4**

THE RIGHT CHILE

The chiles of choice for both the salsa and burger topping are the long, slender, mild New Mexican green chiles. If they're not available, you can use Anaheim chiles or, for a bit more punch and fire, poblano peppers. You can grill the chiles ahead of time (they'll keep, covered, in the refrigerator for several days).

THE RECIPE

1/2 cup roasted New Mexican green chiles, Anaheim chiles, or poblano peppers cut into 1/4-inch strips (4 to 5 chiles; see box below)

4 ounces white Cheddar cheese, coarsely grated (about 1 cup)
1 1/2 pounds ground beef sirloin or chuck
Coarse salt (kosher or sea) and freshly ground black pepper
4 hamburger buns
2 tablespoons olive oil
New Mexican Salsa Verde (recipe follows)

1. Place the chile strips in a serving bowl and stir in the Cheddar. Cover and refrigerate until ready to use.

2. Wet your hands with cold water and divide the ground beef into 4 equal portions. Working quickly and with a light touch, pat each portion into a thick patty. Place the patties on a plate lined with plastic wrap and refrigerate, covered, until ready to grill.

roasting chiles

There are several ways to roast chiles: on a built-in or fireplace grill; in a grill pan; or in a hot, ungreased cast-iron skillet (a contact grill doesn't get hot enough). **MAKES ABOUT 1 1/2 CUPS**

1 1/2 pounds New Mexican green chiles, Anaheim chiles, or poblano peppers

1. Using one of the cooking methods mentioned above, grill the chiles until the skins are black and blistered on all sides, 2 to 3 minutes per side (8 to 12 minutes in all). Transfer the roasted chiles

to a large bowl, cover with plastic wrap (this helps loosen the skins), and let cool to room temperature.

2. Using a paring knife, scrape the skins off the chiles. Cut the chiles in half lengthwise and scrape out the seeds. The chiles are now ready to be used in a recipe.

3. Generously, and I mean generously, season each patty on both sides with salt and black pepper. Grill the burgers, following the instructions for any of the grills in the box at right, until the burgers are cooked through. See the box on page 157 for doneness tests. Remove the burgers and cover to keep warm. Leave the grill on.

4. Brush the cut sides of the hamburger buns with the olive oil. Place the buns on the hot grill, cut side down, and, lowering the temperature if necessary, grill until toasted, 1 to 2 minutes. You may need to work in batches.

5. Place each of the burgers on the bottom half of a bun and top each with a quarter of the chile and cheese mixture. Spoon some *salsa verde* over each, top with the other half of the bun, and serve at once.

if you have a...

CONTACT GRILL: Preheat the grill; if your contact grill has a temperature control, preheat the grill to high. Place the drip pan under the front of the grill. When ready to cook, lightly oil the grill surface. Place the burgers on the hot grill, then gently close the lid. The burgers will be done after cooking 4 to 6 minutes.

GRILL PAN: Place the grill pan on the stove and preheat it to medium-high over medium heat. When the grill pan is hot a drop of water will skitter in the pan. When ready to cook, lightly oil the ridges of the grill pan. Place the burgers in the hot grill pan. They will be done after cooking 4 to 6 minutes per side.

BUILT-IN GRILL: Preheat the grill to high, then, if it does not have a nonstick surface, brush and oil the grill grate. Place the burgers on the hot grate. They will be done after cooking 4 to 6 minutes per side.

FREESTANDING GRILL: Preheat the grill to high; there's no need to oil the grate. Place the burgers on the hot grill. They will be done after cooking about 7 minutes per side.

FIREPLACE GRILL: Rake red hot embers under the gridiron and preheat it for 3 to 5 minutes; you want a hot, 2 to 3 Mississippi fire. When ready to cook, brush and oil the gridiron. Place the burgers on the hot grate. They will be done after cooking 4 to 6 minutes per side.

new mexican salsa verde

This fragrant, mild, green salsa is a staple—no, the very lifeblood—of New Mexican cooking. I've kept it simple, so you can appreciate the flavor of the chiles. This makes a bit more salsa than you can comfortably fit on the burgers. Spoon about two tablespoons on each and serve the rest in a bowl on the side for people to help themselves.
MAKES ABOUT 1 CUP

4 cloves garlic (leave the skins on), skewered on a wooden toothpick or small bamboo skewer

1 cup roasted New Mexican green chiles or Anaheim chiles cut into 1/4-inch strips (8 to 10 chiles; see box on facing page)
2 tablespoons chopped fresh cilantro
2 teaspoons fresh lime juice, or more to taste
1/2 teaspoon ground cumin
1/2 teaspoon dried oregano
Coarse salt (kosher or sea) and freshly ground black pepper

1. Preheat the broiler.

2. Broil the garlic cloves until they are lightly browned and tender, 2 to 3 minutes per side (4 to 6 minutes in all).

3. Scrape any really burnt skin off the garlic. Place the garlic, chile strips,

tip

The secret to a succulent burger is to start with ground beef that's not too lean. I like ground sirloin (or a mixture of ground sirloin and ground chuck) that has about 15 percent fat.

cilantro, lime juice, cumin, oregano, and 4 tablespoons of water in a blender and purée until smooth, scraping down the sides of the blender with a spatula.

4. Transfer the salsa to a saucepan and bring to a gentle simmer over medium heat. Let simmer until thick and flavorful, 5 to 8 minutes, stirring with

a wooden spoon. The salsa should be thick (roughly the consistency of heavy cream) but pourable; add more water as needed. Taste for seasoning, adding more lime juice as necessary and salt and pepper to taste; the salsa should be highly seasoned.

a new cheeseburger

The chief drawback to indoor grilling is that you can't get the smoke flavor associated with grilling over charcoal or wood outdoors. Or can you? By adding bacon and smoked cheddar cheese to the ground beef you end up with a burger bursting with a smoke flavor that's reinforced by a smoky chipotle mayonnaise. The bacon and cheese go right into the meat, not on top, so they keep the burgers moist, even when they're cooked through.

SERVES 4

the great juggling act

A great burger requires using your grill at least twice—to grill the buns and to cook the burgers. If you want to get fancy, you can also grill the onions, peppers, chiles, and/or ham or bacon. All of this is pretty manageable on an outside grill, but it requires some choreography to cook them on an indoor grill, especially a small grill, like a contact grill or grill pan. So here's the proper sequence.

1. First, grill any vegetables you want to use—onions, peppers, chiles. These don't have to be piping hot and can be grilled well in advance.

2. Grill the bacon ahead of time—especially if you plan to crumble it into the ground meat to make the New Cheeseburgers above or the South Carolina pork burgers on page 164. In this case the bacon *should* be cool.

3. Grill the buns or bread. Keep them warm in a cloth-lined bread basket. The exception here is tortillas, which only take a few seconds to warm.

4. Grill the burgers. Keep them warm.

If you have a small indoor grill, work in several batches. There's nothing worse than crowding the grill.

4 thick slices or 6 to 8 thin slices bacon
(4 ounces in all)

1½ pounds ground beef sirloin or chuck

6 ounces smoked cheddar or other
smoked cheese, coarsely grated
(about 1½ cups)

1 clove garlic, minced

Coarse salt (kosher or sea) and plenty of
freshly grated black pepper

4 hamburger buns

2 tablespoons butter (optional), melted

Arugula leaves

Ripe tomato slices

Sweet onion slices

Pickle slices

Chipotle Mayonnaise (recipe follows)

if you have a...

CONTACT GRILL: Preheat the grill; if your contact grill has a temperature control, preheat the grill to high. Place the drip pan under the front of the grill. When ready to cook the burgers, lightly oil the grill surface. Place the burgers on the hot grill, then gently close the lid. The burgers will be done after cooking 4 to 6 minutes.

GRILL PAN: Place the grill pan on the stove and preheat it to medium-high over medium heat. When the grill pan is hot a drop of water will skitter in the pan. When ready to cook, lightly oil the ridges of the grill pan. Place the burgers in the hot grill pan. They will be done after cooking 4 to 6 minutes per side.

BUILT-IN GRILL: Preheat the grill to high, then, if it does not have a nonstick surface, brush and oil the grill grate. Place the burgers on the hot grate. They will be done after cooking 4 to 6 minutes per side.

FREESTANDING GRILL: Preheat the grill to high; there's no need to oil the grate. Place the burgers on the hot grill. The burgers will be done after cooking about 7 minutes per side.

FIREPLACE GRILL: Rake red hot embers under the gridiron and preheat it for 3 to 5 minutes; you want a hot, 2 to 3 Mississippi fire. When ready to cook, brush and oil the gridiron. Place the burgers on the hot grate. They will be done after cooking 4 to 6 minutes per side.

1. Place the bacon in a large heavy skillet and cook over medium-high heat until deeply browned and crisp on both sides, 8 minutes total. Transfer the bacon to a plate lined with paper towels to drain and let cool to room temperature.

2. Crumble or finely chop the bacon, then place it in a mixing bowl. Add the ground beef, cheddar, and garlic, then stir with a wooden spoon to mix. Wet your hands with cold water and divide the meat mixture into 4 equal portions. Working quickly and with a light touch, pat each portion into a thick patty. Place on a plate lined with plastic wrap. Refrigerate, covered, until ready to grill.

3. Season each patty on both sides with salt and pepper. Grill the burgers, following the instructions for any of the grills in the box above, until cooked through. See the box on page 157 for doneness tests.

Remove the burgers and cover to keep warm. Leave the grill on.

4. Brush the cut sides of the hamburger buns with the melted butter, if using. Place the buns on the hot grill, cut side down, and, lowering the temperature if necessary, grill until toasted, 1 to 2 minutes. You may need to work in batches.

5. Place each of the burgers on the bottom half of a bun and top them with arugula, tomato, onion, pickle, and a dollop of the Chipotle Mayonnaise. Top with the other half of the bun and serve at once.

tips

NOTE: Neither a contact grill nor a freestanding grill can grill bacon properly. You'll need to fry the bacon crisp in a skillet, over medium heat for about 5 minutes on the first side and 3 minutes on the second side.

chipotle mayonnaise

Chipotles are smoked jalapeño peppers and they're also one of the few foods I recommend buying canned. The reason is simple—canned chipotles come in an intensely flavorful vinegar sauce called adobo, so when you use the canned peppers you get the added benefit of the sauce. Look for canned chipotles at Hispanic markets and specialty food shops. **MAKES ABOUT ½ CUP**

½ cup mayonnaise
    (preferably Hellmann's)
1 to 2 canned chipotle peppers,
    minced, with 1 tablespoon of
    their adobo sauce
½ teaspoon sweet paprika

Place the mayonnaise, chipotle(s), and paprika in a small nonreactive bowl and whisk to mix. If not serving at once, cover and refrigerate. The mayonnaise will keep for several days, covered, in the refrigerator.

pepper jack burgers
with slow-burn jalapeño sauce

These cheeseburgers acquire Tex-Mex overtones thanks to cumin, cilantro, and cheese—Jack cheese laced with jalapeño peppers. Most cheeseburger recipes call for you to place a slice of cheese on top of the hot burgers, but I like to put the cheese inside, adding grated pepper Jack to the ground beef. The melting cheese keeps the burgers moist, even when they're cooked to medium. **SERVES 4**

1¹/₂ pounds ground beef sirloin or chuck

4 ounces pepper Jack cheese, coarsely grated
 (about 1 cup)

3 tablespoons chopped fresh cilantro

1 teaspoon ground cumin

Coarse salt (kosher or sea) and freshly ground
 black pepper

4 hamburger buns

2 tablespoons extra-virgin olive oil

1¹/₂ cups shredded iceberg lettuce

1 medium-size ripe red tomato, thinly sliced

Pickled jalapeño pepper slices

Slow-Burn Jalapeño Sauce (recipe follows)

1. Place the ground beef, cheese, cilantro, and cumin in a mixing bowl and stir with a wooden spoon to mix. Wet your hands with cold water and divide the beef mixture into 4 equal portions. Working quickly and with a light touch, pat each portion into a thick patty. Season each patty on both sides with salt and pepper, then place on a plate lined with plastic wrap and refrigerate, covered, until ready to grill.

2. Grill the burgers, following the instructions for any of the grills in the box at right, until cooked through. See the box on page 157 for doneness tests. Remove the burgers from the grill and cover to keep warm. Leave the grill on.

3. Brush the cut sides of the hamburger buns with the olive oil. Place the buns on the hot grill, cut side down, and, lowering the temperature if necessary, grill until toasted, 1 to 2 minutes. You may need to work in batches.

4. Place each of the burgers on the bottom half of a bun, then top them with some of the lettuce, tomato, jalapeño pepper slices, and a dollop of Slow-Burn Jalapeño Sauce. Top with the other half of the bun and serve at once.

slow-burn jalapeño sauce

This sauce is a hottie, so use it sparingly. I've given a range of jalapeños: two will give you a baby hot sauce; six a volcanic bruiser. Either way, it will burn low and slow for a while. For an even hotter sauce, leave the seeds in the jalapeños.

MAKES ABOUT ¹/₂ CUP

if you have a...

CONTACT GRILL: Preheat the grill; if your contact grill has a temperature control, preheat the grill to high. Place the drip pan under the front of the grill. When ready to cook, lightly oil the grill surface. Place the burgers on the hot grill, then gently close the lid. The burgers will be done after cooking 4 to 6 minutes.

GRILL PAN: Place the grill pan on the stove and preheat it to medium-high over medium heat. When the grill pan is hot a drop of water will skitter in the pan. When ready to cook, lightly oil the ridges of the grill pan. Place the burgers in the hot grill pan. The burgers will be done after cooking 4 to 6 minutes per side.

BUILT-IN GRILL: Preheat the grill to high, then, if it does not have a nonstick surface, brush and oil the grill grate. Place the burgers on the hot grate. The burgers will be done after cooking 4 to 6 minutes per side.

FREESTANDING GRILL: Preheat the grill to high; there's no need to oil the grate. Place the burgers on the hot grill. The burgers will be done after cooking about 7 minutes per side.

FIREPLACE GRILL: Rake red hot embers under the gridiron and preheat it for 3 to 5 minutes; you want a hot, 2 to 3 Mississippi fire. When ready to cook, brush and oil the gridiron. Place the burgers on the hot grate. The burgers will be done after cooking 4 to 6 minutes per side.

2 to 6 jalapeño peppers, seeded and
    coarsely chopped
1/2 cup chopped fresh cilantro
3 cloves garlic, coarsely chopped
1/2 teaspoon ground cumin
2 tablespoons fresh lime juice, or
    more to taste
1/2 teaspoon coarse salt (kosher or sea),
    or more to taste

Place the jalapeños, cilantro, garlic, cumin, lime juice, salt, and 1/4 cup water in a blender. Purée until smooth, scraping down the sides of the blender with a spatula; add more water as needed for a smooth consistency. Taste for seasoning, adding more lime juice and/or salt as necessary.

barbecue pork burgers
with honey mustard sauce

These smoky burgers were inspired by traditional Carolina pulled pork (shredded smoked pork shoulder). They even contain a version of "brownies"—dark crisp flecks of smoke-roasted pork skin—in this case, browned bits of bacon that are mixed into the ground pork. The burgers are served with a tangy honey mustard sauce, just like you'd find in South Carolina. Think of these pork burgers as Southern barbecue without the wait. **SERVES 4**

THE RECIPE

2 slices bacon
1/2 pounds lean ground pork
1 teaspoon liquid smoke
    (see box on page 179)
1 teaspoon coarse salt (kosher or sea)
1 teaspoon freshly ground black pepper
1 teaspoon sweet paprika

1 teaspoon brown sugar
1/2 teaspoon onion powder
1/2 teaspoon garlic powder
1/4 teaspoon celery seed
8 slices white sandwich bread, toasted
1 cup finely chopped or shredded green cabbage
Honey Mustard Barbecue Sauce (recipe follows)

tip

You can grill the bacon directly on a contact grill. Lay the strips on the grill grate and close the lid. Cook until browned and crisp, 2 to 4 minutes.

1. Place the bacon in a medium-size skillet and cook over medium-high heat until deeply browned and crisp on both sides, 8 minutes total. Transfer the bacon to a plate lined with paper towels to drain and let cool to room temperature.

2. Crumble or finely chop the bacon, then place it in a mixing bowl. Add the pork, liquid smoke, salt, pepper, paprika, brown sugar, onion and garlic powders, and celery seed, then stir with a wooden spoon to mix.

3. Wet your hands with cold water and divide the pork mixture into 4 equal portions. Working quickly and with a light touch, pat each portion into a thick patty. Place the patties on a plate lined with plastic wrap and refrigerate, covered, until ready to grill.

4. Grill the pork burgers, following the instructions for any of the grills in the box at right, until cooked through. See the box on page 157 for doneness tests.

5. Place a burger on a slice of toast. Top it with ¼ cup of the shredded cabbage and a generous dollop (about 2 tablespoons) of Honey Mustard Barbecue Sauce. Top with another piece of toast. Repeat with the remaining burgers and toppings, then serve at once.

if you have a...

CONTACT GRILL: Preheat the grill; if your contact grill has a temperature control, preheat the grill to high. Place the drip pan under the front of the grill. When ready to cook, lightly oil the grill surface. Place the burgers on the hot grill, then gently close the lid. The burgers will be done after cooking 4 to 6 minutes.

GRILL PAN: Place the grill pan on the stove and preheat it to medium-high over medium heat. When the grill pan is hot a drop of water will skitter in the pan. When ready to cook, lightly oil the ridges of the grill pan. Place the burgers in the hot grill pan. They will be done after cooking 4 to 6 minutes per side.

BUILT-IN GRILL: Preheat the grill to high, then, if it does not have a nonstick surface, brush and oil the grill grate. Place the burgers on the hot grate. They will be done after cooking 4 to 6 minutes per side.

FREESTANDING GRILL: Preheat the grill to high; there's no need to oil the grate. Place the burgers on the hot grill. The burgers will be done after cooking about 7 minutes per side.

FIREPLACE GRILL: Rake red hot embers under the gridiron and preheat it for 3 to 5 minutes; you want a hot, 2 to 3 Mississippi fire. When ready to cook, brush and oil the gridiron. Place the burgers on the hot grate. They will be done after cooking 4 to 6 minutes per side.

honey mustard barbecue sauce

In South Carolina barbecue sauce is a sweet but sharp, tangy combination of honey or brown sugar, mustard, and vinegar. If you're used to a sweet, red Kansas City–style sauce, this one will come as a revelation. **MAKES ABOUT 1 CUP**

1 tablespoon unsalted butter

2 slices bacon, cut crosswide into
   1/4-inch slivers

1/2 medium-size onion, finely chopped
   (about 1/2 cup)

1/3 cup honey

1/3 cup Dijon mustard

4 tablespoons cider vinegar, or
   more to taste

Coarse salt (kosher or sea) and freshly
   ground black pepper

1. Melt the butter in a nonreactive saucepan over medium heat. Add the bacon and onion and cook until golden brown, 4 to 5 minutes. Pour off any excess fat (for a richer sauce, leave it in).

2. Add the honey, mustard, and cider vinegar to the saucepan and stir to mix. Reduce the heat to medium-low, bring to a simmer, and cook the sauce until thick and flavorful, 8 to 10 minutes, stirring occasionally with a wooden spoon. Taste for seasoning, adding more vinegar, if necessary, and salt and pepper to taste (see Note).

NOTE: This recipe makes more barbecue sauce than you'll need for 4 burgers. The extra sauce will keep, covered, in the refrigerator for several days and is delicious spooned over hot or cold grilled chicken or sliced pork. Reheat the sauce over low heat before serving.

HONEY

tips

■ Ground lamb is available at butcher shops and more and more frequently at supermarkets. Another good source is a *halal* (Muslim kosher) or Middle Eastern market.

■ For an interesting variation on these burgers, tuck a piece of goat cheese or feta cheese in the center of each before grilling.

lamb burgers
with yogurt cucumber sauce

Grilled ground meat patties are a constant on the world's barbecue trail. The type of meat varies from region to region. Greek grill masters use ground lamb instead of beef, as do those in the Balkans, Asia Minor, the Middle East, and central Asia. These lamb burgers buzz with Greek flavors—garlic, oregano, and mint. A refreshing *tzatziki*—yogurt cucumber dip— is the sauce. To complete the Greek theme, the burgers are served on pita bread instead of buns. **SERVES 4**

THE RECIPE

1½ pounds ground lamb

1 small onion, finely chopped

1 clove garlic, minced

3 tablespoons chopped fresh mint,
   or 2 teaspoons dried mint

3 tablespoons finely chopped fresh
   flat-leaf parsley

1 teaspoon dried oregano (preferably
   Greek)

1 teaspoon coarse salt (kosher or sea),
   or more to taste

1 teaspoon freshly ground
   black pepper

4 pita breads

4 rinsed romaine lettuce leaves

4 paper-thin slices red onion
   (optional)

1 medium-size cucumber, peeled and
   thinly sliced

1 medium-size ripe tomato,
   thinly sliced

Yogurt Cucumber Sauce
   (recipe follows)

1. Place the ground lamb, chopped onion, garlic, mint, parsley, oregano, salt, and pepper in a mixing bowl and stir with a wooden spoon to mix. Wet your hands with cold water and divide the mixture in 4 equal portions. Working quickly and with a light touch, pat each portion into a thick patty. Place the patties on a plate lined with plastic wrap and refrigerate, covered, until ready to grill.

2. Grill the lamb burgers, following the instructions for any of the grills in the box at right, until cooked through. See the box on page 157 for doneness tests.

Remove the burgers and cover to keep warm. Leave the grill on.

3. Place the pita breads on the hot grill, and, lowering the temperature and working in batches, if necessary, grill until toasted, about 1 minute on a contact grill; 1 minute per side on any of the other indoor grills.

4. Cut a slit in each pita. Place a lettuce leaf inside, followed by a burger, an onion slice, if using, some cucumber and tomato slices, and a generous dollop of yogurt sauce. Serve at once.

if you have a...

CONTACT GRILL: Preheat the grill; if your contact grill has a temperature control, preheat the grill to high. Place the drip pan under the front of the grill. When ready to cook, lightly oil the grill surface. Place the burgers on the hot grill, then gently close the lid. The burgers will be done after cooking 4 to 6 minutes.

GRILL PAN: Place the grill pan on the stove and preheat it to medium-high over medium heat. When the grill pan is hot a drop of water will skitter in the pan. When ready to cook, lightly oil the ridges of the grill pan. Place the burgers in the hot grill pan. The burgers will be done after cooking 4 to 6 minutes per side.

BUILT-IN GRILL: Preheat the grill to high, then, if it does not have a nonstick surface, brush and oil the grill grate. Place the burgers on the hot grate. The burgers will be done after cooking 4 to 6 minutes per side.

FREESTANDING GRILL: Preheat the grill to high; there's no need to oil the grate. Place the burgers on the hot grill. The burgers will be done after cooking about 7 minutes per side.

FIREPLACE GRILL: Rake red hot embers under the gridiron and preheat it for 3 to 5 minutes; you want a hot, 2 to 3 Mississippi fire. When ready to cook, brush and oil the gridiron. Place the burgers on the hot grate. The burgers will be done after cooking 4 to 6 minutes per side.

yogurt cucumber sauce

1 medium-size cucumber
1 clove garlic, minced
$^1/_2$ teaspoon coarse salt (kosher or sea),
    or more to taste
1 cup plain whole-milk yogurt
2 tablespoons extra-virgin olive oil
1 tablespoon chopped fresh mint,
    or 1 teaspoon dried mint
Freshly ground black pepper

In keeping with the widespread popularity of the lamb burger, I offer an equally widespread and popular condiment—a garlic-cucumber yogurt sauce known as *tzatziki* in Greece, *cajik* in Turkey, and *raita* in India. For the best results, use whole-milk yogurt. If you can't find it in the supermarket, it's available at natural foods stores or Middle Eastern or Greek grocery stores. **MAKES ABOUT 1$^1/_2$ CUPS**

1. Peel the cucumber and cut it in half lengthwise. Scrape out the seeds with a melon baller or spoon. Coarsely grate the cucumber.

2. Place the garlic and salt in a mixing bowl and mash to a paste with the back of a spoon. Stir in the grated cucumber, yogurt, olive oil, and mint. Taste for seasoning, adding more salt, if necessary, and pepper to taste; the sauce should be highly seasoned.

oaxacan-spiced turkey burgers with chipotle salsa

The southeastern state of Oaxaca is home to some of Mexico's most soulful cooking—moles replete with roasted vegetables, nuts, and chiles; *cecina* (grilled cured pork); *carne asada* (grilled beef); even fire-roasted corn served sizzling

tip

Ground turkey comes in many grades, some quite lean and others unpleasantly fatty. I find that white meat turkey with 8 to 10 percent fat makes the best burgers.

off the embers. These turkey burgers didn't originate in Mexico (although turkey was native to Central America and much prized by the Aztecs), but they are flavored with spices and seasonings that are characteristic of Oaxacan cooking. I think you'll find that the combination of roasted pumpkin, sesame, and cumin seeds makes the burgers irresistible. **SERVES 4**

THE RECIPE

3 tablespoons shelled pumpkin seeds

2 tablespoons sesame seeds

1 teaspoon cumin seeds

1½ pounds lean ground turkey

3 tablespoons finely chopped fresh cilantro

1 scallion, both white and green parts, trimmed and minced

1 clove garlic, minced

1 tablespoon pure chile powder, preferably ancho chile powder

1 teaspoon coarse salt (kosher or sea), or more to taste

1 teaspoon ground coriander

½ teaspoon ground cinnamon

½ teaspoon freshly ground black pepper

4 flour tortillas (each 10 inches)

Chipotle Salsa (page 371)

8 ounces jicama, peeled and cut into matchstick slivers

1 medium-size avocado, peeled, pitted, and diced

1. Heat a small skillet (not a nonstick skillet) over medium heat. Add the pumpkin seeds and cook until fragrant and lightly toasted, 2 to 3 minutes, shaking the pan to ensure even toasting. Transfer the pumpkin seeds to a heatproof mixing bowl. Add the sesame seeds to the skillet and toast until fragrant and lightly browned, 1 to 2 minutes. Transfer the

sesame seeds to the mixing bowl. Add the cumin seeds to the skillet and toast until fragrant and lightly browned, 1 to 2 minutes. Transfer the cumin seeds to the mixing bowl. Let all the seeds cool to room temperature.

if you have a...

CONTACT GRILL: Preheat the grill; if your contact grill has a temperature control, preheat the grill to high. Place the drip pan under the front of the grill. When ready to cook, lightly oil the grill surface. Place the burgers on the hot grill, then gently close the lid. The burgers will be done after cooking 4 to 6 minutes.

GRILL PAN: Place the grill pan on the stove and preheat it to medium-high over medium heat. When the grill pan is hot a drop of water will skitter in the pan. When ready to cook, lightly oil the ridges of the grill pan. Place the burgers in the hot grill pan. The burgers will be done after cooking 4 to 6 minutes per side.

BUILT-IN GRILL: Preheat the grill to high, then, if it does not have a nonstick surface, brush and oil the grill grate. Place the burgers on the hot grate. The burgers will be done after cooking 4 to 6 minutes per side.

FREESTANDING GRILL: Preheat the grill to high; there's no need to oil the grate. Place the burgers on the hot grill. The burgers will be done after cooking about 7 minutes per side.

FIREPLACE GRILL: Rake red hot embers under the gridiron and preheat it for 3 to 5 minutes; you want a hot, 2 to 3 Mississippi fire. When ready to cook, brush and oil the gridiron. Place the burgers on the hot grate. The burgers will be done after cooking 4 to 6 minutes per side.

2. Place the turkey in the bowl with the toasted seeds. Add the cilantro, scallion, garlic, chile powder, salt, coriander, cinnamon, and pepper and stir with a wooden spoon to mix. Wet your hands with cold water and divide the mixture into 4 equal portions. Working quickly and with a light touch, pat each portion into a thick patty. Place the patties on a plate lined with plastic wrap and refrigerate, covered, until ready to grill.

3. Grill the turkey burgers, following the instructions for any of the grills in the box on the previous page, until cooked through. See the box on page 157 for doneness tests. Remove the burgers and cover to keep warm. Leave the grill on.

4. Place the tortillas on the hot grill, and, lowering the temperature and working in batches, if necessary, grill until toasted, about 1 minute on a contact grill; 1 minute per side on any of the other indoor grills.

5. Place a burger on one side of each tortilla. Spoon some Chipotle Salsa over each burger and top with a sprinkling of jicama and avocado. Fold the tortillas over the burgers and serve at once.

thai tuna burgers
with pickled cucumbers and chile peanut tartar sauce

These offbeat tuna burgers are inspired by a Thai fried fish patty called *tod mun pla*. The meaty fish matches up great with a Thai cucumber salad, which stands in for the pickles that go with a conventional hamburger, while the fire-breathing condiment—Chile Peanut Tartar Sauce—makes the standard ketchup quake in the corner. **SERVES 4**

THE RECIPE

FOR THE CUCUMBER SALAD:

2 Kirby (pickling) cucumbers,
   thinly sliced

1/4 medium-size red onion, thinly sliced

1 tablespoon sugar

1 scant teaspoon coarse salt (kosher or sea)

3 tablespoons rice vinegar or distilled
   white vinegar

Freshly ground black pepper

FOR THE BURGERS:

1 1/2 pounds super-fresh red tuna

1 clove garlic, finely chopped

2 teaspoons grated peeled fresh ginger

1 teaspoon sugar

4 fresh basil leaves, thinly slivered

2 tablespoons chopped fresh cilantro

1 Thai chile or serrano pepper, seeded
   and minced (for hotter burgers,
   leave the seeds in)

2 tablespoons fish sauce or soy sauce,
   or more to taste

FOR SERVING:

4 hamburger buns

2 tablespoons Asian (dark) sesame oil

Chile Peanut Tartar Sauce (recipe follows)

1. Make the cucumber salad: Place the cucumbers, onion, sugar, salt, and vinegar in a nonreactive bowl and toss to mix. Season the salad with pepper to taste. Let the salad stand for 1 hour at room temperature, tossing it again once or twice.

2. Make the burgers: Trim any skin or dark or bloody spots off the tuna. Rinse the tuna under cold running water, then blot it dry with paper towels. Finely chop the tuna by hand (you'll get the best con-

sistency this way) or in a food processor. If using a food processor, cut the tuna into 1/2-inch chunks, don't fill the processor bowl more than a quarter full, and run the machine in short bursts.

3. Place the garlic, ginger, and sugar in a mixing bowl and mash to a paste with the back of a spoon. Add the chopped tuna, and the basil, cilantro, Thai chile, and fish sauce and stir with a wooden spoon just to mix. Taste for seasoning, adding more fish sauce as necessary (it's OK to taste high-quality tuna raw). Divide the tuna

if you have a...

CONTACT GRILL: Preheat the grill; if your contact grill has a temperature control, preheat the grill to high. Place the drip pan under the front of the grill. When ready to cook, lightly oil the grill surface. Place the burgers on the hot grill, then gently close the lid. The burgers will be done after cooking about 3 minutes.

GRILL PAN: Place the grill pan on the stove and preheat it to medium-high over medium heat. When the grill pan is hot a drop of water will skitter in the pan. When ready to cook, lightly oil the ridges of the grill pan. Place the burgers in the hot grill pan. The burgers will be done after cooking about 3 minutes per side.

BUILT-IN GRILL: Preheat the grill to high, then, if it does not have a nonstick surface, brush and oil the grill grate. Place the burgers on the hot grate. The burgers will be done after cooking about 3 minutes per side.

FREESTANDING GRILL: Preheat the grill to high; there's no need to oil the grate. Place the burgers on the hot grill. The burgers will be done after cooking about 4 minutes per side.

FIREPLACE GRILL: Rake red hot embers under the gridiron and preheat it for 3 to 5 minutes; you want a hot, 2 to 3 Mississippi fire. When ready to cook, brush and oil the gridiron. Place the burgers on the hot grate. The burgers will be done after cooking about 3 minutes per side.

tips

- Use sushi-quality tuna, so you can serve the burgers medium-rare.

- Fish sauce is a malodorous but tasty condiment made from fermented anchovies. It is available at Asian markets, gourmet shops, and a growing number of super-markets. The best brands come in glass bottles. If fish sauce is unavailable or off-putting, you can substitute soy sauce.

mixture into 4 even portions and shape into patties. Place the patties on a plate lined with plastic wrap and refrigerate, covered, until ready to grill.

4. Grill the tuna burgers, following the instructions for any of the grills in the box on the previous page, until cooked to medium-rare. When done, the burgers will be cooked at the edges but still pink in the center when tested with a knife (unlike hamburgers, it's safe to serve tuna burgers medium-rare). Remove the burgers and cover to keep warm. Leave the grill on.

5. To serve: Brush the cut sides of the buns with the sesame oil. Place the buns on the hot grill, cut side down, and, lowering the temperature if necessary, grill until toasted, 1 to 2 minutes. You may need to work in batches.

6. Spoon some Chile Peanut Tartar Sauce onto the bottom half of each bun. Place a tuna burger on top. Using a slotted spoon, spoon some cucumber salad onto each burger, then top with the other half of the bun and serve at once.

chile peanut tartar sauce

East meets West in this explosively flavorful tartar sauce, which goes great with any sort of grilled seafood. A good tool for grating ginger is a Microplane—a grater that looks like a file with razor-sharp slits. It's also useful for grating lemon zest, the oil-rich yellow rind of the lemon. **MAKES ABOUT 1 CUP**

1 cup mayonnaise (preferably Hellmann's)
1 to 2 Thai chiles or serrano peppers, seeded and minced (for a hotter sauce, leave the seeds in)
2 tablespoons finely chopped dry-roasted peanuts
2 tablespoons finely chopped fresh cilantro
2 teaspoons finely grated peeled fresh ginger
1 teaspoon finely grated lemon zest
2 teaspoons fresh lemon juice, or more to taste
1 tablespoon fish sauce or soy sauce, or more to taste
Freshly ground black pepper

Place the mayonnaise, chile(s), peanuts, cilantro, ginger, lemon zest, lemon juice, and fish sauce in a nonreactive mixing bowl and whisk to mix. Taste for seasoning, adding more lemon juice and/or fish sauce as necessary and pepper to taste. Any leftover sauce will keep, covered, in the refrigerator for up to 3 days.

Is there any better symbol of indoor grilling than a darkly browned, crisp-skinned, plump, juicy, fragrant, spit-roasted chicken? How about a variety of birds, ranging from a mahogany-hued duck to a spit-roasted turkey breast studded with truffled cheese? And when it comes to chicken breasts, contact grills and grill pans keep them succulent, as you'll discover with the tarragon chicken tenders and chicken breasts with feta cheese and fresh mint. In this chapter you'll also discover a beer-can chicken you can cook in a stove-top smoker and the recipe I used to beat Iron Chef Michiba in Tokyo—Victory Chicken.

poultry

rotisserie

the perfect roast chicken (with herbes de provence)

The first thing I ever cooked in a Showtime rotisserie was chicken with *herbes de Provence,* and the results left me dumbfounded. Here was a machine hawked in infomercials and TV shopping shows. The total prep time was less than five minutes, yet the machine turned out a textbook roast chicken— crisp-skinned, handsomely browned, lasciviously moist, and perfectly cooked. Naturally, you can vary the herbs and/or use other seasonings, and in the pages that follow you'll find spit-roasted chickens with other ethnic pedigrees. But when it comes to your basic Sunday-night roast chicken, it's pretty hard to beat this one. **SERVES 2 TO 4**

tip

Herbes de Provence is a traditional herb blend from southeast France. The short list of ingredients includes dried oregano, basil, marjoram, rosemary, and thyme, with at least one kicker— dried lavender for fragrance and sweetness. Good commercial blends are available at specialty food stores and natural food stores.

THE RECIPE

1 chicken (3¹/₂ to 4 pounds)
Coarse salt (kosher or sea) and freshly
    ground black pepper
2 tablespoons herbes de Provence
2 to 3 teaspoons extra-virgin olive oil
Caramelized Onion Sauce
    (recipe follows)

1. Remove the package of giblets from the body cavity of the chicken and set aside for making stock or another use. Remove and discard the fat just inside the body and neck cavities. Rinse the chicken, inside and out, under cold run-

ning water, then drain and blot dry, inside and out, with paper towels (drying is essential to obtaining a crisp skin).

2. Season the neck and body cavities of the chicken with salt and pepper and sprinkle 2 teaspoons of the *herbes de Provence* inside the body cavity and 1 teaspoon inside the neck cavity of the bird. Truss the chicken using one of the methods described in the box on page 177. Brush the outside of the chicken with olive oil. Season the outside of the chicken generously with salt and pepper and sprinkle the remaining 1 tablespoon of *herbes de Provence* over it.

3. When ready to cook, place the drip pan in the bottom of the rotisserie. Skewer the chicken on the rotisserie spit (see sidebar, this page). Attach the spit to the rotisserie and turn on the motor. If your rotisserie has a temperature control, set it to 400°F (for instructions for using a rotisserie, see page 14). Cook the chicken until the skin is crisp and a deep golden brown and the meat is cooked through, 1 to 1½ hours. To test for doneness, use an instant-read meat thermometer: Insert it into the thickest part of a thigh but not so that it touches the spit or a bone. The internal temperature should be about 180°F.

4. Transfer the chicken to a platter or cutting board and remove the bird from the spit. Let the chicken rest for 5 minutes, then untruss it, carve, and serve with Caramelized Onion Sauce.

caramelized onion sauce

Caramelized onions give this sauce a golden color and sweet earthy taste. In keeping with the Provençal theme of the chicken, use a dry, aromatic French vermouth, like Noilly Prat. Crème fraîche is a very thick, slightly sour French cream; look for it in specialty food stores and cheese shops. An equal amount of heavy cream can be used as a substitute. **MAKES ABOUT 1 CUP**

2 tablespoons (¼ stick) unsalted butter
1 medium-size onion, finely chopped
2 cloves garlic, minced
½ cup dry white vermouth
1½ cups chicken stock (preferably homemade)
½ cup crème fraîche or heavy (whipping) cream
Coarse salt (kosher or sea) and freshly ground black pepper

1. Melt the butter in a medium-size saucepan over medium heat. Add the onion and cook until a deep golden brown, 4 to 6 minutes, adding the garlic after 3 minutes and stirring often with a wooden spoon.

2. Add the vermouth and increase the heat to high. Let boil until only about 2 tablespoons of the liquid remain. Add the chicken stock and let boil until only about 1 cup of the liquid remains. Add the crème fraîche and let boil until the sauce is thick and creamy and reduced to about 1 cup. The total cooking time in Step 2 will be between 8 and 10 minutes. Season with salt and pepper to taste; the sauce should be highly seasoned. The sauce can be refrigerated, covered, for up to 4 days. Rewarm it gently in a heavy saucepan.

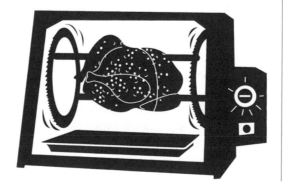

HOW TO PUT A BIRD ON A ROTISSERIE SPIT

It's important when cooking a chicken on the rotisserie to affix it securely to the spit. The Showtime rotisserie has an ingenious double spit, which keeps the bird from spinning loosely. If your rotisserie has a single spit, use the screw-on forks to secure the bird to the spit. Insert one fork in each end and tighten the screw with a fork or pliers to fix it in place. When cooking a single chicken, spit the bird end to end—that is, with the spit going in the neck end and coming out the tail end. When cooking two or more chickens, spit the birds through the sides. Position the birds so head and tail ends alternate.

tips

■ Gordon roasts his chicken in the oven, but the marinade and sauce are great for spit roasting and grilling. If you are using a rotisserie, cook a whole bird. To cook the chicken on a grill, marinate pieces, skin on and bone in, or skinless, boneless breasts, in the garlic mustard marinade instead. You'll need about 1½ pounds of breast meat. Marinate the chicken breasts for 2 hours. You can grill the chicken on a contact grill, built-in grill, freestanding grill, grill pan, or in the fireplace, following the instructions in the recipe on page 183.

■ The easiest way to grate lemon zest is to use a Microplane. Take only the yellow oil-rich outer rind, not the bitter white pith beneath it.

rotisserie

hamersley's lemon mustard chicken

Putting roast chicken on a restaurant menu may not seem innovative these days, but when Gordon Hamersley started serving it at his bistro in Boston's South End back in 1987, serving the down-home dish seemed, well, nothing less than revolutionary. After all, those were the glory days of American nouvelle cuisine (not to mention the financial boom times of the 1980s). But, there are roast chickens and there are roast chickens, and Hamersley's was the very exemplar of the species. Not only was the skin crackling crisp and the meat exceptionally moist, this baby had flavor! Mustard made it spicy; fresh lemon made it piquant; and there was garlic enough to ward off a legion of vampires. I've long since moved away from Boston, but my wife and I make still make an annual pilgrimage to Hamersley's Bistro to savor that fabulous chicken. Here's a version that you can cook on a rotisserie. **SERVES 2 TO 4**

THE RECIPE

3 shallots, coarsely chopped

3 cloves garlic, coarsely chopped

½ cup rinsed, dried, stemmed, coarsely chopped fresh flat-leaf parsley

1 tablespoon herbes de Provence

1 teaspoon dried rosemary

1½ teaspoons coarse salt (kosher or sea)

1 teaspoon freshly ground black pepper

1 teaspoon finely grated lemon zest

2 tablespoons fresh lemon juice

¼ cup Dijon mustard

⅓ cup extra-virgin olive oil

1 chicken (3½ to 4 pounds)

3 thin (¼ inch) lemon slices

3 cloves garlic, peeled

Garlic Lemon Jus (recipe follows)

1. Place the shallots, garlic, parsley, *herbes de Provence,* rosemary, salt, and pepper in a food processor. Run the processor in short bursts to finely chop, then purée these ingredients to a thick, coarse paste. Add the lemon zest, lemon juice, and mustard, then add the olive oil in a thin stream with the motor running and process until a smooth paste forms. Set the marinade aside.

2. Remove the package of giblets from the body cavity of the chicken and set aside for making stock or another use. Remove and discard the fat just inside the body and neck cavities. Rinse the chicken, inside and out, under cold running water, then drain and blot dry, inside and out, with paper towels (drying is essential to obtaining a crisp skin).

3. Place 1 slice of lemon and 1 clove of garlic in the chicken's neck cavity, then place the remaining 2 lemon slices and 2 garlic cloves in the body cavity. Spoon a little of the marinade in the neck and body cavities of the chicken. Place the chicken in a large, heavy-duty, resealable plastic bag and add the remaining marinade. Squeeze the bag to coat the chicken all over with marinade and let marinate in the refrigerator for at least 4 hours, or as long as overnight, turning the bird several times so that it marinates evenly.

4. When ready to cook, place the drip pan in the bottom of the rotisserie. Remove the chicken from the marinade and discard the marinade. Truss the chicken using one of the methods described in the box at right. Skewer it on the rotisserie spit (see sidebar on page 175). Attach the spit to the rotisserie and turn on the motor. If your rotisserie has a temperature control, set it to 400°F (for instructions for

trussing a chicken

Whenever I cook a chicken, I like to truss it first—that is, tie the bird into a compact shape with butcher's string. A trussed chicken browns and cooks more evenly; it looks better and more professional when you serve it. And when you cook a chicken in a countertop rotisserie, trussing is essential, lest a wayward drumstick jam the rotisserie mechanism or come in direct contact with the heating element. There are three ways to truss poultry:

THE HIGH-TECH METHOD: The Showtime rotisserie comes with elasticized string ties (they look like giant white rubber bands) that you can use for trussing. Loop one crosswise around the back end of the bird to hold the legs tight to the body, then another one crosswise around the wings to hold them against the body.

THE CLASSICAL METHOD: Sew the legs and wings to the body, using a trussing needle (an oversize needle) and butcher's string. Hold one leg close to the body of the bird and insert the needle through the thigh, then through the body and out the drumstick on the other side. Now, insert the needle through the wing on that side, then through the body, and out the wing on the other side. Tie the two ends together.

THE BAMBOO SKEWER METHOD: If you don't have any butcher's string handy, hold one leg close to the body and stick a bamboo skewer into the thigh, through the body, and out the drumstick on the other side. Now, insert a second bamboo skewer into the wing on that side, then through the body, and out the wing on the other side. Break off the protruding skewer ends.

using a rotisserie, see page 14). Cook the chicken until the skin is crisp and a deep golden brown and the meat is cooked through, 1 to 1½ hours. To test for doneness, use an instant-read meat thermometer: Insert it into the thickest part of a thigh but not so that it touches the spit or a bone. The internal temperature should be about 180°F.

5. Transfer the chicken to a platter or cutting board and remove the spit. Reserve the drippings for making the *jus*. Let the chicken rest for 5 minutes, then untruss it, carve, and serve with the Garlic Lemon Jus.

**FAT
SEPARATORS**

A fat separator or gravy separator looks like a measuring cup with a spout extending from the very bottom. When you pour the drippings from a roast into it, the fat floats to the top, so you can pour off the pure meat juices from underneath.

garlic lemon jus

A *jus* is a natural gravy—pan drippings enriched chicken broth and flavorings like garlic and lemon, but without any starchy thickeners or cream. Use a fat separator (a measuring cup or gravy boat with the spout attached at its base) to separate the meat drippings from the fat. **MAKES ABOUT 1 CUP**

Drippings from Hamersley's Lemon Mustard
    Chicken or other spit-roasted chicken
About 1¹⁄₂ cups chicken broth
    (preferably homemade)
1 tablespoon unsalted butter
3 cloves garlic, thinly sliced crosswise
1 tablespoon diced seeded rindless
    lemon flesh
1 teaspoon fresh lemon juice
Coarse salt (kosher or sea) and freshly
    ground black pepper

1. Pour the drippings from the drip pan into a fat separator. Wait a few minutes, then pour the drippings into a large measuring cup, stopping when the fat starts to come out. Add enough chicken broth to obtain 1¹⁄₂ cups.

2. Melt the butter in a saucepan over medium heat. Add the garlic and diced lemon and cook until the garlic is lightly browned, 3 to 4 minutes. Add the lemon juice and bring to a boil. Add the chicken broth and drippings. Increase the heat to high, bring to a boil, then let the sauce boil until it is reduced to about 1 cup. Whisk in salt and pepper to taste.

rotisserie

canela and chipotle-brined spit-roasted chicken

The Coach House in Edgartown, Massachusetts, is one of our neighborhood restaurants in the summer. We dine there often to enjoy chef Ryan Hardy's superlative roast chicken. His secret is marinating the chicken overnight in a brine perfumed with canela (Mexican cinnamon) and spicing it up with chipotle peppers. Brining the chicken gives it plenty of flavor while keeping it moist as it grills. You can use this brine not only for chicken and other poultry but also for virtually any other meat, from venison to pork roast (the brine here will cure a 4- to 5-pound roast). **SERVES 2 TO 4**

THE RECIPE

3 tablespoons fennel seeds
1¹/₂ tablespoons aniseed
1¹/₂ tablespoons coriander seed
1¹/₂ tablespoons star anise pieces
1¹/₂ tablespoons hot red pepper flakes
1 tablespoon fresh or dried thyme leaves
1 tablespoon chopped fresh flat-leaf parsley
¹/₂ teaspoon whole cloves
3 canela (see sidebar on page 180) or cinnamon sticks (each about 3 inches)
2 bay leaves
³/₄ cup granulated sugar
¹/₃ cup firmly packed brown sugar
6 tablespoons coarse salt (kosher or sea)
2 quarts warm water
2 to 4 canned chipotle peppers in adobo, with 1 tablespoon juices
8 cloves garlic, peeled
1 teaspoon liquid smoke
1 chicken (3¹/₂ to 4 pounds)

1. Heat a heavy skillet (not a nonstick skillet) over medium heat. Add the fennel seeds, aniseed, and coriander seed and toast until fragrant and just beginning to brown, 2 to 4 minutes. Transfer to a large heatproof mixing bowl. Add the star anise, hot pepper flakes, thyme, parsley, cloves, canela sticks, bay leaves, granulated sugar, brown sugar, salt, water, chipotle peppers, garlic, and liquid smoke to the bowl. Whisk until the sugar and salt dissolve. Let the brine cool to room temperature.

liquid smoke

Some of the recipes in this book call for liquid smoke to impart the flavor we associate with true-blue, cooked-in-a-pit barbecue. Heresy? Treason? Not really. Liquid smoke is a naturally produced product, made from real wood and smoke, and it's been part of the barbecue scene in the United States for the better part of a century.

According to the Dallas-based Colgin Companies, manufacturer of the nation's best-selling liquid smoke, the process begins with a traditional hardwood (hickory, pecan, mesquite, or apple) that is burned in a retort designed to make it smolder without catching fire. The resulting smoke is funneled into a water-cooled condenser, where it liquefies, then it's filtered and mellowed in oak aging tanks. Water, molasses, vinegar, and salt are added to make a redolent, translucent brown liquid with an intense smoke flavor.

Used judiciously, a few drops of liquid smoke can give foods grilled or spit roasted indoors a smoky barbecue flavor. It's a popular ingredient in both commercial and homemade barbecue sauces. According to Colgin, liquid smoke also has antioxidant and antimicrobal properties, which impede the growth of bacteria and the spoilage of meat.

In this book liquid smoke is used in three ways—as an ingredient in brines and marinades; in basting sauces brushed on foods during cooking; and as a flavoring for sauces. Liquid smoke is available in most supermarkets. It does not need to be refrigerated once opened and will keep its robust smoke flavor for at least two years. Two popular brands are Colgin and Wright's.

ABOUT CANELA

Canela—Mexican cinnamon, *Cinnamomum zeylanicum*—is true cinnamon, as opposed to the hard smooth bark of the cassia tree, which is what usually passes for cinnamon in North America. Recognizable by its crumbly, multi-layered bark, canela is spicier and more fragrant than cassia. However, cassia will give you a perfectly tasty bird too. Look for canela at Mexican markets and gourmet shops or see the Mail-Order Sources on page 396.

2. Remove the package of giblets from the body cavity of the chicken and set aside for making stock or another use. Remove and discard the fat just inside the body and neck cavities. Rinse the chicken, inside and out, under cold running water, then drain and blot dry, inside and out, with paper towels.

3. Add the chicken to the brine and place a pot lid or a resealable plastic bag filled with water on top of it to keep it submerged. Or place the chicken and the brine in a large, heavy-duty, resealable plastic bag. Refrigerate, covered, for 24 hours, turning the chicken several times to ensure even brining.

4. When ready to cook, place the drip pan in the bottom of the rotisserie. Drain the chicken, discarding the brine. Truss the chicken using one of the methods described in the box on page 177. Skewer it on the rotisserie spit (see sidebar on page on 175). Attach the spit to the rotisserie and turn on the motor. If your rotisserie has a temperature control, set it to 400°F (for instructions for using a rotisserie, see page 14). Cook the chicken until the skin is crisp and a deep golden brown and the meat is cooked through, 1 to 1½ hours. To test for doneness, use an instant-read meat thermometer: Insert it in the thickest part of a thigh but not so that it touches the spit or a bone. The internal temperature should be about 180°F.

5. Transfer the chicken to a platter or cutting board and remove the spit. Let the chicken rest for 5 minutes, then untruss it, carve, and serve.

VARIATION: You can also brine and grill chicken pieces and skinless boneless breasts. You'll need about 2 pounds chicken pieces or 1½ pounds skinless, boneless breast meat. Brine chicken pieces for 5 to 8 hours; chicken breasts for 3 to 4 hours. You can grill chicken on a contact grill, built-in grill, freestanding grill, grill pan, or in the fireplace, following the instructions in the recipe on page 183.

stove-top smoker

beer-can chicken indoors

Soon after I first published a recipe for beer-can chicken back in 1996, apartment and condo dwellers began asking me how they can make this unique dish indoors. Bake it in the oven, was my response, but I always felt badly that the important element of wood smoke would be lacking. Finally, here's a beer can chicken perfumed with wood smoke that you can cook in the kitchen, thanks to the stove-top smoker. The two-stage roasting process, first in the smoker, then in the oven, gives you crisp skin just like a bird grilled outdoors. **SERVES 2 TO 4**

THE RECIPE

1 chicken (3½ to 4 pounds)
2 tablespoons Basic Barbecue Rub (page 362)
  or your favorite rub
2 teaspoons vegetable oil
1 can (12 ounces) beer
Cooking oil spray (optional)
Kansas City–Style Sweet and Smoky
  Barbecue Sauce (page 374) or
  your favorite commercial sauce
  (optional), for serving

YOU'LL ALSO NEED:
2 tablespoons hickory wood sawdust;
  heavy-duty aluminum foil

1. Remove the packet of giblets from the body cavity of the chicken and set aside for making stock or another use. Remove and discard the fat inside the body and neck cavities. Rinse the chicken, inside and out, under cold running water, then drain and blot dry, inside and out, with paper towels. Sprinkle 1 tablespoon of the rub inside the body and neck cavities of the chicken. Lightly brush the outside of the bird all over with the oil. Sprinkle the remaining 1 tablespoon of rub all over the outside of the chicken.

2. Pop the tab off the beer can. Drink or pour out half of the beer (¾ cup). Using a

church key–style can opener, make 2 additional holes in the top of the beer can. Spoon any remaining rub into the beer can. Don't worry if it foams up: This is normal.

3. Holding the chicken upright, with the opening of the body cavity at the bottom, lower it onto the beer can so the can fits into the cavity. Pull the legs forward to form a sort of tripod, so the bird stands upright. The rear leg of the tripod is the beer can. Tuck the wing tips behind the chicken's back.

4. Set up the smoker (for instructions for using a stove-top smoker, see page 16). Place the sawdust in the center of the bottom of the smoker. Line the drip pan with aluminum foil and place it in the smoker. Lightly coat the smoker rack with cooking oil spray, or use a paper towel dipped in oil, and place the rack in the smoker. Carefully stand the chicken upright on the beer can in the center of the smoker on the rack. Tent the bird with a large sheet of heavy-duty aluminum foil, crumpling and crimping the edges over the outside rim of the smoker bottom to make a tight seal. Try not to let the foil come in contact with the chicken.

SMOKED CHICKEN SANS BEER CAN

Want to make a terrific barbecued, smoked-roasted chicken without the beer can? Using a stove-top smoker and two-step roasting process, it's a cinch. Follow the instructions for beer-can chicken but place the bird breast side up directly on the smoker rack (for a neater appearance, truss the bird first; see box on page 177). Smoke the chicken for 30 minutes, then bake it in a 400°F oven for 40 to 50 minutes.

You can also smoke-roast chicken quarters or pieces. Start with about 2 pounds of chicken. Season it with 2 to 3 tablespoons of barbecue rub, then place the pieces on the smoker rack. They'll be done after smoking for 20 to 30 minutes—you won't need to bake them.

tip

5. Place the smoker over high heat for 3 minutes, then reduce the heat to medium. Smoke the chicken until it has a good smoke flavor, about 30 minutes.

6. Meanwhile, preheat the oven to 400°F.

7. Uncover the chicken and discard the aluminum foil. Place the chicken and beer can, still on the smoker bottom, in the oven and bake the bird until the skin is crisp and golden brown and the chicken is cooked through, 40 to 50 minutes. To test for doneness, insert an instant-read meat thermometer in the thickest part of a thigh but not so that it touches a bone. The internal temperature should be about 180°F.

8. Using two pairs of tongs, carefully transfer the chicken in its upright position on the beer can to a platter. Use one pair of tongs to grab the bird by the beer can just under the butt and the other to grip the bird at the wings. Present the bird to your guests. Let the chicken rest for 5 minutes, then carefully lift it off the beer can. Take care not to spill the hot beer or otherwise burn yourself. (Normally I discard the beer, but some people like to save it for making barbecue sauce.) Halve, quarter, or carve the chicken and serve it with barbecue sauce, if desired, on the side.

victory chicken

In August 2003, I traveled to Tokyo to do a televised barbecue battle with Iron Chef Rokusaburo Michiba. This simple chicken is one of the dishes I won with. As any American pit master knows, the essence of true barbecue is wood smoke. In Japan, I had neither logs nor a smoker, but I figured I could give grilled chicken a bit of the old barbecue magic by basting it with liquid smoke and butter. Will this recipe give you the same results as patiently smoking a whole chicken to a mahogany sheen in a hickory-fired pit? Not exactly. But you will get a delicious bird cooked indoors that's redolent of barbecue spice and smoke flavors. **SERVES 4**

2 whole skinless, boneless chicken breasts (each 12 to 16 ounces), or 4 half breasts (each half 6 to 8 ounces)

2 tablespoons Basic Barbecue Rub (page 362)

2 tablespoons (¼ stick) unsalted butter

1 teaspoon liquid smoke (see box on page 179)

¾ to 1 cup of your favorite barbecue sauce (for a good candidate, see page 374)

1. Trim any sinews or excess fat off the chicken breasts and discard. Rinse the breasts under cold running water, then drain and blot dry with paper towels. Remove the tenders from the chicken breasts (see box on page 191) and set them aside for kebabs or satés (you'll find recipes using tenders on pages 197 and 198). Sprinkle the rub over the chicken breasts on both sides, rubbing it onto the meat with your fingertips. Let the chicken cure in the refrigerator, covered, for 20 minutes.

2. Meanwhile, make the basting mixture: Melt the butter in a small saucepan over medium heat. Remove the saucepan from the heat and stir in the liquid smoke.

3. Arrange the chicken breasts on the grill on a diagonal to the ridges and cook the chicken, following the instructions for any of the grills in the box at right, until cooked through. Use the poke test to check for doneness; the chicken should feel firm when pressed. Or insert an instant-read meat thermometer into the thick part of a breast through one end: The internal temperature should be about 160°F. Baste the chicken on the cooked side after 2 minutes, then baste the other side after 2 more minutes.

4. Transfer the chicken to a platter or plates. Brush any remaining smoky butter over it and serve it with the barbecue sauce of your choice.

if you have a...

CONTACT GRILL: Preheat the grill; if your contact grill has a temperature control, preheat the grill to high. Place the drip pan under the front of the grill. When ready to cook, lightly oil the grill surface. Place the chicken breasts on the hot grill, then close the lid. The chicken will be done after cooking 4 to 6 minutes. You will need to turn the chicken breasts so that you can baste both sides.

GRILL PAN: Place the grill pan on the stove and preheat it to medium-high over medium heat. When the grill pan is hot a drop of water will skitter in the pan. When ready to cook, lightly oil the ridges of the grill pan. Place the chicken breasts in the hot grill pan. They will be done after cooking 4 to 6 minutes per side.

BUILT-IN GRILL: Preheat the grill to high, then, if it does not have a nonstick surface, brush and oil the grill grate. Place the chicken breasts on the hot grate. They will be done after cooking 4 to 6 minutes per side.

FREESTANDING GRILL: Preheat the grill to high; there's no need to oil the grate. Place the chicken breasts on the hot grill. They will be done after cooking 5 to 7 minutes per side.

FIREPLACE GRILL: Rake red hot embers under the gridiron and preheat it for 3 to 5 minutes; you want a hot, 2 to 3 Mississippi fire. When ready to cook, brush and oil the gridiron. Place the chicken breasts on the hot grate. They will be done after cooking 4 to 6 minutes per side.

chicken breasts grilled
with feta and fresh mint

Just a few ingredients—and a bit of ingenuity in combining them—can create a titanic range of flavor. The ingredients in question here, feta cheese and fresh mint, are Greek. You might not normally think of them together, but there's a precedent, a salty Cypriot cheese called Halloumi that's flavored with mint. If you've dismissed skinless, boneless chicken breasts as bland, this dish will make you reconsider. **SERVES 4**

tip

The only remotely tricky part of this recipe is cutting a pocket in each chicken breast half so you can stuff it with feta and mint. It helps if you place the half breast at the edge of a cutting board with the thicker part facing out. Holding the breast flat with the palm of one hand, use a small paring knife to cut a pocket in the side, parallel to the cutting board.

THE RECIPE

2 whole skinless, boneless chicken breasts
  (each 12 to 16 ounces), or 4 half breasts
  (each half 6 to 8 ounces)
1 piece (1½ ounces) feta cheese,
  thinly sliced
8 fresh mint leaves, rinsed, blotted dry,
  and cut into thin slivers
Coarse salt (kosher or sea)
Freshly ground black pepper
1 tablespoon fresh lemon juice
1 tablespoon extra-virgin olive oil
Lemon wedges, for serving

YOU'LL ALSO NEED:
Wooden toothpicks

1. If using whole chicken breasts, cut each in half. Trim any sinews or excess fat off the chicken breasts and discard. Rinse the breasts under cold running water, then drain and blot dry with paper towels. Remove the tenders from the chicken breasts (see box on page 191) and set them aside for kebabs or satés (you'll find recipes using tenders on pages 197 and 198). Place a half breast at the edge of a cutting board. Cut a deep horizontal pocket in the breast, taking care not to pierce the edges. Repeat with the remaining breast halves.

2. Place 2 or 3 slices of feta and a few slivers of mint in the pocket of each chicken breast. Pin the pockets shut with lightly oiled toothpicks. Place the breasts in a nonreactive baking dish just large enough to hold them. Generously season the breasts on both sides with salt and pepper and sprinkle any remaining mint over them. Drizzle the lemon juice and olive oil over both sides of the chicken breasts, patting them onto the meat with your fingers. Let the chicken breasts marinate in the refrigerator, covered, for 20 minutes, turning once or twice.

3. Arrange the chicken breasts on the grill on a diagonal to the ridges and cook the chicken, following the instructions for any of the grills in the box at right, until cooked through. Use the poke test to check for doneness; the chicken should feel firm when pressed. Or insert an instant-read meat thermometer into the thick part of a breast through one end: The internal temperature should be about 160°F.

4. Transfer the chicken breasts to a platter or plates and remove and discard the toothpicks. Serve the chicken at once with lemon wedges.

if you have a...

CONTACT GRILL: Preheat the grill; if your contact grill has a temperature control, preheat the grill to high. Place the drip pan under the front of the grill. When ready to cook, lightly oil the grill surface. Place the chicken breasts on the hot grill, then close the lid. The chicken will be done after cooking 4 to 6 minutes.

GRILL PAN: Place the grill pan on the stove and preheat it to medium-high over medium heat. When the grill pan is hot a drop of water will skitter in the pan. When ready to cook, lightly oil the ridges of the grill pan. Place the chicken breasts in the hot grill pan. They will be done after cooking 4 to 6 minutes per side.

BUILT-IN GRILL: Preheat the grill to high, then, if it does not have a nonstick surface, brush and oil the grill grate. Place the chicken breasts on the hot grate. They will be done after cooking 4 to 6 minutes per side.

FREESTANDING GRILL: Preheat the grill to high; there's no need to oil the grate. Place the chicken breasts on the hot grill. They will be done after cooking 5 to 7 minutes per side.

FIREPLACE GRILL: Rake red hot embers under the gridiron and preheat it for 3 to 5 minutes; you want a hot, 2 to 3 Mississippi fire. When ready to cook, brush and oil the gridiron. Place the chicken breasts on the hot grate. They will be done after cooking 4 to 6 minutes per side.

coffee-brined chicken breasts
with redeye sauce #3

Skinless, boneless chicken breasts are the poultry cut grill jockeys both love and hate. We love convenience (not to mention the fact that they're virtually pure protein with practically no fat). On the down side, they're rather bland in flavor and tend to dry out on the grill. Brining is a great way to

tip

This brine is also well suited for 2 pounds of pork chops, another food that tends to dry out on the grill.

compensate for both of these shortcomings—especially if you use this "redeye" variation on traditional brine. A shot of espresso adds an unexpected flavor (don't worry, it's subtle), along with an inviting mahogany hue. To complete the coffee motif, I propose serving the chicken with an espresso-flavored mustard barbecue sauce. **SERVES 4**

THE RECIPE

if you have a...

CONTACT GRILL: Preheat the grill; if your contact grill has a temperature control, preheat the grill to high. Place the drip pan under the front of the grill. When ready to cook, lightly oil the grill surface. Place the chicken breasts on the hot grill, then close the lid. The chicken will be done after cooking 4 to 6 minutes.

GRILL PAN: Place the grill pan on the stove and preheat it to medium-high over medium heat. When the grill pan is hot a drop of water will skitter in the pan. When ready to cook, lightly oil the ridges of the grill pan. Place the chicken breasts in the hot grill pan. They will be done after cooking 4 to 6 minutes per side.

BUILT-IN GRILL: Preheat the grill to high, then, if it does not have a nonstick surface, brush and oil the grill grate. Place the chicken breasts on the hot grate. They will be done after cooking 4 to 6 minutes per side.

FREESTANDING GRILL: Preheat the grill to high; there's no need to oil the grate. Place the chicken breasts on the hot grill. They will be done after cooking 5 to 7 minutes per side.

FIREPLACE GRILL: Rake red hot embers under the gridiron and preheat it for 3 to 5 minutes; you want a hot, 2 to 3 Mississippi fire. When ready to cook, brush and oil the gridiron. Place the chicken breasts on the hot grate. They will be done after cooking 4 to 6 minutes per side.

1/2 **cup hot brewed espresso**
1/4 **cup coarse salt (kosher or sea)**
1/4 **cup firmly packed dark brown sugar**
4 **lemon slices (each** 1/4 **inch thick)**
1 **tablespoon black peppercorns**
1 **tablespoon mustard seeds**
1 **tablespoon coriander seed**
2 **whole skinless, boneless chicken breasts (each 12 to 16 ounces), or 4 half breasts (each half 6 to 8 ounces)**
2 **tablespoons unsalted butter, melted**
Redeye Sauce #3 (recipe follows)

1. Place the espresso, salt, and brown sugar in a large nonreactive mixing bowl and whisk until the salt and sugar dissolve. Add 3 cups of cool water and the lemon slices, peppercorns, mustard seeds, and coriander seed and stir to mix. Let the brine cool to room temperature.

2. If using whole chicken breasts, cut each breast in half. Trim any excess fat or sinews off the chicken breasts and discard. Rinse the breasts under cold running water, then drain and blot dry with paper towels. Remove the tenders from the chicken breasts (see box on page 191) and set aside for kebabs or satés (you'll find recipes using tenders on pages 197 and 198). Add the chicken breasts to the brine and place a weight, such as a pot lid or plate, on top to keep them submerged. Or place the breasts in a large resealable plastic bag and add the brine. Let the chicken breasts brine in the refrigerator for 2 to 3 hours, turning them twice so they brine evenly.

3. When ready to cook, drain the chicken breasts, discarding the brine. Blot the chicken breasts dry with paper towels. Lightly brush each breast on both sides with the butter.

4. Arrange the chicken breasts on the grill on a diagonal to the ridges and cook the chicken, following the instructions for any of the grills in the box on the facing page, until cooked through. Use the poke test to check for doneness; the chicken should feel firm when pressed. Or insert an instant-read meat thermometer into the thick part of a breast through one end: The internal temperature should be about 160°F.

5. Transfer the chicken to a platter or plates and serve at once with the Redeye Sauce #3 on the side.

redeye sauce #3

This sauce belongs to the great American tradition of redeye gravies—sauces made by using coffee to deglaze a frying pan that was used to cook ham or pork steaks. So why's the sauce called #3? I like coffee barbecue sauces so much, I've created several different versions. You'll find an Asian-influenced recipe, for example, on page 141. **MAKES ABOUT 1 CUP**

1 slice of bacon, thinly slivered
1 shallot, finely chopped
3 tablespoons hot brewed espresso or
    strong coffee
3 tablespoons cider vinegar
¼ cup Dijon mustard
¼ cup firmly packed dark brown sugar
2 tablespoons heavy (whipping) cream
1 tablespoon Worcestershire sauce
Coarse salt (kosher or sea) and
    freshly ground black pepper

1. Place the bacon in a heavy saucepan over medium heat and cook until the fat begins to melt, about 2 minutes, stirring with a wooden spoon. Add the shallot and continue cooking until it and the bacon are golden brown, 2 to 3 minutes.

2. Add the espresso and cider vinegar and bring to a boil over medium-high heat. Stir in the mustard, brown sugar, cream, and Worcestershire sauce, reduce the heat to medium, and let simmer gently until the sauce is thick and flavorful, 5 to 8 minutes. Season with salt and pepper to taste.

DON'T DESERT YOUR POST

Grilling is a quick process, whether you do it indoors or outdoors. For example, in a Foreman contact grill, a chicken breast can go from undercooked (135°F) to overcooked (180°F) in 1 to 2 minutes. When you start grilling, stay by the grill until the food is cooked.

milenko's cumin-crusted chicken
with cucumber cream sauce

This recipe comes from my Yugoslavian friend Milenko Samardzich. Its Balkan roots are apparent in the cumin-garlic-lemon marinade and the sauce, a variation on the cucumber and yogurt or cucumber and sour cream sauces found throughout the eastern Mediterranean. Milenko roasts a whole chicken, which you could certainly do in the rotisserie (see the Variation on the facing page). I've retooled his recipe and used chicken breasts cooked on an indoor grill. **SERVES 4**

THE RECIPE

2 whole boneless chicken breasts
     (each 12 to 16 ounces), or 4 half breasts
     (each half 6 to 8 ounces)
2 cloves garlic, coarsely chopped
1½ teaspoons coarse salt (kosher or sea)
1 teaspoon ground cumin
1 teaspoon ground coriander
½ teaspoon freshly ground black pepper
3 tablespoons extra-virgin olive oil
1 tablespoon fresh lemon juice
Cucumber Cream Sauce (recipe follows)
1 tablespoon finely chopped fresh flat-leaf
     parsley

1. If using whole chicken breasts, cut each in half. Trim any sinews or excess fat off the chicken breasts and discard. Rinse the breasts and under cold running water,

then drain and blot dry with paper towels. Remove the tenders from the chicken breasts (see box on page 191) and set aside for kebabs or satés (you'll find recipes using tenders on pages 197 and 198). Arrange the chicken breasts in a large nonreactive baking dish just large enough to hold them.

2. Place the garlic, salt, cumin, coriander, and pepper in a mortar and, using a pestle, pound them to a paste. Add the olive oil and lemon juice. Alternatively, you can use a blender to purée the ingredients. Pour the spice mixture over the chicken and let marinate for 4 to 6 hours in the refrigerator, covered, turning several times.

3. When ready to cook, drain the chicken breasts well and discard the marinade. Arrange the chicken breasts on the grill on a diagonal to the ridges and cook the chicken, following the instructions for any of the grills in the box at right, until cooked through. Use the poke test to check for doneness; the chicken should feel firm when pressed. Or insert an instant-read meat thermometer into the thick part of a breast through one end: The internal temperature should be about 160°F.

4. Transfer the chicken breasts to a platter or plates. Spoon a few tablespoons of the cucumber sauce on top of each breast. Sprinkle the parsley over the chicken and serve at once with the rest of the sauce on the side.

VARIATION: For a more dramatic rendition of Milenko's chicken (one that gives you lots of crackling crisp skin), roast a whole bird in the rotisserie. A 3½- to 4-pound chicken will serve 4. Make the marinade following the directions in Step 2. Place the chicken in a resealable plastic bag, pour the marinade over it, and let marinate for at least 4 hours, preferably overnight, turning it several times.

When ready to cook, place a drip pan in the bottom of the rotisserie. Drain the chicken and discard the marinade. Truss the chicken; you'll find instructions for doing this on page 177. Skewer the chicken on the rotisserie spit (see sidebar on page 175). Attach the spit to the rotisserie and turn on the motor. If your rotisserie has a temperature control, set it to 400°F (for instructions for using a rotisserie, see page 14). The chicken will be a deep golden brown and cooked through after 1 to 1½ hours. To test for doneness, use an instant-

read meat thermometer: Insert it into the thickest part of a thigh but not so that it touches the spit or a bone. The internal temperature should be about 170°F. Let the chicken rest for 5 minutes before carving. Serve with the cucumber sauce spooned on top and garnished with parsley.

cucumber cream sauce

Turks call it *cacik;* Greeks *tzatziki;* and throughout the eastern Mediterranean and Asia Minor variations of this creamy refreshing cucumber sauce turn up wherever meats are grilled. This sauce owes its richness to sour cream. On page

if you have a...

CONTACT GRILL: Preheat the grill; if your contact grill has a temperature control, preheat the grill to high. Place the drip pan under the front of the grill. When ready to cook, lightly oil the grill surface. Place the chicken breasts on the hot grill, then close the lid. The chicken will be done after cooking 4 to 6 minutes.

GRILL PAN: Place the grill pan on the stove and preheat it to medium-high over medium heat. When the grill pan is hot a drop of water will skitter in the pan. When ready to cook, lightly oil the ridges of the grill pan. Place the chicken breasts in the hot grill pan. They will be done after cooking 4 to 6 minutes per side.

BUILT-IN GRILL: Preheat the grill to high, then, if it does not have a nonstick surface, brush and oil the grill grate. Place the chicken breasts on the hot grate. They will be done after cooking 4 to 6 minutes per side.

FREESTANDING GRILL: Preheat the grill to high; there's no need to oil the grate. Place the chicken breasts on the hot grill. They will be done after cooking 5 to 7 minutes per side.

FIREPLACE GRILL: Rake red hot embers under the gridiron and preheat it for 3 to 5 minutes; you want a hot, 2 to 3 Mississippi fire. When ready to cook, brush and oil the gridiron. Place the chicken breasts on the hot grate. They will be done after cooking 4 to 6 minutes per side.

168 you'll find a more traditional version of the sauce made with yogurt. **MAKES ABOUT 1½ CUPS**

1 regular cucumber, or ½ large hothouse (English seedless) cucumber
1 clove garlic, minced
½ teaspoon ground cumin
½ teaspoon curry powder, or more to taste
½ teaspoon coarse salt (kosher or sea), or more to taste
¼ teaspoon freshly ground black pepper, or more to taste
1 cup sour cream or crème fraîche
2 teaspoons red wine vinegar or fresh lemon juice

1. Peel the cucumber, then cut it in half lengthwise and, using a melon baller or spoon, scrape out the seeds. Cut the cucumber into ½-inch chunks. Place the cucumber, garlic, cumin, curry powder, salt, and pepper in a food processor and process to a smooth paste.

2. Add the sour cream and purée, running the machine in short bursts. Taste for seasoning, adding more curry powder and/or salt as necessary.

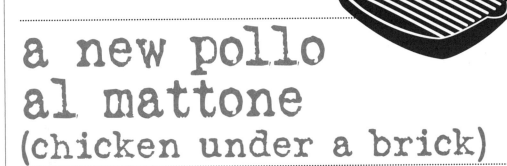

a new pollo al mattone (chicken under a brick)

*P*ollo al mattone (chicken under a brick) is a northern Italian trattoria standby, not to mention a surefire attention grabber, that involves grilling a spatchcocked chicken or a chicken breast under a brick or heavy stone. There are several advantages to this singular method of cooking. The brick presses the bird into the grill grate, giving you killer grill marks and a crisp crust. It also helps the bird stay moist as it grills, and the novelty factor is off the charts. A contact grill can accomplish the same thing. It may not look as cool, but it certainly makes up for this inconvenience. But the technique works on just about any indoor grill. You'll just need to put a weight like a grill press (see sidebar on page 303), a cast-iron skillet, or a small foil-wrapped brick on top of the chicken. **SERVES 4**

THE RECIPE

¹/₃ cup finely chopped fresh flat-leaf
    parsley
1 tablespoon chopped fresh rosemary
2 cloves garlic, minced
1 teaspoon finely grated lemon zest
¹/₂ teaspoon cracked black peppercorns
¹/₂ teaspoon hot red pepper flakes
Coarse salt (kosher or sea)
1 tablespoon Dijon mustard
2 tablespoons freshly squeezed lemon juice
¹/₂ cup extra-virgin olive oil
Freshly ground black pepper
2 whole boneless chicken breasts (each
    12 to 16 ounces), or 4 half breasts
    (each half 6 to 8 ounces)
Lemon wedges, for serving

1. Make the rub: Place 3 tablespoons of the parsley, the rosemary, garlic, lemon zest, cracked pepper, hot pepper flakes, and 1¹/₂ teaspoons of salt in a small bowl and stir to mix. Set aside.

2. Place the mustard in a nonreactive mixing bowl. Whisk in the lemon juice, followed by the olive oil in a thin stream; the mixture should thicken. Whisk in the remaining parsley, then season with salt and pepper to taste. Set half of the mustard mixture aside to use as a sauce.

3. If using whole chicken breasts, cut each in half. Trim any sinews or excess fat off the chicken breasts and discard.

Rinse the breasts under cold running water, then drain and blot dry with paper towels. Remove the tenders from the chicken breasts (see box below) and set aside for kebabs or satés (you'll find recipes using tenders on pages 197 and 198). Place the breasts in a large nonreactive baking dish and sprinkle the rub over

chicken breasts and tenders

Chicken breasts are lean and simple to prepare. Bone-in, skin-on breasts give you the best of all possible worlds. The bones add flavor. Crisp brown skin is the tastiest part of any grilled or roast chicken, and as the fat in the skin melts, it bastes the meat.

If you buy chicken breasts from a butcher shop or natural foods market, it's likely you will be able to find ones with the skin and bones. The cooking time for these will be slightly longer, but the results are worth it. If you prefer to grill skinless, boneless chicken breasts, you can still achieve terrific flavor through the judicious use of marinades, rubs, glazes, and/or basting sauces.

On the underside of each half of a chicken breast is a long, slender, cylindrical muscle called the tender. I like to remove the tenders from the breast and save them for making yakitori, kebabs, and satés. To remove the tender, grab the loose end and gently pull on it, cutting the tender away from the rest of the breast with a paring knife. Most supermarkets sell chicken tenders packaged separately.

There's a tough white tendon that runs the length of a chicken tender. To remove it, place the tender at one edge of a cutting board, tendon side down. Press the end of the tendon against the cutting board with the fingers of one hand. Slide the tip of a boning or paring knife along the tendon, sandwiching it between the blade and the cutting board, then cut off and discard the tendon. You now have a perfect cylinder of chicken for grilling.

if you have a...

on a diagonal to the ridges and cook the chicken, following the instructions for any of the grills in the box at left, until cooked through. Use the poke test to check for doneness; the chicken should feel firm when pressed. Or insert an instant-read meat thermometer into the thick part of a breast through one end: The internal temperature should be about 160°F.

5. Transfer the chicken breasts to a platter or plates. Whisk the reserved sauce to recombine and spoon it over the chicken breasts. Serve at once, with lemon wedges.

NOTE: The traditional *Pollo al mattone* is made with a whole spatchcocked chicken (a bird with the backbone removed, so you can open it out flat, like a book), which means there's lots of skin, the tastiest part of the bird. I've called for boneless breasts here because they're easier to work with, but try to find breasts with the skin on so you still get the crackling crisp exterior of the original. If you're feeling ambitious, you can make this recipe with spatchcocked game hens (see the recipe on page 219 for cooking times).

both sides, patting it onto the chicken with your fingertips. Pour the remaining mustard mixture over the chicken breasts, turning to coat both sides. Let marinate in the refrigerator, covered, for at least 30 minutes, preferably 1 to 2 hours.

4. When ready to cook, lift each chicken breast out of the marinade with tongs and hold it upright until the excess marinade drains off. Discard the marinade. Arrange the chicken breasts on the grill

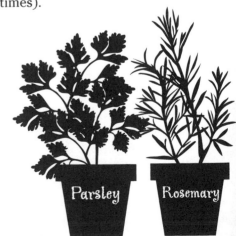

Parsley   Rosemary

chicken "steaks" canary islands

slas Canarias in Miami is one of those homey neighborhood restaurants you want everyone to know about but are loathe to mention to a single soul. The reasons are simple: the great down-home cooking, the congenial waitstaff, the embarrassingly affordable prices, and a dining area that's as clean as an operating room. The restaurant is run by two cousins, Jesus and Santiago Garcia, who named it for the birthplace of their grandfather, the Canary Islands. One of the house specialties is a dish of Nicaraguan origin—a plate-burying chicken "steak" marinated in a mixture that combines the garlic herbal flavor of South American *chimichurri* with the vinegary tang of Spanish Caribbean adobo. Although the chicken tastes best if you marinate it overnight, you're really only looking at about ten minutes of active preparation time. **SERVES 4**

tip

Skirt steak is also great prepared in this manner—indeed it's another Islas Canarias specialty. There's enough marinade for 1½ pounds of skirt steak; you'll find cooking times in the recipe on page 71.

THE RECIPE

2 whole boneless chicken breasts
(each 12 to 16 ounces), or 4 half chicken
breasts (each half 6 to 8 ounces)
Coarse salt (kosher or sea) and freshly ground
black pepper
¼ cup white wine vinegar or red wine vinegar
½ sweet onion, finely diced (about ½ cup)
3 cloves garlic, coarsely chopped
1 teaspoon dried oregano
½ teaspoon ground cumin
¾ cup extra-virgin olive oil
⅓ cup chopped fresh flat-leaf parsley

1. If using whole breasts, cut each breast in half. Trim any sinews or excess fat off the chicken breasts and discard. Rinse the breasts under cold running water, then drain and blot dry with paper towels. Remove the tenders from the chicken breasts (see box on page 191) and set aside for kebabs or satés (you'll find recipes using tenders on pages 197 and 198). Place a breast half between 2 pieces of plastic wrap and gently pound it to a thickness of ½ inch using a meat pounder,

if you have a...

CONTACT GRILL: Preheat the grill; if your contact grill has a temperature control, preheat the grill to high. Place the drip pan under the front of the grill. When ready to cook, lightly oil the grill surface. Place the chicken breasts on the hot grill, then close the lid. The chicken will be done after cooking 4 to 6 minutes.

GRILL PAN: Place the grill pan on the stove and preheat it to medium-high over medium heat. When the grill pan is hot a drop of water will skitter in the pan. When ready to cook, lightly oil the ridges of the grill pan. Place the chicken breasts in the hot grill pan. They will be done after cooking 4 to 6 minutes per side.

BUILT-IN GRILL: Preheat the grill to high, then, if it does not have a nonstick surface, brush and oil the grill grate. Place the chicken breasts on the hot grate. They will be done after cooking 4 to 6 minutes per side.

FREESTANDING GRILL: Preheat the grill to high; there's no need to oil the grate. Place the chicken breasts on the hot grill. They will be done after cooking 5 to 7 minutes per side.

FIREPLACE GRILL: Rake red hot embers under the gridiron and preheat it for 3 to 5 minutes; you want a hot, 2 to 3 Mississippi fire. When ready to cook, brush and oil the gridiron. Place the chicken breasts on the hot grate. They will be done after cooking 4 to 6 minutes per side.

until the salt dissolves. Whisk in the olive oil. Correct the seasoning, adding salt and pepper to taste. The mixture should be highly seasoned. Pour half of this mixture into another nonreactive serving bowl and set aside for use as a sauce. Whisk 2 tablespoons of the parsley into the mixture in the mixing bowl then pour it over the chicken, turning the breasts to coat on both sides. Let the chicken breasts marinate in the refrigerator, covered, for at least 2 hours or as long as overnight, turning them a few times so that they marinate evenly.

3. When ready to cook, drain the chicken breasts well and discard the marinade. Arrange the chicken breasts on the grill on a diagonal to the ridges and cook the chicken, following the instructions for any of the grills in the box at left, until cooked through. Use the poke test to check for doneness; the chicken should feel firm when pressed. Or insert an instant-read meat thermometer into the breast through one end: The internal temperature should be about 160°F. You may need to cook the chicken breasts in more than one batch; cover the grilled chicken with aluminum foil to keep warm until ready to serve.

the side of a heavy cleaver, a rolling pin, or the bottom of a heavy saucepan (this will give the breast a uniform thickness). Repeat with the remaining breast halves. Place the chicken breasts in a large nonreactive baking dish and season them on both sides with salt and pepper.

2. Place the vinegar, onion, garlic, oregano, and cumin in a nonreactive mixing bowl. Add ½ teaspoon of salt and ¼ teaspoon of pepper and whisk

4. Whisk the remaining parsley into the reserved bowl of vinegar mixture. Spoon half of it over the chicken breasts and serve the remainder on the side.

chicken paillards
with "virgin" sauce

Starting with a classic Mediterranean leitmotif, tomato, garlic, basil, and olive oil, this recipe builds to a crescendo of flavor. It does this using the most plebian cut of poultry ever to hit the grill, the skinless, boneless chicken breast. To lend it interest (dare I even say chic?), the chicken breast is pounded into a thin sheet known as a paillard. As for the "Virgin" Sauce, the mixture of fresh tomatoes, basil, garlic, and olive oil may be uncomplicated, but the flavors are as bright as the midday sun. **SERVES 4**

THE RECIPE

2 whole skinless, boneless chicken breasts
(each 12 to 16 ounces), or 4 half breasts
(each half 6 to 8 ounces)
1 clove garlic, minced
3 fresh basil leaves, minced, plus 4 basil sprigs
for garnish
Coarse salt (kosher or sea) and freshly ground
black pepper
2 tablespoons extra-virgin olive oil
"Virgin" Sauce (recipe follows)

1. If using whole chicken breasts, divide them in half. Trim any sinews or excess fat off the chicken breasts and discard. Remove the tenders from the breasts (see box on page 191) and set aside for kebabs or satés (you'll find recipes using tenders on pages 197 and 198). Rinse the breasts under cold running water, then drain (don't blot them dry with paper towels; the breasts should be damp).

Place a breast half between 2 pieces of plastic wrap and gently pound it to a thickness of between $1/4$ and $1/8$ inch using

if you have a...

GRILL PAN: Place the grill pan on the stove and preheat it to medium-high over medium heat. When the grill pan is hot a drop of water will skitter in the pan. When ready to cook, lightly oil the ridges of the grill pan. Place the paillards in the hot grill pan. They will be done after cooking 1 to 2 minutes per side. Use a large spatula to turn them.

BUILT-IN GRILL: Preheat the grill to high, then, if it does not have a nonstick surface, brush and oil the grill grate. Place the

paillards on the hot grate. They will be done after cooking 1 to 2 minutes per side. Use a large spatula to turn them.

FIREPLACE GRILL: Rake red hot embers under the gridiron and preheat it for 3 to 5 minutes; you want a hot, 2 to 3 Mississippi fire. When ready to cook, brush and oil the gridiron. Place the paillards on the hot grate. They will be done after cooking 1 to 2 minutes per side. Use a large spatula to turn them.

tips

■ To seed a tomato, cut it in half crosswise. Working over a bowl, hold a tomato half cut side down and squeeze it between your fingers to wring out the seeds. If necessary, use the tip of a butter knife to help scrape them out.

■ To sliver basil leaves, roll them lengthwise into a tight cylinder, then, using a chef's knife, cut them crosswise into paper-thin slices. Tease the resulting slices apart and you'll have the thin slivers of herb that the French call chiffonade.

a meat pounder, the side of a heavy cleaver, a rolling pin, or the bottom of a heavy saucepan. Repeat with the remaining breast halves.

2. Place the garlic and minced basil, $1/2$ teaspoon of salt, and $1/2$ teaspoon of pepper in a bowl and mash to a paste with the back of a spoon. Stir in the olive oil. Brush each paillard on both sides with the garlic and basil mixture and season lightly with salt and pepper.

3. Cook the chicken paillards, following the instructions for any of the grills in the box on the previous page, until cooked through. Use the poke test to check for doneness; the chicken should feel firm when pressed. You may need to work in more than one batch; cover the grilled paillards with aluminum foil to keep warm until ready to serve.

4. Transfer the paillards to a platter or plates and spoon "Virgin" Sauce over them. Garnish each with a sprig of basil and serve at once.

NOTE: The only even remotely tricky part of this recipe is pounding the chicken breasts into paillards. You can use small boneless whole breasts or large breast halves; whole breasts are easier to work with as they are thinner to begin with.

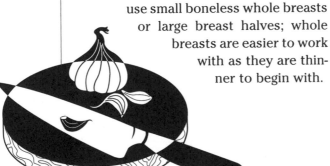

"virgin" sauce (fresh tomato sauce)

The French call this redolent garlic, basil, and tomato condiment *sauce vierge* (literally virgin sauce), perhaps because it's not cooked. It lives or dies by the quality of the ingredients: verdant basil leaves (fresh, of course); tomatoes so luscious and ripe they go splat if you drop them; and olive oil of a noticeably green color and with a fragrance and flavor you can only describe as fruity. The olives in the sauce are not strictly traditional, but they add a nice touch.

MAKES ABOUT 1 CUP

1 clove garlic, minced
$1/2$ teaspoon salt, or more to taste
1 large ripe red tomato (6 to 8 ounces), seeded (see Tips, this page) and cut into $1/4$-inch dice
12 niçoise olives, or 6 black olives, pitted and cut into $1/4$-inch dice
8 fresh basil leaves, thinly slivered (see Tips, this page)
$1/4$ cup extra-virgin olive oil
1 tablespoon red wine vinegar, or more to taste
Freshly ground black pepper

Place the garlic and salt in a nonreactive bowl and mash to a paste with the back of a spoon. Add the tomato, olives, basil, olive oil, and vinegar and stir to mix. Taste for seasoning, adding more salt and/or vinegar as necessary and pepper to taste; the sauce should be highly seasoned.

tarragon chicken tenders

Tarragon and chicken is one of those classic flavor combinations enshrined in French bistro cuisine. The sweet, aniselike taste of tarragon transforms humdrum breast meat into something bright and alluring. Here's a simple version prepared with the leanest, most tender part of the chicken, the slender cylindrical muscle aptly called the tender (for a tip on removing the sinew, see box on page 191). If you are cooking the chicken in a grill pan, you can make a particularly tasty cream sauce by deglazing the grill pan with a little lemon juice and butter. Or if you're using a different indoor grill; make a quick lemon and cream sauce on the stove. **SERVES 4**

THE RECIPE

FOR THE CHICKEN:
1½ pounds chicken tenders
 (12 to 16 tenders)
Coarse salt (kosher or sea) and freshly
 ground black pepper
3 tablespoons chopped fresh tarragon
 leaves, plus 4 whole sprigs
 for garnish
1 teaspoon finely grated lemon zest
2 tablespoons fresh lemon juice
2 tablespoons extra-virgin olive oil

FOR THE SAUCE (OPTIONAL):
2 tablespoons fresh lemon juice
2 tablespoons salted butter
½ cup heavy (whipping) cream

1. Make the chicken: Place the chicken tenders in a nonreactive baking dish just large enough to hold them in a single layer. Season the tenders generously on both sides with salt and pepper. Sprinkle the chopped tarragon and lemon zest all over the tenders, patting them onto the chicken with your fingertips. Drizzle the lemon juice and the olive oil over the tenders and pat them onto the chicken. Let the tenders marinate in the refrigerator, covered, for 10 minutes.

2. When ready to cook, drain the chicken tenders well by lifting one end with tongs and letting the marinade drip off. Discard

tip

Fresh tarragon is available in the produce section of many supermarkets. Even better, if you've got a sunny windowsill or patio, buy a tarragon plant at a nursery and snip off fresh leaves when you need them. Tarragon doesn't dry well—it loses most of its flavor. If you can't find it fresh, choose a different fresh herb, like dill or flat-leaf parsley.

if you have a...

CONTACT GRILL: Preheat the grill; if your contact grill has a temperature control, preheat the grill to high. Place the drip pan under the front of the grill. When ready to cook, lightly oil the grill surface. Place the chicken tenders on the hot grill, then close the lid. The chicken tenders will be done after cooking 3 to 5 minutes.

GRILL PAN: Place the grill pan on the stove and preheat it to medium-high over medium heat. When the grill pan is hot a drop of water will skitter in the pan. When ready to cook, lightly oil the ridges of the grill pan. Place the chicken tenders in the hot grill pan. They will be done after cooking 2 to 3 minutes per side.

BUILT-IN GRILL: Preheat the grill to high, then, if it does not have a nonstick surface, brush and oil the grill grate. Place the chicken tenders on the hot grate. They will be done after cooking 2 to 3 minutes per side.

FREESTANDING GRILL: Preheat the grill to high; there's no need to oil the grate. Place the chicken tenders on the hot grill. They will be done after cooking 3 to 4 minutes per side.

FIREPLACE GRILL: Rake red hot embers under the gridiron and preheat it for 3 to 5 minutes; you want a hot, 2 to 3 Mississippi fire. When ready to cook, brush and oil the gridiron. Place the chicken tenders on the hot grate. They will be done after cooking 2 to 3 minutes per side.

the marinade. Arrange the tenders on the grill on a diagonal to the ridges and cook, following the instructions for any of the grills in the box at left, until the chicken is cooked through. Use the poke test to check for doneness; the chicken should feel firm when pressed. You may need to cook the chicken in more than one batch; cover the grilled tenders with aluminum foil to keep warm until ready to serve.

3. Transfer the chicken tenders to a platter or plates. If making the sauce, place the lemon juice and the butter in a small saucepan or in the grill pan over medium heat. Add the cream and bring to a boil (use a wooden spoon to scrape up the brown bits from between the ridges of the grill pan). Let the sauce boil until thickened, 3 to 5 minutes. Pour the lemon cream sauce over the chicken tenders and serve at once.

chicken tenders
with basil and bacon

To call this recipe easy would be an understatement to say the least, but although it contains only three ingredients, chicken tenders, basil leaves, and bacon slices, it explodes with flavor. The recipe is only a suggestion. Among the many possible variations, you could substitute sun-dried tomatoes or slivers of Parmesan cheese for the basil leaves and use prosciutto or pancetta in place of the bacon. Or, skewer the bacon slices onto the chicken tenders using stalks of rosemary, as described in the salmon recipe on page 227. **SERVES 4**

in the salmon recipe on page 227.

THE RECIPE

1½ pounds chicken tenders
  (12 to 16 tenders)
1 bunch fresh basil, rinsed, shaken dry,
  and stemmed
12 to 16 thin slices bacon (½ to ¾ pound)

YOU'LL ALSO NEED:
Wooden toothpicks or butcher's string

1. Place 1 large or 2 small basil leaves on top of each chicken tender. Wrap each tender and basil in a slice of bacon, then secure the bacon with a toothpick or tie it in place with butcher's string (if you are cooking on a contact grill, you won't need to do this).

2. Cook the bacon-wrapped chicken tenders, following the instructions for any of the grills in the box at right, until the bacon is browned and the chicken is cooked through. Use the poke test to check for doneness; the chicken should feel firm when pressed. You may need to cook the chicken in more than one batch; cover the grilled tenders with aluminum foil to keep warm until ready to serve.

3. Transfer the chicken tenders to a platter or plates and remove and discard the toothpicks or pieces of string, if using. Serve the chicken tenders at once.

tip

When cooking these tenders on a built-in or freestanding grill, don't crowd the grill grate. That way, should the bacon fat cause a flare-up, you can simply move the tenders to another section of the grill.

if you have a...

CONTACT GRILL: Preheat the grill; if your contact grill has a temperature control, preheat the grill to high. Place the drip pan under the front of the grill. When ready to cook, lightly oil the grill surface. Place the chicken tenders on the hot grill, then close the lid. The chicken tenders will be done after cooking 3 to 5 minutes.

GRILL PAN: Place the grill pan on the stove and preheat it to medium-high over medium heat. When the grill pan is hot a drop of water will skitter in the pan. When ready to cook, lightly oil the ridges of the grill pan. Place the chicken tenders in the hot grill pan. They will be done after cooking 2 to 3 minutes per side.

BUILT-IN GRILL: Preheat the grill to high, then, if it does not have a nonstick surface, brush and oil the grill grate. Place the chicken tenders on the hot grate. They will be done after cooking 2 to 3 minutes per side.

FREESTANDING GRILL: Preheat the grill to high; there's no need to oil the grate. Place the chicken tenders on the hot grill. They will be done after cooking 3 to 4 minutes per side.

grilled chicken
with salsa criolla

Chicken isn't the first meat one thinks of at Argentinean restaurants, but when you've had your fill of the local grass-fed beef, grilled chicken topped with a gutsy tomato, bell pepper, and onion sauce is just the ticket. This recipe was inspired by a landmark Buenos Aires chophouse called La Cabaña Las Lilas. On a warm spring day, seated on its terrace overlooking a canal, there's no better spot in Buenos Aires to have lunch. **SERVES 4**

THE RECIPE

if you have a...

CONTACT GRILL: Preheat the grill; if your contact grill has a temperature control, preheat the grill to high. Place the drip pan under the front of the grill. When ready to cook, lightly oil the grill surface. Place the chicken thighs on the hot grill, then close the lid. The chicken will be done after cooking 4 to 6 minutes.

GRILL PAN: Place the grill pan on the stove and preheat it to medium-high over medium heat. When the grill pan is hot a drop of water will skitter in the pan. When ready to cook, lightly oil the ridges of the grill pan. Place the chicken thighs in the hot grill pan. They will be done after cooking 3 to 5 minutes per side.

BUILT-IN GRILL: Preheat the grill to medium-high, then, if it does not have a nonstick surface, brush and oil the grill grate. Place the chicken thighs on the hot grate. They will be done after cooking 3 to 5 minutes per side.

FREESTANDING GRILL: Preheat the grill to high; there's no need to oil the grate. Place the chicken thighs on the hot grill. They will be done after cooking 4 to 6 minutes per side.

FIREPLACE GRILL: Rake red hot embers under the gridiron and preheat it for 3 to 5 minutes; you want a hot, 2 to 3 Mississippi fire. When ready to cook, brush and oil the gridiron. Place the chicken thighs on the hot grate. They will be done after cooking 3 to 5 minutes per side.

8 chicken thighs, with skin and bones
   (about 2 pounds total)
1 tablespoon extra-virgin olive oil
Coarse salt (kosher or sea) and freshly ground
   or cracked black peppercorns
About 1 tablespoon dried oregano
Salsa Criolla (recipe follows)

1. Rinse the thighs under cold running water, then drain and blot dry with paper towels. Place a thigh on a work surface skin side down. Using a sharp paring knife, cut along the length of the thigh bone. Cut the meat away from one end of the bone, then pull or scrape the meat from the bone. Cut the meat away from the other end of the bone. Repeat with the remaining thighs. Discard the bones or set them aside for making stock or another use.

2. Lightly brush the chicken thighs all over with olive oil, then season them generously with salt, pepper, and oregano.

3. Place the seasoned chicken thighs on the grill, skin side down, and cook, following the instructions for any of the grills in the box on the facing page, until cooked through. Use the poke test to check for doneness; the chicken should feel firm when pressed.

4. Transfer the chicken thighs to a platter or plates and serve at once with the Salsa Criolla on top or on the side.

salsa criolla

Salsa criolla—Creole sauce—is one of the two obligatory condiments served whenever Argentineans grill meats. At its most basic, it consists of nothing more than diced tomato, onion, and red bell pepper. Not only is it good with

chicken, it also goes great with grilled steak or pork. So what's the other condiment? *Chimichurri* (you'll find a recipe for my version of it on page 142).

MAKES ABOUT 2 CUPS

1 luscious ripe red tomato, seeded (but not peeled) and cut into 1/4-inch dice

1 small or 1/2 large red bell pepper, seeded and cut into 1/4-inch dice

1 small or 1/2 medium-size onion, cut into 1/4-inch dice

1 tablespoon finely chopped fresh flat-leaf parsley

1/4 cup extra-virgin olive oil

2 tablespoons red wine vinegar

Coarse salt (kosher or sea) and freshly ground black pepper

Place the tomato, bell pepper, onion, parsley, olive oil, and vinegar in an attractive nonreactive serving bowl and toss to mix. Season with salt and pepper to taste. The sauce can be made several hours ahead.

tip

If you want to grill chicken breasts rather than thighs, use four breast halves that weigh between 6 and 8 ounces each and follow the cooking times on page 183.

rotisserie

thai thighs (crisp chicken thighs with honey chile sauce)

The thigh is my favorite part of the chicken for grilling. Its dark meat is rich and tasty, as meat next to the bone always is. It has ample marbling to keep the chicken moist and plenty of

tips

■ Sweet Thai chile sauces are available at Asian markets and many supermarkets. Or use Sriracha, a sweet Thai hot sauce.

■ You can also grill these thighs on any of the grills listed in the box on page 200.

skin to crisp. These facts aren't lost on Thai grill masters either; they transform chicken thighs into splendid barbecue. The seasonings here, garlic, cilantro root, salt, and pepper, are favorites in Esarn, a region in Thailand where grilling is an obsession. And chile-phobes take heart—the sauce, a thick, sweet, garlicky chile condiment, is flavorful but not the least bit fiery. Cooked in a rotisserie basket, chicken thighs couldn't be easier. **SERVES 4**

THE RECIPE

6 cloves garlic, coarsely chopped

3 tablespoons coarsely chopped cilantro roots or leaves (see Note; if using roots, rinse well), plus 4 cilantro sprigs for garnish

2 teaspoons coarse salt (kosher or sea)

1 teaspoon freshly ground white pepper

1 tablespoon vegetable oil

8 chicken thighs, with skin and bones (about 2 pounds total)

1/2 cup Thai chile sauce or Sriracha (see Tips, this page)

1/4 cup honey

3 tablespoons fresh lime juice

Lime wedges, for serving

1. Place the garlic, chopped cilantro, salt, and white pepper in a mortar and, using the pestle, pound to a paste. Stir in the oil. Or, place the garlic, cilantro, salt, and pepper in a food processor and finely chop. With the motor running, add the oil and process until a thick paste forms.

2. Trim any excess fat off the chicken thighs. Rinse the thighs under cold running water, then drain and blot dry with paper towels. Place the chicken and the garlic paste in a mixing bowl and stir to coat evenly. Let the chicken thighs marinate in the refrigerator, covered, for at least 4 hours or as long as overnight.

3. When ready to cook, place the drip pan in the bottom of the rotisserie. Place the chicken thighs in the rotisserie basket and fasten the lid. Attach the basket to the rotisserie spit, then attach the spit to the rotisserie and turn on the motor. If your rotisserie has a temperature control, set it to 400°F (for instructions for using a rotisserie, see page 14). Cook the chicken thighs until golden brown on the outside and cooked through, 30 to 40 minutes. To test for doneness, use an instant-read meat thermometer: Insert it in the thickest part of a thigh but not so that it touches a bone. The internal temperature should be about 170°F.

4. Meanwhile, make the sauce: Place the chile sauce, honey, and lime juice in a nonreactive saucepan, bring to a boil over medium-high heat, and let boil until thick and syrupy, 3 to 5 minutes. The sauce can be served warm or at room temperature.

5. Mound the chicken thighs on a platter or plates. Pour the sauce over them and garnish with the cilantro sprigs. Serve at once, with lime wedges on the side.

NOTE: Thais would flavor the marinade with cilantro roots, available at Asian and Indian markets and at farmers' markets, where bunches of cilantro are sold with the roots still on. You can approximate the flavor with cilantro leaves.

vietnamese grilled chicken sandwiches
with vietnamese slaw

Lunch hour at Lee's Sandwiches would make Grand Central Station's rush hour seem tranquil. Hyperbole? This bakery cafeteria in the heart of Little Saigon in Orange County, California, teems with hungry people in search of unbelievably tasty food for unbelievably cheap prices. Two bucks will buy you a textbook *banh mi,* a kind of Vietnamese sandwich made with a baguette that's steaming hot out of the oven. This one features sweet, garlicky chicken; cool, crunchy carrot slaw; refreshing mint leaves; and thinly sliced jalapeños for an invigorating blast of fire. At Lee's Sandwiches, bread is baked almost continuously (a light in the window goes on when the bread is in the oven). Here's how to make the sandwich on an indoor grill. **SERVES 4**

tip

The Vietnamese, and indeed, most grill jockeys outside the United States, prefer chicken thighs over breasts for grilling (they're more succulent). However, breasts are easier to work with and more widely available—you could certainly use them here. You'll need about 1¼ pounds of half-breasts. Follow the cooking times in the recipe on page 183.

T H E   R E C I P E

FOR THE CHICKEN AND MARINADE:

4 to 6 chicken thighs, with skin and bones
    (1¾ pounds; 4 to 6 thighs; see Note)

¼ cup Asian fish sauce or soy sauce

3 tablespoons fresh lime juice

3 tablespoons sugar

2 cloves garlic, minced

½ teaspoon coarse salt (kosher or sea)

½ teaspoon freshly ground black pepper

FOR THE SANDWICHES:

1 freshly baked loaf of French bread
    (about 24 inches long)

8 Boston lettuce leaves

Vietnamese Slaw (recipe follows)

1 large ripe tomato, thinly sliced

4 paper-thin slices sweet white onion

4 jalapeño peppers, or more to taste,
    sliced very thinly and sharply on
    the diagonal

16 sprigs fresh cilantro

16 fresh mint leaves

1. Prepare the chicken: Trim any excess fat off the chicken thighs but don't remove it all. Rinse the thighs under cold running water, then drain and blot dry with paper towels. Place a thigh on a work surface, skin side down. Using a sharp paring knife, cut along the thin side from one end of the thigh bone to the other. Cut the meat away from one end of the bone, then pull or scrape the meat from the bone. Cut the meat away from the other end of the bone. Remove and discard the skin. Repeat with the remaining thighs. Discard the bones or set them aside for making stock or another use.

2. Place the chicken in a nonreactive baking dish. Place the fish sauce, lime juice, sugar, garlic, salt, and pepper in a nonreactive bowl and whisk until the sugar dissolves. Pour the fish sauce mixture over the chicken and let it marinate, covered, in the refrigerator for 2 to 4 hours, turning the chicken pieces several times so they marinate evenly.

3. Cook the chicken thighs, following the instructions for any of the grills in the box at left, until cooked through. Use the poke test to check for doneness; the chicken should feel firm when pressed.

if you have a...

CONTACT GRILL: Preheat the grill; if your contact grill has a temperature control, preheat the grill to high. Place the drip pan under the front of the grill. When ready to cook, lightly oil the grill surface. Place the chicken thighs on the hot grill, then close the lid. The chicken will be done after cooking 4 to 6 minutes.

GRILL PAN: Place the grill pan on the stove and preheat it to medium-high over medium heat. When the grill pan is hot a drop of water will skitter in the pan. When ready to cook, lightly oil the ridges of the grill pan. Place the chicken thighs in the hot grill pan. They will be done after cooking 3 to 5 minutes per side.

BUILT-IN GRILL: Preheat the grill to medium-high, then, if it does not have a nonstick surface, brush and oil the grill grate. Place the chicken thighs on the hot grate. They will be done after cooking 3 to 5 minutes per side.

FREESTANDING GRILL: Preheat the grill to high; there's no need to oil the grate. Place the chicken thighs on the hot grill. They will be done after cooking 4 to 6 minutes per side.

FIREPLACE GRILL: Rake red hot embers under the gridiron and preheat it for 3 to 5 minutes; you want a hot, 2 to 3 Mississippi fire. When ready to cook, brush and oil the gridiron. Place the chicken thighs on the hot grate. They will be done after cooking 3 to 5 minutes per side.

4. To assemble the sandwiches: Just before serving, cut the bread crosswise into 4 equal pieces. Cut each piece almost in half through the side.

5. Place 2 lettuce leaves on a piece of bread. Place a chicken thigh on top and top with some of the slaw, some tomato slices, an onion slice, some jalapeño slices, and 4 cilantro sprigs and mint leaves. Repeat with the remaining ingredients.

NOTE: If you can find boneless chicken thighs, buy 1¼ pounds and remove the skin. If using preboned thighs, check for pieces of bone and remove any sinews and excess fat.

vietnamese slaw

Made from daikon and carrots, this simple slaw adds crunch and succulence to any sandwich (or for that matter, grilled chicken, meat, or seafood). Daikon is a long, thick, mild-flavored white radish. It's likely to be available in the supermarket produce section—or at an Asian market or natural foods store.

You can serve the slaw right after you've made it, but it will taste better if the ingredients have a few hours to meld together in the refrigerator. You won't use all of the slaw when making the Vietnamese Grilled Chicken Sandwiches. Serve the rest on the side or save it for another meal. **MAKES ABOUT 3 CUPS**

1 daikon (about 12 ounces), peeled
2 medium-size carrots, peeled
4 tablespoons rice vinegar
3 tablespoons sugar, or more to taste
1 teaspoon coarse salt (kosher or sea),
    or more to taste
½ teaspoon freshly ground white pepper

Using the shredding disc of a food processor, a mandoline, or working by hand, cut the daikon and carrots into matchstick slivers and place them in a nonreactive mixing bowl. Add the rice vinegar, sugar, salt, and white pepper. Toss to mix. Let the slaw cure in the refrigerator for at least 30 minutes, ideally 1 to 2 hours. Just before serving, toss the slaw well and taste for seasoning, adding more sugar and/or salt as necessary. The slaw can be refrigerated, covered, for several days.

tips

- The sandwiches will taste even better if you warm the bread in a 400°F oven for about 5 minutes.

- You could streamline this recipe and grill the marinated chicken to serve for lunch or dinner, sans bread or even slaw.

rotisserie

spit-roasted brined turkey

E very fall I embark on a quest to make the perfect Thanksgiving turkey. This has led me over the years from the oven to the grill to the smoker and even to an oversize can of beer. That last resulted in the infamous beer-can turkey, a recipe you'll find in my *Beer-Can Chicken* book. The spit-roasted bird here brings us back indoors to cook in a countertop rotisserie. The brine helps keep the bird plump, moist, and flavorful, while the gentle heat and slow rotation of the turnspit produce a bird with a burnished brown skin. Best of all, once the bird is in the rotisserie, there's nothing to do until it's time to take it out. **SERVES 8 TO 10**

THE RECIPE

1 quart hot water
1 cup coarse salt (kosher or sea)
1 cup firmly packed light brown sugar
3 quarts cold water
2 bay leaves
1 small onion, cut in half
2 whole cloves
1 tablespoon black peppercorns
1 tablespoon coriander seed
4 strips lemon zest
    (each about 1/2 by 11/2 inches)
1 turkey (8 to 10 pounds)

1. Place the hot water, salt, and brown sugar in a large stockpot and whisk until the salt and brown sugar dissolve. Whisk in the cold water. Pin a bay leaf to each

onion half with a clove and add these to the brine. Add the peppercorns, coriander seed, and lemon zest. Let the brine cool to room temperature.

2. Remove the package of giblets from the body cavity of the turkey and set aside for making stock or another use. Remove and discard the fat just inside the body and neck cavities. Rinse the turkey, inside and out, under cold running water, then drain and blot dry, inside and out, with paper towels. Place the turkey in the brine and put a pot lid or resealable plastic bag filled with water on top to keep the bird submerged. Cover the pot, place it in the refrigerator, and let the turkey brine for 24 hours.

3. When ready to cook, place the drip pan in the bottom of the rotisserie. Drain the turkey, discarding the brine. Truss the bird using one of the methods described in the box on page 177. Skewer the turkey on the rotisserie spit (see sidebar on page 175). Attach the spit to the rotisserie and turn on the motor. If your rotisserie has a temperature control, set it to 400°F (for instructions for using a rotisserie, see page 14). Cook the turkey until the skin is crisp and a deep golden brown and the meat is cooked through, 1¾ to 2½ hours. To test for doneness, use an instant-read meat thermometer: Insert it in the thickest part of a thigh but not so that it touches the spit or a bone. The internal temperature should be about 180°F.

4. Transfer the turkey to a platter or cutting board and remove the spit. Let the turkey rest for 5 to 10 minutes, then untruss it, carve, and serve.

This recipe is for a whole turkey, but you could also brine and spit roast a bone-in turkey breast (about 5 pounds) or a turkey roast (a turkey breast that has been rolled into a tight cylinder and tied with butcher's string). The cooking time for bone-in breast would be 1½ to 2 hours. For the rolled boneless breast it would be 1 to 1½ hours.

stove-top smoker

smoked turkey

Necessity, as the saying goes, is the mother of invention. I first made this turkey some fifteen years ago as the result of absent mindedness or, more specifically, forgetting to put the bird in the oven for a family Thanksgiving dinner. With only a couple of hours left before the meal, I threw the turkey in my stove-top smoker, tented it with foil, and cooked it on the stove. I reasoned that the relatively high heat and the sealed-in smoke and steam would cook a ten pound bird in about two hours. It was one of the most succulent turkeys I've ever served. The only shortcoming was the skin, which was somewhat soggy rather than crackling crisp—and that can be remedied by popping the bird in a hot oven (see box on page 139). **SERVES 10 TO 12**

tip

Because of the turkey's size, you'll need to tent the smoker with a large piece of aluminum foil, rather than covering it with its lid.

FOR THE TURKEY:
1 tablespoon coarse salt
    (kosher or sea)
1 tablespoon poultry seasoning
2 teaspoons garlic powder
2 teaspoons freshly ground black pepper
1 turkey (about 10 pounds)
Cooking oil spray (optional)
2 tablespoons (1/4 stick) salted butter
    (optional), melted

FOR THE MADEIRA GRAVY:
2 tablespoons (1/4 stick) salted butter
2 shallots, minced
2 tablespoons flour
1 to 1 1/2 cups turkey or chicken stock
    (preferably homemade)
3 tablespoons Madeira
1/4 cup heavy (whipping) cream
Coarse salt (kosher or sea) and freshly
    ground black pepper

YOU'LL ALSO NEED:
3 tablespoons hickory sawdust;
    heavy-duty aluminum foil

1. Prepare the turkey: Place the salt, poultry seasoning, garlic powder, and pepper in a small bowl and whisk to mix. Set this rub aside.

2. Remove the packet of giblets from the neck or body cavity of the turkey and set aside for making stock or another use. Remove and discard the fat just inside the body and neck cavities. Rinse the turkey, inside and out, under cold running water, then drain and blot dry, inside and out, with paper towels. Sprinkle a third of the rub inside of the body and neck cavities of the bird, then

sprinkle the remaining rub all over the outside, patting it onto the meat with your fingertips.

3. Set up the smoker (for instructions for using a stove-top smoker, see page 16). Place the sawdust in the center of the bottom of the smoker. Line the drip pan with aluminum foil and place it in the smoker. Lightly coat the smoker rack with cooking oil spray, or use a paper towel dipped in oil, and place the rack in the smoker. Truss the bird using one of the methods described in the box on page 177. Arrange the turkey, breast side up, on the rack. Tent the bird with a large sheet of heavy-duty aluminum foil, crumpling and crimping the edges over the outside rim of the smoker bottom to make a tight seal. Try not to let the foil come in contact with the turkey.

4. Place the smoker over high heat for 3 minutes, then reduce the heat to medium. Smoke the turkey until it has absorbed the maximum amount of smoke, about 40 minutes.

5. Meanwhile, preheat the oven to 350°F.

6. Uncover the turkey and discard the aluminum foil. Brush the outside of the turkey with the melted butter, if using. Place the turkey still on the smoker bottom in the oven and bake it until the skin is crisp and golden brown and the bird is cooked through, 1 1/2 to 1 3/4 hours. To test for doneness, use an instant-read meat thermometer: Insert it in the thickest part of a thigh but not so that it touches a bone. The internal temperature should be about 180°F.

7. Transfer the turkey to a platter, cover it loosely with aluminum foil, and let rest for about 10 minutes. Pour the drippings out of the drip pan into a fat separator (see sidebar on page 178) and set aside along with the drip pan; you'll use them when making the Madeira gravy.

8. Make the Madeira gravy: Melt the butter in a saucepan over medium heat. Add the shallots and cook until soft and translucent, about 3 minutes, stirring with a wooden spoon. Add the flour and cook, stirring, until it is a rich golden brown, about 2 minutes. Pour the drippings from the bottom of the fat separator into a large measuring cup, stopping when the fat starts to come out. Add enough turkey stock to obtain 2 cups. Place the drip pan over high heat, add the Madeira, and bring to a boil, scraping the edges and bottom of the pan with a wooden spoon to dislodge any burnt-on drippings.

9. Remove the saucepan from the heat and whisk in the 2 cups stock and drippings, the boiled Madeira, and the cream. Place the saucepan over medium-high heat and gradually bring the gravy to a boil, whisking steadily; it will thicken. Let the sauce simmer briskly until reduced to about 2 cups, about 5 minutes. Taste for seasoning, adding salt and pepper to taste. When serving the Duke and Duchess of Windsor, strain the sauce through a fine-meshed strainer into a sauceboat. Ordinary folks, like me, will probably prefer the gravy with the flavorful bits and pieces still in it. Carve the turkey and serve the gravy on the side.

rotisserie

rum-brined turkey breast
with island spices

At the risk of sounding like more of a curmudgeon than I am, I remember turkey breast back when it was really turkey breast, not the lifeless combination of ground turkey meat, water, and artificial flavorings that's sold as "turkey roll." It's so easy to roast a turkey breast from scratch, it's hard to understand why more people don't do it. A countertop rotisserie makes the task a snap and virtually eliminates the risk of the turkey drying out—even a lean breast. Brining is another way to ensure that the breast will be both flavorful and moist. This dish features a brine with an electrifying West Indian combination of ginger, allspice, Scotch bonnet chile, and rum. **SERVES 8**

tip

■ The turkey breast should be completely submerged during the brining process. Brine it in a tall narrow pot, placing a resealable plastic bag filled with water on top if necessary to keep the turkey submerged.

■ The Scotch bonnet is one of the world's hottest chiles. If you live on the West Coast, you can substitute habaneros or, if you want to skirt the heat issue altogether, simply omit the chile.

2 cups hot water
1¼ cups firmly packed brown sugar
¾ cup coarse salt (kosher or sea)
2½ quarts (10 cups) cold water
1 cup dark rum
3 tablespoons liquid smoke
  (see box on page 179)
3 scallions, both white and green parts,
  trimmed and cut into 2-inch pieces
2 cloves garlic, peeled and gently crushed
  with the side of a cleaver
1 piece (2 inches) fresh ginger, peeled and
  thinly sliced
1 tablespoon dried thyme
½ to 1 Scotch bonnet chile (optional),
  cut in half and seeded
1 tablespoon allspice berries
1 tablespoon black peppercorns
2 whole nutmegs
2 teaspoons whole cloves
1 bone-in turkey breast (about 5 pounds)

YOU'LL ALSO NEED:
Butcher's string

1. Place the hot water, brown sugar, and salt in a large stockpot (it should be large enough to hold the turkey breast and about 1 gallon of brine) and whisk until the salt and brown sugar dissolve. Add the cold water, rum, liquid smoke, scallions, garlic, ginger, thyme, Scotch bonnet, if using, allspice berries, peppercorns, nutmegs, and cloves and whisk to mix.

2. Rinse the turkey breast under cold running water, then place the turkey breast in the brine, making sure it is completely submerged. Let the turkey breast brine in the refrigerator, covered, for 24 hours. You can also brine the breast in a resealable plastic bag.

3. When ready to cook, place the drip pan in the bottom of the rotisserie. Drain the turkey breast, discarding the brine. Skewer the turkey breast on the rotisserie spit. Tie it in one or two places with butcher's string to give it a compact cylindrical shape. Attach the spit to the rotisserie and turn on the motor. If your rotisserie has a temperature control, set it to 400°F (for instructions for using a rotisserie, see page 14). Cook the turkey breast until it is golden brown and cooked through, 1½ to 2 hours. To test for doneness, use an instant-read meat thermometer: Insert it into the thickest part of the breast but not so that it touches the spit or a bone. The internal temperature should be about 170°F.

4. Transfer the turkey breast to a platter or cutting board, remove the spit, and let the turkey rest for 5 to 10 minutes. Cut off and discard the string. Thinly slice the turkey breast off the bones crosswise against the grain. Serve hot or cold.

rotisserie

turkey roast
with truffled cheese

As Americans have sought new sources of protein, turkey has gone from holiday bird to weeknight dinner. And now we have the turkey roast. Made from boned turkey that is rolled into a compact cylinder, it looks and cooks pretty much like a pork loin. As you might imagine, its cylindrical shape makes it ideal for spit roasting. Turkey, especially the white meat, has a tendency to dry out, so you'll need to do two things to keep it moist: Swaddle the roast with pancetta (Italian cured pork belly) or bacon. And stuff the turkey with strips of cheese, which will begin to melt as it spit roasts, basting the turkey from the inside. You can use aged Provolone or Pecorino Romano—both are firm enough to survive spit roasting without completely melting into a puddle. For turkey that's totally over-the-top, go for a truffled cheese, like *caciotta al tartufo* from Umbria or a French or American version (you'll find them at cheese shops or specialty food stores). I think you'll adore the way truffled cheese perfumes the mild-flavored turkey. **SERVES 6**

tip

Chances are turkey roasts are available at your supermarket or local butcher shop. If you want to try making a turkey roast yourself, buy a turkey breast and bone it from the inside so that it stays in one piece: Run the tip of a knife along the inside of the ribs and the sternum, separating them from the meat. Then, starting on one side, roll the turkey breast into a tight cylinder and tie it crosswise with butcher's string. Leave the skin on—it will help keep the meat moist as it cooks.

T H E   R E C I P E

5 to 6 ounces firm truffled cheese, Provolone, or Pecorino Romano
1 turkey roast (about 3 pounds)
Coarse salt (kosher or sea) and freshly ground black pepper
4 slices pancetta or bacon (4 to 6 ounces)

YOU'LL ALSO NEED:
Butcher's string

1. Cut the cheese into 6 strips that are 3 to 4 inches long and $\frac{1}{2}$ inch thick. Cut one end of each strip of cheese on the diagonal to make a sharp point. Using a long sharp slender implement, like a sharpening steel that has been wiped clean with a damp cloth or a long slender carving knife, make 6 tunnels in the roast lengthwise, each about 4 inches long. Insert a strip of cheese into each tunnel, gently pushing it in as far as it will go. Very generously season the roast on all sides with salt and pepper.

2. If using pancetta, unroll it. Arrange four 12-inch lengths of butcher's string on a work surface so that they are parallel and about an inch apart. Place a slice of pancetta on top and in the center of the strings, running perpendicular to them. Set the turkey roast on top of the pancetta so that the pancetta runs along the length of the turkey. Place a slice of pancetta lengthwise on top of the roast.

Press the remaining 2 slices of pancetta against the long sides of the roast. Tie each piece of string around the roast so that it holds the slices of pancetta against the roast and shapes it into a compact cylinder.

3. When ready to cook, place the drip pan in the bottom of the rotisserie. Attach the spit to the rotisserie and turn on the motor. If your rotisserie has a temperature control, set it to 400°F (for instructions for using a rotisserie, see page 14). Cook the roast until it is darkly browned on all sides and cooked through, about 1½ hours. To test for doneness, use an instant-read meat thermometer: Insert it into the roast but not so that it's touching the spit. The internal temperature should be about 170°F.

4. Transfer the turkey roast to a platter or cutting board, remove the spit, and let the roast rest for at least 5 minutes. Cut off and discard the string. Thinly slice the roast crosswise and serve at once topped with the pancetta.

turkey "steaks"
with cranberry kumquat relish

Thanksgiving in a grill pan—that's one way to describe these citrus and coriander rubbed, flash-grilled "steaks" cut from the meaty breast of the turkey and served with a raucously flavorful raw cranberry kumquat relish. But don't wait for Thanksgiving—the entire dish can be made from start to finish in less than a half hour. **SERVES 4**

THE RECIPE

FOR THE LEMON CORIANDER RUB:

2 strips lemon zest (each ½ by 1½ inches; remove them from lemon with a vegetable peeler), coarsely chopped

2 teaspoons coriander seed

2 teaspoons white peppercorns

2 teaspoons coarse salt (kosher or sea)

FOR THE TURKEY "STEAKS":

1½ pounds turkey "steaks" (see box on page 214)

1 to 2 tablespoons extra-virgin olive oil

Frances Raichlen's Cranberry Kumquat Relish (recipe follows)

1. Make the lemon coriander rub: Place the lemon zest, coriander seed, peppercorns, and salt in a spice mill or clean coffee grinder and grind to a fine powder.

2. Prepare the turkey "steaks": Rinse the turkey "steaks" under cold running water, then drain and blot dry with paper towels. Lightly brush each "steak" on both sides with olive oil. Sprinkle both sides with the rub, gently patting it onto the turkey with your fingertips.

3. Cook the turkey "steaks," following the instructions for any of the grills in the box at right, until cooked through. Use the poke test to check for doneness; the turkey should feel firm when pressed. If desired, rotate each turkey "steak" a quarter turn after 1½ minutes to create a handsome crosshatch of grill marks.

4. Transfer the turkey "steaks" to a platter or plates. Place a spoonful of cranberry kumquat relish in the center of each "steak" and serve the remaining relish on the side.

if you have a...

CONTACT GRILL: Preheat the grill; if your contact grill has a temperature control, preheat the grill to high. Place the drip pan under the front of the grill. When ready to cook, lightly oil the grill surface. Place the turkey "steaks" on the hot grill, then close the lid. The "steaks" will be done after cooking 3 to 4 minutes.

GRILL PAN: Place the grill pan on the stove and preheat it to medium-high over medium heat. When the grill pan is hot a drop of water will skitter in the pan. When ready to cook, lightly oil the ridges of the grill pan. Place the turkey "steaks" in the hot grill pan. They will be done after cooking 3 to 4 minutes per side.

BUILT-IN GRILL: Preheat the grill to high, then, if it does not have a nonstick surface, brush and oil the grill grate. Place the turkey "steaks" on the hot grate. They will be done after cooking 3 to 4 minutes per side.

FREESTANDING GRILL: Preheat the grill to high; there's no need to oil the grate. Place the turkey "steaks" on the hot grill. They will be done after cooking 4 to 5 minutes per side.

FIREPLACE GRILL: Rake red hot embers under the gridiron and preheat it for 3 to 5 minutes; you want a hot, 2 to 3 Mississippi fire. When ready to cook, brush and oil the gridiron. Place the turkey "steaks" on the hot grate. They will be done after cooking 3 to 4 minutes per side.

turkey "steaks"

Some butcher shops and supermarket meat departments sell turkey "steaks" and cutlets. Turkey "steaks" are cut across the grain into medallions; turkey cutlets are cut on a sharper diagonal and are slightly thinner. If you can't find turkey "steaks," it's easy to cut your own. To carve them from a bone-in breast, place it bone side down on a work surface and remove the skin. Take out the wishbone: Slide a sharp paring knife or a boning knife under each side of the wishbone, cutting the bottom tips free. Holding the wishbone near the top, twist and pull it until it comes out. Make a lengthwise cut along one side of the breastbone; then, cutting as close to the rib cage as possible, slide the knife down along the bones to release the meat. Repeat on the other side. You should wind up with two flattish cylinders of meat. Cut each breast half crosswise on a shallow diagonal to form ¼- to ½-inch-thick "steaks" or medallions. If you can buy a boneless turkey breast, all you'll need to do is cut it into "steaks."

If you want to make this with turkey cutlets instead, they'll take 1 to 2 minutes per side (1 to 2 minutes total in a contact grill) to cook through.

frances raichlen's cranberry kumquat relish

This is one of the few dishes I learned to make from my mother, who had a definite aversion to cooking. Appropriately, it requires no stove—the cranberries and kumquats are served raw in all their astringent glory. Lest fears of a mouth-puckering tartness deter you from trying the relish, I can assure you that the fruit is mellowed by the addition of brown sugar, honey, and port wine. The relish is pretty amazing with turkey or, for that matter, grilled pork or game. **MAKES ABOUT 2 CUPS**

1 package (12 ounces) fresh cranberries
6 kumquats, or 1 small orange
    (see Note)
½ cup shelled pecans or walnuts
⅓ cup firmly packed light brown sugar
½ teaspoon ground cinnamon,
    or more to taste
3 tablespoons port or dry red wine
2 tablespoons honey, or more
    to taste

Rinse, drain, and pick through the cranberries, removing the stems and discarding any berries with blemishes. Cut each kumquat into quarters and remove the seeds. Place the kumquats and pecans in a food processor and coarsely chop, running the machine in short bursts. Add the cranberries, brown sugar, and cinnamon and coarsely chop. Add the port and honey and pulse the processor just to mix. The relish should have some chew to it. Taste for seasoning, adding more honey and/or cinnamon as necessary.

NOTE: If you want to use an orange in place of the kumquats, cut it into 8 pieces and remove the seeds before adding it to the food processor.

VARIATION: For an unconventional but electrifying touch, add 1 to 2 chopped seeded jalapeño peppers when you purée the cranberries and kumquats.

rotisserie

spit-roasted duck
with star anise and soy

Duck is enjoyed the world over, but when it comes to transforming this fatty fowl into a crisp-skinned, moist, meaty miracle no one can beat Asian grill masters. The recipe here was inspired by a charming book called *Simple Laotian Cooking,* by Penn Hongthong. It's no secret that the dark rich meat of duck calls for sweet flavorings (think of French duckling *à l'orange*). But what makes this so singular is the smoky licorice sweetness of star anise. And when it comes to crisping skin, rendering fat, and keeping meat tender, spit roasting is nearly peerless. **SERVES 2 TO 4**

tips

■ This dish is extremely easy to prepare, but you do need 24 hours for the duck to marinate.

■ As the name suggests, star anise is a star-shaped spice. It's hard, reddish-brown, and about the size of a nickel. Native to southwestern China and northern Vietnam, you'll find it at Asian markets and most specialty food stores. It's a major ingredient in Chinese five-spice powder, so if you can't find star anise (or you've got five-spice powder on hand) you can use 2 teaspoons of the powder instead.

THE RECIPE

1 duck (5 to 6 pounds), thawed if frozen
¹⁄₃ cup soy sauce
3 tablespoons sugar
1 teaspoon coarse salt (kosher or sea)
1 teaspoon freshly ground white pepper
8 whole star anise
3 cloves garlic, peeled and gently crushed
   with the side of a cleaver

1. Remove the packet of giblets from the body cavity of the duck and set aside for another use (save the liver for the yakitori on page 38; the liver can be frozen). Remove and discard the fat just inside the body and neck cavities. Trim off any excess neck skin. Rinse the duck, inside and out, under cold running water, then drain and blot dry, inside and out, with paper towels. Prick the duck skin all over with a sharp fork, such as a carving fork, taking care to pierce only the skin, not the meat. Place the duck in a large resealable plastic bag.

2. Place the soy sauce, sugar, salt, and white pepper in a small bowl and whisk until the sugar and salt dissolve. Stir in the star anise and garlic. Pour this marinade over the duck in the bag and, while forcing the air out of the bag, seal it. Place the bag with the duck in a large bowl and let marinate in the refrigerator for 24 hours, turning the bird several times so that it marinates evenly.

3. When ready to cook, place the drip pan in the bottom of the rotisserie. Drain the duck well, discarding the marinade.

Prick the duck skin again with a sharp fork. Truss the bird using one of the methods described in the box on page 177. Skewer the duck on the rotisserie spit, attach the spit to the rotisserie, and turn on the motor. If your rotisserie has a temperature control, set it to 400°F (for instructions for using a rotisserie, see page 14).

4. Cook the duck until the skin is dark brown and crisp and the meat is tender, about 1¼ hours. To test for doneness, use an instant-read meat thermometer: Insert it in the thickest part of a thigh but not so that it touches the spit or a bone. The internal temperature should be between 160°F for medium and 170°F for medium-well. After about 35 minutes, stop the rotisserie and prick the duck skin once more to help release the fat. To further crisp the skin, if your rotisserie has a pause button, you can stop the spit so that the breast faces the heating element for a few minutes about 5 minutes before the duck is done.

5. Transfer the duck to a platter or cutting board, remove the spit, and let the duck rest for 5 minutes. Untruss the duck, then cut it in half or into quarters, discarding the backbone, and serve at once.

VARIATION: Duck quarters also come out crackling crisp on the outside and tender and moist on the inside when cooked in a contact grill. The trick is to score the skin to help release the fat. To prepare a 5- to 6-pound duck for the contact grill, cut it into quarters: First cut off a leg, running the blade of a chef's knife under the thigh to the joint that attaches the leg to the body. Holding the thigh, lift the leg and snap the thigh bone out of the joint. Continue cutting to the back of the duck to remove the leg. Repeat with the other leg. Place the duck breast side up and, using poultry shears, cut it in half through the breast bone. Cut through the ribs around each breast half. Discard the hind part of the carcass. Cut off and discard the outer 2 tips of each wing.

Using a very sharp knife, score the skin all over in a narrow crosshatch pattern; the cuts should be about ¼ inch apart and go through the skin but not the meat. Make the marinade as described in Step 2 on page 215 and let the duck quarters marinate in the refrigerator for at least 4 hours or long as overnight, turning them several times.

When ready to cook, drain the duck very well, discarding the marinade, and blot dry with paper towels. Lightly brush the duck quarters all over with 1 tablespoon of Asian (dark) sesame oil. Preheat the grill; if your contact grill has a temperature control, preheat the grill to medium-high. Place the drip pan under the front of the grill.

Arrange the duck quarters on the grill skin side up and close the lid. The skin will be crisp and golden brown and the meat will be cooked through in 6 to 8 minutes. If the skin starts to brown too much before the meat is cooked through, place pieces of aluminum foil between the duck skin and the top grill plate to slow the browning.

rotisserie

cesare giaccone's sweet-sour duck

You might not guess it to look at him, but Cesare Giaccone is one of Italy's most celebrated chefs. A cigarette dangles from a mouth framed by a splendid salt-and-pepper moustache. His hands are roughly callused. And, outside of the kitchen the sexagenarian sports the blue trousers and jacket of an Italian laborer. But to dine at his tiny rustic restaurant Da Cesare in the Piedmont village of Albaretto della Torre (near the white truffle capital of Alba) is to experience some of the most extraordinary cooking in Italy. Case in point, this duck: Rosemary, garlic, and shallots make it fragrant; honey and wine vinegar make it sweet-and-sour. My addition here? Spit roasting, which melts out the fat, crisping the skin in the process. **SERVES 2**

tip

Giaccone roasts duck in a time-blackened metal roasting pan in the oven, having first whacked it in half with a mighty meat cleaver. I've recrafted the recipe for the rotisserie; you could spit roast a whole duck, but the result is closer to Giaccone's if you cut the duck into quarters and cook it in the rotisserie basket.

THE RECIPE

FOR THE DUCK:
1 duck (5 to 6 pounds), thawed if frozen
Coarse salt (kosher or sea) and freshly
     ground black pepper
3 cloves garlic, finely chopped
6 large shallots, peeled, 2 thinly sliced,
     the other 4 left whole
2 tablespoons chopped fresh rosemary,
     plus 4 whole rosemary sprigs
1 tablespoon vegetable oil

FOR THE SAUCE:
1 clove garlic, peeled and gently crushed
     with the side of a cleaver
1 sprig fresh rosemary
1/3 cup honey

1/3 cup red wine vinegar
1/2 cup chicken or veal stock
3 tablespoons unsalted butter,
     cut into 1/2-inch pieces
Coarse salt (kosher or sea) and freshly
     ground black pepper

1. Prepare the duck: Remove the packet of giblets from the body cavity of the duck and set aside for another use (save the liver for the yakitori on page 38). Remove and discard the fat just inside the body and neck cavities. Trim off any excess neck skin. Rinse the duck, inside and out, under cold running water, then drain and blot dry, inside and out, with paper towels.

2. Cut the duck into quarters: First cut off a leg, running the blade of a chef's knife under the thigh to the joint that attaches the leg to the body. Holding the thigh, lift the leg and snap the thigh bone out of the joint. Continue cutting to the back of the duck to remove the leg. Repeat with the other leg. Place the duck breast side up and, using poultry shears, cut it in half through the breast bone. Cut through the ribs around each breast half. Discard the hind part of the carcass. Cut off and discard the outer 2 tips of each wing.

3. Lightly score the duck skin, particularly the portion covering the breast: Using a very sharp knife, make cuts in a crosshatch pattern about ¼ inch apart. The idea is to cut through the skin but not the meat. This will help the fat cook out.

4. Place the duck in a baking dish and season it generously on all sides with salt and pepper. Sprinkle the chopped garlic, sliced shallots, and chopped rosemary all over the duck quarters. Drizzle the oil all over the duck, patting it and the garlic, shallots, and rosemary onto the meat with your fingers. Let the duck marinate, covered, in the refrigerator, for 1 to 4 hours.

5. When ready to cook, place the drip pan in the bottom of the rotisserie. Arrange the duck quarters in the rotisserie basket: Place 2 duck quarters skin side down and with the thicker part of each quarter facing the outside of the basket. Place 2 whole shallots between the duck quarters, then place 2 rosemary sprigs on top of each duck quarter. Place the remaining 2 duck quarters on top, skin side up and with the thicker part of each quarter facing the outside of the basket. Place the remaining 2 whole shallots between the top 2 duck quarters. Close the basket tightly.

6. Attach the basket to the rotisserie spit, then attach the spit to the rotisserie and turn on the motor. If your rotisserie has a temperature control, set it to 400°F (for instructions for using a rotisserie, see page 14). Cook the duck until the skin is browned and crisp and the meat is cooked through and tender, 1 to 1¼ hours for well-done duck with crisp skin (if you prefer your duck medium, it will take about 45 minutes). To test for doneness, use an instant-read meat thermometer: Insert it in the thickest part of a thigh but not so that it touches the spit or a bone. The internal temperature should be about 160°F for medium or about 180°F for well-done.

7. Meanwhile, after the duck has cooked for about 30 minutes, make the sauce: Place the crushed garlic clove, rosemary sprig, honey, wine vinegar, and chicken stock in a large, heavy nonreactive saucepan and bring to a boil over high heat. Let boil until reduced by half, 6 to 10 minutes. With the sauce still boiling, whisk in the pieces of butter, then let the sauce boil until thick and syrupy, about 2 minutes longer. Remove and discard the garlic clove and rosemary sprig. Season the sauce with salt and pepper to taste. Keep the sauce warm but not over direct heat until ready to serve. Don't worry if it separates; bring it to a boil just before you are ready to serve and it will come back together.

8. Transfer the duck quarters to a platter or plates, spoon the sauce over them, and serve at once.

game hens tabaka-grilled under a press

I first ate *tabaka,* game hen prepared in the style of the Republic of Georgia, in 1976 at a restaurant in Boston called the Hermitage. I've been hooked on it ever since. The hens were pan fried in clarified butter, and what made them so crisp was the fact that they were cooked under a metal weight (the process is not unlike Tuscan *pollo al mattone*—chicken grilled under a brick; see page 190). Did someone say metal weight? Sounds a lot to me like the configuration of a contact grill, which has a heavy hinged lid and a heating element on the top as well as well as on the bottom. A contact grill gives you the cool pressed look and crisp crust of pan frying a bird under a weight, without all of the fat. And since you're grilling in a controlled environment, there aren't the flare-ups normally associated with live fire. Sounds like a win-win situation to me, especially when you marinate the games hens in a fragrant mixture of citrus juice, cinnamon, and shallots. You

tips

■ Spatchcocking the game hens involves nothing more than removing the birds' backbones and breast bones and opening them flat like a book. Detailed instructions are provided in the recipe. If this seems too daunting, you can substitute a 6- to 8-ounce skinless, boneless chicken breast for each game hen (you'll find cooking times for chicken breasts in the recipe on page 191).

■ For an attractive presentation, spoon the sauce into the well of two serving plates and place the game hens on top.

can also get great results using just about any other indoor grill—you'll just need to place a weight on top of the game hens. **SERVES 2**

THE RECIPE

2 game hens (each about 1 pound)
2 teaspoons coarse salt (kosher or sea)
2 teaspoons freshly ground black pepper

2 teaspoons ground coriander
1 teaspoon ground cumin
1 teaspoon ground cinnamon
1/2 teaspoon hot red pepper flakes
1/2 cup fresh orange juice
1/2 cup dry white wine
2 tablespoons fresh lemon juice
2 tablespoons extra-virgin olive oil
3 tablespoons chopped fresh cilantro
2 shallots, thinly sliced
2 cloves garlic, thinly sliced
4 strips orange zest (each 1/2 by 11/2 inches; remove them with a vegetable peeler)
Fresh dill sprigs or cilantro sprigs, for garnish
Sour Plum Sauce (recipe follows)

if you have a...

CONTACT GRILL: Preheat the grill; if your contact grill has a temperature control, preheat the grill (see Tips on facing page). Place the drip pan under the front of the grill. When ready to cook, lightly oil the grill surface. Place the game hens on the hot grill skin side up, then close the lid. The hens will be done after cooking 8 to 12 minutes. If the skin side starts to brown too much before the hens are cooked through, slide a piece of aluminum foil between them and the grill surface.

GRILL PAN: Place the grill pan on the stove and preheat it to medium over medium heat. When the grill pan is hot a drop of water will skitter in the pan. When ready to cook, lightly oil the ridges of the grill pan. Place the game hens in the hot grill pan, then put a grill press (see box on page 303), a couple of aluminum foil–wrapped bricks, or a heavy cast-iron skillet on top of them. The hens will be done after cooking 5 to 8 minutes per side.

BUILT-IN GRILL: Preheat the grill to medium, then, if it does not have a nonstick surface, brush and oil the grill grate. Place the game hens on the hot grate, then put a grill press (see box on page 303), a couple of aluminum foil–wrapped bricks, or a heavy cast-iron skillet on top of them. The hens will be done after cooking 5 to 8 minutes per side.

FREESTANDING GRILL: Preheat the grill to high; there's no need to oil the grate. Place the game hens on the hot grill, then put a grill press (see box on page 303), a couple of aluminum foil–wrapped bricks, or a heavy cast-iron skillet on top of them. The hens will be done after cooking 6 to 9 minutes per side.

FIREPLACE GRILL: Rake slightly ashed-over (not red hot) embers under the gridiron and preheat it for 3 to 5 minutes; you want a medium, 5 to 6 Mississippi fire. When ready to cook, brush and oil the gridiron. Place the game hens on the hot grate, then put a grill press (see box on page 303), a couple of aluminum foil–wrapped bricks, or a heavy cast-iron skillet on top of them. The hens will be done after cooking 5 to 8 minutes per side.

1. Remove the packet of giblets (if any) from the body cavities of the game hens and set aside for making stock or another use. Remove and discard the fat just inside the body and neck cavities. Rinse the hens, inside and out, under cold running water, then drain and blot dry, inside and out, with paper towels.

2. Spatchcock the game hens: Place a hen breast side down on a work surface. Using poultry shears and starting at the neck end, cut out the backbone by making a lengthwise cut on either side of the bone. Remove and discard the backbone or set it aside for making stock or another use. Open the game hen like a book, skin side down. Using a paring knife, cut underneath each side of the breastbone. Run your thumbs firmly along both sides of the breastbone and white cartilage, then pull these out. Cut off the wing tips and trim off any loose skin. If you are feeling ambitious, turn the bird over (skin side up) and lay it out flat. Make a 1-inch slit in the rear portion of each side of the hen. Reach under the bird and pull the end of each drumstick through the nearest slit to secure it. Spatchcock the remaining game hen the same way.

3. Place the salt, pepper, coriander, cumin, cinnamon, and hot pepper flakes in a small mixing bowl and whisk to mix. Sprinkle this rub all over the spatch-cocked game hens on both sides, dividing it evenly between them and rubbing it onto the meat with your fingertips.

4. Place the orange juice, wine, lemon juice, and olive oil in a nonreactive bowl and whisk to mix.

5. Arrange half of the cilantro, shallots, garlic, and orange zest in the bottom of a nonreactive baking dish just large enough to hold the opened-out hens side by side. Place the hens on top and sprinkle the remaining cilantro, shallots, garlic, and orange zest over them. Pour the orange juice mixture over the game hens. Let the hens marinate in the refrigerator, covered, for at least 2 hours or as long as overnight, turning them several times so they marinate evenly.

6. When ready to cook, lift the hens up with tongs and let the marinade drain off them; discard the marinade. Cook the game hens, following the instructions for any of the grills in the box on the facing page, until they are golden brown and cooked through. You may have to cook the hens in 2 batches. To test for doneness,

use an instant-read meat thermometer: Insert it into the thickest part of a thigh but not so that it touches a bone. The internal temperature should be about 180°F.

7. Transfer the game hens to a platter or plates. Let the hens rest for 2 minutes, then garnish them with dill sprigs and serve with the Sour Plum Sauce on the side.

sour plum sauce

At least two of the world's great grill cultures, Japan and the Republic of Georgia, prize the fruity acidity of underripe plums in condiments for barbecue. The Republic of Georgia is the birthplace of this sauce, which goes by the name *tkemali*. Sour plum sauce is the traditional accompaniment to *tabaka*, game hen cooked under a weight, but it's also good brushed on or served with spit-roasted chicken and grilled fish.

MAKES ABOUT 1 CUP

1/2 pound sour plums, rinsed, stemmed, cut in half, and pitted
1 tablespoon fresh lemon juice, or more to taste
1 tablespoon extra-virgin olive oil
1 large clove garlic, minced
1 teaspoon ground coriander
2 tablespoons finely chopped fresh cilantro
2 tablespoons finely chopped fresh dill, or 2 teaspoons dried dill
1/2 teaspoon coarse salt (kosher or sea), or more to taste
1/4 teaspoon freshly ground black pepper, or more to taste
1/2 teaspoon hot red pepper flakes
1 teaspoon sugar or honey (optional)

tips

■ If making the chicken in a Foreman grill, preheat it to high. If making it in a VilaWare *panini* machine, heat it to medium-high.

■ The traditional plum for *tkemali* is the sour wild fruit called *alycha*. You can use any tart plums, from slightly underripe purple ones to greengages. If your local supermarket is anything like mine, it's probably easier to buy sour plums than sweet ripe ones.

1. Place the plums, lemon juice, olive oil, garlic, coriander, cilantro, dill, salt, black pepper, and hot pepper flakes in a nonreactive saucepan. Add ½ cup of water and bring to a gentle simmer, covered, over medium heat. Cook the sauce until the plums are so tender they fall apart, 5 to 8 minutes.

2. Transfer the sauce to a food processor and purée until smooth. Taste for seasoning, adding more lemon juice, salt, and/or black pepper as necessary; the sauce should be tart and flavorful. If it's too tart, add up to 1 teaspoon of sugar, but just a pinch; the sauce should be quite acidic. *Tkemali* is traditionally served at room temperature. Refrigerated, covered, any leftover sauce will keep for at least 4 days.

tip

As in Game Hens Tabaka-Grilled Under a Press (page 219), the birds are spatchcocked (partially boned and spread open like a book). If this seems overly complicated (it's really quite easy), you can substitute a 6- to 8-ounce skinless, boneless chicken breast for each game hen (you'll find cooking times for chicken breasts in the recipe on page 191).

piri-piri game hens

Here's another bird cooked under a weight, this one from southern Africa. The recipe comes from Zimbabwe, but piri-piri is enjoyed throughout South Africa, Angola, and Mozambique. The dish takes its name from a tiny, fiery chile brought to Africa from Brazil by Portuguese explorers in the sixteenth century. Thus the essence of piri-piri chicken is heat. In the interest of wide acceptance, I've toned it down a bit and called for relatively mild jalapeño peppers, but you can certainly up the ante by using cayenne or Thai chiles—or even Scotch bonnets. **SERVES 2**

THE RECIPE

2 to 4 jalapeño peppers (or as many as you can stand), seeded and coarsely chopped

2 cloves garlic, coarsely chopped

1 piece (1 inch) fresh ginger, peeled and coarsely chopped

1 tablespoon sweet paprika

1½ teaspoons coarse salt (kosher or sea)

½ teaspoon cayenne pepper, or more to taste

½ cup fresh lemon juice (from 2 to 3 lemons)

¼ cup vegetable oil

2 games hens (each about 1 pound)

Lemon wedges, for serving

1. Place the jalapeños, garlic, ginger, paprika, salt, cayenne, lemon juice, and oil in a blender and purée to a smooth paste. If using a food processor, purée the jalapeños, garlic, ginger, paprika, salt, and cayenne first, then, with the motor running, add the lemon juice and oil.

2. Remove the packet of giblets (if any) from the body cavities of the game hens and set aside for making stock or another use. Remove and discard the fat just inside the body and neck cavities. Rinse the hens, inside and out, under cold running water, then drain and blot dry, inside and out, with paper towels.

3. Spatchcock the game hens: Place a hen breast side down on a work surface. Using poultry shears and starting at the neck end, cut out the backbone by making a lengthwise cut on either side of the bone. Remove and discard the backbone or set it aside for making stock or another use. Open the game hen like a book, skin side down. Using a paring knife, cut underneath each side of the breastbone. Run your thumbs firmly along both sides of the breastbone and white cartilage, then pull these out. Cut off the wing tips and trim off any loose skin. If you are feeling ambitious, turn the bird over (skin side up) and lay it out flat. Make a 1-inch slit in the rear portion of each side of the hen. Reach under the bird and pull the end of each drumstick through the nearest slit to secure it. Spatchcock the remaining game hen the same way.

4. Place the spatchcocked game hens in a nonreactive baking dish just large enough to hold them opened out side by side. Pour the jalapeño mixture over the hens, turning them several times to coat with the marinade. Let the game hens marinate in the refrigerator, covered, for at least 4 hours or as long as overnight, tuning them several times so that they marinate evenly.

5. When ready to cook, lift the hens up with tongs and let the marinade drain off them; discard the marinade. Cook the

if you have a...

CONTACT GRILL: Preheat the grill; if your contact grill has a temperature control, preheat the grill (see Tips on page 221). Place the drip pan under the front of the grill. When ready to cook, lightly oil the grill surface. Place the game hens on the hot grill skin side up, then close the lid. The hens will be done after cooking 8 to 12 minutes. If the skin side starts to brown too much before the hens are cooked through, slide a piece of aluminum foil between them and the grill surface.

GRILL PAN: Place the grill pan on the stove and preheat it to medium over medium heat. When the grill pan is hot a drop of water will skitter in the pan. When ready to cook, lightly oil the ridges of the grill pan. Place the game hens in the hot grill pan, then put a grill press (see box on page 303), a couple of aluminum foil–wrapped bricks, or a cast-iron skillet on top of them. The hens will be done after cooking 5 to 8 minutes per side.

BUILT-IN GRILL: Preheat the grill to high, then, if it does not have a nonstick surface, brush and oil the grill grate. Place the game hens on the hot grate, then put a grill press (see box on page 303), a couple of aluminum foil–wrapped bricks, or a heavy cast-iron skillet on top of them. The hens will be done after cooking 5 to 8 minutes per side.

FREESTANDING GRILL: Preheat the grill to high; there's no need to oil the grate. Place the game hens on the hot grill, then put a grill press (see box on page 303), a couple of aluminum foil–wrapped bricks, or a heavy cast-iron skillet on top of them. The hens will be done after cooking 6 to 9 minutes per side.

FIREPLACE GRILL: Rake slightly ashed-over (not red hot) embers under the gridiron and preheat it for 3 to 5 minutes; you want a medium, 5 to 6 Mississippi fire. When ready to cook, brush and oil the gridiron. Place the game hens on the hot grate, then put a grill press (see box on page 303), a couple of aluminum foil–wrapped bricks, or a cast-iron skillet on top of them. The hens will be done after cooking 5 to 8 minutes per side.

tip

While most jalapeño peppers are green, you can also find red ones. These will make the marinade for Piri-Piri-Game Hens look more authentic.

game hens, following the instructions for any of the grills in the box on the previous page, until they are golden brown and cooked through. You may have to cook the hens in 2 batches. To test for doneness, use an instant-read meat thermometer: Insert it into the thickest part of a thigh but not so that it touches a bone. The internal temperature should be about 180°F.

6. Transfer the game hens to a platter or plates. Let the hens rest for 2 minutes, then serve them with lemon wedges.

For people intimidated by cooking fish on an outdoor grill, the contact grill and the grill pan make grilling virtually foolproof. Even if you're an experienced fish griller, this chapter will help you expand your repertory with salmon grilled on rosemary branches, shad roe cooked on a George Foreman grill, and a spectacular tuna loin roasted in a countertop rotisserie. With a stove-top smoker you can enjoy home-smoked salmon with bagels, barbecued shrimp, and for something offbeat, scallops with a poppy seed crust.

seafood

grilled salmon
with a mustard
and brown sugar crust

Here's a recipe that's so simple and easy to make, it's almost embarrassing. It contains only five ingredients, including the fish itself, salt, and pepper, yet it elevates what has become an extremely commonplace fish to an uncommon pleasure. Like most oily fish, salmon is enhanced by acidic sharpness and a touch of sweetness. Here acidic mustard cuts the oiliness of the salmon, while brown sugar reinforces its richness. If you like, you can add a mustard and dill sauce that's a cinch to put together.

SERVES 4

THE RECIPE

4 pieces salmon fillet (each about 6 ounces;
    see box on page 231 and Notes)
Coarse salt (kosher or sea) and freshly ground
    black pepper

1 cup firmly packed dark brown sugar
3 tablespoons Dijon mustard (see Notes)
Sweet Mustard and Dill Sauce
    (optional; recipe follows)

if you have a...

CONTACT GRILL: Preheat the grill; if your contact grill has a temperature control, preheat the grill to high. Place the drip pan under the front of the grill. When ready to cook, lightly oil the grill surface. Arrange the salmon on the hot grill at a diagonal to the ridges, then close the lid. The salmon will be done after cooking 3 to 5 minutes.

FIREPLACE GRILL: Rake red hot embers under the gridiron and preheat it for 3 to 5 minutes; you want a hot, 2 to 3 Mississippi fire. When ready to cook, brush and oil the gridiron. Place the salmon on the hot grate. It will be done after cooking 3 to 5 minutes per side.

1. Run your fingers over the salmon fillets, feeling for bones. Using needle-nose pliers or tweezers, pull out any you find. Rinse the fish under cold running water, then blot it dry with paper towels. Very generously season the salmon on both sides with salt and pepper.

2. Spread the brown sugar out in a large shallow bowl, crumbling it between your fingers or with a fork. Brush or spread each salmon fillet on both sides with the mustard. Dredge both sides of each fillet in the brown sugar, patting it onto the fish with your fingertips. Gently shake off any excess brown sugar; the fish should be fairly thickly crusted.

3. Cook the salmon, following the instructions for any of the grills in the box on the facing page, until the outside is darkly browned and the fish is cooked through. To test for doneness, press the fish with your finger; it should break into clean flakes.

4. Transfer the salmon to a platter or plates and serve at once.

NOTES:

■ I like crisp salmon skin, so I buy fillets with skin, but you can certainly use skinless salmon also. Other oily fish, like arctic char or bluefish, would also be great prepared this way.

■ While I like the sharp flavor of a Dijon or Meaux (grainy) mustard, you can also use a sweet honey mustard or a hot mustard from Düsseldorf.

sweet mustard and dill sauce

This sweet spicy mustard sauce takes its inspiration from Scandinavia, where mustard and dill are popular seasonings for salmon. It goes great with the sweet mustard-crusted salmon. The recipe may give you more sauce than you need. It makes a great dip for grilled vegetables. **MAKES ABOUT 1 CUP**

$1/3$ cup mayonnaise (preferably Hellmann's)
$1/3$ cup sour cream
$1/3$ cup Dijon or Meaux mustard
2 tablespoons chopped fresh dill
1 tablespoon brown sugar
(dark or light), or more to taste
Freshly ground black pepper

Place the mayonnaise, sour cream, mustard, dill, and brown sugar in a small nonreactive bowl and whisk to mix. Taste for seasoning, adding more brown sugar and pepper to taste. The sauce can be refrigerated, covered, for several days.

tip

The hardest thing about this recipe is cleaning a contact grill. Do this while it's hot, using paper towels. Or, if you want to wait until after dinner to clean the grill, reheat it first.

rosemary salmon

This is one of the most novel ways I know to prepare salmon and it fairly explodes with flavor, thanks to the insertion of a whole sprig of rosemary into the very heart of the fillet. In addition to the obvious flavor dividend, it looks cool and the preparation time is less than ten minutes. It's a technique you can apply to a great many grilled foods, from chicken to shrimp to lamb. **SERVES 4**

THE RECIPE

4 rosemary branches (see Note)
4 pieces skinless salmon fillet
(each about 2 inches wide, 3 to 4 inches
long, ¾ to 1 inch thick, and 6 ounces;
see box on page 231)
2 tablespoons extra-virgin olive oil
Coarse salt (kosher or sea) and freshly
ground black pepper

2 cloves garlic, minced
1 teaspoon finely grated lemon zest
Lemon wedges, for serving

1. Strip the leaves off the bottom 4 inches of each rosemary branch (pull them off between your thumb and forefinger) and very finely chop the leaves; you'll use the chopped rosemary to season the salmon.

2. Run your fingers over the salmon fillets, feeling for bones. Using needle-nose pliers or tweezers, pull out any you find. Rinse the fish under cold running water, then blot it dry with paper towels. Skewer each salmon fillet on the bare part of a rosemary branch through the center of a short side (the idea is to create a sort of kebab). Place the fish on a large plate and brush on both sides with the olive oil. Generously season the fish on both sides with salt and pepper.

3. Place the chopped rosemary and the garlic and lemon zest in a small bowl and stir to mix. Sprinkle the rosemary mixture over the salmon on all sides, patting it onto the fish with your fingertips. Let the fish stand at room temperature while you preheat the grill.

if you have a...

CONTACT GRILL: Preheat the grill; if your contact grill has a temperature control, preheat the grill to high. Place the drip pan under the front of the grill. When ready to cook, lightly oil the grill surface. Arrange the salmon on the hot grill at a diagonal to the ridges, then close the lid. It will be done after cooking 3 to 5 minutes.

GRILL PAN: Place the grill pan on the stove and preheat it to medium-high over medium heat. When the grill pan is hot a drop of water will skitter in the pan. When ready to cook, lightly oil the ridges of the grill pan. Arrange the salmon in the hot grill pan at a diagonal to the ridges. The salmon will be done after cooking 3 to 5 minutes per side.

BUILT-IN GRILL: Preheat the grill to high, then, if it does not have a nonstick surface, brush and oil the grill grate. Arrange the salmon on the hot grill so that the exposed ends of the rosemary extend off the grate. The salmon will be done after cooking 3 to 5 minutes per side.

FREESTANDING GRILL: Preheat the grill to high; there's no need to oil the grate. Place the salmon on the hot grill. It will be done after cooking 4 to 6 minutes per side.

FIREPLACE GRILL: Rake red hot embers under the gridiron and preheat it for 3 to 5 minutes; you want a hot, 2 to 3 Mississippi fire. When ready to cook, brush and oil the gridiron. Arrange the salmon on the hot grate at a diagonal to the bars. It will be done after cooking 3 to 5 minutes per side.

Rosemary

4. Cook the salmon, following the instructions for any of the grills in the box on the facing page, until it is just cooked through. To test for doneness, press the fish with your finger; it should break into clean flakes.

5. Transfer the salmon to a platter or plates and serve it with lemon wedges on the side. (Note: You're not meant to eat the rosemary.)

NOTE: Choose a bunch of rosemary with relatively stiff stems. Cut the end of each stem sharply on the diagonal to make a sharp point so it's easy to insert in the salmon. If the stalks aren't stiff enough to pierce the fish, make a starter hole with a bamboo skewer.

tip

The easiest way to grate lemon zest is on a Microplane. They're available at cookware shops.

moroccan salmon

Around my house we have a saying: If something tastes good sautéed, baked, or fried, it will probably taste even better grilled. Consider Moroccan fried fish with *charmoula,* a tangy cilantro cumin sauce. Traditionally, small whole fish like sardines are pan-fried or deep-fried. A contact grill gives you a similar crisp exterior and only a fraction of the fat and mess. You'll also get good results in a grill pan or on a built-in or fireplace grill. I've substituted the more popular and readily available salmon fillets for the whole fish (on page 230 you'll find a Variation using whole sardines). The *charmoula* here does double duty as a marinade and a sauce. **SERVES 4**

T H E   R E C I P E

1/2 cup fresh cilantro leaves

1/2 cup fresh flat-leaf parsley leaves

2 cloves garlic, coarsely chopped

1 teaspoon sweet paprika

1/2 teaspoon coarse salt (kosher or sea),
     or more to taste

1/2 teaspoon freshly ground black pepper

1/2 teaspoon ground coriander

1/2 teaspoon ground cumin

1/2 teaspoon hot red pepper flakes,
     or more to taste

3 tablespoons fresh lemon juice, or more to taste

1/2 cup extra-virgin olive oil

4 pieces salmon fillet or salmon steaks
     (each 6 to 8 ounces; see box on page 231
     and Note)

if you have a...

CONTACT GRILL: Preheat the grill; if your contact grill has a temperature control, preheat the grill to high. Place the drip pan under the front of the grill. When ready to cook, lightly oil the grill surface. Place the salmon on the hot grill, then close the lid. The salmon will be done after cooking 3 to 5 minutes.

GRILL PAN: Place the grill pan on the stove and preheat it to medium-high over medium heat. When the grill pan is hot a drop of water will skitter in the pan. When ready to cook, lightly oil the ridges of the grill pan. Place the salmon in the hot grill pan. It will be done after cooking 3 to 5 minutes per side.

BUILT-IN GRILL: Preheat the grill to high, then, if it does not have a nonstick surface, brush and oil the grill grate. Place the salmon on the hot grate. It will be done after cooking 3 to 5 minutes per side.

FIREPLACE GRILL: Rake red hot embers under the gridiron and preheat it for 3 to 5 minutes; you want a hot, 2 to 3 Mississippi fire. When ready to cook, brush and oil the gridiron. Place the salmon on the hot grate. It will be done after cooking 3 to 5 minutes per side.

1. Place the cilantro, parsley, garlic, paprika, salt, black pepper, coriander, cumin, and hot pepper flakes in a food processor and pulse the machine to finely chop. Add the lemon juice and process until a coarse purée forms. With the motor running, add the olive oil in a thin stream. Taste for seasoning, adding more salt, hot pepper flakes, and/or lemon juice as necessary; the *charmoula* should be highly seasoned.

2. If using salmon fillets, run your fingers over them, feeling for bones. Using needle-nose pliers or tweezers, pull out any you find (you will not need to do this with salmon steaks). Rinse the fish under cold running water, then blot it dry with paper towels. Pour a third of the *charmoula* over the bottom of a nonreactive baking dish just large enough to hold the salmon in one layer. Arrange the salmon pieces on top. Spoon half of the remaining *charmoula* over the fish, then set the rest of the *charmoula* aside. Let the salmon marinate in the refrigerator, covered, for 2 to 4 hours (the longer it marinates, the richer the flavor will be).

3. When ready to cook, drain the salmon and discard the marinade. Cook the salmon, following the instructions for any of the grills in the box at left, until it is browned and cooked through. To test for doneness, press the fish with your finger; it should break into clean flakes.

4. Arrange the salmon on a platter or plates. Stir the remaining *charmoula* to recombine, then spoon it on top of the salmon.

NOTE: I like to leave the skin on salmon fillets; it becomes crisp as it grills. But if you don't care for fish skin, skinless is fine.

VARIATION: You could certainly grill sardines in this manner. Whole gutted sardines will be done after 3 to 5 minutes on a contact grill or 2 to 3 minutes per side on a grill pan, built-in grill, or fireplace grill.

rotisserie

lemon basil salmon "roast"

Think about the attributes that make poultry and meat perfect for spit roasting: a compact cylindrical shape to ensure even cooking and enough fat to cook to a crackling crust and baste the meat as it roasts. A whole chicken or duck fits the bill; ditto rib roasts and boneless pork loins. What may not come to mind immediately is fish, particularly salmon. Yet a salmon "roast," made by tying fillet skin side out, is ideal for spit roasting—it's easy to stuff; the skin becomes wafer crisp; the fish stays moist; and the finished "roast" makes an impressive centerpiece. This recipe is really "about" the salmon, so I've kept the flavoring pretty simple: sliced lemon, fresh basil leaves, salt, and pepper. The recipe looks way more complicated than it really is. You're talking about maybe ten minutes of preparation time. **SERVES 6 TO 8**

wild vs. farmed

It's said that in Colonial New England, salmon was so abundant employment contracts limited how many times each week the cheap fish could be served to indentured servants. The ensuing centuries have brought dwindling supplies and skyrocketing prices. So, when the first large-scale salmon farms began appearing in Maine, the Pacific Northwest, Chile, Scandinavia, and the British Isles by the 1990s, the aquacultured fish seemed like a terrific idea.

Now fish lovers are questioning the quality of farm-raised salmon and whether the bargain is really worth the price. There are three areas of concern: cleanliness, texture, and taste. Consumers are right to be apprehensive about eating salmon from huge farms where the fish are fed chemical-laden food and swim in poorly flushed pens. The salmon are often in such close proximity to each other that the fish must be fed antibiotics to keep them healthy. This has led some wild salmon enthusiasts to call the farmed variety the "chicken of the sea." The color of the fish is controlled as much by pigment in the food they eat as by any other ingredients in their diet. The confined quarters and lack of exercise produce fish with a flabby texture and bland taste.

On the other hand, farmed salmon is abundant and inexpensive. My local supermarket often sells it for $5 or $6 a pound. Wild salmon has a superior flavor and texture, but it's a lot more expensive—as much as $12 or $14 a pound. Depending on the salmon's state of origin (most of it comes from Alaska and the Pacific Northwest), the season is limited.

Even if price and seasonable availability are no object, one is faced with a moral dilemma. Greater demand for wild salmon will inevitably lead to overfishing and dwindling supplies. I personally use wild salmon when I can get it and organic farmed salmon when I can't. One good source for wild salmon is Legal Sea Foods (see Mail-Order Sources on page 396).

tip

You can also spit roast a piece cut crosswise from a whole salmon (picture a very thick salmon steak). Although it will contain bones, it's less work to prepare than assembling a salmon "roast."

Start with a center-cut piece of salmon that's 8 inches long and about 3 pounds. Season the fish with salt and pepper, then place the lemon slices and basil leaves in the hollow that runs down the center. Tuck one long edge of the salmon inside the other and tie the fish in a tight cylinder with butcher's string. Skewer the salmon lengthwise on the spit. The cooking time will be the same as that of the salmon "roast." When you test for doneness, be careful not to touch the spit or a bone with the instant-read meat thermometer.

Carve the salmon crosswise and warn everyone to look out for the bones.

THE RECIPE

1 large piece boneless salmon fillet with skin (about 8 inches long, 7 to 8 inches wide, and 3 pounds; see box on page 231)

2 medium-size lemons

Coarse salt (kosher or sea) and freshly ground black pepper

12 whole basil leaves, rinsed and blotted dry

Lemon Basil Mustard Sauce (recipe follows)

YOU'LL ALSO NEED:
Butcher's string

1. Run your fingers over the salmon fillet, feeling for bones. Using needle-nose pliers or tweezers, pull out any you find. Rinse the fish under cold running water, then blot it dry with paper towels.

2. Cut the rind completely off one lemon and thinly slice the fruit crosswise. Using a fork, remove any seeds. Cut the other lemon into 6 wedges for serving and set aside.

3. Cut the salmon fillet in half lengthwise to create 2 pieces that are about 8 inches long and 3½ to 4 inches wide. Cut four 18-inch pieces of butcher's string. Arrange them on a work surface so that they are parallel and about 2 inches apart. Place 1 piece of salmon skin side down across the strings so that it is perpendicular to and in the center of them. Generously season the meat side of that piece of salmon with salt and pepper. Arrange the lemon slices on the fillet and top with the basil leaves.

4. Generously season the meat side of the remaining piece of salmon fillet with salt and pepper. Place this piece skin side up on top of the first, positioning the thicker end of the top fillet over the thinner end of the bottom piece so the overall thickness of the fish is even. Tie each of the 4 pieces of string together tightly.

5. Cut 2 pieces of string that are about 28 inches long. Loop each piece around the fillets lengthwise and tie them together tightly. Generously season the outside of the fillets with salt and pepper.

6. Place the drip pan in the bottom of the rotisserie. Skewer the salmon "roast" lengthwise on the rotisserie spit. (If the rotisserie has a 2-prong spit, you may need to insert one spit in the top layer and the other in the bottom layer of the "roast.") Attach the spit to the rotisserie and turn on the motor. If your rotisserie has a temperature control, set it to 400°F (for instructions for using a rotisserie, see page 14). Cook the salmon until it is sizzling, crusty, and dark golden brown on the outside and cooked through, 45 to 55 minutes. To test for doneness, insert an instant-read meat thermometer into the center of a fillet but not so that it touches the spit. The internal temperature should be about 130°F.

7. Transfer the "roast" to a platter and remove the spit. Cut off and discard the strings. Cut the "roast" crosswise into 6 even portions and serve with the Lemon Basil Mustard Sauce and the lemon wedges.

lemon basil mustard sauce

Lemon zest and fresh lemon juice give this mustard sauce a bright, clean finish. The sauce would be delectable with just about any sort of grilled fish, shellfish, chicken, or vegetables. **MAKES ABOUT 1½ CUPS**

6 large fresh basil leaves, rinsed and
   blotted dry
1 cup mayonnaise (preferably Hellmann's)
¼ cup sour cream
1½ teaspoons finely grated lemon zest
1 tablespoon fresh lemon juice
2 tablespoons Dijon mustard
1 tablespoon dry mustard, such as Coleman's

1. Roll the basil leaves crosswise into a compact roll, then cut them crosswise into the thinnest possible slices and fluff these with your fingers.

2. Place half of the sliced basil in a nonreactive mixing bowl. Add the mayonnaise, sour cream, lemon zest, lemon juice, Dijon mustard, and dry mustard and whisk to mix. Transfer the sauce to serving bowl(s) and top with the remaining sliced basil.

VARIATION: You probably don't normally think of pairing ham or cheese with fish, but stuffing the salmon "roast" with thinly sliced serrano ham and Manchego cheese makes an unexpectedly delicious combination. Serrano ham is Spain's answer to prosciutto (it's a little sweeter), while Manchego is a firm Spanish sheep's milk cheese from La Mancha. Both are widely available in the United States. You'll need about 2 ounces of each; about 8 slices of serrano ham and 4 slices of Manchego cheese.

stove-top smoker

sunday morning smoked salmon

This is a recipe near and dear to my heart, because I make it once a week. Every Saturday afternoon, I cure a piece of salmon and smoke it in my stove-top smoker. That way, we're sure to have freshly smoked salmon to go with bagels on

Sunday morning. The curing takes about four hours, but the actual preparation time is maybe fifteen minutes. What emerges from the smoker is an amazingly moist, flavorful, hot-smoked salmon that will raise your standards for smoked fish. **SERVES 4 TO 6**

THE RECIPE

1¹/₂ pounds skinless salmon fillet
    (preferably a center cut piece;
    see box on page 231)
1 cup vodka or rum
    (optional; see Tips on facing page)
1 cup firmly packed dark brown sugar

¹/₂ cup coarse salt (kosher or sea)
2 tablespoons freshly ground black pepper
1 tablespoon ground coriander
Cooking oil spray (optional)
Bagels and cream cheese or toast points,
    capers, and sour cream, for serving

YOU'LL ALSO NEED:
1 tablespoon hardwood sawdust

how to smoke in a wok

Long before the advent of the stainless steel stove-top smoker in the West, the Chinese practiced the venerable art of smoking—in a wok. The wok remains the smoker of choice for preparing such Chinese classics as tea-smoked duck, and you can use it to smoke a wide variety of other foods, from salmon to chicken to vegetables. You need a wok, ideally one made of heavy-gauge steel, that has a tightly fitting metal or bamboo lid (metal will give you a better seal). You also need a round wire cake rack that fits snugly in the wok and holds the food 2¹/₂ to 3 inches above the bottom. And you'll need some hardwood sawdust.

I have one wok I use solely for smoking, so I don't bother to line it with aluminum foil. If you want to smoke in your family's wok, cut out a circle of heavy-duty aluminum foil that's a few inches larger than the wok and tightly press it into the wok, shiny side up, to line the inside. Place the sawdust in a pile at the bottom of the wok. Set the wire cake rack inside, then put the food you want to smoke on top of it. Place the wok on a wok ring or directly over a burner and heat it to high.

In a few minutes you'll start to see and smell smoke. When you do, reduce the heat to medium and tightly cover the wok. If the lid doesn't form a snug fit and smoke starts to escape, roll one or two paper towels into a tube, wet them with water, and use these to plug up any gaps. Smoke the food just as you would in a stove-top smoker, following the directions in the recipe. When it's done, discard the sawdust and foil. Make sure the sawdust is completely burned to ash—it's a good idea to douse it with some water. You should never put glowing embers, even faintly glowing ones, in a trash can.

1. Run your fingers over the salmon fillet, feeling for bones. Using needle-nose pliers or tweezers, pull out any you find. Rinse the salmon under cold running water, then blot it dry with paper towels. Place the fish in a nonreactive baking dish just large enough to hold it and pour the vodka, if using, over it. Turn the fillet over. Let marinate in the refrigerator for 20 minutes, turning the fillet twice.

2. Place the brown sugar, salt, pepper, and coriander in a mixing bowl and mix well, breaking up any lumps in the brown sugar with your fingers.

3. Drain the fillet and blot it dry with paper towels. Dry the baking dish. Arrange a third of the sugar mixture in the bottom of the baking dish in the shape of the salmon fillet. Place the fillet on top and cover it with the remaining brown sugar mixture. Cover the baking dish with plastic wrap and let the fish cure in the refrigerator for 4 hours. When it's properly cured, there will be a pool of liquid at the bottom of the baking dish—the liquid the salt has drawn out of the salmon.

4. Rinse the fish under cold water to wash off all the brown sugar mixture, then blot the salmon dry with paper towels.

5. Set up the smoker (for instructions for using a stove-top smoker, see page 16). Place the sawdust in the center of the bottom of the smoker. Line the drip pan with aluminum foil and place it in the smoker. Lightly coat the wire rack with cooking oil spray, using a paper towel dipped in oil. Place the wire rack in the smoker. Place the salmon fillet on the rack with what was the skin side facing down.

6. Cover the smoker and place it over high heat for 3 minutes, then reduce the heat to medium. Smoke the salmon until cooked through, about 18 minutes. To test for doneness, press the fish with your finger; it should break into clean flakes.

7. Transfer the salmon to a wire rack placed over a plate and let it cool to room temperature, then refrigerate, covered, until ready to serve (salmon prepared this way tastes best served chilled). Serve it with bagels and cream cheese or with toast points, capers, and sour cream. The smoked salmon can be refrigerated, covered, for up to 4 days.

tips

■ Salmon sometimes has a fishy flavor, the result of its high oil content. A brief soaking in vodka or another spirit, such as rum, helps remove this. If you like, you can skip this step.

■ As for what kind of wood to use for smoking, I'm partial to cherry but any hardwood, from hickory to alder, will do.

"barbecued" arctic char

"Barbecued" arctic char combines technology and tradition. The recipe starts with a classic rub, applied to the fish to provide that triple blast of salt, spice, and sweetness so characteristic of American barbecue. Its smoke flavor comes from another traditional barbecue ingredient, the sine qua non of Kansas City–style sauce, liquid smoke (for more about liquid smoke, see box on page 179). Add to this the convenience of an indoor grill. But the proof is in the tasting, and this indoor "barbecued" fish has a lot of the smoke and spice of the real McCoy. **SERVES 4**

ARCTIC CHAR

Arctic char is a northern cold-water fish with the vivid orange color of salmon and something of the delicate flavor of trout. If you live in the frost belt or the northeast, you can probably find it at your local fish market. Salmon makes a good substitute.

THE RECIPE

4 pieces skinless arctic char or
    salmon fillet (each about 6 ounces)
2 tablespoons Basic Barbecue Rub
    (page 362)
2 tablespoons olive oil
1 teaspoon liquid smoke
Barbecue Vinaigrette (optional;
    recipe follows)

1. Run your fingers over the fish fillets, feeling for bones. Using needle-nose pliers or tweezers, pull out any you find. Rinse the fish under cold running water, then blot it dry with paper towels. Sprinkle the barbecue rub all over the fish, patting it on with your fingertips. Let the fish cure at room temperature for 10 minutes.

2. Place the olive oil and liquid smoke in a small bowl and stir with a fork. Set the basting mixture aside.

3. Cook the fish, following the instructions for any of the grills in the box at left, until it is just cooked through. To test for doneness, press the fish with your finger; it should break into clean flakes. Start basting the fish with the olive oil mixture after 1 minute and baste both sides at least twice.

4. Transfer the fish to a platter or plates. Spoon the Barbecue Vinaigrette on top, if using, and serve at once.

if you have a...

CONTACT GRILL: Preheat the grill; if your contact grill has a temperature control, preheat the grill to high. Place the drip pan under the front of the grill. When ready to cook, lightly oil the grill surface. Place the fish on the hot grill, then close the lid. The fish will be cooked through after 3 to 5 minutes (if you prefer it pink in the center, cook it a minute or so less). You will need to turn the fish so that you can baste both sides.

GRILL PAN: Place the grill pan on the stove and preheat it to medium-high over medium heat. When the grill pan is hot a drop of water will skitter in the pan. When ready to cook, lightly oil the ridges of the grill pan. Place the fish in the hot grill pan. It will be cooked through after 3 to 5 minutes per side (if you prefer it pink in the center, cook it a minute or so less).

BUILT-IN GRILL: Preheat the grill to high, then, if it does not have a nonstick surface, brush and oil the grill grate. Place the fish on the hot grate. It will be cooked through after 3 to 5 minutes per side (if you prefer it pink in the center, cook it a minute or so less).

FIREPLACE GRILL: Rake red hot embers under the gridiron and preheat it for 3 to 5 minutes; you want a hot, 2 to 3 Mississippi fire. When ready to cook, brush and oil the gridiron. Place the fish on the hot grate. It will be cooked through after 3 to 5 minutes per side (if you prefer it pink in the center, cook it a minute or so less).

barbecue vinaigrette

Conventional barbecue sauce is too thick and heavy to go with fish, but this vinaigrette couples subtlety and finesse with the smoky sweetness of a traditional Kansas City–style barbecue sauce.
MAKES ABOUT 1/2 CUP

1 tablespoon red barbecue sauce (see Note)
1 tablespoon fresh lemon juice
3 tablespoons olive oil
1 tablespoon very finely diced sweet onion
1 tablespoon very finely diced seeded tomato
1 tablespoon very finely diced green bell
    pepper
Coarse salt (kosher or sea) and freshly ground
    black pepper

Place the barbecue sauce in a small non-reactive bowl. Gradually whisk in 2 tablespoons of water and the lemon juice, olive oil, onion, tomato, and bell pepper. Season with salt and pepper to taste. The sauce is best made no more than an hour before serving.

NOTE: If you're feeling ambitious, you can use the made-from-scratch barbecue sauce on page 374 in the vinaigrette. But a good commercial sauce, like KC Masterpiece, will give you fine results too.

the easiest grilled swordfish you'll ever make

I like to think of this dish as a sort of *piccata* of swordfish sizzled on the grill. It may be the easiest grilled fish you ever make, and if it weren't so delectable, I'd be hesitant to share such a streamlined recipe. As with most uncomplicated dishes, the ingredients are of the utmost importance. You'll want ocean-fresh swordfish (the sort caught by harpoon on a day boat, not by a longline trawler), imported Parmigiano-Reggiano cheese (the kind that's sold in a chunk, not pregrated), and real nonpareil capers.

SERVES 4

tip

Any number of fish, from steak fish like tuna and salmon to fillets like cod or mahimahi, can be prepared like this swordfish.

THE RECIPE

4 swordfish steaks (each about ¾ inch thick and 6 ounces)
1½ tablespoons extra-virgin olive oil
Coarse salt (kosher or sea) and freshly ground black pepper

1 tablespoon unsalted butter
¼ cup finely grated Parmesan cheese
2 tablespoons drained capers
Lemon wedges, for serving

if you have a...

CONTACT GRILL: Preheat the grill; if your contact grill has a temperature control, preheat the grill to high. Place the drip pan under the front of the grill. When ready to cook, lightly oil the grill surface. Place the fish steaks on the hot grill, then close the lid. The fish steaks will be done after cooking 4 to 6 minutes.

GRILL PAN: Place the grill pan on the stove and preheat it to medium-high over medium heat. When the grill pan is hot a drop of water will skitter in the pan. When ready to cook, lightly oil the ridges of the grill pan. Place the fish steaks in the hot grill pan. They will be done after cooking 3 to 5 minutes per side.

BUILT-IN GRILL: Preheat the grill to high, then, if it does not have a nonstick surface, brush and oil the grill grate. Place the fish steaks on the hot grate. They will be done after cooking 3 to 5 minutes per side.

FREESTANDING GRILL: Preheat the grill to high; there's no need to oil the grate. Place the fish steaks on the hot grill. They will be done after cooking 4 to 6 minutes per side.

FIREPLACE GRILL: Rake red hot embers under the gridiron and preheat it for 3 to 5 minutes; you want a hot, 2 to 3 Mississippi fire. When ready to cook, brush and oil the gridiron. Place the fish steaks on the hot grate. They will be done after cooking 3 to 5 minutes per side.

1. Rinse the swordfish under cold running water, then blot it dry with paper towels. Lightly brush each swordfish steak on both sides with the olive oil and season generously with salt and pepper.

2. Cook the fish steaks, following the instructions for any of the grills in the box at left, until they are nicely browned and cooked through, rotating each steak a quarter turn after 1½ minutes to create a handsome crosshatch of grill marks. To test for doneness, press the fish with your finger; it should break into clean flakes.

3. Transfer the swordfish steaks to a platter or plates. Stick the butter on the end of a fork and rub it over the top of each steak. Sprinkle the Parmesan and capers over the fish and serve at once with lemon wedges.

grilled swordfish
with lemon basil butter

This is the sort of dish a grill pan excels at—simply grilled fish with a vibrantly flavorful compound butter. The pan's raised ridges give you razor-sharp grill marks (not to mention the charring characteristic of outdoor grilling). Swordfish prepared this way also turns out great cooked on a contact or built-in grill, or cooked in a fireplace. The result is anything but dry, thanks to an herb-scented compound butter that moistens the swordfish as it melts on top. **SERVES 4**

4 swordfish steaks (each about ¾ inch thick
   and about 6 ounces)
1 tablespoon extra-virgin olive oil
1 teaspoon finely grated lemon zest
   (see Note)
1 teaspoon coarse salt (kosher or sea)
1 teaspoon freshly ground white or
   black pepper
Lemon Basil Butter (recipe follows)

1. Rinse the swordfish under cold running water, then blot it dry with paper towels. Lightly brush each swordfish steak on both sides with the olive oil. Place the lemon zest, salt, and white pepper in a small bowl and stir to mix. Season the fish on both sides with the lemon zest mixture, patting it onto the steaks with your fingertips. Let the swordfish cure for 15 minutes.

2. Cook the fish steaks, following the instructions for any of the grills in the box at right, until they are nicely browned and cooked through, rotating each steak a quarter turn after 1½ minutes to create a handsome crosshatch of grill marks. To test for doneness, press the fish with your finger; it should break into clean flakes.

3. Transfer the fish to a platter or plates. Place 1 tablespoon or a ½-inch-thick slice of the Lemon Basil Butter on each hot swordfish steak and serve at once.

NOTE: The best tool for grating lemon zest (the oil-rich yellow outer rind of the fruit) is a Microplane. They're available at most cookware shops.

NOT JUST FISH

This recipe should be viewed as an indoor grilling strategy as well as a great dish. Any firm-fleshed or steak fish can be grilled this way and served with a flavored butter—swordfish, tuna, salmon, cod, grouper, or arctic char, to name a few (for that matter, you can grill and serve chicken breasts, turkey, pork or veal medallions, and steaks in a similar fashion).

if you have a...

CONTACT GRILL: Preheat the grill; if your contact grill has a temperature control, preheat the grill to high. Place the drip pan under the front of the grill. When ready to cook, lightly oil the grill surface. Place the fish steaks on the hot grill, then close the lid. The fish steaks will be done after cooking 3 to 5 minutes.

GRILL PAN: Place the grill pan on the stove and preheat it to medium-high over medium heat. When the grill pan is hot a drop of water will skitter in the pan. When ready to cook, lightly oil the ridges of the grill pan. Place the fish steaks in the hot grill pan. They will be done after cooking 3 to 5 minutes per side.

BUILT-IN GRILL: Preheat the grill to high, then, if it does not have a nonstick surface, brush and oil the grill grate. Place the fish steaks on the hot grate. They will be done after cooking 3 to 5 minutes per side.

FREESTANDING GRILL: Preheat the grill to high; there's no need to oil the grate. Place the fish steaks on the hot grill. They will be done after cooking 4 to 6 minutes per side.

FIREPLACE GRILL: Rake red hot embers under the gridiron and preheat it for 3 to 5 minutes; you want a hot, 2 to 3 Mississippi fire. When ready to cook, brush and oil the gridiron. Place the fish steaks on the hot grate. They will be done after cooking 3 to 5 minutes per side.

lemon basil butter

Compound butters are some of the world's best condiments for grilled food. They're easy to make and have a long freezer life, so you can always have some on hand for an impromptu grill session. This compound butter made with lemon and basil is a great way to dress up just about anything hot off the grill. The half cup it makes is twice as much as you'll need for the grilled swordfish. Freeze it in two batches. You'll find recipes for three more compound butters on pages 366 and 367.

MAKES ABOUT ½ CUP

You'll find recipes for three more compound butters on pages 366 and 367.

8 tablespoons (1 stick) unsalted butter, at room temperature
8 fresh basil leaves, rinsed and stemmed
1 clove garlic, coarsely chopped
1 teaspoon finely grated lemon zest
1 tablespoon fresh lemon juice
1 tablespoon capers, drained
Coarse salt (kosher or sea) and freshly ground black pepper

Place the butter, basil, garlic, lemon zest, lemon juice, and capers in a food processor and process until smooth. Season with salt and pepper to taste. If you are using the compound butter immediately, spoon dollops on the grilled fish. If you are preparing the butter ahead, spoon it onto 2 pieces of plastic wrap and roll each into a tight cylinder, twisting the ends of the plastic wrap closed like a Tootsie Roll. Refrigerate or freeze the butter until firm. The flavored butter can be refrigerated for up to 5 days or frozen for 3 months. To use, unwrap the butter and cut off ½-inch crosswise slices.

tip

While it may seem odd to call for unsalted butter and then add salt, the reason is simple—the capers are quite salty, so this keeps the salt in check.

contact grill

sesame seared tuna

The flavor of sesame is a perfect partner for rich beefy tuna, a combination pioneered by Wolfgang Puck at his groundbreaking restaurant Chinois on Main in Santa Monica and picked up by countless chefs around the country. The nutty crust of black and white sesame seeds is stylishly minimalist, and the dish goes together in no time. I suggest serving the tuna *tataki* style—seared on the outside, rare inside, with a wasabi sauce for dipping. **SERVES 4**

4 tuna steaks (each 1¼ to 1½ inches thick and about 6 ounces)

3 tablespoons Asian (dark) sesame oil

Coarse salt (kosher or sea) and freshly ground black pepper

¼ cup white sesame seeds

¼ cup black sesame seeds, or more white

Cooking oil spray

Wasabi "Cream" Sauce (recipe follows)

1. Trim any skin or dark or bloody spots off the tuna. Rinse the tuna under cold running water, then blot it dry with paper towels. Brush the tuna steaks on both sides with 2 tablespoons of the sesame oil and season them generously on both sides with salt and pepper. Place both the white and black sesame seeds in a shallow bowl and stir to mix. Dredge each tuna steak in the sesame seeds, coating both sides, and patting the seeds onto the fish with your fingertips. Lightly drizzle the remaining 1 tablespoon of sesame oil over both sides of the tuna.

2. Preheat the contact grill (for instructions for using a contact grill, see page 3); if your contact grill has a temperature control, preheat the grill to high. Place the drip pan under the front of the grill.

3. When ready to cook, lightly coat the grill surface with cooking oil spray. Place the sesame-crusted tuna steaks on the hot grill, then gently close the lid. Grill the tuna until cooked to taste, 2 to 4 minutes for rare. Test for doneness using the poke method: A rare tuna steak will be quite soft, with just a little resistance.

4. Transfer the tuna to a platter or plates and serve at once, with the Wasabi "Cream" Sauce drizzled over the top or served on the side.

VARIATION: If you have a grill pan with shallow ridges, like the one made by Calphalon, you can sear the tuna in it. The tuna steaks will be cooked to rare after 2 to 4 minutes per side.

wasabi "cream" sauce

Wasabi is commonly but incorrectly described as Japanese horseradish. True wasabi is a member of the mustard family, and this scaly tan root with its pale green flesh, is now being grown in Oregon. Fresh wasabi is expensive and hard to find, but you can probably find wasabi powder at your supermarket or natural foods store. That's what I call for here. The sauce would be great not only with tuna but also with salmon, swordfish, scallops, chicken breasts, lamb, or steaks. **MAKES ABOUT ½ CUP**

SO FRESH

You want to buy sushi-quality tuna for this recipe— the sort of fish so fresh you don't mind eating it rare or raw in the center. And if you want to serve the tuna rare, look for steaks that are at least 1¼ inches thick.

tip

Black sesame seeds are a particular variety of sesame seed—look for them at Japanese markets, natural foods stores, and in the foreign food section of many supermarkets. If you can't find them, use more white sesame seeds; the tuna won't look quite as stunning, but the taste will still be fantastic.

tip

For a dramatic presentation, spoon the Wasabi "Cream" Sauce into a squirt bottle and squirt decorative zigzags of the sauce over the grilled fish.

1 tablespoon wasabi powder
1 tablespoon cold water
6 tablespoons mayonnaise
    (preferably Hellmann's)
2 teaspoons soy sauce
2 teaspoons fresh lemon juice

1. Place the wasabi powder in a small non-reactive mixing bowl. Add the water and stir to form a thick paste. Let the wasabi paste sit for 5 minutes.

2. Add the mayonnaise, soy sauce, and lemon juice to the wasabi paste and whisk to mix. The sauce can be refrigerated, covered, for several days.

blackened tuna
with cajun tartar sauce

Indulge me in a stroll down memory lane. The year is 1984, the place Inman Square in Cambridge, Massachusetts. I'm the restaurant critic for *Boston* magazine, and I've just had my first taste of blackened redfish. My cicerone to the glories of Cajun cuisine is John Silberman, acolyte of New Orleans' legendary Paul Prudhomme and founder of an unassuming storefront eatery called the Cajun Yankee. The pleasure of eating there was directly proportional to my dread of writing about it, for I knew the moment the review hit the stands a table at his tiny restaurant would become almost as hard to come by as an audience with the pope. Today, of course, some Cajun cooking is so ubiquitous it's practically a cliché, but I still remember the eye-stinging thrill

CAJUN SPICE FROM SCRATCH

Cajun seasoning is widely available, of course, but many commercial brands contain MSG and who knows what else. It's easy to make your own (see ingredient list, facing page); use it to flavor the fish and the tartar sauce.

of my first bite. Silberman now runs a restaurant in Cambridge called Magnolias. His blackened tuna is brilliant cooked on an indoor grill. **SERVES 4**

THE RECIPE

1 tablespoon coarse salt (kosher or sea)

1 tablespoon garlic powder

1 tablespoon onion powder

1 tablespoon sweet paprika

1 tablespoon dried oregano

2 teaspoons dried thyme

2 teaspoons freshly ground black pepper

1 teaspoon freshly ground white pepper

1 teaspoon cayenne pepper

4 tuna steaks (each 1 to 1¼ inches thick and 6 ounces; see Note)

2 tablespoons (¼ stick) unsalted butter, melted

Lemon wedges, for serving

Cajun Tartar Sauce (recipe follows)

1. Place the salt, garlic and onion powders, paprika, oregano, thyme, black and white peppers, and cayenne in a small bowl and stir to mix. Set the Cajun seasoning aside.

2. Trim any skin or dark or bloody spots off the tuna. Rinse the tuna under cold running water, then blot it dry with paper towels. Brush each tuna steak on both sides with the butter. Set aside 1 tablespoon of the Cajun seasoning for the Cajun Tartar Sauce. Sprinkle about ½ teaspoon of the remaining Cajun seasoning on each side of the tuna steaks, patting it onto the fish with your fingertips. Store any leftover Cajun seasoning in an airtight jar away from heat or light; it will keep for several months.

3. Cook the tuna steaks, following the instructions for any of the grills in the box below, until cooked to taste, rotating each steak a quarter turn after 1 minute on each side to create a handsome crosshatch of grill marks. Test for doneness using the poke method: A medium-rare tuna steak will be gently yielding.

4. Transfer the tuna to a platter or plates. Serve with lemon wedges and Cajun Tartar Sauce on the side.

if you have a...

CONTACT GRILL: Preheat the grill; if your contact grill has a temperature control, preheat the grill to high. Place the drip pan under the front of the grill. When ready to cook, lightly oil the grill surface. Place the tuna steaks on the hot grill, then close the lid. The tuna will be cooked to medium-rare after 3 to 5 minutes.

GRILL PAN: Place the grill pan on the stove and preheat it to medium-high over medium heat. When the grill pan is hot a drop of water will skitter in the pan. When ready to cook, lightly oil the ridges of the grill pan. Place the tuna steaks in the hot grill pan. They will be cooked to medium-rare after 3 to 5 minutes per side.

BUILT-IN GRILL: Preheat the grill to high, then, if it does not have a nonstick surface, brush and oil the grill grate. Place the tuna steaks on the hot grate. They will be cooked to medium-rare after 3 to 5 minutes per side.

FIREPLACE GRILL: Rake red hot embers under the gridiron and preheat it for 3 to 5 minutes; you want a hot, 2 to 3 Mississippi fire. When ready to cook, brush and oil the gridiron. Place the tuna steaks on the hot grate. They will be cooked to medium-rare after 3 to 5 minutes per side.

NOTE: If you want to serve the tuna rare in the center, pick steaks that are at least 1¼ inches thick. Of course, any steak fish, from sword to cod, can be grilled in this fashion, or you could grill Prudhomme's original choice—redfish.

cajun tartar sauce

Why make your own tartar sauce? Well, for starters, you can leave out all the sugar that mars commercial sauces. And you can kick up the spice as hot as your tongue will bear. Any leftover sauce will keep for up to a week in the refrigerator. **MAKES ABOUT 1 CUP**

¾ **cup mayonnaise (preferably Hellmann's)**
3 **tablespoons Cajun mustard or Dijon mustard**
1 **tablespoon minced shallot**
1 **tablespoon minced pickled or fresh jalapeño pepper**
1 **tablespoon minced pimiento-stuffed olives**
1 **tablespoon fresh lemon juice, or more to taste**
1 **tablespoon Cajun seasoning (reserved from the Blackened Tuna, previous page)**
1 **teaspoon Crystal hot sauce, or other hot sauce, or more to taste**

Place the mayonnaise, mustard, shallot, jalapeño, olives, lemon juice, Cajun seasoning, and hot sauce in a small nonreactive mixing bowl and whisk to mix. Taste for seasoning, adding more lemon juice and/or hot sauce as necessary.

grilled tuna
with green peppercorn sauce

When tuna became the beef of the '90s, this tuna dish, handsomely branded with grill marks on the outside, rare and suave within, became the new "steak" au poivre. And no one makes it better than Christian Ville, chef and co-owner of the popular Le Bouchon du Grove restaurant in Coconut Grove. Founded by Christian's cousin, Georges-Eric Farge, Le Bouchon is the quintessential French bistro—perfect in every last detail, down to the white lace curtains, the zinc bar, and the playing of

tip

Green peppercorns are the unripe fruit of the pepper tree. They're often sold bottled in brine. Look for green peppercorns at specialty food stores. If you buy dried green peppercorns, add them with the wine in Step 1 to soften.

"La Marseillaise" every time someone celebrates a birthday. As for the tuna, if you like your fish peppery and seared on the outside and sushi rare in the center, this is your ticket. **SERVES 4**

2 tablespoons (¼ stick) unsalted butter

2 shallots, minced

⅓ cup dry white wine

1 cup bottled clam juice or fish stock

1 cup heavy (whipping) cream

1 tablespoon Cognac

1½ teaspoons cornstarch

2 tablespoons drained green peppercorns
   (see Tips on facing page)

1 teaspoon fresh lemon juice

Coarse salt (kosher or sea)

4 tuna steaks (each 1¼ to 1½ inches thick
   and about 6 ounces)

2 to 3 teaspoons extra-virgin olive oil

Freshly ground black pepper

1. Melt the butter in a heavy nonreactive saucepan over medium heat. Add the shallots and cook until soft and translucent but not brown, 1 to 2 minutes. Add the wine, increase the heat to high, and bring to a boil. Let boil until the wine is reduced by half, about 2 minutes. Add the clam juice, bring to a boil, and boil until about 1 cup of liquid remains, about 5 minutes. Add the heavy cream, bring to a boil, and boil until slightly reduced, about 3 minutes.

2. Place the Cognac and the cornstarch in a small bowl and whisk until the cornstarch dissolves, then whisk the Cognac mixture into the cream mixture. Bring to a boil and boil for 1 minute; the sauce should thicken slightly. Remove the saucepan from the heat and whisk in the green peppercorns and lemon juice. Season with a little salt to taste. The sauce can be prepared up to an hour ahead and kept in a warm place.

3. Trim any skin or dark or bloody spots off the tuna. Rinse the tuna under cold running water, then blot it dry with paper towels.

if you have a...

CONTACT GRILL: Preheat the grill; if your contact grill has a temperature control, preheat the grill to high. Place the drip pan under the front of the grill. When ready to cook, lightly oil the grill surface. Place the tuna steaks on the hot grill, then close the lid. The tuna will be cooked to rare after 2 to 4 minutes.

GRILL PAN: Place the grill pan on the stove and preheat it to medium-high over medium heat. When the grill pan is hot a drop of water will skitter in the pan. When ready to cook, lightly oil the ridges of the grill pan. Place the tuna steaks in the hot grill pan. They will be cooked to rare after 2 to 4 minutes per side.

BUILT-IN GRILL: Preheat the grill to high, then, if it does not have a nonstick surface, brush and oil the grill grate. Place the tuna steaks on the hot grate. They will be cooked to rare after 2 to 4 minutes per side.

FREESTANDING GRILL: Preheat the grill to high; there's no need to oil the grate. Place the tuna steaks on the hot grill. They will be cooked to rare after 3 to 5 minutes per side.

FIREPLACE GRILL: Rake red hot embers under the gridiron and preheat it for 3 to 5 minutes; you want a hot, 2 to 3 Mississippi fire. When ready to cook, brush and oil the gridiron. Place the tuna steaks on the hot grate. They will be cooked to rare after 2 to 4 minutes per side.

4. When ready to cook, lightly brush the tuna steaks with olive oil on both sides and generously season them with salt and pepper. Cook the tuna steaks, following the instructions for any of the grills in the box on the previous page, until cooked to taste, rotating each steak a quarter turn after 1 minute on each side to create a handsome crosshatch of grill marks. Test for doneness using the poke method: A rare tuna steak will be quite soft, with just a little resistance.

5. Spoon the peppercorn sauce onto a platter or plates. Arrange the tuna steaks on top and serve at once.

rotisserie

garlic and rosemary studded tuna "roast"

Once you wrap your mind around the concept of cooking fish on a rotisserie, there's no limit to the possibilities. Which brings us to this Sicilian-inspired tuna "roast," made by spit roasting a garlic and rosemary studded tuna loin in a rotisserie. If you like, you can also add anchovies—the practice of pairing the salty, pungent flavor of anchovies with tuna or roast meat dates back to ancient Roman times, when *garum* and *liquamen,* both sauces made from pickled, fermented fish, were widely used as seasonings and condiments. If you like anchovies—or even if you just tolerate them—try them in this roast. I'm sure you'll appreciate the salty bursts of flavor they impart to the tuna. **SERVES 8 TO 10**

2 large fresh rosemary sprigs

1 tuna loin (about 4½ pounds)

3 cloves garlic, cut into matchstick slivers

5 anchovy fillets (optional), drained,
    blotted dry, and cut crosswise into
    ¾-inch pieces

Coarse salt (kosher or sea) and freshly
    ground black pepper

2 tablespoons extra-virgin olive oil

Anchovy Cream Sauce (recipe follows)

YOU'LL ALSO NEED:
Butcher's string

1. Break the rosemary into 12 to 15 small sprigs, each with 3 or 4 leaves on it.

2. Trim any skin or dark or bloody spots off the tuna. Rinse the tuna under cold running water, then blot it dry with paper towels. Using the tip of a paring knife, make about 36 small holes ½ inch deep in the tuna on all sides, about 1½ inches apart. Gently twist the knife to widen each hole. Insert garlic slivers in one third of the holes, rosemary sprigs in another third, and pieces of anchovy, if using, in the remaining holes (if not using anchovies, use more garlic and rosemary).

3. Cut 4 pieces of butcher's string, and tie the tuna crosswise tightly in 4 places to give it a compact, cylindrical shape. Season the tuna generously on all sides with salt and pepper and drizzle the olive oil over it, rubbing it onto the fish. The tuna can be prepared to this stage up to 4 hours ahead and refrigerated, covered— indeed, the flavor will be richer if you stud it several hours ahead.

4. When ready to cook, place the drip pan in the bottom of the rotisserie. Skewer the tuna lengthwise on the rotisserie spit. Attach the spit to the rotisserie and turn on the motor. If your rotisserie has a temperature control, set it to 400°F (for instructions for using a rotisserie, see page 14).

5. Cook the tuna until it is browned on all sides and cooked to taste, about 40 minutes for very rare inside, 50 minutes for medium-rare, or 1 hour for medium. To test for doneness, insert an instant-read meat thermometer into the center of the tuna loin but not so that it touches the spit. The internal temperature should be about 80°F for very rare, 85°F for medium-rare, or 90°F for medium (the temperature will rise by about 10 degrees as the tuna rests).

6. Transfer the tuna to a platter or cutting board, remove the spit, and let the fish rest for 5 minutes. Cut off and discard the strings. Slice the tuna loin crosswise and serve with the Anchovy Cream Sauce.

VARIATIONS: Consider jumping food groups—garlic, rosemary, and anchovy taste equally great in spit-roasted beef rib roast or pork loin. For weights and cooking times, see page 38 for beef rib roast and page 92 for pork loin.

tips

■ A tuna loin is a cylindrical cut about 8 inches long and 4 to 5 inches in diameter. It's what tuna steaks are cut from. Your fishmonger or supermarket fish department should have no problem finding you one if you call ahead of time. If you want to serve the tuna rare or medium-rare in the center, buy sushi-quality fish.

■ On the West Coast, you can often find small tuna loins that look like half of a pork tenderloin. These can be studded with garlic, rosemary, and anchovies, as described in the recipe at left. Grilled on a contact grill, they'll be medium-rare after 2 to 4 minutes. Cooked in a grill pan or on a built-in or fireplace grill, they'll be medium-rare after 2 to 4 minutes per side.

anchovy cream sauce

This creamy sauce takes its inspiration from the *bagna cauda* of the Piedmont in northwest Italy. The name literally means hot bath; actually, it's a sort of fondue into which raw vegetables are dipped. Don't be alarmed by the seemingly large quantities of garlic and anchovies—the lengthy simmering mellows the brash flavors of both into an exquisitely silky cream sauce. **MAKES ABOUT 1½ CUPS**

2 cups heavy (whipping) cream
3 cloves garlic, peeled and gently flattened
    with the side of a cleaver
4 anchovy fillets, drained and blotted dry
¾ teaspoon finely grated lemon zest
Freshly ground black pepper
4 tablespoons (½ stick) unsalted butter

1. Place the cream, garlic, anchovies, and lemon zest in a heavy saucepan over medium heat. Bring to a simmer and simmer gently until the cream is reduced to about 1½ cups, 8 to 12 minutes, stirring from time to time with a wooden spoon. Season with pepper to taste.

2. Place the sauce in a blender or food processor and purée until smooth. Just before serving, return the sauce to the saucepan and bring to the barest simmer over medium-low heat. Whisk in the butter. Taste for seasoning, adding more pepper as necessary.

tips

▪ When grilling in a grill pan, it's best to keep the seasonings simple. Full-scale marinades have a way of dripping onto the pan between the grill ridges and creating a smoky mess.

▪ *Skordalia* can also be made with walnuts instead of almonds.

greek cod with skordalia

Cod was once America's most popular fish (not to mention its first commercial export). In recent years, its moist, flaky, delicate white flesh has been passed over in favor of darker, more full-flavored fish, like salmon and tuna. This recipe features cod steaks handsomely seared in a grill pan, served with an *aïoli*-like garlic sauce called *skordalia,* a sauce of great antiquity enjoyed in the age of Socrates. **SERVES 4**

THE RECIPE

FOR THE SKORDALIA:

3 slices white sandwich bread, crusts cut off

3 cloves garlic, coarsely chopped

3 tablespoons blanched almonds, coarsely
    chopped

1 tablespoon red wine vinegar

1 tablespoon fresh lemon juice

1/3 cup extra-virgin olive oil

Coarse salt (kosher or sea) and freshly ground
    white pepper

A tiny pinch of cayenne pepper

FOR THE FISH:

4 cod steaks (each about ¾ inch thick and
    8 ounces)

1½ tablespoons extra-virgin olive oil
    (preferably Greek)

Coarse salt (kosher or sea) and freshly ground
    white pepper

1 teaspoon dried oregano

2 tablespoons fresh lemon juice

1 tablespoon finely chopped fresh flat-leaf
    parsley

Lemon wedges, for serving

1. Make the *skordalia:* Place the slices of bread in a mixing bowl and add enough warm water to cover. Let the bread soak for 5 minutes, then drain it well in a colander. Hold the bread in your hands and squeeze it well to extract any excess liquid.

2. Place the soaked bread and the garlic, almonds, wine vinegar, lemon juice, and olive oil in a blender (for a smooth sauce, you must use a blender, not a food processor). Run the machine until a creamy purée forms, scraping down the

sides of the blender several times with a rubber spatula. Season with salt, white pepper, and cayenne to taste; the *skordalia* should be highly seasoned.

3. Prepare the fish: Rinse the cod under cold running water, then blot it dry with paper towels. Lightly brush the cod steaks on both sides with olive oil, then season them generously on both sides with salt and white pepper. Crumble the oregano between your fingers and sprinkle it all over the fish. Sprinkle the fish with lemon juice on both sides, patting it onto the cod with your fingertips.

if you have a...

CONTACT GRILL: Preheat the grill; if your contact grill has a temperature control, preheat the grill to high. Place the drip pan under the front of the grill. When ready to cook, lightly oil the grill surface. Place the fish steaks on the hot grill, then close the lid. The fish will be done after cooking 3 to 5 minutes.

GRILL PAN: Place the grill pan on the stove and preheat it to medium-high over medium heat. When the grill pan is hot a drop of water will skitter in the pan. When ready to cook, lightly oil the ridges of the grill pan. Place the fish steaks in the hot grill pan. They will be done after cooking 3 to 5 minutes per side.

BUILT-IN GRILL: Preheat the grill to high, then, if it does not have a nonstick surface, brush and oil the grill grate. Place the fish steaks on the hot grate. They will be done after cooking 3 to 5 minutes per side.

FREESTANDING GRILL: Preheat the grill to high; there's no need to oil the grate. Place the fish steaks on the hot grill. They will be done after cooking 4 to 6 minutes per side.

FIREPLACE GRILL: Rake red hot embers under the gridiron and preheat it for 3 to 5 minutes; you want a hot, 2 to 3 Mississippi fire. When ready to cook, brush and oil the gridiron. Place the fish steaks on the hot grate. They will be done after cooking 3 to 5 minutes per side.

4. Cook the fish steaks, following the instructions for any of the grills in the box on the previous page, until nicely browned and cooked through. To test for doneness, press the fish with your finger; it should break into clean flakes.

5. Transfer the cod to a platter or plates. Top each fish steak with a dollop of *skordalia* and sprinkle parsley over it. Serve the lemon wedges and any remaining *skordalia* on the side.

monkfish
in the style of da ivo

Da Ivo is the sort of restaurant every visitor dreams of discovering in Venice, with a cubbyhole of a dining room built over a canal. Passing gondoliers float by close enough to reach in the window for a glass of wine. Presiding over this tiny fiefdom is Tuscan-born Natale Ivo, who has lived in Venice since the 1960s. Grumpy and world-weary in the way of many Venetians, Ivo is still passionate enough about his cuisine to pull out a bottle of unfiltered olive oil from his native Tuscany or a pear of supernatural ripeness.

Ivo says he has the only charcoal grill in Venice, and he takes no small pride in it. Ivo uses a technique I've never seen anywhere else. He crusts his seafood with bread crumbs (no egg, no batter) prior to grilling. It requires a gentle fire and constant supervision to grill the fish without burning the bread crumbs. Then, the fish is served with nothing more than gorgeous olive oil flavored with garlic and parsley. **SERVES 4**

tip

For the bread crumbs, Ivo uses untoasted crumbs made from day-old white bread with the crusts cut off. You can make your own by pulsing chunks of stale bread in a food processor.

4 monkfish steaks (each about ¾ inch thick
    and 6 to 8 ounces)
1 to 2 tablespoons extra-virgin olive oil
Coarse salt (kosher or sea) and freshly ground
    black pepper
1½ cups bread crumbs
Parsley and Garlic Sauce (recipe follows)
Lemon wedges, for serving

1. Rinse the monkfish steaks under cold running water, then blot them dry with paper towels. Lightly brush the monkfish on both sides with olive oil, then season it generously on both sides with salt and pepper. Place the bread crumbs in a wide shallow bowl. Dredge each monkfish steak in bread crumbs on both sides, shaking off the excess.

2. Cook the monkfish, following the instructions for any of the grills in the box at right, until the crumbs are crusty and golden brown and the fish is cooked through. To test for doneness, press the fish with your finger; it should break into clean flakes.

3. Transfer the monkfish to a platter or plates and spoon a little of the Parsley and Garlic Sauce over each piece. Garnish with lemon wedges and serve at once with the remaining sauce on the side.

parsley and garlic sauce

Da Ivo's simple sauce contains only four ingredients—commonplace ingredients at that. It requires little more in the way of technique than chopping and stirring. Alas, neither you nor I will be able to duplicate Da Ivo's sauce for love or money. Not unless we could buy the garlic and parsley at Venice's legendary Rialto Market the morning we plan to make it, and not unless our olive oil, extra virgin and unfiltered, of course, comes from a tiny farm in Tuscany. Garlic and parsley taste different in Italy. Ditto for olive oil. But, if you use the best olive oil and freshest flat-leaf parsley and garlic you can find, your sauce will come close. It's good with any sort of grilled fish or shellfish, chicken, or veal. **MAKES ABOUT 6 TABLESPOONS**

if you have a...

CONTACT GRILL: Preheat the grill; if your contact grill has a temperature control, preheat the grill to high. Place the drip pan under the front of the grill. When ready to cook, lightly oil the grill surface. Place the monkfish on the hot grill, then close the lid. The fish will be done after cooking 4 to 6 minutes.

BUILT-IN GRILL: Preheat the grill to medium-high, then, if it does not have a nonstick surface,

brush and oil the grill grate. Place the fish steaks on the hot grate. They will be done after cooking 4 to 6 minutes per side.

FIREPLACE GRILL: Rake red hot embers under the gridiron and preheat it for 3 to 5 minutes; you want a medium-hot, 4 Mississippi fire. When ready to cook, brush and oil the gridiron. Place the fish steaks on the hot grate. They will be done after cooking 4 to 6 minutes per side.

GREEN GARLIC

When garlic is less than fresh, it develops a green shoot in the center of the cloves. This can be bitter. To avoid this, cut the cloves in half lengthwise and cut out and discard the green part.

1 clove garlic, finely chopped

1/2 teaspoon coarse salt (kosher or sea)

6 tablespoons extra-virgin olive oil (preferably unfiltered)

2 to 3 tablespoons finely chopped, rinsed and stemmed fresh flat-leaf parsley

1. Place the garlic and salt in a small mixing bowl and mash to a paste with the back of a spoon.

2. Add the olive oil and parsley and whisk to mix. Serve the sauce within 30 minutes.

ginger lime halibut

A contact grill is perfect for cooking halibut. Its delicate white flesh is prone to stick to conventional grills, and its fragility makes it challenging to turn. On a contact grill, all you have to do is close the lid. On other grills, oil the grate well (freestanding grills don't even need that) and use a large spatula for turning the fish. The halibut here is marinated in an East-West combination of ginger, lime juice, soy sauce, and olive oil that's boiled down to make a sensational sauce. **SERVES 4**

THE RECIPE

1 piece (2 inches) peeled fresh ginger

1 clove garlic, peeled

1 to 2 limes

1/4 cup soy sauce

1/4 cup extra-virgin olive oil

1/4 teaspoon freshly ground black pepper

4 skinless halibut fillets (each 6 to 8 ounces)

1 tablespoon butter

1. Using a Microplane or a fine grater, grate the ginger and garlic into a nonreactive mixing bowl. Grate the lime for 1/2 teaspoon of zest and add it to the bowl. Juice the limes: measure 1/4 cup of juice

and add it to the bowl with the soy sauce, olive oil, and pepper and whisk to mix.

2. Rinse the halibut under cold running water, then blot it dry with paper towels. Arrange the fish in a nonreactive baking dish just large enough to hold it in one layer. Pour the ginger and lime marinade over the halibut, turning to coat both sides. Cover the baking dish with plastic wrap and let the fish marinate in the refrigerator for at least 30 minutes or as long as 4 hours, turning the fish several times (the longer the you marinate the

tip

Halibut is widely available on the West Coast (Alaska is a large supplier), and its popularity is growing on the East Coast. Other fish that would be good prepared this way include striped bass, sea bass, and bluefish.

fish, the richer the flavor will be, but even if you only have a half hour, you'll still get plenty of flavor).

3. When ready to cook, drain the marinade from the fish, straining it into a saucepan. Bring the marinade to a boil over high heat and let boil until thick and syrupy, about 5 minutes. Whisk in the butter. If you are using a built-in grill, freestanding grill, or fireplace grill, set aside ¼ cup of the boiled marinade for basting the halibut (you don't baste the fish on a contact grill or in a grill pan). You'll serve the rest of the marinade as a sauce.

4. Cook the halibut, following the instructions for any of the grills in the box at right, until nicely browned and cooked through. To test for doneness, press the fish with your finger; it should break into clean flakes.

5. Transfer the halibut to a platter or plates and serve at once, spooning the remaining boiled marinade on top.

if you have a...

CONTACT GRILL: Preheat the grill; if your contact grill has a temperature control, preheat the grill to high. Place the drip pan under the front of the grill. When ready to cook, lightly oil the grill surface. Place the halibut on the hot grill, then close the lid. The fish will be done after cooking 3 to 5 minutes.

GRILL PAN: Place the grill pan on the stove and preheat it to medium-high over medium heat. When the grill pan is hot a drop of water will skitter in the pan. When ready to cook, lightly oil the ridges of the grill pan. Be sure the halibut is well drained, then place it in the hot grill pan. It will be done after cooking 3 to 5 minutes per side.

BUILT-IN GRILL: Preheat the grill to high, then, if it does not have a nonstick surface, brush and oil the grill grate. Place the halibut on the hot grate. It will be done after cooking 3 to 5 minutes per side. Baste the halibut one or two times with some of the boiled marinade.

FREESTANDING GRILL: Preheat the grill to high; there's no need to oil the grate. Place the halibut on the hot grill. It will be done after cooking 4 to 6 minutes per side. Baste the halibut one or two times with some of the boiled marinade.

FIREPLACE GRILL: Rake red hot embers under the gridiron and preheat it for 3 to 5 minutes; you want a hot, 2 to 3 Mississippi fire. When ready to cook, brush and oil the gridiron. Place the halibut on the hot grate. It will be done after cooking 3 to 5 minutes per side. Baste the halibut one or two times with some of the boiled marinade.

pancetta-grilled halibut
with pancetta sage vinaigrette

Halibut is one of the most appealing fish to grace a table—bone white; mild, even sweet in flavor; with a fine, delicate texture that's always tender. In the Italian-inspired recipe here, the halibut is grilled sandwiched between thin slices of pancetta and sage leaves, which add flavor, prevent the fish from sticking to the grate, and keep it from drying out. Despite the relatively few ingredients, the halibut explodes with flavor. **SERVES 4**

THE RECIPE

10 thin slices pancetta (8 to 10 ounces total;
     see Note)
4 skinless halibut fillets (each 6 to 8 ounces)
1 bunch fresh sage, or basil for people who
     don't like sage, rinsed and stemmed
Coarse salt (kosher or sea) and freshly ground
     black pepper
2 teaspoons drained capers
1 tablespoon sherry vinegar or red wine vinegar
1 tablespoon fresh lemon juice
5 tablespoons hazelnut oil or extra-virgin
     olive oil

YOU'LL ALSO NEED:
Butcher's string

1. Place 2 slices of the pancetta in a small skillet over medium-high heat and fry until browned and crisp, about 3 minutes. Transfer the cooked pancetta to a paper towel to drain, then cut it into thin slivers. Place the slivered pancetta in a small nonreactive mixing bowl and set aside until you make the vinaigrette.

2. Rinse the halibut under cold running water, then blot it dry with paper towels. Place 4 slices of pancetta on a plate or work surface. Place 3 sage leaves on top of each slice of pancetta. Generously season the halibut pieces on both sides with salt and pepper and place one piece on top of each slice of pancetta. Arrange 3 sage leaves on top of each piece of fish, then cover each with a slice of pancetta. Tie the pancetta onto the halibut with butcher's string, wrapping it around the fish as you would tie ribbon on a gift package (if you are using a contact grill, you don't need to do this).

if you have a...

CONTACT GRILL: Preheat the grill; if your contact grill has a temperature control, preheat the grill to high. Place the drip pan under the front of the grill. When ready to cook, lightly oil the grill surface. Place the halibut bundles on the hot grill, then close the lid. The fish will be done after cooking 3 to 5 minutes.

GRILL PAN: Place the grill pan on the stove and preheat it to medium-high over medium heat. When the grill pan is hot a drop of water will skitter in the pan. When ready to cook, lightly oil the ridges of the grill pan. Place the halibut bundles in the hot grill pan. They will be done after cooking 3 to 5 minutes per side.

BUILT-IN GRILL: Preheat the grill to high, then, if it does not have a nonstick surface, brush and oil the grill grate. Place the halibut bundles on the hot grate. They will be done after cooking 3 to 5 minutes per side.

FIREPLACE GRILL: Rake red hot embers under the gridiron and preheat it for 3 to 5 minutes; you want a hot, 2 to 3 Mississippi fire. When ready to cook, brush and oil the gridiron. Place the halibut bundles on the hot grate. They will be done after cooking 3 to 5 minutes per side.

3. Using a spatula, carefully transfer the halibut bundles to the hot grill. Cook the halibut, following the instructions for any of the grills in the box at left, until the pancetta is lightly browned and the fish is cooked through. To test for doneness, press the fish with your finger; it should break into clean flakes.

4. Meanwhile, make the vinaigrette: Finely chop enough sage to obtain 1 tablespoon and add it and the capers to the slivered pancetta. Add the vinegar and lemon juice and whisk to mix. Whisk in the hazelnut oil in a thin stream, then season with salt and pepper to taste.

5. Transfer the fish to a platter or plates, remove and discard the string, if using, and serve at once, spooning the vinaigrette on top.

NOTE: Pancetta is Italian pork belly, cured in a way similar to prosciutto. It's

sold in round slices, which are just the right size for sandwiching the fish. Pancetta doesn't have a smoke flavor like American bacon, a plus when grilling a delicate fish like halibut. However, you could certainly use bacon and still wind up with a very appealing dish.

tips

■ If you have a contact grill, cooking the pancetta for the vinaigrette on it before you put on the fish will save you from having to wash a skillet and also greases the grill.

■ If halibut is unavailable, turbot, cod, haddock, sea bass, or even salmon can be prepared this way.

grilled sea bass
with miso glaze

Sea bass burst upon the food scene in the United States in the mid-1990s. We were hooked after the first bite. We prized the pearl white flesh and delicate flavor and the way the fish stayed moist no matter how long you cooked—or even overcooked—it. Before long, this once exotic fish from the deep, cold waters off Chile became an American staple. Sea bass is ideal for grilling: It doesn't fall apart, like so many white fish do on the grill, and it keeps its succulence even when exposed to a high dry heat. The contact grill, which cooks from both top and bottom, is ideal for sea bass. But other indoor grills will work well too. In this

tips

recipe, inspired by chef Nobu Matsuhisa of New York City's legendary Nobu, the mild sweet flavor of the sea bass is reinforced by a sweet miso marinade that doubles as a glaze. **SERVES 4**

THE RECIPE

1¹/₂ pounds sea bass fillets
¹/₂ cup sake
¹/₂ cup mirin (sweet rice wine)
1 cup white miso (see box on page 357)
5 to 6 tablespoons sugar
1 teaspoon finely grated lemon zest
¹/₄ teaspoon freshly ground white pepper

1. Rinse the sea bass under cold running water, then blot it dry with paper towels. Cut the fish sharply on the diagonal into ³/₄-inch-thick slices.

2. Place the sake and mirin in a nonreactive saucepan over high heat and bring to a boil. Let boil for 2 minutes to cook out the alcohol. Lower the heat to medium-low and whisk in the miso, sugar, lemon zest, and white pepper. Let simmer gently until thick and creamy, about 5 minutes. Remove the pan from the heat and let the marinade cool to room temperature. Pour half of the miso mixture into a non-reactive baking dish just large enough to hold the fish slices in one layer.

3. Arrange the fish slices in the baking dish on top of the marinade. Spoon the remaining marinade on top. Cover the baking dish with plastic wrap and let the fish marinate in the refrigerator for at least 6 hours, preferably for 24.

4. When ready to cook, remove the fish from the marinade with tongs, letting each piece drain a little (it's OK to have some marinade on the fish). Discard the marinade. Cook the fish, following the instructions for any of the grills in the box at left, until nicely browned and cooked through. To test for doneness, press the fish with your finger; it should break into clean flakes.

5. Transfer the fish to a platter or plates and serve at once.

if you have a...

CONTACT GRILL: Preheat the grill; if your contact grill has a temperature control, preheat the grill to high. Place the drip pan under the front of the grill. When ready to cook, lightly oil the grill surface. Place the fish on the hot grill, then close the lid. The fish will be cooked through after 6 to 8 minutes.

BUILT-IN GRILL: Preheat the grill to high, then, if it does not have a nonstick surface, brush and oil the grill grate. Place the fish on the hot grate. It will be cooked through after 4 to 6 minutes per side.

FREESTANDING GRILL: Preheat the grill to high; there's no need to oil the grate. Place the fish on the hot grill. It will be cooked through after 5 to 7 minutes per side.

FIREPLACE GRILL: Rake red hot embers under the gridiron and preheat it for 3 to 5 minutes; you want a hot, 2 to 3 Mississippi fire. When ready to cook, brush and oil the gridiron. Place the fish on the hot grate. It will be cooked through after 4 to 6 minutes per side.

contact grill

sea bass
in a potato crust

When potato-crusted sea bass began turning up in American restaurants in the late 1990s it was hard to say which made bigger waves, the bass or the crust. Technically speaking, this fish from the icy waters off the coast of Chile is not a bass (it's more correctly referred to as the Patagonian toothfish and belongs to the *Nototheniidae* family), but its mild, sweet flavor is the real deal. As for the crust, the tasty overlapping slices of potato are meant to look like fish scales. You don't need restaurant-quality sauté skills or artery-clogging doses of butter to prepare this eye-catching dish at home—it just takes a little patience and a contact grill. **SERVES 4**

THE RECIPE

1 large baking potato (12 to 14 ounces), peeled

4 pieces skinless sea bass fillet (each about 4 inches long, 3 inches wide, and 1 inch thick)

About 4 tablespoons (1/2 stick) unsalted butter, melted

Coarse salt (kosher or sea) and freshly ground black pepper

1/4 cup finely chopped fresh chives (optional)

Cooking oil spray

5 tablespoons heavy (whipping) cream

YOU'LL ALSO NEED:

8 pieces parchment paper (each 6 by 5 inches)

1. Using a mandoline, the slicing blade of a food processor, or a sharp knife wielded with a very steady and precise hand, cut the potato crosswise into very thin (1/8-inch) slices; you should have between 40 and 48. Place the potato slices in a colander, rinse them with cold water, and spread them out on paper towels to dry.

2. Rinse the fish under cold running water, then blot it dry with paper towels.

3. Using a pastry brush, spread a generous 1/2 teaspoon of butter over a piece of parchment paper to within 1/2 inch of the edge and sprinkle a little salt and pepper over it. Arrange 4 or 5 potato slices on

tip

To make them easier to handle, I assemble the potato crusts on parchment paper. Then I top each piece of fish with another piece of parchment and cook it between the pieces of paper. The instructions for putting everything together probably look more complicated than they actually are; you should be able to have the fish ready to cook in less than 15 minutes.

top of the buttered parchment paper so that they overlap to form an oval that is roughly 5 inches long and 4 inches wide. Spread about ¾ teaspoon of butter over the potato slices and sprinkle 1 teaspoon of the chives on top, if using.

4. Season 1 piece of fish on both sides with salt and pepper and place it in the center of the oval of potato slices. Spread about ¾ teaspoon butter over the fish and sprinkle 1 teaspoon of the chives on top, if using. Arrange 4 or 5 more potato slices so that they overlap to form an oval that covers the piece of fish. Spread about ¾ teaspoon of butter over the potatoes, then place a piece of parchment paper on top. Repeat until all the remaining pieces of parchment paper, potato slices, and fish have been used. Set aside the remaining 4 teaspoons of chives, if using; you'll use these when making the cream sauce. The potato-crusted fish can be prepared to this stage several hours ahead and refrigerated, covered.

5. Preheat the grill (for instructions for using a contact grill, see page 3); if your contact grill has a temperature control, preheat the grill to high. Place the drip pan under the front of the grill.

6. When ready to cook, lightly coat the grill surface with cooking oil spray. Leaving the potato-crusted

fish between the pieces of parchment paper, arrange them on the hot grill and close the lid. Grill until the potato slices are nicely browned and the fish is cooked through, 7 to 10 minutes. To test for doneness, press the fish with your finger; it should break into clean flakes. You may need to cook the fish in more than one batch; transfer the grilled fish, still in the parchment paper, to a 250°F oven to keep warm. If you have cooked all the fish in one batch, transfer it in the parchment to a platter or cutting board, and cover it with aluminum foil to keep warm.

7. Make the sauce: Pour the liquid from the drip pan into a heavy saucepan and place it over high heat. Add the cream and bring to a boil. Let the sauce simmer briskly until it is thick and creamy, about 3 minutes. Remove the saucepan from the heat and stir in the remaining chives, if using. It's unlikely the sauce will need more salt and pepper, but taste for seasoning, adding either as necessary.

8. To serve, peel the top pieces of parchment paper off the potato crusts and discard them. Using a spatula, slide the fish and potato crusts off the bottom pieces of parchment paper and transfer them to a platter or plates. Spoon the cream sauce around the potato-crusted fish and serve at once.

OLIVE OIL

dilled trout
with georgian walnut sauce

According to Greek mythology, Prometheus gave man the gift of fire in the Caucasus Mountains, which is now where you find the Republic of Georgia. To this day, Georgians love all manner of grilled fare, enhancing their barbecue with an unexpected palate of flavors that includes walnuts, plums and other tart fruits, cilantro, dill, hot peppers, and even molasses made from pomegranates. This recipe features trout stuffed with lemon and dill, served with a creamy walnut sauce fragrant with coriander and garlic, a sort of Georgian pesto. It sounds exotic and tastes terrific—and it's very easy to make. **SERVES 4**

THE RECIPE

4 trout (each 12 ounces to 1 pound),
   cleaned
Coarse salt (kosher or sea) and freshly
   ground black pepper
2 tablespoons extra-virgin olive oil
16 fresh dill sprigs
1 lemon, sliced paper-thin crosswise, seeded,
   rind cut off
Georgian Walnut Sauce (recipe follows)

YOU'LL ALSO NEED:
Wooden toothpicks or butcher's string

1. Rinse the trout, inside and out, under cold running water, then blot them dry with paper towels. Using a sharp knife, make 2 or 3 cuts to the bone in the thickest part of each side of each trout.

2. Season the cavity of each trout with salt and pepper. Drizzle a little olive oil (about 1/2 teaspoon) in the cavity of each fish and add 2 of the dill sprigs and a couple of lemon slices (set aside 4 lemon slices for garnish). Brush the outsides of the trout with the remaining olive oil and season generously with salt and pepper. Place a dill sprig on top of each fish lengthwise. Pin the fish cavities shut with toothpicks or tie them closed with butcher's string (if you are using a contact grill, you won't need to do this). Let the fish marinate in the refrigerator, covered, for about 15 minutes.

3. Cook the fish, following the instructions for any of the grills in the box below, until cooked through. To test for doneness, press the fish with your finger; it should break into clean flakes. You may have to grill the trout in batches.

4. Transfer the trout to a platter or plates. Spoon a little Georgian Walnut Sauce over each or place dollops of sauce on the side. Garnish each fish with a sprig of dill and a lemon slice and serve at once with the rest of the sauce on the side.

VARIATION: I call for whole trout here, but you could certainly substitute boneless trout fillets or fillets of salmon or arctic char. You'll need four fillets that weigh about 6 ounces each. Cut a pocket in the side of each piece of fish and stuff the dill and lemon in it, then tie the fillets closed with butcher's string. The cooking time for

fillets will be 3 to 5 minutes per side, or 3 to 5 minutes in all on a contact grill.

georgian walnut sauce

Walnuts are one of the cornerstones of Georgian cuisine, prized for their earthy flavor, healthful oils, and ability to make rich, creamy sauces without starchy thickeners. Think of this sauce as a sort of walnut pesto. **MAKES ABOUT 1 CUP**

1¼ cups shelled walnuts
2 cloves garlic, coarsely chopped
1½ teaspoons ground coriander
1 teaspoon hot or sweet paprika
½ teaspoon coarse salt (kosher or sea), or more to taste
½ teaspoon freshly ground black pepper, or more to taste
2 tablespoons fresh lemon juice, or more to taste
3 tablespoons finely chopped fresh dill

1. Place the walnuts, garlic, coriander, paprika, salt, and pepper in a food processor. Process to a smooth paste, scraping down the side of the bowl several times with a spatula. Add the lemon juice and process to mix.

2. With the processor running, add enough water in a thin stream to form a smooth creamy sauce (you'll need between ½ and ¾ cup water). Add the dill and process in short bursts just to mix. Taste for seasoning, adding more salt, pepper, and/or lemon juice as necessary; the sauce should be richly flavored. Any leftover sauce can be refrigerated, covered, for up to 3 days.

if you have a...

CONTACT GRILL: Preheat the grill; if your contact grill has a temperature control, preheat the grill to high. Place the drip pan under the front of the grill. When ready to cook, lightly oil the grill surface. Place the trout on the hot grill, then close the lid. The fish will be done after cooking 5 to 8 minutes.

GRILL PAN: Place the grill pan on the stove and preheat it to medium over medium heat. When the grill pan is hot a drop of water will skitter in the pan. When ready to cook, lightly oil the ridges of the grill pan. Place the trout in the hot grill pan. They will be done after cooking 5 to 8

minutes per side (use a spatula to turn the fish).

BUILT-IN GRILL: Preheat the grill to high, then, if it does not have a nonstick surface, brush and oil the grill grate. Place the trout on the hot grate. They will be done after cooking 5 to 8 minutes per side (use a spatula to turn the fish).

FIREPLACE GRILL: Rake red hot embers under the gridiron and preheat it for 3 to 5 minutes; you want a hot, 2 to 3 Mississippi fire. When ready to cook, brush and oil the gridiron. Place the trout on the hot grate. They will be done after cooking 5 to 8 minutes per side (use a spatula to turn the fish).

rotisserie

bacon-grilled trout
with lemon and dill

I first made a version of this dish on my *Barbecue University* TV show. I wanted to demonstrate how you could grill whole fish over an open fire, in this case on a charcoal grill without a grate. The secret was to use a fish basket, an ingenious device that lets you turn the basket with the fragile fish inside. Now I've transferred the recipe to another sort of grilling basket—the flat wire basket used in countertop rotisseries. The smoky flavor of the bacon cooks right into the fish, giving you that campfire flavor indoors. **SERVES 2**

THE RECIPE

2 whole trout (each 12 to 16 ounces)
Coarse salt (kosher or sea) and freshly
    ground black pepper
1 lemon
6 fresh dill sprigs, rinsed, or 8 fresh basil
    leaves, if dill is unavailable
4 slices bacon

YOU'LL ALSO NEED:
4 pieces butcher's string, each about
    6 inches long (optional)

1. Rinse the trout, inside and out, under cold running water, then blot dry, inside and out, with paper towels. Season the cavity of each trout with salt and pepper.

2. Cut the lemon in half lengthwise. Cut one half crosswise into paper-thin slices, discarding the ends. Remove any seeds

with a fork. Cut the other half lemon into quarters lengthwise to make lemon wedges for serving and set aside.

3. Place the lemon slices and dill sprigs in the cavity of each fish, dividing them evenly between them. Place 2 slices of bacon on a work surface and place a trout on top of each. Place the 2 remaining slices of bacon on top of the fish. If you like, you can secure the bacon to the trout by tying it crosswise with 2 pieces of butcher's string. Carefully place the bacon-covered trout in the rotisserie basket perpendicular to the spit and close it tightly.

4. When ready to cook, place the drip pan in the bottom of the rotisserie. Attach the basket to the rotisserie spit,

tips

■ **Where can you find fresh trout? If you live up north or in one of the Great Lakes or mountain states, your fishmonger may carry it. When I'm in Miami, I order it by mail (see Mail-Order Sources on page 396).**

■ **I like the look of whole roasted fish, so I cook trout with its head and tail. You can also prepare boneless trout fillets by tying two together. If you want to cook the whole trout on a contact grill or in a grill pan, you'll find cooking times in the recipe on page 259.**

■ **You'll get the best flavor if you use an artisanal apple wood–smoked bacon. One good brand is Nueske's Hillcrest Farm (see Mail-Order Sources on page 396).**

then attach the spit to the rotisserie and turn on the motor. If your rotisserie has a temperature control, set it to 400°F (for instructions for using a rotisserie, see page 14). Cook until the bacon is golden brown and the trout is cooked through, 20 to 30 minutes. To test for doneness, insert a slender metal skewer into the center of a trout for 20 seconds: It should come out hot to the touch. Or use the flake test: Press the fish with your finger; it should break into clean flakes.

5. Remove the spit from the rotisserie and transfer the trout to a platter or plates. Remove and discard the string, if using. Serve the trout with the lemon wedges.

VARIATION: You can spit roast or grill fillets of salmon or arctic char using the same flavorings. Start with 2 skinless pieces that are about 4 inches long, 2 to 3 inches wide, and 1 inch thick and weigh 6 to 8 ounces each. Cut a pocket in one side of each and stuff it with some of the lemon and dill. Place each stuffed fillet on a slice of bacon and top each with one of the remaining slices of bacon. Secure the bacon to the fillets by tying them up like a gift package, using butcher's string. Spit roasted in a rotisserie basket, the fillets will be done after 15 to 20 minutes. Cooked on a contact grill, they will be done after 3 to 5 minutes; in a grill pan, it will take 3 to 5 minutes per side.

contact grill

shad roe by george

When the George Foreman grill came out, it was embraced by college students, retirees, and convenience-seeking and health-minded home cooks. Serious foodies tended to want nothing to do with it. I myself was a skeptic until it dawned on me that the grill's unique heat configuration—cooking food from both top and bottom simultaneously—might be useful for delicate or easily burned dishes, like shad roe.

The egg sacs of the silvery shad are a great springtime delicacy, coupling the delicate flavor of caviar with the buttery richness of foie gras. Shad roe tends to spatter and even explode when pan fried. A contact grill gives it the requisite crisp exterior without soiling your stove. If you've never had shad roe before,

tips

■ Shad roe is in season in February through April and is sold at fishmongers in the mid-Atlantic states and New England. Roe comes with a pair of lobes. One good source is CT River Shad (see Mail-Order Sources on page 396). Try to buy shad roe with both lobes intact.

■ If you'd prefer to cook the shad roe in a grill pan, you'll find instructions in the Variation on the facing page.

you're in for a revelation, and if you're already a believer, you'll be astonished by how easy it is to cook on a contact grill. **SERVES 2 AS AN APPETIZER, 1 AS A MAIN COURSE; CAN BE MULTIPLIED AS DESIRED**

THE RECIPE

1 pair shad roe (6 to 8 ounces)
Coarse salt (kosher or sea) and freshly
    ground black pepper
About 1/4 cup flour
4 slices bacon (preferably thick,
    artisanal smoked bacon)
1 heaping tablespoon drained capers
Cooking oil spray
Lemon wedges, for serving

1. Gently separate the shad roe into 2 lobes (pull them apart with your fingers). Trim off any loose veins or membranes. Rinse the roe under cold running water to remove any bloody spots, then pat the roe dry with paper towels. Generously season each lobe on both sides with salt and pepper.

2. Line a large shallow bowl with paper towels, then spoon the flour into it. Arrange 2 slices of bacon on a large plate. Dip each lobe of shad roe in the flour, coating it on both sides, then shake off the excess. Arrange a lobe of roe lengthwise on top of each slice of bacon. Spoon 1 teaspoon of the capers on top of each lobe of roe, then place one of the remaining slices of bacon lengthwise on top of each. You'll use the remaining teaspoon of capers as garnish.

3. Preheat the grill (for instructions for using a contact grill, see page 3) if your contact grill has a temperature control,

preheat it to high. Place the drip pan under the front of the grill.

4. When ready to cook, lightly coat the grill surface with cooking oil spray. Lift each lobe from underneath (grab the ends of the slices of bacon) and place it on the hot grill, then close the lid. Grill until the bacon is crisp and golden brown and the shad roe is cooked through (it will feel firm when pressed with your finger), 5 to 8 minutes.

5. Transfer the shad roe to plates and sprinkle the remaining capers over it. Serve with lemon wedges.

VARIATION: To cook shad roe in a grill pan, prepare it as described in Steps 1 and 2, then, using 3 pieces of butcher's string, tie a slice of bacon onto the top and bottom of each lobe. Preheat the grill pan to medium over medium heat—you'll get the best results if you use a grill pan that has shallow ridges, like a Calphalon. When the grill pan is hot a drop of water will skitter in the pan. When ready to cook, lightly oil the ridges of the grill pan. Arrange the roe in the hot grill pan on a diagonal to the ridges. Place a grill press (see page 303) on top of the roe. The shad roe will be cooked through after 5 to 8 minutes per side. Sprinkle 1 teaspoon of capers over the roe before serving it with lemon wedges.

salt and pepper shrimp

Here's a grilled rendition of a Vietnamese classic, salt and pepper shrimp (the original is usually deep fried). The mega dose of salt, pepper, and fresh lime juice creates an electrifying and surprisingly complex dipping sauce. It's the perfect counterpoint to simply grilled shrimp. **SERVES 4**

THE RECIPE

if you have a...

CONTACT GRILL: Preheat the grill; if your contact grill has a temperature control, preheat the grill to high. Place the drip pan under the front of the grill. When ready to cook, lightly oil the grill surface. Place the shrimp on the hot grill, then close the lid. The shrimp will be done after cooking 2 to 3 minutes.

GRILL PAN: Place the grill pan on the stove and preheat it to medium-high over medium heat. When the grill pan is hot a drop of water will skitter in the pan. When ready to cook, lightly oil the ridges of the grill pan. Place the shrimp in the hot grill pan. They will be done after cooking 1 to 3 minutes per side.

BUILT-IN GRILL: Preheat the grill to high, then, if it does not have a nonstick surface, brush and oil the grill grate. Place the shrimp on the hot grate. They will be done after cooking 1 to 3 minutes per side.

FREESTANDING GRILL: Preheat the grill to high; there's no need to oil the grate. Place the shrimp on the hot grill. They will be done after cooking 2 to 4 minutes per side.

FIREPLACE GRILL: Rake red hot embers under the gridiron and preheat it for 3 to 5 minutes; you want a hot, 2 to 3 Mississippi fire. When ready to cook, brush and oil the gridiron. Place the shrimp on the hot grate. They will be done after cooking 1 to 3 minutes per side.

FOR THE SHRIMP:
1½ pounds extra-large shrimp in
   their shells (see Note)
1½ teaspoons coarse salt (kosher or sea)
1½ teaspoons freshly ground black pepper
1 tablespoon vegetable oil

FOR THE SAUCE:
½ cup fresh lime juice
1 tablespoon coarse salt (kosher or sea)
1 tablespoon freshly ground black pepper

1. Prepare the shrimp: Rinse the shrimp under cold running water, then blot them dry with paper towels. Using kitchen shears, cut the shell of each shrimp lengthwise down the back. Using the tip of a metal skewer or a paring knife, pull out the vein. Place the shrimp in a large mixing bowl. Sprinkle the salt and pepper over them and toss to mix. Add the oil and stir to coat evenly. Let the shrimp marinate in the refrigerator, covered, for 30 minutes to 1 hour.

2. Make the sauce: Place the lime juice, salt, and pepper in a small nonreactive mixing bowl and whisk until the salt dissolves. Divide the sauce among 4 small attractive bowls.

3. Cook the shrimp, following the instructions for any of the grills in the box on the facing page, until just cooked through. When done, the shrimp will turn pinkish white and will feel firm to the touch.

4. Transfer the shrimp to a platter or plates. Serve the salt and pepper lime juice on the side, for dipping.

NOTE: When you order salt and pepper shrimp in Vietnam, the shrimp come whole, heads on, and a great part of the pleasure of eating them lies in peeling the shrimp and sucking the juices. It's virtually impossible to buy shrimp with the heads on in most parts of this country, but you can approximate some of the same tactile pleasure by grilling the shrimp in the shells. This has the added advantage of keeping the shrimp extra moist. Of course, if you're serving this dish to more fastidious eaters, you'll want to start with peeled and thoroughly deveined shrimp.

sweet soy shrimp

Shrimp has a tendency to dry out on the grill. In the West we combat this by basting the shellfish with garlic butter or oil. Asian grill masters use a sweet salty seasoning of honey, sugar, Chinese five-spice powder, and soy sauce. Here these ingredients give shrimp a double blast of flavor—first as a marinade, then boiled down to make a glaze. **SERVES 6 TO 8 AS AN APPETIZER, 4 AS A MAIN COURSE**

THE RECIPE

1½ pounds extra-large shrimp, peeled and deveined
2 tablespoons sugar
1½ teaspoons Chinese five-spice powder
1 teaspoon freshly ground black pepper
⅓ cup soy sauce
3 tablespoons Chinese rice wine or dry sherry

3 tablespoons honey
2 tablespoons Asian (dark) sesame oil
1 scallion, trimmed, white part gently crushed with the side of a cleaver, green part finely chopped and set aside for garnish
1 tablespoon toasted sesame seeds (see Note), for garnish

tips

■ Sweet Soy Shrimp calls for Shaoxing, Chinese smoky rice wine, which has smoky overtones reminiscent of Scotch whisky and sherry. It is frequently available at Asian markets, natural foods stores, or some supermarkets. Dry sherry and Japanese sake make good substitutes.

■ Chinese five-spice powder is a blend of spices, including star anise, fennel, cinnamon, pepper, and cloves. If you can't find five-spice powder, you can use ¼ teaspoon aniseed or fennel seeds and ¼ teaspoon cinnamon.

if you have a...

CONTACT GRILL: Preheat the grill; if your contact grill has a temperature control, preheat the grill to high. Place the drip pan under the front of the grill. When ready to cook, lightly oil the grill surface. Place the shrimp on the hot grill, then close the lid. The shrimp will be done after cooking 2 to 3 minutes. You will need to turn the shrimp so that you can baste both sides.

GRILL PAN: Place the grill pan on the stove and preheat it to medium-high over medium heat. When the grill pan is hot a drop of water will skitter in the pan. When ready to cook, lightly oil the ridges of the grill pan. Place the shrimp in the hot grill pan. They will be done after cooking 1 to 3 minutes per side. Use the boiled marinade sparingly when basting, taking care not to drip a lot of it into the grill pan. After it has cooled down, soak the grill pan in hot water to loosen any burnt-on marinade.

BUILT-IN GRILL: Preheat the grill to high, then, if it does not have a nonstick surface, brush and oil the grill grate. Place the shrimp on the hot grate. They will be done after cooking 1 to 3 minutes per side.

FREESTANDING GRILL: Preheat the grill to high; there's no need to oil the grate. Place the shrimp on the hot grill. They will be done after cooking 2 to 4 minutes per side.

FIREPLACE GRILL: Rake red hot embers under the gridiron and preheat it for 3 to 5 minutes; you want a hot, 2 to 3 Mississippi fire. When ready to cook, brush and oil the gridiron. Place the shrimp on the hot grate. They will be done after cooking 1 to 3 minutes per side.

scallion white and stir to mix. Let the shrimp marinate in the refrigerator, covered, for 1 to 2 hours.

2. Place a strainer over a heavy saucepan and drain the shrimp marinade into it. Discard the scallion white. Let the marinade come to a boil over high heat, then boil until thick and syrupy, 3 to 5 minutes.

3. Cook the shrimp, following the instructions for any of the grills in the box at left, until just cooked through. When done, the shrimp will turn pinkish white and will feel firm to the touch. Baste each side of the shrimp once with some of the boiled marinade.

4. Transfer the shrimp to a platter or plates and drizzle the remaining boiled marinade over them. Sprinkle the sesame seeds and scallion greens on top and serve at once.

NOTE: To toast sesame seeds, place them in a dry cast-iron or other heavy skillet (don't use a nonstick skillet for this). Cook the sesame seeds over medium heat until they are fragrant and just beginning to brown, about 3 minutes, shaking the skillet to ensure that they toast evenly. Transfer the toasted sesame seeds to a heatproof bowl to cool.

1. Rinse the shrimp under cold running water, then blot them dry with paper towels. Place the shrimp in a large nonreactive mixing bowl, add the sugar, five-spice powder, and pepper, and stir to coat evenly. Add the soy sauce, rice wine, honey, sesame oil, and

peanut shrimp
with southeast asian dipping sauce

This dish fairly crackles with Southeast Asian flavors, although I can't promise you'll find this exact rendition in Thailand, Cambodia, or Vietnam. Rather, it's a combination of Southeast Asian ingredients that makes a quick-to-prepare shrimp you can sizzle on a grill. For an extra layer of flavor, not to mention a fun way to eat shrimp with your fingers, wrap the shellfish in lettuce and mint leaves before dipping them in the sauce. **SERVES 4**

THE RECIPE

1½ pounds extra-large shrimp, peeled
   and deveined
Coarse salt (kosher or sea) and freshly
   ground black pepper
2 cloves garlic, minced
¼ cup finely chopped fresh cilantro
¼ cup finely chopped roasted peanuts
1 tablespoon Asian fish sauce
1 tablespoon vegetable oil
1 bunch fresh mint, rinsed, shaken or
   spun dry, and torn into sprigs
1 head Boston lettuce, separated into
   individual leaves, rinsed,
   and spun dry
Vietnamese Dipping Sauce
   (recipe follows)

1. Rinse the shrimp under cold running water, then blot them dry with paper towels. Place the shrimp in a mixing bowl and season them well with salt and pepper,

stirring to coat evenly. Add the garlic, cilantro, and 2 tablespoons of the peanuts and stir to mix. Add the fish sauce and vegetable oil and toss to coat evenly. Let the shrimp marinate in the refrigerator, covered, for 15 minutes.

2. Arrange the mint sprigs and lettuce leaves on a platter.

3. When ready to cook, drain the shrimp and discard the marinade. Cook the shrimp, following the instructions for any of the grills in the box on the following page, until just cooked through. When done, the shrimp will turn pinkish white and will feel firm to the touch.

4. Transfer the shrimp to a platter or plates and sprinkle the remaining 2 tablespoons of peanuts over them. To eat,

tips

■ The easiest way to finely chop peanuts is in a food processor, but run the machine in short bursts or you'll wind up with peanut butter.

■ Fish sauce is a malodorous but delicious condiment made from pickled anchovies. Look for a brand in a glass bottle, or substitute soy sauce if fish sauce is unavailable or too off-putting.

if you have a...

CONTACT GRILL: Preheat the grill; if your contact grill has a temperature control, preheat the grill to high. Place the drip pan under the front of the grill. When ready to cook, lightly oil the grill surface. Place the shrimp on the hot grill, then close the lid. The shrimp will be done after cooking 2 to 3 minutes.

GRILL PAN: Place the grill pan on the stove and preheat it to medium-high over medium heat. When the grill pan is hot a drop of water will skitter in the pan. When ready to cook, lightly oil the ridges of the grill pan. Place the shrimp in the hot grill pan. They will be done after cooking 1 to 3 minutes per side.

BUILT-IN GRILL: Preheat the grill to high, then, if it does not have a nonstick surface, brush and oil the grill grate. Place the shrimp on the hot grate. They will be done after cooking 1 to 3 minutes per side.

FREESTANDING GRILL: Preheat the grill to high; there's no need to oil the grate. Place the shrimp on the hot grill. They will be done after cooking 2 to 4 minutes per side.

FIREPLACE GRILL: Rake red hot embers under the gridiron and preheat it for 3 to 5 minutes; you want a hot, 2 to 3 Mississippi fire. When ready to cook, brush and oil the gridiron. Place the shrimp on the hot grate. They will be done after cooking 1 to 3 minutes per side.

wrap a shrimp and a couple of mint leaves in a lettuce leaf, then dip it in the Vietnamese sauce.

vietnamese dipping sauce

Nuoc cham is an electrifying sauce that accompanies virtually all Vietnamese grilling (virtually all Vietnamese food, for that matter). A small bowl of it contains the universe of Vietnamese flavors—the sweetness of sugar, the acidity of fresh lime juice, the musky saltiness of fish sauce, the pungency of garlic, and the heat of fresh chile. For information on fish sauce, see the Tips on page 267. **MAKES ABOUT 1 CUP**

2 cloves garlic, minced
3 tablespoons sugar
1 small or 1/4 to 1/2 large carrot,
    cut into hair-thin slivers
    (for about 1/4 cup; see Note)
1/4 cup Asian fish sauce
1/4 cup fresh lime juice (from 2 limes)
3 tablespoons rice vinegar
1 Thai chile or serrano pepper, thinly sliced

1. Place the garlic and sugar in a mixing bowl and mash with the back of a spoon. Add the carrot, stir, and let stand until the carrot softens, about 10 minutes.

2. Add the fish sauce, lime juice, rice vinegar, and 1/4 cup of water to the carrot mixture and stir until the sugar dissolves. Divide the sauce among 4 tiny serving bowls, then float some chile slices on top. The sauce is best served the day it's made.

NOTE: The easiest way to cut hair-thin slivers of carrot is first to shave the carrot into paper-thin slices with a vegetable peeler. Cut the carrot slices into 2-inch lengths. Stack the slices on top of each other, then slice them lengthwise into hair-thin strands.

tapas bar shrimp
with garlic, parsley, and chiles

L a Casa del Abuelo ("grandfather's house") is one of Madrid's most atmospheric *tapas* bars. It's a tiny storefront with handmade ceramic tiles and a timeworn marble bar where you eat standing up. Since it opened in the early 1900s, La Casa has served only two dishes: *gambas al ajillo* (shrimp sizzled with garlic, parsley, and spicy guindilla chiles) and *gambas a la plancha* (shrimp sizzled in the shells on a griddle). The mounds of shrimp shells on the floor attest to La Casa's popularity—despite the limited menu. A *plancha* is a sort of griddle, and if you were to place a second hot griddle on top of it, you'd have a contact grill, the inspiration for the recipe that follows. But don't worry, you can cook a very tasty version using any sort of indoor grill.

SERVES 6 TO 8 AS AN APPETIZER, 4 AS A MAIN COURSE

tips

■ Casa del Abuelo uses supernaturally sweet Atlantic shrimp, which are cooked and served in the shells. The closest equivalent in the United States would be the sweet shrimp from the coast of Maine or spot prawns from the Pacific Northwest. But even shrimp of lesser pedigree will give you good results.

■ The pepper of choice in Madrid is the guindilla, a small, smoky, fiery dried chile. You can substitute dried chipotle pepper or hot red pepper flakes.

THE RECIPE

1½ pounds extra-large shrimp, peeled and deveined (see Note)
Coarse salt (kosher or sea) and freshly ground black pepper
2 cloves garlic, finely chopped
¼ cup finely chopped fresh flat-leaf parsley
½ to 1 teaspoon crumbled guindilla chile or dried chipotle pepper, or ½ to 1 teaspoon hot red pepper flakes
4 tablespoons extra-virgin olive oil (preferably Spanish)
Lemon wedges, for serving

1. Rinse the shrimp under cold running water, then blot them dry with paper towels. Place the shrimp in a large bowl and season them generously with salt and pepper. Stir in the garlic, 3 tablespoons of the parsley, the crumbled guindilla, and 2 tablespoons of the olive oil. Let the shrimp marinate in the refrigerator, covered, for 15 to 30 minutes.

2. Cook the shrimp, following the instructions for any of the grills in the

if you have a...

CONTACT GRILL: Preheat the grill; if your contact grill has a temperature control, preheat the grill to high. Place the drip pan under the front of the grill. When ready to cook, lightly oil the grill surface. Place the shrimp on the hot grill, then close the lid. The shrimp will be done after cooking 2 to 3 minutes.

GRILL PAN: Place the grill pan on the stove and preheat it to medium-high over medium heat. When the grill pan is hot a drop of water will skitter in the pan. When ready to cook, lightly oil the ridges of the grill pan. Place the shrimp in the hot grill pan. They will be done after cooking 1 to 3 minutes per side.

BUILT-IN GRILL: Preheat the grill to high, then, if it does not have a nonstick surface, brush and oil the grill grate. Place the shrimp on the hot grate. They will be done after cooking 1 to 3 minutes per side.

FREESTANDING GRILL: Preheat the grill to high; there's no need to oil the grate. Place the shrimp on the hot grill. They will be done after cooking 2 to 4 minutes per side.

FIREPLACE GRILL: Rake red hot embers under the gridiron and preheat it for 3 to 5 minutes; you want a hot, 2 to 3 Mississippi fire. When ready to cook, brush and oil the gridiron. Place the shrimp on the hot grate. They will be done after cooking 1 to 3 minutes per side.

box at left, until just cooked through. When done, the shrimp will turn pinkish white and will feel firm to the touch.

3. Transfer the shrimp to a platter or plates. If you have used a contact grill, pour any liquid in the drip pan over the shrimp. Drizzle the remaining 2 tablespoons of olive oil over the shrimp, sprinkle the remaining 1 tablespoon of parsley on top, and serve at once with lemon wedges.

NOTE: If you like to peel your own shrimp at the table, leave the shells on and devein the shrimp as described in Step 1 on page 264.

stove-top smoker

barbecued shrimp
in a stove-top smoker

Here's a barbecued shrimp that's worthy of the name, thanks to a mustard and paprika barbecue rub and the hickory smoke from a stove-top smoker. In the style of Buffalo wings, right at the end the shrimp are tossed with a mixture of melted butter and hot sauce. **SERVES 4**

THE RECIPE

2 teaspoons sweet paprika

2 teaspoons sugar

2 teaspoons coarse salt (kosher or sea)

1 teaspoon dry mustard

1 teaspoon freshly ground black pepper

1 teaspoon chili powder

$1/4$ teaspoon celery seed

1 to $1^1/2$ pounds jumbo shrimp, peeled and
    deveined

2 teaspoons vegetable oil

Cooking oil spray (optional)

2 tablespoons ($1/4$ stick) salted butter

1 tablespoon of your favorite hot sauce
    (I like Crystal hot sauce from Louisiana)

YOU'LL ALSO NEED:

1 tablespoon hickory sawdust

1. Place the paprika, sugar, salt, mustard, pepper, chili powder, and celery seed in a small bowl and whisk to mix the rub.

2. Rinse the shrimp under cold running water, then blot them dry with paper towels. Place the shrimp and rub in a large mixing bowl and toss to mix. Add the oil and stir to coat evenly. Let the shrimp marinate in the refrigerator, covered, for 30 minutes to 1 hour.

3. When ready to cook, set up the smoker (for instructions for using a stove-top smoker, see page 16). Place the sawdust in the center of the bottom of the smoker. Line the drip pan with aluminum foil and place it in the smoker. Lightly coat the smoker rack with cooking oil spray, or use a paper towel dipped in oil, and place the rack in the smoker. Arrange the shrimp on the rack at least $1/4$ inch apart. Cover the smoker and place it over high heat for 3 minutes, then reduce the heat to medium. Smoke the shrimp until just cooked, 10 to 12 minutes. When done, the shrimp will turn pinkish white and will feel firm to the touch.

4. Meanwhile, melt the butter in a small saucepan over medium-high heat. Add the hot sauce, bring it to a boil, and let boil about 10 seconds.

5. Transfer the shrimp to a bowl or platter. Pour the butter mixture on top and stir to mix. Serve at once, with plenty of cold beer.

tips

■ One quick and easy way to devein shrimp is by inserting a metal skewer or the tine of a fork into the rounded part of the back, about $1/4$ inch deep. Hook the vein on the tip and gently pull to remove it.

■ You can also smoke the shrimp on the stove-top in a wok. You'll find instructions for doing this on page 234.

not your ordinary grilled scallops

Randall's Ordinary, in North Stonington, Connecticut, may not be the oldest inn in North America, but people have been cooking in its massive stone hearth since 1685. Today, you can see how our country's founders cooked over live fire, for hearth cookery remains the inn's focal point. It's still done by chefs in linen shirts and knee britches, using antique gridirons, "spiders" (frying pans with legs to hold them above the coals), reflecting ovens, and turnspits, many of them as old as the inn itself. Hearth-cooked scallops are something of a house specialty, cooked with butter and garlic over a smoky oak fire. If you've got a fireplace, by all means grill the scallops in it—the smoke flavor will be remarkable. If you don't, I've modified the recipe so you can cook the scallops on a contact, built-in, or freestanding grill.

SERVES 4

if you have a...

CONTACT GRILL: Preheat the grill; if your contact grill has a temperature control, preheat the grill to high. Place the drip pan under the front of the grill. When ready to cook, lightly oil the grill surface. Place the scallops on the hot grill, then close the lid. The scallops will be done after cooking 2 to 4 minutes.

BUILT-IN GRILL: Preheat the grill to high, then, if it does not have a nonstick surface, brush and oil the grill grate. Arrange the scallops on the hot grill so that the exposed ends of the skewers extend off the grate. The scallops will be done after cooking 2 to 3 minutes per side.

FREESTANDING GRILL: Preheat the grill to high; there's no need to oil the grate. Place the scallops on the hot grill. They will be done after cooking 3 to 4 minutes per side.

FIREPLACE GRILL: Rake red hot embers under the gridiron and preheat it for 3 to 5 minutes; you want a hot, 2 to 3 Mississippi fire. When ready to cook, brush and oil the gridiron. Place the scallops on the hot grate. They will be done after cooking 2 to 3 minutes per side.

THE RECIPE

1½ pounds large sea scallops

Coarse salt (kosher or sea) and freshly ground
   black pepper

1½ to 2 tablespoons sweet paprika

4 tablespoons (½ stick) unsalted butter

2 cloves garlic, minced

2 tablespoons minced fresh chives
   or scallion greens

1 cup dried bread crumbs
   (preferably homemade)

2 tablespoons chopped fresh flat-leaf
   parsley (optional)

Lemon wedges, for serving

YOU'LL ALSO NEED:

About 4 metal skewers (10 to 12 inches long),
   or 6 to 8 bamboo skewers (8 inches long)

1. Pull off and discard the small crescent-shaped muscle from the side of any scallop that has one (it's noticeably tougher than the rest of the scallop). Rinse the scallops under cold running water, then drain them and blot them dry with paper towels. Place 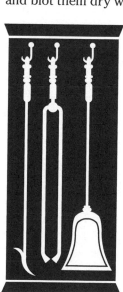 the scallops on a plate and generously sprinkle both sides with salt, pepper, and paprika. Thread the scallops onto skewers. (If you are cooking the scallops on a contact grill, you don't need to skewer them.)

2. Melt the butter in a small frying pan over medium heat. Add the garlic and chives and cook until fragrant but not brown, 2 to 3 minutes. Brush the scallops all over with some of the garlic butter mixture.

3. Place the bread crumbs in a large shallow bowl. Dredge the scallops a few at a time in the bread crumbs to coat the tops and bottoms, gently shaking off the excess.

4. Cook the scallops, following the instructions for any of the grills in the box on the facing page, until golden brown and just cooked through. When done the scallops will be opaque and feel firm to the touch but just barely; they shouldn't feel hard.

5. Transfer the scallops to a platter or plates. Pour any remaining garlic butter over them and sprinkle the parsley on top, if using. Serve the scallops at once with lemon wedges.

When buying scallops, look for bright, clean-smelling specimens. Avoid scallops sitting in a pool of milky liquid—they've most likely been frozen.

scallops howard stern

Radio talk show czar Howard Stern is a huge grill buff, running his oversize outdoor Viking gas grill like a race car at the Indy 500. Yes, I appeared on his show, and yes, I gave him a private barbecue class. I'd planned to show him how to make rosemary and prosciutto grilled scallops, but Howard doesn't eat red meat. He did have some smoked salmon in the refrigerator— the inspiration for these Scallops Howard Stern. **SERVES 6 AS AN APPETIZER, 4 AS A MAIN COURSE**

THE RECIPE

1½ pounds large sea scallops (14 to 16)
Coarse salt (kosher or sea) and freshly
    ground black pepper
12 to 14 ounces very thinly sliced
    smoked salmon
About 24 fresh rosemary sprigs
    (each 3 to 4 inches long)
2 tablespoons extra-virgin olive oil
1 medium-size lemon

1. Pull off and discard the small crescent-shaped muscle from the side of any scallop that has one (it's noticeably tougher than the rest of the scallop). Rinse the scallops under cold running water, then drain and blot them dry with paper towels. Season the scallops lightly with salt, generously with pepper.

2. Cut the smoked salmon into strips just large enough to wrap around the edge of

the scallops, about ¾ inch wide and 3½ to 4 inches long.

3. Place a scallop flat on a work surface. Wrap a piece of salmon around the edge, then skewer it through the side with a rosemary sprig (the idea is to pin the salmon to the scallop with the rosemary). Repeat until all the remaining scallops have been wrapped in salmon. Arrange the scallops on a plate or in a nonreactive baking dish.

4. Place the olive oil in a small nonreactive bowl. Finely grate about ½ teaspoon of lemon zest (the yellow oil-rich outer rind) over the olive oil. Add 1 tablespoon of lemon juice and stir with a fork, then brush the lemon oil over both sides of each scallop. Let the scallops marinate in the refrigerator, covered, for 15 minutes.

5. Cook the scallops, following the instructions for any of the grills in the box at right, until golden brown and just cooked through. When done the scallops will be opaque and feel firm to the touch but just barely; they shouldn't feel hard.

6. Transfer the scallops to a platter or plates and serve at once.

if you have a...

CONTACT GRILL: Preheat the grill; if your contact grill has a temperature control, preheat the grill to high. Place the drip pan under the front of the grill. When ready to cook, lightly oil the grill surface. Place the scallops on the hot grill, then close the lid. The scallops will be done after cooking 2 to 4 minutes.

BUILT-IN GRILL: Preheat the grill to high, then, if it does not have a nonstick surface, brush and oil the grill grate. Arrange the scallops on the hot grill so that the exposed ends of the rosemary sprigs extend off the grate. The scallops will be done after cooking 2 to 3 minutes per side.

FREESTANDING GRILL: Preheat the grill to high; there's no need to oil the grate. Place the scallops on the hot grill. They will be done after cooking 3 to 4 minutes per side.

FIREPLACE GRILL: Rake red hot embers under the gridiron and preheat it for 3 to 5 minutes; you want a hot, 2 to 3 Mississippi fire. When ready to cook, brush and oil the gridiron. Place the scallops on the hot grate. They will be done after cooking 2 to 3 minutes per side.

contact grill

poppy seed-crusted scallops
with lemon cream sauce

These poppy seed–crusted scallops come from my stepson, Jake, executive chef of the restaurant Pulse at the Sports Club/LA in Rockefeller Center in New York. Like many revolutionary dishes, it's astonishingly simple, but the contrast of textures and flavors—the crunchy, nutty poppy seeds, the soft, smooth briny scallops—will take your breath away. The gentle pressure of a contact grill is perfect for pressing the poppy seeds into the scallops. **SERVES 4**

THE RECIPE

1½ pounds large sea scallops
2 tablespoons (¼ stick) unsalted butter, melted
Coarse salt (kosher or sea) and freshly ground black pepper
¾ cup poppy seeds, spread out in a shallow bowl
Cooking oil spray
Lemon Cream Sauce (recipe follows)

YOU'LL ALSO NEED:
Parchment paper (optional; see Tips)

1. Pull off and discard the small crescent-shaped muscle from the side of any scallop that has one (it's noticeably tougher than the rest of the scallop). Rinse the scallops under cold running water, then drain and blot dry with paper towels. Lightly brush each scallop on both sides with the butter. Generously season each scallop on both sides with salt and pepper.

2. Dredge the scallops a few at a time in the poppy seeds to coat the tops and bottoms, gently shaking off the excess.

3. Preheat the grill (for instructions for using a contact grill, see page 3); if your contact grill has a temperature control, preheat the grill to high. Place the drip pan under the front of the grill.

4. When ready to cook, lightly coat the grill surface with cooking oil spray. Place the scallops on the hot grill and gently close the lid. Grill the scallops until just cooked through, 2 to 4 minutes. When done the scallops will be opaque and feel firm to the touch but just barely; they shouldn't feel hard.

5. Spoon the Lemon Cream Sauce over 4 plates. Place the scallops on top and serve at once.

lemon cream sauce

Do lemon, cream, and Parmesan cheese seem like odd companions for poppy seeds? All are used in cooking—sometimes combined in a single dish—in the Trentino–Alto Adige, in northeastern Italy, where the Italian Alps border Austria. Jake's cooking tends to be Asian inspired, but he's ecumenical enough to grab good food pairings from anywhere. The sauce is the perfect accompaniment for his poppy seed–crusted scallops. **MAKES ABOUT ¾ CUP**

1¼ cups heavy (whipping) cream
4 strips lemon zest
    (each about ½ by 1½ inches)
⅓ cup freshly grated Parmigiano-Reggiano cheese
Coarse salt (kosher or sea) and freshly ground black pepper

tips

■ On contact grills with deep ridges the poppy seeds have a tendency to fall off the scallops. You can prevent this by placing pieces of parchment paper between the plate of the grill and the scallops.

■ The zest is the oil-rich yellow outer rind of the lemon; remove it from the fruit in thin strips with a vegetable peeler.

■ For the cheese, use genuine imported Parmigiano-Reggiano.

Place the cream and lemon zest in a heavy saucepan over medium-high heat and let simmer briskly until reduced to about ¾ cup, 5 to 8 minutes, stirring from time to time. Remove the strips of lemon zest with a fork and discard them. Whisk in the Parmigiano-Reggiano and let simmer until it melts, about 2 minutes. Season with salt and pepper to taste. Keep the sauce warm at the back of the stove or in a pan of warm but not boiling water until ready to serve.

grilled scallops
with sweet corn sauce

Scallops are, perhaps, the sweetest of all shellfish—especially the large, meaty bivalves that are harvested one by one by fishermen in scuba gear and appropriately named diver scallops. So, it's fitting that the sweet, briny shellfish should be served with a Mexican sweet corn sauce, inspired by a soup traditionally served in Oaxaca. The dish looks great and tastes even better. If it helps timing wise, the sauce can be prepared ahead. **SERVES 4**

THE RECIPE

1 tablespoon butter
¼ Vidalia or other sweet onion or
    white onion, coarsely chopped
2 cloves garlic, raw or grilled
    (page 373, Step 1), coarsely chopped
5 ears corn (see Note)
¾ cup evaporated milk
2 tablespoons chopped fresh cilantro,
    plus cilantro sprigs for garnish
½ teaspoon sugar, or more to taste

Coarse salt (kosher or sea) and freshly
    ground white pepper
1½ pounds diver or large sea scallops
1 tablespoon walnut oil, hazelnut oil,
    or extra-virgin olive oil

1. Melt the butter in a small saucepan over medium heat. Add the onion and raw garlic, if using, and cook until soft and translucent, 3 to 4 minutes.

tip

Look for diver scallops at premium fish markets or order them by mail; you'll find sources on page 396.

if you have a...

CONTACT GRILL: Preheat the grill; if your contact grill has a temperature control, preheat the grill to high. Place the drip pan under the front of the grill. When ready to cook, lightly oil the grill surface. Place the scallops on the hot grill, then close the lid. The scallops will be done after cooking 2 to 4 minutes.

GRILL PAN: Place the grill pan on the stove and preheat it to medium-high over medium heat. When the grill pan is hot a drop of water will skitter in the pan. When ready to cook, lightly oil the ridges of the grill pan. Place the scallops in the hot grill pan. They will be done after cooking 2 to 3 minutes per side.

BUILT-IN GRILL: Preheat the grill to high, then, if it does not have a nonstick surface, brush and oil the grill grate. Place the scallops on the hot grate. They will be done after cooking 2 to 3 minutes per side.

FREESTANDING GRILL: Preheat the grill to high; there's no need to oil the grate. Place the scallops on the hot grill. They will be done after cooking 3 to 4 minutes per side.

FIREPLACE GRILL: Rake red hot embers under the gridiron and preheat it for 3 to 5 minutes; you want a hot, 2 to 3 Mississippi fire. When ready to cook, brush and oil the gridiron. Place the scallops on the hot grate. They will be done after cooking 2 to 3 minutes per side.

tip

Walnut and hazelnut oils are available at specialty food stores. Their distinctive flavors will reinforce the sweetness of the scallops. But olive oil works fine too.

2. If using raw corn, remove the husks. Cut the kernels off the corn cobs, using lengthwise strokes of a chef's knife, and measure 1½ cups. Set the remaining corn kernels aside for a garnish.

3. Place the corn kernels, cooked onion, cooked or grilled garlic, and the evaporated milk, chopped cilantro, and sugar in a blender and blend until a smooth purée forms. Transfer the corn mixture to a saucepan and bring to a gentle simmer over medium heat. Let the corn sauce simmer gently until thick, creamy, and richly flavored, 4 to 8 minutes, stirring occasionally with a wooden spoon. Taste for seasoning, adding more sugar as necessary and salt and white pepper to taste. For a particularly velvety-smooth sauce, pour it through a fine-meshed strainer. (I usually don't do this, preferring a more rustic sauce.) The corn sauce can be prepared up to 3 days ahead and refrigerated, covered. Rewarm it over medium-low heat, then taste for seasoning, adding more salt and/or pepper as necessary.

4. Pull off and discard the small crescent-shaped muscle from the side of any scallop that has one (it's noticeably tougher than the rest of the scallop). Rinse the scallops under cold running water, then drain and blot them dry with paper towels. Brush the scallops all over with the walnut oil and season them generously with salt and white pepper.

5. Cook the scallops, following the instructions for any of the grills in the box at left, until just cooked through. When done the scallops will be opaque and feel firm to the touch; they should not feel hard.

6. Spoon the corn sauce onto a platter or plates. Arrange the grilled scallops on top and sprinkle the reserved corn kernels over them. Garnish with cilantro sprigs and serve at once.

NOTE: Grilling the corn will give the sauce an extra layer of flavor. To do this, follow the instructions on page 330 but baste the corn with plain melted butter rather than soy butter. If you're the sort of person who plans ahead, you may want to do this when you've got the grill out for another meal. But if you're in a hurry, you can make a highly tasty sauce using raw fresh corn kernels.

The grill was the original toaster, as you surely know if you've ever tasted Italian bruschetta cooked the traditional way—grilled in the fireplace, rubbed with garlic, and drizzled with olive oil. So it should come as no surprise that the sandwich reaches its apotheosis on the indoor grill. At least three great sandwich cultures back me on this: France, the source of the *croque monsieur;* Italy, home of *panini;* and Cuba, with its pressed sandwiches. Here's a complete course on grilling breads and sandwiches, from garlic-grilled lavash and a lobster Reuben sandwich to a cutting-edge BLT.

breads and sandwiches

the real bruschetta

Certain foods are indelibly fixed in memory. Such was my first taste of Italian bruschetta. The place was a tiny restaurant in San Gimignano in Tuscany. It was utterly unremarkable in terms of menu or decor, except that there was a freestanding hearth in the center of the dining room where a white-haired master tended a small Tuscan grill set over a mound of glowing oak embers. To make bruschetta, he hand cut slices of saltless Tuscan bread and lightly charred them on the gridiron (bruschetta takes its name from the Italian word *bruscare,* to burn). He rubbed each hot, crusty slice with raw garlic, sprinkled it with coarse sea salt and cracked black peppercorns, and drizzled unfiltered Tuscan olive oil over it. Bruschetta has become popular to the point of cliché in the United States, and I'd wager most Americans think what makes it bruschetta is a topping of diced tomatoes. Here's the real deal, and when grilled in your fireplace there's no better grilled bread on the planet.

MAKES 8 PIECES

if you have a...

GRILL PAN: Place the grill pan on the stove and preheat it to medium-high over medium heat. When the grill pan is hot a drop of water will skitter in the pan. When ready to cook, lightly oil the ridges of the grill pan. Place the bread in the hot grill pan. It will be done after cooking 1 to 3 minutes per side.

BUILT-IN GRILL: Preheat the grill to high, then, if it does not have a nonstick surface, brush and oil the grill grate. Place the bread on the hot grate. It will be done after cooking 1 to 3 minutes per side.

FREESTANDING GRILL: Preheat the grill to high; there's no need to oil the grate. Place the bread on the hot grill. It will be done after cooking 2 to 4 minutes per side.

FIREPLACE GRILL: Rake red hot embers under the gridiron and preheat it for 3 to 5 minutes; you want a hot, 2 to 3 Mississippi fire. When ready to cook, brush and oil the gridiron. Place the bread on the hot grate. It will be done after cooking 1 to 3 minutes per side.

tip

8 slices (1/2 inch thick) Tuscan bread
4 cloves garlic, peeled and cut in half
    crosswise
Coarse salt (kosher or sea) and cracked or
    freshly ground black pepper
Extra-virgin olive oil in a small bottle or
    cruet

1. Cook the bread following the instructions for any of the grills in the box on the facing page, until golden brown and toasted. Don't take your eyes off the grill, as the bread can burn quickly. You may need to grill the bread in batches.

2. Rub one side of each slice of bread with the

cut side of a piece of garlic. Generously sprinkle that side with salt and pepper, then drizzle olive oil over it. Eat at once.

VARIATIONS: The Catalonians in southeastern Spain make a dish similar to bruschetta, but in addition to the garlic, they rub the grilled bread with the cut side of a luscious, red ripe tomato half before seasoning it with salt and pepper and drizzling olive oil over it.

For a thoroughly American barbecue twist on this Italian classic, rub the grilled bread with smoked garlic (you'll find the recipe on page 368), using 1 to 2 cloves for each slice.

The chief challenge when making bruschetta will be finding saltless Tuscan bread, which tastes insipid by itself but is glorious when grilled, rubbed with garlic, and sprinkled with salt. Look for loaves at Italian bakeries or, if you're feeling ambitious, you can make your own following a recipe in an Italian baking book, such as *The Italian Baker* by Carol Field. If you can't find Tuscan bread, substitute a dense country-style loaf and cut back on the salt.

garlic bread grilled indoors

Long, slender slices of bread, redolent of olive oil, garlic, and Parmesan and toasted audibly crisp on the grill—there's nothing like grilled garlic bread. It's super easy to prepare on a variety of indoor grills. To maximize the surface area exposed to the garlic and grill, slice the bread lengthwise as well as crosswise. **MAKES 12 PIECES**

THE   RECIPE

if you have a...

CONTACT GRILL: Preheat the grill; if your contact grill has a temperature control, preheat the grill to high. Place the drip pan under the front of the grill. When ready to cook, lightly oil the grill surface. Place the bread on the hot grill, then close the lid. The bread will be done after cooking 3 to 5 minutes.

GRILL PAN: Place the grill pan on the stove and preheat it to medium-high over medium heat. When the grill pan is hot a drop of water will skitter in the pan. When ready to cook, lightly oil the ridges of the grill pan. Place the bread in the hot grill pan. It will be done after cooking 1 to 3 minutes per side.

BUILT-IN GRILL: Preheat the grill to high, then, if it does not have a nonstick surface, brush and oil the grill grate. Place the bread on the hot grate. It will be done after cooking 1 to 3 minutes per side.

FREESTANDING GRILL: Preheat the grill to high; there's no need to oil the grate. Place the bread on the hot grill. It will be done after cooking 2 to 4 minutes per side.

FIREPLACE GRILL: Rake red hot embers under the gridiron and preheat it for 3 to 5 minutes; you want a hot, 2 to 3 Mississippi fire. When ready to cook, brush and oil the gridiron. Place the bread on the hot grate. It will be done after cooking 1 to 3 minutes per side.

1 loaf French bread
   (18 to 20 inches long; see Note)
2 to 3 cloves garlic, coarsely chopped
1/3 cup extra-virgin olive oil
2 tablespoons chopped fresh flat-leaf parsley
   (optional)
1/2 cup finely grated Parmigiano-Reggiano
   cheese

1. Using a long serrated knife, cut the bread crosswise into thirds; the lengths should be just a little shorter than the grill plates. Turn each piece on its side and cut it lengthwise into 4 broad thin slices.

2. Squeeze the garlic through a garlic press into a small bowl or place it in a bowl and mash it to a paste with the back of a wooden spoon. Add the olive oil and parsley, if using, and stir to mix. Brush the pieces of bread on both sides with the garlic oil.

3. Cook the garlic bread, following the instructions for any of the grills in the box at left, until browned and crisp. Don't take your eyes off the grill, as the bread can burn quickly. You may need to grill the bread in batches.

4. Sprinkle the Parmesan on the hot bread and serve at once. (If you are using a contact grill, you can sprinkle the Parmesan over the bread while it is still on the grill, after it has cooked for 2 minutes; it will cook right into the bread.)

NOTE: Any crusty baguette will work handily here.

VARIATIONS: There are many ways to customize the garlic bread recipe. You can substitute butter for the olive oil or grated Manchego cheese for the Parmesan. You can use roasted or smoked garlic (see page 368) in place of the fresh. Or top the bread with sliced sage leaves or prosciutto. Whichever topping you choose, serve the bread the minute—no, the second—it comes off the grill.

contact grill

tostadas (cuban toasts)

How does the day begin for tens, maybe hundreds of thousands, of Miamians—and certainly me? With *café con leche* and a *tostada. Café con leche* is Cuban caffe latte—strong, mud-black espresso stirred to a thick paste with a tooth-rattling dose of sugar and lightened with steamed whole milk. Into this blissful mixture you dip an 8-inch-piece of Cuban bread that's been slathered with butter and flattened and toasted wafer crisp in a *plancha,* a Cuban sandwich press. The result is a riot of textures and flavors: the sugary coffee; the salty butter; the crusty bread, which softens to a comforting pap the longer you dunk it in your coffee. It's as much a part of the south Florida experience as beignets dipped in chicory-flavored coffee are in New Orleans, and it's one of the best things about living in Miami. Contact grills work a lot like a *plancha;* you can use them to make not only *tostadas* but also a variety

cuban coffee

Strong, black, sweet Cuban coffee is the fuel that powers Miami. Every morning and throughout the day, Miamians of all ethnic backgrounds stop at gas stations and luncheonettes, sandwich shops and neighborhood markets for what is surely some of the best and most reasonably priced coffee in the United States.

Cuban coffee is brewed in espresso machines from dark-roast beans (the most popular brands are Pilon and Bustelo). The one thing all Cuban coffee drinks have in common is sugar—lots of it. Here are the options you're likely to encounter at a Miami coffee shop.

CAFE CUBANO OR CAFECITO: A shot of very strong, very sweet espresso.

COLADA: A large shot of *café cubano* served with four to six thimble-size plastic cups, so you can share it with your friends or officemates.

CAFE CORTADITO: A shot of sweetened espresso with a little hot steamed whole milk added—the Cuban equivalent of an Italian *macchiato.*

CAFE CON LECHE: The Cuban version of cappuccino or café au lait: sweetened espresso with hot milk added in a ratio of $1/2$ or 1 part milk to 1 part coffee, for an *oscuro,* a dark or strong *café con leche;* or more commonly, 2 parts milk to 1 part coffee. This is the coffee of choice for dipping your *tostada* into.

tip

To be strictly authentic, you'd use Cuban bread for *tostadas* (see sidebar on page 309). If you live in an area with a large Cuban community, you'll be able to find it at a neighborhood market or supermarket. But *tostadas* can also be made with a soft supermarket French bread or for that matter even a proper crusty baguette.

of Cuban sandwiches (see pages 309 through 311). Serve *tostadas* with *café con leche,* c*affe latte,* or *café au lait.* It's the next best thing to breakfast in Miami. **SERVES 2; CAN BE MULTIPLIED AS DESIRED**

T H E   R E C I P E

2 pieces (8 inches long) Cuban bread or
　　French bread
2 to 3 tablespoons salted butter,
　　at room temperature
Cooking oil spray

1. Preheat the grill (for instructions for using a contact grill, see page 3); if your contact grill has a temperature control, preheat the grill to high. Place the drip pan under the front of the grill.

2. Slice each piece of bread almost in

half the long way and open it up like a book. Spread the cut side with most of the butter and fold the bread back together. Spread the outside of each piece of bread with the remaining butter.

3. When ready to cook, lightly coat the grill surface with cooking oil spray. Arrange the bread on the hot grill so that it is perpendicular to the ridges, then close the lid. Grill the bread until the outside is browned and crisp, 3 to 4 minutes. Serve at once.

garlic lavash
(cracker bread on the grill)

Lavash is a flat bread found throughout Armenia, the Caucasus, Iran, and Afghanistan. Thanks to its paper thinness, you can grill it cracker crisp in less than a minute. Its mild flavor (a cross between that of pita and matzo) makes it a perfect foil for any number of toppings—herbs, cheese, roasted peppers, even ground lamb. That's not all: You can grill it open face, topped like a pizza; or fill it like a quesadilla. Serve lavash whole or break it into crisp shards to scoop up salsas or dips. **SERVES 4**

2 pieces lavash (see Note)
1½ tablespoons extra-virgin
   olive oil
Coarse salt (kosher or sea)
Coarsely ground black pepper or
   hot red pepper flakes
2 cloves garlic, finely chopped

1. Lightly brush each piece of lavash on both sides with the olive oil and sprinkle salt, pepper, and garlic over them.

2. Cook the lavash, following the instructions for any of the grills in the box at right, until lightly browned and crisp. Don't take your eyes off the grill, as the lavash can burn quickly. You may need to grill the lavash in batches.

3. Transfer the lavash to a wire rack and let it cool enough to handle, then break it into large pieces. The lavash can be served hot or at room temperature. In the unlikely event that you have any left over, it can be stored in an airtight tin or plastic bag for up to 2 days.

if you have a...

CONTACT GRILL: Preheat the grill; if your contact grill has a temperature control, preheat the grill to high. Place the drip pan under the front of the grill. When ready to cook, lightly oil the grill surface. Place the lavash on the hot grill, then close the lid. The bread will be done after cooking 2 to 3 minutes.

BUILT-IN GRILL: Preheat the grill to high, then, if it does not have a nonstick surface, brush and oil the grill grate. Place the lavash on the hot grate. It will be done after cooking 30 seconds to 1 minute per side.

FREESTANDING GRILL: Preheat the grill to high; there's no need to oil the grate. Place the lavash on the hot grill. It will be done after cooking 1 to 2 minutes per side.

FIREPLACE GRILL: Rake red hot embers under the gridiron and preheat it for 3 to 5 minutes; you want a hot, 2 to 3 Mississippi fire. When ready to cook, brush and oil the gridiron. Place the lavash on the hot grate. It will be done after cooking 30 seconds to 1 minute per side.

NOTE: Look for lavash in the bread or Middle Eastern food section of the supermarket. Better still, you may be able to find freshly baked lavash in a Middle Eastern market. You want fresh, pliable lavash, not dry ones. The lavash I use are about 10 inches square.

parmesan and rosemary lavash

Here's how grilled lavash would taste if it were prepared by a northern Italian—with Parmesan cheese, of course. Use crumbled dried rosemary if fresh is not available. **SERVES 4**

if you have a...

CONTACT GRILL: Preheat the grill; if your contact grill has a temperature control, preheat the grill to high. Place the drip pan under the front of the grill. When ready to cook, lightly oil the grill surface. Place the lavash on the hot grill, then close the lid. The bread will be done after cooking 2 to 3 minutes.

BUILT-IN GRILL: Preheat the grill to high, then, if it does not have a nonstick surface, brush and oil the grill grate. Place the lavash on the hot grate. It will be done after cooking 30 seconds to 1 minute per side.

FREESTANDING GRILL: Preheat the grill to high; there's no need to oil the grate. Place the lavash on the hot grill. It will be done after cooking 1 to 2 minutes per side.

FIREPLACE GRILL: Rake red hot embers under the gridiron and preheat it for 3 to 5 minutes; you want a hot, 2 to 3 Mississippi fire. When ready to cook, brush and oil the gridiron. Place the lavash on the hot grate. It will be done after cooking 30 seconds to 1 minute per side.

sprinkle the rosemary and Parmesan cheese over them.

2. Cook the lavash, following the instructions for any of the grills in the box at left, until lightly browned and crisp. Don't take your eyes off the grill, as the lavash can burn quickly. You may need to grill the lavash in batches.

3. Transfer the lavash to a wire rack and let it cool enough to handle, then break it into large pieces. The lavash can be served hot or at room temperature. In the unlikely event that you have any left over, it can be stored in an airtight tin or plastic bag for up to 2 days.

2 pieces lavash (see Note on page 285)
2 tablespoons (¼ stick) butter, melted
2 tablespoons finely chopped fresh rosemary
¼ cup finely grated Parmesan cheese

1. Lightly brush each piece of lavash on both sides with the butter and then

sesame scallion lavash

Sesame-dotted scallion bread is classic in Chinese dim sum. This grilled version, made with lavash, is a lot less oily and easier to make. **SERVES 4**

THE RECIPE

2 pieces lavash (see Note on page 285)

2 tablespoons Asian (dark) sesame oil

1 scallion, both white and green parts,
    minced (about 2 tablespoons)

1 tablespoon white sesame seeds

1 tablespoon black sesame seeds,
    or more white

1. Lightly brush each piece of lavash on both sides with the sesame oil and then sprinkle the scallions and sesame seeds over them.

2. Cook the lavash following the instructions for any of the grills in the box at right, until lightly browned and crisp. Don't take your eyes off the grill, as the lavash can burn quickly. You may need to grill the lavash in batches.

3. Transfer the lavash to a wire rack and let it cool enough to handle, then break it into large pieces. The lavash can be served hot or at room temperature. In the

if you have a...

CONTACT GRILL: Preheat the grill; if your contact grill has a temperature control, preheat the grill to high. Place the drip pan under the front of the grill. When ready to cook, lightly oil the grill surface. Place the lavash on the hot grill, then close the lid. The bread will be done after cooking 2 to 3 minutes.

BUILT-IN GRILL: Preheat the grill to high, then, if it does not have a nonstick surface, brush and oil the grill grate. Place the lavash on the hot grate. It will be done after cooking 30 seconds to 1 minute per side.

FREESTANDING GRILL: Preheat the grill to high; there's no need to oil the grate. Place the lavash on the hot grill. It will be done after cooking 1 to 2 minutes per side.

FIREPLACE GRILL: Rake red hot embers under the gridiron and preheat it for 3 to 5 minutes; you want a hot, 2 to 3 Mississippi fire. When ready to cook, brush and oil the gridiron. Place the lavash on the hot grate. It will be done after cooking 30 seconds to 1 minute per side.

unlikely event that you have any left over, it can be stored in an airtight tin or plastic bag for up to 2 days.

contact grill

wisconsin "rarebit"

Wisconsin may have the world's best-kept cheese secret. Sure, everyone knows that untold tons of pleasant, vivid orange commercial cheddar come from the Badger State. What you may not realize is that contemporary Wisconsin cheese makers are turning out some astonishing farmstead cheeses— silken mascarpones, buttery monastery-style cheeses, and crumbly blues worthy of Stilton. You can even find cave-ripened cheddars, aged for five years until they are tooth-tinglingly sharp. Which brings us to rarebit, a dish of British origin that's fallen somewhat out of fashion in recent years. Traditional Welsh rarebit is a sort of cheese and ale fondue served over toasted bread (just the snack for a hapless hunter whose rabbit got away). Here's a "rarebit" you can make a lot more quickly on a contact grill (Foreman-type or *panini* machine). **SERVES 2; CAN BE MULTIPLIED AS DESIRED**

THE RECIPE

4 very thin slices dense white
    sandwich bread
1¹⁄₂ tablespoons unsalted butter,
    at room temperature or melted
1 tablespoons English hot mustard or
    Dijon mustard, or more to taste
Worcestershire sauce
4 to 6 ounces Wisconsin cheddar, sliced as
    thinly as possible (about 6 slices)
Cooking oil spray

1. Preheat the grill (for instructions for using a contact grill, see page 3); if your contact grill has a temperature control, preheat the grill to high. Place the drip pan under the front of the grill.

2. Using a knife or pastry brush, spread or brush the slices of bread on one side with the butter. Place 2 slices of bread on a work surface buttered side down, then spread the top of each with the mustard. Sprinkle a few drops of Worcestershire sauce over the mustard. Arrange the slices of cheddar on top, trimming them

so that they come just to the edges of the bread. Place the cheese trimmings in the center of the sandwiches. Place the remaining 2 slices of bread on top, buttered side up.

3. When ready to cook, lightly coat the grill surface with cooking oil spray. Using a spatula, transfer the sandwiches to the hot grill and gently close the lid. Grill the sandwiches until the bread is nicely browned and the cheese is melted, about 5 minutes. Serve at once.

tips

■ These sandwiches will be highly tasty made with any Wisconsin cheddar and absolutely amazing prepared with a cave-aged five-year-old, like the cheddar from Carr Valley Cheese Company (see Mail-Order Sources on page 396).

■ Rarebit is traditionally served on dense white sandwich bread, but don't rule out rye, wheat berry, or whole wheat bread.

contact grill

dutch "rarebit"

This sandwich was inspired by a trip to Amsterdam, a city of amazing beauty (seventeenth-century town houses overlooking canals), astonishing open-mindedness, and plenty of great food. The Dutch can boast of their remarkably piquant cheeses, hams of great character, and bread so dark, rich, and grainy a slice is almost a meal in itself. Put these together in a contact grill (Foreman-type or *panini* machine) and you get a grilled cheese sandwich you won't soon forget.

SERVES 2; CAN BE MULTIPLIED AS DESIRED

THE RECIPE

**4 slices (about 1/2 inch thick) dark country
     rye bread or whole wheat bread**
**1 1/2 tablespoons unsalted butter,
     at room temperature or melted**
**1 tablespoon Dutch, German, or Dijon mustard,
     or more to taste**
Worcestershire sauce
**2 to 3 ounces thinly sliced smoked ham,
     such as Westphalian or Black Forest
     (about 6 slices)**
**2 to 3 ounces thinly sliced Leyden or other
     Dutch cheese (about 4 slices)**
6 cornichons, thinly sliced lengthwise
Cooking oil spray

1. Preheat the grill (for instructions for using a contact grill, see page 3); if your contact grill has a temperature control, preheat the grill to high. Place the drip pan under the front of the grill.

2. Using a knife or pastry brush, spread or brush the slices of bread on one side with the butter. Place 2 slices of bread on a work surface buttered side down, then spread the top of each with the mustard. Sprinkle a few drops of Worcestershire sauce over the mustard. Arrange the slices of ham on the bread, followed by the slices of cheese, trimming both so that they come just to the edges of the bread. Place the trimmings in the center of the sandwiches. Top each sandwich with half of the cornichon slices. Place the remaining 2 slices of bread on top, buttered side up.

3. When ready to cook, lightly coat the grill surface with cooking oil spray. Using a spatula, transfer the sandwiches to the hot grill and gently close the lid. Grill the sandwiches until the bread is nicely browned and the cheese is melted, about 5 minutes. Serve at once.

tips

■ You're probably familiar with the Dutch cheeses Gouda and Edam, but there are dozens of others to choose from, including the cumin seed or caraway studded Leyden, which makes an astonishingly fragrant sandwich. Look for it and other Dutch cheeses at cheese or specialty food stores.

■ Cornichons are very tiny, very sour pickles. If the supermarket doesn't carry them, a specialty food store will be your source, or substitute thinly sliced pickled onions.

contact grill

sage derby "rarebit"

Sage Derby (pronounced "dar-bee") is one of England's most distinctive cheeses—a cheddary, green-veined cow's milk cheese that owes its herbal flavor to the addition of chopped sage. Sage is a classic herb for poultry, my inspiration for a "rarebit" made with sage Derby and sliced turkey. **SERVES 2; CAN BE MULTIPLIED AS DESIRED**

tips

■ For best results, use a farmhouse sage Darby—Steven Jenkins, author of the *Cheese Primer,* recommends Kirkby Malzeard Dairy's, which is sometimes labeled Tuxford & Tebbutt.

■ As for the turkey, it should be carved from a whole turkey or turkey breast (no turkey roll, please)— the sort of turkey you'd get from a good deli or roast yourself.

THE RECIPE

4 slices (about ½ inch thick) dense white
   sandwich bread
1½ tablespoons unsalted butter,
   at room temperature or melted
1 tablespoon English mustard, or more to taste
2 to 3 ounces thinly sliced roast or smoked
   turkey (about 6 slices)
2 to 3 ounces thinly sliced sage Derby cheese
   (about 4 slices)
Cooking oil spray

1. Preheat the grill (for instructions for using a contact grill, see page 3); if your contact grill has a temperature control, preheat the grill to high. Place the drip pan under the front of the grill.

2. Using a knife or pastry brush, spread or brush the slices of bread on one side with the butter. Place 2 slices of bread on a work surface buttered side down, then spread the top of each with the mustard. Arrange the slices of turkey on the bread followed by the slices of cheese, trimming both so that they come just to the edges of the bread. Place the trimmings in the center of the sandwiches. Place the remaining 2 slices of bread on top, buttered side up.

3. When ready to cook, lightly coat the grill surface with cooking oil spray. Using a spatula, transfer the sandwiches to the hot grill and gently close the lid. Grill the sandwiches until the bread is nicely browned and the cheese is melted, about 5 minutes. Serve at once.

contact grill

a new blt:
with bacon, leicester cheese, and green tomato

F ew things can beat the perfection of a BLT, but this grilled cheese sandwich comes close. The ingredients are key. The bacon should be thickly sliced, naturally cured, and corn cob or wood smoked (one good brand, Nueske's Hillcrest Farm, is available by mail order; see page 396). The cheese, Leicester, from central England, is sharp, orange, and Cheddarlike, with a sweet, spicy flavor; look for it at cheese or specialty food shops. To provide the requisite crunch and acidity, the tomato should be hard and green. **SERVES 2; CAN BE MULTIPLIED AS DESIRED**

THE RECIPE

4 slices (about ¹/₂ inch thick) green tomato,
    cut crosswise from 1 large tomato
Coarse salt (kosher or sea) and freshly
    ground black pepper
4 slices bacon (about 4 ounces total),
    each slice cut crosswise in half
Cooking oil spray
4 slices (about ¹/₂ inch thick) dense white
    sandwich bread
1¹/₂ tablespoons salted butter,
    at room temperature or melted
1 to 2 tablespoons mayonnaise
    (optional)
4 ounces thinly sliced Leicester cheese
    (about 6 slices)

1. Preheat the grill (for instructions for using a contact grill, see page 3); if your contact grill has a temperature control, preheat the grill to high. Place the drip pan under the front of the grill.

2. Generously season the tomato slices with salt and pepper. Place 2 pieces of bacon on a work surface side by side and place a tomato slice on top. Top the tomato slice with 2 pieces of bacon. Repeat with the remaining pieces of bacon and tomato slices.

3. When ready to cook, lightly coat the grill surface with cooking oil spray. Using a spatula, transfer the bacon and tomato slices to the hot grill and close the lid. Grill until the bacon is browned and the tomato is tender, 4 to 6 minutes. Using a

tip

For an interesting variation on the recipe, substitute Canadian bacon for the bacon, Livarot (an odiferous French cheese) for the Leicester, and a ripe red tomato for the green. The result will still be a BLT—but with an entirely different personality.

spatula, transfer the tomatoes and bacon to a plate. Leave the grill turned on.

4. Using a knife or pastry brush, spread or brush the slices of bread on one side with the butter. Place 2 slices of bread on a work surface buttered side down, then spread the top of each with mayonnaise, if using. Arrange 2 grilled bacon and tomato bundles on each slice of bread, cutting them as needed so that they cover the bread. Arrange the slices of cheese on top, trimming them so that they come just to the edges of the bread.

Place the cheese trimmings in the center of the sandwiches. Place the remaining 2 slices of bread on top, buttered side up.

5. When ready to cook, lightly coat the grill surface again with cooking oil spray. Using a spatula, transfer the sandwiches to the hot grill and gently close the lid. Grill the sandwiches until the bread is nicely browned and the cheese is melted, about 5 minutes. Let the sandwiches cool slightly (fresh tomatoes get very hot when grilled), then serve.

contact grill

classic croque monsieur

The classic sandwich of the French café, *croque monsieur* is two slices of buttered bread filled with ham and cheese and cooked on a griddle or in a sandwich press until golden and crusty. Did someone say sandwich press? How about using a contact grill, which has the added advantage of creating grill marks? The preparation may sound simple, but unless you use the proper ingredients in the right proportions, you'll wind up with a fast-food cliché. First, there's the bread—the French would use *pain de mie,* a crustless, dense-grained white bread. Country-style white bread works great on this side of the Atlantic; to be strictly authentic, cut off the crusts. Next, the ham: No molded, boiled ham product, but real ham, ideally smoked or at the very least baked. (Hint: If it comes in perfectly square or rectangular slices, it's probably not real ham.) A smoked Vermont or honey-baked ham would be ideal. Finally, the cheese. Tradition calls for Gruyère—a sharp, tangy cheese from the French or Swiss Alps, which has a nutty sweetness. Look for it at a specialty food store, cheese shop, or a good supermarket cheese department. **SERVES 2; CAN BE MULTIPLIED AS DESIRED**

THE RECIPE

4 slices (about 1/2 inch thick) dense
    white sandwich bread, crusts cut off
    and discarded
2 tablespoons (1/4 stick) salted butter,
    at room temperature or melted
2 ounces thinly sliced smoked or
    baked ham (about 6 slices)
2 ounces Gruyère cheese, grated
    (about 1/2 cup)
Freshly ground black pepper
Cooking oil spray
Mornay Sauce (optional; recipe follows)

1. Preheat the grill (for instructions for using a contact grill, see page 3); if your contact grill has a temperature control, preheat the grill to high. Place the drip pan under the front of the grill.

2. Using a knife or pastry brush, spread or brush both sides of the slices of bread with the butter, buttering one side of each slice more heavily than the other. Place 2 slices of bread on a work surface with the less heavily buttered side facing up. Arrange the ham slices on top, trimming them so that they come just to the edges of the bread. Place the ham trim-

mings in the center of the sandwiches. Sprinkle the Gruyère over the ham, dividing it evenly between the 2 sandwiches and spreading it out to the edges of the bread. Sprinkle some pepper over the sandwiches. Place the remaining 2 slices of bread on top, with the more heavily buttered side facing up.

3. When ready to cook, lightly coat the grill surface with cooking oil spray. Using a spatula, transfer the sandwiches to the hot grill and gently close the lid. Grill the sandwiches until the bread is browned and crisp and the cheese is melted, about 5 minutes. Serve at once with Mornay Sauce, if desired.

mornay sauce

This simple French cheese sauce is often spooned over croque monsieur and other pressed sandwiches. The mustard isn't strictly traditional, but I like the way it counterpoints the richness of the cheese. I like to use equal parts

tips

■ Some restaurants crown their *croque monsieur* with Mornay sauce (a cheese-flavored béchamel). It might seem like gilding the lily, but if you want to try it, there's a recipe for Mornay Sauce here.

■ To turn the sandwich into a *croque madame,* cut a hole in the top slice and crack in an egg before grilling.

Gruyère and Parmesan cheese, but to simplify the recipe you could use straight Gruyère. **MAKES ABOUT 1 CUP**

1½ tablespoons unsalted butter
1½ tablespoons flour
1 cup whole milk
¼ cup (about 1 ounce) coarsely grated
    Gruyère cheese
½ cup (about 1 ounce) coarsely grated
    Parmesan cheese
1 teaspoon Dijon mustard
Coarse salt (kosher or sea) and freshly
    ground black pepper
A pinch of freshly grated nutmeg
    (optional)

1. Melt the butter in a heavy saucepan over medium heat. Remove the saucepan from the heat and whisk in the flour.

Return the saucepan to the heat and cook until the flour and butter are sizzling but not brown, about 2 minutes, whisking constantly.

2. Remove the pan from the heat and gradually whisk in the milk. Return the saucepan to the heat and gradually bring the mixture to a boil, whisking steadily, about 3 minutes. Let the sauce simmer for 3 minutes, whisking steadily.

3. Whisk in the Gruyère and Parmesan and cook until melted, 1 to 2 minutes, whisking steadily. Add the mustard and season the sauce with salt and pepper to taste and just a pinch of nutmeg, if desired. Serve the Mornay Sauce at once or keep it warm on the back of the stove until ready to use.

contact grill

croque
with roquefort and walnuts

Roquefort, the salty, tangy French blue cheese made with sheep's milk, has an affinity for walnuts. If you live near an artisanal bakery, you may be able to find walnut bread. If not, use white bread and add walnuts to the Roquefort mixture. **SERVES 2; CAN BE MULTIPLIED AS DESIRED**

tip

The best ham for this recipe would be a smoked, cured ham, like Bayonne ham from France or Westphalian or Black Forest ham from Germany. Look for these at specialty food stores or, in a pinch, substitute prosciutto.

2 ounces Roquefort cheese (about
  ½ cup crumbled), at room temperature
2½ tablespoons salted butter, at room
  temperature
2 tablespoons coarsely chopped toasted
  walnuts (optional; see sidebar)
Freshly ground black pepper
4 slices (about ½ inch thick) walnut bread
  or dense white sandwich bread
2 ounces very thinly sliced smoked ham
  (about 6 slices)
Cooking oil spray

1. Preheat the grill (for instructions for using a contact grill, see page 3); if your contact grill has a temperature control, preheat the grill to high. Place the drip pan under the front of the grill.

2. Place the Roquefort in a mixing bowl and mash it to a paste with a fork. Add 1 tablespoon of the butter and the walnuts, if using, and stir to mix. Season with pepper to taste.

3. Spread the remaining 1½ tablespoons of butter on one side of the slices of bread, dividing it evenly among them. Place 2 slices of the bread on a work surface, buttered side down. Arrange the ham slices on top, trimming them so that they come just to the edges of the bread. Place the ham trimmings in the center of the sandwiches. Spoon the Roquefort mixture on top, dividing it evenly between the 2 sandwiches and spreading it out to the edges of the bread. Place the remaining 2 slices of bread on top, buttered side up.

4. When ready to cook, lightly coat the grill surface with cooking oil spray. Using a spatula, transfer the sandwiches to the hot grill and gently close the lid. Grill the sandwiches until the bread is browned and crisp and the cheese is melted, about 5 minutes. Serve at once.

toasting walnuts

To toast walnuts, place them in a dry cast-iron or other heavy skillet (don't use a nonstick skillet for this). Cook the walnuts over medium-high heat until fragrant and lightly browned, 3 to 4 minutes, shaking the skillet to ensure that they toast evenly. Transfer the toasted walnuts to a heatproof bowl to cool.

contact grill

goat cheese and tomato croque

Here's a meatless, Mediterranean-inspired *croque monsieur*. The goat cheese, tomato, and basil filling will play pinball with your taste buds. You can use either sun-dried tomatoes or fresh ones—or even a mixture of both. Warning: Fresh tomatoes

tip

The first sun-dried tomatoes to reach America from Italy were cured in oil, obscenely expensive, and exquisitely, explosively flavorful. Today, most sun-dried tomatoes are industrially processed and sold dry, but you can approximate the intense flavor of the original Italian product by plumping the tomatoes in boiling water, then tossing them with garlic and oil. If you can find oil-cured tomatoes, available at Italian markets, specialty food stores, and well-stocked supermarkets, you won't need to do this.

absorb a lot of heat as they grill. Let the sandwich cool slightly before taking a bite, so you don't burn your tongue. **SERVES 2; CAN BE MULTIPLIED AS DESIRED**

THE RECIPE

8 sun-dried tomato halves, or 1 medium-size
　　luscious ripe red tomato
1½ tablespoons extra-virgin olive oil, plus
　　1 tablespoon more if using air-dried
　　tomatoes
½ cup (4 ounces) soft goat cheese,
　　such as Montrachet, at room
　　temperature
Freshly ground black pepper
4 slices (about ½ inch thick) French bread,
　　cut sharply on the diagonal
6 fresh basil leaves, slivered
Cooking oil spray

1. If using oil-cured sun-dried tomatoes, drain them well. If using air-dried tomatoes, place them in a heatproof bowl, add boiling water to cover, and let soak for 20 minutes. Drain well and toss with 1 tablespoon of olive oil. Coarsely chop the sun-dried tomatoes. If using a fresh tomato, thinly slice it.

2. Place the goat cheese in a mixing bowl and mash with a wooden spoon until smooth. Season the cheese with pepper to taste. If using sun-dried tomatoes, add them to the cheese and stir to mix.

3. Preheat the grill (for instructions for using a contact grill, see page 3); if your contact grill

has a temperature control, preheat the grill to high. Place the drip pan under the front of the grill.

4. Brush the oil on one side of each slice of bread. Place 2 slices of bread on a work surface, oiled side down. Spoon the goat cheese mixture on top, dividing it evenly between the 2 sandwiches and spreading it out to the edges of the bread. If using fresh tomatoes, arrange them on the cheese mixture. Place half of the basil leaves on each sandwich. Place the remaining 2 slices of bread on top, oiled side up.

5. When ready to cook, lightly coat the grill surface with cooking oil spray. Using a spatula, transfer the sandwiches to the hot grill and gently close the lid. Grill the sandwiches until the bread is browned and crisp and the cheese is melted, about 5 minutes. Serve at once.

contact grill

croque
with gouda and mushroom hash

The French call this earthy mushroom hash duxelles, and it's an appellation rich with associations. It pays tribute to the Marquis d'Uxelles, patron of the great seventeenth-century chef François Pierre de La Varenne (he became the namesake of the French cooking school, La Varenne, where I trained in Paris in the 1970s). It's pretty hard to beat the combination of grilled cheese and mushrooms, especially mushrooms flavored with Cognac and shallots and cooked down to concentrate their woodsy flavor. **SERVES 2; CAN BE MULTIPLIED AS DESIRED**

THE RECIPE

FOR THE MUSHROOM HASH:
12 ounces fresh mushrooms, stemmed
  and wiped clean with damp paper towels
1 teaspoon fresh lemon juice
1 tablespoon salted butter or extra-virgin
  olive oil
2 to 3 large shallots, minced
  (for about ½ cup)
1 clove garlic, minced
1½ tablespoons Cognac
2 tablespoons finely chopped fresh
  flat-leaf parsley
Coarse salt (kosher or sea) and freshly
  ground black pepper

FOR THE CROQUES:
4 slices (about ½ inch thick)
  dense white sandwich bread or
  whole wheat bread

2 tablespoons (¼ stick) salted butter,
  at room temperature or melted
2 ounces thinly sliced aged Gouda cheese
  (about 6 slices)
Cooking oil spray

1. Make the mushroom hash: Cut any large mushrooms into quarters; cut smaller ones in half. Place the mushrooms and lemon juice in a food processor and finely chop, running the machine in short bursts and working in several batches if necessary, so you don't crowd the bowl. Do not overprocess or you'll reduce the mushrooms to mush.

2. Melt the butter in a frying pan over medium heat. Add the shallots and garlic and cook until just beginning to brown,

tip

Mushroom hash is traditionally made with commonplace white or button mushrooms, but you can jazz it up by using any exotic mushrooms, from shiitakes to morels, or a mixture of mushrooms.

about 3 minutes, stirring with a wooden spoon. Add the Cognac and bring to a boil; it will evaporate almost immediately, leaving a flavorful residue. Add the mushrooms and the parsley and increase the heat to high. Cook until all the mushroom juices have evaporated and the mixture is thick and concentrated, 4 to 6 minutes, stirring with a wooden spoon. Taste for seasoning, adding salt and pepper to taste; the mushroom hash should be highly seasoned. Let cool to room temperature, then refrigerate, covered, until ready to use. The recipe can be prepared up to a day ahead to this stage.

3. Preheat the grill (for instructions for using a contact grill, see page 3); if your contact grill has a temperature control, preheat the grill to high. Place the drip pan under the front of the grill.

4. Make the *croques*: Using a knife or pastry brush, spread or brush both sides of the slices of bread with the butter, buttering one side of each slice more heavily than the other. Place 2 slices of bread on a work surface, with the less heavily buttered side facing up. Arrange the cheese slices on top, trimming them so they come just to the edges of the bread. Place the cheese trimmings in the center of the sandwiches. Spoon the mushroom mixture on top, dividing it evenly between the 2 sandwiches and spreading it out to the edges of the bread. Place the remaining 2 slices of bread on top, with the more heavily buttered side facing up.

5. When ready to cook, lightly coat the grill surface with cooking oil spray. Using a spatula, transfer the sandwiches to the hot grill and gently close the lid. Grill the sandwiches until the bread is browned and crisp and the cheese is melted, about 5 minutes. Serve at once.

contact grill

croque bernardin (grilled cheese with smoked salmon on brioche)

Once you understand the principle of putting together a *croque monsieur,* there's no limit to the combinations you can come up with. The grilled cheese and smoked salmon sandwich here was inspired by Eric Ripert, the überchef of Le Bernardin in Manhattan. There are many possibilities for smoked salmon here—Irish, Norwegian, or from Maine. Just be sure it's cold smoked and thinly sliced. **SERVES 2; CAN BE MULTIPLIED AS DESIRED**

THE RECIPE

4 thin (no more than ½ inch thick) slices
    brioche (see Note)
1½ tablespoons butter, melted
2 ounces thinly sliced smoked salmon
    (about 6 slices)
1 thin slice lemon
2 ounces Gruyère cheese, sliced paper-thin
    (about 8 slices)
Cooking oil spray

1. Preheat the grill (for instructions for using a contact grill, see page 3); if your contact grill has a temperature control, preheat the grill to high. Place the drip pan under the front of the grill.

2. Using a pastry brush, brush the slices of brioche on one side with the butter. Place 2 slices of brioche on a work surface, buttered side down. Arrange the salmon slices on top, trimming them so that they come just to the edges of the bread. Place the salmon trimmings in the center of the sandwiches.

3. Seed the lemon slice and remove and discard the rind. Finely chop the lemon, then sprinkle it over the salmon, dividing it evenly between the 2 sandwiches. Arrange the slices of Gruyère on top, trimming them so that they come just to the edges of the bread. Place the cheese trimmings in the center of the sandwiches. Place the remaining 2 slices of brioche on top, buttered side up.

4. When ready to cook, lightly coat the grill surface with cooking oil spray. Using a spatula, transfer the sandwiches to the hot grill and gently close the lid. Grill the sandwiches until the bread is browned and crisp and the cheese is melted, about 5 minutes.

NOTE: Ripert would use brioche, a French bread rich in butter and eggs. French bakeries frequently sell brioche in loaf form. If not, look for it in the familiar *tête*—head—shape, which you can cut into slices. In a pinch, you could substitute thinly sliced challah or sandwich bread.

contact grill

a new panini caprese

Used to describe a salad made with fresh mozzarella, tomatoes, and basil, *caprese* means in the style of Capri. (The salad has become almost as ubiquitous as Caesar salad.) There are also *panini caprese* made with the same ingredients and generally served without being grilled. I like the intense, concentrated flavor of sun-dried tomatoes for these *panini,* but you can certainly use slices of fresh tomato instead. The *panini* are also delicious made with goat cheese in place of the mozzarella. **SERVES 2; CAN BE MULTIPLIED AS DESIRED**

THE RECIPE

FOR THE SUN-DRIED TOMATOES:

8 air-dried sun-dried tomato halves
　　(see Tip on page 296)
2 cups boiling water
2 tablespoons extra-virgin olive oil
1 clove garlic, peeled and gently flattened
　　with the side of a cleaver
Freshly ground black pepper

FOR THE PANINI:

4 ounces fresh mozzarella, drained and
　　cut into 1/4-inch-thick slices
2 soft Italian rolls, split
8 to 12 large fresh basil leaves, rinsed and
　　shaken dry
1 1/2 tablespoons salted butter,
　　at room temperature or melted
Cooking oil spray

1. Prepare the sun-dried tomatoes: Place the tomatoes in a heatproof bowl, pour the boiling water over them, and let soak for 20 minutes. Drain the tomatoes in a colander, squeezing them to press out the water. Transfer the tomatoes to a cutting board and cut them crosswise into thin slivers. Place the tomato slivers in a bowl and stir in the olive oil and garlic. Season with pepper to taste. Let the tomatoes marinate for 30 minutes. Discard the garlic clove. The tomatoes can be prepared up to a day ahead and stored at room temperature.

2. Preheat the grill (for instructions for using a contact grill, see page 3); if your contact grill has a temperature control, preheat the grill to high. Place the drip pan under the front of the grill.

3. Make the *panini*: Arrange half of the mozzarella slices on the bottom half of each roll, trimming them so that they come just to the edge of the rolls. Place the cheese trimmings in the center of the *panini.* Top with the marinated tomatoes and basil, then cover with the top half of the rolls. Using a knife or pastry brush,

spread or brush the outside of the rolls with the butter.

4. When ready to cook, lightly coat the grill surface with cooking oil spray. Using a spatula, transfer the *panini* to the hot grill and close the lid. Grill the *panini* until the rolls are crusty and golden brown and the cheese is melted, about 5 minutes (see Tip on facing page). Cut the *panini* in half on the diagonal and serve at once.

contact grill

prosciutto and fontina panini

This is one of Italy's simplest grilled *panini,* and it's one of the best. Fontina is a buttery, delicately pungent and piquant cheese from the Piedmont in northern Italy, recognizable by the stenciled purple circle with a mountain in the center of its rind. (Be sure to use imported Italian Fontina; the American version tastes downright bland next to the real thing.) Paired with salty prosciutto, you get the ultimate ham and cheese sandwich. **SERVES 2; CAN BE MULTIPLIED AS DESIRED**

THE RECIPE

4 slices dense white sandwich bread

1¹/₂ tablespoons salted butter,
    at room temperature or melted

2 to 3 ounces thinly sliced prosciutto
    (about 12 slices)

2 to 3 ounces thinly sliced Fontina cheese
    (about 4 slices)

Coarsely ground or cracked black pepper

Cooking oil spray

tip

These *panini* would traditionally be made with *pane a cassetta,* a dense, crustless white sandwich bread similar to French *pain de mie* (both are baked in a covered pan, which impedes the formation of a crust). The closest thing in the United States is a dense white sandwich bread with the crusts cut off—not that *panini* with the crusts on is such a terrible thing.

panini

Visit a busy bar or café in an Italian metropolis at lunchtime and this is what you'll see: trays of handsome sandwiches, layered with mozzarella, prosciutto, or olive paste, basil, or anchovies (to name just a few of the most popular ingredients), piled high and awaiting a quick blast of heat on a *panini* machine before being devoured by hordes of hungry, hurried patrons.

The *panini* machine is a glorified contact grill—two ridged heated metal plates attached by a hinge at the back (in fact the *panini* machine may have been the inspiration for American contact grills, like the ubiquitous George Foreman). Its squared-off raised ridges apply broad, closely spaced, tack-sharp grill marks. *Panini* machines are made primarily of stainless steel, not plastic, so they look like serious grilling devices. Most have thermostatic heat controls, enabling the temperature to be adjusted for some serious high-heat grilling.

But while the machine is sophisticated, the sandwiches are simplicity itself, featuring just a couple of ingredients—mozzarella and olive paste, for example, or Fontina and prosciutto. Perfect *panini* are golden brown and handsomely striped with grill marks. Crisp on the outside and hot and melting on the inside, they're thin enough that you can nibble on them comfortably. As with so much Italian cooking, the focus is on the quality of the ingredients.

Panini literally means little breads or rolls. Technically speaking, a *panino* has come to mean a sandwich made on a roll, while a *tramezzino* is a sandwich made with sliced bread. Either can be served grilled or uncooked. *Toast* refers to a grilled sandwich made on sliced bread. However, practically speaking, at least in the United States, *panini* means any Italian-style grilled sandwiches, and that's how I'm using the term in this book.

Italians make *panini* with several different types of bread, including *ciabatta*, which translated means slipper and is named for its shape, and *pane a cassetta*, a sort of sandwich bread. Although it's common practice in North America, Italians do not generally make *panini* with focaccia. Whatever the bread, it's brushed lightly with butter or olive oil before being grilled, which makes the crust crackling crisp.

You can make fine *panini* on a regular contact grill, such as the George Foreman, but to get the true *panini* look you need a *panini* machine, with its distinctive closely spaced ridges that produce grill marks that are about ¼ inch apart. One machine available in the United States and made for home use is VillaWare's Uno *panini* grill (see Mail-Order Sources on page 396).

Starting on page 300 you'll find classic *panini*, followed by some contemporary interpretations. Feel free to try your own combinations of ingredients—just remember, when making *panini*, less is more.

1. Preheat the grill (for instructions for using a contact grill, see page 3); if your contact grill has a temperature control, preheat the grill to high. Place the drip pan under the front of the grill.

2. Using a knife or pastry brush, spread or brush the slices of bread on one side with the butter. Place 2 slices of bread on a work surface buttered side down and arrange the slices of prosciutto on them followed by the slices of cheese, trimming both so that they come just to the edges of the bread. Place the trimmings in the center of the sandwiches. Generously sprinkle pepper over the sandwiches. Place the remaining 2 slices of bread on top, buttered side up.

3. When ready to cook, lightly coat the grill surface with cooking oil spray. Using a spatula, transfer the *panini* to the hot grill and close the lid. Grill the *panini* until the bread is crusty and golden brown and the cheese is melted, about 5 minutes (see the Tip on page 300). Cut the *panini* in half on the diagonal and serve at once.

contact grill

mozzarella and olive paste panini

Remember the first time you tasted real mozzarella? Not the rubbery stuff entombed in plastic—I'm talking about fresh mozzarella, a cheese that retains the sweetness of fresh milk with the barest, most delicate edge of piquancy. Once almost impossible to find outside of Italian markets, fresh mozzarella is now widely available at specialty food stores, natural foods stores, and many supermarkets. You know it's the real thing if it comes packed in water. Fresh mozzarella is perfect paired with olive paste to make vivid, vibrant black-and-white *panini*.

SERVES 2; CAN BE MULTIPLIED AS DESIRED

THE RECIPE

FOR THE OLIVE PASTE:
1 cup pitted black olives
2 teaspoons drained capers (optional)
1 clove garlic, coarsely chopped (optional)
1 anchovy fillet (optional), patted dry and
 coarsely chopped
1/2 teaspoon hot red pepper flakes (optional)
About 1 tablespoon olive oil
Coarsely ground or cracked black peppercorns

FOR THE PANINI:
4 slices (about 1/2 inch thick) dense white
 sandwich bread
1 1/2 tablespoons salted butter,
 at room temperature or melted
4 ounces fresh mozzarella, drained and
 cut into 1/4-inch slices
Cooking oil spray

1. Make the olive paste: Place the olives and capers, garlic, anchovy, and/or hot pepper flakes, if using, in a food processor and coarsely chop. Add enough oil to process into a thick coarse paste. Season with black pepper to taste.

2. Preheat the grill (for instructions for using a contact grill, see page 3); if your contact grill has a temperature control, preheat the grill to high. Place the drip pan under the front of the grill.

3. Make the *panini:* Using a knife or pastry brush, spread or brush the slices of bread on one side with the butter. Place 2 slices of bread on a work surface buttered side down and spread half of the olive paste

tips

over them. Arrange half of the slices of mozzarella on each slice of bread, trimming them so that they come just to the edges of the bread. Place the cheese trimmings in the center of the *panini.* Spread the remaining olive paste on the unbuttered side of the remaining 2 slices of bread, then place these on top of the *panini,* buttered side up.

4. When ready to cook, lightly coat the grill surface with cooking oil spray. Using a spatula, transfer the *panini* to the grill and close the lid. Grill the *panini* until the bread is crusty and golden brown and the cheese is melted, about 5 minutes (see Tip on page 300). Cut the *panini* in half on the diagonal and serve at once.

VARIATION: For a colorful version of Mozzarella and Olive Paste Panini, substitute a sun-dried tomato paste for the olive paste made in Step 1 on page 303. Soak 3 ounces of air-dried tomato halves as described in Step 1 on page 300, draining them thoroughly. (You'll have about 1¼ cups of tomatoes; if you have oil-packed sun-dried tomatoes, you will not need to soak them.) Coarsely chop the tomatoes, then place them in a food processor. Add 3 coarsely chopped fresh basil leaves, 1 coarsely chopped garlic clove, 2 teaspoons of drained capers, and ½ teaspoon freshly ground black pepper and process until finely chopped. Add 1 to 2 tablespoons of olive oil—enough to form a thick coarse paste. You'll end up with about 1 cup of sun-dried tomato paste. It can be refrigerated, covered, for several days and would be good with all manner of grilled meat.

contact grill

mozzarella and anchovy panini

I first sampled this sandwich at a neighborhood bar in the Giudecca, a residential island in Venice (and also home to the Cipriani hotel). The brusque counterpoint of salty anchovy and sweet mozzarella was as compelling as the contrast of crusty grilled bread and meltingly soft, gooey cheese. For an interesting appetizer, you could serve these *panini* cut into strips or quarters, atop the grilled tomato sauce on page 372. I think of this as the grilled version of mozzarella *in carozza* (literally, in a carriage).

SERVES 2; CAN BE MULTIPLIED AS DESIRED

THE RECIPE

4 slices (about 1/2 inch thick) dense white
    sandwich bread
1 1/2 tablespoons unsalted butter,
    at room temperature or melted
4 ounces fresh mozzarella, drained and
    cut into 1/4-inch-thick slices
12 to 16 anchovy fillets (about 1 ounce),
    drained well and blotted dry
Cooking oil spray

1. Preheat the grill (for instructions for using a contact grill, see page 3); if your contact grill has a temperature control, preheat the grill to high. Place the drip pan under the front of the grill.

2. Using a knife or pastry brush, spread or brush the slices of bread on one side with the butter.

Place 2 slices of bread on a work surface buttered side down and arrange half of the slices of mozzarella on each slice of bread, trimming them so that they come just to the edges of the bread. Place the cheese trimmings in the center of the *panini*. Arrange the anchovy fillets on top side-by-side, placing 6 to 8 on each of the *panini*. Place the remaining 2 slices of bread on top, buttered side up.

3. When ready to cook, lightly coat the grill surface with cooking oil spray. Using a spatula, transfer the *panini* to the grill and gently close the lid. Grill the *panini* until the bread is crusty and golden brown and the cheese is melted, about 5 minutes (see Tip on page 300). Cut the *panini* in half on the diagonal and serve at once.

tip

For the best results, use oil-packed anchovies (drain them well and blot them dry with paper towels) and a fresh artisanal mozzarella. Look for mozzarella that is sold in liquid and is sweet with the scent of fresh milk.

contact grill

panini
with goat cheese, capers, and roasted peppers

Goat cheese and roasted peppers have become part of the American flavor palate. The counterpoint of sweet smoky roasted bell peppers and sourish, chalky, tangy goat cheese remains irresistible, as you'll discover with these crusty *panini*.

SERVES 2; CAN BE MULTIPLIED AS DESIRED

tip

The options for goat cheese range from soft, mild, log-shaped ones, like Montrachet, to sharper, stronger, soft-ripened cheeses. The milder kind goes particularly well with roasted peppers.

THE RECIPE

4 ounces goat cheese, cut crosswise
    into ¼-inch slices
2 soft Italian rolls, split
2 roasted red or yellow bell peppers
    (see Variation on page 329), peeled,
    seeded, and cut into strips
1 tablespoon drained capers
2 to 3 tablespoons extra-virgin olive oil
Coarse salt (kosher or sea) and freshly
    ground black pepper
Cooking oil spray

1. Preheat the grill (for instructions for using a contact grill, see page 3); if your contact grill has a temperature control, preheat the grill to high. Place the drip pan under the front of the grill.

2. Place half of the slices of goat cheese on the bottom half of each roll, making sure they don't stick out over the edge. Top with the strips of bell pepper and the capers. Drizzle 1½ teaspoons of olive oil

on top of the *panini*, then season them with salt and black pepper and cover with the top half of the rolls. Lightly brush the outside of the rolls with olive oil.

3. When ready to cook, lightly coat the grill surface with cooking oil spray. Using a spatula, transfer the *panini* to the grill and close the lid. Grill the *panini* until the rolls are crusty and golden brown and the cheese is melted, about 5 minutes (see Tip on page 300). Cut the *panini* in half on the diagonal and serve at once.

contact grill

polenta "panini"

Polenta and *panini*—two great reasons to love Italy and two great reasons to fire up your grill. This recipe brings them together in a sort of grilled ham and cheese sandwich made with prosciutto and Fontina cheese and golden rounds of polenta instead of bread. Loosely inspired by Viana La Place's colorful book *Panini, Bruschetta, Crostini,* it makes an interesting appetizer, a light first course, or a side dish. **SERVES 4**

THE RECIPE

1 package (18 ounces) precooked
   polenta
5 ounces very thinly sliced prosciutto
   (about 20 slices)
8 ounces very thinly sliced Fontina cheese
   (about 16 slices; see Note)
8 to 10 fresh sage leaves
3 tablespoons unsalted butter, melted,
   or extra-virgin olive oil
Coarse salt (kosher or sea) and freshly
   ground black pepper
Cooking oil spray

1. Cut the polenta crosswise into ¼-inch-thick slices. Place half of the slices on a work surface and top them with the prosciutto (it's OK if the prosciutto sticks over the edge a little). Top the prosciutto with the Fontina. Place a sage leaf in the center of the *"panini,"* then cover with the remaining round of polenta. The recipe can be prepared several hours ahead to this stage. Cover the *"panini"* with plastic wrap and store in the refrigerator.

2. Preheat the grill (for instructions for using a contact grill, see page 3); if your contact grill has a temperature control, preheat the grill to high. Place the drip pan under the front of the grill.

3. Lightly brush the *"panini"* on both sides with the melted butter. Season both sides with salt and pepper.

4. When ready to cook, lightly coat the grill surface with cooking oil spray. Place the *"panini"* on the hot grill and *gently* close the lid. Grill the *"panini"* until golden brown and the cheese is melted, about 5 minutes. Transfer to a platter or plates and serve at once.

NOTE: Fontina is a piquant, buttery, rich cheese from northern Italy—look for it at specialty food stores. For an American rendition of the *"panini,"* substitute white Cheddar or Jack cheese.

tip

For ease in preparation, use ready-made polenta, sold in plastic tubes in supermarkets.

contact grill

"midnighter" sandwiches (medianoches)

Italians aren't the only people to have built a sandwich culture around a contact grill. The Cuban sandwich is the Spanish Caribbean answer to *panini,* and whether you enjoy it in Miami or Havana, it will always come buttery and crusty on the outside, hot and moist inside, and flat enough to bite into comfortably. The most famous Cuban sandwich is the *medianoche,* the midnighter, a regal combination of roast pork, cooked ham, Swiss cheese, and sliced pickles served on a small elongated sweet roll. Smaller than the formidable *pan con lechón* (page 311) or the Cubano (facing page), this is a sandwich that, in theory at least, you can eat after a movie or show without going to bed with indigestion.

SERVES 2; CAN BE MULTIPLIED AS DESIRED

tips

■ You'll need roast pork for the "Midnighter" Sandwiches. On page 94, you'll find a recipe for Cuban–style roast pork, but you can also use regular oven-roasted pork.

■ The traditional bread for a *medianoche* is a soft, sweet roll with a flavor like challah. And challah makes a good substitute.

THE RECIPE

About 2 tablespoons salted butter,
    at room temperature
2 soft, slightly sweet rolls
    (each 6 to 7 inches long), split, or
    4 slices (about 1/2 inch thick) challah
1 generous tablespoon mayonnaise
1 generous tablespoon mustard
    (I like to use Dijon)
4 ounces thinly sliced Swiss cheese
    (about 6 slices)
3 ounces thinly sliced roast pork
    (about 6 slices)
1 dill pickle, thinly sliced

3 ounces thinly sliced baked or smoked ham
    (about 6 slices)
Cooking oil spray

YOU'LL ALSO NEED:
2 pieces parchment paper or aluminum foil
    (each 16 by 12 inches)

1. Preheat the grill (for instructions for using a contact grill, see page 3); if your contact grill has a temperature control, preheat the grill to high. Place the drip pan under the front of the grill.

2. Lightly butter the outside of the rolls. Spread the mayonnaise on the cut side of the bottom half of the rolls. Spread the mustard on the cut side of the top half of the rolls. (If using slices of challah, spread one side of each with the butter, then spread the mayonnaise on the unbuttered side of 2 slices and the mustard on the unbuttered side of the remaining 2 slices.) Place the Swiss cheese on top of the bottom (mayonnaise-covered) half of the rolls and top it with the roast pork. Place the pickle slices on top of the top (mustard-covered) half of the rolls and top them with the ham. Leave the sandwich halves open.

3. Lightly brush the 2 pieces of parchment paper with butter. Place 1 piece buttered side up on a work surface, with one of the long edges closest to you. Arrange the 2 halves of 1 sandwich on the left side of the piece of parchment paper, then fold the parchment paper over them.

Repeat with the remaining sandwich halves and piece of parchment paper.

4. When ready to cook, lightly coat the grill surface with cooking oil spray. Arrange the paper-wrapped sandwiches on the hot grill at a diagonal to the ridges and close the lid. Grill the sandwiches until the rolls are crusty and golden brown and the cheese is melted, about 5 minutes. Leave the grill turned on.

5. Unwrap the sandwiches and assemble them: Place the top halves on the bottom halves, bread side up. Place the sandwiches back on the grill and cook for 30 seconds, pressing on the grill to flatten them.

6. Cut each sandwich in half sharply on the diagonal (this is how it's done at Miami's Cuban sandwich shops) and serve at once.

contact grill

el cubano especial (cuban two-ham and roast pork sandwiches)

Like many businesses in Miami, the Latin American Cafeteria began as a tiny mom-and-pop shop specializing in Cuban sandwiches and grew into a multimillion-dollar restaurant chain. When you want to experience the Cuban sandwich in all

CUBAN BREAD

Cuban bread—*pan cubano*—is a cousin of the French baguette, with several important distinctions. It contains lard, which is added for flavor; it's much puffier and softer than French bread; and it's deliberately underbaked so a dark brown crust doesn't form. This may seem odd until you know that most Cuban bread is destined to be cooked a second time on a *plancha* (a sandwich press). The soft texture allows the bread to compress into a crisp sandwich, while the anemic crust browns without burning.

If you live in an area with a large Cuban community (like south Florida or Union City, New Jersey), you may be able to buy *pan cubano*. Otherwise, this is a good time to use the puffy, elongated loaves sold as "French" or "Italian" bread at your local supermarket. If you use one of these to make sandwiches, scoop out a little of the doughy center first.

tips

its glory, look for one of the half-dozen Latin American Cafeterias in greater Miami. The basic layout is a U-shaped counter with a raised platform in the center on which sandwich makers practice their craft like high priests at some culinary altar. Up and down go the sandwich presses, turning out dozens, make that hundreds, of sandwiches an hour. Hanging from the ceiling is an ingredient you might be surprised to find at a Cuban sandwich shop—Smithfield ham—but this sweet, salty, dry-cured ham is an essential ingredient in the house specialty: El Cubano Especial. Think of it as the ultimate paean to pork, a belt-loosening sandwich made with roast pork, baked ham, and Smithfield ham, with just a little melted Swiss cheese to hold it together.

SERVES 2; CAN BE MULTIPLIED AS DESIRED

THE RECIPE

About 2 tablespoons salted butter, at room temperature
1 loaf Cuban bread (see sidebar on page 309) or French bread, cut crosswise into 2 pieces (each about 10 inches long) and split
3 ounces thinly sliced roast pork; be sure to include some of the dark-brown outside bits
3 ounces thinly sliced Smithfield ham (about 8 slices)
2 ounces thinly sliced Swiss cheese (about 4 slices)
3 ounces thinly sliced baked or smoked ham (about 8 slices)
Cooking oil spray

YOU'LL ALSO NEED:
2 pieces parchment paper or aluminum foil (each 16 by 12 inches)

1. Preheat the grill (for instructions for using a contact grill, see page 3); if your contact grill has a temperature control, preheat the grill to high. Place the drip pan under the front of the grill.

2. Lightly butter the outside of the bread. Place the pork on the bottom half of the bread, then top it with the Smithfield ham. Place the cheese on the top half of the bread and cover it with the baked ham. Leave the sandwich halves open.

3. Lightly brush the 2 pieces of parchment paper with butter. Place 1 piece buttered side up on a work surface, with one of the long edges closest to you. Arrange the 2 halves of 1 sandwich on the left side of the piece of parchment paper, then fold the parchment paper over them. Repeat with the remaining sandwich halves and piece of parchment paper.

4. When ready to cook, lightly coat the grill surface with cooking oil spray. Arrange the paper-wrapped sandwiches on the hot grill at a diagonal to the ridges and close the lid. Grill the sandwiches until the bread is crusty and golden brown and the cheese is melted, about 5 minutes. Leave the grill turned on.

5. Unwrap the sandwiches and assemble them: Place the top halves on the bottom halves, bread side up. Place the sandwiches back on the grill and cook for 30 seconds, pressing on the grill to flatten them.

6. Cut each sandwich in half crosswise, then cut each half in half lengthwise and serve at once.

grilling meat sandwiches

So, how do you make the perfect Cuban sandwich or grinder—one where the cheese fully melts, the cold cuts and meats are steaming hot, and the bread is crusty and browned but not burnt? Well, it takes more than simply putting the sandwich on your contact grill. Enter Marta Sanchez, the Boaco, Nicaragua–born coffee and sandwich diva of the L&A Market, a combination gas station, wine shop, and café that serves as my daily breakfast stop. Marta makes simply the best *café con leche* in Miami, and the writing of this book was fueled by many a cup of her perfect strong, sweet, dark, creamy brew.

When it comes time to make the *medianoche* ("midnighter"; page 308) or Cubano (mixed pork; facing page) sandwiches that feed legions of Miamians at lunchtime,

Marta uses a grilling technique found at many Miami sandwich shops. She puts the two halves of the sandwich open-faced on buttered parchment paper, with the meat on top of the cheese. Then she puts the sandwich, paper and all, in the sandwich press with another piece of buttered parchment paper on top. The butter crisps the bread and sizzles the meat while the cheese melts. (The parchment paper has the added advantage of keeping the grill clean.) When everything is heated through, Marta simply folds the two halves of the sandwich shut, guaranteeing a crisp crust, hot meat, and melted cheese every time. The technique works well for all kinds of sandwiches made with meat and cold cuts, including the grinders on page 316 and muffulettas on page 317.

contact grill

cuban roast pork sandwiches

Whenever visiting food dignitaries come to Miami, I take them to El Palacio de los Jugos. Part juice bar, part produce market, and part food court, the colorful, boisterous "Juice Palace" embodies the Spanish Caribbean soul of Miami. The first concession you encounter on the left when you enter is a roast pork vendor with the best *pan con lechón* (roast pork sandwiches) in Miami. This is not a sandwich to make when you're feeling ambivalent about your appetite, but if you're hungry—real hungry—nothing else quite hits the spot.

SERVES 2; CAN BE MULTIPLIED AS DESIRED

T H E   R E C I P E

1 loaf Cuban bread (see the sidebar on page 309) or French bread, cut crosswise into 2 pieces (each about 10 inches long) and split

1½ tablespoons salted butter, at room temperature or melted

8 to 10 ounces chopped or thinly sliced roast pork (about 10 slices); be sure to include some of the dark brown outside bits

1 small sweet white onion, sliced paper-thin

4 to 6 tablespoons Cuban Garlic, Cumin, Citrus Sauce (recipe follows)

Cooking oil spray

1. Preheat the grill (for instructions for using a contact grill, see page 3); if your contact grill has a temperature control, preheat the grill to high. Place the drip pan under the front of the grill.

2. Using a knife or pastry brush, spread or brush the outside of the pieces of bread with the butter. Place half of the roast pork slices on the bottom half of each piece of bread and top with the onion slices. Spoon 2 to 3 tablespoons of the Cuban Garlic, Cumin, Citrus Sauce over each sandwich, then cover with the top half of the rolls.

3. When ready to cook, lightly coat the grill surface with cooking oil spray.

Arrange the sandwiches on the hot grill at a diagonal to the ridges and close the lid. Grill the sandwiches until the bread is crusty and golden brown and the pork is heated through, about 5 minutes (see Tip on page 300). Cut each sandwich in half sharply on the diagonal (this is how it's done at Miami's Cuban sandwich shops) and serve at once.

cuban garlic, cumin, citrus sauce

Here's my version of *mojo* (pronounced "MO-ho"), Cuba's answer to vinaigrette—a pungent fried-garlic sauce perfumed with cumin and oregano and spiked with piquant *naranja agria*—sour orange—juice. In Miami, you can buy bottled *mojo* at any supermarket, but the homemade version is always better. And you can customize it, using lime juice, lemon juice, or even grapefruit juice in place of the sour orange juice. This recipe

tip

Roast pork is essential for this sandwich, and on page 94 there's a recipe for Cuban-style pork shoulder cooked in a rotisserie. Or you can use oven-roasted° pork.

makes more than you need for the Cuban Roast Pork Sandwiches on page 311, but the sauce keeps well, and you'll want to spoon it over every imaginable meat, from grilled steaks to spit-roasted pork. **MAKES ABOUT 1 CUP**

1/3 cup extra-virgin olive oil

5 cloves garlic, finely chopped

3 tablespoons chopped fresh cilantro
    or flat-leaf parsley

1/2 cup sour orange juice, or 1/3 cup fresh lime
    juice and 2 tablespoons fresh orange juice

1/2 teaspoon ground cumin

1/2 teaspoon dried oregano

Coarse salt (kosher or sea) and freshly
    ground black pepper

1. Heat the olive oil in a deep nonreactive saucepan over medium heat. Add the garlic and cilantro and cook until just beginning to brown, 2 to 3 minutes. Do not let them burn.

2. Immediately stir in the sour orange juice, cumin, oregano, and 2 tablespoons of water and bring to a boil. Let the sauce boil until the sour orange juice loses its sharpness, about 2 minutes. Season with salt and pepper to taste; the *mojo* should be highly seasoned. Let cool to room temperature before using. I like to keep the *mojo* in a bottle or jar so I can shake it well when I'm ready to use it. It can be refrigerated for several days.

tip

The sour orange is a citrus fruit that looks like an orange, only it's greenish in color. Its flavor is akin to a lime with a hint of orangy sweetness. If you live in an area with a large Spanish Caribbean community, you can probably find it at the supermarket. Lime juice with a squeeze of fresh orange juice will approximate the flavor.

contact grill

a new elena ruz, with turkey, cranberries, and cream cheese

This is one of the most curious sandwiches to come off a contact grill. While the combination of roast turkey, cream cheese, and cranberry sauce may sound odd, it's quite delicious. The original Elena Ruz, made with turkey, cream cheese, and strawberry jam on toast, is a sandwich named for a Havana socialite of the 1920s. A little less sugary than strawberry jam, cranberry sauce makes this a great sandwich to assemble with Thanksgiving leftovers. **SERVES 2; CAN BE MULTIPLIED AS DESIRED**

tips

■ Use roast turkey or roast turkey breast for these sandwiches, not turkey roll. Smoked turkey makes an even richer, if less conventional, Elena Ruz. There are several good recipes on pages 206 through 212.

■ To make a traditional Elena Ruz sandwich, substitute strawberry preserves for the cranberry sauce.

THE RECIPE

2 soft sandwich rolls (each 6 to 7 inches long), split, or 2 pieces (each about 8 inches long) French bread, split

1½ tablespoons salted butter, at room temperature or melted

3 ounces cream cheese (6 tablespoons), at room temperature

4 ounces thinly sliced roast or smoked turkey (about 12 slices)

6 tablespoons cranberry sauce or cranberry jelly, at room temperature

Cooking oil spray

1. Preheat the grill (for instructions for using a contact grill, see page 3); if your contact grill has a temperature control, preheat the grill to high. Place the drip pan under the front of the grill.

2. Using a knife or pastry brush, spread or brush the outside of the rolls with the butter. Spread half of the cream cheese on top of the bottom half of each roll. Arrange the slices of turkey on top of the cream cheese, dividing them evenly between the 2 sandwiches and trimming them so that they come just to the edge of the rolls. Place the turkey trimmings in the center of the sandwiches. Spoon the cranberry sauce on top of the turkey, dividing it evenly between the 2 sandwiches. Cover the sandwiches with the top half of the rolls.

3. When ready to cook, lightly coat the grill surface with cooking oil spray. Arrange the sandwiches on the hot grill at a diagonal to the ridges and close the lid. Grill the sandwiches until the rolls are crusty and golden brown and hot in the center, about 5 minutes (see Tip on page 300). Cut each sandwich in half sharply on the diagonal and serve at once.

contact grill

guava and queso blanco sandwiches

This sandwich came to light chiefly in my imagination (I've certainly never seen it on a menu), and yet it's inspired by a snack eaten by thousands of Miamians each morning. The snack—coffee break fare—features a sweet, perfumed slice of guava paste and a slab of salty *queso blanco* or cream cheese baked together in a puff pastry envelope or deep fried in an empanada. What makes the combination work is the contrast of the sweet, musky guava with the piquant cheese, and there's no reason the two can't be enjoyed in a grilled sandwich. Especially when the sandwich is made with puffy Cuban bread, which compresses into a crisp crust when cooked on a contact grill. **SERVES 2; CAN BE MULTIPLIED AS DESIRED**

THE RECIPE

2 pieces (each about 8 inches long)
  Cuban bread (see sidebar on page 309)
  or soft French bread, split
1½ tablespoons salted butter,
  at room temperature or melted
4 ounces cream cheese (½ cup), at room
  temperature, or 4 ounces queso blanco,
  cut into ¼-inch-thick slices
4 ounces guava paste (see Note), cut into
  ¼-inch-thick slices (about 8 slices)
Cooking oil spray

1. Preheat the grill (for instructions for using a contact grill, see page 3); if your contact grill has a temperature control, preheat the grill to high. Place the drip pan under the front of the grill.

2. Using a knife or pastry brush, spread or brush the outside of the pieces of bread with the butter. Spread half of the cream cheese on the bottom half of each roll. (If using *queso blanco,* arrange half of the slices on the bottom half of each roll, trimming them so that they come just to the edges of the bread. Place the cheese trimmings in the center of the sandwiches.) Arrange the slices of guava paste on top, then cover the sandwiches with the top half of the rolls.

3. When ready to cook, lightly coat the grill surface with cooking oil spray. Arrange the sandwiches on the hot grill at a diagonal to the ridges and close the lid. Grill the sandwiches until the bread is crusty and golden brown and the cheese is melted, about 5 minutes (see Tip on page 300). Cut each sandwich in half sharply on the diagonal and serve at once.

NOTE: Guava paste is a sort of thick crimson jelly made from the fragrant tropical fruit. When I say thick, I mean it—it's thick enough to slice, the way you would jellied cranberry sauce. The best guava paste comes in round flat cans (there's a cheaper version sold in rectangular slabs in cardboard boxes, but it tends to fall apart when grilled). One good, widely available brand is Goya.

tip

For cheese, there are two options: cream cheese, which is now favored by many first- and second-generation Hispanics, or *queso blanco,* a firm, salty white cheese that makes your teeth squeak when you bite into it. Queso blanco is available at Hispanic markets and at a growing number of supermarkets. The contrast of flavor with the guava paste is more dramatic when you use *queso blanco.* Paired with cream cheese the effect is more subtle.

contact grill
grinders

I n the 1970s, my folks lived in Williamstown, Massachusetts. On my first visit home from college, I discovered the western Massachusetts version of what up until then I had called a hoagie—the grinder. (Elsewhere in the United States this oversize sandwich made with an assortment of cold cuts, such as ham, salami, and mortadella; cheese; and hot peppers also goes by the names submarine, hero, and Italian sandwich.) What was new to me about this grinder was that it was baked in a pizza oven. The result was a crisp roll stuffed with melting cheese and sizzling hot cold cuts. A grinder that has been cooked on a contact grill is easier to eat because it's flatter, but it's every bit as crusty and delectable as the original. **SERVES 2; CAN BE MULTIPLIED AS DESIRED**

tip

Mortadella is an Italian sausage similar to bologna; capocolla is a spicy shoulder ham. Both will be available at Italian delis, if they're not at the supermarket.

THE RECIPE

2 tablespoons (¼ stick) salted butter,
    at room temperature
2 hoagie or submarine rolls, split
2 tablespoons mayonnaise
2 ounces thinly sliced Provolone cheese
    (about 4 slices)
2 ounces thinly sliced capocolla or
    baked ham (about 6 slices)
2 ounces thinly sliced Italian salami
    (about 6 slices)
2 tablespoons hot pepper relish (optional)
¼ head iceberg lettuce, cored and shredded
    paper-thin with a chef's knife or in a food
    processor
1 medium-size tomato, very thinly sliced
A few paper-thin slices sweet onion (optional)
1 to 4 pickled hot peppers, thinly sliced
    (optional; see Note)

2 ounces thinly sliced mortadella
    (about 6 slices)
Cooking oil spray

YOU'LL ALSO NEED:
2 pieces parchment paper or aluminum foil
    (each 16 by 12 inches)

1. Preheat the grill (for instructions for using a contact grill, see page 3); if your contact grill has a temperature control, preheat the grill to high. Place the drip pan under the front of the grill.

2. Lightly butter the outside of the rolls. Spread 1 tablespoon of the mayonnaise on the bottom half of each roll. Layer half of the Provolone, capocolla, and salami on the bottom half of each roll in that order, making sure that they don't stick out over the edges.

3. Spread 1 tablespoon of the hot pepper relish, if using, on the top of each roll and top each with half of the lettuce and tomato, the onion and hot peppers, if using, and the mortadella in that order, making sure that they don't stick out over the edges. Leave the sandwich halves open.

4. Lightly brush the 2 pieces of parchment paper with butter. Place 1 piece, buttered side up, on a work surface with one of the long edges closest to you. Arrange the 2 halves of 1 sandwich on the left side of the piece of parchment paper, then fold the paper over them. Repeat with the remaining sandwich halves and piece of parchment paper.

5. When ready to cook, lightly coat the grill surface with cooking oil spray. Arrange the paper-wrapped sandwiches on the hot grill at a diagonal to the ridges and close the lid. Grill the sandwiches until the bread is crusty and golden brown and the cheese is melted, about 5 minutes. Leave the grill turned on.

6. Unwrap the sandwiches and assemble them, covering the bottom halves with the top. Place the sandwiches back on the grill and cook for 30 seconds, pressing on the grill to flatten them. Cut each sandwich in half crosswise and serve at once.

NOTE: You want hot peppers pickled in vinegar or brine—the kind that come in a jar.

contact grill

grilled muffulettas

The muffuletta is New Orleans' answer to a submarine sandwich. Legend credits its invention to Salvatore Lupo, founder of the Central Grocery, a landmark Italian food store on Decatur Street in the French Quarter (it takes its name from a round loaf of Sicilian bread). The idea of grilling a muffuletta comes not from New Orleans (where the very notion would probably smack of heresy) but from one of our neighborhood

tips

restaurants on Martha's Vineyard, Alchemy on Main Street in Edgartown. The inspiration for grilled muffuletta may be the grinder of western Massachusetts (see page 316) or it may be the Italian practice of grilling a simple cheese or prosciutto sandwich on a *panini* machine. Either way, what results is a splendid new take on a New Orleans classic. **SERVES 2; CAN BE MULTIPLIED AS DESIRED**

■ In New Orleans, muffulettas are made with a crusty, chewy, round, sesame seed–dotted bread. I'm going to suggest a rather unorthodox substitute here—a kaiser roll (I like the way a *panini* machine flattens kaiser rolls to produce a crunchy crust).

■ Traditional tasso is spicy smoked Louisiana pork. Look for it at specialty food stores or see Mail-Order Sources on page 396. You can substitute spiced or smoked ham.

THE RECIPE

2 tablespoons extra-virgin olive oil
2 kaiser rolls, split
3 ounces thinly sliced sharp Provolone cheese
    (about 4 slices)
2 ounces thinly sliced tasso or smoked ham
    (about 6 slices)
A few paper-thin slices sweet onion
1/2 cup New Orleans Olive Relish
    (recipe follows)
2 ounces thinly sliced prosciutto
    (about 6 slices)
2 ounces thinly sliced Italian salami
    (about 6 slices)
Cooking oil spray

YOU'LL ALSO NEED:
2 pieces parchment paper or aluminum foil
    (each 16 by 12 inches)

1. Preheat the grill (for instructions for using a contact grill, see page 3); if your contact grill has a temperature control, preheat the grill to high. Place the drip pan under the front of the grill.

2. Drizzle 1½ teaspoons of the olive oil over the inside and outside of each roll.

Layer half of the Provolone and tasso on the bottom half of each roll. Layer half of the onion, ¼ cup of the olive relish, and half of the prosciutto and salami on the top half of each roll in that order. Leave the sandwich halves open.

3. Oil the 2 pieces of parchment paper with the remaining 1 tablespoon of olive oil. Place 1 piece, oiled side up, on a work surface with one of the long edges closest to you. Arrange the 2 halves of 1 sandwich on the left side of the piece of parchment paper, then fold the parchment paper over them. Repeat with the remaining sandwich halves and piece of parchment paper.

4. When ready to cook, lightly coat the grill surface with cooking oil spray. Arrange the paper-wrapped sandwiches on the hot grill and close the lid. Grill the sandwiches until the bread is crusty and golden brown and the cheese is melted, about 5 minutes. Leave the grill turned on.

5. Unwrap the sandwiches and assemble them, covering the bottom halves with the top. Place the sandwiches back on the grill and cook for 30 seconds, pressing on the grill to flatten them. Cut each sandwich in half and serve at once.

new orleans olive relish

It's the tangy olive relish that makes a muffuletta a muffuletta (without it, the sandwich is pretty much like a hoagie or submarine). Feel free to vary the basic proportions of the ingredients to come up with the flavor you like best. Some versions of the relish include pickled carrots, cauliflower, and onions, and of course you can add any of these. This recipe makes more than you'll need for two muffulettas. It's great spooned over just about everything that's grilled—I'm sure you won't have any trouble finding a use for what's left over. **MAKES ABOUT 1 CUP**

¹⁄₂ cup pimento-stuffed green olives
¹⁄₂ cup pitted black olives or kalamata olives
1 celery rib, coarsely chopped
1 clove garlic, coarsely chopped
2 tablespoons finely chopped fresh flat-leaf parsley
2 teaspoons drained capers
1 pickled hot pepper, coarsely chopped, or ¹⁄₂ teaspoon hot red pepper flakes
¹⁄₂ teaspoon dried oregano
2 tablespoons extra-virgin olive oil
1 tablespoon red wine vinegar, or more to taste
Freshly ground black pepper

Place the green and black olives, celery, garlic, parsley, capers, hot pepper, and oregano in a food processor and coarsely or finely chop them, running the machine in short bursts. (The olive mixture can be whatever texture you prefer; just don't purée it.) Add the olive oil and vinegar and pulse the machine just to mix. Taste for seasoning, adding more vinegar as necessary and black pepper to taste. The relish will keep for several weeks stored in a glass jar in the refrigerator.

contact grill

classic reubens

The Reuben is the apotheosis of the American melting pot— corned beef, Swiss cheese, German sauerkraut, Russian dressing, and rye bread—brought together, so the story goes, by Arnold Reuben, owned of Reuben's Restaurant in New York City. The year was 1914, according to Reuben's daughter in a story

THE REUBEN SANDWICH

Reuben sandwiches are widely available and frequently ghastly—the result of improperly sliced corned beef, inferior cheese, soggy sauerkraut, and/or commercial Russian dressing. The corned beef should be sliced paper-thin across the grain. The cheese should be true Emmentaler, imported from Switzerland and recognizable by its sweet nutty flavor. The sauerkraut should be barrel-fresh or from a jar or bag, never canned. It should be drained in a colander, then pressed with the back of a spoon to wring out the juices. As for the Russian dressing, it's so easy to prepare from scratch, there's really no reason not to make your own.

told in *The Dictionary of American Food & Drink,* by John Mariani. The occasion was a visit by a vaudeville actress named Annette Seelos. Reuben created the legendary sandwich for Seelos but decided (perhaps after tasting it) to name it for himself. Not that you can blame him, because the combination of sweet, salty, and sour, of crisp, chewy, gooey, is unique in the annals of sandwiches.

SERVES 2; CAN BE MULTIPLIED AS DESIRED

THE RECIPE

4 slices dark rye bread or marbled
    rye bread
2 tablespoons (¼ stick) salted butter,
    at room temperature or melted
¼ cup Russian Dressing (recipe follows)
3 ounces corned beef, sliced paper-thin
    across the grain (about 8 slices)
3 ounces thinly sliced Emmentaler cheese
    (about 4 slices)
⅔ cup drained sauerkraut
1 dill pickle, thinly sliced (not traditional,
    but an interesting way to top off the
    sandwich)
Cooking oil spray

1. Preheat the grill (for instructions for using a contact grill, see page 3); if your contact grill has a temperature control, preheat the grill to high. Place the drip pan under the front of the grill.

2. Using a knife or pastry brush, spread or brush the slices of bread on one side with the butter. Place 2 slices of bread on a work surface buttered side down, then spread the top of each with 1 tablespoon of the Russian Dressing. Arrange the slices of corned beef on the bread, fol-

lowed by the slices of cheese, trimming both so that they come just to the edges of the bread. Place the trimmings in the center of the sandwiches. Spoon ⅓ cup of the sauerkraut over each sandwich, spreading it out to the edges of the bread. Top each sandwich with half of the pickle slices. Spread the unbuttered side of the remaining 2 slices of bread with the remaining 2 tablespoons of Russian dressing, dividing it evenly between them, then place them on top of the sandwiches, Russian Dressing side down.

4. When ready to cook, lightly coat the grill surface with cooking oil spray. Using

a spatula, transfer the sandwiches to the hot grill and gently close the lid. Grill the sandwiches until the bread is browned and crisp and the cheese is melted, about 5 minutes. Cut each sandwich in half and serve at once.

russian dressing

Despite the name, Russian Dressing is an American condiment made by combining mayonnaise with chili sauce and pickle relish. This recipe makes more than you'll need for two Reubens—

it's good to have the dressing on hand for dipping or spreading on other sandwiches. It will keep for several days in the refrigerator. **MAKES ABOUT 1 CUP**

⅔ **cup mayonnaise (preferably Hellmann's)**
¼ **cup chili sauce or ketchup**
2 tablespoons sweet pickle relish
Freshly ground black pepper

Place the mayonnaise, chili sauce, and pickle relish in a small nonreactive bowl and stir or whisk to mix. Season with pepper to taste.

tip

By chili sauce, I mean the sweet red condiment similar to ketchup; one widely available brand is Heinz. For an exotic Reuben, you could substitute a hotter sauce, like the Thai Sriracha.

contact grill
lobster reubens

Most people come to the legendary Joe's Stone Crab in Miami Beach for—you guessed it—stone crabs. When you've had your fill of this delectable crustacean, you might try one of the restaurant's lesser-known specialties. Joe's Stone Crab uses Florida lobster, a.k.a. spiny lobster, to make its Reubens, but the sandwiches are equally delectable made with Maine lobster or, for that matter, crab. **SERVES 2; CAN BE MULTIPLIED AS DESIRED**

THE RECIPE

4 slices light rye bread
2 tablespoons (¼ stick) salted butter, at room temperature or melted
¼ **cup Russian Dressing (this page)**

3 ounces thinly sliced Emmentaler cheese (about 4 slices)
3 ounces cooked lobster meat, thinly sliced
⅔ **cup drained sauerkraut (see Note)**
Cooking oil spray

tip

Joe's Stone Crab cooks its Reubens on a giant gas grill. First two slices of bread are grilled open-faced, with a slice of cheese atop each. Then the lobster and sauerkraut are added and the sandwich is assembled. Keep this procedure in mind if you want to make the sandwich on a built-in or free-standing grill.

1. Preheat the grill (for instructions for using a contact grill, see page 3); if your contact grill has a temperature control, preheat the grill to high. Place the drip pan under the front of the grill.

2. Using a knife or pastry brush, spread or brush the slices of bread on one side with the butter. Place 2 slices of bread on a work surface buttered side down, then spread the top of each with 1 tablespoon of the Russian Dressing. Arrange half of the slices of Emmentaler on the bread, trimming them so that they come just to the edges. Place the cheese trimmings in the center of the sandwiches. Top each sandwich with half of the lobster meat.

3. Spoon ⅓ cup of the sauerkraut over each sandwich, spreading it out to the edges of the bread. Arrange the remaining slices of Emmentaler on top of the sandwiches, trimming the edges to fit. Spread the unbuttered side of the remaining 2 slices of bread with the remaining 2 tablespoons of Russian Dressing, dividing it evenly between them, then place them on top of the sandwiches, Russian Dressing side down.

4. When ready to cook, lightly coat the grill surface with cooking oil spray. Using a spatula, transfer the sandwiches to the hot grill and gently close the lid. Grill the sandwiches until the bread is browned and crisp and the cheese is melted, about 5 minutes. Cut each sandwich in half and serve at once.

NOTE: For the best results, use barrel-fresh sauerkraut or sauerkraut from a jar, not canned, and drain it in a colander.

contact grill

a new egg in the hole

A camp breakfast classic, egg in the hole is an egg fried in a slice of bread that has a hole cut in the center. The traditional recipe presents a major challenge—turning the concoction over without breaking the egg yolk. Enter the contact grill, which makes a very nifty fried egg sandwich that you don't have to turn. What else is new about this egg in the hole? For an upscale touch, I've made it with a quail egg and brioche instead of ordinary white bread. To round out the flavors, I add Canadian bacon and cheese. For something even more decadent, you can sprinkle a little truffle oil on top. **MAKES 8; SERVES 2 TO 4 AS AN APPETIZER, 2 AS A LIGHT MAIN COURSE**

THE RECIPE

16 thin slices (about 1/4 inch thick) brioche or French bread (each slice should be 2 1/2 to 3 inches in diameter or square)

2 to 3 tablespoons butter, melted

8 thin slices (3 to 4 ounces) white Cheddar, Jack, or Gruyère cheese, cut to just fit the bread

8 thin slices (3 to 4 ounces) Canadian bacon, ham, or prosciutto, cut to just fit the bread

Cooking oil spray

8 quail eggs (see Note)

Coarse salt (kosher or sea) and freshly ground black pepper

Truffle oil (optional)

1. Preheat the grill (for instructions for using a contact grill, see page 3); if your contact grill has a temperature control, preheat the grill to high. Place the drip pan under the front of the grill.

2. Using a round cookie cutter or a piping bag tip, cut a 1-inch hole in the center of 8 of the slices of brioche. Brush the other 8 slices on one side with some of the butter and place them on a work surface, butter side down. Place a slice of cheese on top of each buttered slice of brioche, then top with a slice of Canadian bacon. Place the remaining slices of bread on top of the Canadian bacon and brush the tops with the remaining butter.

3. When ready to cook, lightly coat the grill surface with cooking oil spray. Arrange the sandwiches on the hot grill with the holes facing up. (You may need to work in batches.) For fully cooked quail eggs, add them to the sandwiches now. The shells of quail eggs are a little tougher to crack than chicken eggs; using a sharp knife, crack off the top 1/4 inch of one, then pour out the egg into the hole in a sandwich. Repeat with the remaining eggs. Gently lower the lid and grill the sandwiches until the bread is golden brown and the cheese is melted, about 5 minutes. If you like

tip

If your bakery doesn't carry brioche, you can make eggs in the hole with a soft, fat loaf of French bread, but don't use a crusty baguette.

your egg yolks runny, let the sandwiches grill for 2 minutes, then add the quail eggs.

4. Transfer the sandwiches to a platter or plates and season each with a little salt and pepper. Sprinkle each sandwich with a few drops of truffle oil, if desired, and serve at once.

NOTE: Quail eggs are available at specialty food stores and many supermarkets. If you like your yolks a little runny, add the eggs halfway through the grilling process. If you like them well-done, add the eggs when you put the sandwiches on the grill.

Whether you're flame charring bell peppers like an Argentinean pit master or sizzling bacon-crusted sweet potatoes or squash with Asian spices, there's nothing like an indoor grill. Some of the more unexpected techniques here include roasting onions and potatoes in a fireplace, spit roasting artichokes or Belgian endive, and giving corn the Japanese treatment— grilled with sesame soy butter. Tired of the conventional potato salad? Try the smoked potato salad with a Peruvian chile cheese sauce. Indoor grilling will give you a whole new take on vegetables.

vegetables and sides

rotisserie

artichokes on a spit

Push the envelope and think out of the box—these are two of the mottos I try to cook by and live by, and they certainly hold for indoor grilling. Even artichoke leaves (normally tough except at their base) acquire a singed, smoky, waferlike crispness, so you can munch on them whole, thanks to the steady radiant heat and slow rotation of a rotisserie. All with little more effort than the push of a button. **SERVES 2 TO 4**

THE RECIPE

**2 large globe artichokes
(1½ to 2 pounds total)
1 lemon, cut in half
3 cloves garlic, cut into matchstick
slivers
4 to 6 tablespoons extra-virgin
olive oil
Coarse salt (kosher or sea) and freshly
ground black pepper
Saffron Aïoli (optional; recipe follows)**

1. Using kitchen shears, cut off and discard the spiny tips of the artichoke leaves. Cut the bottom ¼ inch off each stem but leave the rest of the stem intact. Using a sharp knife, cut each artichoke lengthwise in quarters. Using a grapefruit spoon or melon baller, scrape out the fibrous part in the center of each arti-

choke. Rub all of the cut parts of the artichokes with lemon juice to prevent discoloring.

2. Place 3 or 4 slivers of garlic between the leaves of each artichoke quarter, then generously brush the artichokes with olive oil, dabbing it between the leaves. Season the artichokes very liberally with salt and pepper. Arrange the artichoke quarters in a flat rotisserie basket so that the stem ends are on the inside and will be perpendicular to the spit. Close the basket tightly.

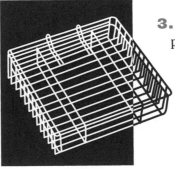

3. When ready to cook, place the drip pan in the rotisserie. Attach the basket to the rotisserie spit, then attach the spit to the rotisserie and turn on the motor. If your rotisserie has a temperature control, set it to 400°F (for instructions for using a rotisserie, see page 14).

4. Cook the artichokes until they are a deep golden brown on the outside and tender inside, 50 minutes to 1 hour. To test for doneness, insert a skewer in an artichoke; it should pierce the heart easily. Transfer the artichokes to a platter or plates and serve at once with the Saffron *Aïoli,* if desired.

saffron aïoli

Garlic mayonnaise—*aïoli*—is the great condiment of Provence. Here it's perfumed with another evoca-tive Mediterranean flavoring: saffron. Buy saffron threads rather than powder; they're more likely to be pure saffron. **MAKES ABOUT 1 CUP**

¼ teaspoon saffron threads
2 teaspoons hot water
2 to 3 cloves garlic, mashed to a paste
1 cup mayonnaise (preferably Hellmann's)
Tiny pinch of cayenne pepper
Freshly ground white pepper

Crumble the saffron threads between your fingers into a small mixing bowl. Add the water and let soak for 5 minutes. Add the garlic, mayonnaise, and cayenne and whisk to mix. Season with white pepper to taste. The *aïoli* can be refrigerated, covered, for up to 3 days.

tip

While I've provided a tasty saffron and garlic mayonnaise as a sauce here, you may find spit-roasted artichokes so flavorful you don't want to serve them with anything more than some melted butter— or nothing at all.

rotisserie

prosciutto-wrapped belgian endive

Most of the Belgian endive that's consumed in the United States is served raw, sliced in salads. In Europe, especially in France and the Benelux countries, people also enjoy this crisp, slender, white, pleasantly bitter member of the lettuce family cooked. Spit roasting produces an effect similar to braising endive, which is the cooking method preferred in Europe. Here the endive is stuffed with Gouda cheese before being wrapped in tangy prosciutto. **MAKES 8; SERVES 4 TO 8**

THE RECIPE

1 slice (¼ inch thick; about 2 ounces)
    aged Gouda or other firm cheese
8 Belgian endives
8 thin slices prosciutto (about 2 ounces)

YOU'LL ALSO NEED:
Butcher's string

1. Cut the cheese into 8 long thin strips; each should be about ½ inch shorter than the endive and ¼ inch wide.

2. Cut each endive lengthwise into quarters, cutting to *but not through* the root end (the idea is to open up the endive like an elongated tulip). Place a piece of Gouda in the center of each endive, trimming off any cheese that sticks out. Tightly wrap each endive crosswise in a slice of prosciutto, then tie it in place with 2 pieces of butcher's string.

3. Arrange the endives in a flat rotisserie basket so that they will be perpendicular to the spit. Close the basket tightly.

4. When ready to cook, place the drip pan in the bottom of the rotisserie. Attach the basket to the rotisserie spit, then attach the spit to the rotisserie and turn on the motor. If your rotisserie has a temperature control, set it to 400°F (for instructions for using a rotisserie, see page 14). Cook the endives until they are crusty and golden brown on the outside and soft inside, 40 minutes to 1 hour. Use a skewer to test for doneness; it should pierce the endive easily. Transfer the endive to a platter or plates and serve at once.

VARIATIONS: Think of this recipe as a jumping-off point. You can stuff the endive with any of a number of cheeses, such as Taleggio or Cheddar. For that matter, you could wrap it in bacon or pancetta instead of prosciutto.

tip

The endives tend to shrink and rattle around in the rotisserie basket as they cook. I've called for eight so you can tightly pack the basket.

buenos aires grilled bell peppers

There's nothing like live fire to heighten a bell pepper's natural sweetness while imparting a haunting smoke flavor. But don't take my word for it—just ask grill masters from countries as diverse as Japan, Turkey, Italy, and Argentina. The red bell pepper is the belle of the ball in Buenos Aires, where it's grilled whole over live coals, then served on the stem, with nothing more than a drizzle of olive oil and a whisper of garlic— or sometimes just all by itself. Grilling peppers in the fireplace most closely approximates what you'd get at an Argentinean steakhouse. You can also use a built-in grill. **SERVES 4**

THE RECIPE

4 large red bell peppers
2 tablespoons extra-virgin olive oil
1 to 2 cloves garlic, minced
Coarse salt (kosher or sea) and
    coarsely ground black pepper

1. Cook the bell peppers, following the instructions for either of the grills in the box at right, until darkly browned on all sides, turning with tongs. Brown the 4 sides of the peppers, then brown the tops and bottoms. You don't need to burn the skin to peel it, as you would with Italian grilled peppers.

2. Transfer the peppers to a platter. Drizzle a little olive oil over each and sprinkle them with garlic. Season the peppers with salt and pepper and serve warm. The peppers will need to be cored and seeded at the table.

if you have a . . .

BUILT-IN GRILL: Preheat the grill to high, then, if it does not have a nonstick surface, brush and oil the grill grate. Place the bell peppers on the hot grate. They will be done after cooking 3 to 5 minutes on each side (12 to 20 minutes in all) and 1 to 2 minutes on the top and the bottom.

FIREPLACE GRILL: Rake red hot embers under the gridiron and preheat it for 3 to 5 minutes; you want a hot, 2 to 3 Mississippi fire. When ready to cook, brush and oil the gridiron. Place the bell peppers on the hot grate. They will be done after cooking 3 to 5 minutes on each side (12 to 20 minutes in all) and 1 to 2 minutes on the top and the bottom.

VARIATION: For a slightly more elaborate presentation, grill the bell peppers until they are completely charred. Let the peppers cool slightly, then scrape off the skin. Cut them in half, remove the core and stem, and scrape out the seeds. Cut the peppers into 1-inch strips and arrange them on a plate. Drizzle the olive oil over them, top with the garlic, and season with salt and pepper. For extra punch, add diced anchovies. The peppers (try this with yellow, orange, or green peppers, too) can be served warm or at room temperature.

tip

The Japanese grill their corn husked and cut into pieces or broken in half. The reason is simple: Most Japanese grills are relatively tiny, and shucked, halved corn takes up less room. It's a useful method when cooking on an indoor grill, too.

grilled corn
with soy butter and sesame

Grilled corn is found all along the world's barbecue trail—seasoned with lime juice and chiles in India, mayonnaise and grated cheese in Mexico, and of course, sweet butter, salt, and pepper here in the United States. Soy butter is what Japanese grill masters use to baste corn. It goes great with American varieties, like white corn from Cape Cod or silver shoe peg from the Eastern Shore of Maryland. **SERVES 4**

THE RECIPE

if you have a...

GRILL PAN: Place the grill pan on the stove and preheat it to medium-high over medium heat. When the grill pan is hot a drop of water will skitter in the pan. When ready to cook, lightly oil the ridges of the grill pan. Arrange the ears of corn in the hot grill pan so that they are parallel to the ridges. The corn will be done after cooking 2 to 3 minutes per side (8 to 12 minutes in all).

BUILT-IN GRILL: Preheat the grill to high, then, if it does not have a nonstick surface, brush and oil the grill grate. Arrange the ears of corn on the hot grate so that they are parallel to the ridges. The corn will be done after cooking 2 to 3 minutes per side (8 to 12 minutes in all).

FREESTANDING GRILL: Preheat the grill to high; there's no need to oil the grate. Arrange the ears of corn on the hot grate so that they are parallel to the ridges. The corn will be done after cooking 3 to 4 minutes per side (12 to 16 minutes in all).

FIREPLACE GRILL: Rake red hot embers under the gridiron and preheat it for 3 to 5 minutes; you want a hot, 2 to 3 Mississippi fire. When ready to cook, brush and oil the gridiron. Arrange the ears of corn on the hot grate so that they are parallel to the ridges. The corn will be done after cooking 2 to 3 minutes per side (8 to 12 minutes in all).

3 tablespoons unsalted butter

1 scallion, both white and green parts, finely chopped

2 tablespoons soy sauce

4 ears sweet corn, shucked and cut or broken in half crosswise

1 tablespoon toasted sesame seeds (see Note)

1. Melt the butter in a saucepan over medium heat. Add the scallion and cook until it loses its rawness, about 1 minute (you don't want the scallion to brown). Stir in the soy sauce and remove the saucepan from the heat.

2. Cook the corn, following the instructions for any of the grills in the box at left, until nicely browned on all sides, basting it with a little of the soy butter. Use a light touch as you baste; you don't want to drip a lot of butter into the grill.

3. Transfer the corn to a platter. Brush it with any remaining soy butter, sprinkle the sesame seeds over it, and serve at once.

NOTE: To toast sesame seeds, place them in a dry cast-iron or other heavy skillet (don't use a non-stick skillet for this). Cook the sesame seeds over medium heat until lightly browned, about 3 minutes, shaking the skillet to ensure that they toast evenly. Transfer the toasted sesame seeds to a heatproof bowl to cool.

rotisserie

bacon-grilled corn

Bacon-grilled corn turns up from time to time at American barbecues, but I'll wager you've never before seen it spit roasted. The method has several advantages: As it slowly spins the bacon becomes crisp without burning. The bacon fat keeps the corn moist without the risk of flare-ups. (Did I mention that this is a great way to rid the bacon of most of its fat?) And, the bacon imparts an amazing smoky flavor to the corn. **SERVES 4**

THE RECIPE

4 slices smoky bacon
4 ears sweet corn, shucked

1. Hold a piece of bacon by the ends and gently pull on it to stretch it. Starting at one end, wrap a piece of bacon around an ear of corn in a spiral, like the red stripe on a candy cane. Repeat with the remaining bacon and corn.

2. Arrange the bacon-wrapped ears of corn in a flat rotisserie basket so that they will be perpendicular to the spit. Close the basket tightly.

tips

■ For the best results, use an artisanal smoked bacon—bacon that's been smoked, not just injected with brine and smoke flavoring. You'll find it often at farmers' markets. One good brand available by mail order is Nueske's Hillcrest Farm (see page 396).

■ If you're using a large rectangular basket or your basket doesn't close tightly, it's a good idea to tie the bacon to the corn at both ends and in the middle with butcher's string.

3. When ready to cook, place the drip pan in the bottom of the rotisserie. Attach the basket to the rotisserie spit, then attach the spit to the rotisserie and turn on the motor. If your rotisserie has a temperature control, set it to 400°F (for instructions for using a rotisserie, see page 14). Cook the corn until the bacon is crisp and golden brown and the corn is browned and tender, 30 to 40 minutes.

4. Transfer the corn to a platter or plates and serve at once.

eggplant
in the style of argentina

Argentineans are about the most relentless carnivores on the planet; it's not uncommon for people there to eat beef twelve or thirteen times a week. But there are at least two grilled vegetables that turn up just about everywhere Argentinean grass-fed beef sizzles over blazing coals: *morrones* (red bell peppers; see page 328 for a recipe) and oregano-scented grilled eggplant. The seasonings are simple—basically the Argentinean spice rack consists of salt, pepper, oregano, bay leaves, parsley, and perhaps hot paprika. The rub adds flavor, and the basting mixture keeps the eggplant moist as it grills. And, grilling eggplant makes it seared on the outside and tender inside—in short, everything grilled eggplant should be. **SERVES 4**

tip

If you are cooking the eggplant on a contact grill, place a sprig of parsley on top of each slice and it will grill right into the eggplant.

THE RECIPE

1 eggplant (about 1 pound), cut crosswise into ½-inch-thick slices

¼ cup extra-virgin olive oil

Coarse salt (kosher or sea) and freshly ground black pepper

3 cloves garlic, minced

1½ teaspoons dried oregano

1 teaspoon hot red pepper flakes

1. Lightly brush the eggplant slices on both sides with about 2 tablespoons of the olive oil and season them very generously with salt and black pepper. Place the garlic, oregano, and hot pepper flakes in a small bowl and stir to mix, then sprinkle about half of this mixture on the eggplant slices on both sides, patting it onto the eggplant with your fingertips. Add the remaining 2 tablespoons of olive oil to the bowl with the garlic mixture, stir to mix, and set aside to use for basting the eggplant.

2. Cook the eggplant, following the instructions for any of the grills in the box at right, until it is nicely browned and very tender; it should feel soft when poked with your finger. Brush the eggplant slices once or twice with the garlic-oil mixture as they grill.

3. Transfer the grilled eggplant to a platter or plates and serve at once.

if you have a...

CONTACT GRILL: Preheat the grill; if your contact grill has a temperature control, preheat the grill to high. Place the drip pan under the front of the grill. When ready to cook, lightly oil the grill surface. Place the eggplant on the hot grill, then close the lid. The eggplant will be done after cooking 3 to 6 minutes.

GRILL PAN: Place the grill pan on the stove and preheat it to medium over medium heat. When the grill pan is hot a drop of water will skitter in the pan. When ready to cook, lightly oil the ridges of the grill pan. Place the eggplant in the hot grill pan. It will be done after cooking 3 to 6 minutes per side.

BUILT-IN GRILL: Preheat the grill to high, then, if it does not have a nonstick surface, brush and oil the grill grate. Place the eggplant on the hot grate. It will be done after cooking 3 to 6 minutes per side.

FREESTANDING GRILL: Preheat the grill to high; there's no need to oil the grate. Place the eggplant on the hot grill. It will be done after cooking 4 to 7 minutes per side.

rotisserie

fennel
with honey and
sherry vinegar sauce

Fennel has been described as licorice-flavored celery, and this anise-flavored vegetable, with its bulbous white base, is delectable cooked on the rotisserie. The slow, gentle roasting softens its fibrous flesh, and the honey and sherry vinegar marinade keeps it from drying out. Because fennel is a hard and dense vegetable, I recommend marinating it overnight. **SERVES 4**

T H E   R E C I P E

1/4 cup extra-virgin olive oil

1/4 cup sherry vinegar

1/4 cup honey

Coarse salt (kosher or sea) and freshly
    ground black pepper

2 large fennel bulbs, trimmed (see Note)

1. Place the olive oil, sherry vinegar, and honey in a large nonreactive mixing bowl and whisk until well mixed. Season with a little salt and pepper.

2. Cut each fennel bulb into quarters lengthwise. Add the fennel to the marinade and stir to coat evenly. Let the fennel marinate in the refrigerator, covered, overnight. Gently stir the fennel from time to time so that it marinates evenly. You can also marinate the fennel in a resealable plastic bag.

3. Drain the marinade off the fennel into a heavy nonreactive saucepan and set aside. Arrange the fennel quarters in a flat rotisserie basket so that they will be perpendicular to the spit. Close the basket tightly.

4. When ready to cook, place the drip pan in the bottom of the rotisserie. Attach the basket to the rotisserie spit, then attach the spit to the rotisserie and turn on the motor. If your rotisserie has a temperature control, set it to 400°F (for instructions for using a rotisserie, see page 14). Cook the fennel until it is browned and very tender, about 1 hour.

5. Meanwhile, make the sauce: Bring the marinade to a boil over medium-high heat and let boil until thick, syrupy, and reduced by about a third, 8 to 12 minutes. Taste for seasoning, adding more salt and/or pepper as necessary.

6. Transfer the fennel to a serving dish, spoon the sauce over it, and serve at once.

NOTE: Fennel sometimes comes with its long, slender stems and feathery leaves attached. These are delectable cut into salads. Or add them to the grill when you cook fish. Cut the stems off flush with the top of the fennel bulb.

portobello "bool kogi"
with sesame, soy, and garlic

One of Korea's national dishes (dare I say treasures?), *bool kogi* is thinly shaved beef that's grilled after marinating in a sweet-salty-nutty mixture of sugar, soy sauce, sesame oil, and hefty doses of garlic. The sugar caramelizes during the grilling process, giving the meat a candylike sweetness (to learn how to prepare beef steak in this fashion, see page 79). I've always thought of mushrooms as the beef of the vegetable world, so the notion of a portobello *bool kogi* shouldn't come as a complete surprise. Serve this as a vegetarian entrée or as an intensely flavorful side dish. **SERVES 4**

THE RECIPE

4 medium-size portobello mushrooms
    (each 4 to 5 inches across and
    5 to 8 ounces)
2 scallions, both white and green parts,
    trimmed and minced
1/2 cup soy sauce
1/3 cup sake or cream sherry
1/4 cup plus 1 tablespoon Asian (dark)
    sesame oil
1/4 cup sugar
3 cloves garlic, minced
2 tablespoons sesame seeds (optional)
1 teaspoon Korean chile powder or
    hot paprika (optional)
1/2 teaspoon freshly ground black pepper

1. Using a paring knife, trim the stems off the portobellos. Wipe the caps clean with a damp paper towel (don't rinse them, or they'll become soggy). Place the mushroom caps in a nonreactive baking dish just large enough to hold them or in a resealable plastic bag.

2. Set aside 2 tablespoons of the minced scallion greens for garnish.

3. Place the remaining scallions and the soy sauce, sake, sesame oil, sugar, garlic, sesame seeds, chile powder, if using, and pepper in a nonreactive mixing bowl, whisk until the sugar dissolves, and pour the mixture over the portobellos. Let the mushrooms marinate in the refrigerator, covered, for 4 to 6 hours, turning them several times so that they marinate evenly.

tip

I call for portobello mushrooms here because I like their generous size (with a little imagination, a portobello looks like a burger). However, any kind of mushroom can be marinated and grilled this way. You'll need about 1 1/2 pounds.

if you have a...

CONTACT GRILL: Preheat the grill; if your contact grill has a temperature control, preheat the grill to high. Place the drip pan under the front of the grill. When ready to cook, lightly oil the grill surface. Place the portobellos on the hot grill rounded side up, then close the lid. The mushrooms will be done after cooking 4 to 6 minutes.

GRILL PAN: Place the grill pan on the stove and preheat it to medium-high over medium heat. When the grill pan is hot a drop of water will skitter in the pan. When ready to cook, lightly oil the ridges of the grill pan. Place the portobellos in the hot grill pan. They will be done after cooking 4 to 6 minutes per side.

BUILT-IN GRILL: Preheat the grill to high, then, if it does not have a nonstick surface, brush and oil the grill grate. Place the portobellos on the hot grate. They will be done after cooking 4 to 6 minutes per side.

FREESTANDING GRILL: Preheat the grill to high; there's no need to oil the grate. Place the portobellos on the hot grill. They will be done after cooking 5 to 7 minutes per side.

FIREPLACE GRILL: Rake red hot embers under the gridiron and preheat it for 3 to 5 minutes; you want a hot, 2 to 3 Mississippi fire. When ready to cook, brush and oil the gridiron. Place the portobellos on the hot grate. They will be done after cooking 4 to 6 minutes per side.

4. Drain the portobellos, pouring the marinade into a heavy nonreactive saucepan. Bring the marinade to a boil over high heat and let boil until syrupy and reduced by about a third, 3 to 5 minutes. You'll use this as a sauce.

5. Cook the portobellos, following the instructions for any of the grills in the box at left, until browned and tender.

6. Transfer the portobellos to a platter or plates. Spoon the sauce and, if cooked in a contact grill, any juices that collected in the drip pan over the mushrooms. Sprinkle the reserved scallion greens on top and serve at once.

rotisserie

spit-roasted onions
with balsamic honey glaze

tip

You don't need a "designer" onion, like a Vidalia or Maui; even everyday yellow or white onions come out candy sweet after spit roasting.

The more I use the rotisserie, the more I marvel at its ability to bring out the richness and sweetness of vegetables, especially roots and tubers. Case in point—spit-roasted onions. Roasting onions in their skin adds color and flavor. So does the olive oil, balsamic vinegar, and honey marinade, which gets boiled down into a thick, syrupy sauce. I don't mean to be immodest, but these may be the best onions you've ever tasted.

SERVES 4 (UNLESS YOU'RE REALLY HUNGRY)

¼ **cup extra-virgin olive oil**
¼ **cup balsamic vinegar**
¼ **cup honey**
**Coarse salt (kosher or sea) and freshly
    ground black pepper**
2 large onions

1. Place the olive oil, balsamic vinegar, and honey in a large nonreactive mixing bowl and whisk until well mixed. Season with a little salt and pepper.

2. Cut each onion lengthwise into quarters, leaving the skin on and the root end intact. Add the onions to the marinade and stir to coat evenly. Let the onions marinate in the refrigerator, covered, for at least 2 hours, preferably overnight. Gently stir the onions from time to time so that they marinate evenly. You can also marinate the onions in a resealable plastic bag.

3. Drain the marinade off the onions into a heavy nonreactive saucepan and set aside. Place the onion quarters in a flat rotisserie basket and close it tightly.

4. When ready to cook, place the drip pan in the bottom of the rotisserie. Attach the basket to the rotisserie spit, then attach the spit to the rotisserie and turn on the motor. If your rotisserie has a temperature control, set it to 400°F (for instructions for using a rotisserie, see page 14). Cook the onions until they are dark brown and very tender, 50 minutes to 1 hour. Use a skewer to test for doneness; it should pierce an onion easily.

5. Meanwhile, make the sauce: Bring the marinade to a boil over medium-high heat and let boil until thick, syrupy, and reduced by about a third, 8 to 12 minutes. Taste for seasoning, adding more salt and/or pepper as necessary.

6. Transfer the onions to a serving dish, spoon the balsamic vinegar sauce over them, and serve at once.

onions in the fireplace

Roast whole onions in the fireplace and the smoke and fire flavors they take on are breathtaking. There are two ways you can do this. Start with four onions in their skins.

To roast onions in front of the fire, first make four doughnut-shaped rings from crumpled aluminum foil (you'll use these to hold the onions upright). The rings should be about 2 inches across. Cut the top ½ inch off each onion; leave the root ends intact. Set the onions, cut side up, on the foil rings. Place a pat of butter or drizzle a little olive oil on top of each onion, then season them generously with salt and pepper. Place the onions on the foil rings right in front of the fire, at the edge of the fireplace or on its floor, so they are about 10 inches away from the embers. Roast the onions until the skins darken and the onions are soft, 12 to 15 minutes per side (48 minutes to 1 hour in all), turning them with tongs.

To roast onions in the embers, leave the onions whole. Rake out a mound of embers and place the onions on top. Shovel more embers and ash over the onions to cover them. Roast the onions until the skins blacken and the onions are soft, 20 to 40 minutes.

I like to serve the onions right in their burnt skins. You can spoon the soft, moist interior out of the charred shell; it's rather like eating a soft-boiled egg. The Parmesan Cream Sauce on page 345 would make a good accompaniment. Or make a balsamic vinegar and honey glaze by combining the ingredients as described in Step 1 at left, then bringing them to a boil over medium-high heat and boiling them until you have about ½ cup.

contact grill

pieces of eight #1 (garlicky green plantains)

The plantain is a jumbo cooking banana and a staple throughout Latin America. When green (unripe), it tastes starchy and bland—rather like a potato. As it ripens from yellow to black, it becomes sweeter, eventually acquiring a taste that could well be described as that of a candied banana. Once considered an exotic ethnic food, with the Latinization of the American diet plantains have become widely available. Which brings us to a dish of South American origin—*patacones*—plantain "coins," named for an old Spanish gold currency. I call them pieces of eight. Traditionally, *patacones* are deep-fried twice: First the slices are cooked until soft enough to be flattened slightly; then they're fried a second time to render them golden brown and crisp. You can achieve a similar effect using a contact grill with a lot less fuss, mess, and best of all, a lot less fat. Here's a garlic-rich version of pieces of eight—made with green plantains. On the next page you'll find a candy-sweet version made with ripe plantains. **SERVES 4 TO 6**

tip

Plantains can be eaten at any of three stages of ripeness: *verde*, green and hard; *pintón*, yellow and semisweet; and *maduro*, black, soft, and sweet. Use green plantains or greenish-yellow plantains for Pieces of Eight #1.

THE RECIPE

2 green plantains
Ice cubes
2 to 3 tablespoons extra-virgin olive oil,
    or 2 tablespoons (¼ stick) butter, melted
2 cloves garlic, minced
2 tablespoons finely chopped fresh cilantro
    or flat-leaf parsley
Coarse salt (kosher or sea) and freshly ground
    black pepper
Cooking oil spray

1. Cut the ends off the plantains. Make three shallow slits through the peel running the length of each plantain. Use the tip of the knife only and cut just through the peel, not the flesh of the plantain. Place the plantains in a large bowl, add cold water to cover and a couple of ice cubes, and let soak for 20 minutes. This will help loosen the peel from the plantains.

2. Remove the peels by sliding your thumb inside the slits. Cut the plantains crosswise into slices about ¾ inch thick. Place the plantain slices in a mixing bowl and sprinkle the olive oil, garlic, and cilantro over them. Season with salt and pepper and toss gently to mix.

3. Preheat the grill (for instructions for using a contact grill, see page 3); if your contact grill has a temperature control, preheat the grill to high. Place the drip pan under the front of the grill.

4. When ready to cook, lightly spray the grill surface with cooking oil spray. Place the plantain slices on the hot grill; if they start to slide down to the low end, prop up that end of the grill with a plate. Close the lid. Set the mixing bowl aside. Grill the plantains until lightly browned and beginning to soften, 3 to 4 minutes.

5. Leaving the grill on, return the plantains to the bowl with the garlic oil and toss to mix. Place the plantains back on the grill and firmly close the lid, slightly flattening the plantains. Continue grilling the plantains until they are nicely browned and tender, 3 to 4 minutes longer. Transfer the grilled plantains to a platter or plates and serve at once (I like to serve the plantains out of the bowl that held the garlic oil).

pieces of eight #2 (grilled sweet plantains)

Every once in a while, if you're lucky, you stumble upon a recipe that's bold and different enough to be hailed as an innovation. I hesitate to claim such a discovery as my own, but my wife believes these *maduros,* sweet grilled ripe plantains, are truly revolutionary. Grilling gives ripe plantain "coins" the candy sweetness of fried plantains, one of Miami's most popular side dishes, without the mess and grease of deep-fat frying.

SERVES 4 TO 6

tip

You need fully ripe plantains for Pieces of Eight #2. If you live in an area with a large Hispanic community, you'll probably be able to find them— look for plantains with skins that are yellowish black to fully black. Otherwise, you can buy green plantains and let them ripen at room temperature until they are yellowish black; it will take a week to ten days.

if you have a...

CONTACT GRILL: Preheat the grill; if your contact grill has a temperature control, preheat the grill to high. Place the drip pan under the front of the grill. When ready to cook, lightly oil the grill surface. Place the sliced plantains on the hot grill; if they start to slide to the low end, prop that end of the grill up with a plate. Close the lid. The plantains will be done after cooking 3 to 5 minutes.

GRILL PAN: Place the grill pan on the stove and preheat it to medium-high over medium heat. When the grill pan is hot a drop of water will skitter in the pan. When ready to cook, lightly oil the ridges of the grill pan. Place the sliced plantains in the hot grill pan. They will be done after cooking 3 to 5 minutes per side.

BUILT-IN GRILL: Preheat the grill to medium-high, then, if it does not have a nonstick surface, brush and oil the grill grate. Place the sliced plantains on the hot grate. They will be done after cooking 3 to 5 minutes per side.

FIREPLACE GRILL: Rake red hot embers under the gridiron and preheat it for 3 to 5 minutes; you want a medium-hot, 4 Mississippi fire. When ready to cook, brush and oil the gridiron. Place the sliced plantains on the hot grate. They will be done after cooking 3 to 5 minutes per side.

2 ripe plantains
2 to 3 tablespoons extra-virgin olive oil, or unsalted ($\frac{1}{4}$ stick) butter, melted
Coarse salt (kosher or sea) and freshly ground black pepper

1. Cut the ends off the plantains. Make three shallow slits through the peel running the length of each plantain. Use the tip of the knife only and cut just through the peel, not the flesh of the plantain. Remove the peels and cut the plantains crosswise into slices about $\frac{3}{4}$ inch thick if using a contact grill, or sharply on the diagonal in $\frac{1}{4}$-inch-thick slices if using another indoor grill.

2. Place the plantain slices in a mixing bowl. Sprinkle the olive oil over them, season with salt and pepper, and gently toss to mix.

3. When ready to cook, remove the plantains from the mixing bowl and set the bowl aside. Cook the plantain slices, following the instructions for any of the grills in the box at left, until they are a dark golden brown and very tender. After the plantains have cooked for 2 minutes, brush them with any olive oil that is left in the mixing bowl.

4. Transfer the grilled plantain slices to a platter or plates and serve at once.

rotisserie

new potatoes
with rosemary and garlic

've long been a partisan of cooking potatoes on the grill. On an outdoor grill, you use the indirect method, cooking the spuds next to, not directly over, the fire. Indoors you can achieve a similar effect in a countertop rotisserie. After being marinated with garlic and rosemary, the potatoes are spit roasted in a rotisserie basket. The result is potatoes with a savory, crisp outside and a creamy inside. To achieve the same effect in the oven, you'd probably need to use a whole stick of butter. **SERVES 4**

THE RECIPE

1½ pounds baby red potatoes
2 cloves garlic, minced
3 tablespoons chopped fresh rosemary
    leaves, or 1½ teaspoons dried
    rosemary
Coarse salt (kosher or sea) and freshly
    ground black pepper
2 tablespoons extra-virgin olive oil

1. Scrub the potatoes under cold running water and cut out any blemishes. Blot the potatoes dry with paper towels, then place them in a large mixing bowl. Add the garlic and rosemary to the potatoes, season them generously with salt and pepper, and stir with a wooden spoon to coat evenly. Add the olive oil and stir to mix. Let the potatoes marinate in the refrigerator, covered, for at least 5 minutes or up to 6 hours.

2. When ready to cook, place the drip pan in the bottom of the rotisserie. Place the potatoes in a flat rotisserie basket and close it tightly. Attach the basket to the rotisserie spit, then attach the spit to the rotisserie and turn on the motor. If your rotisserie has a temperature control, set it to 400°F (for instructions for using a rotisserie, see page 14).

3. Cook the potatoes until golden brown and very tender, about 40 minutes. Use a skewer to test for doneness; it should pierce the potatoes easily. Transfer the potatoes to a platter or plates and serve.

tip

You can season and cook the potatoes right away, but for a really perfumed flavor, let them marinate with the rosemary and garlic for 4 to 6 hours.

fireplace grill

potatoes
roasted in ashes

EMBERS VS. ASHES?

There are at least two ways to roast root vegetables in a fireplace: in the embers and in the ashes. The difference between the two is something like the difference between direct grilling and indirect grilling outdoors with cooking in the embers more akin to grilling using the direct (ideal for onions) method and cooking in ashes more like grilling using the indirect (well suited to potatoes) method. The ashes serve as a sort of insulator to keep the embers from scorching the potato skins. If you're planning on roasting in ashes, it's a good idea to save some from previous fires in a metal bucket, so you always have plenty on hand.

Centuries ago, the hearth was a focal point of the home—a primary source of light and heat and the means for cooking. Potatoes and other root vegetables roasted in the ashes were a staple (think of van Gogh's painting *The Potato Eaters*). The Spanish had their *papas en las cenizas* (potatoes roasted in the ashes). The French had their luxurious *truffes sous la cendre* (truffles cooked under ashes). Beyond the romance of roasting vegetables in the fireplace, there are two gustatory advantages: The fire imparts a subtle smoke flavor as it slowly and gently roasts the potatoes and it produces an extraordinary soft, creamy texture. **SERVES 4**

THE RECIPE

4 large baking potatoes
 (12 to 14 ounces each)
Sweet butter or extra-virgin olive oil
Sour cream or crème fraîche
Finely chopped fresh chives
Coarse salt (kosher or sea) and freshly
 ground black pepper

YOU'LL ALSO NEED:
Ashes; a fireplace shovel; a natural
 bristle paintbrush

1. Scrub the potatoes under cold running water and blot dry with paper towels. Prick each potato in several places with a fork.

2. Light wood in the fireplace and let it burn down to glowing embers (for instructions for grilling in a fireplace, see page 12).

3. When ready to cook, rake a 1-inch layer of embers in one part of the fireplace. Shovel a 1-inch layer of ash on top. Arrange the potatoes on top of the ashes; shovel 1 inch of ash over them, then shovel a 1-inch layer of embers on top of the ash. Roast the potatoes until cooked through, 40 minutes to 1 hour. Use a long slender metal skewer to test for doneness. When the potatoes are fully cooked, the skewer will pierce them easily.

4. Place butter, sour cream, and chives in attractive serving bowls and set aside.

5. Shovel the embers and ash off the potatoes and remove them with tongs, shaking off the excess ash. Transfer the potatoes to a heatproof platter. Brush off any remaining ash with the paintbrush. Cut a lengthwise slit in the top of each potato and squeeze the sides to open the potatoes up. Pile butter, sour cream, and chives into the potatoes, then season with salt and pepper and serve.

VARIATIONS: Sweet potatoes, boniatos (Caribbean sweet potatoes), and large onions would all also be delicious roasted in ashes. For that matter, so would green plantains. All will take between 40 minutes and 1 hour to cook through.

truffles in the ashes

OK, so you've won the lottery—here's how a nineteenth-century Frenchman would have spent the money. Invest in as many black truffles as you can, ideally four to five truffles for each person you plan to serve. Select ones that are about 1 inch in diameter and 4 to 5 ounces each. (By truffles, I mean *Tuber melanosporum,* the aromatic French black truffle, which is in season in the fall and winter.) If the truffles have not already been cleaned, scrub them under cold running water with a stiff-bristled brush and pat them dry with paper towels.

To roast the truffles, rake out 1 inch of embers in one part of the fireplace and shovel a 1-inch layer of ash on top. Arrange the truffles on the ashes; shovel 1 inch of ash over them, then shovel a 1-inch layer of embers on top of the ash. The truffles will be cooked through and just tender after 12 to 20 minutes (when the truffles are done, a metal skewer will pierce them easily). Remove the truffles from the pile of ashes and brush off any remaining ash. Serve them with nothing more than a glass of gorgeous Bordeaux.

stove-top smoker

papas a la huancaína (peruvian potato salad)

Potatoes in the style of Huancayo, a city about a hundred miles east of Lima, may well be the world's best potato salad. Don't act surprised: Peru is the birthplace of the potato, and this Andean nation is home to more than two hundred species. What makes the salad unique is a creamy,

tips

■ *Queso blanco* is a salty white cheese available in Hispanic markets and a growing number of supermarkets. If you can't find it, you can achieve a similar effect by combining white Cheddar or feta and Muenster.

■ *Aji amarillo* is one of the defining flavors of Peruvian cuisine— a pugnacious piquant yellow chile that is sold dried, ground, puréed, or whole in jars. Look for it in Hispanic or specialty food stores or see Mail-Order Sources on page 396. There's no exact substitute for *aji amarillo,* but a mixture of smoked or hot paprika and turmeric comes close.

■ You can also smoke the potatoes in a wok. You'll find instructions for doing this in the box on page 234.

piquant, spicy sauce made with salty white cheese and Peruvian chiles. In my version the potatoes are smoked, resulting in an extraordinary juxtaposition of flavors and textures. **SERVES 4**

THE RECIPE

Cooking oil spray (optional)
1½ pounds baby new potatoes (white or red; see Note), rinsed, scrubbed, and blotted dry with paper towels
2 teaspoons extra-virgin olive oil
Coarse salt (kosher or sea) and freshly ground black pepper
1 hard-cooked egg, peeled
6 ounces queso blanco (see Tips), or 3 ounces each white Cheddar and Muenster, cut into ½-inch cubes
1 to 2 teaspoons ground aji amarillo (see Tips), 2 to 4 bottled or frozen aji amarillo, 2 to 3 teaspoons aji amarillo paste, or 1 teaspoon smoked or hot paprika
1 tablespoon fresh lemon juice, or more to taste
¼ teaspoon ground turmeric (½ teaspoon if you're using paprika)
½ cup evaporated milk
¼ cup canola oil
4 Boston lettuce leaves
¼ cup black olives

YOU'LL ALSO NEED:
1½ tablespoons oak or apple sawdust

1. Set up the smoker (for instructions for using a stove-top smoker, see page 16). Place the sawdust in the center of the bottom of the smoker. Line the drip pan with aluminum foil and place it in the smoker.

Lightly coat the smoker rack with cooking oil spray, or use a paper towel dipped in oil, and place the rack in the smoker.

2. Place the potatoes in a large bowl and toss them with the olive oil, then season them with salt and pepper. Place the potatoes on the smoker rack. Cover the smoker and place it over high heat for 3 minutes, then reduce the heat to medium. Smoke the potatoes until tender (they should be easy to pierce with a knife), 30 to 40 minutes. Transfer the smoked potatoes to a wire rack to cool.

3. Cut the egg into ¼-inch slices. Place the egg, *queso blanco, aji amarillo,* lemon juice, turmeric, evaporated milk, and canola oil in a blender or food processor and purée until smooth. Taste for seasoning, adding more lemon juice as necessary and salt and pepper to taste; the sauce should be highly seasoned.

4. Line a platter or 4 plates with the lettuce leaves and place the smoked potatoes on top. Spoon the sauce over them. Garnish with the olives and serve at once.

NOTE: The potatoes should be 1 to 1½ inches in diameter. You can use larger potatoes if you cut them in half or quarter them.

rotisserie

shallots
with parmesan cream sauce

Like onions, shallots contain a lot of sugar and become candy sweet when spit roasted. Their flavor is even more complex than an onion's, with earth tones that hint at leek and garlic. In this recipe, spit-roasted shallots are paired with a Parmesan-flavored béchamel sauce to make a sort of deconstructed gratin.

SERVES 4

THE RECIPE

1¹/₂ pounds shallots
1¹/₂ tablespoons extra-virgin olive oil
Coarse salt (kosher or sea) and freshly
   ground black pepper
Parmesan Cream Sauce
   (recipe follows)

1. If using large shallots, cut them in half; leave smaller shallots whole. Place the shallots in a mixing bowl and add the oil. Season with salt and pepper, then toss to coat. Place the shallots in a flat rotisserie basket and close it tightly.

2. When ready to cook, place the drip pan in the bottom of the rotisserie. Attach the basket to the rotisserie spit, then attach the spit to the rotisserie and turn on the motor. If your rotisserie has a temperature control, set it to 400°F (for instructions for using a rotisserie, see page 14). Cook the shallots until they are darkly browned on the outside and very tender, 40 minutes to 1 hour. Use a

skewer to test for doneness; it should pierce a shallot easily.

3. Cut any whole shallots in half. Serve the shallots in the skins with the Parmesan Cream Sauce spooned over them. To eat, scoop the shallots out of the skin.

parmesan cream sauce

This is a cayenne-spiked béchamel sauce enriched with freshly grated Parmesan cheese. When my dietician stepdaughter, Betsy, is around, I make it with skim milk. When she isn't, I use half-and-half or light cream. **MAKES ABOUT 1 CUP**

tip

You can spit roast medium-size shallots (ones that are about the size of walnuts) or large ones that have been cut in half. In either case, leave the skins on; as they brown they give the shallot a nice flavor.

1¹/₂ tablespoons salted butter

1¹/₂ tablespoons flour

1 cup skim milk, whole milk, half-and-half,
or light cream, or a mixture of any
of these

¹/₃ to ¹/₂ cup freshly grated Parmigiano-
Reggiano cheese

Coarse salt (kosher or sea) and freshly
ground white pepper

A pinch of freshly grated nutmeg

A pinch (just a pinch) of cayenne pepper

1. Melt the butter in a small heavy saucepan over medium-high heat. Add the flour and cook until the mixture bubbles and the flour has lost its raw smell, about 2 minutes, whisking steadily. Do not let the flour brown.

2. Remove the saucepan from the heat and whisk in the milk. Return the pan to the heat, bring the sauce to a simmer, and let simmer 3 to 5 minutes, whisking often. The sauce will thicken after about a minute, but you want to cook it for 3 to 5 minutes so it loses the floury taste.

3. Reduce the heat to low, whisk in the Parmesan cheese, and cook, stirring, until the cheese melts. Season with salt, white pepper, nutmeg, and cayenne to taste. Serve the sauce no more than 15 minutes after it's made; keep it warm at the back of the stove until ready to serve.

fire-roasted shallots

Like onions, shallots can be roasted in the fireplace. Start with large shallots, ones that weigh a little more than an ounce apiece, and don't peel them. There are two ways to roast them.

Place whole shallots on a brick right in front of the fire, at the edge of the fireplace, or on its floor, so they are about 10 inches away from the embers. Roast the shallots until the skins blacken and the shallots are soft, 5 to 8 minutes per side (10 to 16 minutes in all), turning with tongs.

Or, make a pile that is roughly half ash and half embers. Nestle the shallots in the embers and roast them until they are blackened and soft, 10 to 15 minutes in all.

To serve, scrape off the burnt skins (don't worry about removing every last bit) and serve the shallots with the Parmesan Cream Sauce (this page) or drizzle some olive oil and few drops of balsamic vinegar over them and season them with salt and pepper.

grilled squash
with herbes de provence

Here's a simple way to cook summer squash, and if you've ever found these watery vegetables to be lacking in flavor, you'll love the way an indoor grill can caramelize the squash and concentrate its flavor. *Herbes de Provence* is a blend of Mediterranean herbs. You can buy it pre-blended at specialty food stores, or make your own following the recipe in my *Barbecue! Bible Sauces, Rubs, and Marinades.* **SERVES 2 TO 4**

2 yellow squashes or zucchini (12 to 14 ounces total)
1 to 2 tablespoons extra-virgin olive oil
Coarse salt (kosher or sea) and freshly ground black pepper
2 tablespoons herbes de Provence
1 to 2 cloves garlic (optional), minced

1. Trim the ends off the squash. Cut each squash lengthwise into ¹⁄₂-inch-thick slices if you are using a contact grill; cut each into ¹⁄₄-inch-thick slices if using any of the other indoor grills (see Note). Lightly brush each slice on both sides with olive oil, then season on both sides with salt and pepper. Sprinkle the *herbes de Provence* and garlic, if using, over both sides of the squash.

2. Cook the squash, following the instructions for any of the grills in the box at right, until they are golden brown and tender.

3. Transfer the grilled squash to a platter or plates and serve at once.

NOTE: Squash can be cooked on any sort of indoor grill, but whether you slice it thick or thin depends upon the kind of grill you are using. The key to cooking squash on a contact grill is to slice it thick enough so that both sides will come in contact with the grill—ideally about ¹⁄₂ inch thick. If you are grilling squash in a grill pan, on a built-in or freestanding grill, or in the fireplace, you'll get the best browning and the richest flavor if you slice it thin (about ¹⁄₄ inch thick).

if you have a...

CONTACT GRILL: Preheat the grill; if your contact grill has a temperature control, preheat the grill to high. Place the drip pan under the front of the grill. When ready to cook, lightly oil the grill surface. Place the squash on the hot grill, then close the lid. The squash will be done after cooking 3 to 5 minutes.

GRILL PAN: Place the grill pan on the stove and preheat it to medium-high over medium heat. When the grill pan is hot a drop of water will skitter in the pan. When ready to cook, lightly oil the ridges of the grill pan. Place the squash in the hot grill pan. It will be done after cooking 2 to 4 minutes per side.

BUILT-IN GRILL: Preheat the grill to high, then, if it does not have a nonstick surface, brush and oil the grill grate. Place the squash on the hot grate. It will be done after cooking 2 to 4 minutes per side.

FREESTANDING GRILL: Preheat the grill to high; there's no need to oil the grate. Place the squash on the hot grill. It will be done after cooking 3 to 5 minutes per side.

FIREPLACE GRILL: Rake red hot embers under the gridiron and preheat it for 3 to 5 minutes; you want a hot, 2 to 3 Mississippi fire. When ready to cook, brush and oil the gridiron. Place the squash on the hot grate. It will be done after cooking 2 to 4 minutes per side.

asian-spiced grilled squash

Most grilled squash recipes receive what might be called the Thanksgiving treatment—a sweet spice rub or basting sauce that likely includes cinnamon, nutmeg, allspice, honey, and/or brown sugar. Here's an Asian take on grilled squash, featuring garlic, sesame seeds, and soy sauce. These savory seasonings bring out the natural sweetness of the squash, without turning it into something that could double as dessert.

SERVES 4

if you have a...

CONTACT GRILL: Preheat the grill; if your contact grill has a temperature control, preheat the grill to high. Place the drip pan under the front of the grill. When ready to cook, lightly oil the grill surface. Place the squash on the hot grill, then close the lid. The squash will be done after cooking 4 to 6 minutes. You will need to turn the squash so that you can baste both sides.

GRILL PAN: Place the grill pan on the stove and preheat it to medium-high over medium heat. When the grill pan is hot a drop of water will skitter in the pan. When ready to cook, lightly oil the ridges of the grill pan. Place the squash in the hot grill pan. It will be done after cooking 2 to 3 minutes per side. Use the butter mixture sparingly when basting, taking care not to drip a lot of it into the grill pan. After it has cooled down, soak the grill pan in hot water to loosen any burnt-on butter mixture.

BUILT-IN GRILL: Preheat the grill to medium-high, then, if it does not have a nonstick surface, brush and oil the grill grate. Place the squash on the hot grate. It will be done after cooking 2 to 3 minutes per side.

FREESTANDING GRILL: Preheat the grill to high; there's no need to oil the grate. Place the squash on the hot grill. It will be done after cooking 3 to 4 minutes per side.

FIREPLACE GRILL: Rake red hot embers under the gridiron and preheat it for 3 to 5 minutes; you want a medium-hot, 3 to 4 Mississippi fire. When ready to cook, brush and oil the gridiron. Place the squash on the hot grate. It will be done after cooking 2 to 3 minutes per side.

THE RECIPE

1½ pounds butternut or other winter squash
2 tablespoons (¼ stick) unsalted butter
2 cloves garlic, minced
1 scallion, both white and green parts, minced
1 tablespoon black or white sesame seeds
2 tablespoons maple syrup
1 tablespoon soy sauce

1. Peel the squash and remove and discard the seeds. Cut the squash crosswise into ½-inch-thick slices if you are using a contact grill; cut it into ¼-inch-thick slices if you are using any of the other indoor grills.

2. Place the butter in a small saucepan and melt it over medium heat. Add the garlic, scallion, and sesame seeds and cook until the garlic has lost its rawness, about 1 minute; do not let the garlic brown. Stir in the maple syrup and soy sauce, bring to a boil, and let boil for 30 seconds.

3. When ready to cook, brush the squash slices on both sides with some of the butter mixture. Cook the squash, following the instructions for any of the grills in the box on the facing page, until browned and tender; it should be easy to pierce with a knife. Baste the squash once or twice with the garlic mixture as it cooks.

4. Transfer the squash to a platter or plates and serve at once, spooning any remaining butter mixture and, if cooked in a contact grill, any juices that collected in the drip pan over it.

tips

■ You could use any orange-fleshed winter squash for this recipe. I call for butternut, which is the easiest to peel. Acorn or Hubbard squash would give you interesting-looking arched slices.

■ For a great look, use black sesame seeds, which are available at Asian markets and natural foods stores. If you can't find them, white sesame seeds will work just fine.

contact grill

a new candied yam

Conventional grills are great for cooking vegetables with a high moisture content, like peppers and mushrooms. But what about dense root vegetables, like yams and potatoes? The direct, relatively mild heat of a contact grill is perfect for producing tubers that are caramelized on the outside and tender without being mushy inside. My wife, Barbara, who tends to be a bit of a skeptic when it comes to indoor grilling, pronounced these the best candied yams she's ever tasted. **SERVES 4**

THE RECIPE

2 large yams (about 1½ pounds total)
2 tablespoons (¼ stick) salted butter
2 tablespoons maple syrup

¾ cup sugar, in a large shallow bowl
Cooking oil spray

tips

■ I like garnet yams, tubers with a rich flavor and vivid reddish orange hue, for this recipe. You could also use conventional sweet potatoes.

■ Some people like to add ground cinnamon or nutmeg to the sugar. If you want to try this, use ½ teaspoon of either spice.

1. Peel the yams and cut them crosswise into ½-inch-thick slices (thick enough to give you grill marks on both sides). Discard the pointy ends.

2. Melt the butter in a small saucepan over medium-high heat. Stir in the maple syrup, bring to a boil, and let boil until it becomes thick and syrupy, about 30 seconds. Remove the saucepan from the heat. Using a pastry brush, brush each yam slice on both sides with the butter mixture, then dip both sides in the sugar, shaking off the excess.

3. Preheat the grill (for instructions for using a contact grill, see page 3); if your contact grill has a temperature control, preheat the grill to high. Place the drip pan under the front of the grill.

4. When ready to cook, lightly coat the grill surface with cooking oil spray. Place the yam slices on the hot grill on a diagonal to the ridges and close the lid. Grill until browned on the outside and tender inside (they'll be easy to pierce with a knife), 6 to 8 minutes.

5. Transfer the yams to a platter or plates and serve at once, spooning any juices that collected in the drip pan over them.

contact grill

bacon-grilled yams

I 've always been a sucker for the sweet salty counterpoint of bacon and maple syrup. And I'm not alone in this—the traditional Vermont breakfast, a specialty of the Inn at Sawmill Farms in West Dover, consists of bacon and eggs poached in maple syrup. That was my inspiration for these sweet, smoky, bacon-grilled yams. From eggs with bacon and maple syrup to yams with bacon and maple syrup is a bit of a leap, but one you'll be glad you made. **SERVES 4**

THE RECIPE

2 large yams (about 1½ pounds total)
8 thick slices bacon (about 8 ounces total),
    cut in half crosswise

¼ cup maple syrup
Cooking oil spray

1. Peel the yams and cut them lengthwise into 8 slices, each about ½ inch thick. Place 8 pieces of bacon on a work surface. Brush one side of the yam slices with some of the maple syrup, then place each, syrup side down, on a piece of bacon. Brush the tops of the yam slices with some of the maple syrup and place the remaining pieces of bacon on them.

2. Preheat the grill (for instructions for using a contact grill, see page 3); if your contact grill has a temperature control, preheat the grill to high. Place the drip pan under the front of the grill.

3. When ready to cook, lightly coat the grill surface with cooking oil spray. Using a spatula, transfer the bacon and yam slices to the hot grill, then close the lid. Grill the yams until the bacon is crisp and browned and the yams are tender inside (they'll be easy to pierce with a knife), 6 to 8 minutes.

4. Transfer the yams to a platter or plates, pour the remaining maple syrup over them, and serve at once.

tip

You'll want to use an artisanal smoked bacon for this yam recipe. Vermont abounds with small smokehouses. One good brand that's available by mail order is Harrington's of Vermont (see page 396).

rotisserie

chile-rubbed sweet potatoes

Once you get into rotisserie roasting, anything is fair game, even sweet potatoes. The gentle rotation and steady heat produce sweet potatoes with a crisp skin and an exceptionally buttery interior. The recipe here features a spicy Southwestern-style rub made with chile powder, cumin, and cinnamon. **SERVES 4**

tip

For the best results, choose long, slender sweet potatoes or yams that will fit in the rotisserie basket. In our house, we're partial to garnet yams, distinguished by their dark reddish-orange color and concentrated, rich-flavored flesh.

THE RECIPE

2 teaspoons pure chile powder
1 teaspoon coarse salt (kosher or sea)
1/2 teaspoon freshly ground black pepper
1/2 teaspoon ground cumin
1/4 teaspoon ground cinnamon
4 sweet potatoes (about 1 1/2 pounds total)
1 1/2 tablespoons extra-virgin olive oil or
    butter, melted
Cooking oil spray

1. Place the chile powder, salt, pepper, cumin, and cinnamon in a large mixing bowl and whisk to mix.

2. Scrub the sweet potatoes under cold running water and blot them dry with paper towels. Brush the sweet potatoes all over with the olive oil. Add the sweet potatoes to the bowl with the rub and stir to coat evenly.

3. Lightly coat a flat rotisserie basket with cooking oil spray. Arrange the sweet potatoes in the rotisserie basket so they will be perpendicular to the spit. Close the basket tightly.

4. When ready to cook, place the drip pan in the bottom of the rotisserie. Attach the basket to the rotisserie spit then attach the spit to the rotisserie and turn on the motor. If your rotisserie has a temperature control, set it to 400°F (for instructions for using a rotisserie, see page 14). Cook the sweet potatoes until they are crusty and golden brown on the outside and soft inside, 40 minutes to 1 hour. Use a skewer to test for doneness; it should pierce a sweet potato easily.

5. Transfer the sweet potatoes to a platter or plates and serve at once.

VARIATIONS: For sweet spit-roasted sweet potatoes with a candylike crust, mix 1/2 cup of sugar, 1 tablespoon of ground cinnamon, 1/2 teaspoon coarse salt, and 1/2 teaspoon freshly ground black pepper in a broad shallow bowl. Brush 4 long, slender sweet potatoes with 2 tablespoons of maple syrup. Roll the sweet potatoes in the cinnamon sugar to coat them all over, then cook them in the rotisserie as described in Steps 3 and 4 at left.

Parmesan cheese brings out the savory qualities of sweet potatoes. Place 1/2 cup finely grated Parmesan in a large shallow bowl. Brush 4 long, slender sweet potatoes with 2 tablespoons of melted unsalted butter and season them all over with coarse salt and freshly ground black pepper. Roll the sweet potatoes in the Parmesan to coat them all over, then cook them in the rotisserie as described at left.

sage and garlic grilled tomatoes

Tomatoes are great for grilling. The searing heat caramelizes the tomato's natural sugars. Tomatoes readily absorb the flavors of herbs and other seasonings, and their shocking red color looks terrific on a plate along with grilled poultry, seafood, or beef. The tomatoes can be grilled on any sort of indoor grill—for that matter, you could also smoke them in a stove-top smoker, as described in the Smoked Gazpacho recipe on page 51.

SERVES 4 TO 6

THE RECIPE

6 plum tomatoes (about 1¼ pounds),
    cut in half lengthwise
2 tablespoons extra-virgin olive oil
Coarse salt (kosher or sea) and cracked
    black pepper
3 cloves garlic, minced
1 tablespoon finely chopped fresh sage,
    plus 12 whole fresh sage leaves

1. Brush the tomato halves all over with olive oil. Season them generously all over with salt and pepper, then sprinkle the

if you have a...

CONTACT GRILL: Preheat the grill; if your contact grill has a temperature control, preheat the grill to high. Place the drip pan under the front of the grill. When ready to cook, lightly oil the grill surface. Arrange the tomato halves on the hot grill, cut side up, then close the lid. The tomatoes will be done after cooking 4 to 6 minutes.

GRILL PAN: Place the grill pan on the stove and preheat it to medium-high over medium heat. When the grill pan is hot a drop of water will skitter in the pan. When ready to cook, lightly oil the ridges of the grill pan. Arrange the tomato halves, cut side down, in the hot grill pan on a diagonal to the ridges. The tomatoes will be done after cooking 4 to 6 minutes per side. Rotate the tomatoes a quarter turn after grilling 2 minutes on the first side to create a handsome crosshatch of grill marks.

BUILT-IN GRILL: Preheat the grill to high, then, if it does not have a nonstick surface, brush and oil the grill grate. Arrange the tomato halves, cut side down, on the hot grate on a diagonal to the

ridges. The tomatoes will be done after cooking 4 to 6 minutes per side. Rotate the tomatoes a quarter turn after grilling 2 minutes on the first side to create a handsome crosshatch of grill marks.

FREESTANDING GRILL: Preheat the grill to high; there's no need to oil the grate. Arrange the tomato halves, cut side down, on the hot grate on a diagonal to the ridges. The tomatoes will be done after cooking 5 to 7 minutes per side. Rotate the tomatoes a quarter turn after grilling 2 minutes on the first side to create a handsome crosshatch of grill marks.

FIREPLACE GRILL: Rake red hot embers under the gridiron and preheat it for 3 to 5 minutes; you want a hot, 2 to 3 Mississippi fire. When ready to cook, brush and oil the gridiron. Arrange the tomato halves, cut side down, on the hot grate on a diagonal to the ridges. The tomatoes will be done after cooking 4 to 6 minutes per side. Rotate the tomatoes a quarter turn after grilling 2 minutes on the first side to create a handsome crosshatch of grill marks.

garlic and chopped sage over them. Press a whole sage leaf in the center of the cut side of each tomato half. Set any leftover olive oil aside.

2. Cook the tomatoes, following the instructions for any of the grills in the box on the previous page, until nicely browned.

3. Transfer the tomatoes to a platter or plates and drizzle any remaining olive oil over them. Serve at once.

VARIATIONS: This recipe calls for fresh sage because I like its earthy flavor and I also like the way the whole leaves look when grilled into the tomato halves. If you don't like or can't find sage, you can achieve a similar effect with small sprigs of fresh rosemary, tarragon, thyme, flat-leaf parsley, or another herb.

You can also grill small whole plum tomatoes this way. Skewer the sage leaves onto the tomatoes with wooden toothpicks.

tofu teriyaki

Tofu and soy sauce are both made from soybeans, so it's not surprising they come together in a dish that's almost as popular in Japan as hot dogs are in the United States. If you find tofu bland, this sweet and salty made-from-scratch teriyaki sauce is your ticket. To round out the flavors, the tofu is dotted with toasted sesame seeds and chopped scallions.

SERVES 4 TO 6

tips

■ Mirin is a sweet Japanese rice wine. Depending upon where you live, you may find it at Asian markets, natural foods stores, or liquor stores. Or you can use another 1/2 cup of sake and add 1 1/2 tablespoons of sugar.

■ If you're in a hurry, you can certainly use a commercial teriyaki sauce instead of making your own.

THE RECIPE

FOR THE TERIYAKI SAUCE:
1 scallion, white part only, trimmed and gently flattened with the side of a cleaver
1 clove garlic, peeled and gently flattened with the side of a cleaver
2 slices peeled fresh ginger (each 1/4 inch thick)
1/2 cup sake
1/2 cup mirin (sweet rice wine)
3 tablespoons sugar

6 tablespoons soy sauce
1 teaspoon cornstarch dissolved in 2 teaspoons water

FOR THE TOFU:
2 packages (about 2 pounds) extra-firm tofu, drained
2 tablespoons toasted sesame seeds (see Note)
1 scallion, green part only, very thinly sliced crosswise

1. Make the teriyaki sauce: Place the scallion white, garlic, ginger, sake, mirin, and sugar in a small, heavy nonreactive saucepan and bring to a boil over high heat. Let boil until reduced by about one quarter, 3 to 5 minutes. Add the soy sauce, reduce the heat to medium, and let the sauce continue to boil until syrupy, 3 to 5 minutes.

2. Stir the cornstarch and water until smooth, then whisk into the simmering teriyaki sauce. Let the sauce continue to simmer for about 30 seconds; it should thicken slightly. Strain the teriyaki sauce into a heatproof bowl and let cool to room temperature. The teriyaki sauce can be made several hours or even a day ahead and refrigerated, covered. Let it return to room temperature before using.

3. Prepare the tofu: Cut each piece of tofu crosswise into ¹⁄₂-inch-thick slices. Place the tofu slices in a nonreactive baking dish just large enough to hold them in one layer. Pour two thirds of the teriyaki sauce over the tofu, turning it to coat both sides. Set the remaining teriyaki sauce aside. Let the tofu marinate in the refrigerator, covered, for 30 minutes to 1 hour.

4. Cook the tofu, following the instructions for any of the grills in the box at right, until golden brown.

5. Transfer the tofu to a platter or plates and drizzle the reserved teriyaki sauce over it. Sprinkle the sesame seeds and scallion greens on top of the tofu and serve at once.

NOTE: To toast sesame seeds, place them in a dry cast-iron or other heavy

if you have a...

CONTACT GRILL: Preheat the grill; if your contact grill has a temperature control, preheat the grill to high. Place the drip pan under the front of the grill. When ready to cook, lightly oil the grill surface. Place the tofu on the hot grill, then close the lid. The tofu will be done after cooking 3 to 5 minutes.

GRILL PAN: Place the grill pan on the stove and preheat it to medium-high over medium heat. When the grill pan is hot a drop of water will skitter in the pan. When ready to cook, lightly oil the ridges of the grill pan. Drain the tofu well, then place it in the hot grill pan. The tofu will be done after cooking 3 to 5 minutes per side. After it has cooled down, soak the grill pan in hot water to loosen any burnt-on teriyaki sauce.

BUILT-IN GRILL: Preheat the grill to high, then, if it does not have a nonstick surface, brush and oil the grill grate. Place the tofu on the hot grate. It will be done after cooking 3 to 5 minutes per side.

FREESTANDING GRILL: Preheat the grill to high; there's no need to oil the grate. Place the tofu on the hot grill. It will be done after cooking 4 to 6 minutes per side.

FIREPLACE GRILL: Rake red hot embers under the gridiron and preheat it for 3 to 5 minutes; you want a hot, 2 to 3 Mississippi fire. When ready to cook, brush and oil the gridiron. Place the tofu on the hot grate. It will be done after cooking 3 to 5 minutes per side.

skillet (don't use a nonstick skillet for this). Cook the sesame seeds over medium heat until lightly browned, about 3 minutes, shaking the skillet to ensure that they toast evenly. Transfer the toasted sesame seeds to a heatproof bowl to cool.

ELEPHANT GARLIC

Elephant garlic is just what it sounds like—a head of garlic that's the size of a softball. It's perfect for making grilled garlic chips. You don't have to do this, but the chips really round out the sandwiches.

"barbecued" tofu sandwiches

Some years ago my wife, Barbara, and stepdaughter, Betsy, became vegetarians. Their decision was temporary, but it did force me to serve barbecued tofu sandwiches on Super Bowl Sunday. A quick baste of butter and liquid smoke gives tofu the requisite smoky flavor. **SERVES 4**

THE RECIPE

if you have a...

CONTACT GRILL: Preheat the grill; if your contact grill has a temperature control, preheat the grill to high. Place the drip pan under the front of the grill. When ready to cook, lightly oil the grill surface. Place the tofu on the hot grill, then close the lid. The tofu will be done after cooking 4 to 7 minutes. You will need to turn the tofu when basting.

GRILL PAN: Place the grill pan on the stove and preheat it to medium-high over medium heat. When the grill pan is hot a drop of water will skitter in the pan. When ready to cook, lightly oil the ridges of the grill pan. Place the tofu in the hot grill pan. It will be done after cooking 3 to 5 minutes per side. Take care not to drip a lot of barbecue sauce into the grill pan. After it has cooled down, soak the grill pan in hot water to loosen any burnt-on barbecue sauce.

BUILT-IN GRILL: Preheat the grill to high, then, if it does not have a nonstick surface, brush and oil the grill grate. Place the tofu on the hot grate. It will be done after cooking 3 to 5 minutes per side.

FREESTANDING GRILL: Preheat the grill to high; there's no need to oil the grate. Place the tofu on the hot grill. It will be done after cooking 4 to 6 minutes per side.

FIREPLACE GRILL: Rake red hot embers under the gridiron and preheat it for 3 to 5 minutes; you want a hot, 2 to 3 Mississippi fire. When ready to cook, brush and oil the gridiron. Place the tofu on the hot grate. It will be done after cooking 3 to 5 minutes per side.

2 packages (about 2 pounds) extra-firm or firm tofu (see Notes), drained

1½ tablespoons unsalted butter

2 teaspoons liquid smoke (see box on page 179)

2 tablespoons of your favorite barbecue rub (for some options, see pages 362 through 364)

2 cloves elephant garlic, sliced very thinly crosswise

1 tablespoon extra-virgin olive oil

Coarse salt (kosher or sea) and freshly ground black pepper

About ½ cup of your favorite barbecue sauce (for one option, see page 374)

8 Boston lettuce leaves

4 kaiser rolls or buns, split

1 luscious, ripe red tomato, thinly sliced

1 dill pickle, thinly sliced

1. Cut each piece of tofu crosswise into ½-inch-thick slices. Melt the butter in a small saucepan over medium heat and stir in the liquid smoke. Lightly brush the slices of tofu on both sides with the butter mixture. Sprinkle the barbecue rub all over the tofu.

2. Preheat the oven to 350°F; you'll use it to brown the garlic (see Notes).

3. Place the garlic slices in a small bowl, add the olive oil, and toss to coat. Season the garlic with salt and pepper. Spread the slices of garlic out on a rimmed baking sheet. Bake the garlic until crisp and golden brown, 5 to 10 minutes.

4. Cook the tofu, following the instructions for any of the grills in the box on the facing page, until sizzling and deeply browned, basting it with ¼ cup of the barbecue sauce when it has turned golden brown on both sides.

5. Place 2 lettuce leaves on the bottom half of each roll. Top with the grilled tofu, followed by some garlic, tomato, and pickle slices. Spoon the remaining ¼ cup of barbecue sauce over the tofu. Top with the other half of the roll and serve at once.

NOTES:

■ You need extra-firm or firm tofu for this recipe, preferably not silken. You're likely to find it in the produce section of the supermarket.

■ If you have a contact grill you can brown the garlic slices on it instead of in the oven. Preheat the grill to high. The garlic will be done after 2 to 3 minutes. If you're grilling the tofu on a contact grill, press the slices of garlic into the top and bottom of the slices of tofu and they will grill right into the tofu.

on tofu and miso

Tofu and miso are soy products that originally came from Asia. Tofu is sold in white or ivory-colored blocks; miso comes in the form of an aromatic paste. Both are used for grilling—tofu as grill fare itself; miso in glazes and barbecue sauces. Tofu and miso are mainstays of Japanese grilling and make valuable additions to any indoor griller's repertory.

Native to China and wildly popular in Japan, many excellent brands of tofu are now made in North America. Tofu is also called bean curd—an apt metaphor, as to make it, soymilk is separated into "curds," which are strained and pressed into the familiar cobblestone-shaped cakes.

There are two basic types of tofu: regular and silken. Regular tofu is firmer and drier than the soft and custardlike silken tofu. Regular tofu works the best for grilling, as silken is so creamy it tends to fall apart on the grill. Both regular and silken tofu come in several styles, including extra-firm, firm, and soft. Extra-firm is the sturdiest and best for grilling. (Many grill masters like to press tofu under a skillet for an hour or so to firm it up before grilling.) Tofu is available in the produce section of most supermarkets and, of course, in Asian markets and natural foods stores.

Miso is a highly nutritious, flavorful paste made from cultured (fermented) soybeans, grains, and salt. The mixture is aged in cedar kegs for a period of months or even years. The flavor is sui generis, but if you imagine the concentrated flavor of well-aged Parmesan cheese and the intense salty tang

of a bouillon cube (only much better tasting) combined with the creamy richness of peanut butter, you will begin to get the idea.

Like tofu, miso comes in a variety of styles and grades, some sold in plastic tubs, others in plastic-wrapped pouches. Many come from Japan, but there are excellent misos made in North America. Look for them in the produce section of your supermarket, natural foods store, or at a Japanese market. Miso should be refrigerated and keeps for several months.

Some of the major styles of miso include:

■ **White miso** (also called *shiro miso*) is a mild, white, sweet miso made from soybeans and white rice. *Saikyo miso* is a very sweet white miso that's especially well suited to grilling.

■ **Yellow miso** (also called *shinshu miso*) is similar to white miso but a little yellow in color and saltier in flavor.

■ **Brown rice miso** (also called *genmai miso*) is made with soybeans, brown rice, and salt. It's sandy colored, salty, and intensely flavored, thanks to being aged one and a half to two years.

■ **Red miso** (also called *aka miso*) is a darker miso made with soybeans, rice, and salt. This is an all-purpose miso often used to make miso soup.

■ **Barley miso** (also called *mugi miso*) is a dark, reddish brown miso made from soybeans, barley, and salt. It's smooth to chunky in texture, with a rich, earthy flavor often described as having chocolate and coffee overtones.

stove-top smoker

smoked tofu

Vegetarians, the health conscious, and lovers of Asian food need no inducement to eat tofu. Here's a reason for the rest of us: Tofu absorbs spice and smoke flavors as readily as ribs or brisket do. This tofu "ham," which is brined and smoked, has character, even soul—not to mention a depth of flavor that will take skeptics by surprise. You know the many health benefits of eating tofu. The taste is also pure pleasure. **SERVES 4 TO 6**

tips

■ The texture of the "ham" will vary depending on the sort of tofu you use. Silken tofu will have a creamy, almost custardy consistency. It's extremely fragile, so you'll need to handle it with care. Conventional tofu is drier and firmer. Both come in extra-firm and firm varieties, and both are delectable.

■ You can also smoke the tofu in a wok. You'll find instructions for doing this in the box on page 234.

THE RECIPE

2 cups cool water
1/4 cup firmly packed light brown sugar
2 tablespoons coarse salt (kosher or sea)
1 teaspoon black peppercorns
1 teaspoon mustard seeds
1/4 teaspoon whole cloves
1/2 cinnamon stick (about 1 1/2 inches)
2 bay leaves
2 strips lemon zest (each about 1/2 by
    1 1/2 inches)
2 packages (about 2 pounds) extra-firm
    or firm tofu, drained
Cooking oil spray (optional)

YOU'LL ALSO NEED:
1 1/2 tablespoons cherry or apple wood
    sawdust

1. Place the water, brown sugar, salt, peppercorns, mustard seeds, cloves, cinnamon stick, bay leaves, and lemon zest in a deep narrow mixing bowl and whisk until the salt and sugar dissolve.

2. Add the tofu, making sure it is completely submerged, and let brine in the refrigerator, covered, for 6 to 8 hours. You can also brine the tofu in a resealable plastic bag.

3. Set up the smoker (for instructions for using a stove-top smoker, see page 16). Place the sawdust in the center of the bottom of the smoker. Line the drip pan with aluminum foil and place it in the smoker. Lightly coat the smoker rack with cooking oil spray, or use a paper towel dipped in oil, and place the rack in the smoker. Drain the tofu well and blot dry with paper towels. Place the tofu on top of the smoker rack.

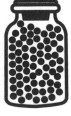

4. Cover the smoker and place it over high heat for 3 minutes, then reduce the heat to medium. Smoke the tofu until lightly browned, 15 to 20 minutes.

5. Transfer the smoked tofu to a plate and let cool to room temperature. Refrigerate the tofu until ready to serve, then cut it crosswise into thin slices. The smoked tofu can be served chilled or at room temperature. It can be refrigerated, covered, for up to 5 days.

parmesan-crusted polenta

Polenta is Italian cornmeal mush. If you think that sounds plebian, wait until you taste it grilled. In the old days, making polenta required an arm-numbing hour of stirring the polenta pot, and if you wanted to grill it, the polenta had to chill for a half day. Today, you can have grilled polenta in no time, thanks to the advent of ready-made polenta sold in plastic tubes. Serve grilled polenta as an appetizer or side dish, or pair it with the Grilled Tomato Sauce on page 372 for a satisfying main course. **SERVES 4**

tip

Buy Parmigiano-Reggiano cheese and grate it just before you are ready to use it. To grate the cheese in a food processor, cut it into ½-inch chunks. Then, using the metal chopping blade, add the chunks of cheese to the processor bowl while the motor is running.

THE RECIPE

1 package (18 ounces) precooked polenta
Coarse salt (kosher or sea) and freshly ground black pepper
3 tablespoons unsalted butter, melted
1 cup fresh finely grated Parmigiano-Reggiano (about 4 ounces), in a shallow bowl
Grilled Tomato Sauce (optional; page 372), for serving

1. Cut the polenta crosswise into ½-inch-thick slices and season each on both sides with salt and pepper. Brush each piece on one side with melted butter, then dip it into the Parmesan to thickly crust it, shaking off any excess. Brush the other side of the polenta rounds with melted butter, then dip this side in the Parmesan, again shaking off the excess.

if you have a...

CONTACT GRILL: Preheat the grill; if your contact grill has a temperature control, preheat the grill to high. Place the drip pan under the front of the grill. When ready to cook, lightly oil the grill surface. Place the polenta rounds gently on the hot grill, then close the lid. The polenta will be done after cooking 3 to 5 minutes.

GRILL PAN: Place the grill pan on the stove and preheat it to medium-high over medium heat. When the grill pan is hot a drop of water will skitter in the pan. When ready to cook, lightly oil the ridges of the grill pan. Place the polenta rounds in the hot grill pan. They will be done after cooking 3 to 5 minutes per side.

BUILT-IN GRILL: Preheat the grill to high, then, if it does not have a nonstick surface, brush and oil the grill grate. Place the polenta rounds on the hot grate. They will be done after cooking 3 to 5 minutes per side.

FREESTANDING GRILL: Preheat the grill to high; there's no need to oil the grate. Place the polenta rounds on the hot grill. They will be done after cooking 4 to 6 minutes per side.

FIREPLACE GRILL: Rake red hot embers under the gridiron and preheat it for 3 to 5 minutes; you want a hot, 2 to 3 Mississippi fire. When ready to cook, brush and oil the gridiron. Place the polenta rounds on the hot grate. They will be done after cooking 3 to 5 minutes per side.

Place the Parmesan-crusted polenta on a plate lined with plastic wrap as they are coated.

2. Cook the polenta, following the instructions for any of the grills in the box at left, until it is golden brown and heated through. Use a metal spatula to turn the polenta.

3. Transfer the polenta rounds to a platter or plates. Sprinkle any remaining Parmesan on top and serve at once with the Grilled Tomato Sauce, if desired.

A lot of what takes grilled food over the top are seasonings like rubs, basting mixtures, barbecue sauces, and salsas. This brief chapter includes the basic recipes that should be in every indoor grill master's repertory and fills you in on just when to use them. Here you'll learn how to make four of my favorite all-purpose rubs, not to mention three flavored butters for basting and serving. Once you've tried my Grilled Tomato Sauce and Smoked Tomato Salsa, your notion of red sauces will never be quite the same. When it comes to the basics of grilling—indoors or out—it's all about flavor.

basics

basic barbecue rub

Virtually all the recipes in this book call for freshly ground black pepper. The reason is simple—freshly ground peppercorns have a robust and decisive flavor that is far superior to commercial ground pepper. But reaching for a pepper mill every time you need pepper is time consuming and inefficient—especially when large quantities are called for. What I do is grind a handful or so of whole peppercorns in a spice mill or coffee grinder once a week and store the ground pepper in a sealed jar. Even after a week, it retains the vibrancy of freshly ground pepper, and you can grab a pinch or spoonful whenever you need it.

This is about my umpteenth version of a rub that lies at the heart of American barbecue—the four-four rub, which contains just four ingredients: salt, pepper, paprika, and sugar. Simple but sufficient to turn any beast that walks, bird that flies, or fish that swims into splendid barbecue. I think you'll like the way the flavored salts, cumin, and oregano round out its richness. Figure on using two to three teaspoons of rub per pound of meat. **MAKES ABOUT 2/3 CUP**

THE RECIPE

3 tablespoons sweet paprika

3 tablespoons brown sugar
   (either light or dark is OK)

1 1/2 tablespoons freshly ground black pepper

1 tablespoon garlic salt

1 tablespoon onion salt

1 tablespoon celery salt

1 teaspoon ground cumin

1 teaspoon dried oregano

Place the paprika, brown sugar, pepper, garlic salt, onion salt, celery salt, cumin, and oregano in a small mixing bowl and whisk to mix, breaking up any lumps in the brown sugar with your fingers. Store the rub in an airtight jar away from heat or light; it will keep for at least 6 months.

all-purpose smoky barbecue rub

I've been tinkering with this rub for the better part of a decade. Brown sugar makes it sweet; black pepper and paprika make it fiery; and the celery seed, garlic, and onion give it an aromatic earthiness that goes well with all manner of meat and poultry, seafood, and even tofu. Figure on using two to three teaspoons of rub per pound of meat. **MAKES ABOUT 1 CUP**

1/3 cup firmly packed dark brown sugar
1/4 cup hickory smoked salt
1/4 cup sweet paprika
2 tablespoons freshly ground black pepper
1 tablespoon garlic flakes
1 tablespoon onion flakes
1 teaspoon celery seed

Place the brown sugar, smoked salt, paprika, pepper, garlic flakes, onion flakes, and celery seed in a small bowl and whisk to mix, breaking up any lumps in the brown sugar with your fingers.

Store the rub in an airtight jar away from heat or light; it will keep for at least 6 months.

NOTE: Use this recipe as a basic guide, not a formula to be slavishly followed to the quarter teaspoon. For example, if you like a spicier rub, substitute hot paprika for the sweet paprika. Or for a Texas touch, add 2 tablespoons of chili powder.

tip

I've called for hickory-smoked salt in the all-purpose rub to give you some of the smoky flavor you'd get on an outdoor grill. Smoked salt is available at most supermarkets, but you can certainly use regular salt instead.

lone star barbecue rub

Texas rubs are considerably more spicy and less sweet than Southern and Midwestern rubs. They're based on pure chile powder and spiced up with oregano, cumin, coriander, and cinnamon. This rub goes great on beef, pork, and poultry. Figure on using two to three teaspoons of rub per pound of meat.

MAKES ABOUT 1 CUP

ON GARLIC,
ONION, AND
BAY LEAVES

Dried garlic and
onion are com-
mon ingredients in
traditional American
barbecue rubs. They
taste different from
the fresh bulbs—
milder and sweeter—
but lack the pungency
of fresh. Dried garlic
and onion come in
three forms:

■ **POWDERED:** The
most finely ground,
it's the consistency
of flour. Also used to
flavor what is sold as
garlic or onion salt.

■ **GRANULATED:**
Somewhat more
coarsely ground, it's
the consistency of
cornmeal. Also used
in flavored salts.

■ **FLAKES:** Quite
coarse, these come in
tiny chips, like what
you find on garlic or
onion bagels.

At least one recipe
in this book calls for
ground bay leaf. You
can find ground bay
leaves in most well-
stocked supermarkets,
or see Mail-Order
Sources (page 396).
To make your own,
crumble a few dried
bay leaves and grind
them in a spice mill;
store in a sealed jar.

THE RECIPE

1/2 cup ancho chile powder (see Note)
1/4 cup coarse salt (kosher or sea)
2 tablespoons freshly ground black pepper
2 tablespoons dried oregano
1 tablespoon garlic powder
1 tablespoon onion powder
2 teaspoons ground cumin
1 teaspoon ground coriander
1 teaspoon ground cinnamon

Place the chile powder, salt, pepper, oregano, garlic powder, onion powder, cumin, coriander, and cinnamon in a small bowl and whisk to mix. Store the rub in an airtight jar away from heat or light; it will keep for at least 6 months.

NOTE: For the best results, use a pure chile powder ground from ancho or New Mexico chiles. See Mail-Order Sources on page 396 for a source.

cajun rub

Commercial Cajun rub is widely available, of course, but it's easy to make from scratch and you can skip the MSG found in many brands. With three types of pepper—black, white, and cayenne—this blend isn't exactly mild mannered, but there's a lot more going on here in the way of aromatics than heat. Figure on using two to three teaspoons of rub per pound of meat. **MAKES ABOUT 3 TABLESPOONS**

THE RECIPE

1 tablespoon coarse salt (kosher or sea)
1 tablespoon sweet paprika
1 teaspoon freshly ground black pepper
1 teaspoon freshly ground white pepper
1/2 teaspoon dried thyme
1/2 teaspoon dried oregano
1/2 teaspoon granulated onion (see sidebar)
1/2 teaspoon granulated garlic
   (see sidebar)

1/4 teaspoon ground bay leaf (see sidebar)
1/4 teaspoon cayenne pepper

Place the salt, paprika, black pepper, white pepper, thyme, oregano, granulated onion and garlic, bay leaf, and cayenne in a small bowl and whisk to mix. Store the rub in an airtight jar away from heat or light; it will keep for at least 6 months.

the three windows of flavor

A great deal of confusion surrounds the subject of rubs, marinades, bastes, barbecue sauces, butters, and salsas. Just how and when do you use them? Keep the Three Windows of Flavor in mind and you'll get it right every time. The Three Windows refers to the three stages when you can add flavor to grilled or smoked foods: before cooking; while it cooks; and after the food comes off the grill. Here's how it works.

THE FIRST WINDOW: BEFORE GRILLING

This is when you apply seasonings to raw foods. You'll find three types in this book: rubs, marinades, and brines.

Rubs are often mixtures of herbs, spices, and/or salt and can be either dry or wet, like a paste. You can apply a rub right before you grill, in which case it acts like a seasoned salt. Or you can apply it several hours or even a day ahead, in which case it will cure meat in addition to seasoning it. Rubs are especially well suited to fatty foods, such as ribs or brisket, although they also go well with lean foods, like chicken breasts. Rubs are particularly useful when you want to cook in a grill pan (marinades tend to gather in the bottom of the pan and burn).

Marinades are wet seasonings that often include an oil (such as olive or sesame oil), an acid (such as vinegar or lemon juice), and aromatics (such as garlic, onion, ginger, scallions, and/or fresh or dried herbs). The larger or tougher the food, the longer you need to marinate it. While you might marinate shrimp for half an hour, you'd marinate a leg of lamb overnight. Marinades are great for lean foods, like chicken breasts or shrimp, helping them retain their moisture as they grill.

Brines are a special kind of marinade based on salt, water, and frequently sugar. Brines are used to cure meats and seafood prior to grilling or smoking. They help meat retain moisture as it grills.

THE SECOND WINDOW: DURING GRILLING

Next come seasonings you apply to foods while they cook. There are three kinds: bastes, mop sauces, and glazes. Bastes often contain oil or butter, not to mention a broad range of flavorings from lemon, to herbs, to spirits. They're brushed on chicken breasts, chops, fish, shrimp, and fruit (to name just a few things) as they sizzle on the grill. The fat in a baste helps keep the food moist.

A mop sauce is a more liquid mixture that is traditionally swabbed on foods with a barbecue mop. Mop sauces tend to be based on vinegar, beer, coffee, or other thin liquids and usually contain little or no sugar. Mops are generally used with foods that cook slowly, like briskets, ribs, and pork shoulders. The lack of sugar keeps mop sauces from burning during prolonged cooking.

Glazes are also applied during the second stage. They usually contain some sort of sweetener (honey, sugar, or jam, to name a few examples). Glazes cook to a sweet, often sticky crust as they grill.

THE THIRD WINDOW: AFTER GRILLING

These flavorings are applied once food comes off the grill or rotisserie. A short list would include compound butters, salsas, chutneys, relishes, and barbecue sauces. The searing heat of the grill has already worked its magic—these preparations are designed to round out or counterpoint the flavor.

Compound butters are flavored butters meant to be dolloped on hot food right before it's served. As they melt, they mix with the meat juices to form a sort of sauce. The flavoring possibilities are limitless: You can use any combination of herbs, spices, cheese, chiles, and/or citrus you like.

Salsas, chutneys, and relishes are usually served chilled or at room temperature and add a contrast in temperature to food hot off the grill. All three contain vinegar, lemon or lime juice, or some other acidic ingredient, which helps cut the richness of meat.

You may be surprised to find barbecue sauce in the third flavoring category, but I'm adamant that it should be applied toward the end of cooking or after the food is done. You don't want the sugar in the sauce to burn on the grill.

PUTTING IT ALL TOGETHER

So now you know just when to use a rub or marinade, baste or mop sauce, and compound butter or barbecue sauce. Each is good on its own. You can also use them together to produce complex layers of flavor. For example, you might put rub on a chicken breast, baste it with melted butter and liquid smoke as it grills, then serve it with a sweet smoky barbecue sauce. This is what I did to make Victory Chicken (page 182). There are no hard and fast rules. Feel free to experiment and let your imagination—and your taste buds—be your guide.

parmesan, sage, and pepper butter

Compound butter flavored with Parmesan, sage, and black pepper is good with swordfish, or, for that matter, almost any other grilled fish and chicken or veal chops. For the best results, use imported Parmigiano-Reggiano cheese from northern Italy; it will have the words *Parmigiano-Reggiano* stamped into the rind. A half cup is double what you need when serving four. Freeze the butter in two batches. **MAKES ABOUT ½ CUP**

THE RECIPE

8 tablespoons (1 stick) unsalted butter, at room temperature
¼ cup freshly grated Parmigiano-Reggiano cheese
4 fresh sage leaves, thinly slivered, or 1 teaspoon crumbled dried sage
1 tablespoon cracked black pepper
Coarse salt (kosher or sea)

Place the butter, Parmigiano-Reggiano, sage, and pepper in a food processor and process until well blended and creamy. Season with salt to taste. If you are preparing the butter ahead, spoon it onto 2 sheets of plastic wrap, dividing it evenly between them. Roll each into a tight cylinder, twisting the ends of the plastic wrap closed like a Tootsie Roll. Refrigerate or freeze the butter until firm. The flavored butter can be refrigerated for up to 5 days or frozen for 3 months. To use, spoon about 1 tablespoon on top of each serving or unwrap the butter and cut off ½-inch crosswise slices.

curried onion butter

Lend grilled fish an Indian or West Indian accent with this aromatic butter—curry powder and caramelized onions are common in both parts of the world. The butter is particularly good with salmon, swordfish, and chicken breasts. The recipe makes enough for eight servings, so you'll probably want to divide it in half before freezing it. **MAKES ABOUT ½ CUP**

THE RECIPE

8 tablespoons (1 stick) unsalted butter,
    at room temperature
1 small onion, sliced paper-thin
2 teaspoons curry powder
1 teaspoon mustard seeds (preferably black)
Coarse salt (kosher or sea) and freshly ground
    black pepper

1. Melt 2 tablespoons of the butter in a nonstick frying pan over medium heat. Add the onion, curry powder, and mustard seeds and cook until the onion is soft and turns a dark golden brown, about 10 minutes. You'll probably need to lower the heat as the onion starts to brown to keep it from burning. Transfer the onion mixture to the bowl of a food processor and let cool to room temperature.

2. Add the remaining 6 tablespoons of butter to the food processor and process until well mixed and creamy. Taste for seasoning, adding salt and pepper to taste.

3. If you are preparing the butter ahead, spoon it onto 2 sheets of plastic wrap, dividing it evenly between them. Roll each into a tight cylinder, twisting the ends of the plastic wrap closed like a Tootsie Roll. Refrigerate or freeze the butter until firm. The flavored butter can be refrigerated for up to 5 days or frozen for 3 months. To use, spoon about 1 tablespoon on top of each serving or unwrap the butter and cut off ½-inch crosswise slices.

tip

Black mustard seeds are available at Indian markets. If you can't find them, substitute yellow or white mustard seeds.

chipotle lime butter

When fire and smoke are in order, this compound butter flavored with chipotles and lime fits the bill. It's great with grilled shrimp, tuna, pork chops, or chicken breasts. You'll have enough flavored butter for about eight servings.
MAKES ABOUT ½ CUP

THE RECIPE

1 to 2 canned chipotle peppers, cut in half lengthwise, seeded (for a hotter butter, leave the seeds in), and chopped

1 clove garlic, minced

1/2 teaspoon grated fresh lime zest

2 teaspoons fresh lime juice, or more to taste

8 tablespoons (1 stick) unsalted butter, at room temperature

Coarse salt (kosher or sea)

Place the chipotle(s), garlic, lime zest, lime juice, and butter in a food processor and process until well mixed and creamy. Taste for seasoning, adding more lime juice as necessary, and season with salt to taste. If you are preparing the butter ahead, spoon it onto 2 sheets of plastic wrap, dividing it evenly between them. Roll each into a tight cylinder, twisting the ends of the plastic wrap closed like a Tootsie Roll. Refrigerate or freeze the butter until firm. The flavored butter can be refrigerated for up to 5 days or frozen for 3 months. To use, spoon about 1 tablespoon on top of each serving or unwrap the butter and cut off 1/2-inch crosswise slices.

stove-top smoker

smoked garlic

If I were to name the single most important flavoring on the world's barbecue trail, there's no question it would be garlic. From Buenos Aires to Baku to Bali, it's hard to think of a dish that isn't perfumed in some way with this aromatic root. Given the smoking mania of Americans, it was only a matter of time until someone decided to roast garlic in a smoker. The process improves an already good flavor in two key ways—the slow gentle heat mellows the pungency and brings out the root's sweetness, while the smoke transforms the garlic in a way you'd never expect. **MAKES 2 HEADS**

tips

2 heads garlic
Cooking oil spray (optional)

YOU'LL ALSO NEED:
**Wooden toothpicks; 1¹/₂ tablespoons
oak or hickory sawdust**

1. Break the garlic into cloves. Cut the root ends off of each, then peel the cloves (see Note). Skewer the garlic on toothpicks, 3 to 4 cloves per toothpick.

2. Set up the smoker (for instructions for using a stove-top smoker, see page 16). Place the sawdust in the center of the bottom of the smoker. Line the drip pan with aluminum foil and place it in the smoker. Lightly coat the smoker rack with cooking oil spray, or use a paper towel dipped in oil, and place the rack in the smoker. Place the skewered garlic on the rack.

3. Place the smoker over high heat for 3 minutes, then reduce the heat to medium. Smoke the garlic until lightly browned and tender, 15 to 20 minutes. When done the cloves should be soft when pressed between your thumb and forefinger.

4. Transfer the smoked garlic to a plate and let cool, then remove and discard the toothpicks. The smoked garlic can be refrigerated in a sealed jar for several weeks.

NOTE: One easy way to peel garlic is to gently crush it with the side of a cleaver, then slip off the skin. Alternatively, you can roll it in a garlic peeler, a flexible plastic tube.

■ What can you do with smoked garlic? Well, for starters, nibble it on its own. Or, spread it on bruschetta (see page 280) or use it to make garlic bread. Purée it with chickpeas to make an unbelievably flavorful hummus. Mash it with mayonnaise to create a smoked garlic aïoli. Soak a few cloves in olive oil and you have a fabulous baste or salad dressing. Stick a few cloves on a toothpick and add them to a martini . . . the uses are endless.

■ You can also smoke the garlic in a wok. You'll find instructions for doing this in the box on page 234.

stove-top smoker

smoked tomato salsa

Salsa has a natural affinity for fire. Since Aztec times, Mexican salsa makers have flame-charred tomatoes, onions, peppers, and other salsa ingredients to add an extra layer of flavor. This recipe takes the process one step further by smoking the vegetables in a stove-top smoker. The salsa is great served with tortilla chips or, even better, grilled bread (see the bruschetta recipe on page 280). **MAKES 1¹⁄₂ CUPS**

THE RECIPE

(see the bruschetta recipe on page 280)

tips

■ The idea here is to smoke the vegetables without really cooking them through. You want them to stay crisp and juicy. For this reason, the vegetables are smoked quickly—in 10 minutes or less.

■ The vegetables can also be smoked in a wok. You'll find instructions for doing this in the box on page 234.

6 plum tomatoes (about 1¹⁄₄ pounds), cut in half lengthwise

2 to 4 jalapeño peppers, stemmed, halved, and seeded (for a hotter salsa, leave the seeds in)

1 ear corn, shucked

¹⁄₄ Vidalia or other sweet white onion, peeled

2 cloves garlic, peeled and skewered on a wooden toothpick

3 tablespoons finely chopped fresh cilantro

2 tablespoons fresh lime juice, or more to taste

Coarse salt (kosher or sea) and freshly ground black pepper

YOU'LL ALSO NEED:

1¹⁄₂ tablespoons hickory or other hardwood sawdust

1. Set up the smoker (for instructions for using a stove-top smoker, see page 16). Place the sawdust in the center of the bottom of the smoker. Line the drip pan with aluminum foil and place it in the smoker. Place the smoker rack in the smoker. Arrange the tomato and jalapeño halves, cut side up, on the rack. Add the corn, onion, and garlic and cover the smoker. Place the smoker over high heat for 3 minutes, then reduce the heat to medium. Smoke the vegetables until they are heavily smoked (they'll be coated with a light brown film) but still raw in the center, 8 to 10 minutes.

2. Transfer the smoked vegetables to a cutting board and let cool to room temperature. Cut the tomatoes, onions, and jalapeños into 1-inch pieces. Cut the garlic cloves in half. Cut the kernels off the corn cob using lengthwise strokes of a chef's knife.

3. Place the smoked vegetables in a food processor and coarsely chop them, running the machine in short bursts. Add the cilantro and lime juice. Taste for seasoning, adding more lime juice as necessary and salt and pepper to taste; the salsa should be highly seasoned. The salsa tastes best the day it's made but can be refrigerated, covered, for several days.

chipotle salsa

Not only is this grilled vegetable and chipotle salsa great with the Oaxacan turkey burgers (see page 168), it's tasty with almost any Mexican-style grilled meat or seafood. The indoor grill master has several options for grilling the vegetables: grill pan, built-in grill, or fireplace grill. You can even roast them in a hot unoiled cast-iron skillet. **MAKES ABOUT ¾ CUPS**

THE RECIPE

6 tomatillos (about 8 ounces total), husked

5 plum tomatoes (about 12 ounces total)

4 cloves garlic, skewered on a wooden toothpick or small bamboo skewer

1 small onion, cut into quarters

1 to 2 canned chipotle peppers (see Note) with 2 teaspoons of their adobo sauce, or more to taste

3 tablespoons chopped fresh cilantro

1 tablespoon fresh lime juice, or more to taste

½ teaspoon sugar, or more to taste

Coarse salt (kosher or sea) and freshly ground black pepper

1. Grill the tomatillos, tomatoes, garlic, and onion, in batches if necessary, following the instructions for any of the grills in the box at right, until darkly browned on all sides.

2. Transfer the grilled vegetables to a cutting board and let cool. Scrape any really burnt skin off the vegetables but leave most of it on; the dark spots will add color and character.

3. Cut the vegetables into 1-inch pieces and purée in a food processor, adding the

if you have a...

GRILL PAN OR CAST-IRON SKILLET: Place the grill pan or skillet on the stove and preheat it to medium-high over medium heat. When the pan is hot a drop of water will skitter in the pan. Place the tomatillos, tomatoes, garlic, and onion in the hot pan and cook, turning as necessary (you will most likely have to work in batches). The tomatillos, tomatoes, and onion will be done after cooking 3 to 5 minutes per side; the garlic will be done after 2 to 4 minutes per side.

BUILT-IN GRILL: Preheat the grill to high, then, if it does not have a nonstick surface, brush and oil the grill grate. Place the tomatillos, tomatoes, garlic, and onion on the hot grate. The tomatillos, tomatoes, and onion will be done after cooking 3 to 5 minutes per side; the garlic will be done after 2 to 4 minutes per side.

FIREPLACE GRILL: Rake red hot embers under the gridiron and preheat it for 3 to 5 minutes; you want a hot, 2 to 3 Mississippi fire. When ready to cook, brush and oil the gridiron. Place the tomatillos, tomatoes, garlic, and onion on the hot grate. The tomatillos, tomatoes, and onion will be done after cooking 3 to 5 minutes per side; the garlic will be done after 2 to 4 minutes per side.

chipotles with their adobo and the cilantro, lime juice, and sugar. Taste for seasoning, adding more adobo, and/or sugar and salt and pepper to taste. The salsa will keep, covered, in the refrigerator for up to 3 days.

NOTE: Chipotle peppers (smoked jalapeños) reinforce the smoke flavor of this grilled vegetable salsa. I generally avoid canned foods, but chipotles are an exception because the peppers come packed in a spicy vinegar sauce called adobo, which gives them even more flavor.

tip

For the maximum flavor, grill the vegetables over oak or hickory embers in a fireplace. You can also char the vegetables on another indoor grill, but if you do, you may want to "cheat" and add ½ teaspoon liquid smoke to the sauce.

grilled tomato sauce

Like soup, tomato sauce is one of the dishes you're least likely to think of grilling. But there's a powerful reason to try this sauce. Beyond the mere novelty factor, grilling imparts a gutsy smoke flavor to the sauce and heightens the natural sweetness of the vegetables. Don't take just my word for it: For thousands of years, Mexicans have grilled tomatoes, onions, and peppers to make rich-tasting salsas. I've adapted the technique to make an exceptionally flavorful tomato sauce. Serve the sauce over grilled polenta (see page 359), with any simple grilled fish or chicken breasts, or with just about any cooked pasta.

MAKES ABOUT 3½ CUPS

THE RECIPE

5 luscious, ripe red tomatoes
    (2 to 2¼ pounds total), cut in half
    crosswise and stem ends removed
1 medium-size white onion, peeled and
    cut into quarters
1 rib celery
4 cloves garlic, peeled and skewered on
    a wooden toothpick or small bamboo
    skewer
3 tablespoons extra-virgin olive oil
1 teaspoon dried oregano
½ teaspoon hot red pepper flakes
1 bay leaf
6 fresh basil leaves
Coarse salt (kosher or sea) and freshly
    ground black pepper
¼ to ¾ cup chicken stock, vegetable
    stock, or water (optional)

1. Cook the tomatoes, onion, celery, and garlic, following the instructions for any of the grills in the box at right, until nicely browned. You may need to cook the vegetables in more than one batch.

2. Transfer the grilled vegetables to a plate and let cool. Finely chop the onion, celery, and garlic by hand or in a food processor (if using a food processor, run the machine in spurts). Heat the olive oil in a large nonreactive saucepan over medium heat. Add the chopped onion, celery, and garlic, the oregano, hot pepper flakes, and bay leaf and cook until lightly browned, 4 to 5 minutes.

3. Coarsely purée the tomatoes and their juices with the basil in a food processor. Add the tomato mixture to the saucepan with the vegetables. Bring to a

simmer over medium heat, then let the sauce simmer gently until thick and richly flavored, 8 to 10 minutes. Season with salt and black pepper to taste. The sauce should be thick but pourable. If it's too thick, add a little stock or water. Remove and discard the bay leaf. The sauce can be refrigerated, covered, for up to 4 days or frozen for up to 2 months. Let the sauce come to room temperature, then reheat it in a nonreactive saucepan over medium heat, stirring often.

if you have a...

GRILL PAN: Place the grill pan on the stove and preheat it to medium-high over medium heat. When the grill pan is hot a drop of water will skitter in the pan. When ready to cook, lightly oil the ridges of the grill pan. Arrange the tomatoes, cut side up, and the onion, celery, and garlic in the hot grill pan. The tomatoes and onion quarters will be done after cooking 3 to 5 minutes per side. The celery and garlic will be done after cooking 2 to 4 minutes per side.

BUILT-IN GRILL: Preheat the grill to high, then, if it does not have a nonstick surface, brush and oil the grill grate. Arrange the tomatoes, cut side up, and the onion, celery, and garlic on the hot grate. The tomatoes and onion quarters will be done after cooking 3 to 5 minutes per side. The celery and garlic will be done after cooking 2 to 4 minutes per side.

FREESTANDING GRILL: Preheat the grill to high; there's no need to oil the grate. Arrange the tomatoes, cut side up, and the onion, celery, and garlic on the hot grill. The tomatoes and onion quarters will be done after cooking 4 to 6 minutes per side. The celery and garlic will be done after cooking 3 to 5 minutes per side.

FIREPLACE GRILL: Rake red hot embers under the gridiron and preheat it for 3 to 5 minutes; you want a hot, 2 to 3 Mississippi fire. When ready to cook, brush and oil the gridiron. Arrange the tomatoes, cut side up, and the onion, celery, and garlic on the hot grate. The tomatoes and onion quarters will be done after cooking 4 to 6 minutes per side. The celery and garlic will be done after cooking 3 to 5 minutes per side.

tip

Brown sugar is darker and more richly flavored, of course, than granulated sugar—the result of adding molasses to the sugar. Dark brown sugar contains more molasses than light, so it's marginally more flavorful. But both have an earthy, malty flavor that beats white sugar hollow. In most spice rub and barbecue sauce recipes, light brown sugar will work almost as well as dark. So, if you have only one variety on hand, it's not worth rushing to the store to buy the other—especially if a recipe calls for only a couple of teaspoons.

kansas city–style sweet and smoky barbecue sauce

When most Americans speak of barbecue sauce, they're thinking of a thick, sweet, smoky condiment with just a faint edge of vinegar—in short, the sort of sauce people in Kansas City have claimed as their own for decades. Here's a quick homemade version. **MAKES 3 CUPS**

THE RECIPE

2 cups ketchup, or more to taste
1/4 cup molasses, or more to taste
1/4 cup cider vinegar, or more to taste
1/4 cup Worcestershire sauce, or more to taste
3 tablespoons brown sugar, or more to taste
2 tablespoons prepared mustard, or more to taste
1 tablespoon dry mustard, or more to taste
2 teaspoons liquid smoke, or more to taste
1 teaspoon garlic powder, or more to taste
1 teaspoon onion powder, or more to taste
1/2 teaspoon freshly ground black pepper, or more to taste

1. Place the ketchup, molasses, cider vinegar, Worcestershire sauce, brown sugar, prepared mustard, dry mustard, liquid smoke, garlic powder, onion powder, and pepper in a heavy nonreactive saucepan and whisk to mix. Slowly bring the sauce to a boil over medium heat. Let the sauce simmer gently until thick and richly flavored, about 10 minutes, whisking several times.

2. Taste for seasoning, adding more of any of the ingredients you may desire. Transfer the hot sauce to glass jars. Tightly cover the jar and let the sauce cool to room temperature. Once the jar is opened, refrigerate the sauce; it will keep for several months.

When I was growing up, a grilled dessert meant marshmallows roasted (or often incinerated) over a campfire. How times have changed! Today, there's no limit to the desserts you can cook on the grill—from banana *"tostones"* (dredged in cinnamon sugar), to port wine–basted grilled plums (cooked on whole cinnamon sticks), to fresh pineapple chunks grilled on vanilla beans. That's not to say you should ignore the s'more, and you'll learn how to make marshmallows from scratch and grill pound cake s'mores on a contact grill. When it comes to bringing a meal to a dramatic close, there's nothing like the grill for cooking dessert.

desserts

maple-glazed bananas

Grilling enhances the sweetness of most fruits—especially bananas, which develop haunting nuances of candy and caramel. What you may not have realized (I certainly hadn't until I started writing this book) is that the process works great on a variety of indoor grills. Depending on your tolerance (enthusiasm?) for decadence, you can serve these grilled bananas by themselves, topped with vanilla ice cream, and/or with chocolate or caramel sauce drizzled over them. **SERVES 4**

tip

You can use either brown sugar or confectioners' sugar when grilling these bananas. Brown sugar will give you more flavor. Confectioners' sugar caramelizes better.

THE RECIPE

if you have a...

CONTACT GRILL: Preheat the grill; if your contact grill has a temperature control, preheat the grill to high. Place the drip pan under the front of the grill. When ready to cook, lightly oil the grill surface. Arrange the bananas, cut side up, on the hot grill, positioning them so that they are perpendicular to the ridges, then close the lid. The bananas will be done after cooking 3 to 5 minutes. The amount of caramelization you'll get will depend upon your particular contact grill.

GRILL PAN: Place the grill pan on the stove and preheat it to medium-high over medium heat. When the grill pan is hot a drop of water will skitter in the pan. When ready to cook, lightly oil the ridges of the grill pan. Place the bananas, cut side down, in the hot grill pan and cook them 2 to 4 minutes, then turn them over and cook for about 2 minutes.

BUILT-IN GRILL: Preheat the grill to high, then, if it does not have a nonstick surface, brush and oil the grill grate. Place the bananas, cut side down, on the hot grate and cook them 2 to 4 minutes, then turn them over and cook for about 2 minutes.

FIREPLACE GRILL: Rake red hot embers under the gridiron and preheat it for 3 to 5 minutes; you want a hot, 2 to 3 Mississippi fire. When ready to cook, brush and oil the gridiron. Place the bananas, cut side down, on the hot grate and cook them 2 to 4 minutes, then turn them over and cook for about 2 minutes.

4 bananas (see Note)

3 tablespoons maple syrup

6 to 8 tablespoons dark brown sugar
   or confectioners' sugar

Ground cinnamon

6 tablespoons Hot Fudge Sauce
   (optional; page 393)

6 tablespoons Cinnamon Caramel Sauce
   (optional; page 394)

Vanilla ice cream (optional), for serving

1. Place the bananas on a work surface and cut each in half lengthwise (leave the skins on). Brush the cut sides with the maple syrup and generously sprinkle brown sugar over them. Lightly dust the cut sides of the bananas with cinnamon.

2. Cook the bananas, following the instructions for any of the grills in the box at left, until the cut side is caramelized to a dark golden brown and the fruit starts to pull away from the peel.

3. Transfer the grilled banana halves still in their skins to a platter or plates and place a scoop of vanilla ice cream alongside, if desired. Drizzle Hot Fudge Sauce and/or Cinnamon Caramel Sauce over all, if desired.

NOTE: The best bananas for grilling will be just shy of ripe and have firm yellow skins but won't have any of the tiny brown "sugar" spots that indicate the bananas are completely ripe.

contact grill

banana "tostones"
with cinnamon rum whipped cream

Green plantains that are deep-fried, flattened in a wooden press, and then refried are a staple throughout the Caribbean and Central America. They're called *tostones* (see box on page 378), and from this starchy appetizer or side dish to grilled pressed banana *"tostones"* for dessert is a bit of a stretch, but one eminently worth making. And this is one dessert that your trusty contact grill really excels at (for a version made on a built-in or a fireplace grill, see the following page). The icing on the cake, as it were, is a rum-scented whipped cream. **SERVES 4**

THE RECIPE

FOR THE WHIPPED CREAM:
1 cup heavy (whipping) cream
3 tablespoons confectioners' sugar
1 tablespoon dark rum
1 teaspoon ground cinnamon

FOR THE BANANAS:
²/₃ cup granulated sugar

1 tablespoon ground cinnamon
2 teaspoons very finely grated lemon or lime zest
4 bananas, chilled in the refrigerator for 1 hour
4 tablespoons (¹/₂ stick) unsalted butter, melted
Cooking oil spray
Fresh mint sprigs (optional), for garnish

tip
Use a Microplane or the fine side of a box grater to grate the citrus zest.

flattening "tostones"

Banana *"tostones"* can be cooked on a built-in grill or in the fireplace, but you'll need to flatten the bananas first. Cut the bananas crosswise into 1-inch slices, place them upright between two pieces of plastic wrap, and gently flatten them with the side of a cleaver, a small skillet, or a meat pounder. The banana slices should be about 1/2 inch thick. Brush the flattened banana slices with melted butter before dipping them in the cinnamon sugar.

To cook *"tostones"* on a built-in grill, preheat the grill to high, then if it does not have a nonstick surface, brush and oil the grill grate. Place the flattened banana slices on the hot grate. They will be sizzling and darkly browned after cooking 2 to 4 minutes per side.

To cook *"tostones"* on a fireplace grill, rake red hot embers under the gridiron and preheat it for 3 to 5 minutes; you want a hot, 2 to 3 Mississippi fire. When ready to cook, brush and oil the gridiron. Place the flattened banana slices on the hot grate. They will be sizzling and darkly browned after cooking 2 to 4 minutes per side.

1. Make the whipped cream: Place the cream in a chilled mixer bowl or in a large metal bowl. Beat with a mixer until soft peaks form, starting on the slow speed and gradually increasing the speed to high. The total beating time will 6 to 8 minutes. When soft peaks have formed, add the confectioners' sugar, rum, and cinnamon. Continue beating the cream until stiff peaks form, about 2 minutes longer. Don't overbeat the cream or it will start to turn to butter. The cinnamon rum whipped cream can be made several hours ahead. Refrigerate it, covered, until ready to serve.

2. Prepare the bananas: Place the granulated sugar, cinnamon, and lemon zest in a shallow bowl and stir to mix.

3. Preheat the grill (for instructions for using a contact grill, see page 3); if your contact grill has a temperature control, preheat the grill to high. Place the drip pan under the front of the grill.

4. Meanwhile, peel the bananas and cut each crosswise into 1-inch pieces. Dip the ends of each piece of banana in the melted butter, then in the cinnamon sugar, shaking off the excess.

5. When ready to cook, lightly coat the grill surface with cooking oil spray. Arrange the pieces of banana upright on the grill. Lower the lid, pressing down to flatten the bananas. Grill the bananas until they are crusty and golden brown, 3 to 5 minutes. After 2 minutes, lift the lid, brush the tops of the bananas with any remaining butter, and sprinkle any remaining cinnamon sugar over them.

6. Place the banana *"tostones"* on plates. Garnish each serving with a large dollop of cinnamon rum whipped cream and a mint sprig, if using, and serve at once.

grilled peaches
with bourbon caramel sauce

T he peach is one of my preferred fruits for grilling. The searing
heat turns the peach juices and sugar into a luscious golden
caramel that cooks right into the fruit. This is singularly easy
to accomplish on a contact grill, but other indoor grills will do
the trick too. **SERVES 4**

THE RECIPE

4 large ripe peaches (see Note)
2 tablespoons (¼ stick) unsalted butter, melted
1 cup firmly packed dark brown sugar,
    crumbled between your fingers into a
    shallow bowl
1 pint vanilla or peach ice cream
Bourbon Caramel Sauce (recipe follows)
4 fresh mint sprigs, for garnish

1. Cut each peach in half along the crease.
Twist the peach halves in opposite directions to separate them. Remove and discard the pits. Cut ¼ inch off the rounded
part of each peach half to expose the
flesh. Brush the cut parts of the peach
halves with the melted butter. Dip both
sides of the peach halves in the brown
sugar, pressing gently on them to crust
them with sugar, then shake off the excess.

2. Cook the peaches, following the
instructions for any of the grills in the box
at right, until bubbling and golden brown.

3. To serve, scoop the vanilla ice cream
into 4 martini glasses or small bowls.

if you have a...

CONTACT GRILL: Preheat
the grill; if your contact grill has a
temperature control, preheat the
grill to high. Place the drip pan
under the front of the grill. When
ready to cook, lightly oil the grill
surface. Place the peaches, pit side
up, on the hot grill, then close the
lid. The peaches will be done after
cooking 3 to 5 minutes.

GRILL PAN: You can cook
the peaches in a grill pan, but be
prepared for lots of smoke as the
sugar burns on the bottom of the
pan. Place the grill pan on the
stove and preheat it to medium-
high over medium heat. When
the grill pan is hot a drop of water
will skitter in the pan. When ready
to cook, lightly oil the ridges of
the grill pan. Place the peaches,
pit side down, in the hot grill pan.

They will be done after cooking
3 to 5 minutes per side. After it has
cooled down, soak the grill pan in
hot water to loosen any burnt-on
brown sugar.

BUILT-IN GRILL: Preheat
the grill to high, then, if it does
not have a nonstick surface, brush
and oil the grill grate. Place the
peaches, pit side down, on the hot
grate. They will be done after
cooking 3 to 5 minutes per side.

FIREPLACE GRILL: Rake
red hot embers under the gridiron
and preheat it for 3 to 5 minutes;
you want a hot, 2 to 3 Mississippi
fire. When ready to cook, brush
and oil the gridiron. Place the
peaches, pit side down, on the
hot grate. They will be done after
cooking 3 to 5 minutes per side.

Place 2 peach halves on top of each serving and, if you have cooked the peaches
in a contact grill, pour any juices that

have collected in the drip pan over them. Spoon the Bourbon Caramel Sauce over the peaches, then garnish each serving with a mint sprig and serve at once.

NOTE: You need lasciviously ripe peaches for this recipe—the sort that are squeezably soft and fragrant enough to smell from the next room. Be sure to use freestone peaches, the kind that have loose pits that can easily be removed.

bourbon caramel sauce

Peaches are the premier fruit of the South, where that most American of liquors, bourbon, is the preferred spirit. Served with grilled peaches, this luscious caramel sauce brings them together. Or, for a tropical touch, you could use dark rum. **MAKES ABOUT 1 CUP**

1/2 cup firmly packed dark brown sugar
3 tablespoons light corn syrup
3 tablespoons bourbon
2 tablespoons (1/4 stick) unsalted butter
1/4 cup heavy (whipping) cream

Place the brown sugar, corn syrup, bourbon, and butter in a heavy saucepan over medium-high heat. Bring to a boil and let boil until dark, thick, and syrupy, about 5 minutes. Stir in the cream and let boil until the sauce is thick and syrupy, 3 to 5 minutes. You can serve the sauce either warm or at room temperature. The sauce can be refrigerated, covered, for several weeks. Reheat it over medium heat, whisking it well.

cinnamon plums
with port sauce

These grilled plums look cool—and taste even better—thanks to the unusual skewers they're cooked on: whole cinnamon sticks. A cinnamon-scented port sauce does double duty as a baste. You can use any kind of indoor grill, but apply the port sauce sparingly when you are basting to minimize the chance of smoke and flare-ups. **SERVES 4**

FOR THE PORT SAUCE:

1 cup port

2 whole cloves

2 strips lemon zest
 (each about 1/2 by 11/2 inches)

1 cinnamon stick (3 inches)

3 tablespoons sugar, or more to taste

11/2 teaspoons cornstarch

1 tablespoon fresh lemon juice

FOR THE PLUMS:

4 large ripe plums (see Notes)

8 cinnamon sticks (each 3 inches)

8 strips lemon zest
 (each about 1/2 by 11/2 inches)

Vanilla ice cream or yogurt, for serving

4 fresh mint sprigs, for garnish

1. Make the port sauce: Place the port in a heavy nonreactive saucepan. Stick the cloves into the strips of lemon zest and add them to the port, along with the cinnamon stick and the sugar. Gradually bring to a boil over high heat, then let boil until slightly reduced and just beginning to become syrupy, 3 to 5 minutes.

2. Dissolve the cornstarch in the lemon juice and gradually stir it into the port mixture. Reduce the heat to medium and let the sauce simmer until it thickens, 1 to 2 minutes. Strain the sauce into a heat-proof bowl and let cool to room temperature. The sauce can be refrigerated, covered, for several days.

3. Prepare the plums: Cut each in half along the crease. Twist the plum halves in opposite directions to separate them. Remove and discard the pits. Cut each

plum half in half. Using a metal skewer and working from the pit side, make a hole in the center of each plum quarter. Skewer two plum quarters through these holes on each cinnamon stick, skin side to cut side, placing a strip of lemon zest between each 2 quarters. The recipe can be prepared several hours ahead to this stage.

4. Cook the plum kebabs, following the instructions for any of the grills in the box below, until they are sizzling and

if you have a...

CONTACT GRILL: Preheat the grill; if your contact grill has a temperature control, preheat the grill to high. Place the drip pan under the front of the grill. When ready to cook, lightly oil the grill surface. Place the plum kebabs on the hot grill, then close the lid. The plums will be done after cooking 4 to 6 minutes. You will need to turn the kebabs so that you can baste them all over with the port sauce.

GRILL PAN: Place the grill pan on the stove and preheat it to medium-high over medium heat. When the grill pan is hot a drop of water will skitter in the pan. When ready to cook, lightly oil the ridges of the grill pan. Place the plum kebabs in the hot grill pan. They will be done after cooking 3 to 5 minutes per side. Use the port sauce sparingly when basting the plums, taking care not to drip a lot of it into the grill pan. After it has cooled down, soak the grill

pan in hot water to loosen any burnt-on port sauce.

BUILT-IN GRILL: Preheat the grill to high, then, if it does not have a nonstick surface, brush and oil the grill grate. Place the plum kebabs on the hot grate. They will be done after cooking 3 to 5 minutes per side.

FREESTANDING GRILL: Preheat the grill to high; there's no need to oil the grate. Place the plum kebabs on the hot grill. They will be done after cooking 4 to 6 minutes per side.

FIREPLACE GRILL: Rake red hot embers under the gridiron and preheat it for 3 to 5 minutes; you want a hot, 2 to 3 Mississippi fire. When ready to cook, brush and oil the gridiron. Place the plum kebabs on the hot grate. They will be done after cooking 3 to 5 minutes per side.

golden brown. As the plums grill, baste them lightly with a little of the port sauce.

5. To serve, scoop vanilla ice cream into 4 martini glasses, wine goblets, or small bowls. Place 2 plum kebabs on top of each scoop of ice cream and spoon the remaining port sauce over them. Garnish with the mint sprigs and serve at once.

NOTES:

■ Almost any type of plum is good grilled. I like big, fleshy, freestone purple plums (freestone refers to a fruit that's easy to pit).

■ The zest is the oil-rich outer yellow rind of the lemon. Remove it in the thinnest possible strips, using a vegetable peeler or paring knife.

contact grill

pears belle hélène on the grill

During my student days in Paris, *poires belle Hélène* was one of my favorite desserts. It may not sound terribly extravagant these days, but the combination of poached pears, vanilla ice cream, chocolate sauce, and toasted almonds is perfect in its understated simplicity. In this version, fresh pears are thickly crusted with chopped almonds, which toast right into the fruit on the contact grill. **SERVES 4**

THE RECIPE

1 pint vanilla ice cream in a cylindrical
    or rectangular paper container,
    frozen solid
1¼ cups blanched slivered almonds
¼ cup sugar
2 ripe Anjou or Comice pears
½ lemon

2 tablespoons (¼ stick) unsalted butter,
    melted
Cooking oil spray
Warm Chocolate Sauce
    (recipe follows)
4 fresh mint sprigs, for garnish

1. Peel the carton off the ice cream. Cut the block of ice cream crosswise into 4 even slices. Place one in the center of each of 4 dessert plates or shallow bowls and place in the freezer.

2. Place the almonds and sugar in a food processor and finely chop, running the machine in short bursts. Place the chopped almond mixture in a shallow bowl.

3. Stem the pears and cut out the blossom ends. Peel the pears, then rub the lemon all over them to prevent them from browning. Cut each pear lengthwise into 4 slices, each about ½ inch thick, then rub the lemon over the cut edges. Using a melon baller or paring knife, cut the seeds and cores out of the centers of the middle slices. Brush the pear slices on both sides with the butter. Dip both sides of the pear slices in the chopped almond mixture, pressing gently on them to crust them with nuts.

4. Preheat the grill (for instructions for using a contact grill, see page 3); if your contact grill has a temperature control, preheat the grill to high. Place the drip pan under the front of the grill.

5. When ready to cook, lightly coat the grill surface with cooking oil spray. Place the pear slices on the grill and close the lid. Grill until the almonds are golden brown, 3 to 5 minutes.

6. To serve, arrange 2 pear slices overlapping on each bed of ice cream. Spoon the Warm Chocolate Sauce on top, then garnish each serving with a mint sprig and serve at once.

warm chocolate sauce

This simple chocolate sauce contains only three ingredients, so the quality of the chocolate is paramount. Use a dark bittersweet or semisweet chocolate. I'm partial to that made by Scharffen Berger from San Francisco (see Mail-Order Sources on page 396). **MAKES ABOUT 1 CUP**

6 tablespoons heavy (whipping) cream
6 ounces bittersweet or semisweet chocolate, coarsely chopped
½ teaspoon vanilla extract

Place the cream in a heavy saucepan over high heat and bring just to a boil. Stir in the chocolate and lower the heat to the lowest setting. Cook just until the chocolate melts, 2 to 4 minutes. Stir in the vanilla extract. Keep the sauce warm until serving by placing the saucepan in a pan of simmering water.

tips

■ The traditional fruit for pears *belle Hélène* would be Anjou or Comice pears. The pears should be ripe and sweet. Give them the "Charmin test." Gently squeeze them between your thumb and forefinger; when ripe they should be gently yielding.

■ Rather than being quartered in wedges, the pears here are cut in flat slices. This maximizes the surface area of the fruit that's exposed to the grill.

grilled pineapple #4

I love the way grilling caramelizes pineapple. I love the smart look of bold dark grill marks against the pineapple's golden flesh. I love it so much, this is the fourth grilled pineapple dessert to appear in one of my cookbooks, and the recipe has a particularly nostalgic origin. It comes from one of my classmates from Sudbrook Junior High School, Marlene Rodman, who resurfaced in my life serendipitously almost forty years later as a videographer for Maryland Public Television and part of the crew for my *Barbecue University* TV show. **SERVES 6**

THE RECIPE

if you have a...

CONTACT GRILL: Preheat the grill; if your contact grill has a temperature control, preheat the grill to high. Place the drip pan under the front of the grill. When ready to cook, lightly oil the grill surface. Place the pineapple slices on the hot grill, then close the lid. The pineapple will be done after cooking 4 to 6 minutes.

GRILL PAN: Place the grill pan on the stove and preheat it to medium-high over medium heat. When the grill pan is hot a drop of water will skitter in the pan. When ready to cook, lightly oil the ridges of the grill pan. Place the pineapple slices in the hot grill pan. They will be done after cooking 4 to 6 minutes per side. After it has cooled down, soak the grill pan in hot water to loosen any burnt-on brown sugar.

BUILT-IN GRILL: Preheat the grill to high, then, if it does not have a nonstick surface, brush and oil the grill grate. Place the pineapple slices on the hot grate. They will be done after cooking 4 to 6 minutes per side.

FREESTANDING GRILL: Preheat the grill to high; there's no need to oil the grate. Place the pineapple slices on the hot grill. They will be done after cooking 5 to 7 minutes per side.

FIREPLACE GRILL: Rake red hot embers under the gridiron and preheat it for 3 to 5 minutes; you want a hot, 2 to 3 Mississippi fire. When ready to cook, brush and oil the gridiron. Place the pineapple slices on the hot grate. They will be done after cooking 4 to 6 minutes per side.

1 ripe golden pineapple
2 large eggs
1 teaspoon ground cinnamon
1/4 teaspoon ground cloves
1 cup firmly packed light brown sugar,
    crumbled between your fingers
    into a wide shallow bowl
Coconut or vanilla ice cream
    (optional), for serving

1. Cut the rind off the pineapple and cut the fruit crosswise into 1/2-inch slices. Using a round pastry tip or melon baller, remove the core from each slice to make pineapple rings.

2. Crack the eggs into a small bowl. Add the cinnamon and cloves and beat with a fork until well mixed.

3. When ready to cook, brush the egg mixture on the pineapple using a pastry brush. Dip each pineapple slice in the brown sugar, then pat it with your fingertips to thickly and evenly crust the pineapple on both sides. Shake off any excess brown sugar.

4. Cook the pineapple slices, following the instructions for any of the grills in the box on the facing page, until golden brown. You may need to cook the pineapple in more than one batch.

5. Transfer the grilled pineapple to plates or bowls and serve at once. Coconut or vanilla ice cream makes a great accompaniment.

vanilla-grilled pineapple
with dark rum glaze

Vanilla and pineapple are both New World foods that much impressed Columbus and Cortés. They come together here in an offbeat dessert that features pineapple chunks grilled on pieces of vanilla bean. The idea, beyond the undeniable novelty factor—and you should never underestimate the novelty factor—is that the long, slender spice perfumes the kebabs from the inside out and gives you something flavorful and unexpected to chew on. **SERVES 4 TO 6**

THE RECIPE

1 ripe golden pineapple
6 to 8 vanilla beans (see Note)
1 bunch fresh mint, rinsed, shaken dry, and stemmed
1/4 cup firmly packed dark brown sugar
1/4 cup dark rum

3 tablespoons heavy (whipping) cream
2 tablespoons (1/4 stick) unsalted butter
Pinch of salt
Vanilla ice cream or pineapple sorbet, for serving

PICKING PINEAPPLE

The fruit of choice for these recipes is the golden pineapple. How do you know when one is ripe and sweet? The color of the rind is one indicator; the more golden the rind, the sweeter the fruit. Another is the aroma; if the fruit is fragrant, chances are it's ripe and ready to eat.

if you have a ...

CONTACT GRILL: Preheat the grill; if your contact grill has a temperature control, preheat the grill to high. Place the drip pan under the front of the grill. When ready to cook, lightly oil the grill surface. Place the pineapple kebabs on the hot grill, then close the lid. The pineapple kebabs will be done after cooking 6 to 9 minutes. You will need to turn the kebabs so that you can baste them all over with the glaze.

GRILL PAN: Place the grill pan on the stove and preheat it to medium-high over medium heat. When the grill pan is hot a drop of water will skitter in the pan. When ready to cook, lightly oil the ridges of the grill pan. Place the pineapple kebabs in the hot grill pan. They will be done after cooking 2 to 3 minutes per side (6 to 9 minutes in all). Use the rum glaze sparingly when basting the pineapple kebabs, taking care not to drip a lot of it into the grill pan. After it has cooled down, soak the grill pan in hot water to loosen any burnt-on glaze.

BUILT-IN GRILL: Preheat the grill to high, then, if it does not have a nonstick surface, brush and oil the grill grate. Place the pineapple kebabs on the hot grate. They will be done after cooking 2 to 3 minutes per side (6 to 9 minutes in all).

FREESTANDING GRILL: Preheat the grill to high; there's no need to oil the grate. Place the pineapple kebabs on the hot grill. They will be done after cooking 3 to 4 minutes per side (9 to 12 minutes in all).

FIREPLACE GRILL: Rake red hot embers under the gridiron and preheat it for 3 to 5 minutes; you want a hot, 2 to 3 Mississippi fire. When ready to cook, brush and oil the gridiron. Place the pineapple kebabs on the hot grate. They will be done after cooking 2 to 3 minutes per side (6 to 9 minutes in all).

3-inch pieces. Using a metal skewer, make a hole through the side of each pineapple chunk. Skewer two chunks of pineapple through these holes on each piece of vanilla bean, placing a mint leaf between the chunks.

2. Place the brown sugar, rum, cream, butter, and salt in a heavy saucepan and bring to a boil over high heat. Let the rum glaze boil until thick and syrupy, about 5 minutes, stirring with a wooden spoon.

3. Cook the pineapple kebabs, following the instructions for any of the grills in the box at left, until they are nicely browned on all sides, turning with tongs. As the pineapple kebabs grill, baste them lightly with a little of the glaze.

4. To serve, scoop vanilla ice cream into martini glasses or small bowls. Place a couple of pineapple kebabs on top. Spoon any remaining glaze over them and serve at once.

NOTE: If you have the choice, buy the long, slender vanilla beans from Madagascar rather than the short, stubby vanilla beans from the Caribbean.

1. Peel and core the pineapple and cut it into 1½-inch chunks. Cut the vanilla beans sharply on the diagonal into roughly

grilled pound cake
with pineapple "salsa" and tequila whipped cream

'**ve** said it before, and I'll say it again—the grill was the original toaster. And there's nothing like a quick sizzle on the grill to transform ordinary pound cake into a singular, even extraordinary dessert. Especially when paired with a pineapple "salsa" and tequila-scented whipped cream. **SERVES 4**

T H E   R E C I P E

¾ **cup heavy (whipping) cream**
3 tablespoons confectioners' sugar
¼ **teaspoon ground cinnamon**
1 tablespoon tequila (preferably gold)
8 slices pound cake (each ½ **inch thick)**
2 to 3 tablespoons unsalted butter, melted
Pineapple "Salsa" (recipe follows)
4 fresh mint sprigs, for garnish

1. Place the cream in a chilled mixer bowl or in a large metal bowl. Beat with a mixer until soft peaks form, starting on the slow speed and gradually increasing the speed to high. The total beating time will be 6 to 8 minutes. When soft peaks have formed, add the confectioners' sugar, cinnamon, and tequila. Continue beating the cream until stiff peaks form, about 2 minutes longer. Don't overbeat the cream or it will start to turn to butter. The tequila whipped cream can be made several hours ahead. Refrigerate it, covered, until ready to serve.

if you have a...

CONTACT GRILL: Preheat the grill; if your contact grill has a temperature control, preheat the grill to high. Place the drip pan under the front of the grill. When ready to cook, lightly oil the grill surface. Place the slices of pound cake on the hot grill, then close the lid. The pound cake will be done after cooking 2 to 4 minutes.

GRILL PAN: Place the grill pan on the stove and preheat it to medium-high over medium heat. When the grill pan is hot a drop of water will skitter in the pan. When ready to cook, lightly oil the ridges of the grill pan. Place the slices of pound cake in the hot grill pan. They will be done after cooking 2 to 4 minutes per side.

BUILT-IN GRILL: Preheat the grill to high, then, if it does not have a nonstick surface, brush and oil the grill grate. Place the pound cake slices on the hot grate. They will be done after cooking 2 to 4 minutes per side.

FREESTANDING GRILL: Preheat the grill to high; there's no need to oil the grate. Place the pound cake slices on the hot grill. They will be done after cooking 3 to 5 minutes per side.

FIREPLACE GRILL: Rake red hot embers under the gridiron and preheat it for 3 to 5 minutes; you want a hot, 2 to 3 Mississippi fire. When ready to cook, brush and oil the gridiron. Place the pound cake slices on the hot grate. They will be done after cooking 2 to 4 minutes per side.

2. Lightly brush each slice of pound cake with butter on both sides. Cook the pound cake, following the instructions for any of the grills in the box on the previous page, until lightly toasted. If desired, rotate each slice a quarter turn after 1 minute to create a handsome crosshatch of grill marks. You may need to cook the pound cake slices in more than one batch.

3. Place the pound cake slices on plates. Top each serving with a spoonful of Pineapple "Salsa" and a dollop of tequila whipped cream, garnish with a sprig of mint, and serve at once.

pineapple "salsa"

This "salsa" is actually a sort of fruit salad, but it does contain the quintessential salsa ingredients, lime juice and jalapeño peppers. The jalapeños are certainly unexpected, but they have an interesting way of intensifying the sweetness of the pineapple.

MAKES ABOUT 2 CUPS

2 cups fresh pineapple cut into $1/2$-inch cubes

3 tablespoons thinly slivered fresh mint or lemon verbena

1 to 2 jalapeño peppers (preferably red), seeded and minced (for a hotter "salsa," leave the seeds in)

2 tablespoons fresh lime juice, or more to taste

1 tablespoon light brown sugar, or more to taste

Place the pineapple, mint, jalapeño(s), lime juice, and brown sugar in a nonreactive mixing bowl, but don't mix them until 5 minutes before you are ready to serve. Taste for seasoning, adding more lime juice and/or brown sugar as necessary.

VARIATION: Slivered mint keeps this "salsa" in the realm of a salad. If you really want to push the limits try substituting chopped fresh cilantro for the mint.

pound cake s'mores

Here's what would happen if you crossed pound cake with a s'more. Indoor grills do a great job of melting the chocolate and marshmallow, and you can customize the recipe in an almost infinite number of ways, adding mint leaves or guava paste, for example, or a thick smear of Nutella or caramel sauce (you'll find a recipe on page 394). Create your favorite variation and post your recipe on the Barbecue Board (www.barbecuebible.com). I originally conceived this recipe for a contact grill, but in fact these s'mores can be made in a grill pan or on other indoor grills. For a high-tech "cookout," place a contact grill or a freestanding grill in the center of the table. Then, have everyone assemble and cook their s'mores to order. **MAKES 8 S'MORES; SERVES 4 TO 8**

THE RECIPE

8 to 10 ounces very good bittersweet
    chocolate in thin bars
8 marshmallows (see Notes)
1 to 2 tablespoons confectioners'
    sugar
16 slices pound cake
    (each ¼ inch thick)
1 bunch lemon verbena (see Notes) or
    mint, rinsed, dried, stemmed, and
    thinly slivered, or 3 tablespoons
    thinly slivered candied ginger
    (optional)
3 tablespoons unsalted butter,
    melted

1. If necessary, break the chocolate bars into 8 rectangles; each should be about the size of a slice of pound cake.

2. Using a slender knife, cut the marshmallows crosswise into ¼-inch slices; dust the knife with confectioners' sugar first to keep the marshmallow from sticking.

3. Arrange 8 slices of the pound cake on a platter and top each with a piece of chocolate, some marshmallow slices, and some lemon verbena and/or candied ginger, if using, in that order. Top with the remaining slices of pound cake. The s'mores can be prepared sev-

eral hours ahead to this stage. Keep covered with plastic wrap until ready to cook.

if you have a...

CONTACT GRILL: Preheat the grill; if your contact grill has a temperature control, preheat the grill to high. Place the drip pan under the front of the grill. When ready to cook, lightly oil the grill surface. Arrange the s'mores on the hot grill on a diagonal to the ridges, then close the lid. The s'mores will be done after cooking 3 to 5 minutes. As the s'mores cook, press down on the lid of the grill *very* gently.

GRILL PAN: Place the grill pan on the stove and preheat it to medium-high over medium heat. When the grill pan is hot a drop of water will skitter in the pan. When ready to cook, lightly oil the ridges of the grill pan. Place the s'mores in the hot grill pan on a diagonal to the ridges. The s'mores will be done after cooking 2 to 4 minutes per side. After it has cooled down, soak the grill pan in hot water to loosen any burnt-on marshmallow.

BUILT-IN GRILL: Preheat the grill to medium-high, then, if it does not have a nonstick surface, brush and oil the grill grate. Place the s'mores on the hot grate on a diagonal to the ridges. They will be done after cooking 2 to 4 minutes per side.

FREESTANDING GRILL: Preheat the grill to high; there's no need to oil the grate. Place the s'mores on the hot grill on a diagonal to the ridges. They will be done after cooking 3 to 5 minutes per side.

FIREPLACE GRILL: Rake red hot embers under the gridiron and preheat it for 3 to 5 minutes; you want a medium-hot, 4 Mississippi fire. When ready to cook, brush and oil the gridiron. Place the s'mores on the hot grate on a diagonal to the ridges. They will be done after cooking 2 to 4 minutes per side.

tips

4. When ready to cook, brush the pound cake s'mores on both sides with the butter. Cook the s'mores, following the instructions for any of the grills in the box on the previous page, until they are toasted and golden brown and the chocolate and marshmallows have melted. If cooking in a grill pan or on a built-in, free-standing, or fireplace grill, use a spatula to turn the s'mores. Serve at once.

NOTES:
■ Buy the largest marshmallows you can find.
■ Lemon verbena is a green leafy herb with a lemony flavor.

VARIATION: Make chocolate caramel s'mores by substituting chocolate cake for the pound cake and *dulce de leche* for the chocolate bars. *Dulce de leche* is a milk caramel. It's available canned and in jars. You'll find it in Latino markets and specialty food stores. These s'mores will definitely be gooey and amazing!

cast-iron braziers

the ultimate s'mores (in the style of the blackwolf run)

Contemporary chefs have deconstructed and reconstructed the s'more in some of the nation's trendiest dining rooms. Of course they have made the recipe appropriately upscale, featuring artisanal marshmallows in unconventional shapes, "designer" graham crackers, and sophisticated chocolate sauces instead of commercial candy bars. You still toast everything to order, only now it's over tiny cast-iron braziers filled with Sterno.

The s'mores served at the Blackwolf Run, a rustic lodge that's part of the American Club hotel and resort in Kohler, Wisconsin, are a case in point. The marshmallows—2½-inch squares of pure paradise, are the first innovation. The graham crackers are actually pecan-flavored whole wheat and rye flour cookies. And there are two sauces: caramel *and* homemade hot fudge. To prepare these s'mores at home takes a not inconsiderable amount of time, but it makes for some of the best s'mores on the planet. **MAKES 20 LARGE S'MORES; FIGURE ON 2 PER PERSON**

THE RECIPE

FOR THE MARSHMALLOWS:
Cooking oil spray
1 cup confectioners' sugar, sifted
1/2 cup cold water
3 tablespoons (3½ envelopes)
    unflavored gelatin
2 cups granulated sugar
1/2 cup light corn syrup
1/2 cup hot water
1/4 teaspoon salt
Whites from 2 large eggs
1 teaspoon vanilla extract, rose water,
    orange flower water, or
    Grand Marnier

FOR THE PECAN GRAHAM COOKIES:
1 cup granulated sugar
2/3 cup coarsely chopped pecans
    (about 3 ounces)
1¹/3 cup whole wheat flour
1/2 cup rye flour
1¹/2 teaspoons baking powder
1 teaspoon baking soda
1 teaspoon ground cinnamon
1/4 teaspoon salt
8 tablespoons (1 stick) cold
    unsalted butter, cut into
    1/2-inch pieces
1 large egg

Yolks from 2 large eggs
1 tablespoon molasses
1 tablespoon honey
1 teaspoon vanilla extract

FOR THE S'MORES:
Hot Fudge Sauce (recipe follows)
Cinnamon Caramel Sauce (page 394)

YOU'LL ALSO NEED:
One 8-by-12- or 9-by-13-inch baking dish
    (metal or glass); candy thermometer;
    2 greased baking sheets;
    20 bamboo skewers; cast-iron
    braziers and Sterno
    (see sidebar on page 392)

1. Make the marshmallows: Lightly coat the bottom and sides of the baking dish with cooking oil spray. Dust the bottom and sides with 2 to 3 tablespoons of the confectioners' sugar.

WORTH THE EFFORT

Before you decide that no dessert that takes up five pages of text is worth the work, please know that this one can be divided and conquered. For example, you can make the marshmallows, cookies, and even the sauces several days ahead. For that matter, you can make your own marshmallows but use your favorite store-bought cookies or graham crackers. You can substitute hot fudge sauce from a jar, or even skip the sauces altogether— the marshmallows and pecan cookies are extraordinary just by themselves.

BRAZIERS

Finding individual braziers may be a challenge. Look for them at Asian markets or see the Mail-Order Sources on page 396. You want cast-iron braziers that are about 5 inches tall and 4 to 5 inches across—the sort that once were used to cook tiny shish kebabs at Polynesian restaurants. Cans of Sterno provide the flame and heat. Up to four people can share one brazier. You could also toast the marshmallows in your fireplace, in which case you'll need long, flameproof skewers. Or you can toast the s'mores in the fireplace.

2. Place the cold water in the bowl of a stand mixer or metal mixing bowl. Sprinkle the gelatin over the water, gently stir it with a fork, and let stand until spongy, 5 minutes.

3. Meanwhile, place the granulated sugar, corn syrup, hot water, and salt in a large heavy saucepan over high heat and stir to mix. Cover the saucepan and bring to a boil, then cook until clear, about 2 minutes. Uncover the saucepan and, using a natural bristle pastry brush dipped in cold water, wash any sugar crystals down from the side of the saucepan. Attach a candy thermometer to the side of the saucepan and let the sugar mixture boil until it registers 240°F on the candy thermometer, 6 to 8 minutes. Remove the saucepan from the heat and pour the sugar mixture into the gelatin mixture. Stir with a wooden spoon until the gelatin dissolves.

4. Using a mixer, beat the sugar and gelatin mixture at high speed until thick, white, creamy, and nearly tripled in volume, 8 to 10 minutes. It will look like Marshmallow Fluff.

5. Place the egg whites in another mixer bowl or metal bowl and beat until soft peaks form, starting on the slow speed for about 2 minutes, then beating on medium for about 4 minutes, and finally on high for 1 to 2 minutes; the total beating time will be about 8 minutes.

6. Add the beaten egg whites and the vanilla to the gelatin mixture, beat just to mix, then spoon into the prepared baking dish. Smooth the top with a spatula. Sift ¼ cup of the confectioners' sugar evenly over the top. Refrigerate the marshmallow, uncovered, until firm, at least 3 hours and up to 24 hours.

7. To cut out the marshmallows, run the tip of a paring knife around the inside of the baking dish to loosen the marshmallow. Generously dust a work surface with confectioners' sugar. Place the remaining confectioners' sugar in a mixing bowl. Turn the marshmallow out onto the dusted work surface, shaking the baking dish if necessary to release it. Using a sharp knife, cut the marshmallow into 4 lengthwise rows and 5 crosswise rows to make 20 marshmallows. Place 2 or 3 marshmallows in the bowl with the confectioners' sugar and gently toss to coat all sides. Repeat with the remaining marshmallows. Stored in an airtight container at a cool room temperature the marshmallows will keep for at least a week. Place pieces of plastic wrap between the layers of marshmallows.

8. Preheat the oven to 375°F.

9. Make the pecan graham cookies: Place the granulated sugar and the pecans in a food processor fitted with the metal blade and process to a coarse powder, running the machine in short bursts. Add the whole wheat flour, rye flour, baking powder, baking soda, cinnamon, and salt and process to mix. Add the butter and process in short bursts until the mixture feels fine and crumbly, like cornmeal. Add the egg, egg yolks, molasses, honey, and vanilla and process in short bursts until the mixture comes together into a smooth dough.

10. Pinch off 1-inch pieces of dough and roll them into balls. Arrange the balls of dough about 2 inches apart on the greased baking sheets. With lightly moistened fingers, flatten the balls to make 2-inch round circles (you'll have about 40). Bake the cookies until golden brown and lightly cracked on top, about 12 minutes. Let the cookies cool for about 5 minutes on the baking sheets, then, using a spatula, transfer them to wire racks to cool completely. The cookies can be made up to 3 days ahead and stored in an airtight container.

11. Place a can of Sterno in each brazier and light it.

12. Make the s'mores: Skewer each marshmallow on 2 parallel bamboo skewers. Toast the marshmallows over the braziers until browned to taste.

13. Place each toasted marshmallow on a pecan graham cookie. Top with spoonfuls of hot fudge and caramel sauce, then another cookie. It doesn't get much better than this!

hot fudge sauce

Hot fudge sauce is a treat anytime—especially when it's homemade. Tradition calls for it to be cooked in a doubler boiler, but if you're an impatient, Type A person (like I am), you can cook the whole shebang directly in a heavy saucepan. Work over low to moderate heat—just don't let the sauce boil. **MAKES 1½ CUPS**

¼ cup unsweetened cocoa powder
½ cup sugar
½ cup heavy (whipping) cream
¼ cup light corn syrup
3 ounces unsweetened chocolate, coarsely chopped
2 tablespoons (¼ stick) unsalted butter
1 teaspoon vanilla extract
A pinch of salt

1. Place the cocoa powder and sugar in the top of a double boiler or in a metal mixing bowl over a saucepan of briskly simmering water. Whisk until well mixed. Add the cream and corn syrup and whisk to mix. Cook the cream mixture over briskly simmering water until thick and creamy, 3 to 5 minutes, whisking steadily.

2. Add the chocolate, butter, vanilla, and salt, stir to mix, and cook until the chocolate and butter are melted and the sauce is smooth and creamy, 2 to 3 minutes. Keep the sauce warm until ready to serve. The sauce can be refrigerated, covered, for several weeks. Let it come to room temperature, then reheat it in a double boiler before serving.

cinnamon caramel sauce

Maybe you've never thought about making caramel sauce from scratch, but nothing could be easier. You cook sugar until it's golden brown, then dissolve it in heavy cream. The cinnamon isn't traditional, but I like the way it rounds out the flavor. **MAKES ABOUT 1½ CUPS**

¾ cup sugar
3 tablespoons hot water
⅔ cup heavy (whipping) cream
½ teaspoon ground cinnamon

1. Place the sugar and hot water in a heavy saucepan and gently stir with a wooden spoon to mix. Cover the saucepan, place it over high heat, and bring to a boil. Let the sugar mixture boil until clear, about 1 minute. Using a natural bristle pastry brush dipped in cold water, wash any sugar crystals down from the side of the saucepan.

2. Uncover the saucepan and let the sugar mixture cook until thick and deep golden brown, 5 to 8 minutes. You can gently shake the pan so the sugar cooks evenly, but don't stir it.

3. Remove the saucepan from the heat and add the cream and cinnamon. Stand back—it will bubble and hiss. Return the saucepan to the heat and let the sauce simmer until it is thick and creamy, about 3 minutes, stirring to mix with a wooden spoon. Let the caramel sauce cool to room temperature before serving. The sauce can be refrigerated, covered, for several weeks. Let it return to room temperature before serving.

approximate equivalents

1 STICK BUTTER = 8 tbs = 4 oz = ½ cup

1 CUP ALL-PURPOSE PRESIFTED FLOUR OR DRIED BREAD CRUMBS = 5 oz

1 CUP GRANULATED SUGAR = 8 oz

1 CUP (PACKED) BROWN SUGAR = 6 oz

1 CUP CONFECTIONERS' SUGAR = 4½ oz

1 CUP HONEY OR SYRUP = 12 oz

1 CUP GRATED CHEESE = 4 oz

1 CUP DRIED BEANS = 6 oz

1 LARGE EGG = about 2 oz or about 3 tbs

1 EGG YOLK = about 1 tbs

1 EGG WHITE = about 2 tbs

Please note that all conversions are approximate but close enough to be useful when converting from one system to another.

weight conversions

US/UK	METRIC	US/UK	METRIC
½ oz	15 g	7 oz	200 g
1 oz	30 g	8 oz	250 g
1½ oz	45 g	9 oz	275 g
2 oz	60 g	10 oz	300 g
2½ oz	75 g	11 oz	325 g
3 oz	90 g	12 oz	350 g
3½ oz	100 g	13 oz	375 g
4 oz	125 g	14 oz	400 g
5 oz	150 g	15 oz	450 g
6 oz	175 g	1 lb	500 g

liquid conversions

U.S.	IMPERIAL	METRIC
2 tbs	1 fl oz	30 ml
3 tbs	1½ fl oz	45 ml
¼ cup	2 fl oz	60 ml
⅓ cup	2½ fl oz	75 ml
⅓ cup + 1 tbs	3 fl oz	90 ml
⅓ cup + 2 tbs	3½ fl oz	100 ml
½ cup	4 fl oz	125 ml
⅔ cup	5 fl oz	150 ml
¾ cup	6 fl oz	175 ml
¾ cup + 2 tbs	7 fl oz	200 ml
1 cup	8 fl oz	250 ml
1 cup + 2 tbs	9 fl oz	275 ml
1¼ cups	10 fl oz	300 ml
1⅓ cups	11 fl oz	325 ml
1½ cups	12 fl oz	350 ml
1⅔ cups	13 fl oz	375 ml
1¾ cups	14 fl oz	400 ml
1¾ cups + 2 tb	15 fl oz	450 ml
2 cups (1 pint)	16 fl oz	500 ml
2½ cups	20 fl oz (1 pint)	600 ml
3¾ cups	1½ pints	900 ml
4 cups	1¾ pints	1 liter

oven temperatures

F	GAS MARK	C	F	GAS MARK	C
250	½	120	400	6	200
275	1	140	425	7	220
300	2	150	450	8	230
325	3	160	475	9	240
350	4	180	500	10	260
375	5	190			

Note: Reduce the temperature by 20°C (68°F) for fan-assisted ovens.

grills

Calphalon
P.O. Box 583
Toledo, Ohio 43697
(800) 809-7267
www.calphalon.com
Grill pans

Camerons Smoker
P.O. Box 60220
Colorado Springs,
    Colorado 80960
(888) 563-0227
www.cameronssmoker.com
Stove-top smokers

tabletop braziers

Small, Sterno-fueled braziers,
sometimes called s'mores
makers, are available
from Bed Bath & Beyond:
(800) 462-3966,
www.bedbathandbeyond.com;
and Target: (800) 440-0680,
www.target.com.

George Foreman
Salton
1801 North Stadium
    Boulevard, Columbia,
    Missouri 65202
(866) 372-5866
www.biggeorge.com
www.salton.com
Contact grills

Jenn-Air
Maytag Customer Service
240 Edwards Street
Cleveland, Tennessee
    37311
(800) 688-1100
www.jennair.com
Stoves with built-in grills

Le Creuset
P.O. Box 67
Early Branch, South Carolina
    29916
(877) 273-8738
www.lecreuset.com
Grill pans and panini presses
    (grill presses)

Lodge Manufacturing Co.
P.O. Box 380
South Pittsburg, Tennessee
    37380
(423) 837-7181
www.lodgemfg.com
Cast-iron grill pans and
    grill presses

Ronco
P.O. Box 4052
Beverly Hills, California
    90213
(800) 486-1806
www.showtimerotisserie.com
Countertop rotisseries

SpitJack
1 Oak Hill Road, Worcester,
    Massachusetts 01609
(800) 755-5509
www.spitjack.com
Tuscan grills and fireplace
    rotisseries

Sur La Table
Seattle Design Center
5701 Sixth Avenue South,
    Suite 486
Seattle, Washington
    98108
(800) 243-0852
www.surlatable.com
Tuscan grills

T-Fal
2121 Eden Road
Millville, New Jersey
    08332
(800) 395-8325
www.t-falusa.com
Freestanding grills

Thermador
5551 McFadden Avenue
Huntington Beach,
    California 92649
(800) 656-9226
www.thermador.com
Stoves with built-in grills

Viking
111 Front Street,
    Greenwood,
    Mississippi 38930
(888) 845-4641
www.vikingrange.com
Stoves with built-in grills

VillaWare
18901 Euclid Avenue, No. 1
Cleveland, Ohio 44117
(866) 484-5529
www.villaware.com
Panini machines (contact
    grill), grill pans, and
    stove-top smokers

Wolf Appliance Company
P.O. Box 44848
Madison, Wisconsin 53744
(800) 332-9513
www.subzero.com
Stoves with built-in grills
    (Wolf retail sales is a
    subdivision of Sub-Zero
    Freezer Company)

Zojirushi
6259 Bandini Boulevard
Commerce, California 90040
(800) 733-6270
www.zojirushi.com
Freestanding grills

sawdust

Camerons Smoker
P.O. Box 60220
Colorado Springs,
    Colorado 80960
(888) 563-0227
www.cameronssmoker.com
Wood chips

W W Wood, Inc.
P.O. Box 398
1799 Corgey Road
Pleasanton, Texas 78064
(830) 569-2501
www.woodinc.com
Smoking chips

ingredients

A Couple of Basketcases
2035 NE 151st Street
North Miami, Florida 33162
(305) 945-0500
www.acoupleofbasketcases.
    com
Oils, vinegars, and Asian
    ingredients, among other
    things

mail-order sources

Brugger Brothers
3868 NE 169th Street, Unit 401
North Miami Beach, Florida
    33160
(800) 949-2264
www.din.net/talamanca
Talamanca peppercorns,
    my favorite kind

Carr Valley Cheese Company
S3797 County G
La Valle, Wisconsin 53941
(800) 462-7258
www.carrvalleycheese.com
Cheese, including aged
    Wisconsin cheddar

The Chile Shop
109 East Water Street
Santa Fe, New Mexico 87501
(505) 984-0737
www.thechileshop.com
Chiles and spices, including
    New Mexican chile
    powder, Mexican and
    Southwestern ingredients

CT River Shad
48 Maple Street
Chester, Connecticut 06412
(203) 589-5863
www.ctrivershad.com
Shad roe

Dean & DeLuca
P.O. Box 2259
Wichita, Kansas 67201
(800) 221-7714
www.deandeluca.com
All manner of oils, vinegars,
    condiments, spices, and
    so on

Frieda's
4465 Corporate Center Drive,
    Los Alamitos, California
    90720
(800) 241-1771
www.friedas.com
Unusual fruits and
    vegetables, including a
    variety of fresh and dried
    chiles

Harrington's of Vermont
210 East Main Street
Richmond, Vermont 05477
(802) 434-4444
www.harringtonham.com
Cob-smoked bacon, hams,
    and smoked meats

iseafood.com
Grand Central Market
New York, New York 10017
(516) 208-9066
www.iseafood.com
Fish and shellfish, including
    trout, wild salmon, and
    diver scallops

Jamaica Groceries & Spices
9587 SW 160th Street
Miami, Florida 33157
(305) 252-1197
www.jamaica.n.v.switchboard
    .com
Caribbean ingredients

Jamison Farm
171 Jamison Lane
Latrobe, Pennsylvania
    15650
(800) 237-5262
www.jamisonfarm.com
Artisanal lamb

Kalustyan's
123 Lexington Avenue
New York, New York
    10016
(800) 352-3451
www.kalustyans.com
Herbs and spices, including
    aji amarillo and ancho
    chile powder, East Indian
    ingredients

Kitchen Market
218 Eighth Avenue
New York, New York
    10011
(888) 468-4433
www.kitchenmarket.com
Chiles and spices, including
    ancho chile powder and
    aji amarillo

La Tienda
3701 Rochambeau Drive
Williamsburg, Virginia
    23188
(888) 472-1022
www.tienda.com
Pimentón (smoked paprika)

Legal Sea Foods
One Seafood Way
Boston, Massachusetts 02210
(800) 328-3474
www.legalseafoods.com
Fish and shellfish, including
    wild salmon

Magic Seasoning Blends
824 Distributors Row
Harahan, Louisiana
    70123
(800) 457-2857
www.chefpaul.com
Cajun products, including
    tasso (smoked pork)

Marché aux Delices
P.O. Box 1164
New York, New York
    10028
(888) 547-5471
www.auxdelices.com
Truffles and exotic
    mushrooms

Melissa's
P.O. Box 21127
Los Angeles, California
    90021
(800) 588-0151
www.melissas.com
Unusual fruits, vegetables,
    and spices, including
    canela

Mo Hotta Mo Betta
P.O. Box 1026
Savannah, Georgia 31402
(800) 462-3220
www.mohotta.com
Hot sauces, barbecue sauces,
    and chili powders

Nueske's Hillcrest Farm
Rural Route #2,
    P.O. Box D
Wittenberg, Wisconsin
    54499
(800) 392-2266
www.nueske.com
Artisanal bacon

Old Chatham Sheepherding
    Company
155 Shaker Museum Road
Old Chatham, New York
    12136
(888) 743-3760
www.blacksheepcheese.com
Camembert-style cheese

The Oriental Pantry
423 Great Road
Acton, Massachusetts
    01720
(800) 828-0368
www.orientalpantry.com
Asian ingredients

Pendery's
1221 Manufacturing Street
Dallas, Texas 75207
(800) 533-1870
www.penderys.com
Herbs and spices, including
    ground bay leaves

Peppers
Rehoboth Outlets #3
1815 Ocean Outlets
Rehoboth Beach, Delaware
    19971
(800) 998-3473
www.peppers.com
Hot sauces

Recchiuti Confections
Ferry Building Marketplace
One Ferry Building,
    Shop #30
San Francisco, California
    94111
(800) 500-3396
www.recchiuticonfections.com
Chocolate and marshmallows

Scharffen Berger Chocolate
    Maker
914 Heinz Avenue
Berkeley, California 94710
(800) 930-4528
www.scharffenberger.com
Chocolate

Smithfield Hams
P.O. Box 250
Portsmouth, Virginia
    23705
(800) 926-8448
www.smithfieldhams.com
Hams and bacon

The Spice House
1031 North Old World
    Third Street
Milwaukee, Wisconsin
    53203
(414) 272-0977
www.thespicehouse.com
Herbs and spices, including
    Greek oregano and
    pimentón (smoked
    paprika)

Vosges Haut-Chocolat
858 West Armitage, #185
Chicago, Illinois 60614
(888) 301-9866
www.vosgeschocolate.com
Marshmallows